The Bewildered Herd

The Bewildered Herd

Media Coverage of International Conflicts & Public Opinion

B. A. Taleb

iUniverse, Inc.
New York   Lincoln   Shanghai

The Bewildered Herd

Media Coverage of International Conflicts & Public Opinion

iUniverse, Inc.

For information address:
iUniverse, Inc.
2021 Pine Lake Road, Suite 100
Lincoln, NE 68512
www.iuniverse.com

ISBN: 0-595-32686-2

Printed in the United States of America

To my parents & family.

"The Way means including the people to have the same aim as the leadership, so that they will share death and share life, without fear of danger."

—Sun Tzu, The Art of War

Acknowledgments

Acknowledgments and appreciation are made to all those authors, researchers, journalists, and media outlets quoted or referred to in this book and whose work and contributions were essential for its completion. Profound appreciation and gratitude is also the due right of all those journalists and reporters who continue to seek the truth and to be objective, sometimes at the expense of their own lives.

Contents

List of Illustrations

Graphics

Diagrams

Maps

Expiatory Notes

List of Tables

Introduction

The leading figure of public opinion research, Walter Lippmann, used a very significant expression to refer to the majority of people in a democratic society. They were called "The Bewildered Herd". The two words that constitute this term, used by Lippmann, are quite interesting. The word "herd" signifies "group thinking" and is far from the individual free-thinking and free-choice which characterises the basic theoretical components of modern democracies. The other word "bewildered" suggests amazement, enchantment, and lack of connection with reality. If this is what the majority is, then what is the role of the minority?. Is the minority in a society the one who conditions this majority so that it will blindly follow like a "herd" while being "bewildered" in the process? Is the government the all-wise and all-knowing minority, the media the bewildering agent, and public opinion the "bewildered herd", particularly during an international crisis or conflict?.

Over the last few decades, the growth in the importance of the role of media as an actor within any given society is, to say the least, simply astonishing. The growth in this role within human society also means an increasing ability to influence a society's choices and attitudes, due to the media's ability to influence public opinion.

Although many studies have been conducted to shed the light on the issues of public opinion formation and even more studies on the media itself, few have attempted to connect the two issues and to include a comprehensive analysis of the sociological, political, economic, and psychological dimensions of this relationship. An aspect of media conduct and ability remains, furthermore, quite unveiled. This mysterious aspect is that which relates to understanding the role and effect of the media during an international crisis or conflict. This book, hence, attempts to understand, clarify, and present reasons that determine the media's pattern of behaviour vis-à-vis an international crisis, the reasons behind this pattern of behaviour, and the impact of the media's coverage of an international crisis or conflict on domestic and world public opinion.

The first part of this work examines the relationship between media, national, and international politics. It, therefore, constitutes an important element for a comprehensive understanding of the type of relations that exist between the media, on one hand, and both national and international politics on the other. This first part of the book attempts, for a start, to shed a light on the transformation in both the

1

form and role of media, starting from the 19th century media and up to the media in its present form and role. This transformation did not simply take place out of the blue. It occurred due to various factors and developments. At one point, it was simply shaped by the innovations in communication technologies taking place. At another, it was shaped by the political situation prevailing in its corresponding era. What is even more interesting is to see how and under which conditions this role of the media was also significantly influenced by globalisation.

Another section of part one of this work tackles the delicate issue of the relationship between national media and national politics. For the media, especially nowadays, have come to be more worthy of being designated as the "fourth estate". Indeed, it would be intriguing to see the manifestations of national politics within the national media and how the media, for its part, performs its "supposed" role of surveillance of the political establishment within a given country. It is yet even more interesting to examine the influence of the political establishment on the media's orientations and whether such an influence is "so different" or not, between an authoritarian and a democratic system of government.

Similar to the relationship between national media and national politics, an important aspect discussed at this point is the relation that exists between national media and international politics. For it is certainly beneficial to see if there is some sort of reflection in the national media of international political tendencies and, indeed, whether, on the other hand, those international political tendencies are affected, and to what extent, by the national media's attitudes in certain leading world countries.

Nowadays, however, formal or official bodies are not the only actors to reckon with, within a given society. The past decade has witnessed the emergence of a new actor who's growth and influence on society and political decision-making are growing at a very fast pace. This new actor is that which is commonly referred to as the "civil society" and which is, in the most obvious of cases, represented by Non-Governmental Establishments. One of the sections of this book, is, thus, dedicated to a discussion of the relationship between the media and this new social actor. What would seem also interesting to find out is whether the media, for its part, is somehow affected or guided by the most used and relied upon tool nowadays to measure public opinion towards issue. This tool is known as the opinion polls. If the media is supposed to influence public opinion, it can also be influenced by public opinion. It is, hence, useful to see if it is, why it is, and to what extent this influence on the media can go.

One of the issues that is vital to discuss, to better understand the transformation and the current role of the media as an active actor in society, is that which relates to the relationship between national media and what has come to be known as trans-national media. From a simple first examination of semantics, a first essential difference between the two types of media is immediately found. For whereas national media is that which is normally bound by the boundaries of the country in which it exists, trans-national media is that type of media, which transcends state boundaries. The difference in the resources, scope, and influence of the two types is, hence, easy to understand. What is more interesting to examine, however, would be the type of relationship, which exists between these two types of media. It is important to stress, at this point, that these two represent "types" of media and not "outlets". The difference in reference, should, thus, be always kept in mind.

To avoid falling in the error of a hasty and, indeed, simplistic labelling of this relationship between trans-national and national media as a Master/Slave type of relationship, a thorough examination of this relationship is conducted. This examination tackles the issue in its various aspects and forms. For, to be able to understand the influence of trans-national media on national media, it is essential to examine this influence in certain forms, under which, it is most likely to exist. The linguistic influence, political orientation, and source dependence are, therefore, taken as being most representative of this influence trans-national media might have on national media.

Notwithstanding this, trans-national media is not simply suspected of influencing just the national media in any given country. Indeed, what is most remarkable and "frightening" in our present day is that boundaries of countries, except for conditioning the physical movement of humans and merchandise, have become obsolete, due to the revolution in communication, transmission, and reception technologies. Trans-national media reaches, hence, not only the national media within the boundaries of a receiving or "host country", but is also received by and destined for the population of this country as well. This fact stipulates that it is indispensable to see the impact that this trans-national media can have on the public opinion of the receiving audience in the host country. Similar to the method, according to which the influence of trans-national media on national media is examined, the study of the impact of trans-national media on public opinion in host countries is done by studying the individual forms of this influence. The aspects discussed in this part relate to the psychological and sociological behavioural effect of trans-national media on public opinion in host countries. Specifically, there is a discussion of the effect of repetition on the receiving audience in host countries, the dependence on international news coverage, and, finally, the selection and presentation of international news within the national media of host countries.

Media's role in public opinion formation is established in many aspects of daily life. For instance, it is quite indispensable for advertisers to use the media to promote their products. It is also important for politicians, during electoral campaigns for example, to use the media as a tool to influence public opinion and orient it in their favour. Likewise, the public, in general, depends to a large extent on the media for its orientation on certain issues. All of this is a fact that is quite established and taken for granted in daily life. Indeed, the media has become so integrated in daily human life that it is practically unthinkable that a society can imagine itself existing without it. The media informs and entertains and, lately, began doing both at the same time. A good term that describes the recent merger of these two concepts of the media function is "infotainement". The media seems to have realized that the message passes more effectively if the information presented to the public is not rigid but one that is framed in an attractive manner, and the public, due to a natural human trait in them, seem to be attracted more by what is more "flashy". This seems to be taking place on all levels of information diffusion and public issues. The danger is that what is "flashy" is often deceiving as well.

Out of all these types of information, which can influence public opinion, perhaps none is more sensitive than the type and form of information presented to the public cornering an international conflict or crisis. This is precisely the objective of this book. It takes one of the most important events that can take place on the international scene, namely an international crisis or conflict, and attempts to evaluate the mechanisms and impact of national media coverage of this crisis or conflict on domestic public opinion. It also discusses the reasons behind the different attitudes the media can adopt vis-à-vis an international crisis, compared to the attitude it might adopt vis-à-vis another. Understanding this impact of international crisis coverage on public opinion is important, not simply for pure academic reasons, but also for humanitarian and ethical ones, as well. An international crisis or conflict also means that a humanitarian tragedy is taking place. It also means that ethics, not just of journalists, but also of other people are involved. It is, indeed, difficult to conceive that with all the progress humanity has made so far, there are still, to borrow the expression of Edward S. Herman and Noam Chomsky "worthy and unworthy victims". It is, thus, imperative to know if there are really a distinction between "worthy" and "unworthy" victims, and how and why does this distinction exist in the media coverage, and, subsequently, in the attitudes of public opinion.

An international crisis is an extremely important event, due to various reasons. The word crisis itself can be understood as a disruption of the natural order of things. When this disruption of the usual order takes place, a number of interests are at stake. The most known of these interests are the strategic national interests of countries, such as their economic, political, or security interests which can be affected by this disruption of the usual order. Indeed, it can be said that the reaction to the crisis itself, on a state level, depends largely on the extent to which the national interests of this state are affected by the events of this crisis. This is why countries tend to react differently to the same international crisis. Some countries would tend to be more involved than others in one crisis, while those other countries, might be, for their part, more involved in another international crisis. The rules of *realpolitik* seem to perfectly explain the reaction of states to different international crises and conflicts. What is, hence, interesting to find out is whether there exists a sort of *realpolitik* determining the different media reactions to these international crises as well, and whether there are common grounds where the determinants of reaction of both state and media converge vis-à-vis an international crisis, to what degree, and in what form. What is yet, even more important to understand, is whether public opinion, during an international crisis, is conditioned by the media, why, and to what extent.

The third section of the first part of this work is dedicated to this issue. It tackles the role played by the media during an international crisis or conflict. This section of the book is divided into parts that examine the various aspects of this role, as well as examining the interests of the state, where this media exists, in this international crisis. The first element to discuss in this section relates to the expected role of the media during an international crisis. For the media is expected, during an international crisis, to perform the role of coverage. Yet, in doing this, it is also expected to assume objectivity. It is also interesting to see the effect of technological innovations on the media's role of transmission of an international crisis. It is, furthermore, necessary to see if the media tends to assume a role of under-exposure or over-exposure of an international crisis and why.

After discussing its supposed role, it is important to see if the media has certain interests involved in an international crisis, and in which manner. It can be assumed that the media can have four types of interests in the coverage of an international crisis or conflict. There are the pure journalistic interests in covering news; there are sometimes social interests, economic interests, and even political interests. The media can have one of these types of interests or, in some occasions, all of these interests might exist at the same time.

This role of the media is also shaped and affected by the national interests of the country in which this media exists. The media, being an element and an actor in the society it exists within, is susceptible to be affected by the domestic social reaction to the international crisis in question. Therefore, a discussion of the national interests that might affect and shape the media's attitude towards the international crisis would take into consideration the national or governmental interests in this crisis, as well as the society's interest, represented by the various forms of affinities this society might have concerning this international crisis or conflict.

One of the behaviours that the media seems to adopt in its coverage attitude towards an international crisis is adopting some sort of a unformed pattern in coverage that is particular to each international crisis or conflict, and that seems to be adopted almost by the totality of media outlets and forms. It seems appropriate to label this behaviour "the domino's syndrome" in media coverage of international crises. What is important to know is whether, first, such behaviour does really exist, and, second, whether it is caused by the international political tendencies towards each international crisis.

A theory is stronger when it is backed by a valid experience. This experience is what part two of this book is about. It is a study of the overage of the conflicts in Bosnia and in Chechnya by the printed media of two democratic countries (France and the United States), and this coverage's impact on public opinion tendencies in both countries.

A clarification is required on the reasons underlying the specific choice of the crisis in Bosnia and Chechnya. In fact, this choice was made due to several similarities, though not totally visible at first sight, between the Bosnia and the Chechnya crises. First, there is the similarity of religion. Both Chechens and Bosnians are predominantly Muslims. Second, both crises took place in the immediate post Cold-War era. Third, both crises were sparked by a referendum calling for independence. Fourth, both Bosnia and Chechnya were forcefully assimilated to an ethnically and religiously "foreign" state structure. Bosnia was included in the multi ethno-religious artificial structure of former Yugoslavia. Chechnya, for its part, was forced during several periods of its history to form a part of Tsarist Russia, the Soviet Union, and recently, the Russian Federation. Fifth, both crises involved considerable human loses and suffering. Sixth, in both cases, the quest for independence was crushed by massive, central or central-backed, military force. Furthermore, both crises took place in the Western hemisphere, one in the heart of European soil and the other not very far in Euro-Asia. Finally, in both cases, international organisations were proven to be rather helpless or inactive. In the case of Bosnia, the UN demonstrated its inability to effectively put an end to the conflict. In the case of Chechnya, even the voice of protest of the UN was and is almost inexistent, and other, than the Organisation of Security and Cooperation in Europe, concern over the humanitarian tragedy in Chechnya hardly existed. For all of these reasons, the choice for comparison fell on the crises of Bosnia and Chechnya.

This does not mean that the two conflicts were totally similar. Certain differences can, undeniably, be identified between the case of Bosnia and that of Chechnya. The first of these differences relates to the parties to each conflict. For, whereas the Bosnian conflict was a multilateral one, the one in Chechnya is predominantly bilateral. In Bosnia, the conflict involved different political entities (Serbia, Croatia, Bosnia) while that of Chechnya involved only the Russian Federation and the Republic of Chechnya. The second difference between the two conflicts relates to the development of the nature of the conflict itself. In Bosnia, the conflict soon developed to become a global one where the UN,

NATO, major European powers, and major world powers were involved. On the other hand, the conflict in Chechnya remained primarily one where only the Russian Federation's forces and the Chechen are involved. The third difference that can be found is one, which has to do with the weight of history of the two regions on international affaires. Historic experience of the results of conflicts in Bosnia are much more imposing on the collective world memory than those of the conflicts in and over Chechnya. It is the conflict of the Balkans, after all, that served as the trigger for the first global disastrous war in human history. Furthermore, a distinction can be made between the two conflicts concerning the use and direction of terrorism as a political tool. In Bosnia, terrorism, even historically, was confined to the region and, generally, its landscape did not bypass the frontiers to neighbouring Balkan republics. On the other hand, terrorism in the case of Chechnya, operations targeting Russian civilians are often conducted inside Russia itself. Finally, it is fair to say that the conflict in Bosnia rapidly became an open one while that of Chechnya remained predominantly a "locked conflict". The conflict of Bosnia was internationalised and became open to, not only international interventions of different parties, but also to various interests of world powers. On the other hand, the conflict of Chechnya remains closed in a vicious circle that only contains the Russian Federation and the Chechens with no other outside power allowed to enter this circle, except, perhaps, for the recent introduction of an Islamic dimension of the conflict which turned Chechnya into a destination land of Jihad.

To better understand the media attitudes in the United States and France towards the two crises, a comprehensive methodology is applied in the conduct of this case study. The first factor taken into consideration is that which is related to the respective national interests of both the United States and France vis-à-vis each of the two crises. It is necessary to start with an analysis of the national interests of both countries. The necessity stems from the need to have an answer to the question of whether the media coverage in the United States and in France is affected or not by these national interests, why, and, if they are affected, then to what extent can national interests of a country shape its national media's attitudes.

An important point to remind of is that both countries chosen have an essential shared similarity. They are both democratic states by excellence. The choice of the media of two democratic states is not done without a valid reason. Indeed, it is known that media in authoritarian or non-democratic systems of government normally perform nothing more than a propaganda function. Therefore, a comparison between the attitudes of media in a democratic state and the attitudes of media in a non-democratic one would not have been useful for this book's purposes. The second reason for the choice of two democratic countries is an attempt to answer the question of whether the media, even in a democratic state, would also tend, consciously or unconsciously, to adopt some sort of a clandestine propaganda pattern particularly during an international crisis which, at the end, would not be much different from the overt propaganda function of media in non-democratic states. The question is quite sensitive to aboard for it concerns the essence and meaning of democracy, free thought, and free choice itself. Another reason for the choice of these two countries is the fact that both are leaders of particular political philosophy and doctrine in the conduct of their foreign policy. Indeed, both countries often diverged on various occasions in their positions towards different international affaires. Moreover, it was interesting to see the effect of geographic proximity on national interests and foreign policy decisions of the two countries.

To be able to try and provide an answer to this question, a thorough examination of the French and United States' printed media coverage of the two crises is done. The case study, hence, proceeds by examining the manner in which the printed media in both countries covered the crisis in Bosnia and the crisis in Chechnya. This analysis takes into consideration the terminology used in coverage, the images used, the intensity or repetition of coverage, the placement of each crisis's coverage within the printed media, and the involvement and attitudes of the journalists who were most involved in the coverage of these two crises. The examination also takes into consideration the effect of trans-national media on the coverage attitudes of the printed media in the United States and in France vis-à-vis the two crises in question. The case study would then attempt to aboard the effects of such coverage on the domestic public opinion vis-à-vis each crisis in both countries, and to see if public opinion attitudes in both countries corresponded to their respective national media's coverage of the two crises.

The third and final part of this book concerns an essential part that should render this analysis of the media coverage of international conflicts and public opinion more complete. Part three is the ethical and theoretical discussion element of this book. For, in the third part, there is an analysis of media coverage of international crises, and how this coverage is torn between the various involved interests and the desired "objectivity" ideal of the media in democratic societies of government.

The first section of this last part of the book is dedicated to a discussion of the use of the media as a political tool. It would be, indeed, interesting to understand if the media is, and can actually be, used as an effective tool for attaining political interests and how can this usage take place at the time of an international crisis. It would be interesting to see if there is a deliberate pattern of over-exposing or under-exposing of an international crisis or conflict for political ends. It would also be useful to know, during an international crisis, if there is convergence between media interests and the interests of the "political machine". Furthermore, an important portion of this section relates to a well-known fact about media function in democratic societies. This function is actually, what earned the media to be labelled as the "fourth estate". A principal reason behind its labelling as the "fourth estate", other than its ability to influence public opinion, is the role of surveillance of the governmental establishment, which the media often tends to assume. The question is whether the media not only surveys but is also surveyed by the governmental establishment.

The second part of the final part, specifically, relates to the influence of media coverage of international crises on public opinion. In this section some important questions are posed. Undeniably, a favourable public opinion is a very desired objective of any democratic government, when possible. For this is the essence of democratic systems. It is the principal that it is the public who chooses its government and who has, thus, a great say in its government's polices. Thus, in a democracy, the public is the one that governs through its chosen representatives. At least, this is the ideal situation. In more realistic conditions, the reality is somewhat different. For even if the government does not totally respond to public opinion, this government is only quite rarely changed. This is because it is impossible to condition governmental conduct to public opinion, but it is possible to do the opposite. It is, indeed, much more practical and feasible to condition public opinion to its government than to condition the government to public opinion. In other words, it is not possible to give the public the power to govern, or to decide the future of a country, but it is possible to make this public have the "illusion" that it is actually the one who governs. Thus, it is not realistic to have a completely favourable public opinion for any government. Yet, a wise government, in a democratic society, is naturally supposed to acquire favorable public opinion for its polices. After all, the least that this government would want to have on its back is a hostile public opinion that might end its mandate to govern. This is important because more favourable public opinion translates into more legitimacy for this government's decisions. Therefore, it is always necessary to try to win this public opinion. If there is an international crisis where vital, national interests are involved, a more solid and favourable public opinion is needed. If this favourable public opinion does not initially exist or is totally indifferent, it should be created and conditioned to give legitimacy to the governments' eventual involvement in this crisis or conflict. This might sound like a propaganda behaviour adopted in times of war. However, it is not one. For, a propaganda behaviour is a conscious one that is performed directly by state, or by state related institutions, such as its army. A propaganda behaviour can be applied to the media glorifying its government and diabolising its enemies directly in authoritarian or non-democratic regimes. What takes place with the media behaviour during an international crisis in democratic systems is more of a convergence of interests and quite a number of other elements, which result in a behaviour, that, though subtle, exhibits similarities with the propaganda behaviour of the media in authoritarian systems. What is also different is the society where the media operates. For, a society in an authoritarian system has practically no outside source of information other than what is fed to it by its national state controlled media. This is why it is easier to influence public opinion in authoritarian systems. The possibility of having different sources of information in democratic systems makes this influence a bit more difficult to have. Another point of difference is that which is related to mentalities existing in each of the two types of societies. For whereas citizens in a non-democratic states are preconditioned to think only what the all-knowing and all-wise state thinks, those in democratic societies always reclaim free-thought and free-choice. Nonetheless, whether this free-thinking and free-choice actually exist and is not merely an illusion in democratic societies remains an issue of debate. The second section of the final part of this work relates to a discussion of these issues. It tries to find out why and how public opinion can serve as a source of legitimacy for the political establishment. It also tries to discover whether the public is influenced by the media coverage because it is dependent on its coverage. It is also interesting to see the limitations, in a democratic society, of media influence on public opinion.

The most renowned accusation of media seems to be that which relates to its objectivity. These accusations and this debate on the objectivity of media, especially during an international crisis or conflict, can be labelled as "the media's crisis of objectivity". It is interesting, hence, to understand this crisis and to examine its reasons. One of these reasons is quite apparent, though. It is an inherent belief that the media's freedom is without limits and, thus, can achieve this objectivity if it really wants to. Yet, there are, especially during an international conflict or crisis, factors that can be termed as "objective" limitations on media coverage. It is useful to find out what these "objective" limitations on media coverage of an international crisis or conflict are, and how do these limitations contribute to the media's crisis of objectivity. It is also interesting to know how the independence of media contributes to this crisis of objectivity, and in which manner. These are the issues discussed In the last and final section of this book.

Part One:

The Relationship between Media, National and International Politics

1.1. The Place of Media in the International and National Political Fabric

1.1.1. The Transformation of the Role of the Media

It is perhaps interesting to examine the transformation of the role of the media over the last hundred years or so. This transformation has been affected and influenced by a number of variables and innovations that affected the media during this period. New technological innovations, wars, the emergence of new social theories and struggles have certainly helped shape and transform the role of the media over the last hundred years.

1.1.1.1. 19th Century Media

A number of evolutions, social factors and tendencies characterized the nineteenth century. Some prefer to call the nineteenth century the age of romantics. Others on the other hand might refer to it as the age where civil wars and social claims began to emerge.

The media, in the nineteenth century, was overwhelmingly represented by newspapers. Radio, television and other forms of present time media did not exist at the time. However, nineteenth century newspapers did not exactly take the form of the newspapers we have today. Indeed, the majority of those were weeklies or semi-weeklies. In addition, the pages were much less (4-8 pages).

It is not just the difference in form that differentiates nineteenth century newspapers from present day ones, it's also the difference in content and objectives. The great majority of these newspapers were highly partisan. In fact, several of them were funded by political parties. As far as the content is concerned, nineteenth century newspapers generally provided their readers with a combination of articles: local news, some national and international news, fiction and poetry, and sensational stories.

Nineteenth century newspapers typically devoted between half and three-quarters of its pages to advertising. This may be attributed to the fact that it was hard to collect subscription fees, even when these fees were sometimes goods or services.

Among the pages devoted to articles, most items were about "events"—local, national or international happenings—as opposed to "ideas"—discussions of citizenship, works of moral uplift, and the like. The event articles were noticeably slanted towards the local and the political.

National and international news was mostly obtained via news brokers or by simply copying extracts that appeared in other newspapers. This naturally led to the fact that several newspapers might come up with the same article.

As far as journalists are concerned, most of them were essentially propagandists for political parties. The role of journalists became that of objective reporters and investigators only after newspapers became independent of direct political control in the mid-19th century, a period that saw the work of some of the most celebrated journalists, including Sir Henry Morton Stanely[1] and William Howard Russell[2]. The late nineteenth century witnessed the introduction of sensational journalism (the yellow press) mainly in the United States of America which, greatly increased circulation.

The first academic courses providing training in journalism were established around the beginning of the 20th century. Awareness of the social responsibilities of journalists and the new specialized demands of radio and television broadcasting increased this trend towards professionalism. Thus, in the 19th century, the media played the role of a partisan for political and intellectual elites.

1.1.1.2. Global Wars Media.

The term "global wars" refers to the two great wars (The First and the Second World Wars). By definition, wartime is different from periods of peace and regular activity. In wartime all efforts would be made to ensure the victory over the adversary.

---

[1]   Stanley, Sir Henry Morton, 1841–1904, Anglo-American journalist and empire builder, b. Denbigh, Wales. Originally named John Rowlands, he took the name of his adoptive father in New Orleans, where Stanley went in 1857. After fighting on both sides in the American Civil War, he drifted into journalism. His coverage of Lord Napier's Abyssinian campaign in 1868 for the New York Herald won him journalistic fame, and the *Herald* commissioned him to go to Africa to find David Livingstone. Stanley located the great explorer on Lake Tanganyika on Nov. 10, 1871, addressing him with the famous words, "Dr. Livingstone, I presume?"

[2]   Sir William Howard Russell (1820-1907). William Howard Russell was the first and one of the most famous of war correspondents in history. He made his great reputation in the Crimean War of 1854-55 reporting for the London Times. He received the name "Bull Run" Russell in America while covering the Civil War.

In the First as well as in the Second World Wars, the world was divided into two camps each claiming higher morality and rights over the other. In this sense, the media at the time was used to contribute to the war effort mainly through emphasising the aspects of patriotism and the rightfulness of one camp over the other.

But war in itself needed, to be won, an enormous support from the people inside. They had to be convinced that they should contribute to the war effort, that their cause is just and that going to war is not a bad decision but a glorious one. It is interesting to note, in this respect, that propaganda war to support the war effort was more conducted in one's own country mostly through the help of renowned writers, photographers, poster designers and journalists. The example of the American president Woodrow Wilson is worth mentioning to illustrate this notion. Wilson was elected on the slogan "He Kept Us out of War". Yet in 1917 this fact changed when the United States decided to enter The First World War.

Wilson had two problems at hand. The first one was to find a way to convince the American people to fight a war so far away. The second was to find a way to finance the war. He found the answer to his two problems in the person of the American journalist Muckraker George Creel[3]. Creel managed to convince the American people of the justness of the war and of financing the war effort by buying Wilson's Liberty War Bonds.

---

3   George Creel (1876-1953) headed the U.S. propaganda effort during World War One. Creel's career began as a newspaper reporter in 1894 for the *Kansas City World*. By the time the U.S. entered World War One in April 1917 Creel had begun to establish something of a reputation as an investigative journalist (or 'muckraker' to some), having in the interim acted as editor for the *Rocky Mountain News* (1911). He was chosen to head Wilson's Committee on Public Information (CPI) in 1917, although given his outspokenness his selection was controversial among Wilson's Republican opponent (notably Henry Cabot Lodge, Wilson's ongoing political nemesis). While Creel acted to reduce the level of anti-German feeling in the country over the course of the following two years with unbiased news reporting, he nevertheless devoted his not inconsiderable energies to ensuring full public backing for the U.S. war effort. To this end he extended the scope of his remit from Wilson to include all aspects of the U.S. media, including film, posters, music, paintings and cartoons. Creel also arranged for the recruitment of 75,000 so-called 'Four Minute Men'—people who volunteered to speak for four minutes in public locations around the country in favour of the war effort). Domestically however Creel's irascible outspokenness ensured he found enemies among Wilson's conservative opponents, including Lodge. If anything, Creel's aggressive campaigning on behalf of Wilson for the latter's Fourteen Points galvanised U.S. home opposition, and certainly contributed to the ultimate rejection in Congress of the Treaty of Versailles.

It is worth motioning to say that the First World War witnessed the emergence of military magazines such as *The Stars and Strips*. This weekly saw the light on the 8th of February 1918. Its circulation began with less than 300,000 copies and eventually reached more than 520,000, produced by a staff of some 300 army personnel[4]. The nature of this magazine and its mandate led only to one objective. This was to boast the moral of the American troops stationed in Europe during the First World War[5].

Thus, patriotism was probably the driving journalistic force of this period. Yet, if wartime and war effort has unified the entire society of a given nation during the First World War, this wasn't the case in the years that followed. It is actually after the end of the war that we can see the emergence of conflict and competition amongst the media branches of the time. This conflict and competition led, perhaps, to more diversity and to les monotheistic journalism approaches.

One reflection of this emerging competition can be seen in what Gwenyth L. Jackaway calls "the press-radio war"[6]. At the beginning, Jackaway explains, and in the early 1920's, radio was the latest "craze" and many of the newspaper publishers at the time did not feel at all threatened by this new invention. On the contrary, she explains that they saw in it an opportunity to draw profit by featuring stories about this new technology. Jackaway explains that as radio became a subject of growing interest to the public, newspapers responded by running more stories about it. Some newspapers went even further, devoting several pages, or even, on the weekends, an entire magazine section to radio. Some of the most powerful newspapers of the time in the United States like *The Los Angeles Times* and the *Chicago Tribune* owned their own radios[7]. The conflict started in the mid-1920's when journalists started to express concern that radio posed a serious threat to their business. At the time, most radio broadcasters were dependant on newspapers for their supply of news items because they lacked the personnel and the equipment to do the news collecting themselves. This fact let to what Jackaway calls "the radio-press war" which lasted from 1924–1939.

Yet, again and with the change of circumstances, competition is to be forgotten to the benefit of unified efforts with the outbreak of the Second World War on the 3rd of September 1939. According to Nicholas John Cull, the spirit of that period (The Second World War) "required the government to mobilize all groups

---

4   See Alfred E. Cornbeise, <u>The Stars and Strips: Doughby's Journalism in World War I</u>, Greenwood Press, Westport, CT, 1984, pp. 3-7.

5   Ibid, pp. 97-98.

6   See Gwenyth L. Jackaway, <u>The Media at War: radio Challenge to the Newspapers, 1924-1939</u>, Greenwood, Westport, CT, 1995, pp.14-16.

7   Idem.

behind a war effort that generated millions of posters, words and images, all aimed at including as many Americans as possible in what came to be called the war effort"[8]. Cull explains that, both in Europe and the United States alike, the focus was on a new more effective type of media (The Movies) or what he calls "the era's most effective medium of popular culture". Films proved at the time their effective role in promoting patriotism. Nonetheless, movie productions did not go uncensored. Cull states that, throughout the war, the studios output was negotiated in the United States by the Office of War Information (OWI); the United State's government's propaganda agency. The OWI was headed at the time by Elmer Davis[9] who, according to cull, insisted that this agency's only goal was to "tell the truth" though he also believed that "the easiest way to propagandise people is to let a propaganda theme go in through an entertainment picture when people do not realize they are being propagandised"[10].

This boom of the cinema industry as the new tool informing and guiding the people took place simultaneously in all countries concerned by the war situation. For instance, Anthony Aldgate states that "the period of the Second World War was a time of relative prosperity for the British film industry"[11]. He adds, "The war was definitely to prove a golden age as far as domestic films were concerned"[12]. Like in the United States, the film industry in Britain was linked with the British Ministry of Information. This, however, is quite understandable in wartime and was done to ensure the well functioning of the national propaganda during a war situation.

---

8   See Nicholas John Cull, <u>Selling War: the British Propaganda Campaign Against American "Neutrality" in World War II</u>, Oxford University Press, New York, 1995, pp. 1-7.

9   Elmer Davis (1890–1958) was a US radio announcer & news commentator. During the war years, radio listeners tuned in regularly to hear Elmer Davis report and analyse the day's events. On one occasion he presented the details of the sighting of an unidentified submarine within the U.S. safety (neutrality) zone by announcing, "Of course the safety zone declaration doesn't say that belligerent war ships must keep out; only that they mustn't do any fighting. But what are they there for? American neutrality is a serious matter. It seems a pity that it threatens to provide the war with comic relief…" An example of Davis' tough-minded talk was his broadcast recommending the government disseminate news under one organization. This would prompt FDR to create the OWI, or Office of War Information, which Davis would be asked to head.

10   Ibid.

11   See Anthony Aldgate, <u>The British Can Take It: The British Cinema in the Second World War</u>, Edinburgh University Press, Edinburgh, 1994, pp. 2-4.

12   Ibid.

It is interesting to note the new developments in media form, content and tools during the period from 1914 to 1944. For in this period technological innovations and inventions came to play the greater role. Nevertheless, and despite this technological advancement, from limited four pages newspapers to motion pictures passing by the radio, the political tendencies and the state dominance has proven to be vital in the functioning and orientation of the media machine in any given country involved in one of those two great wars. Again this is understandable since irregular situations produce most of the time deformed developments. During the period examined in this part, media's behaviour is proven to have been fluctuating according to the situation or the circumstances. It is, thus, fair to say that the media's behaviour and role in peaceful times differs from its role and behaviour in crisis or wartime times.

1.1.1.3. Cold War Media

The role of media in the Cold War era was reflection of what some writers call "the cold war culture"[13]. The media in this period where the world was divided into two main camps was sort of a platform for the diffusion of this Cold War Culture. The media, in this era, was mainly characterised by two main things: rhetoric and propaganda. This took place not only within the media of the two Cold War protagonists but also within the media of the countries that orbited the United States and the Soviet Union.

It can be said that fear and diabolising of the other and the presentation of a nuclear attack as the ultimate end that everyone should be prepared to was the ultimate theme of this Cold War Culture. The media in that time was a mere instrument of propaganda. Furthermore, distinction between the media and the government hardly existed. Everyone was supposed to work for the cause of national interest. Guy Oakes states, for example, "Survival Under Atomic Attack was the first of many media—government publications and films, newspaper and magazine articles, radio and television scripts, interviews and speeches, and even novels—that employed the conventionalisation argument in order to diminish the horrifying aspects of nuclear weapons"[14]. Other than fear of being accused of being called anti-nationalist, the media in the Cold War era seemed to have sought to impress the government to be accorded more privileges. This was

---

13   See for instance Guy Oakes, The Imaginary War: Civil Defense and American Cold War Culture, Oxford USNew York, 1994. Also see Peter J. Kuznick and James Burkhart Gilbert, Rethinking Cold War Culture, Smithsonian Institution Press, 2001.

14   See Guy Oakes, op. cit., p. 54.

mostly apparent at the heights of the threat of Cold War. In the United States, for instance, "Newspapers, magazines, radio, and television competed to gain government certification for their publications and broadcasts on civil defence as an official national security seal of approval"[15]. In the Soviet Union, political total control of media was more apparent to an extent that some would call the explosion of the Chernobyl nuclear reactor on the 25th-26th of April 1986 the first "real media" event in the USSR[16]. The problem with the apparent political control on media performance in both camps seems to have resulted in a lack of media credibility. Indeed, aggressive propaganda can sometimes lead to alienation of the audience. The need show less direct government control of the media in order to be more convincing and to look more "objective" as manifested even in a system as centralised as the USSR was. A good example of this was the creation of the Novosti Press Agency (*Agentsvo Pechati Novosti—APN*) on the 3rd of April, 1961 in the USSR by Khrushchev as a "response to TASS's poor performance as an international promoter of Soviet interests[17]" because "TASS's blatant association with the Soviet government minimized its credibility as a source of objective information, and that TASS's dour, bureaucratic style of journalism would not "sell" the Soviet Union in consumer-oriented markets abroad"[18].

Media employed by the political power in each camp was the perfect weapon of the Cold War. For, in itself, the Cold War was a confrontation between two camps that stopped short of an all out war. Yet, even without all out combat, the Cold War "like its "hot" counterpart, is a contest. It is a contest between competing systems as represented, for example, by the Soviet Union and the United States. It is a contest involving such tangibles as geography, markets, spheres of influence, and military alliances, as well as such intangibles as public opinion, attitudes, images, expectations, and beliefs about whatever system is currently in ascendancy"[19]. The importance of media in this Cold War stemmed from the importance of gaining public opinion to the cause of one camp or the other. Martin J. Medhurst states, in this respect, "The currency of Cold War combat— the tokens used in the contest—is rhetorical discourse: discourse intentionally designed to achieve a particular goal with one or more specific audience. While

---

15   Ibid., p. 41.

16   See John W. Young, <u>Cold War Europe, 1945-1991: A Political History</u>, Arnold, London, 1996, p.227.

17   See Jennifer Turpin, <u>Reinventing the Soviet Self: Media and Social Change in the Former Soviet Union</u>, Praeger Publishers, Westport, CT., 1995, p.19.

18   Idem.

19   See Martin J. Medhurst, <u>Cold War Rhetoric: Strategy, Metaphor, and Ideology</u>, Michigan State University Press, East Lansing, MI., 1997, p.19.

the weapons of a hot war are guns, bombs, missiles, and the like, Cold War weapons are words, images, symbolic actions, and, on occasion, physical actions undertaken by covert means"[20].

Media, during the Cold War era, was both creator and representative of the culture of the era. It was employed by the political power in each camp as an instrument of this Cold War. Fear of and diabolising the other camp was the common trait of media during the Cold War. Total control of the media, although more apparent in the Soviet Union and its camp, also characterized the situation of the media in the adversary camp.

1.1.1.4. Post Cold War Media

The Cold War can rightfully be considered as a struggle for global influence between the United States and the Soviet Union. To achieve this global domination, the two countries employed a variety of methods, all short of a direct, all-out attack on each other's homelands. The methods they used included the creation of rival alliances, the extension of military and economic aid to client states and would-be client states, a massive and expensive arms race, propaganda campaigns, espionage, and guerrilla-warfare.

The Cold War was also one of the longest conflicts in human history, over seventy years in duration, with periodic lulls in the level of hostility. It was also the widest in scope of all the world's wars. Indeed, it was fought on every continent on the globe and even in space, considering the space race. The Cold War was also one of the costliest of the world's conflicts, not only in numbers of lives lost but also in resources expended. In the end, the Soviet Union collapsed, and communism, at least in the form that existed in the Soviet Union, expired.

The presidency of George Bush, who succeeded Ronald Reagan in January 1989, witnessed the end of the Cold War, the collapse of communism in Eastern Europe, and the disintegration of the Soviet Union itself. During Bush's presidency, the development of a new, post-Cold War relationship between the United States and what would become the successor states to the Soviet Union began. The new relationship would be characterized by cooperation rather than the confrontation that had been the hallmark of the Cold War.

Ironically, considering the important role that he would play in building the new Soviet-American relationship, Bush was slow to pick up the baton of détente. Gorbachev, in his speech before the United Nations on December 7, 1988, had challenged the then president-elect to end the Cold War. Not only did he announce a massive, unilateral reduction of Soviet armed forces and the withdrawal of ten

---

20   Idem.

divisions from Eastern Europe, he also challenged the United States to cooperate with the Soviet Union in resolving conflicts around the world, particularly in Afghanistan, Cambodia, Nicaragua, and Angola. Gorbachev also recommended that a revived United Nations should be the instrument of superpower cooperation in creating a new world order.

With this new concept (The New World Order) came another concept that is worth mentioning in this respect. This new concept is that of World Opinion. Franck Louis Rusciano defines this concept by saying that it's "the consensus that implies that nations generally share an opinion regarding proper behaviour in the international sphere, while the threat of isolation implies that nations are willing to act upon this consensus to punish errant nations or leaders"[21]. This can also mean that world opinion can be modelled according to international political directions and tendencies. In this respect, it can be regarded as a legitimatising political tool.

Lusciano conducted a very interesting comparative study around this concept in comparing the reference to this World Opinion in two newspapers covering the Gulf War. The purpose of Lusciano's study was to establish whether the perspective of World opinion and the usage of this term differed in an American newspaper (*The New York Times*) and a third World newspaper (*The Times of India*). Lusciano's conclusion was that while the two dailies tended to be very similar in their perspective on World opinion in this crisis, there were considerable differences that underscore the relative positions of the United States and India in the international community.

Lusciano's study and findings are quite interesting. They confirm the fact that the view depends actually on the viewer. In short, the way we perceive things depends largely on our feelings, needs, and aims. Lusciano mentions an interesting example of which can illustrate this idea. He mentions an image shown on television of the Iraqi president Saddam Hussein in the first eight weeks of the Gulf War crisis in which Saddam Hussein is shown on television with two British children being held in Baghdad. For the Iraqis this image was intended to illustrate the humane treatment of the westerners barred from leaving Baghdad. Yet, for the majority of the world media, it represented a tyrannical and cruel image of the Iraqi president.

The use of media to influence and alter public opinion has, thus, intensified in the post Cold War era. Some, however, might argue that this use of the media to influence public opinion suffered no change since the times of the Cold War. This is not exactly correct and for two reasons. The first is that anti-communist

---

21   See Robert E. Denton and Frank Louis Rusciano, <u>The Media and the Persian Gulf War</u>, Praeger Publishers, Westport, CT, 1993,pp.71-77.

and anti-liberal rhetoric was quite distinguishable during the period of the cold War and can easily be identified as propaganda. There was no such thing as consensus and world opinion. It was one camp against the other. The other reason is that the use of television to manipulate domestic and world public opinion by spotlighting a certain image really showed its effect in the post cold War era, especially with the coverage of the Gulf crisis and war. It is after the fall of the Berlin Wall that television proved itself to be a highly effective instrument of war. This advantage of the television over other types of media such as the printed media or the radio as an effective tool of altering public opinion is, of course, attributed to its technological characteristics. It is television that combines the image, the sound and the narration all at the same time. Ideas and suggestions can be implanted in the audience's minds more easily than worlds or voice alone can do.

Nevertheless, even with the New World Order and the end of the Cold War, the question of media freedom was not dealt with in the same way everywhere. Even with the end of communist threat and the *Perestroika* and *Glasnost*, the media wasn't entirely free from state intervention and censorship. Robert E. Denton explains that the problem with the media in democratic societies is to keep a balance between providing adequate information for informed citizen action (i.e. approval or disapproval) and the security and integrity of the national interests[22]. This naturally is even more evident in less or non-democratic countries. A good example of this can be seen in the way the Soviet Union's media dealt with the Chernobyl nuclear disaster of 1986 at the time of the *Perestroika* and *Glasnost* i.e. at the very end of the Cold War. In this respect, Marlyn J. Young and Michael K. Launer examine news coverage that appeared in three Soviet daily newspapers and on Soviet television from the day of the explosion until May the 14 when president Gorbachev addressed the nation. They state that there was a government's decision to conduct a continuous campaign in the press media, radio, and television in which government officials, scientists and health officials all aimed at reinforcing the official position of the Soviet government. Over the three years that followed the accident, Marlyn J. Young and Michael K. Launer claim, the aim of the government was to provide evidence according to which the Chernobyl tragedy was reconstructed as a triumph of technology and human courage under the guiding hand of the communist Party. They add that "the original glasnost initiative was a response to a complex of policy problems that the Party chairman viewed as insoluble without consensus formation. As such, it represented an innovative application of traditional Leninist thinking: The functions

---

22   Ibid. p. 27.

of the media were to "change the ethical and moral outlook of the population" and "rouse [the people] to contribute to the economic goals of the leadership"[23].

The role of the media in the post Cold War era can be said to have changed considerably. The introduction of new concepts such as the New World Order and, with it, the consciousness of the importance of World Opinion and the fear of exclusion or isolation are some of the most important characteristics of this transformation in the role of media. The emergence of television as an effective media tool to alter public opinion is another characteristic of this era. One can argue as well that the example of the Gulf War in this era announced the arrival of an interesting behaviour of the media which consists in spotlighting the world's opinion on a certain crisis situation in the world.

1.1.1.5. Tran-national Media: The New Actor on the International Scene

In the past years, a new and highly efficient actor has emerged on the international scene. Indeed, it is astonishing to contemplate the transformation of the spectrum of media coverage and audience from that geographically limited within the transmitting country to that were the audience is mainly a cross-border one. The BBC World Wide broadcasting service, CNN, NBC, TV5...etc. are mere examples of such new trans-national and cross-border media giants.

What probably contributed to the emergence of such a trans-national media is the development that occurred in the communication and journalistic theories over the years. Indeed, nowadays such theories are largely based on economic theories where there are consumers, market, production and competition for the market shares. Even such economic connotations were not always the same applied in all cases. For instance, Alan Thomas, in a 1960 study of the Canadian media, tries to establish the distinction between three notions that basically could mean the same thing (the audience, the market and the public)[24].

Thomas states that the evolution of Canadian broadcasting was dominated by the interaction between these different names of the receiving end. Thomas explains that the market is characterized by attention to things rather than people. He argues that this concept is by nature more attentive to private enterprises than to the interests of the state as a whole. On the other hand, the public, according to Thomas, is identified with the state and the community. Thomas explains, for instance, that Canada's problem was how to create a genuine public

---

23   See Marlyn J. Young and Michael K. Launer, "Redefining Glasnost in the Soviet Media", <u>Journal of Communications</u>, vol. 41, no. 2, 1991, pp. 102-105.

24   See Alan Thomas M, Audience, "Market and Public-An Evaluation of Canadian Broadcasting", <u>Canadian Communications</u>, vol.1, N°1, 1960, pp.16-47.

out of separate geographic (as well as linguistic and cultural) communities: The audience, for Thomas, is made up of members of the public as well as the market when they are tuned in. As such, and unlike the public or the market, the audience is wholly a creation of broadcasting and does not exist without it.

The transformation of the role and objectives of trans-national media through the public transmission services all over the world cannot go unnoticed. For example, traditionally, public service broadcasting has been expected to represent the national as opposed to the foreign. Nowadays these conceptual categories are reflected in terms of the local and the global. Global cultural industries recognize this by developing products targeted to "niche markets". Public broadcasting has a different role, which it seeks to fulfil principally by conceiving its audience as a public rather than a market.

In order to fully understand the scope of the effect and influence of the trans-national media, it is important to examine what's called "a trans-national company or cooperation". Richard A. Gershon defines the trans-national corporation (TNC) as a "nationally based company with overseas operations in two or more countries". For him, one distinctive feature of the trans-national corporation (TNC) is that strategic decision making and the allocation of resources is predicated upon economic goals and efficiencies with little regard to national boundaries[25]. Gershon explains that what distinguishes the trans-national media corporations (TNMCs) from other types of TNCs is that the principle product being sold is information and entertainment. The trans-national media corporation has become a salient feature of today's global economic landscape.

Another important consideration, for Gershon, is that today's TNMCs and trans-national telecommunications corporations (TNTCs) are highly differentiated in their approach to business. The business strategies and corporate culture of today's TNMCs and TNTCs are often a direct reflection of the person (or persons) who were responsible for developing the organization and its business mission[26]. Today's media companies continue to grow and expand. Indeed the challenges of staying globally competitive become increasingly difficult. Such a behaviour of competition has engendered a new competitive spirit that cuts across nationality and economic class. Its what Gershon calls "a new form of economic Darwinism", characterized by a belief that size (and complementary strengths) is crucial to business survival[27]. Hence, it can be argued that trans-national media, with its

---

25   See Richard A. Gershon, "The Trans-national Media Corporation: Environmental Scanning and Strategy Formulation"; Journal of Media Economics. vol. 13, N°. 2, 2000, PP. 81–95.

26   Ibid.

27   Idem.

extension and structure, can sometimes crush local or domestic media. It can also be said that personal tendencies and objectives of the trans-national media's management can highly affect the conduct and positions of the trans-national media itself.

It is essential to note that the extraordinary growth of TNMC[28]s in the latter part of the 1980s has had a profound influence over the international sale and distribution of media products and services. H. Mowlana claims that the TNMC has become one of the chief organizers and manufacturers of the international flow of communication. The TNMC is capable of promoting and distributing a set of messages that effectively bypasses traditional channels of communication, including family, church, and schools. The messages of advertising, television, and film are often culturally laden and can sometimes promote political attitudes and social beliefs that are contrary to the values of the host nation and its domestic culture[29]. The power of the TNMC has become so evident that they have become the new target of criticism and accusations. Indeed, the terms media or (cultural) imperialism that were once so popular in the 1970s has given way to a more revised thinking about the role of western media exports. This opinion is advocated by McAnany & Wilkinson who state that the United States and western media are no longer the primary targets for such research and investigation. Instead, the TNMC has become more of the focus on issues of political hegemony and cultural influence. According to them, the TNMC has become the dominant force in the production, sale, and distribution of international media products[30]. The predominant role and size of the use media exports cannot be ignored in this respect. Accordingly, many countries in the world have introduced legislations and barriers to try to limit the influence of the U.S. media industries on other countries and nations of the world and to limit the extent of this new cultural imperialism.

It is obvious then that the trans-national mass media companies have come to take a primary role on the international scene. This fact is evident in the effect of such media on the world public behaviour. Such an effect can be seen in the threats to the traditional state sovereignty such a trans-national mass media can pose. Indeed, the tendency is to always seek to create a bigger and more influential trans-national mass media cooperation or company all the time. This is evident in the numerous merger and acquisition operations between mass media companies. This also shows that size in media does matter, as far as its influence is concerned.

---

28   Trans-National Media Corporations.

29   See H. Mowlana," The new sovereigns: Multinational Corporations as World Powers", <u>Englewood Cliffs</u>, NJ, 1975, pp. 77-90.

30   See McAnany, E., & Wilkinson, K., "From Cultural Imperialists to Takeover Victims", <u>Communication Research</u>, vol. 19, N°.6, 1992, pp. 724-748.

1.1.2. The Relationship Between National Media and National Politics

The relationship between national media and national politics is an interesting relationship indeed. It is a relationship that can be looked at as a rebel oppressor relationship from the point of view of the media and as a trustee-minor relationship from the point of view of the political establishment. It is quite interesting to examine the real nature of this relationship and to see whether the nature of the government system has any real effect on the nature of the relationship between the national media and the government.

1.1.2.1. National Political Tendencies and Media Manifestations

It is important to note the fact that national politics do actually manifest themselves via the domestic media in any given country. This of course is done to enhance political decisions and orientations of the governing authorities. It might, however, be argued that such a model of behaviour in which the media is actually a direct tool of the politicians can only be found in non-democratic or autocratic countries. This is not the case. In fact such behaviour can also be found in countries that have a long tradition of democratic practice.

According to Robert M. Entman[31] journalists in the United States, for instance, cannot be void of their own personal feelings and political tendencies. This, according to Entman results in a situation where some political, economic, or social facts and events are emphasized and not others, influencing by the process the public opinion. For his part, Matthew Robert Kerbel explains the manner in which the media cover presidential campaigns in the United States using the example of frames. He states that between quite a number of manifestations relating to an election campaign such as petition writing, voting, letter writing or any of the other activities related to election campaigns in a democracy, the press might choose to concentrate on one aspect of those instead of others. Instead, he argues that the media would present the election as a mere quest for power by candidates. After consuming this coverage, the audience experiences the campaign in these terms. In essence, Kerbel says, the press is determining the frame of reference—the frame—within which we can make sense of the disparate information emanating from election campaigns. He compares the frame provided by media coverage with a window frame, the scene through which will vary depending upon the size, placement, and clarity of the window as well as upon where the

---

31   Entman, Robert M., <u>Democracy without Citizens: Media and the Decay of American Politics</u>, Oxford University Press, New York, 1989,.PP. 30-31.

viewer is standing while looking out. Similarly, the manner in which information is conceptualised in news stories, Kerbel explains, will influence how that information is understood[32]. Thus, the manner through which a fact is presented can affect the manner in which this fact is perceived.

There is, however, no globally accepted definition of news frame or framing although the ones that exist indicate, in general, similar characteristics. For instance, news frames are "conceptual tools which media and individuals rely on to convey, interpret and evaluate information" [33]. For others, frames set the parameters "in which citizens discuss public events"[34]. They are "persistent selection, emphasis, and exclusion"[35]. For some, framing is selecting "some aspects of a perceived reality" to enhance their salience "in such a way as to promote a particular problem definition, causal interpretation, moral evaluation, and/or treatment recommendation"[36]. For others, frames are to help audiences "locate, perceive, identify, and label" the flow of information around them[37] and to "narrow the available political alternatives" [38]. To overcome these diverse interpretations, the simplest solution is probably to consider frames as a manner of perception.

Framing effects are also a somewhat controversial issue. Some claim that framing effects are "changes in judgment engendered by subtle alterations in the definition of judgment or choice of problems"[39]. Others define framing effect as "one in which salient attributes of a message (its organization, selection of content, or thematic structure) render particular thoughts applicable, resulting in their activation and use in evaluations" [40]. Experiments with question wording, for example, show that the framing of choices can have profound consequences for respondents'

---

32   See Matthew Robert Kerbel, <u>Remote & Controlled: Media Politics in a Cynical Age</u>, Westview Press, Boulder, CO., 1998, pp. 59-65.

33   See Neuman, W. R., Just, M. R., & Crigler, A. N, <u>Common knowledge</u>, University of Chicago Press, Chicago, 1992, p. 60.

34   See G. Tuchman, <u>Making News, Free Press</u>, New York, 1978, p. IV.

35   See T. Gitlin, <u>The Whole World is Watching, : Mass Media in the Making and the Unmaking of the New Left</u>, University of California Press, Berkeley, 1980, p.7.

36   See Robert M. Entman, "Framing: Towards the Clarification of a Fractured Paradigm", <u>Journal of Communications</u>, vol. 43, N°. 3., 1993, p.53.

37   See E. Gofman, <u>Frame Analysis: An Assay on the Organization of Experience</u>, Harper &Row, New York, 1974, p. 21.

38   See Tuchman, <u>Op. Cit.</u>, p.156.

39   See S. Iyangar & Kinder D.R., <u>News that Matters</u>, University of Chicago Press, Chicago, 1987, p. 816.

40   See Price, V., et al, "Switching Frames of Thought: The Impact of News Frames on Readers", <u>Communication Research</u>, vol.24, 1997, p. 486.

perception of risk [41]. Here again and to reach a simplified understanding, it can be said that framing a news item would shape the audience's reaction to that item.

As far as types of frames are concerned, five main news frames have been identified in numerous studies. These are the Conflict Frame, the Human Interest Frame, the Economic Consequences Frame, the Morality Frame and the Responsibility Frame.

For its part, the Conflict Frame stresses the conflict between individuals, groups, or institutions as a means of capturing audience attention. Some studies found that the media draw on a few central frames for reporting a range of issues and that conflict was the most common in the handful of frames in U.S. news[42]. Others have also noted that discussion in the news between political elites often reduces complex substantive political debate to overly simplistic conflict. For instance, presidential election campaign news in the U.S. is framed largely in terms of conflict[43]. Some writers suggest that, due to this emphasis on conflict, the news media have often been criticized for inducing public cynicism and mistrust of political leaders[44].

The Human Interest frame induces a human face or an emotional perspective to the presentation of an event, issue, or problem. Neuman et al. described this as the "human impact" frame, and, next to conflict, found it to be a common frame in the news[45]. Indeed, the market for news being more and more competitive, journalists are finding it harder to come up with news that captures the audiences interest. In this sense, framing news in human interest terms is one way to achieve this. In fact, such a frame refers to an effort to personalize the news, dramatize or "emotionalise" the news, in order to capture and retain audience interest.

The Economic Consequences Frame is that which reports an event, a problem, or an issue in terms of its economic consequences on the individual, group, institution, region, or country. Neuman et al. identifies it as a common frame in the news[46]. Some writers emphasize that the wide impact of an event is an important news value, and economic consequences are often considerable[47]. This is

41   See D. Kahneman, & Tversky, A., "The Psychology of Preferences", Scientific American, N° 246, 1982, pp. 6-42.

42   See Neuman et al., op. cit., pp.61-62

43   See T. Patterson, Out of Order, Knopf, New York, 1993.

44   See J. Cappella & Jameson, K., Spiral of cynicism, Oxford University Press, New York, 1997.

45   See Neuman et al., op cit.

46   Ibid.

47   See D.,Graber, Mass Media and American Politics, CQ Press, Washington, DC, 1993.

quite natural since all individuals in a society are generally attentive to the stability of their economic situation.

As far as it is concerned, the Morality Frame places the event, problem, or issue in the context of religious tenets or moral prescriptions. Due to the professional nature of objectivity, journalists usually refer to moral frames indirectly (through quotation or inference, for instance) by having someone else raise the question. For instance, a newspaper could use the views of an interest group to raise questions about sexually transmitted diseases. A story like that may contain moral messages or offer specific social prescriptions about how to behave. However, Neuman et al found this frame to be more common in the minds of audiences than in the content of news. They, notwithstanding, identified this frame as among the several used in reporting[48].

The Responsibility Frame introduces an issue or a problem in such a way as to attribute responsibility for its cause or solution to either the government or to an individual or a group. Notwithstanding the fact that the existence of a responsibility frame in the news has not been measured explicitly, the U.S. news media have been credited with (or blamed for) shaping public understanding of who is responsible for causing or solving key social problems, such as poverty[49]. For instance, Iyengar argues that television news—by covering an issue or problem in terms of an event, instance, or individual (episodically) rather than in terms of the larger historical social context (thematically)—encourages people to offer individual level explanations for social problems[50]. Therefore, for him, the poor woman on welfare is held responsible for her fate, rather than the government or the system.

An excellent study has been done, in this respect, concerning the news framing in European media by Holli A. Semetko and Patti M. Valkenburg[51]. They investigated the prevalence of 5 news frames identified in earlier studies on framing and framing effects: attribution of responsibility, conflict, human interest, economic consequences, and morality. They, furthermore, content analysed 2,601 newspaper stories and 1, 522 television news stories in the period surrounding the Amsterdam meetings of the European Heads of State in 1997. The results of their study indicates that, overall, the attribution of responsibility frame was most

---

48   See Neuman et al.,op. cit., p.75.

49   See S. Iyangar & Kinder D.R.,op. cit.

50   See S. Iyangar, Is Anyone Responsible: How Television Frames Political issues, University of Chicago Press, Chicago, 1991.

51   See Holli A Semetko and Patti M. Valkenburg, "Framing European Politics: A Content Analysis of Press and Television News", Journal of Communication, vol. 50.N° 2, 2000, pp.93-109.

commonly used in the news, followed by the conflict, economic consequences, human interest, and morality frames, respectively. The study also indicates that the use of news frames depended on both the type of outlet and the type of topic. Furthermore, most significant differences were not between media (television vs. the press) but between sensationalists vs. serious types of news outlets. In addition, sober and serious newspapers and television news programs more often used the responsibility and conflict frames in the presentation of news, whereas sensationalist outlets more often used the human-interest frame.

Manifestations of politics in the media are, thus, a natural thing through different frames of course. In fact, what Entman says about the fact that journalists cannot distance themselves from their personal feelings or political convictions is quite understandable. If one looks at the picture as a whole, the idea of "framing" the issues for the consumer also makes sense, since all media have their own political convictions that are inherent to them and different from others. It is the case, then, that one ends up seeing the picture in different frames depending on the media that presents it and its own motivations and convictions.

This example of the election campaigns is a good reflection of the manifestations of politics in national media. In our days, more than ever before, candidates go before the people through the mass media rather than in person[52]. In fact, the information in the mass media becomes the only contact many have with politics. The pledges, promises, and rhetoric encapsulated in news stories, columns, and editorials constitute much of the information upon which a voting decision has to be made. Most of what people know comes to them "second" or "third" hand from the mass media or from other people[53]. Although the evidence that mass media deeply change attitudes in a campaign is far from conclusive,[54] the evidence is much stronger that voters learn from the immense quantity of information available during each campaign[55]. People, of course, vary greatly in their attention to mass media because some are more influenced than others by the media in their convictions.

52   See Bernard R. Berelson, Paul F. Lazarsfeld, and William N. McPhee, Voting, University of Chicago Press, Chicago, 1954, p. 234.

53   See Kurt Lang and Gladys Engel Lang, "The Mass Media and Voting", in Bernard Berelson and Morris Janowitz, eds., Reader in Public Opinion and Communication, 2d ed., New York, Free Press, 1966, p. 466.

54   See Berelson et al., op. cit., p. 223; Paul F. Lazarsfeld, Bernard Berelson, and Hazel Gaudet, The People's Choice, Columbia University Press, New York, 1948, p. xx; and Joseph Trenaman and Denis McQuail, Television and the Political Image, Methuen and Co., London, 1961, pp. 147, 191.

55   See Bernard C. Cohen, The Press and Foreign Policy, Princeton University Press, Princeton, 1963, p. 120.

There is in fact a very important function of the media that has to be explored in this respect. This function is called the Agenda-Setting function of the media. Cohen has an interesting way of describing this function of the media. He says that "the press may not be successful most of the time in telling people what to think, but it is stunningly successful in telling its readers what to think about"[56]. Indeed, while the mass media have little influence on the direction or intensity of attitudes, it is hypothesized that the mass media set the agenda for each political campaign influencing the salience of attitudes towards the political issue.

An excellent example of this agenda-setting function of the media is that referred to by Maxwell McCombs. McCombs includes a study done to determine the agenda-setting capacity of the mass media in the 1968 presidential campaign. This study attempted to match what a city in the United States (Chapel Hill) voters said were key issues of the presidential campaign, with the actual content of the mass media they were exposed to during the campaign[57]. Two main adjectives were given to the news coverage of the campaign: major and minor news. The distinction between major or minor news depended on the kind of media used (printed or television). In short, the study considered that major events in television were any story 45 seconds or more in length and/or one of the three lead stories. In newspapers, a major item was any story, which appeared as the lead on the front page or on any page under a three-column headline in which at least one-third of the story (a minimum of five paragraphs) was devoted to political news coverage. In news magazines, it was any story more than one column or any item, which appeared in the lead at the beginning of the news section of the magazine. As far as editorial page coverage of newspapers and magazines was concerned, any item in the lead editorial position (the top left corner of the editorial page) plus all items was considered a major one.

The findings of the study was that the over-all major item emphasis of the selected mass media on different topics and candidates during the campaign (see Table 1 below) indicates that a considerable amount of campaign news was not devoted to discussion of the major political issues but rather to analysis of the campaign itself.

---

56 Idem, p.13.
57 See Maxwell McCombs & Donald Show, <u>Agenda Setting: Readings on Media, Public Opinion, and Policymaking</u>, Lawrence Erlbaum Associates, Hillsdale, NJ. 1991, pp. 17-25.

Table 1: Major Mass Media Reports on Candidates and Issues, By Candidates.

Quoted Source

The Issues	Nixon	Agnew	Humphrey	Muskie	Wallace	Lemay	Total
Foreign Policy	7	%9	%13	%15	%2	%-	10%
Law and Order	5	13	4	-	12	-	6
Fiscal Policy	3	4	2	-	-	-	2
Public welfare	3	4	(*b	5	2	-	2
Civil Rights	3	9	(*)b	0	4	-	2
Other	19	13	14	25	11	-	15

The Campaign

Polls	1	-	-	-	1	-	(*)b
Campaign Events	18	9	21	10	25	-	19
Campaign Analysis	25	17	30	30	35	-	28

Other Candidates

Humphrey	11	22	-	5	1	-	5
Muskie	-	-	-	-	-	-	-
Nixon	-	-	11	5	3	-	5
Agnew	-	-	(*)b	-	-	-	(*)b
Wallace	5	-	3	5	-	-	3
Lemay	1	-	1	-	4	-	1
Total Percent	101	%100	%99c	100	%100	%-	98%
Total Number	188	23	221	20	95	11	558

Source :Maxwell McCombs & Donald Show , Agenda Setting: Readings on Media, Public Opinion, and Policymaking, Lawrence Erlbaum Associates, Hillsdale, NJ. 1991, p.20.
A=Coverage of Lemay amounted to only 11 major Items during the September 12-October 6 period and are not Individually Included in the percentages; they are included In the total column.
B=Less than .05 per cent.
C=Does not sum to 100% because of rounding

The findings of this survey may alter the ideas of people who think of campaign news as being primarily about the issues. For instance, 35% percent of the major news coverage of the candidate Wallace was composed of this analysis ("Has he a chance to win or not?'). For the candidates Humphrey and Nixon the figures were, respectively, 30 % and 25 %. At the same time, table one indicates also the relative emphasis of candidates speaking about each other. The candidate Agnew, for example, apparently spent more time attacking the candidate Humphrey (22 % of the major news items about Agnew) than did Nixon (11 % of the major news about Nixon). Curiously enough, the over-all minor item emphasis of the mass media on these political issues and topics closely paralleled that of major items.

Although as, Mcombs and Show put it, the existence of an agenda-setting function of the mass media is not proved by the correlations reported in this study, the evidence is in line with the conditions that must exist if agenda-setting by the mass media does occur[58]. They add "Interpreting the evidence from this study as indicating mass media influence seems more plausible than alternative explanations. Any argument that the correlations between media and voter emphasis are spurious—that they are simply responding to the same events and not influencing each other one way or the other-assumes that voters have alternative means of observing the day-to-day changes in the political arena. This assumption is not plausible"[59].

Political manifestations in the media are, thus, a normal behavior and if correlation does exist this means that both the media and the audience affect, react, and possibly change their behavior because of each other all the time. These manifestations can be the result of this agenda setting function of the media and are usually manifested via one or more of the so far identified media frames.

1.1.2.2. The Media's Role of Surveillance of the Governmental Establishment

One of the most important roles of the media is that of surveillance of the governmental or political establishment's actions, policies and decisions. This role is essential to the media's existence and one of the main reasons behind its calling the "fourth estate". It is interesting to know if such a role actually exists. And if it does exist how far can it apply to the current relationship between the national media and the governmental establishment.

This role of the media as the "fourth estate" or an agent of the social change didn't always exist as such. In fact, it developed with the development of the media itself. John Eldridge et al.[60] explains, for instance, that traditional interpretations of the development of the mass media in Britain depicts a struggle by the press to gain its freedom from the state and political interests in the British society. This struggle was won in the middle of the 19th century with the cancellation of the 'taxes on knowledge[61]. After the cancellation of these taxes, the press was seen as being a check on government or what has come to be called the "fourth estate".

John Eldridge et al.[62] further suggest that, according to this view of history, new media further develop the ways in which the media and communications

---

58   Maxwell McCombs & Donald Show, op. cit., p.25.

59   Idem.

60   See John Eldridge et al, The Mass Media and Power in Modern Britain, Oxford University, Oxford, 1997, pp.10-25.

61   These largely were taxes on newspapers and periodicals which raised their prices beyond the reach of the vast majority of the British people

62   See John Eldridge et al., op. cit.

industries can contribute to the extension of democracy. Therefore, the birth of the cinema and the wireless, for example, in the first half of the twentieth century and the post-war emergence of television helped to expand mass democracy and the democratic process.

However, those who fear the impact of mass communications on the society do not share this view. For them, the development of the mass media is not a steady march toward more freedom but a history of constantly changing forms of control. The partisans of this view argue that the media is more of agencies of social control, in the hands of an established authority or a dominant class who can manage and manipulate the emergence of mass opinion and mass democracy to serve their purposes. According to this context, the middle of the 19th century did not witness the establishment of the freedom of the press, but rather a change from state control to market control of mass communication. An example of those is J. Curran, who, in his account of the struggle for the cancellation of the taxes on knowledge, explained this as the main objective of many of those involved in the campaign against the press taxes[63].

The accent was on the role the press would play in the engineering of social consent. The birth of the wireless service, seventy-five years later, was accompanied by similar concerns about the power of the media on the society and the masses. For instance, the Committee for Imperial Defence[64] considered that the

---

63   See J. Curran, <u>Capitalism and Control of the Press 1900-1975</u>, Edward Arnold, London, 1977.

64   The Middle East, already an area of immense strategic importance during the 1920s and 1930s, assumed even greater significance as the Second World War approached. The discovery and exploitation of large oil resources had already brought the region to the attention of the world's major powers, all of whom were faced with growing demands for oil from industry, increasingly mechanised armies, and (most importantly for Britain) their Navies. Britain, being the dominant colonial force in the area with colonies, mandates and protectorates in Egypt, Anglo-Egyptian Sudan, British Somaliland, Iraq, Palestine, Trans-Jordan, Aden, Kuwait and Muscat and Oman, was obviously keen to keep a close watch on events both in the Middle East, and further a field. The scramble for oil rights (involving American, British, Dutch and French companies amongst others) was exacerbated by the Arab Revolt in Palestine, a reaction to British support for a Jewish homeland, and increasing demands for greater autonomy throughout the region. The Committee of Imperial Defence (CID) was established in 1902, as an advisory body with no executive powers. With the assistance of numerous sub-committees (such as the Oil Board and the Middle East Sub-Committee) it advised the Cabinet and government departments on both general principles and on detailed issues. The Prime Minister was its Chairman and only permanent member.

emergence of broadcasting had 'incalculable significance for political stability[65]. The Committee was afraid of the power of the new medium to act as an instrument of propaganda and worked strongly against allowing any private individual with sufficient funds to broadcast. According to N. Pronay and Spring[66], this was a risk that the Committee felt impossible to take. Here again the best solution to this dilemma was that the new medium should be placed in trusted hands.

For their part, John Eldridge et al, say that the conceptualisation of the mass media as being either the 'fourth estate' or 'agencies of social control' is an oversimplification. They suggest that the role of the mass media in any period in time is largely shaped by factors particular to that period under consideration as well as the medium under study. Furthermore, according to them, further detailed examination means that such conceptualisations become more complex and qualified. Nevertheless, they explain that history does show that central to any debate about the power of the media is an understanding of the countervailing pulls on the mass media as the representatives of the public, the public opinion, and the masses and as the agents of control exercised by the state and the dominant institutions in society. This, they explain, has raised questions throughout history about the impact of the mass media on their audience, the nature and extent of censorship, the power of owners to influence the content of the media, and the relationship between the media and their audience[67].

The question is at this point, does the British model of development of the media and its relationship with the government apply to all other systems of government or countries. Some scholars[68] identified as much as four theories concerning the government-media relationship. These four theories are the authoritarian, libertarian, communist, and social responsibility perspectives theory. Although they are presented as distinctive sets of relationships, the basic distinction is that which exists between authoritarian and libertarian views. The remaining two are considered variations and/or compromises along this fundamental dichotomy.

The opinions concerning these theories are as controversial as they are many. Siebert et al.[69] consider, for instance, that in an authoritarian system the governing regime is the highest authority. Its task is to direct the citizenry whom the

---

65   See N. Pornay and Spring D. W., (eds.), <u>Propaganda, Politics and Film 1918-45</u>,
      Macmillan, London, 1982, p. 13.

66   Idem.

67   See John Eldridge et al, <u>op. cit.</u>

68   See Michael D. Mansfield and Dan D. Nimmo, <u>Government and the News Media:
      Comparative Dimensions</u>, Baylor University Press, Waco, TX., 1982, p.1-9.

69   See F. S. Siebert et al., <u>Theories of the Press</u>, University of Illinois Press, Urbana,
      1956.

political system considers as a group of people not in themselves competent to make self-governing decisions. In this sense, the role of mass communication, and certainly of the news media, is to support the governing regime and the elite who make the decisions. Since the national government decides who can and cannot exercise the journalistic privilege, press freedom extends only so far as the regime is willing to permit.

On the other hand, a libertarian or democratic system is one that is open, nondirective, and pluralist in character. The idea in this case is that of a citizenry of rational beings, possessed with individual rights, and competent for self-government. In this sense, the role of the press would be to provide sort of a free marketplace of ideas where through competition" truth can be discovered". In this context J. C. Merrill explains that the libertarian viewpoint has evolved over the years to include the general notion of the news media as being the "fourth branch of government". This translates into an independent, free institution whose task is to inform the public about their government, whether or not such reporting is supportive of the government's policies[70].

The third theory is the communist one. According to this theory, the governing regime in such a political system is the Communist Party. Some scholar label this theory as a a variant of the authoritarian one. In such a system, the media is a tool of the party. Its role in this case is to provide support of the regime's decisions and ideology.

The fourth theory is that called the social responsibility one. It is, to some scholars, a variant of the libertarian one. The role of the media's responsibility is to serve the public interest and promote the social good and the social welfare. In an ideal situation, the media can achieve this aim in a self-regulating fashion. However, if it did not, the intervention of the government in the name of the public good may take place.

There is an important default to the Siebert et al. model. It would be indeed difficult to distinguish the boundaries between political systems. They are to say the least ambiguous. It is, thus, difficult to apply the four theories exactly as the dominant representations of government-media relation's model. For instance, would the communist model apply to countries of Eastern Europe? And now with the collapse of the communist regime in Russia, how would such a model apply?. In addition, quite a number of regimes of third world countries and of current Eastern European states have a mixture of socialist and authoritarian characteristics.

The media's role of surveillance of the governmental establishment is a role that has different variations and appearances. It varies according to the government or the regime to be surveyed. In other words, the extent of this role depends

---

70   See J. C. Merrill, The Imperative of Freedom, Hastings House, New York, 1974.

on the extent given to the press by the governing regime. Furthermore, the media's role as the "fourth estate" or an agent of the social change for the "social good of the public" can sometimes be undermined or censored by the government or the regime for the "greater good of the nation" or, in other terms, the higher national interest of the state. This can take place regardless of the type of regime or political system of the country.

1.1.2.3. Government Influence on National Media

The influence of the government or the political establishment on the national media cannot be ignored. Though this influence might be unnoticeable in democratic systems of government, it is quiet apparent in authoritarian or dictatorial ones. It is necessary, therefore, to examine the influence of the government on the media in both types of government.

Notwithstanding the fact that it's rarely apparent, the influence of a democratic government on its media does actually exist. Michael W. Mansfield has included a marvellous collection of studies of the relationship between different "democratic" governments in the world and the media in those countries[71]. An interesting example of this can be found in the study conducted by David G. Boyce of the British government and the British News Media[72]. Boyce's choice of the British media as a subject of this study was that it was in Britain that the classic doctrines governing the relationship between the government and the media were formulated in particular in the late 18th and early 19th centuries. The aim of his study was to examine a situation where a liberal government tries to combine its advocating of a free press with what Boyce calls its "watching of the public interests".

Boyce explains that in an ideal situation, from a liberal theorists' point of view, a democratic government would set aside and let the free press communicate to a free people. This means that there would be no constraints on the media's role of expressing itself. Yet, this is not the case. In his study of the British media, Boyce explains that economic factors had an enormous effect in the imposition of constraints on the British press in the early 19th century. The press, which paid its various taxes and duties to the state, was suffering from the competition of the unstamped, illegal, and radical press, which flourished in the political ferment of England after Waterloo. The argument at the time was that by reducing press taxation, the government would encourage investments in the newspaper markets and direct the flow of advertising to the most favourable newspapers. Boyce explains that it was a convincing argument for the government that the free

---

71   Michael W. Mansfield, op. cit.
72   Ibid, pp.79-88

market would help favour certain newspapers over others. With the repeal of the last remaining "tax on knowledge"[73] in 1861, the way was opened for the press to become big business. For now it is logical to think that with economic well being of a newspaper came naturally a political independence, which would give it more of a right to be labelled as the fourth estate. Yet, economic factors were not the only elements in which a press can be influenced.

It is interesting to know that governments in the 19th century were prepared to drop legislative control of the press. This wasn't the only method of control governments had. Indeed, there were other means of influencing journalists, by an exchange of information, for example, or by assiduous cultivation of well-disposed editors. In fact, in the early 20th century, as some newspapers ran into increasingly acute financial difficulties under competition from Lord[74] Northcliffe's mass appeal press, there was always the chance to inject sums of money from party funds. Such expedients did not always ensure loyalty, but at least they kept politicians in touch with newspapers; and newspaper editors gratefully received contributions, while at the same time insisting that they were independent political figures[75].

As far as the new media is concerned, Boyce explains that Wireless broadcasting began in the United Kingdom in 1920. Two years later the Marconi company[76] began to provide regular broadcast services. In 1922 the Post Office authorised a British Broadcasting Company to start work, replacing the Marconi company, and consisting of representatives of the major wireless companies, with the smaller companies invited to join. Until 1926, Boyce emphasizes, the BBC was not a public body; but neither was it an ordinary commercial enterprise. In fact, the shares of the Post Office were restricted to 7½ percent. Meanwhile the government set up a committee under the chairmanship of Sir Frederick Sykes[77] to examine the financial, organizational, and national implications of the new medium. Its deliberations were shaped by a number of factors: by the example of the United States, where a free-for-all in the broadcasting world had quickly produced a "cacaphony of the air"; and by the feeling that to allow financing from

---

73   This was actually the name of the tax on newspapers at the time.
74   Alfred Charles William Harmsworth, later Alfred Lord Northcliffe (1865-1922) was a British newspaper pioneer who revolutionised magazine and newspaper publishing in Britain in the early years of the twentieth century, and who wielded significant political power through the medium of his popular dailies.
75   See Boyce, D. G., Curran, J., & Wingate, P., Newspaper History: From the 17th Century to the Present Day, London: Constable, 1978. pp. 19-40.
76   Marconi House was opened on 25 March 1912 on the Strand. Marconi House was later to house the 2L0 transmitter, which began broadcasting for an hour daily on 11 May 1922 before the formation of the BBC.
77   Sykes, Sir Frederick Hugh (1877-1954) Knight Major General

advertisements would inevitably lower standards. It was this fear of what wireless could do to the people, if not properly supervised, that helped shape the final form of the BBC, a form recommended by the Crawford Committee[78] in 1926. Smith explains in this respect that The BBC was to be a public corporation, "acting as Trustee for the national interest," led by a board of governors, under a chairman appointed by the Crown. He adds that its ultimate controller would be a government official, the Postmaster General, who issued wireless licences and collected licence fees[79]. Yet, the BBC's first Charter did not contain any prohibitions or restrictions on its work.

With this obvious legitimate freedom in the Charter of the BBC, it is logical to expect that it would be totally free from government control in the pursuing of its business and its political orientations. This, however, was not the case. Indeed, several examples can be given of the British governments intervention in the cooperation's work can be given. An interesting example of this can actually be seen in the intervention of Sir Winston Churchill in 1926 to prevent the BBC from holding a debate over a general strike, which he regarded as illegal. Moreover, the British government pressured the BBC not to give permission to a spokesman from the trade union. When, in fact, the BBC tried to intervene an present an editorial of the situation, the Postmaster General objected saying that such editorials should be referred to him first for approval.

An important issue at hand here for its relevance to this research's subject is the role of the BBC at the time of crisis. This role was quite evident in the Second World War. The reason behind the importance of the role of an establishment, such as the BBC, at the time stems from the speed in which it can transmit and disseminate the information in times of crisis, which gave it an excellent edge over newspapers. Boyce explains that this role was so vital to the British government at

---

78 The British Broadcasting Company was founded in 1922 when the government licensed the six major radio manufacturers and some smaller ones to form a limited company. It was agreed that a licence fee collected by the Post Office and payable by anyone owning a receiver should finance it (Cain 9). In 1925, however, the first government license was to expire. By this time, the manufacturers focused more on competing with one another to sell their wireless sets than on the company's programming output and, on the other hand, the Post Office, as a public body expressed reluctance to collect the licence fees on behalf of a private company. Owing to the circumstances mentioned above, the government created a committee, under the leadership of the Earl of Crawford to carry out a close analysis on the future of broadcasting in Britain. It became known as the Crawford Committee and was required to report in 1926

79 See Smith, A. (Ed.), <u>British Broadcasting</u>, David & Charles, Newton Abbott, 1974. pp.50-55

the time. He also emphasizes the fact that it was important for the British government that the BBC does not look as the government propaganda machine and that it would enjoy as much credibility as possible[80]. One of the most important illustrations of the government's realisation of the power of the BBC during times of crisis can be seen in the establishment in 1935 of the Ministry of Information, which was meant to be sort of a censoring machine of the BBC's conduct.

Indeed, there are numerous examples of the British government's interventions in the work of the BBC, which illustrate the relationship that exists between these two institutions. For its role the BBC was trying to conserve its role as the "fourth estate" while the government could not abandon its role as the deciding body and the one that knows better the national interests of the country. This debate was quite evident through out the 1970's and 1980's with a number of controversial programs on the BBC such as "A Question of Ulster" in which a number of representatives of northern Ireland were interviewed on British TV. The debates over such issues of the freedom of the press and the national interests of the state had their contribution in the appearance of what Boyce calls "the Social Responsibility theory" of the press[81]. This theory meant, in short, that journalism is so important that it can't be left to journalists alone. This notion, of course, can be related back to the one that existed in the 1920's concerning the "irresponsible press".

It is obvious from the example of the British media situation that there is actually a control of the state or the political establishment over the performance of the media and its orientations. The example of the British media was given to illustrate the fact that the press or the media can be restrained and oriented even in one of the most democratic systems in the world. Indeed, it's not just in autocratic, dictatorial or undemocratic systems of government that such control exists. Of course, the argument of the degree of control or intervention can always be advanced to support the position of democratic systems. It might be, rightfully, claimed that the liberties of the press or the media in democratic societies cannot be compared to the liberties that exist in non-democratic systems. Nonetheless, though this might be true, it is not a question of how much liberty is there, it's actually a question restrictions to that liberty, whether they exist or not. In that sense the question of the social responsibility or the national responsibility of the media arises.

In a sense, the question can be summed in one equation:-Which is more important a free media or the national interests of the state?. In an ideal situation, however, the national interests of a state would be the same as those of the media. This is rarely the case. In fact, the truth as they say always hurts. States would

---

80   Ibid.
81   Idem.

always have some sort of control over there media regardless whether those states were democratic or not. States would always intervene, if they have to, to direct or redirect the media and will continue to censor when it is in there interests to censor. It is, indeed, difficult with this logic to still label the media as the "fourth estate" since it's "sovereignty" is jeopardized automatically by the sovereignty of the state or the state system in power.

1.1.3. National Media and International Politics

The relationship between national media and international politics can be regarded in two main ways. The first of these means of examining this relationship is to study the effect of the international political orientations on the domestic or national media. This would perhaps help clarify some of the domestic media's positions or points of view vis-à-vis certain issues or international crisis. On the other hand, the other way of looking at this relationship would possibly help clarify the effect of the national media on international politics. In other words, would the media orientations of the media of a certain country help shape or orient global political orientations?.

1.1.3.1. The Effect of International Political Tendencies on Domestic Media Orientations

The effects that the international political environment or political tendencies can have on the domestic media orientations are quite evident. Yet, the problem is to give a clearer and a more adequate definition and identification of these elements that affect the domestic media coverage of international news.

H. Denis Wu in an interesting study concerning international news coverage in 38 countries mentions two levels of analysis according to which news coverage in domestic media can be examined[82]. The first level is called the "gatekeeper" level. According to Wu, this level of examination suggests the existence of a process of newsgathering and distribution that is conducted by a chain of gatekeepers, who apply a set of traditional news values that reflect a collective judgment of what is newsworthy and what is not. Wu states that gatekeepers tend to select information that reflects unexpectedness, proximity, conflict, discrepancy, and prominence. According to this level of analysis, the news over-represents events that occur close to home or incidents that are disruptive or that feature well-known or powerful people.

---

82   See H. Denis Wu, "The Systematic Determinants of International News Coverage: A Comparison of 38Countires", Journal of Communications, vol.50, N°2., pp.110-130.

The other level of analysis mentioned by Wu is the larger one and that which concerns the international level[83]. According to this level, trans-national information flow is a reflection and a constituent of the larger global system, which in turn is latently structured by the world's politics, economy, and culture. Wu suggests that "In many ways, international news transmission continues to reflect the earlier imperial system in which news agencies follow national flags, armies, and traders"[84]. In addition, Wu explains that larger Western nations, which have the resources to maintain their own systems of newsgathering, tend to distribute resources strategically. Accordingly, reporters are typically assigned to foreign locales with pleasant amenities or to those regions with traditional and current links to their home country. Consequently, news is expected to follow reporters' postings.

Notwithstanding, Wu presents a number of what he calls the "systemic factors that are likely to result in an increase of news coverage. These factors include trade, territorial size, cultural ties, communication resources and physical distance. All of these can be categorized under the umbrella of "systemic factors"[85]. According to Wu, systemic factors influence the volume and content of news that flows from various parts of the world and determine the "menu" of international news available to gatekeepers.

Wu's study systematically examined nine systemic variables that may exert influence on the amount of international news coverage in host countries[86]. He explains that the variables can be organized into three broad categories. The first of those categories of traits is that related to the traits of the country such as population, degree of press freedom, geographic size, and economic power. The second category relates to interactions and relatedness between host and guest countries such as the geographic distance, shared language, volume of trade, and past colonial ties. The third of these categories include the logistics of news gathering such as the presence of international news agencies.

For their part, J. Galtung and M.H. Ruge argue that as far as national traits are concerned, economic, social, political, and geographic characteristics of nations determine the amount and the nature of coverage one country receives in another

---

83   Idem.

84   Ibid, P.110.

85   Wu defines Systemic Factors as" the distinctive traits of individual nations, as well as the magnitude of interaction between any two nations in the context of the global system". Ibid. p.111.

86   Wu identifies Host Countries as the countries that cover the news media of other countries. On the other hand, Guest Countries are those countries that are covered in the news media of other countries.

country's news media[87]. Other researchers such as K.E. Rosengren suggest that other factors such as population, trade and geographic distance affect the amount of news a country would receive in another country's media[88]. However, the degree of influence of each factor varies according to the country being examined. For instance, T. J. Ahern, in a study concerning the foreign news coverage in U.S. newspapers, found that trade and GNP, together with political relations with the U.S., can account for almost 60% of the variance in predicting the number of articles published in three elite U.S. newspapers. He also notes that factors such as location, population, and political system were found to matter as well, but not as significantly as the aforementioned factors[89]. Another study concerning this time Canadian media and conducted by H.G. Kariel and L.A. Rosenvall reaches the conclusion that "eliteness" of nations was the most significant factor, followed by population, trade, and GNP[90]. Examining the coverage of another geographic sphere, J. Charles, L. Shore, and R. Todd studied the coverage of eighteen African nations in *The New York Times*. The outcome of their study indicated that economic ties (trade) and population determined the amount of news coverage, whereas stories that involved violence tended to get front-page treatment[91].

The other category of factors determining coverage of foreign news in domestic media is that Wu describes as "Interactions and relatedness". In this respect, some studies suggested that nations that have a colonial tie have more attention in the domestic media. An example of studies that support this hypothesis is that conducted by T. Nnaemeka and J. Richstad[92] who surveyed nineteen newspapers of the Pacific region and found that news originating from Oceania[93] received the primary emphasis in the region's media. They reached the conclusion that one

---

87   See J. Galtung and M.H. Ruge, "The Structure of Foreign News", Journal of Peace Research, N°2, 1965, pp.64-91. Galtung and Ruge conceptualised the structural theory of foreign news. Their research investigated the influence of national traits on the flow of foreign news across borders and constituted the bases for many later studies dealing with this issue.

88   See K.E. Rosengren, "Four Types of Tables", Journal of Communications, vol.27, N°1,1977, pp.67-75.

89   See T. J. Ahem, Jr., "Determinants of Foreign Coverage in U.S. Newspapers", In R.L. Stevenson and D.L.Shaw (eds.), Foreign News and the New World Information Order, Iowa State University Press, Ames, 1984, pp. 217-236.

90   See H.G. Kariel and L.A. Rosenvall, "Factors Influencing International News Flow", Journalism Quarterly, N°61, 1984, pp. 509-516.

91   See J. Charles, L. Shore, and R.Todd, "*The New York Times* Coverage of Equatorial and Lower Africa", Journal of Communication, vol. 29,N°2, 1979, pp. 148-155

92   See T. Nnaemeka and J. Richstad, "Structured Relations and Foreign News Flow in the Pacific Region", Gazette, N°26, 1980, pp. 235-258.

93   Oceania includes Australia, New Zealand, and islands of the Pacific.

third of foreign news in that region came from North America and Western Europe. In addition, the press in each of the three Pacific territories (Australia, New Zealand, and islands of the Pacific) devoted far more news to their respective centres[94] than their immediate neighbours. The conclusion of this study was that the pattern of news flow in the region was vertical rather than horizontal.

As a support of the findings of the above study of the Pacific region, old colonial ties were also found to be an important factor in determining the volume of news flow. An example of this is the study conducted by W.A.E. Skurnik in which six African newspapers with distinct ideological orientations were used to test determinants of foreign news coverage[95]. Skurnik found that, other than colonial ties, regionalism and national interests were also found as significant factors.

Another study tempted to examine the coverage of Arab and African nations in 24 newspapers in Asia and Western Europe. In his study, L.E. Atwood examined 24 newspapers from 12 countries in Asia and Western Europe. He concludes that African and Arab countries tended to get covered with more stories in the press of the same colonial group. Interestingly enough, there appeared to be two types of emphasis regarding the colonial power at hand. For the Commonwealth countries, trade news dominated the international news agendas while, for the French Community countries, cultural news was emphasized[96].

As far as the effect of language is concerned, it was found to be another decisive element among the cultural factors that filter information and news flow. For their part, H. G., Kareil, and L.A., Rosenvall used cluster analysis to examine language's impact on Canadian dailies' coverage[97]. Their findings showed that French-language and English-language newspapers fall perfectly into distinctly separate groups. Nevertheless, the study indicates that the extent to which different coverage is carried out between the two cultural realms is more significant among the English-language newspapers than among the French-language counterparts.

Another issue to investigate here would be that relating to cultural and geographic proximity as far as international news coverage is concerned. Using U.S. newspapers as the study sample, M. A. Johnson examined the determinants of circulation size, cultural proximity, and geographic proximity as far as the coverage of

---

94   The centres concerning these regions are here the U.S. for Australia, the U.K. for New Zealand and France for the Islands of the Pacific.

95   See W.A.E. Skurnik, "Foreign News Coverage in Six African Newspapers, The potency of national Interests", Gazette, 28, 1981, pp. 117-130.

96   See L.E. Atwood, Old Colonial Ties and News Coverage in Africa, Paper presented to the International Communication Association annual convention, Honolulu, HI, US. May 1985.

97   See H. G., Kareil, and L. A. Rosenvall, "Cultural affinity displayed in Canadian Daily Newspapers", Journalism Quarterly, N° 60, 1983, pp. 431-436.

Mexico is concerned[98]. Johnson found that the quantity of Mexican coverage is influenced not only by the size of the newspaper (circulation), but also by the cultural proximity factor.

The overall result of these studies mentioned-above clearly suggest that the international news coverage is not equal everywhere. Indeed, not only is it unequal at the level of the states but most of the time it is unequal at the level of regions within one state who might be differently affected by the outside geopolitical or economic factors.

H. Denis Wu's[99] study of the coverage of world news in domestic media supports these findings. According to his study, the United States was on top of the list of countries covered in domestic media. It is the most covered country in the world. Based on his study, Johnson presents a list (table 2) of the top 20 countries covered as international news in the domestic media of guest countries. The determinant here is the number of news stories pertaining to each country in the domestic media of the guest countries.

Table 2: The Top 20 Countries in the World's Media

Nation	n	n/total	%
Australia	399	0.0116	1.16
Austria	321	0.0094	0.94
Bosnia and Herzegovina	1518	0.0443	4.43
Brazil	304	0.0089	0.89
China	1354	0.0395	3.95
France	2916	0.085	8.50
Germany	1245	0.0363	3.63
India	468	0.0136	1.36
Iraq	349	0.0102	1.02
Israel	711	0.0207	2.07
Italy	1068	0.0311	3.11
Japan	838	0.0244	2.44
Russia	1850	0.0539	5.39
South Africa	420	0.0122	1.22
Spain	642	0.0187	1.87
Sweden	499	0.0146	1.46
Switzerland	356	0.0104	1.04
Turkey	344	0.0100	1.00
U.K.	2135	0.0623	6.23
U.S.	6067	0.1769	17.69

* See H. Denis Wu, The Systematic Determinants of International News Coverage: A Comparison of 38 Countires, Journal of Communications, vol. 50, N°2., p.122.

---

98   See M. A., Johnson, "Predicting News Flow from Mexico", <u>Journalism and Mass Communication Quarterly</u>, vol.74, N°2, 1997, pp. 315-330.

99   See H. Denis Wu, <u>Op. Cit.</u>

As Wu explains the findings of this study reflect "the pre-eminent status of the U.S. on the world stage"[100]. Furthermore, the top ten countries on the list suggest that those countries with enormous economic and political clout tend to be emphasized in the press. Wu explains that, other than being a world power, the only alternative means to be spotlighted in the world press is to have some large-scale, disruptive incidents. He indicates that this was the case of Bosnia, for example.

Wu concludes, "The phenomenon of the press's concentration on the world elites perhaps is not entirely unexpected. After all, powerful players set up game rules and dictate the repertoire of actions performed on the world stage, thus affecting the rest of the less powerful countries. The topics to which the majority of international news hole is devoted—international politics, trans-national trade, military conflict, and domestic politics—also evidently reflect that news from abroad provides the function of surveillance. Thus, it makes a lot of sense for most countries to monitor closely the moves of the few elites. In so doing, they could take necessary steps to protect their own national interests should something emergent or threatening occur"[101].

To sum up then, the international political situation or environment, immensely, affect the orientations of the national or the domestic media. The degree in which a country is covered in the media of a guest country depends on factors such as the political relations, economic relations, geographic proximity, cultural proximity, language pertinence, the existence of news agencies…etc. It also depends on the agenda-sitting intentions of the news agencies. Only an abnormal incident on the world stage can focus the media spotlights on that area where the incident takes place. Notwithstanding, the coverage of this abnormal incident depends as well on the well of the "powerful players" as Wu put it.

1.1.3.2. The Effect of National Media on International Politics

In certain situations domestic or national media of a powerful nation can shape the political orientations at an international level. This might take place first through the effect that this national media can have on the government of its country. Thus, affecting the foreign policy orientations of this country and in doing that affecting, by the process, the country's positions vis-à-vis an international issue.

There are two good examples of the national media's ability to affect the foreign policy of the government and by doing that affect the position of the country vis-à-vis international issues. The two examples in this case pertain to the media of the United States. The first example has to do with the understanding of

---

100 Ibid, p.126.
101 Ibid, p.127.

the United States' government of the situations in the Third World. The second example is that of the American media coverage of the U.S. army soldiers being dragged in the streets of Mogadishu.

William A. Dorman explains that the fact that Americans know very little about developing countries combined with the failure of the press to present a true independent analysis of the situations in these countries, Americans are more likely to accept policies charted by the White House rather than those that local Third World conditions might suggest. He adds that over the years, the United States has supported a string of arguably disastrous regimes in countries ranging from Guatemala and Chile to Pakistan and South Korea and that those who have suffered under leaders of such regimes come to associate their plight with the perceived patron of these dictators[102]. This is quite true. The press has an enormous influence on foreign policy, since it serves as the primary source of information and impressions for both the general public and political leaders. Robert B. Albritton and Jarol B. Manheim explain that as a consequence of this situation the media report can become not only the stuff of public perceptions and expressions but also the very stuff of policy as well support this notion[103]. William A. Dorman suggests, however, that this is not to be understood as a "media conspiracy" to manipulate the news and opinions but as the result of a number of factors such as economic, political, or professional constraints that keep the Third World coverage within a narrow range[104]. George Gerbner and George Marvanyi explain, in this context, that the American press devotes less space and time to the Third World than the press of any other major power[105]. This, however, can also be attributed to the elevated costs of news-gathering abroad, the tendency to generalise rather than examine the specific situation of each country, and the fact that media tends to reinforce the foreign policy of the country. Indeed, the foreign policy establishment clearly decides the meanings of words and symbols and labels.

Consequently, the U.S. administration's vision often comes to be received opinion, reinforcing White House policy. For example, the U.S. press was willing to echo Washington's vastly overblown assessment of the importance of the Tudeh (communist) party in Iran, making it seem the only alternative to the Shah and critics of this view were constantly ignored. In addition, the U.S. media followed

---

102 See William A. Dorman, "Peripheral Vision: U.S. Journalism and the Third World", <u>World Policy Journal</u>, Vol.3, N° 3.,1986, p.419.

103 See Robert B. Albritton and Jarol B. Manheim, "News of Rhodesia: The Impact of a Public Relations Campaign", <u>Journalism Quarterly</u>, No. 60, 1983, p. 622.

104 See William A. Dorman, <u>Op. Cit.</u>, P. 421.

105 See George Gerbner and George Marvanyi, "The Many Worlds of the World's Press", <u>Journal of Communication</u>, N°. 27, 1977, pp. 52-61.

Washington's lead in its admiration of the power of Anwar el-Sadat after the famous Camp David Peace Accords, even with the growing indications that he was losing touch with his people, just as the Shah of Iran had. Similarly, and in the Middle East, Arab countries that take the United States' side in international conflicts, purchase U.S. arms, and allow American capital investment are constantly labelled by the U.S. media as "moderate," while those Arab states that do not are termed "radical".

This idea is best illustrated by the U.S. media's treatment of Iran under Shah Mohammad Reza Pahlavi and its reaction to the revolution there. Since the 1953 CIA assisted coup against Premier Mohammad Mosaddeq and until the Islamic Revolution of 1979, the mainstream U.S. press easily accepted the news frames provided by policymakers and the Shah's supporters in the United States. Indeed, the Shah continued and for a long time to be depicted as a popular, modern ruler whose regime was stable and provided a model for Third World development. Consequently, the American public misjudged Iran which was a "decisive power in the Persian Gulf…whether ruled by the Shah or the Ayatollah Khomeini"[106].

Actually, Iran first received significant U.S. media attention after Mosaddeq's nationalization of the oil industry during the early 1950s. Richard W. Cottam, even states that "the distortions of the Mosaddeq era, both in the press and in academic studies, border on the grotesque.[107]" Despite the fact that Mosaddeq was a remarkable, popular and courageous politician, he was negatively portrayed in U.S. publications. For instance, the Time describes him as "by Western standards an appalling caricature of a statesman"[108]. For its part, the Washington Post describes him as a "fanatical strong man[109]. *The New York Times* even goes further in saying that he is a "dictator only by proxy from a murderous mob"[110]. During the six months preceding Mosaddeq's ouster, the mainstream media demonstrated more concern for the consent of Iran's governed than it did during the subsequent 25 years of the Shah's rule. Over that period, the prestige press described the Shah as a "dictator" or "dictatorial" only a few times.

The second example illustrating the relation between the national media and the foreign policy orientations of the United States is that of the episode of the CNN coverage of the intervention in Somalia (1992–93). As Margaret H. Belknap

---

106   See Amos Perlmutter, "Squandering Opportunity in the Gulf", Wall Street Journal, October 3, 1983.

107   See Richard W. Cottam, Nationalism in Iran, University of Pittsburgh Press, Pittsburgh, 1979, p. 2.

108   See The Time, January 7, 1952, p. 20.

109   See The Washington Post, August 1, 1953.

110   See *The New York Times*, August 9, 1952.

explains "Somalia was an example of careful planning for involvement of the media. Some thought it was too well planned. As the marines arrived on a Somali beach that looked more like a movie set than a real beach, it appeared as though the marines were posturing before the cameras under bright television lights"[111].

Many researchers have come up with a concept describing the effect of television transmission on military and foreign policy decisions in the United States. Indeed, as Belknop puts it, the new challenge for military commanders since the Vietnam war has become to command their units before a television camera[112]. She continues, "today, commanders at all levels can count on operating "24/7"1 on a global stage before a live camera that never blinks. This changed environment has a profound effect on how strategic leaders make their decisions and how war fighters direct their commands"[113]. The concept that describes this effect, at least as far as the United States is concerned, is called the "CNN effect" (see Table 3).

Table 3: Conceptual Variations of the CNN Effect

Operations Other Than War Accelerant	Media shortens decision-making response time. Television diplomacy evident. During time of war, live, global television offer potential security-intelligence risks. But media may also be a force multiplier, method of sending signals. Evident in most foreign policy issues to receive media attention.
Impediment	Two types: 1. Emotional, grisly coverage may undermine morale. Government attempts to sanitize war (emphasis on video game war), limit access to the battlefield. 2. Global, real-time media constitute a threat to operational security.
Agenda Setting Agency	Emotional, compelling coverage of atrocities or humanitarian crises reorder foreign policy priorities. Somalia, Bosnia and Haiti said to be examples.

Source: Steven Livingston, "Clarifying the CNN Effect: An Examination of Media Effect According to the Military Intervention", online Research Paper for the Harvard Public Policy, p. 4.

In 1992 President Bush's decision to station troops in Somalia after viewing media coverage of starving refugees was sharply questioned in the United States. The argument concerned the existence or not of a real threat to U.S. interests there. The controversy also included a debate on whether or not the CNN was deciding were the military would go next. Less than a year later, President

---

111   See Margaret H. Belknap, "The CNN Effect: Strategic Enabler or Operational Risk?", Found on the Internet in Pdf.
      Form at http://carlisle-www.army.mil/usawc/Parameters, P. 7.
112   Ibid, p.1.
113   Idem.

Clinton's decision to withdraw US troops after scenes were televised of a dead American serviceman being dragged through the streets of Mogadishu seemed to confirm the power of CNN. Indeed, opinion polls conducted after this episode found out that half of those interrogated on the issue didn't approve of President Clinton's handling of the situation in Somalia[114].

Other researchers suggest that the post cold war interventions are mostly based on humanitarian concerns resulting from real time coverage of the situation. For instance, Jessica Mathews explains states that "the process by which a particular human tragedy becomes a crisis demanding a response is less the result of a national weighing of need or of what is remediable than it is of what gets on nightly news shows"[115]. This opinion is also shared by James Schlesigner who explains that in the post Cold War era "national policy is determined by the plight of Kurds or the starvation in Somalia as it appears on the screen"[116]. However, Steven Livingston explains that the majority of humanitarian operations are done without media attention. He adds that the U.S. has, for example, shipped 12000 tons of food for Somalia in 1991 well before the media's interest in the crisis in that country in March of the following year[117].

Nevertheless, the extent of media influence on the public policy of the United States in a debateable issue. It is true that media coverage affects public opinion not just in the United States but everywhere else in the world. However, the elements on each case should be taken into considerations. For the response of media and its ability to cover and transmit to the public depends not only on its well or agenda setting but also on the conditions that it has to deal with. Steven Livingston presents different scenarios and conditions that media deals with in the United States and that depends on the kind of intervention that the United States is undertaking (Table 4). For him, each intervention has its own considerations and effects on the public opinion in the United States.

---

114   See B. Drummond Ayers, "A Common Cry Across the U.S.: Its Time to Exist", _The New York Times_, October 9, 1993, p.1.

115   See Jessica Mathews," Policy Vs TV", <u>The Washington Post</u>, March 8, 1994, p. A19.,

116   See James Schlesinger, "Quest for a Post-Cold War Foreign Policy", <u>Foreign Affairs</u>, Winter 1992. On-line without pagination.

117   See Steven Livingston, "Clarifying the CNN Effect: An Examination of Media Effect According to the Military Intervention", online Research Paper for the Harvard Public Policy, P. 8. Found at <u>www.ksg.harvard.edu/presspol/publications/pdfs/70916_R-18.pdf</u>

Table 4: Intervention Types and Accompanying Media Considerations

Type of Intervention	Policy Goals and Objectives	Likely Media Interest	Government Policy	Likely Media Effects	Public Opinion
Conventional Warfare	Destruction of Enemy and his war fighting capabilities	Extremely high.	High degree of attempted media control, "Indexed" news.	Accelerant, Impediment (both types).	High public interest and attentiveness to it.
Strategic Deterrence	Maintain Status Quo. Ex. Cold War, Korean Peninsula	Moderate to high interest. Routinized coverage.	Routine News interaction. White House Dcd, State briefings, etc.	During stability, little effect. Accelerate during periods of instability.	Scrutiny only by attentive public. Expansion of base during instability.
Tactical Deterrence	Meet challenge to Status Quo. Ex. Desert Shield. PRC-Taiwan, March 1996.	Moderate to high interest but episodic.	Controlled but cooperative. Force multiplier.	All three effects but not necessarily injurious.	Attentive public scrutiny. Latent public opinion a concern to policy makes.
SOLIC	Counterterrorism, Hostage rescue, specialised operations.	High interst, particularly hostage situations, some terrorism.	Secrecy, Barring all access.	Impediment (Operational Security Risk)	Little to no public awareness in most cases.
Peace Making	Third Party imposition of political solution by force of arms . Ex. Somalia, Yugoslavia.	High interest at initial stages of operation. Variation afterward .Dependant on level of stability.	Volatile conditions, danger in reporting, access with risk impediment (both types).	Attentive public scrutiny. Latent public opinion a concern to policy makers.	
Peace Keeping	Bolster and accepted political solution by presence of third party.	Moderate Interest unless accord is destabilised.	Generally unrestricted access to theatre of operations.	Impediment (emotional impediment most likely).	Attentive public scrutiny. Latent public opinion a concern to policy makers.
Imposed Humanitarian Operations	Forceful, a political aid policy.	Law moderate interest unless violence occurs.	Volatile conditions, reporting risk.	Impediment (emotional most likely). Attentive public scrutiny. Latent public opinion a concern to policy makers.	
Consensual Humanitarian Operations	Agreed humanitarian assistance.	Initial operation met by moderate to law interest.	Un restricted even encouraged media coverage.	Media effect unlikely.	Attentive public scrutiny.

Source: Steven Livingston, <u>Op. Cit.</u>, p.12.

Whether its through approving the decisions of the government or through the effect it can have on the domestic public opinion, the national media can affect the orientations of the foreign policy of a certain country and consequently its position on the international level. If, moreover, this country is a leading world power, as it is the case of the United States, such an influence is a very important element in the examination of the positions of that country vis-à-vis the international issues.

1.1.4. National Media and Non-State Actors

It is important to examine at this level the relation between the national or domestic media and the non-state actors such as the civil society and the NGO's. Indeed, the roles and importance of these two non-state actors has been developing over the last decades. It is necessary, therefore, to study the interaction between the national media and those two actors. Another element to be verified at this stage would be the effect of the public opinion polls on the national media orientations. For, nowadays, public opinion polls are an important element serving both as a regulator and as a navigator of the media and of the government.

1.1.4.1. National Media, the Civil Society and NGO's

As far as it is concerned, the concept of *Civil Society* is one that has been used by political philosophers centuries ago. This concept is, however, complex and its definition is largely debated. The term itself (Civil Society) has resurfaced in the post-Cold War era. Indeed, this concept is sometimes difficult to understand. Yet, though there are a number of conflicting definitions, there is widespread agreement that during the past few decades, civil society receded and political/commercial society advanced in terms of their impact on people's lifestyles.

In general terms, the Civil Society can be said to be the representation of the voluntary participation. On the other end of the equation, the state can be viewed as the representation of the power of coercion. Furthermore, some consider that civil society extends only to non-profit organisations. Others see it as including only self-organising communities of common interest. Some have even went further in the extent of civil society to include all forms of non-governmental cooperation including big business, while yet others define it to exclude all forms of institutionalised human activity. For instance, Michael Walzer provides the following definition of civil society: "The words "civil society" name the space of un-coerced human association and also the set of relational networks-formed for the sake of family, faith, interest, and ideology—that fill this space. Central and East European dissidence flourished within a highly restricted version of civil society, and the first task of the new democracies created by the dissidents, so we are told, is to rebuild the networks: unions, churches, political par-ties and movements, cooperatives, neighbourhoods, schools of thought, societies for promoting or preventing this and that. In the West, by contrast, we have lived in civil society for many years without knowing it. Or, better, since the Scottish Enlightenment, or since Hegel, the words have been known to the knowers of such things but they have rarely served to focus anyone else's attention. Now writers in Hungary, the former Czechoslovakia, and Poland invite us to think about how this social formation is secured and invigorated"[118]. Thus, civil society can be a very complex and contested term. It can be said to be referring to all people, their activities and their relationships that are not part of the governmental establishment. Moreover, it can also be used to describe all processes other than government and economic activity.

For its part, non-governmental organization or NGO, as a term, was practically unused prior to the formation of the United Nations. For instance, in 1910, around 132 international NGOs met under the name of the Union of International Associations. Quite a number of these bodies, at that time, called themselves international institutes, international unions or simply international organizations.

It is interesting to note, in this respect, that the first draft of the UN Charter did not mention maintaining co-operation with private bodies. Yet, after a lot of lobbying done by groups mainly originating from the United States, this situation was rectified at the 1945 San Francisco Conference, which established the UN. Their efforts helped introduce a provision for strengthening and formalizing the relations with private organizations previously maintained by the League of Nations and also enhance the UN's role in economic and social issues. Additionally, the efforts resulted in the upgrade of the status of the Economic and Social Council ECOSOC[119] of the UN to that of a "principal organ" of the international organisation. In this respect, new terminology was introduced to govern the ECOSOC's relationship with two types of international organizations. Consequently, under Article 70 of the UN Charter, "specialized agencies, established by intergovernmental agreement" could "participate without a vote in its deliberations", while under Article 71 "non-governmental organizations" could have "suitable arrangements for consultation". Thereafter, the term "specialized agencies" and the term "NGOs" became technical UN jargon. However, and unlike much UN jargon, the term, NGO, started being largely used, in the early 1970s.

The controversy over the extent of the term of Civil Society is also applicable, as far as NGO's are concerned. Indeed, quite a number of diverse types of bodies are described as being NGOs. This may stem from the fact that there is no generally accepted definition of the term NGO. In addition, the term can have diverse meanings in different circumstances.

With this in mind, identifying non-governmental organisations can be a difficult thing indeed. Notwithstanding, some fundamental features are used for

---

118   See Michael Walzer, <u>Toward a Global Civil Society</u>, Berghahn Books, Providence R.I., 1998, pp. 7-8.

119   In fact, the Economic and Social Council ECOSOC one of the 'principal organs' specified in the UN Charter and the body to which NGOs are accredited.

identification purposes. First, an NGO should be independent from the control of any government. Second, an NGO should not be constituted as a political party. Third, an NGO should strictly be a non-profit organisation. Finally, an NGO should not be a criminal group or involved in any violent activity, or adopt violent methods to achieve its purposes.

However, it is important to mention that the above-mentioned conditions are generally applicable simply because they conform to the conditions for recognition of NGO's by the United Nations. In practice, the theses distinctions are not always clear. In fact, some NGOs may be identified with a political party. Also, many NGOs depend on commercial activities for profit or income, notably consultancy contracts or sales of publications. Furthermore, and as a small percentage of NGO's, some may be associated with violent political activities and protests. Generally speaking, therefore, an NGO can be regarded as an independent voluntary association of people acting together on a continuous basis, for some common purpose, other than achieving government office, making money or illegal activities. This view of NGO's is particularly important with respect to their active involvement in humanitarian assistance to victims of international conflicts and crisis. For certainly, being declared as an independent body working for humanitarian means, would give the NGO's two main advantages. The first advantage is that of being considered neutral from the conflicts protagonists. The second, is that their independence and their declared neutrality gives NGO's more freedom to act during international conflicts.

Recently, some controversy relating to the structure and nature of NGO's was raised. Some tend to see organizations, and especially the hierarchical ones, as conservative and oppressive. Subsequently, NGOs came to be considered by some as being a part of the established order. Such a point of view can be defined by the fact that some prominent NGOs have a long history, a complex structure, a technical literature and a leadership who is in more in contact with global politics than with the members or advocates of the organisation itself.

This sort of controversy over the nature of NGO's and their structure and conduct can be contrasted with what has come to be called the 'new social movements'. For, contrary to the image of NGO's, the "new social movement" structures are depicted as dynamic, innovative and non-hierarchical structures.

The term "movement" is very important in this respect. It implies the political impact of mass action, by a very large number of people. Additionally, the term" movement" indicates the importance and the role of the individual person in individually seeking to defend his objectives. One of the best examples of these social movements is that of the Labour Movement who's origins go back to nineteenth century[120]. Indeed, references to the "new social movements" such as those calling for peace, women's rights, development, the environment and anti-racism go back to the early 1960's. The innovation of the new social movements stems from the fact that they are not based on race, sex, or religion and also from the new techniques used in mobilizing the masses. Their power of assembling and mobilizing the masses was clearly indicated during the Seattle Ministerial Conference of the WTO[121] in December 1999. There, the anti-globalisation movement proved its extreme efficiency in disturbing the proceedings of the WTO Conference. One very important result of the mass protests of these new social movements is their ability to withdraw the media's attention. Indeed, media coverage of the new social movements protests are constant. This gives the new social movements a say in directing the media's attitudes to the social objectives of such movements.

It is important to indicate that the 1990's were extremely significant for the Civil Society, NGO's and the social movements. During those years, certain developments have led to the reinforcement of the concept of Civil Society. To begin with, there was the advancement in global communication facilities. Second, the fall of communist regimes in Eastern Europe and the military dictatorships in developing countries promoted participation in the new democratic systems. Third, many UN conferences resulted in an unprecedented scale of global public engagement with intergovernmental events. Furthermore, the UN aimed to neutralize the effect of the unilateralisme of the United States by appealing to global civil society as a source of legitimacy for international co-operation.

An important aspect to discuss at this stage, and that is relevant to the research at hand, would be the relationship between the NGO's and the media in crisis and conflict situations. Indeed, NGOs and social movements have learned to harness the power of the media, especially the power of intense TV coverage of a conflict as a way to generate significant cash flows from both governments and the public, especially from donations based on images of misery and human tragedies.

---

120   For instance, in Great Britain, the concentration of people in cities and factories led to working-class consciousness, to labour unions, and to demands for a wider franchise. Initially, those demands met with unflinching opposition. Later, the British aristocracy agreed to Reform. Reform included a broadening of the franchise, in several steps; the adoption of legislation designed to protect the labouring classes; and repeal of the Corn Laws. By the late nineteenth century, British workers had organized a strong trade union movement, though not without strikes and violence. In the wake of the Taff Vale decision of 1901, in which the courts held that companies could sue unions for money lost during strikes, the trade unions turned to the creation of an effective working-class political party, the Labour Party. By 1906, the Liberal, Conservative, and Labour parties were all competing for the working man's vote.

121   The World Trade Organisation.

Notwithstanding, there is a point of view saying that the TV coverage of international conflicts, especially the humanization effects, distort and sometimes damage conflict management and secret diplomacy efforts to resolve the conflict. For instance, Peter Walker explains that the kind of military response prompted up to now by TV coverage in particular is usually not the most effective one. He states "Rapid and radical shifts in the nature of international disaster response have left agencies reeling"[122]. He goes further in explaining that while such humanitarian intervention operations carry the kind of high profile demanded by politicians to satisfy the public's need to "do something", which in turn is an outcome of the TV intense coverage, they are no longer effective or appropriate[123]. Nick Cater is also as this opinion that impulsive intervention resulting from TV coverage of the conflict is counter-productive, despite the fact that its beneficial for NGO's in terms of donations and funding for their activities[124].

A good example supporting this hypothesis of impulsive responses can be seen in the long-term result of the immediate international response to the spread of cholera in Goma[125] in the aftermath of the Rwanda genocide in 1994. The immediate action of installing camps at the time seemed very appropriate. Yet, the result was a Gaza-style refugee camp, which gradually took on the air of permanent structures. Consequently, resulted in the creation of a new crisis of fiefdoms, criminality, and social misery. The report of The Steering Committee for Joint Evaluation of Emergency Assistance to Rwanda states that "ad hoc decisions that were not always in line with sound operating principles and resulted in skewed emphasis on some relief activities at the expense of others"[126]. Such

---

122   See Peter Walker, "Disasters debate: Whose disaster is it anyway? Rights, responsibilities and standards in crisis", research paper delivered to the World Disasters Report 1996 review conference, 23 May 1996.

123   See Peter Walker, "Should soldiers get off the humanitarian front line? Disasters, armies and the new world disorder", research paper delivered to the World Disasters Report 1996 review conference, 23 May 1996.

124   See Nick Cater, "Why does the media always get it wrong in disasters: Stereotypes, standards and free helicopter rides", research paper delivered to the review conference on 23 May 1996 launching World Disasters Report 1996 by the International Federation of Red Cross and Red Crescent Societies (IFRC). London: Oxford University Press, 1996.

125   In 1994, an outbreak of dysentery and cholera in refugee camps in Goma(a city the Democratic Republic of Congo) killed 50 000 people who were fleeing genocide in Rwanda.

126   See "The International Response to Conflict and Genocide: Lessons from the Rwanda", Experience by the Steering Committee for Joint Evaluation of Emergency Assistance to Rwanda. Published by the Danish Foreign Ministry, Vol. E, 1996. p. 66

claims go unnoticed by the NGO's and other humanitarian organisations who persist in reclaiming high-profile media coverage of events in conflicts or looming conflicts around the world. Trevor Lines explains that the results of this are sometimes desperate attempts by the NGO's to attract journalists' attention and, by consequence, funding to often forgotten conflicts[127]. However, the need for the media to effectively cover a conflict and its humanitarian dimensions always remains. Indeed, the role of NGO's as a media provocateur in drawing attention to forgotten, current, and future conflicts can be criticised but it can be more praised and appreciated at the same time.

The role of the Civil Society, NGO's, and the new social movements has certainly been reinforced during the past few years. New technological, political and regional development have provided such non-state organisations with an immense power to mobilize the masses. By consequence, it has also drown the attention of and influenced the conduct of the media. Indeed, the media cannot be indifferent to the attitudes of these non-state actors and vice versa. The breakthrough can come if some sort of understanding and cooperation is established to govern the relationship between the media and these popular movements in order to be the most effective in addressing the humanitarian consequences of human conflicts and crisis.

1.1.4.2. Public Opinion Polls and their Influence on the Media

The influence that opinion public opinion polls have on the orientations of the media in any given country is an important issue to examine. Indeed, the polling practice has become one of the corner stones of the daily life in modern democratic societies, upon which a huge amount of decision-making is dependant. Studying, following, and interpreting public opinion has, thus, become one of the most important functions of the media.

To start with it is important to examine the relationship between the polling practice and public opinion. In other words, it is important to see whether public polls really reflect public opinion. In fact, there are three views describing the research about the relationship between public opinion and polling. These are the populist, the critical, and the constructionist views.

The populist view suggests that opinion polls can effectively express the will of the people and facilitate democratic policymaking, provided they are conducted appropriately. Opinion polls are thought to measure attitudes and beliefs of individuals that, consequently, reflect opinions of the larger public if the appropriate instruments and methods are used.

---

127   See Trevor Lines, "Liberia, who cares?", Letter from the field by <u>Trevor Lines in a bulletin of UK Medecins sans Frontières, May 1996.</u>

Generally speaking, the populist view stresses the individual level of analysis and emphasizes the importance of objective measurement. This view depends on four assumptions. First, the direction of communication flow runs, generally, from the bottom to the top or, in other words, from the governed to the governors. Second, public opinion can be separated from the actions of political institutions and understood instead as an aggregation of individual attitudes, beliefs, and preferences. Third, this aggregation of individuals constitutes a public. Fourth, individuals have consistent and non-contradictory values, attitudes, and beliefs that can be measured by polls.

Some scholars regarded polls as essential to understanding public opinion. For Instance, George Gallup (the founder of the American Institute of Public Opinion AIPO) considers polls to be virtually synonymous with public opinion. Gallup considers polls as a means for citizens to hold the government accountable to their desires[128]. Other researchers, such as F. H. Allport, claim that populist public opinion is public because it involves, primarily, consideration of public affairs[129]. Others such as V.O. Key, for example, argues that the "technique of the sample survey permitted the determination, with some accuracy, of the distribution of opinions within the population"[130]. According to this view, opinions are traits of individuals, and the locus of public opinion lies within the individual's memory and is retrieved in response to survey questions.

For its part, the critical view theory explaining the relationship between public opinion and opinion polls constitutes a sort of criticism to the populist view of public opinion and polling. The critical view of public opinion maintains that polls are unsuitable to measure public opinion because both polls and publics are manipulated by elites seeking to gain power and to domesticate the potentially transformative power of collective public action. Generally speaking, this view depends on social and macro-economic levels of analysis as well as on theories of power and domination. Indeed, quite a number of scholars focus on how elites use public opinion polls to manage and control public opinion. For example, B. Ginsberg talks of several means through which public opinion polls contribute to the management of popular attitudes by elites. He calls these the "domestication

---

128   See Gallup, G. & Rae, S., The Pulse of Democracy, Simon & Schuster, New York, 1940, p.13.

129   See F. H. Allport, "Toward a Science of Public Opinion", Public Opinion Quarterly, Vol.1, 1937, pp. 7-23.

130   See Key, V. O., Jr.," Public Opinion and Democratic Politics",. In B. Berelson and M. Janowitz (Eds.), Reader in Public Opinion and Communication, (2nd ed.) Free Press. New York, 1966, p. 125.

of mass beliefs"[131]. Ginsberg adds" polling is the spearhead of this vast opinion-management apparatus. Though it cannot guarantee success, polling allows governments a better opportunity to anticipate, regulate, and manipulate popular attitudes"[132]. Similarly, S. Herbst examines how polls serve multiple functions in society. According to him these functions go from surveillance and social control to symbolic communication and rationalization[133]. Furthermore, Herbst recognizes the inherently democratic appeal of polls to treat all opinions equally and to turn what is an elusive phenomenon into a seemingly concrete, instrumental "fact." However, Herbst cautioned that polling has replaced rather than increased other democratic forms of communicating opinions in or about public life[134].

Other researchers, writing within this line of thought, such as J. Habermas describe public opinion as a "fiction of constitutional law" that legitimises the authority of the state by appealing to the mythical sovereignty of the people without actually, or in practice, doing so[135]. For his part, C. Christians argues that contemporary media and public opinion polls function as a kind of covert sociological propaganda that undermines rational, discourse-based democratic processes[136].

The third line of thought describing the relationship between public opinion and polls is the constructionist one. It shares with the critical perspective the consideration of public opinion polling as a mechanism of managed democracy. However, unlike the critical approach, though, this line of thought does not conceptualise public opinion as an existing phenomenon that can be either perceived or obscured by different instrumentalities. For the constructionists, public opinion is as epiphenomenal, as arising out of the process of social and communicative interaction. Generally speaking, the constructionist line of thought relates to communication-oriented questions about public opinion. It concentrates on language and symbolic processes as the unit of analysis and asks questions about the social construction of reality.

---

131 See B. Ginsberg, "How Polling Transforms the Public". In M. Margolis & G. Mauser (Eds.), _Manipulating Public Opinion: Essays on Public Opinion as a Dependent Variable,_ CA: Brooks/Cole, Pacific Grove, 1989. p.293.

132 Idem.

133 See Herbst, S., "On the Disappearance of Groups: 19th-and early 20th-Century Conceptions of Public Opinion"., In T. L. Glasser & C. T. Salmon (Eds.), Public Opinion and the Communication of Consent, Guilford Press, New York, 1995, pp. 89-104.

134 Idem.

135 See Habermas, J., The Structural Transformation of the Public Sphere, MIT Press, Cambridge, MA, 1989.

136 See C. Christians, "Propaganda and the Technological System", In T. L. Glasser & C. T. Salmon (Eds.), Public Opinion and the Communication of Consent, Guilford Press, New York, 1995, pp. 156-174.

The constructionist view relies on two assumptions. First, political will cannot exist independently of social and political discourses because it is socially constructed through language. Second, attitudes and opinions are situated, contingent, and emergent. Therefore, what distinguishes constructionist from critical work is the extent to which the former emphasizes the central role played by language in the symbolic construction of reality.

Like the previous two lines of thought, the constructionist view has its scholars and advocates. For instance, W. Lippmann is largely credited as the first scholar of mass communication to explore the extent to which public opinion is socially constructed. Observing that people experience the world primarily through the "pictures in our heads," he explored the dimensions and origins of those pictures, from stereotypes to newspaper reports, in symbolic communication[137]. For his part, M. Edelman argues that real public opinion does not exist; but rather, it is socially constructed in and through the processes of language and social interaction[138]. Like M. Edelman, W. L. Bennett explored the persuasive impact of symbols, myths, and metaphors on public opinion[139]. Starting from the premise that symbols enable us to "create the world we live in". He also argues that the means according to which an issue is defined and presented to the public could affect the intensity, distribution, and expression of opinion[140].

Assuming that public opinion polls actually reflect the public opinion, the relationship between the polling practice and journalists is very important to discuss at this point. To begin with, public opinion polls give journalists a means of writing about the popular will and sentiments by providing information that was gathered directly and in the aggregate from relatively large groups of citizens. This utility of opinion polls is clearly described by James Bryce, when talking about American public opinion in the 19th century. Bryce notes that the nineteenth-century American press served "as an index and mirror of public opinion"[141]. Second, and as A.H. Cantril notes the advances in the polling techniques enabled polling societies to provide their media sponsors with more information about

---

137   See W. Lippmann, Public Opinion, Free Press, New York, 1922.

138   See M. Edelman, "Contestable Categories and Public Opinion", Political Communication, N°10, 1993, pp. 231-242.

139   See W. L., Bennett, "Constructing Publics and their Opinions", Political Communication, N°10,1993, pp. 101-120.

140   See W. L.Bennett, Myth, "Ritual, and Political Control", Journal of Communication, Vol. 30, N° 4, 1980, pp.166-179.

141   See James Bryce, The American Commonwealth, Macmillan and Company, London, 1891,p.265.

larger geographic segments of the public on a more timely basis[142]. Third, and as K. A. Frankovic observes, the technological advances of the last two decades made it possible to gather this information even more rapidly, thus allowing the media to report it ever more quickly[143]. Fourth, polls allow journalists a quasi-objective, proactive role in the news-making process. Indeed, it can be said that conducting polls and reporting on poll-based information to represent the public's opinions, preferences, and intentions allows journalists to assume relatively well their "fourth estate" function. As Paul J. Lavrakas & Michael W. Traugott put it "this is information that comes from a qualitatively unique source that is independent of the media's other political sources such as elected officials and other politicians, their campaign staffers and supporters, lobbyists, and other special interest groups— and this is another reason polling information appeals to journalists"[144].

One good example of the influence of opinion polls on political tendencies can be seen in the role of the public polls of 1998 and early 1999 in the United States which showed consistent and strong majority support for keeping President Clinton in office. In fact the news formulated about the will of the majority of the American people reduced the strength of the congressional Republicans and bolstered the congressional Democrats in the House impeachment and Senate trial processes[145]. Indeed, if such information about the American public's preferences was not available to Congress and to the American people, there would have been a much higher possibility that the U.S. Congress would have removed the president from office or that he would have resigned before being required to leave office.

The importance of public opinion polls to the media in a democracy is thus a vital one. Yet this role that opinion polls play and that enables the media to better perform its role of surveillance requires a number of prerequisites. First, the media should be certain that the information they provide truly reflects the public opinion. Second, the media should be sure that analysing the data coming out of the opinion polls is done as accurately as possible. Finally, the media should report as accurately as possible these findings to its public. Nevertheless, it is important to mention that opinion polls have not proven to reflect the public's opinion in a one hundred percent accurate manner. Indeed, sometimes results come contrary to what the opinion polls predict.

---

142 See A.H. Cantril, <u>The Opinion connection: Polling, Politics and the Press</u>, Congressional Quarterly Press, Washington D.C., 1991.

143 See K. A. Frankovic, <u>News Media Polling in a Changing Technological Environment</u>, Northwestern University, Evanston, 1994.

144 See Paul J. Lavrakas & Michael W. Traugott, <u>The Election Polls, the News Media and Democracy</u>, Chatham House Publishers, New York, 2000, p. 4.

145 Ibid, p.5.

1.2. National and Trans-national Mass Media

Perhaps the first distinction that can be noted to distinguish between national and trans-national media in terminology terms would be that of geography. For whereas national media is restricted within the geographic borders of a certain country, trans-national media is, by definition, that which transcends this geographic barrier. With this virtue of being able to transcend geographic barriers, it would be interesting to study the influence that trans-national media can have on both the national or domestic media and on the domestic public opinion. This effect is quite important especially in the current age of speed and globalisation and curiously enough in one where there is a new search of national identities. Victor Sampedro describes this situation saying that" modern age has disconnected people from geographic regions, traditional spheres of home, place, and identity." He adds that this has "cast them into a new environment"[146].

1.2.1. The Influence of Trans-national Mass Media on National Media

William H. Meyer explains that the business of news and information is central to the concept of capitalism in Western countries. He adds, "Capitalism has always been an "information system" as well as a system of finance and production". According to him the worldwide information network became quickly a fundamental support for the development of international capitalism[147].

The trans-national news corporations are influenced by certain norms that have to do with economic conditions. In fact, the task of gathering news from around the world required certain financial resources. The costs of such venture were initially covered by industrialists, who were interested in gathering international information in order to promote and look after their own business and projects. Nevertheless, the high costs, stipulate that no single newspaper would be

---

146   See Victor Sampdro, "Grounding the Displaced: Local Media Reception in a Transnational Context", Journal of Communications, vol.48, N°2, 1998, pp. 125-144.
147   See William H. Mayer, Transnational Media and World Development: The Structure and Impact of Imperialism, Greenwood Press, New York, 1988, pp.17-23. The book of William Mayer has an interesting study of the conception of news in the West and that which exists in third world countries.

able to support the financial burden even with the support of industrialists. This was how the first news agencies were first created. They would take care of the gathering of news from around the globe and distributing it afterwards to subscribed customers for a fee.

Around the year 1855, three international news agencies were established: *Wolff* in Germany, *Havas* (later *Agence France Press*) in France and Reuters in London. The competition between these agencies was enormous, although Reuters took the lead in most occasions. For instance, although Reuters was primarily established to transmit financial news to bankers and investors, it established in 1890 a Special Service specialised in what was called then "sensational journalism". This type of journalism concentrates on attractive stories of crime and disasters and departs from the patterns of substantial news and information. Indeed, in the early years of international news reporting, competition was so severe and those agencies, which did not follow the popular trends such as that of sensationalism, soon went out of the competition.

According to Anthony Smith, international news agencies at the time supplied two types of foreign news to two types of customers. Financial customers or communities were supplied with "instant, exact and copious commercial and political information" which had enormous importance for their overseas business. On the other hand, the other news market consisted of "a large number of smaller newspapers whose readers wanted romantic headings, big stories and not too much substance"[148].

Yet this competition between the major international news agencies at the time did not mean that there weren't any points of agreement between them. This is far from being true. In fact, as early as 1870, the so called Ring Combination (*Havas*, *Wolff* and Reuters) had divided the world into regions where each member has exclusive rights to collect and sell news in his areas. Reuters had exclusive rights to all areas of the British Empire, the Middle East, and most of Asia. *Havas* had the rights to the areas of the French Empire as well as Latin America. *Wolff*, for its part, was limited to Central Europe. This club of agencies was enlarged in 1900 with the entrance of The New York Associated Press (later the Associated Press). Smith, however, explains that this club came to an end in 1934 with the emergence of old rivalries between the agencies[149].

The fact that international news agencies formed at one point of their history a sort of a cartel with an internal agreement to divide the "market" is a clear indication

---

148 See Smith Anthony, <u>The Geopolitics of Information: How Western Culture Dominates the World</u>, Oxford University Press, New York, 1980, p. 77.

149 Ibid., pp. 81-82.

of the influence of such agencies. Nowadays, other international news companies are providing news and information mainly to an" international consumer". These trans-national media companies can transmit their information directly to the consumer and by doing so could have a direct influence on him or can do that via providing their information to the national media in different countries. If the national media depend largely on the flow of information and news from trans-national corporations, then it would be interesting to examine the different effects that this trans-national flow of information and news can have on the national or domestic media.

1.2.1.1. Linguistic Influence

Discussing the linguistic influence of trans-national media is an important element in the process of determining the impact of trans-national media on the national or domestic media. Indeed, language is the principal mediator of cultural, economic, and political encounters. In this respect, the global pattern of language use illustrates the complex processes of "linguistic globalisation". Generally, the globalisation of languages can be defined as a process by which some languages are increasingly used for international communication and others are disappearing.

Nevertheless, as language use is easily politicised, it is somewhat difficult to reach general agreement about the effects of globalisation on languages. Statistically speaking, at the beginning of the 15th century, about 15,000 languages were spoken. Gradually, and over the last 400 to 500 years, the number of known languages became approximately 6,800. Out of these, only a few comprise the dominant languages in international communication. And of all those languages, English stems out as the dominant language of global communication.

Nowadays, English is said to be the most widely used language for international and intercultural communication. As explained in Diagram 1 below, the globalisation of languages have contributed to the consecration of English as the global language of communications.

Diagram 1: The Globalisation of Languages

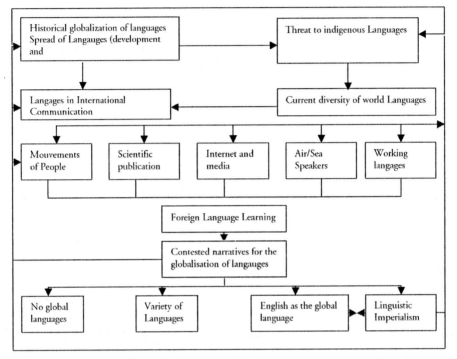

Source: "Globalisation of Languages", <u>Globalisation Research Centre</u>, Online document with pagination, p.4.

Thus, as far as international communication is concerned, English is the dominant language. Indeed, being dominant also labels, English as the "hegemonic" or the "neocolonialist" language. This status gives English the ability to create sort of a discriminatory situation between those who speak it and those who don't and enables it also to control many aspects of the daily life of the great majority of the world's population.

The examples of the communication and linguistic inequity resulting from the hegemony of English are many. For instance, W.J. Coughlin (an American journalist) presents what he calls as the *Mokusatsu* mistake that caused the atomic bombing of Hiroshima and Nagasaki. Coughlin claims that the Japanese Prime Minister's response of *Mokusatsu* to the demand of complete surrender by the United Allies, was misinterpreted to mean "reject" the demand, causing the then the American President, Harry Truman, to order the atomic bombing. Coughlin says that

Mokusatsu actually means both "ignore" and "no comment in Japanese."[150] An idea that can be deducted out of this misinterpretation of the Japanese word is that in the English-dominated Japan-U.S. communication, the Americans always have the control of semantics under which the subtle nuances of the Japanese semantics are "ignored" or "overlooked." Thus, generally speaking, in the English-dominated communication. English speakers are in a position to control communication to their own advantage.

Another important consequence of the dominance of one language over the others is what Ngugi wa Thiong'o calls the "Colonization of the Consciousness". According to him, the colonization of the mind is a result of the domination of the colonizer's language over the language of the colonized. The process described by Ngugi wa Thiong'o takes place as follows: first the destruction or the deliberate undervaluing of a other people's culture, art, religions, history, education, and literature and second, the conscious elevation of the language of the colonizer. Ngugi wa Thiong'o explains that the hegemony over a people's language by the languages of the colonizing nations is crucial to the domination of the mental universe of the colonized.[151] Accordingly, linguistic domination leads to the control of mentalities and is, thus, constitutes an important colonizing element.

However, while the hegemony of English as an element of neo-colonialism occurs at the level of international interpersonal communication, the hegemony of English as the global media language occurs at the level of international mass communication. This leads to results such as cultural and media imperialism, Americanisation of global culture, the unequal flow of international news and information, and the hegemony of English in the Internet. In short, the dominance of English operates as a means of promoting globalisation. Some researchers point our that the hegemony of English in mass international communication is a mere reflection of the free globalisation of world affairs. For instance, A. Pennycook, explains that "its widespread use (English) threatens other languages; it has become the language of power and prestige in many countries, thus acting as a crucial gatekeeper to social and economic progress; its use in particular domains, especially professional, may exacerbate different power relationships and may render these domains more inaccessible to many people; its position in the world gives it a role also as an international gatekeeper, regulating the international flow of people; it is closely linked to national and increasingly non-national forms of culture and knowledge that are dominant in the world; and it is also bound up

---

150 See W.J. Coughlin, "The great Mokusatsu mistake: Was this the Deadliest Error of Our Time", <u>Harper's Magazine</u>, vol. 206, N°.1234, 1053, pp. 31-40.

151 See Ngugi wa Thiong'o, <u>Decolonising the Mind: The Politics of Language in African Literature</u>, James Carey, London, 1981, p. 160.

with aspects of global relations, such as spread of capitalism, development aid and the dominance particularly of North American media"[152]. Another scholar, Roland Robertson, refers in this respect to what he calls "the crystallization of the entire world as a single place" and "the compression of the world and the intensification of consciousness of the world as a whole"[153].

Some researchers claim that Anglo-Americanisation of the world culture is the most serious problem caused by globalisation and one which is based on the Anglo-American monopoly of the global market of information and entertainment. Indeed, It appears that the hegemony of American cultural products is evident in the entire global market of international mass communication. This inevitably results in the "ideological control" of the world population, especially by the United States. Consequently, American ways of feeling and thinking become more visible and influential as American cultural and information products are massively diffused all over the world.

1.2.1.2. Political Orientation

Of the many effects that the trans-national mass media has on the domestic or local media, its political orientation impact is one of the most important of these effects. Although this is essential effect of trans-national mass media on the domestic one, it is by far not the easiest one to detect.

If the trans-national media is to have a political impact on the domestic or local media orientations in developed countries, then its logical to assume that such an influence would be much more visible in less developed countries, especially in the domestic media of former colonies. One of the most intrusting studies conducted in this area of influence of the trans-national media is that of William H. Meyer. He examines the findings from comparing the trans-national media's impact on six local newspapers[154]. These are mainly three English-language African dailies (the *Daily Nation* (Nairobi, Kenya), the Zimbabwe *Herald*, and the *Times of Zambia*) and three Latin American ones *(Excelsior* (Mexico City), *La Nacion,* and *La Prensa* (both from Buenos Aires).

The criteria used by Meyer for the selection of his sample study of domestic newspapers are fairly elaborated by him. From every country represented in the study, the newspaper with the largest daily circulation which ranged from

---

152   See A. Pennycook, <u>Cultural Politics of English as an International Language</u>, Longman, London, 1994, p.13.

153   See Roland Robertson, <u>Globalisation: Social Theory and Global Culture.</u>, Sage, London, 1992, p.8.

154   See William H. Meyer, <u>op. cit.</u>, pp. 41-44.

235,000 to 65,000 daily copies, as well as papers which are regarded as the most influential, are chosen as the study material. In addition, all the newspapers had little or no rural circulation and were mostly limited to urban elites, who are said to be allegedly stimulated by Western media and who are said to desire a more westernised culture and a more Western style goods[155]. Meyer, furthermore, distinguishes between two types of news in his study. These are what he calls "Spot News" and "Developmental News" or "Developmental Journalism". He states," Spot news is generally regarded as raw facts about diplomacy, wars, crime, unrest, and disasters. Developmental news is not just news about modernization or other forms of development. The style known as developmental journalism attempts to imbue all news stories with the links between a raw data-event and projects of economic or political modernization. Developmental journalism also addresses the historical background and long-range implications of an isolated event"[156]. This type of distinction is quite helpful in identifying the type of news projected to the audience and in estimating their later impact on this audience. It is important because it is central to the type of manipulation used to shape the domestic media, especially in developing and least developed countries. Indeed, if the majority of news items provided to the domestic media by the TNNA's (Transnational News Agencies) are merely the news item with no proper analysis, then most of the news items covered can go unnoticed or underestimated. Furthermore, if this desire for "westernisation" mentioned by Meyer is a strong one, then its logical to assume that most journalists in the developing countries and least developed ones are very much likely to follow the analysis of the TNNA's of the news items presented or covered.

Indeed, Meyer's study revealed a pattern in which trans-national media co-operations or trans-national media agencies (TNNA's) primarily provide spot news values for domestic newspapers in the developing countries. For instance, Table 5 distinguishes between the news items according to their source TNNA vs. national and regional (non-aligned) services vs. local correspondents and stringers. In addition, the coverage from each source in this table of findings is further broken down according to subject matter. Thus, the categories of Diplomatic Relations, War, and Crime and Unrest (spot news categories) are depicted as the primary items provided by the trans-national media. On the other hand, and according to these findings, developmental news items are depicted as originating mostly from national/regional newswires and local coverage sources.

---

155   Idem.
156   Ibid., pp.45-46.

Table 5: Topics According to Source (Percentages)

	DIPLOMATIC RELATIONS	CRIME & UNREST	WARS & MILITARY	DISASTER	DEVELOPMENT
SAMPLE =	A84/A85	A84/A85	A84/A85	A84/A85	A84/A85
AFP	16/11%	35/21%	13/18%	4/ 5%	6/ 0%
AP	19/14%	17/28%	17/ 2%	10/ 9%	2/ 5%
Reuters	27/20%	19/15%	14/ 9%	4/ 6%	6/ 2%
UPI	22/ 0%	22/50%	11/ 0%	0/ 0%	0/ 0%
National/ Regional	20/24%	16/ 6%	12/ 3%	8/21%	20/15%
Paper's Reporter	39/17%	4/ 3%	2/ 3%	0/ 3%	27/23%
SAMPLE =	LA85	LA85	LA85	LA85	LA85
AFP	11%	21%	0%	4%	0%
AP	12%	14%	7%	5%	1%
Reuters	21%	10%	21%	5%	5%
UPI	13%	14%	14%	1%	1%
National/ Regional	15%	3%	7%	0%	8%
Paper's Reporter	18%	5%	13%	0%	5%
A84 = Africa, 1984					
A85 = Africa, 1985					
LA85 = Latin America, 1985					

Source: William H. Meyer, *Transnational Media and Third World Development: The Structure and Impact of Imperialism, Op. Cit.* p.52.

Adopting a slightly different methodology, Meyer gives a more sophisticated treatment of the issue of the kind of news items supplied to domestic media by trans-national news agencies (Table 6). According to this new methodology, the columns are divided into TNNA (Big Four) news sources and non-TNNA sources (national or regional newswires and local correspondents). Additionally, the row concerning Spot News contains all stories coded originally as diplomacy, unrest and crime, domestic politics (from other nations), wars, or disasters. On the other hand, Developmental News items are only those in which either the subject was one of national modernization or over half of the item was devoted to the developmental journalistic style. Finally, the category of (Other) contains mostly social, cultural, or scientific news and a few human-interest stories[157].

---

157   Idem. P.52.

Table 6: Spot News Versus Development Reporting

AFRICA (1984)		
	TNNA	LOCAL-REGIONAL
SPOT NEWS	N = 194 (85%)	N = 41 (57%)
DEVELOPMENTAL REPORTS	N = 11 (5%)	N = 17 (24%)
OTHER	N = 24 (10%)	N = 14 (19%)
TOTALS	229 (100%)	72 (100%)
chi-square = 29.72; significant at less than .001 level		
AFRICA (1985)		
	TNNA	LOCAL-REGIONAL
SPOT NEWS	N = 134 (73%)	N = 54 (55%)
DEV. NEWS	N = 5 (3%)	N = 20 (20%)
OTHER	N = 45 (24%)	N = 25 (25%)
TOTALS	184 (100%)	99 (100%)
Chi-square = 25.53; significant at least than .001		
LATIN AMERICA (1985)		
	TNNA	LOCAL-REGIONAL
SPOT NEWS	N = 173 (59%)	N = 161 (55%)
DEV. NEWS	N = 3 (1%)	N -= 14 (5%)
OTHER	N = 119 (40%)	N = 115 (40%)
TOTALS	295 (100%)	290 (100%)
Chi-square = 7.57; significant at .02		
D.F. = 2		

Source: William H. Meyer, Op. Cit. p.53.

This table also shows the fact that news items from TNNA's tend to centre on Spot News and not on the development ones. Spot News being mostly diplomatic news items, foreign wars and crimes, it is logical to assume that TNNA's help in preserving the political status quo in certain countries. By focusing on foreign news in their supply and analysis and not on the reception areas where sometimes political change and improvement is most needed, the trans-national media can be said to be helping to maintain a certain political order in the world. Consequently, spotlighting one country or political system and ignoring others who are, sometimes, in a much worst situation, is one of the most important manifestations of this political manipulation of trans-national media. Furthermore, the fact that trans-national media forms a club or a cartel with its own political and economic agenda (as previously indicated in this research) adds to this assumption that one of the most important impacts of trans-national ᵕedia is manipulation and that one of the most important aspects of this manipᵕon is the political orientation of the domestic media.

In this respect, quite a number of studies revolve around the question whether this trans-national media actually works to preserve the status quo or whether it works to incite social and political change in different countries. The responses to this question vary considerably. Yet the general approved fact is that news itself "suggests a general outlook on the world", "an ideology", and "a frame of interpretation"[158]. However, the question remains on whether ethics of journalists or even economic considerations would allow trans-national news agencies to dominate the moods of thinking of both other journalists and audiences to a high degree. Some researchers have attempted to answer this question by referring to the theory of the trans-national news agencies' clientele theory. For instance, Meyer explains that "international news agencies historically have catered to the needs and tastes of two consumer groups. Political and economic elites are provided with news that affects their vested interests. On the other hand, the general public is provided with news that satisfies desires for the unusual and sensational"[159]. This elite clientele is referred to by as well Peter Golding who explains that the "historical process" which contributed to "the development of news as a service to elite groups" has resulted in a situation in which "the basic goals and values which surround journalism refer to the needs and interests" of elites[160]. However, since the media needs a broader audience and not simply elites to gain profits, Golding explains that reporting must depend on common social values and assumptions in order to reach a mass audience[161]. Thus, it can be said that the media also needs to be socially and politically conscience of the needs of its new clientele (the masses) to stay in business. This, in turn, would allow it less room to move as a manipulator.

The influence of trans-national media on the political orientations of the domestic media is a very subtle issue to discuss. The fact that no media would easily admit that it is politically oriented by another media, adds to the difficulty in the discussion. For, journalists tend to proud themselves of their independence of any outside manipulations. Yet, the political orientation effect remains. It can manifest itself through the type of news and analysis provided to domestic media by the trans-national media. It can also manifest itself by the emphasis that trans-national media exerts sometimes to effect the social or political change in one country or area and not others. The fact that the trans-national media forms sort

---

158   See Elihu Katz, and Tamas Szecsko (eds.), <u>Mass Media and Social Change</u>, Sage, Beverly Hills, California, 1981, p.7.

159   See William H. Meyer, <u>op. cit</u>, p.23.

160   See Peter Golding, "The Missing Dimension—News Media and the Management of Social Change," In Katz and Szecsko, <u>op. cit.</u>, p.79.

161   Idem. pp. 63-82.

of a cartel with its own interests can also be added to the argument that domestic media is politically oriented to act or react in a certain manner. Indeed, the trans-national media's original clients were mostly the elite and they have their own economic and political interests to be catered for. To stay in business, the trans-national media was obliged to set the elite's priority on top of its list.

Nonetheless, nowadays the historical social, political, and economic realities oblige the trans-national media to be also conscience of the social aspirations and political needs of its new clients; the masses. This later fact added to the journalist's individual sense of their role as being objective and as "the voice of the people" makes political orientation of the domestic media by the trans-national media companies less effective, particularly in developed countries. Unfortunately, in developing and least developed countries, this political orientation is still quite effective. It is effective mainly because of the dependence on trans-national news agencies for news and because of the "westernisation" aspirations of the elites in those countries. This suggests a sort of a cultural imperialism of the domestic media by the trans-national one, notably the respective ex-colonial power. It also rises to a vision of a centre and periphery situation in the international information system in which the ex-colonial power is the centre and its ex-colonies are periphery of this centre.

To continue this argument of the trans-national media's political orientation of the domestic media, an important tool of this manipulation power of the trans-national media has to be examined. This manipulation tool is that of dependency on the trans-national media for sources of foreign news items.

1.2.1.3. Source Dependence

The dependence of domestic media on trans-national media as a source for foreign news items is important to discuss. This dependence allows the trans-national media to be more effective in its impact on the domestic media orientations. For the purposes of this research, a comparison between the findings of William H. Meyer's[162] study and that of Jan Servaes[163] seems appropriate. These two studies both concern an examination of news coverage in newspapers, usually influential ones. The differences, however, between the two studies have to be underlined. As far as it is concerned, William H. Meyer's study is about news coverage in general

---

162   See William H. Meyer, op. cit.

163   See Jan Servaes," European Press Coverage of the Grenada Crisis"; Journal of Communication, vol.41, N°4, 1991, pp.29-41. This study would be further referred to in the next sections of this research and in particular those relating to the media 's and other interests in covering an international conflict or crisis.

and not merely pertinent to the coverage of a certain news item or event. Furthermore, Meyer's study is about news coverage in developing countries. On the other hand, Jan Servaes's study is about a specific event (newspapers' coverage of the Grenada invasion). In addition, his study concerns the six most prestigious newspapers in six developed countries. Nevertheless, the part in Servaes's study concerning the sources of news can be a good contrast to the same part of Meyer's study.

For his part, Meyer explains that the imbalances in the news flow between the western countries' press and that of the developing of the less developed ones is usually regarded in two ways. The first one is that imbalances of news flows are a simple expression of the dependency of developing countries' media on the Western media for sources of news items. The other way of regarding this imbalance is to see it as an attempt by the media of developing countries to blindly copy Western media. Meyer goes even further in his analysis of the causes and consequences of these two forms of interpreting this imbalance. He argues' we could call this an imbalance in the form of journalistic westernisation. The two forms of imbalance are also interrelated. The imbalance of media dependency is said to lead to the homogenisation of the world's presses. As LDC's[164] are bombarded by media fare from the West, they come to see the world through Western eyes and adopt Western values. To evaluate charges of an imbalance fairly, one must look at both areas (e.g., dependency, westernisation)"[165]. Concerning the second form of this imbalance in the news flow, Meyer explains (table 7) that the newspapers examined in his study concentrate on the coverage of international news.

Table 7: Percentage of All News for International Reporting

AFRICA						LATIN AMERICA		
D. Nation		Herald		Times		Excelsior	La Nacion	*La Prensa*
1984/85		84/85		84/85		1985	1985	1985
ISSUE								
1.	15%	33%	11%	21%	21%	37%	32%	31%	39%
2.	23%	24%	36%	27%	31%	45%	38%	35%	35%
3.	24%	23%	18%	34%	39%	52%	32%	22%	22%
4.	31%	28%	26%	39%	26%	31%	32%	27%	16%
5.	22%	43%	23%	33%	31%	31%			

Source: William H. Meyer, <u>Op. Cit.</u> p.47.

---

164   Least Developed Countries.
165   See William H. Meyer, <u>Op. Cit.</u>, P.47.

According to table 6, the newspapers covered in Meyer's study allocated between 11 % and 52 % of all news items covered to reports on international affairs, with average coverage ranging from 23 % to 39 %[166]. Another interesting finding of this study is that most of the newspapers covered in the African, Asian and Latin American regions all show a tendency to follow the direction of western media in their focus on certain regions and areas (Table 8)[167].

Table 8: Regions Covered in African and Latin American Presses

	AFRICA				LATIN AMERICA	
	(1984)		(1985)		(1985)	
	N	%	N	%	N	%
REGION						
Africa	197	47%	192	41%	10	1%
Asia	33	8%	62	13%	40	6%
Latin America	13	3%	17	4%	291	42%
Middle East	32	8%	32	7%	21	3%
United States	37	9%	33	7%	137	20%
USSR/ E. Europe	11	2%	19	4%	39	6%
Western Europe	89	21%	99	21%	152	22%
Other	8	2%	12	3%	6	1%
Third World	162	39%	182	39%	239	34%
Third W. + Other	122	29%	124	26%	223	32%
Non-Third World	136	32%	163	35%	241	34%

Source: William H. Meyer, <u>Op. Cit.</u> p.48.

As far as dependency on foreign sources is concerned, Meyer explains (table 9) that that 56 percent to 76 percent of all identifiable sources in all sex newspapers were attributed to the biggest four Western international news agencies. Meyer argues that other studies indicated that this pattern is repeated in other areas of the Third World[168].

---

166   Idem.
167   Idem.
168   Ibid, p. 50.

Table 9: Newswires Identified as Sources

	AFRICA					
	(1984)			(1985)		
Wire Service	N	%		N	%	
TNNA:						
Agence France Presse	69	16%	(23%)	38	9%	(13%)
Associated Press	42	10%	(14%)	57	13%	(19%)
Reuters	110	26%	(36%)	87	20%	(29%)
United Press International	9	2%	(3%)	2	.5%	(1%)
NON-TNNA:						
Local/Regional Services	27	7%	(9%)	33	8%	(11%)
Special Services	4	1%	(1%)	13	3%	(4%)
Paper's Own Reporter	45	11%	(15%)	66	16%	(22%)
Paper's Own Reporter	45	11%	(15%)	66	16%	(22%)
(rather than a wire service)						
No Source Identified	114	27%		131	31%	
	LATIN AMERICA					
	(1985)					
		N			%	
TNNA:						
Agence France Presse		57			10%	(11%)
Associated Press		104			18%	(19%)
Reuters		19			3%	(4%)
United Press International		116			20%	(22%)
NON-TNNA:						
Local/Regional Services		158			27%	(29%)
Special Services		42			7%	(8%)
Paper's Own Reporter		42			7%	(8%)
No Source Identified		44			7%	

Source: William H. Meyer, <u>Op. Cit.</u> p.50.

Those later findings on the dependence of local media in the developing countries on the trans-national media for news sources differ from the findings of Jan Servaes. The study of Servaes concerning sources of news for six prestigious European newspapers indicates that 54 % of the articles on the crisis in Grenada were written by individual editorial staff members or newspapers' own correspondents (table 10)[169].

---

169   See Jan Servaes, <u>op. cit.</u>, p. 37.

Table 10: Sources for articles on Grenada in six European newspapers, by percent

Source	LM %	NZZ %	Times %	FAZ %	NRC %	EP %	Total %
Staff member or correspondent	43	39	75	57	43	60	54
Agency							
U.S.	11	27	5	21	5	8	12
European	14	43	7	11	4	10	10
Caribbean	5	10	2	3	1	3	4
Combined	8	7	2	8	45	13	43
Subtotal	38	58	16	42	55	34	39
Unspecified	19	3	9	1	2	6	7
Total	100	100	100	100	100	100	100
n =	(89)	(88)	(127)	(67)	(80)	(84)	(535)

LM = Le Monde; NZZ = Neue Zurcher Zeitung; FAZ = Frankfurter Allgerneine Zeltung; NRC = NRC-Handelsblad; EP = El Pais

Source: Jan Servaes, « European Press Coverage of the Grenada Crisis", Journal of Communication, vol.41, N°4, 1991, p. 37.

Interestingly enough, in Servaes's study, 39% of the articles have a news agency as a source. Furthermore, a third of those articles combine different reports of this news agency. However, a slight preference is apparent for U.S. news agencies (especially Associated Press) over European ones. Seraves's study also indicates that most coverage of the Grenada crisis was provided by each paper's staff (75 %for the *Times*, 60 % for *El Pais,* and 57 % for the *Frankfurter Allgemeine Zeitung.* For their part, the *Neue Zurcher Zeitung* and the *NRC-Handelsblad* were maily dependent on foreign news agencies (58 % for the *Frankfurter Allgemeine Zeitung* and 55 % for the *NRC-Handelsblad).* These differences in the findings between the two studies are interesting. They can, however, be explained by different notions. The first one is economic. In Jan Servaes's study, most newspapers were probably financially capable of sending their own reporters to cover the story. On the other hand, the economic situation of the media in developing and least developed countries explains their inability to expedite their own correspondents in different areas around the world. Another explanation of this difference in the dependence on trams-national media sources can be referred to the nature of the coverage examined in the two cases. In Meyer's case, the study concerns the coverage in general while in Serbaes's study the study is about the coverage of a specific news item. It can, thus, always be argued that an international crisis is an event that would normally draw exceptional attention and would consequently incite a newspaper to send its own reporter to cover such an event. This explanation is quite logical. Nonetheless, the fact that the German newspaper the *Frankfurter Allgemeine Zeitung* and the Dutch *NRC-Handelsblad* are, in fact, the only two newspapers in Servaes's study to exhibit a slight dependence on trans-national media sources for their news items concerning the Grenada crisis coverage indicates another important factor. This factor is that of interests in the news item. Indeed, the other four newspapers in Servaes's study are all newspapers of countries (the UK, France, Spain, Swiss) who had some sort of interest (to different degrees) in Grenada. Consequently, it can be said that the interest in the item itself, taken apart from economic considerations, can be a good explanation of the fact that some domestic media are less dependant for their news on tarns-national media sources than others. According to this logic, less dependency on outside sources means more interest in the event covered and vice versa.

Another important aspect in this discussion of the domestic media dependency on trans-national media for sources is raised by the two studies mentioned above. This aspect revolves around the determinants of the domestic media's choice of the trams-national media on which it will be dependent for sources. For Meyer, newswire stories on international relations, as reported in the Kenyan, Zambian, and Zimbabwean press, 29 % to 36 % (the largest single group) came from the British newswire (Reuters) and 41 % of all global news in the Latin American press originates from the two U.S. trams-national news agencies. According to Meyer, this is explainable by the former colonial ties and spheres of influence. Indeed, in the case of the African countries, it is interesting to learn that the three were former British colonies. As far as Latin America is concerned, it is explainable by the fact that Latin America is subject to the sphere of influence of the United States[170]. Servaes carries this analysis even further. He adds other factors to this choice of the source of the news item in the case of the European newspapers. He argues that the European newspapers generally obtained information" from an agency with which they have some linguistic, journalistic, and certainly also ideological affinity"[171]. Servaes explains that the *Neue Zurcher Zeitung* and the *Frankfurter Allgemeine Zeitung* used U.S. agencies, *Le Monde* and the *Times* used European agencies, and the *NRC-Handelsblad* and that *El Pais* had no clear preference. Another factor added by Servaes is what he calls "the management style o" of the newspaper. He argues that the selection of sources may be related to the newspapers' management style such as *Le Monde* which used a widely spread correspondent net and filled its news holes through an exchange agreement with *Agence France Presse*) or the British the *Times* which depicted a direct involvement and interest in the subject to be covered. Indeed, all

---

170   See William H. Meyer, op. cit, p.51.
171   See Jan Servaes, op. cit., p.37.

of these factors might intervene to determine the choice of the news sources. Yet, in the case of the domestic media in developing and least developed countries, these factors seem to be irrelevant compared to the colonial or political hegemonic explanatory factor of the direction of the news flow which might lead to a strong consideration of a media centre and periphery behavioural theory.

1.2.2. The Influence of Trans-national Mass Media on Domestic Public Opinion

The influence of trans-national media is certainly not limited to its influence on the local media. Its influence extends to that of the domestic public opinion in the host countries. This influence on domestic public opinion can be effectuated via two main means. The first one is the direct one. In this case trans-national media influences local public opinion directly when the public in the host country is directly exposed to the trans-national media transmission. The second means of influence is the indirect one. In this case the influence of trans-national media is effectuated through its influence on the domestic media and, consequently, on the domestic public opinion.

In both cases, however, the ways through which such influence on the domestic public opinion can take place is better explained with the use of three main frames of analysis. The frames are those of the repetition, dependence on international news and that of the selection and presentation of the international news items.

1.2.2.1. The Effect of Repetition

Repetition of a certain message usually leads to a more persuasive effect of that message on the mind. In this respect, the emphasis that the trans-national media can give, sometimes, in its coverage of a certain conflict or crisis rather than others and the repetition of specific line of thought can alter, affect and even reverse the public opinion. However, repetition itself could be ineffective if the repeated message was not presented in certain acceptable ways to the human mind. In this respect, three main means of persuasion through repetition can be identified. These are the use of repeated metaphors, the media's use of repletion as part of its agenda-setting function and what some researchers tend to label as the media's priming effect.

As far as the repetition of metaphors is concerned, some researchers have already mentioned their greater ability to persuade compared to their literal equivalents. This is due to the traditional distinctions between literal and figurative language. Literal language, as opposed to figurative language, has traditionally been seen as conveying the "proper" or "true" meaning of words[172]. Other studies attempt, furthermore, to explain why metaphors are more persuasive than literal language for persuasion purposes. Some think that a metaphor incites the imagination by indicating the similarities between concepts that would alternatively remain hidden if only literal language was used. Other views suggest that more cognitive resources are needed to understand metaphors which, in turn, incites a person to adopt most of his/her cognitive resources to understanding the "difficult" message. Consequently, he or she would have fewer resources left to counter argue against the message advocacy leading to more persuasion. Another means by which the use of metaphors can add to the persuasion effects is the fact that communicators who use metaphors are usually judged more positively. This translates into an additional credibility of the sources.

The media use of such metaphors can, hence, be said to be quite useful for effective persuasion purposes. In fact, an audience is expected to encounter metaphors in all forms of media whether printed, audio, visual or audio-visual. However, some researchers stress that the use of metaphors can be more effective in some media forms over others. For instance, Read et al. argue that reading, compared to listening, allows for more processing time as well as multiple reviews of the message. On the other hand, listening allows to process a message only once in a limited amount of time[173]. Thus, attention should be given to the linguistic form of the message diffused by the media especially the trans-national one. Indeed, if such metaphors are constantly repeated, the effect on the mind can would be that more metaphors gives less time to think because each metaphor needs time to analyse. Consequently, public opinion can be directed to think in a certain desired manner.

The other form of repetition used by the trans-national media to affect public opinion is that which is related to the agenda-setting function of the media. Denis MaQuail argues that agenda-setting is the expression of a correspondence between the order of importance given in the media to issues and events and the order of significance attached to the same issues and events by the public and politicians[174]. Repetition is an important element of this agenda-setting function of the media. For instance, Severin & Tankard indicate that by employing

---

172   See J. W., Bowers, & Osborn, M. M.," Attitudinal Effects of Selected Types of Concluding Metaphors in Persuasive Speeches", <u>Speech Monographs</u>, N°33, 1966, pp. 147-155.

173   See Read et al., "When is the Federal Budget Like a Baby? Metaphor in Political Rhetori"c, <u>Metaphor and Symbolic Activity</u>, N°5, 1990, pp 125-149.

174   See Denis MaQuail, <u>Mass Communication Theory: An Introduction</u>, Sage, London, 1994, p. 256

repeated news coverage, the media have the capability to raise the importance of certain issues in the public's mind[175]. They also indicate that this would set the agenda for what political matters people consider important[176]. This illustrates the influence that the media can have one the public opinion through repetition. Such repetition, used by the trans-national media and targeted to a worldwide audience more and more receptive (the new technological advances of reception and transmission) would certainly produce the same effect.

As with the case of metaphors, repetition in this case by the media relies on the assumption that most of the audience does not have detailed knowledge of the subject matter and that that it does not take into consideration all what it knows when making its decisions or opinions. In this respect, D. E. Alger explains that by attracting attention to some aspects of politics at the expense of others, the media can help to set the terms by which political judgments are reached[177]. However, he also argues that a number of other studies have criticized this effect of the repletion on the public opinion because they did not specifically demonstrated a causal connection between media agendas and the public's agendas nor showed strong statistical correlations[178]. Although this type of criticism exists, the fact remains that repetition is an essential element of the media to affect public opinion and carry out its agenda-setting function.

The third form of repletion, which may have a bearing on the public opinion, is that labeled by some researchers as the priming effect of the media. It two is related to the agenda-setting function of the media. The theory of priming has its origins in cognitive psychology. It is derived from the associative network model of human memory, in which an idea or concept is stored as a node in the network and is related to other ideas or concepts by semantic paths. Z. Pan and G.M. Kosicki, explain that priming refers to the process of activation of a node in this network, which may serve as a filter, an interpretive frame, or a premise for further information processing or judgment formation[179]. As far as the media is concerned, priming is an essential reformulation of this psychological process that offers an explanation of how media information is stored and retrieved in the human mind. In fact, media activate related thoughts, and consequently behavior, through this network of mental relationships. In this respect, Byron Reeves

---

175   See W.J. Severin, & Tankard, J.W., <u>Communications Theories: Origins, Methods, and Uses in the Mass Media</u>, Longman, New York: 1997, p. 249.

176   Ibid, P.252.

177   See D.E. Alger, <u>The Media and Politics, Prentice Hall</u>, New Jersey, 1989, p.127.

178   Ibid, 126.

179   See Z. Pan, & Kosicki, G.M.," Priming and Media Impact on the Evaluations of the President's Performance", <u>Communication Research</u>, N°24, 1997, p. 9.

explains that the extent of these relationships is determined by semantic associations between concepts in the human memory and the frequency with which the links have been used[180]. Thus, primarily priming is targeted towards the human mind and the human memory. It, thus, has an enormous effect on the formulation of individual and consequently public opinion.

An interesting study on the priming effects on public opinion was conducted by Pan and Kosicki. They examine how the two most important issues during the last three years of the presidency of George Bush (the Persian Gulf War and the economic recession in the United States) were related to the sharp rise and fall of public opinion about Bush's performance. They based their research on the assumption that voters were paying attention to media representation of Bush's performance as far as those two major issues are concerned. They explain that "heavy exposure to media coverage of a dominant issue leads to a stronger and/or more frequent activation of the thought elements related to the issue"[181]. They concluded that increased media priming effects can be attributed to increased media exposure[182]. Thus, increased media exposure of a certain issue can lead to a change in the public opinion on that issue. What applies to national media in this case can certainly be applicable as well to trans-national media. Exposure in this respect can take place on a wider range and affect a maximum of audience. In fact, the public opinion targeted in the case of the trans-national media is what has come to be known as the World Opinion.

Repetition, therefore, is an important means by which the media can influence public opinion. This repetition can be done through the constant emphasis of certain news and events and more subtly through the use of metaphors. Applied to the trans-national media, this assumption of the effects of the media repetition is quite applicable as well. With the new technological innovations and the access of the trans-national media to audiences in distant and remote parts of the world, using repletion in news coverage especially with metaphors and priming emphasis helps the trans-national media in shaping and modelling the public attitudes and the public opinion in different host countries.

---

180   See Byron Reeves, 1996, "Hemispheres of scholarship: Psychological and other Approaches to Studying Media Audiences". In Hay, J., Grossberg, L., and Wartella, E. (Eds.), The Audience and Its Landscape (pp. 265-279), Co, 1996, Westview Press. Boulder,

181   See Z. Pan, & Kosicki, G.M, op. cit., p.11.

182   Ibid.

1.2.2.2. The Dependence on International News

The dependence and need for international news is certainly one of the most important attributes of the trans-national media's influence on the domestic public opinion in host countries. Three main issues play a vital role in the discussion of this dependence on international news and its subsequent effect on the domestic public opinion. These are the technological innovations in the media diffusion and reception industries and the enormous exclusivity the trans-national media has in this area and the lack of press freedom in most world countries.

The technological innovations have enabled trans-national news corporations to capture an audience's attention in even the most remote areas and countries of the world. Nowadays, people in many countries receive daily 24-hour transmission of CNN, CBS, Fox, Reuters…etc. Using television, radio or the Internet, these trans-national media companies transmit either in English or sometimes in another major world language to audiences that in some cases have become addicted to their daily habits of checking the transmission of one or more of those corporations.

During an international crisis, this addiction to the info transmitted by the trans-national media increases. The CNN phenomenon during the Gulf War of 1990-91 is a clear example of this technological dominance, exclusive access and transmission some trans-national media have. Indeed, because of its performance in the Gulf War, CNN can be said to have been an active part in the development of a major international crisis. Indeed, the impact of the CNN coverage of the Gulf War was substantial. Claude Moisy explains that "the impact on the international community was such that the expression "global live coverage" was widely accepted as the description of what had happened and as the definitive hallmark of CNN"[183]. On the other hand, other researchers argue that the power of a network television such as CNN should not be over estimated because of a certain coverage of an international crisis, which can be considered as an isolated fortunate event leading to a considerable increase of the audience. For instance, Richard Parker estimates CNN International viewership at much less than 1% of the world population"[184]. This seems to be quite true for two reasons. The first one is that most audiences prefer to receive the foreign news in their own language. The second is that, since its mostly in a foreign language, the audience would be naturally limited to the audience group which is competent in or capable to understand that language. This group in most world countries constitutes the elite, which is by definition a minority of the population of any country.

---

183   See Claude Moisy, "The Foreign News Flow in the Information Age", <u>Discussion Paper N° D-23</u>, Johan F. Kennedy School of Government, November 1996, P.5.

184   See Richard Parker, <u>Mixed Signals: The Prospects for Global Television News,</u> The Twentieth Century Fund, New York, 1995.

If major network televisions such as CBS or CNN are not the main suppliers of foreign news to the world audience, it is because such a function is still filled by the traditional trans-national newswire services. They have been the main purveyors of foreign news to the world media since their creation in the mid-nineteenth century, mainly the three biggest ones (AP, AFP, Reuters). Indeed, their composition and benefits are enormous (Table 11).

Table 11: Relative Dimension of the Three GNWs (1993)

	AP	Reuters	AFP
Revenue ($M)	355	2,810	204
Expenses	353	2,240	207
Income	2	570	(3)
Empolyees	c.3,000	11,300	c.2,000
Total bureaus	226	126	130
Foreign bureaus	91	c.100	105
Total journalists	1,400	1,350	1,160
Journalists abroad	310	615	560

Source : Claude Moisy, <u>Op. Cit.</u>, p.6.

Those three major trans-national media corporations account for the majority of foreign news collection and distribution throughout the world. To do that, they rely on networks of news producing bureaus that no other type of news organizations or companies maintain to gather their foreign news items and on a network of worldwide autonomous telecommunication systems to distribute their services to their clients. According to Claude Moisy, these trans-national media have between 90 and 100 full-fledged bureaus (an office with at least one permanent staff journalist) outside their home base or original country. Additionally, the number of professional journalists (news writers and photographers) working in these foreign bureaus varies between 300 and 600 depending on the administrative status granted to their local personnel[185]. The volume of foreign news items produced and distributed by these media is quite impressive compared to that produced by well-known television networks. Claude Moisy explains" the three agencies produce 400 and 500 news items every day (not counting multiple versions in different languages) on all aspects of world activities: political, social, economic, cultural, sport, etc. Even the most "domestic" service of AFP, for instance, the French language general wire distributed to the French media (around 150,000 words daily), contains on the average 35% foreign news. The English language wire for Europe (120,000

---

185   See Claude Moisy, <u>op. cit.</u>, p.7.

words), contains more than 50% non-European news. The Associated Press, a wire in the United States, dominated as it is by the heavy demand of its members for national and regional news, can carry up to a hundred foreign stories a day. By comparison, CNN (including CNN International) never brings more than twenty foreign stories a day to its viewers, if for no other reason than the much higher cost of producing and transmitting video news"[186]. The almost incredible grip that transnational media has on the foreign news production and distribution allows it a very influential position in directing and controlling the public opinion. More than the exclusivity these media have in the production and supply of foreign news because of their own enormous information infrastructure, their ability to make others more dependent on their foreign news supply is also supported by other factors such as the degree of press freedom in the world and the decline of printed media.

The freedom of the press can be said to have improved during the past few years, especially in Easter Europe, some parts of Africa and Latin America due to the fall of the Berlin Wall and the introduction of a pluralist political system in most of those countries. Foreign newsgathering for correspondents of trans-national media has become much easier than it was before in these countries. In the past, the governments of these countries impeded cooperation with foreign journalists for different reasons and for charges that can go as far as accusing those who provide foreign journalists with information of being spies or collaborators. Notwithstanding, the majority of these countries have not yet fully independent and free media outlets. Most of the countries in the Middle East, for instance, have not yet allowed private television or radio stations. Even if such stations are allowed, they are mostly controlled by the state. Most of the news broadcasted would, therefore, be reflecting the government's point of view. In most of these countries, the main portion of the news bulletin would be for local news and usually for activities of the countries' leaders. Consequently, foreign news items have to be searched for elsewhere. Sometimes, news items about the country itself would be looked for in the broadcasting of an outside media company or agency simply because it reflects more objectivity than the constant subjective image given by the state owned media. It can be said, thus, that audiences in such countries are very much reliant on foreign news items produced and distributed by the trans-national media corporations. Lack of press or media freedom is, thus, an added advantage to the transnational media's ability in modelling public opinion worldwide.

The trans-national media has both the exclusivity and the circumstantial advantages to make it the major supplier and distributor of foreign news items. This would allow it an enormous ability to form and direct public opinion worldwide.

---

186   Idem.

1.2.2.3. The Selection and Presentation of International News in National Media

An important means by which trans-national media can influence domestic public opinion is through the process in which foreign news items are selected and presented in domestic media. The selection and presentation process actually depends on three main elements. These are the domestic media's internal structure and advocated policy, its editorial structure and the journalistic standards and views involved.

Ideally, any media should be an independent unit choosing the kind and the amount of foreign news items to be presented through it. However, this selection is not totally free from various considerations. This in turn can lead to some imbalances in foreign news coverage. For instance, Johan Eldrige explains that in most domestic media around the world there is a clear shortage of stories about Africa[187]. Yet, today most journalists admit that the selection process is so limiting in itself. Some refer to this restrictive process as the traditional view criteria. Suzan D. Moeller explains that it is usually that which answers such questions such as whether the foreign news items is new, prominent, significant or controversial?[188]. Obviously, the more the foreign news item or story satisfies this criteria the more its chances of being selected. However, understanding the choice of the story to be published requires a comprehension of the process of the news production itself. Some researchers indicate that the final choice made by journalists and editors was already made when the news item itself was produced and that the production of meaning in society is itself is a factor in the choice of news items[189]. Interestingly enough, many studies have indicated how concentration and homogeneity in perspective confines news agencies coverage to a small and similar selection of the news[190]. The idea here is that the news items selected are deemed to be so because of their original choice and production. If the process is looked upon as a straight line one then trans-national media agencies producing the foreign news item also determine its choice in the domestic media. Logically, this assumption is justifiable. The trans-national media have no interest in producing a foreign news item that would have little or no chance of being selected for presentation at the domestic media's end.

---

187 See John Eldrige, <u>Getting the Message: News, Truth and Power</u>, Ruthledge, London: 1993

188 See Susan D. Moeller, <u>Compassion Fatigue. How the Media Sell Disease, Famine, War and Death,</u> Routledge, New York, 1999.

189 See Gaye Tuchman, Making News, <u>op. cit.</u>, p. 215.

190 See Chris Paterson, "Global Battlefields", in Oliver Boyd-Barret, Terhi Rantanen, <u>The Globalization of News,</u> Sage, London, 1998, p. 95.

One of the important factors to be discussed at this point is that pf the domestic media's structure and policy. This structure and policy would certainly reflect on the choice of the foreign news item presented. In this respect, governmental regulations concerning the media are quite significant. Kevin Williams explains that the degree of governmental regulation of the print and electronic media significantly affects both the utilization of technology and the degree of competition and concentration of the media[191]. Indeed, the technological advances and innovations especially the Internet have profoundly affected the regulatory possibilities of governments. However, there is also an advantage to governments in these new technologies. For instance, the internet allows the government to bypass the media by offering the public direct access to news and documentation.

Another important aspect of media policy in many countries is the issue of economic integration. It has pushed the media business towards larger and larger units, due to the degree of internationalisation. In some countries press support is still a factor in maintaining the life of smaller papers. this in terms of audiovisual and, particularly television, has led to a rapid deregulation of state control, and,consequently, created a multitude of new channels and alternative news programs for the domestic public. As far as the printed media is concerned, the increased cost of newspaper production has led to a wave of mergers and consolidations. This naturally led to an increase in the competition among all types of media for advertising revenue and for viewers and readers.

Moreover, foreign news editors have to ensure that more than a small elite of the audience are interested in foreign news. They have to be aware of the fact that sometimes how the story is told is a very important consideration. Foreign news has to be dramatic and easily accessible. Presenting the foreign news item in a dramatic way and making it more accessible to the audience is also part of the competitive strategy of each media to distinguish itself from other media.

Another important factor in this equation of foreign news selection and presentation in domestic media is that which has to do with the editorial structure of the domestic media concerned. This structure revolves around the organisation of the foreign news production, the fact whether the foreign news section is a separate on integrated unit within another department, the availability of staff members for foreign news and the sources for these foreign news items.

Generally speaking, foreign news has a separate unit of production in most media. The technological advances have certainly fortified this independence of foreign news sections inside different media. Nowadays, everyone in a news organisation can have access on the screen to the international news items by the

---

191   See Kevin Williams, <u>Get me a Murder a Day: A History of Mass Communication in Britain</u>, Arnold, London, 1998.

click of a button. Additionally, communication costs both in terms of phone or satellite transmissions have substantially decreased.

The developments in the editorial structure of foreign news departments in the domestic media are interesting. In the past, foreign news departments were essentially staffed with people having a special kind of qualifications and interests. For instance, the staff had to know foreign languages and be willing to travel. Nowadays, the majority of foreign news is available in English, a language which the great majority of journalists are competent in, precisely because the great majority of foreign news items are diffused in English. Consequently, there is no more need to have very special group of people in the department of foreign news.

Another important development has to do with the concept of foreign news itself In the past, foreign news was defined as having only to do with political and economic events in foreign countries, especially those that have an impact on the domestic media's country. Taylor explains that to a large extent foreign news used to be merely diplomatic news[192]. This has certainly changed in today's media. Nowadays, journalists tend to write about much more aspects when they are reporting foreign news items, particularly social and cultural aspects. Consequently, the selection process becomes harder to determine which news item to select and to determine which priority to give this news item in presenting it.

The third factor in the equation of foreign news selection and presentation in domestic media is that which is related to the journalistic standards and professional values: In other words, a sense of what is a good and a bad story for a journalist has become a part of the journalists professionalism. The pressure for journalists to have more sellable stories leads to more competition and to the fact that foreign news stories are becoming more and more shorter in domestic media.

The process in which foreign news items are chosen and presented in domestic media is a complicated one indeed. The recent developments both in media technologies and in journalistic practices makes the criteria through which the foreign news items are chosen and presented in domestic media a more and more selective one. In this process of selection and presentation of foreign news items, the production of news items by the trans-national media is very significant. For often the initial news item production predestines it to be chosen and presented or not in domestic media. This allows the trans-national media an enormous influence in preconditioning the journalists of the domestic media. Consequently, this power of the foreign news selection and presentation process adds to the trans-national media's ability to control domestic public opinion.

---

192   See Phillip M. Taylor, <u>Global Communications, International Affairs and the Media since 1945</u>, Routledge, London, 1997, pp. 58-75.

1.3. International Crises and Media Coverage

The relationship existing between the media and international crisis or conflicts is an interesting one indeed. It can be said that an important change took place in the media's coverage of international crisis in the post cold war period. During the time of the Cold War, local conflicts or civil wars were simply labelled as part of the communist-democratic struggle, where the Soviet Union and its allies supported one side while the United States and its allies supported the other.

The first important test to this labelling of local conflicts came with the outbreak in the war in the ex-Yugoslavia. These wars depended more on mobilizing ethnic or religious affinities, their principal victims were the civilians in the adversary camps, and they were usually marked by ethnic cleansing, genocide and massive immigrations. Some studies estimate the number of civil wars in 1995 at around thirty[193]. In such wars, the survival of the ethnic or religious group was usually used as the key element of mobilizing the group. In such situations, local media was usually used to serve such purposes as enflaming hatred. However, it is also important to mention in this respect that the media can play a role of prevention of such conflicts. Indeed, international media in particular can focus the attention on the situation in a certain region in the world prior to the outbreak of hostilities. By doing so, the media can play a preventive role and not simply a post-action one. Unfortunately, however, such behaviour from the part of the media rarely takes place in spite of the fact that there are usually notable indications of the eventuality of a conflict' before its actual outbreak[194]. This would, however, be an ideal situation where the economic and profit interests of the media doesn't count.

The image the media projects of such conflicts, after their outbreak, is very important as a determinant of the international reactions to be taken. In fact, the method of focusing on the conflict would mobilize the world's public opinion and, thus, lead to an intervention in the conflict area. This intervention, however, and as far as states are concerned does not only depend on the humanitarian necessity of intervention but on other elements as well. This kind of debate is usually raised within the intervening state. A good example of this would be the debate over the US policy in Somalia, Bosnia, Haiti, and Central Africa. The U.S. Defence Secretary in 1994 explains this kind of internal debate

---

193   See Larry Minear, et al., <u>The News Media, Civil War, and Humanitarian Action</u>, Boulder, CO, Lynne, 1996, p.39.

194   See for instance Francoise Hampson book, <u>Incitement and the Media: Responsibility of and for the Media in Conflicts in the Former Yugoslavia</u> by. Colchester, Essex, 1993.

inside the United States. He distinguishes between three types of situations. The first one is a situation where there are "vital" interests for the United States which, thus, justifies the risk of a military action. The Second, is what he labels as "important but not vital" national interests and, in which, force can be used more selectively. The third of these situations is the "humanitarian" interests one. In this last situation, force should be used only if needed to deal with a catastrophe[195]. Clearly, and through this statement of the U. S. Defence Secretary, intervention for humanitarian purposes figures at the very end of the United States' priority list.

Notwithstanding, there is evidence that the media effect has its immediate effect on political decisions of intervention for humanitarian reasons. For instance, the Bush Administration sent forces to Mogadishu, after the diffusion of the starvation images there, to help distribute food aid to starving Somalis. Ironically enough, the same media coverage was the reason for these forces to withdraw when, pictures of a dead US Army Ranger being dragged in Mogadishu forced the Clinton Administration to withdraw the U. S. forces. This double-edged effect of the media coverage was well described at the time by John Shattuck the U.S. Assistant Secretary of State for Human Rights and Democracy who states "The media got us into Somalia and then got us out"[196]. This effect of media coverage of international crisis and conflicts is, however, highly debatable. The U.S. National Security Adviser Anthony Lake disclosed in March 1996, a seven-point list of national interests that might lead to a U.S. use of force. Contrary to the earlier policy of action in the Balkans, the new list hardly touched conflict prevention created by the new generation of sub-state conflicts[197]. Interestingly enough, Lake's list disregarded any emotive power of TV and media coverage of international crisis situations.

Some journalists tend to support the logic of Lake's list. For instance, Warren Strobel, a journalist at the Washington Times, claims that TV coverage "hold no power to force US policymakers to intervene in a civil conflict where there is no clear national interest." He explains that news reports are likely to prompt a government response only when government officials are themselves undecided about what policy to follow in a crisis situation and when the costs of intervening

---

195 See Minear, et al., <u>Op. Cit.</u>, P.17.

196 See John Shattuck, "Human Rights and Humanitarian Crises: Policy-Making and the Media," in Rotberg and Weiss, <u>From Massacres to Genocide</u>, Brookings Institution Press,1996, p. 174.

197 See the speech of the U.S. National Security Adviser Anthony Lake at George Washington University, 8 March 1996<u>"Principles Governing US Use of Force."</u>.

are relatively low[198]. Curiously enough, other studies tend to question the effect of coverage of international crisis on public attitudes. This idea is illustrated in a study made by the Times Mirror Centre for The People and the Press. The outcome was that the month-to-month pattern of US reporting of he Bosnian war over the period (1991-1994) didn't correspond to the changes in the level of public interest in the crisis over the same period of time[199]. Indeed, it is often difficult to understand the role of media coverage of an international crisis if such coverage is considered separately from other factors.

Although images of TV coverage of an international conflict or crisis cannot be questioned in their effect on the viewer, the thing to be done differs and depends on other interests of the intervening state or group of states. One basic thing for the TV images or the coverage to come to existence is that they have to be there in the first place. One important element relating to this discussion of the role of media in the international crisis is that related to what has come to labelled as the "CNN effect".

For his part, however, James A. Baker III questions the credibility of the CNN coverage especially when it comes to its sources of information[200]. They, according to him, are often ill-informed and based on false assumptions. However, some decision makers in the United States such as the former U.S. Defence Secretary William Perry, confirms the power of the "CNN effect" and "the images that pursue him from office to hotel room to home"[201]. This attitude of U.S. officials is, further, supported by the statement of the former U.S. State Department spokesman Nicholas Burns who says: "The challenge for us in government is to balance the need to feed the beast of television against the more natural and wise human instinct to reflect before speaking"[202]. Thus, the effect of the TV images of the coverage of the international conflict or crisis is a highly debatable issue, at least as far as its effect on the decision making is concerned.

---

198   See Warren P. Strobel, "The Media and U.S. Policies Toward Intervention," in Chester A. Crocker and Fen Osler Hampson, Managing Global Chaos, United States Institute of Peace Press, Washington, DC.,1996, p. 358.

199   See Andrew Kohut and Robert C. Toth, "The People, the Press, and the Use of Force", in United States and the Use of Force in the Post-Cold War Era, The Aspen Institute, Queenstown, Maryland:, 1995, p.149.

200   See James A. Baker III, "Report First, Check Later", interviewed by Marvin Kalb, Harvard International Journal of Press/Politics, Vol. 1, N°. 2, Spring 1996, p. 3.

201   See Marvin Kalb, "The Pentagon and the Press", Harvard International Journal of Press/Politics, Vol. 1, N°. 1, Winter 1996, p. 121.

202   See Nicholas Burns, "Talking to the World About American Foreign Policy", Harvard International Journal of Press/Politics, Vol. 1, N°. 4, Fall 1996, p. 12.

Another important scope of view is to see the negative psychological or frustrating effect of the media coverage on the political and public attitudes. Some writers explain, for instance, that as far as Africa is concerned, negative reporting from Africa by the U.S. media erodes the domestic constituency for US involvement in tile continent. Michael Clough argues that this fact explains the low amount of US assistance to the African continent[203]. Warren Strobel's explains the negative frustrating effect of media coverage of human tragedies saying that the images diffused "add to the viewer's frustration and cynicism about the ability of his or her government to do anything about the world's seemingly unsolvable and ever-present problems"[204]. Though this negative effect might be true, the effects of non-coverage can be much more negative.

The relationship between the media and international crisis is, thus, a debatable one. Media coverage can be used for preventive purposes prior to the outbreak of hostilities. This use of media is, unfortunately, not yet effective probably for audience and economic reasons. Whether the media coverage of tragic human conflicts can have an effective impact on a state's intervention decision is also a debatable issue. What is certain though, is that there is a close relationship between the media coverage and the reactions to international crisis. How much can that mobilize state or public reactions is also a debatable issue.

1.3.1. The Role of the Media in International Crises

The role of media during international crisis is a critical role indeed. For it is primarily through the media that one gets the picture of the situation during international crisis. This window through which the situation during an international crisis is depicted can be better understood through an analysis of the fundamental composites underlying the role of the media in covering an international crisis. These composites are those of transmission, the role of coverage itself, the role of objectivity and the role of spotlighting and underestimation of an international crisis.

---

203   See Michael Clough, "The Africa Question: Should the U.S. Get Involved?", <u>Los Angeles Times</u> (November 3, 1996), P.2

204   See Warren P. Strobel, "TV Images May Shock But Won't Alter Policy," <u>Christian Science Monitor</u>, December 14, 1994.

1.3.1.1. The Role of Transmission: Technological Innovations and Their Effect on Media Coverage

One of the most important roles of the media is that of transmission. The performance of this role to its fullest depends, however, on the availability and efficiency of the transmission media. In the past few years, the technological revolution and the innovations in the media transmission materials and equipment have certainly had their impact on the media's coverage of events around the world.

Historically speaking and during the past two centuries, the great majority of international news originated from England and the United States. Indeed, the BBC World Service Radio was the premier radio service. Until the 1990's, the most effective method of transmission was the short-wave radio. For their part, printed media carried detailed wire service stories across the world. Their limitation, however, was that their distribution was limited to urban areas and that they were limited to those who can read them. Until the last decade of the 20th century, people in most parts of the earth had only one or two national television channels. Furthermore, and in many places, television was three decades old at the most.

The first major break through was at the end of the 1980s and the beginning of the 1990s when technological developments, combined with the vision of Ted Turner, (the founder of CNN) created the first global TV, where viewers all over the world could watch events live as they happen in most parts of the world. The effect of this new innovation was best described by George Winslow who said "Tiananmen Square television footage, the Berlin Wall falling, and the Persian Gulf War coverage convinced broadcasters that international news could be a 'ratings bonanza. These events and similar forced news organizations to beef up their global coverage".[205] At the same time, other nations around the world followed suit. For example, at the end of the 1980s, many European countries began to expand upon their limited public broadcasting and offer commercial television stations. Robert E. Burke (president of Worldwide Television News WTN), described this opening up of the European market by saying "There's a large part of the world just peeking out from under government regulation, a huge number of people who speak many languages. In 1989 and 1990 when Eastern Europe began to open up, business for us changed overnight. It used to take six months to get a visa to do a story for a week, now, we set up permanent bureaus. That's good news for a news agency. Those people are well-served."[206]

---

205   See Carla Brooks Johnston, <u>Global News Access: The Impact of New Communications Technologies</u>, Praeger Publishers, Westport, CT., 1998, p. 58.

206   Ibid.

Today, a new term has come to describe this multitude of technological inno-vations in media transmission. This term is The Global Village. Indeed, within this village almost everything is connected by the information superhighway. This meant that even small TV companies would make new efforts to enable their viewers, even in faraway areas, to receive such global information. Even when sophisticated satellite receivers are not available to certain people around the world, hand-made crafted ones are usually fabricated.

Yet, with this revolution in media transmission technologies come two new ideas. The first one is that it is becoming more in the interest of the global or multinational global companies to respond, understand and reflect the needs of the countries or regions it covers or where it is located. This is done to attract more audience to its transmission. The second new idea is that such areas, coun-tries or regions require programmes that are adapted to their needs, culture and language. It is normal, therefore, to see lots of "local" versions of global news agencies or channels such as CNN Europe for instance.

The new technologies of transmission meant primarily a more rapid means of transmission. Indeed, one of the essential goals of the global media channels is to transmit the event before the others do. This naturally would earn the news trans-mitter more credibility and consequently more audience. A good example of such speed of coverage would be the television coverage of the Falkland Islands War in 1982 and the end of the Marcos regime in the Philippines in 1986. In both exam-ples, world direct broadcast satellite (DBS) technologies signified a revolution in the newsgathering business. The reason is that Satellite pictures can be transmit-ted instantly and can be sold anywhere. If need may call for it, local broadcasters could put on a soundtrack giving the news item the locally acceptable spin.

The development of satellite transmission took place via a number of steps. Initially international TV and data communication was carried on INTELSAT satellites and relied on COMSAT earth stations in the United States and on gov-ernment-owned earth stations in other countries. INTELSAT itself is a system of satellites owned by a consortium of 119 countries[207]. In 1962, the United States President John F. Kennedy initiated the Communications Satellite Act.In 1974 the Soviet Union created another satellite network (INTERSPUTNIK)[208]. Since then many countries have launched their own communication satellites into space. What is extraordinary is that while the initial satellite use was primarily for military purposes, scientific exploration, and meteorological use, the civilian communications industry soon began growing at a previously unimaginable pace.

---

207   See http://www.intelsat.int/cmc/bcaster/bc0996.html.
208   See Raymond Akwule, <u>Global Telecommunications</u>, Focal Press, London, 1992, p. 72.

Indeed, as computer and video technologies begin to merge and as cellular phone use expands, it will be increasingly difficult to segregate visual transmission from voice and data transmission. The progress in this technology is tremendous. Carla Brooks Johnston explains that" in the 1970s, one to five communications satellites were launched per year. In the late 1990s, seventy to eighty will be launched in one year. By 2011, there will be about ninety-five launched that year"[209]. She adds that" the industry is dominated by three main companies: Lockheed, Lorrall, and Hughes"[210].

Another important technological breakthrough relating to media transmission is that of fibre optic technology. This technology was first tested for video transmission in 1980. By the late 1980s, utility companies started to replace the traditional coaxial cable with fibre optic cables. The result was that by 1991 around 300 cities in the United States were connected by fibre optic cables in addition to a number of specific corporate, government, and communication routes throughout the world. Here two the progress was fast and impressive. For instance, In developing parts of the world, technologies were completely bypassed as whole countries went from virtually no telephone system to fibre optic systems.

This fast expansion of the utilisation of this technology has its technical and economic reasons. First, fibre optic technology can transmit high-quality voice, data, image, and video in two-way communication at a cheaper rate and in a more accessible, more flexible manner than satellite transmission. Second, with the use of fibre optic technology privacy of transmission is possible. Third, the customer using fibre optics for video transmission won't have the mechanical worries of arranging the location, the equipment, and the satellite time; because these mechanics will be built into the system.

One of the other important elements in this technological revolution of media transmission innovations is that of Digital Compression. This is possibly a major breakthrough since TV is a heavy user of the radio frequency spectrum. Thus, before Digital Compression, each channel occupied the space of several hundred radio channels. In fact what Digital does is that it consolidates space and makes it possible to have more channels in the same space. Before Digital, TV picture frames were sent each 1/25th of a second, with the space in between containing only minor movement modifications. In addition, much of the picture doesn't change from one frame to the next. In fact, it is possible to state that as much as 98% of what is sent can be redundant. Digital compression, therefore, means to sift out what's not redundant. This process can be done digitally with silicon chips similar to those used in a high-speed computer. Furthermore, sending a

---

209   op. cit., p.60.
210   ibid.

program by satellite is highly expensive because of the cost of transponder space. Thus, If the signal is sent digitally, as much as eight or more times the number of channels over one transponder can be sent, thereby greatly limiting the cost.

The effect of these new technological innovations on the media coverage, especially of international crisis goes without saying. Indeed, in less than a decade CNN, BBC's World Service TV, and Rubert Murdoch's[211] BSky-B and STAR TV have reached into living rooms across the globe with their "live" news. At the same time, the traditional wholesalers of news and information such as Reuters and AP have joined Worldwide Television News (WTN) to sell wholesale video to broadcasters.

It can be said that the existence of an international crisis actually helped some of those media news giants when they were first launched. For instance, CNN launched the global TV news era with its unforgettable live news coverage of the crisis on the spot (Peter Arnett showing the world live missile attacks over Baghdad). Similarly, the BBC's World Service TV (WSTV) was launched in 1991. WSTV was propelled by the impact CNN was having as result of its Gulf War coverage. In addition, Rupert Murdoch's B-Sky-B news coverage in Europe also began on the heels of the Persian Gulf War in 1991. In 1993, Murdoch solidified his northern hemisphere coverage with the purchase of the controlling interest in STAR TV in Asia. In less than a decade a revolution had occurred. These newsmakers are well aware that in many parts of the world a picture is, indeed, worth a thousand words, especially during a crisis time. Recently, Al-Jazeera exclusive transmission of the events in Afghanistan in the aftermath of the September 11th 2001 attacks pushed it into the frontline of media giants. Indeed, quite a number of media news companies had to sign agreements with this channel to share the exclusivity of certain of its news items.

Thus, it can be said that the technological innovations during the past decades have immensely contributed to the news coverage all over the world. More news is covered and it is covered faster. Nevertheless, the issue remains of whether all issues are covered equally, objectively and accurately?. If not, it is important to know why such differences in the considerations and characteristics of the news coverage exist.

---

211   Murdoch, Rupert (Keith Rupert Murdoch), born in 1931–, Australian-American publishing magnate. Combining sensationalist journalism with aggressive promotion, he established a worldwide communications empire that includes powerful holdings in Australia and New Zealand; the prestigious *Times* of London and other British papers; and, in the United States, HarperCollins book publishers, the New York *Post*, and *TV Guide.* He also acquired 20th Century Fox film studios and home video and built the Fox Television network, as well as television stations in Australia. His other communications ventures include direct-broadcast satellite television and cable networks. He became a U.S. citizen in 1985.

1.3.1.2. The Role of Coverage

One of the most important and even essential roles of the media is its role of coverage. The media is vital because it conveys tales and stories of daily life, comments on our behaviour, daily livelihood, what is happening inside and outside the borders and human reactions to it. In short, it is sort of a feedback on daily actions and sentiments. In this respect, the media coverage of an international crisis or conflict is extremely important.

The reasons for which the coverage of such exterior far-away crisis and conflicts is important is that it is important to understand first what is happening in order to know how to react. If the coverage of the international crisis exists, it would convey an idea of the conflict situation, its causes and its effects. In an ideal situation, if accurate coverage exists, dealing with the international crisis or conflict would be more effective. Moreover, if it is covered correctly, coverage of an international conflict for instance may act as a preventive factor to avoid repeating the same crisis in the country or in its region. A good example of this use of coverage is that of the coverage of ethnical or religious sub-state wars in countries where there is a multiethnic or a multi-religious social fabric.

Yet, ideal situations are virtually inexistent. In fact, on several occasions, the media failed to fulfil its role of coverage vis-à-vis international crisis and conflicts. An example of such failure is the coverage of the tragic situation and the massacres in Burundi during the period 1993-1996. A failure that ended in the disinterest of the international community in the tragic events taking place in Burundi during that period. Actually, the first major breakthrough that drew attention to the situation there came in July of 1996 with a news item in the International Herald Tribune announcing the massacre of 304 persons in Bugendana in a single ethnic attack[212]. Thereafter, the Burundi president took refuge in the U.S. Embassy and the Tutsi took hold of the army. Only then did the international community start to fear the outbreak of acts of genocide[213]. The result of this late coverage was inaction. The UN even tried to harness the media to put moral pressure on the world powers in order to provide logistical and political commitment to its peacekeeping operation there (using the example of the genocide earlier in Rwanda in 1994 and the non-response of the Western powers to prevent it as a historical stimulant for action).

212　See "Toll at 304 in Burundi attack," Agence France Press, International Herald Tribune, 22 July 1996.

213　See "Burundi Slides Towards Civil War" by Michela Wrong, The Financial Times, 27 July 1996.

Kofi Anan, the then head of the Peace Keeping Operations of the UN was quoted as saying "We have to move very quickly before everything blows up in our faces. History will judge us rather severely for Rwanda, and I don't think we can repeat that experience in Burundi"[214]. Obviously, even when covered, not all international crisis merit intervention, according to the world powers calculations of interests. Minear, et. al., explains that, as far as Rwanda was concerned, a steering committee that was set up to evaluate the international response to the crisis there blamed the media for not realizing the extent of the genocide and massacres in that country. He quotes the committee saying: "the overall failure of the media to accurately and adequately report on a crime against humanity significantly contributed to international disinterest in the genocide, and hence to the inadequate response"[215]. Media then can be held responsible for not covering a international crisis situation properly.

A number of elements should be considered in performing the role of coverage. These include the role of explanation, avoiding dramatization, identifying causes of the crisis, understanding the language and culture of the conflict area and avoiding stereotyping.

It is quite important when covering an international crisis to provide an adequate analysis or explanation of the events being covered. In order to be fully understandable a covered event (like an ethnic killing for instance) should be explained and placed into its right context for the receiver of the coverage to have a better understanding of the coverage of the event.

Another element that should be considered, in order for the media to better perform its coverage role, is that relating to avoiding exaggerating or over-dramatizing of the covered items. Indeed, coverage of the crisis in Bosnia for instance, was often criticized for exaggerating the casualties on the Muslim side. Yet, the others claim that without this kind of dramatizing bigger tragedies might take place. Nik Gowing, gives two good examples of the effectiveness of dramatized coverage. These are the predicament of Kurdish refugees driven from Iraq to southern Turkey after the Gulf War in the early 1991 and the Bosnian Muslims herded into *Srebrenica* in April 1993[216]. Indeed, in both these situations, the emotional TV coverage had a positive political impact inciting the international community to take quick action.

---

214   See Kofi Annan interview on <u>BBC World TV News</u>, 24 July 1996.

215   See Minear, et. al., <u>op. cit.</u>, p.97.

216   See Nik Gowing, <u>Real-Time Television Coverage of Armed Conflicts and Diplomatic Crises: Does it Pressure or Distort Foreign Policy Decisions?</u>, Harvard University, Cambridge, MA., 1994.

For a better coverage of the international crisis, historical and political causes of the conflict should be clearly explained. This, for instance, was particularly important to stress in the former Yugoslavia and Rwanda. As far as the coverage of events in the former Yugoslavia is concerned, it was important to know the historical reasons behind the hatred between Serbs, Croats and Muslims. As far as Rwanda is concerned, journalists, who weren't quite familiar with the events that preceded the massacres there, were inclined to suggest, as Fergal Keane explains, "that the genocide was the result of some innate inter-ethnic loathing that had erupted into irrational violence....Much of the coverage of Rwanda in the early days neglected the part that power and money had played in the calculations of those who launched the genocide"[217]. This is quite important in international crisis coverage since the understanding of the causes helps to present the situation in its right and proportional context.

Good coverage of international crisis should also include an adequate preparation for reporters who cover the events in terms of language and area studies. This, however, could be hindered by the lack of funding for such preparation. Nevertheless, the recent diversification of conflicts and international crisis demands some sort of area specialisation. Different aspects of this preparation for journalists are those related to training in international law, international humanitarian law, and the Geneva conventions. With such preparation, reporters can identify more precisely the nature of the event they are covering whether, for instance, it relates to a war crime, genocide or any other infringement of international law.

The media has, thus, a fundamental role to play in covering international crisis. Yet, in order for this role to be fully effective, certain conditions have to be met. The most important of these is that the media should not ignore its responsibility for the coverage of an international crisis. For the coverage itself to be more effective, good preparation for reporters, avoiding dramatisation and a good understanding of the historical and political roots of the conflict are essential.

1.3.1.3. The Role of Objectivity

A very important role of the media is that of objectivity. The media has to be as objective as possible in its coverage of international crisis. Maintaining this role, however, is not at all an easy thing to do. The difficulty of being objective stems from the fact that in an international crisis different parties are involved. Each of these parties has its own interests, claims and beliefs. In short, each thinks his actions are justified. Thus, no matter how objective the media coverage of the crisis event is, there will always be some sort of dissatisfaction with it from one

---

217   See Fergal Keane, <u>Season of Blood: A Rwandan</u>, Viking, London, 1995, pp.6-7.

side or the other. Indeed, the debate on media objectivity during international crisis is an endless one.

The first example of these debates is that revolving around the media coverage of the crisis in Bosnia. For while some claim that the coverage of the crisis in Bosnia was totally partial others declare totally the opposite. Martin Bell, for instance suggests that, in Bosnia, journalists embarked on crusades and were so partial in their coverage of the events there. He explains that their impartiality was due to their own personal outrage at Serb aggressions there[218]. This view is also that of General Sir Michael Rose of Britain, UNPROFOR commander in Bosnia (1994-95). He criticizes the media partiality with the Bosnian government saying that "It is of course quite understandable that a government struggling for survival should have a propaganda machine...It is not understandable that the international media should become part of that machine. Mischievous distortion of reality can only undermine the work of those who are pursuing the path towards peace"[219]. In fact, most critics of the media coverage partiality in Bosnia came from UN officials. Nit Cowing explains that many of the UN officials "questioned the picture painted by the media" in Sarajevo"[220]. On the other hand, some UN officials praised the Media coverage of the events of Bosnia and Rwanda as well. Richard Goldstone, the South African judge who served as the first chief prosecutor for the United Nations war crimes tribunals for Rwanda and the former Yugoslavia, states that he felt "very warm gratitude and appreciation for the attention that the press gave to war. crime prosecutions". He adds, "Without the media there wouldn't have been ad hoc tribunals at all. The media built up public pressure for them"[221]. Thus, there are contradictory views especially by the UN officials of the ground in Bosnia of the objectivity of the news coverage there. This might be understandable in the sense that if the media coverage did actually show atrocities committed, while the UN military personnel were stationed in Bosnia, then it would mean a critic to the UN's own inefficiency in preventing such atrocities.

In fact, there is a solid explanation for this animosity between the UN and the media concerning the coverage of the crisis in Bosnia. First of all, it should be kept in mind that most of the journalists assigned to Bosnia were veteran foreign

---

218 See Martin Bell, In Harms Way, Hamish Hamilton, London, 1995, p. 273.

219 See David Owen, Balkan Odyssey, New York, Harcourt Brace and Company, New York,1995, p.119.

220 See Nit Cowing, "Instant Pictures, Instant Policy: Is Television Driving Foreign Policy?", The Independent, July 3, 1994, p. 14

221 See Richard Goldstone, remarks at a news conference in Washington, DC, October 2, 1996.

correspondents. Most of them previously covered such wars and conflicts in Southeast Asia, Africa, Afghanistan, Central America, and the Persian Gulf. They were, hence, experienced journalists and not easy to manipulate as far as covering international crisis is concerned. In addition to this fact, it has to be remembered that there was an impression amongst journalists that UN officers in Bosnia were often hostile towards the reporters. Another factor explaining this animosity is that the media and the UN Command had different and sometimes conflicting, responsibilities and agendas in Bosnia. The UN personnel there were mostly soldiers. They had orders to follow and were mostly there to distribute humanitarian assistance. Unlike the media they did not have the inherent ability to present a vision of the events in the crisis as the media did.

Moreover, both and the UN personnel were claiming impartiality in their work. However, their own visions of impartiality were different. For their part, the UNPROFOR[222] would be impartial by referring to the different sides of the conflict. This actually reflected the nature of the UNPROFOR there, which can be resumed in being sort of a buffer zone or an acceptable mediator between the conflicting sides. On the other hand, the journalists' vision of objectivity is not connected to the necessity of being accepted by the conflicting sides. For the journalists, their objectivity was telling the truth as they saw it and regardless whether this truth would make them unacceptable to one side or the other.

It is worth mentioning in this respect that the meaning of impartiality itself, as far as the UN Peace Keeping Operations is concerned is a controversial issue. For instance, Adam Roberts claims that impartiality in UN peacekeeping "is no longer interpreted to mean, in every case, impartiality between the parties to a conflict. In some cases, the UN may, and perhaps should, be tougher with one party than another or give more aid to one side than another." However, he adds that another standard might be followed, based on "...the idea that the UN represents a set of interests, values, and tasks that are distinct in some respects from those of any one belligerent party. In some peacekeeping operations, impartiality may mean hoc impartiality/try between the belligerents, but impartiality in carrying out UN Security Council decisions"[223]. In fact, this disagreement of the

---

222   United Nations Protection Force, Initially established in Croatia to ensure demilitarisation of designated areas. The mandate was later extended to Bosnia and Herzegovina to support the delivery of humanitarian relief, monitor "no fly zones" and "safe areas". The mandate was later extended to the former Yugoslav Republic of Macedonia for preventive monitoring in border areas.

223   See Adam Roberts, "The Crisis in UN Peacekeeping" in A. Crocker and Fen Olster Hampson, Managing Global Chaos, United States Institute of Peace Press, Washington, DC: 1996, p. 315.

concept of impartiality in UN Peace Keeping Operations even caused tensions between the United States and the UN over the UN handling of the situation in Bosnia. Susan L. Woodward, for example, who served as the former political adviser to UN envoy Yasushi Akashi, states that the UNPROFOR was revolted when it was required by the United States and NATO to diverge from its mandate of impartiality in order to take sides with the Bosnian government against the Bosnian Serbs[224]. For their part, the U.S. officials often criticized the UN for being passive with Serb outrageousness. For instance, an internal U.S. State Department report published in *The New York Times* accuses the UN Command in Sarajevo of seeking "to appease the Serb militias". The report continues, "within Serb-controlled territories, it is the Serb 'authorities,' not the UN, who decide how and to whom relief will be distributed"[225]. This controversy over the concept of impartiality between the U.S. and NATO on one side and the UN on the other is quite understandable since both had different agendas and interests in Bosnia. The UN viewed the crisis from its position as a peacekeeper and a mediator mandated by the world community and working within the limits of international law. On the other hand, the U.S. and NATO pressed for action because inaction could have caused a spill over of the conflict to the European continent.

The debate over the objectivity of the media coverage in the Bosnian crisis also took place between journalists themselves. Martin Bell, for instance, explains the moral and emotional pressures that journalists go through while covering international crisis and conflicts, He claims that surrounded by human tragedies, it is extremely difficult for journalists as humans to be impartial[226]. For her part, CNN's Christiane Amanpour helped to keep Bosnia as a major issue on U.S. TV news with her emotional presentations. She even became renowned as the "Queen of the Sarajevo press corps"[227]. She was also famous for what Ed Vulliamy calls "her defiance of bland 'neutrality' in the coverage of genocide"[228]. Amnapour's vision of objectivity "means giving all sides a fair hearing—not treating all sides the same—particularly when all sides are not the same. When you are

---

224 See Susan L. Woodward, <u>Implementing Peace in Bosnia and Herzegovina: A Post-Dayton Primer and Memorandum of Warning</u>, The Brookings Institution, Washington, DC:, 1996, pp.22-23.

225 See Michael R. Gordon, "U.S. Finds Serbs Skim 25% of Bosnian Aid", *The New York Times*, January13, 1993.

226 See Martin Bell, "Testament of an Interventionist", <u>British Journalism Review</u>, Vol. 4, N°. 4, 1993, p. 9.

227 See Ed Vulliamy, "TV Giants Vie To Lure 'Brit Packer'", <u>The Observer</u>, 19 May 1996, p. 23.

228 Ibid.

in a situation like Bosnia, you are an accomplice—an accomplice to genocide"[229]. Another journalist, Roy Gutman, supports Amanpour's view. He says, "I do not believe the fairness doctrine applies equally to victims and perpetrators"[230].On the other side of the equation, others simply denounced the impartiality and lack of the objectivity of the media in the Bosnian crisis. Peter Brock, for instance, who explains that in 1992, the majority of the media had become "so mesmerised by their focus on Serb aggression" that any principle of balance and objectivity evaporated.[231] There is obviously much argument amongst the journalists themselves about the objectivity of their coverage of the Bosnian crisis. Yet, it is always important to remember two things. The first is that journalists are humans who are susceptible to be emotionally involved or affected by what they are supposed to be covering objectively. Second, that there are always interests for the journalists and the media companies in presenting their stories in a particular manner. This has naturally to do with audiences and revenues. The explanation is simple since most audiences would identify with what they see as the victim more than the perpetrators themselves.

It is, thus, extremely difficult for the media to be objective in its coverage of the international conflict or crisis. Sometimes, it is because there are different functions for the media and for the diplomats and sometimes it is because there are different interests for both. Yet, most importantly, it is difficult for journalists not to project their own personal convictions and views in their coverage.

1.3.1.4. The Role of Over Exposure or Under-Exposure of The International Crisis

Deciding whether to over or under expose an international crisis is one of the most important roles or functions of the media. In other words, it is the media, which decides that emphasis should be given to one crisis or conflict over another. It is important, hence, to examine the basis on which such decision-making or selection of emphasis is done. The media's role in exposing and clarifying crisis and conflict situations is vital. The United Nations' Secretary-General Kofi Annan explains," Peacekeeping operations depend for their support on

---

229   See Dina Rabinovitch, "The Million Dollar Action Woman", The Guardian, 6 July 1996.

230   Sherry Ricchiardi, "Exposing Genocide", American Journalism Review, June 1993, pp. 32-36.

231   See Peter Brock, "Dateline Yugoslavia: The Partisan Press", Foreign Policy, N°. 93, Winter 1993, p. 4.

widespread public awareness of the conflicts, and we are committed to doing everything we can to facilitate the work of the media"[232].

In fact, there are quite a number of factors that shape and direct the media's reaction to an international crisis or conflict. Many journalists observed that in the age of video, if there is no picture, there is no story. Christopher Young, for example, states, "situations which cannot be captured on film, or to which photographer cannot get access, tend to be under-reported"[233]. On the opposite side of the equation, he adds' visually dramatic, acute events (such as battles or bombings) receive more coverage, while longer-term, wide-spread situations (such as famine or poverty) get less...while the Gulf War got extensive coverage, the deaths of over 140,000 Bangladeshis due to spring flooding went virtually unreported"[234]. This is a very interesting factor indeed. Due to the technological advancement in media technology, it can be said that the images in our present time have much more credibility than words. This is quite normal, as far as human nature is concerned, since people usually tend to believe more and be affected more by what they can see happening for themselves. This also leads to another consequence, which is that of competition between the media for coverage. If the conflict is interesting and visually transmissible, the news companies usually compete on sending their reporters as fast as possible for coverage in order to be the first on the ground and get a journalistic scope.

Another important factor to be considered in media emphasis on the coverage of some conflicts and not others is that there is a preference for news items where there is a side representing the "good" and another representing the "bad". For instance, the war between Iraq and Iran resulted in hundreds of thousands of casualties and was of an enormous strategic importance foe the Middle East, yet it received relatively little media coverage in Western media. In that war, both parties were regarded as "bad" by the Western public and thus there was no moral victory to be awaited of good over bad. On the other hand, the *Mujahdeen* during the war against the Soviet occupation of Afghanistan were regarded as "freedom fighters" and thus more media coverage was allocated to their struggle. This, of course, can also be explained by the East-West antagonism at the time.

Additionally, giving priority to the coverage of the international crisis as a prime news item does not simply depend on chaotic calculations of the media. In other words, the priority of the news items presented is not a random choice

---

232   See Roger Cohen, "In Bosnia, The War That Can't Be Seen", *The New York Times*, December 25, 1994, E4.

233   See Christopher Young, "The Role of Media in International Conflict", Canadian Institute for Peace and Security, Working Paper N°. 38, 1991.

234   Ibid.

affair. In fact, such priority is governed by what is called "the news cycle". It is, thus, important to understand the nature of the news cycle.

The news cycle simply means that the time span for showing or presenting news items on primetime TV is very important. The consequence is that due to the speed by which things are done, many subjects of foreign news drop out of competition. Indeed, data and video images are updated and replaced rapidly. This means that a news item, that is not updated rapidly turns, is considered old news. Thus, the news cycle tends to change subjects all the time dropping some from competition while bringing others to the top of the list.

A good example of this, would be the covering of the TWA Boeing 747 disaster in July 1996[235] which was soon eclipsed by the conflict in Burundi. These events in Burundi and the subsequent coup were, themselves, and then relegated to virtually zero coverage by the bombing at the Atlanta Olympics[236]. Subsequently, international pressure concerning the conflict in Burundi dwindled, even with the continuation of ethnic cleansing[237]. This is a very good example of the jingling of foreign news items according to their updating.

To constantly satisfy this news cycle, journalists and editors have to search permanently for competitive domestic or international news items. In some occasions, and when there are no domestic political activity (for instance in vacation periods) there is what is called a "lull" in the news cycle. During that lull, emphasis can be given to sending reporters abroad to search for interesting and worthy news items and coverage. One of the good examples of the effect of this lull in the news cycle is given by Nik Gowing. He explains that late July 1993 coincided with the start of midyear vacations worldwide. In that time, he argues, the news cycle is slow. He, further explains, that the BBC presented the story of Irma, a young girl in Sarajevo who had been severely paralysed by shrapnel lodged in her brain. Because of the international news vacuum at the time, Irma's plight grabbed emotive media attention worldwide. Consequently, the media clamour created public-opinion pressure, forcing the British prime minister to mount an

---

235   The Boeing 747, bound for France, took off from JFK International Airport. Moments later, it burst into flames and plummeted into the waters off Long Island, New York. The disaster resulted in the loss of 230 lives. At first, it was believed a bomb caused the explosion. Thorough investigation concluded that the cause was a mechanical malfunction leading to an explosion in the fuel tank.

236   On July 27, 1996 a nail-packed bomb goes off at the Atlanta Olympics, killing one person and injuring more than 100 others.

237   See for instance, David Orr, "Hutu rage grows against Burundi's new Tutsi ruler", The Independent, 30 July 1996 and also Louise Tunbridge, "Killings by Tutsi-led-army fuel violence in Burundi: coup has provoked a vicious cycle of revenge", The Daily Telegraph, 30 July 1996.

airlift, primarily to evacuate Irma, with intense media attention[238]. Some journalists criticised the BBC coverage of this story compared with the on-going Bosnian tragedy that is running on a much larger and more terrifying scale. For instance, Martin Bell, was amazed by the British government's reaction to the girl's story. He states, "that the BBC on that Tuesday should devote more than half of one of its main news programmes to the plight of a single five-year-old girl struck me as daft…"I felt like a humble foot soldier in an army whose high command had taken leave of its senses"[239]. Bell seems to be correct in his criticism since sometimes domestic affairs and the news cycle produce quite a good alibi for governments not to act, when it comes to an international crisis or conflict. Indeed, governments which have little interest in making a more positive engagement in a conflict or a crisis use media indifference for doing as little as possible.

Nik Gowing explains, in this respect, that a consequence of this would be that diplomats, military, or officials in a country should expect that sometimes they would be confronted with sudden public resentment because of the media coverage of a conflict and that sometimes that nothing would happen, even if there was a conflict going on involving human tragedies[240]. He also presents two examples of a direct cause and effect relation of media emphasis on a conflict and a crisis. He argues that the predicament of Kurdish refugees who were driven from Iraq to southern Turkey after the Gulf War in early 1991 as well as the Bosnian Muslims predicament in Srebrenica in April 1993 had emotive TV coverage which lead in both cases to a political impact. On the other hand, he explains that TV coverage in Rwanda and in the early weeks of the unfolding conflict in the former Yugoslavia did not have any political impact[241]. This, certainly, explains the power of the media in over or under exposing a crisis.

Thus, the media's role of emphasising or not emphasising a conflict is a very vital one. Indeed, the nature and degree of such emphasis can lead to a political impact to intervene in the conflict. Under or over exposure of a crisis depends on a number of factors such as the existence of emotive images of the conflict to be transmitted, the moral partition between the "good" and the "bad" parties of the conflict and the determinants of the news cycle. However, it also depends on other factors such as the media's own interests in the coverage of the international crisis and the interests of the states involved as well.

---

238   See Nik Gowing, <u>Real-Time Television Coverage of Armed Conflicts and Diplomatic Crises: Does it Pressure or Distort Foreign Policy Decisions?</u>, Joan Shorenstein Barone Centre, John F. Kennedy School of Government. Cambridge, MA: Harvard University, 1994, p. 80.

239   See Martin Bell, In Harm's Way, <u>op. cit.</u>, p. 143

240   See Nik Gowing, Real-Time Television Coverage, <u>op. cit.</u>, p. 20

241   Ibid.

1.3.2. Media Interests in Covering International Crisis

Why would a media cover an international crisis?. Or to put it more clearly, why would one media cover an international crisis more attentively than another media?. The answer to these questions can be explained through an examination of the interests involved in the coverage of international crisis for the media. These interests range from pure journalistic interests to political interests passing by social and economic ones

For this part of this research an interesting study would be frequently used as a milestone in discussing the media interests in covering international crisis. This study is conducted by Jan Servaes[242]. Servaes compares in this study the coverage of six European newspapers of the Grenada Crisis. In order to examine whether the European press coverage of the Grenada Crisis revealed different interprative frameworks across national cultures, Servaes selected six major newspapers. These are the German *Frankfurter Allgemeine Zeitung,* the French *Le Monde,* the Swiss *Neue Zurcher Zeitung,* the Dutch *NRC-Handelsblad,* the Spanish *El Pais,* and the British *Times.* The selection of these newspapers is explained by the fact that they are opinion leaders for their respective political, economic, cultural, and intellectual constituencies. According to the Servaes, the *Times* and the *Frankfurter Allgemeine Zeitung* are labelled "conservative," *Le Monde* and *El Pais* "progressive," and the *NRC-Handelsblad* and the *Neue Zurcher Zeitung* are labelled somewhere in between.

The choice of Servaes also depends on the fact that elite newspapers usually give much more attention to foreign and feature news items than other dailies. The reason is that they have a network of correspondents, which makes them less dependent on the news supply of the international news agencies. Servaes also explains that the coverage of foreign events for these newspapers is at least quantitatively large enough to speak of a policy[243].

As far as the duration covered by this comparative study is concerned, it covered all issues of the above newspapers covering the Grenada Crisis from October 13, 1984 (the day when the leader of Grenada, Maurice Bishop, was put under house arrest) through November 20, 1984 (five days after the interim government was installed and Grenada presumably entered a new era). One interesting issue in Servaes' study is the special attention paid to the four days of the press ban (October 25-29, 1984) which was imposed by the United States concerning the situation in Grenada. As shown in table 12 below, the comparative study of Servaes revealed quite a number of differences in the coverage of this crisis.

---

242 See Jan Servaes, "European Press Coverage of the Grenada Crisis", <u>Journal of Communication</u>, vol. 41, N°4., 1991, pp. 29-41.

243 Ibid., p.31.

Table 12: Attributes of articles on Grenada in six European newspapers, by percent

Article	LM %	NZZ %	Times %	FAZ %	NRC %	EP %	Total %
Placement							
On page 1	17	16	26	25	28	12	24
On page 2	0	56	0	41	3	16	18
Length							
Long	21	18	31	27	35	43	29
Medium	61	48	65	64	64	56	60
Short	18	34	5	9	1	1	11
Use of primary sources	43	39	79	57	43	60	54
Includes opinion							
Feature	66	92	44	22	36	19	48
Editorial	7	2	19	19	9	29	14
Combined	0	0	0	16	0	6	3
With illustrations	2	9	18	7	35	20	16
n =	(89)	(88)	(127)	(67)	(80)	(84)	(535)

*LM = Le Monde; NZZ = Neue Zurcher Zeitung; FAZ = Frankfurter Allgemeine Zeitung; NRC = NRC-Handelsblad; EP = El Pais .

*Source: Jan Servaes, Op. Cit., p. 32.

Servaes's study depends on the principal that the internal measures of news value are the total number of news items, news paging, the size of the news items, the use of primary or secondary sources, the presence of journalistic opinion, and the presence of illustrations and photographs. However, Saervaes explains that measuring the total surface spent on a subject may not lead to comparability since the size of an article also depends on the newspaper's own make-up and layout (for instance, the size of headlines and blank spaces). In addition, placing the international news item on the front page of the newspaper loses its importance as a determinant if the international news appears on fixed pages of the newspaper.

Similarly, Servaes explains that problems may arise in analysing the themes emphasized in the editorial content since news coverage and the comment or opinion on an issue or event often overlap or may not be strictly divisible. In addition and as far as illustrations and photography is concerned, Servaes clarifies that "additional diagrams or pictures give no uniform indication of the importance of the subject, because, for example, *Le Monde* does not publish a lot of pictures, and the *Neue Zurcher Zeitung* and the *Frankfurter Allgemeine Zeitung* are very economical with pictures"[244].

---

244   Ibid. p.32.

According to Table 12, the story of the invasion of Grenada in the six selected newspapers is told in 535 articles. Of that total number of article, seventeen percent were in *Le Monde*, 16 percent in the *Neue Zurcher Zeitung*, 24 percent in the *Times*, 13 percent in the *Frankfurter Allgemeine Zeitung*, 15 percent in the *NRC-Handelsblad*, and 16 percent in *El Pais*. In addition, twenty percent of all the articles appeared on the front page of the newspapers concerned and 18 percent on the second page. Furthermore, and according to this table, ten percent can be considered short (less than 50 sq. cm), 60 percent medium (51-300 sq. cm), and 30 percent long (more than sq. 301 cm). As far as news sources are concerned, primary sources (correspondents or journalists from the paper's own editorial staff) were used in 54 percents of the articles. Significantly, about half of the articles examined included either a positive or negative opinion within a de facto account of events and 14 percent were coded as purely opinion pieces. Finally, most articles (85 percent) were not illustrated or didn't have photographs.

Thus, with this study in mind, this part of the research would attempt to answer the question of the interests that the media have in covering an international crisis. Indeed, the understanding of these interests and "motives" would give a clearer explanation of the framing of foreign events and, in particular, crisis events in the national media.

1.3.2.1. Pure Journalistic Interests

It is somewhat difficult to define what pure journalistic interests really are. These interests, however, are certainly related to the ethics of journalism and to its idealistic side. These interests can be grouped under main categories such as searching for the truth, trying to make a difference, and getting one's own point of view through to the audience. These also have to do with journalism's ethics. In times of international crisis and conflicts, these interests become more complicated to identify, especially when there are human tragedies involved in the coverage. It is mainly difficult to identify and to assert because of the debate of whether journalists in conflict times should be emotionally involved with the people they cover or to be strictly professional and emotionally indifferent to what they witness. It is, furthermore, difficult because sometimes reporting atrocities can re-raise tensions and hinder the peace efforts.

One of the most impartial things to remember is that journalists are human beings. As such, they are bound to react "humanly" to things they witness. Journalists have a moral role to report what they truly perceive as humans to their audience. After all this would help journalists feel their coverage of a conflict can help affect or even change the course of things. For instance, one of the journalists who became famous for revealing the Serb-run concentration camps in Bosnia (Roy

Gutman) states about his coverage of the conflict in Bosnia and how he hopes it would save human lives "you've got to do everything m your power to stop these things…and exposing it is one of the best ways to do it"[245]. Yet, some writers suggest that this emotional attachment to the event journalists are covering and their desire to feel they are making a difference, can easily transform into a sort of an interventionist position. In this respect, Martin Bell states that "all the reporters who work regularly on the Bosnian beat are, at least privately, interventionist…surrounded by so much misery and destruction, it is humanly difficult to be anything else"[246]. Other researchers, however, insist that journalists should maintain emotional detachment when covering a conflict. For instance, Marvin Kalb who affirms that some journalists covering the conflict in Bosnia wrote their stories "for the specific purpose of affecting national policy". For him, this compromises the media's role of objectivity. However, Kalb admits that sometimes the aim for journalists might justify the means. He adds, "this may be understandable though still regrettable. But if reporters are now to adopt a moral attitude toward their stories, then the public is almost certain to be short-changed"[247]. Kalb's criticism is somewhat unreasonable. It is practically impossible for journalists to detach themselves from their nature as humans. As humans, they have their own interpretations and they are bound to take sides and even to try to change things if they can.

Bob Greene is of this view. He argues that most journalists choose their profession "because it was an opportunity to effect change for good. You never did it for money, because you knew it was the poorest paying job in the world.…[But]…you can try to work for what is presumed to he good, if nothing else, by bringing accurate information to people"[248]. This is also the view of Ed Vulliamy, a famous war correspondent, who on the contrary was more effective in his writing because of his declared affinity with the Muslims during the conflict in Bosnia. He explains, "I am one of those reporters who cannot see this as 'just another story' from which I must remain detached, and in which I must be neutral"[249]. Thus, one of the most important journalistic interests can be said to be that for journalists to covey the truth and try to change the course of things if they can by their coverage of the conflict.

---

245   See Sherry Ricchiardi, "Exposing Genocide. For What'?", <u>American Journalism</u>, *June* 1993, p.34

246   See Martin Bell, Testament of an Interventionist, <u>OP. Cit.</u> p.9.

247   See Marvin Kaib, <u>The Nixon Memo: Political Respectability, Russia, and the Press</u>, The University of Chicago Press, Chicago, 1994, p.93.

248   See "Interview with Bob Greene", <u>Media Studies Journal</u>, Vol.10, N°.4, Fall 1996, p.99

249   See Ed Vulliamy, "This War Has Changed My Life", <u>British Journalism Review</u>, Vol. 4, N°. 2, 1993, p. 5.

Putting the emphasis on the human tragedies in an international conflict or crisis is not an odd behaviour for the media. This is quite evident in table 13 below, where the emphasis of the six newspapers in Jan Servaes's study of the European newspapers' coverage of the Grenada crisis is on the human loses. Table 13 shows that the recurrences of themes emphasising human deaths in that crisis had the lion share (16%) of all the themes of the articles of the six newspapers covering the crisis.

Table 13: Themes of articles on Grenada In six European newspapers (n 535)

Theme	LM n	NZZ n	Times n	FAZ n	NRC n	EP n	Total n	%
Grenada events								
Bishop	7	4	8	4	8	8	39	4
Coard	3	2	3	1	3	8	20	2
Invasion deaths	22	26	45	11	27	27	158	16
Political situation	15	11	26	22	14	18	106	10
Revolutionary Military Council	5	4	6	1	4	7	27	3
Interim government	2	7	42	2	2	2	27	3
Execution of Bishop	5	3	4	3	6	3	24	2
Curfew	0	0	3	2	4	0	9	1
Secret documents	1	2	0	1	0	0	4	0
Prisoners	4	5	2	0	4	2	17	2
Grenada police	2	0	2	0	1	0	5	0
Weapons	1	1	2	1	1	0	4	0
Mass grave	0	0	1	1	3	3	8	1
Pull out of troops	1	2	2	1	1	0	7	1
Reconstruction	0	0	4	0	1	0	2	0
U.S.views								
Official U.S. position	20	19	22	17	23	20	121	12
U.S. as peace-keeping force	11	8	45	4	8	9	55	5
Opposition in U.S.	2	6	4	0	2	1	4	0
Evacuation	2	6	4	0	2	4	15	2
Other responses								
Cuba/Communist	23	22	47	11	15	22	110	11
British	4	7	20	9	6	4	50	5
Caribbean	3	6	44	4	7	1	35	3
Foreign political actors/ governments	10	6	8	44	6	6	50	5
United Nations	5	6	7	2	4	3	27	3.
Church	0	1	0	2	0	0	3	0
Non-political actors	3	3	8	6	2	4	26	3
Legal aspects	3	4	6	3	2	1	16	2
Media	2	4	2	1	1	5	15	1
Other	6	8	5	4	2	4	29	3
Total	160	166	245	129	157	158	1,013	16

*Up to two themes could be coded perarticle. LM= LeMonde; NZZ= Neue Zurcher Zeitung; FAZ = Frankfurter Allgemeine Zeltung; NRC = NRC-Handelsbiad; EP = El Pais

*Source: Jan Servaes, op. cit., p. 35.

Another important interest of journalists is to give their own opinion of the situation when covering a conflict. Other than being interested in getting the story or the news item before others, journalists are also interested in giving their own analysis of the situation. In other words, they are interested in declaring their understanding of the international crisis or the conflict to the audience. This is quite important since it is through the media that the majority of people get their understanding of the international conflict.

In this respect, Servaes's study explains that the majority of the newspapers involved with the Grenada crisis coverage present a rather uniform view of the conflict within an East-West context most of the time[250]. Servaes explains that generally "Grenada coverage in all six papers frames the story as an East-West conflict with the United States concerned foremost with Communist "danger" and less interested in Grenada itself"[251]. However, the study indicates that there are differences as far as the editorial opinions between the six newspapers concerning the crisis are concerned.

Pure journalistic interests are hard to define. Each journalist has his or her own journalistic interests. These can often be translated into moral responsibility. Journalists have an interest in being the first to transmit their understanding of the situation during an international crisis or conflict to their audience. Additionally, they have an interest in that what they convey to their audience is the truth as they conceive it to be. Additionally, journalists have an interest in conveying their own point of view of the conflict and, by doing so, to try to change things on the ground. Yet, pure journalistic interests are not the only interests the media have in covering an international crisis.

1.3.2.2. Social Interests

The role of the media as an agent of the social change is a very important one. One of the most fundamental roles of journalists is to be socially effective. In other words, journalists are people who convey ideas to the public or the audience and by doing so they occupy an influential position as far as affecting or changing the public's opinion or ideas vis-à-vis certain issues.

Similarly, during the coverage of an international crisis, the media can pass certain social messages to raise, for instance, social awareness about the gravity of the humanitarian situation in the crisis area. It can also prompt an interventionist policy or action to settle a deteriorating humanitarian situation due to a conflict. The media has an essential social interest in covering an international crisis. Since one

---

250   See Jan Servaes, op. cit., pp. 35-36.
251   Ibid, p.36.

of its functions is to be an active influential part of the society in which it exists, the media is conscience of the importance of being an active actor. By its coverage of an international crisis, the media can display its ability to provoke an interventionist policy from the part of the state or a change of the society's attitude towards the conflict.

Indeed, the media has to be close to the society's pulse and to do that it has to reflect the society's interests and to create, reshape or redirect these interests. This media can rejoice itself of achieving these social interests on two levels. These are the state foreign policy level and the popular level. On the state level, the media can sometimes proud itself of being the instigator of an interventionist policy that would put an end to the suffering of innocent populations in conflicts. On the popular level, it can proud itself by raising popular consciousness about the humanitarian dimension of an international crisis and, thus, prompt public opinion to act and maybe, in its turn, pressure the government to act as well.

An essential field in which the media has social interest of being able to affect a change is that of the domestic public level. This is quite natural and actually expected from a media in a democratic society and for different reasons. First, the media apparatus itself is composed of members of the society. The reflections of this society's composition and mentality are, thus, bound to be noticed in the media of that society. Second, the media in a democratic society is supposed to be able to reflect the pulse of the society it exists within. If the media wants to be accepted by the society it exists within, and to be consequently able to effect the desired social change, it has to reflect social concerns that are identified with by the majority of the society. Finally, the media has a social interest in exhibiting its ability to mobilize the public opinion, to act sometimes to pressure, or even in some cases, contrary to the foreign policy decisions of the state vis-à-vis an international crisis.

The media has always been an active organ of any society. It's conduct can enormously affect social behaviours concerning many issues related to the society in which it exists. The media can do that via the messages it sends to the society it is living in. Some researchers claim that these messages are actually shaped in certain formats which are dictated by the technology and economic structures that influence a particular medium of communication. This, for instance, can have a considerable influence on the political life of the state[252]. In other cases, some researches found that the media in a society has a great influence on the perception of risks and perils[253]. Sometimes, the exaggeration of risk can lead to undesired

---

252   See D.L Altheide,.An Ecology of Communication: Cultural Formats of Control, Aldine de Gruyter, New York, 1995.

253   See D. Kone, & Mullet, E., "Societal Risk Perception and Media Coverage", Risk Analysis, N° 14, 1994, pp.21-24.

complications in a society. For instance, some studies refer to a heated debate in Denmark that was a consequence of the media's exaggeration of the risk of not removing certain material(asbestos) in that country, although later studies indicated that it was better if such material was left in place and not removed[254]. Thus, the social role and interests of the media for local social life and politics are quite important. For what the media do is to shape the social reactions to issues relating to that society. They, thus, have an interest in assuming this role of social "watchdog" of the society.

On the state's foreign policy level, the ability of the media to influence policy by playing on the humanitarian dimension of a conflict is quite interesting. The media can frame the emphasis on the suffering populations and the human tragedies prompting an action from the government in some cases. This was the case of the Kurdish humanitarian crisis of the 1991[255]. Martin Shaw explains, for instance, that the media coverage of the 1991 Kurdish crisis was framed so as to instigate world-leading countries to apt for an interventionist policy. He states that 'the graphic portrayal of human tragedy and the victims' belief in Western leaders was skilfully juxtaposed with the responsibility and the diplomatic evasions of those same leaders'[256]. However, other researchers argue that the media influence in provoking an interventionist policy by emphasising the humanitarian tragedy dimension of a conflict is not governed by the media coverage as such but by whether or not there is a stated foreign policy directive vis-à-vis the crisis itself[257]. The issue, thus, seems to be debatable. Yet, it seems that the nature of the crisis itself can shape the effect that the humanitarian media coverage of an international crisis can have on whether or not a state should adopt an interventionist policy. Indeed, most of the time it is not enough to focus on the humanitarian dimension of a crisis to make governments do something about it.

---

254 See Agner Fog, "Mass Media and Democracy Crisis", online document with pagination, p.2.

255 In 1990, Iraq invaded Kuwait and the Gulf War which followed further weakened the economic and social situation inside the country. Military defeat at the hands of the US-led coalition was followed by a period of internal instability prompting population movements in the Kurdish north as well as widespread suffering in southern parts of the country.

256 See Martin Shaw, Civil Society and Media in Global Crises, St Martin's Press, London, 1996, p. 88

257 See Piers Robinson, "The News Media and Intervention: critical media coverage, policy uncertainty and air power intervention during humanitarian crisis", Paper for the Political Studies Association-UK 50th Annual Conference, London, 10-13 April 2000.pp.1-11.

An interesting example, in this respect, is the case of the US military intervention in Somalia in 1992-3 (Operation Restore Hope[258]). Indeed, several writers claim that this operation was imitated by the pressure on politicians caused by media intensive coverage of the suffering populations in Somalia[259]. Yet, others explain that the part of coverage Somalia received prior to President Bush's decision to intervene in that country on November 25, 1992[260] was unmentionable. This might be true but the fact remains that media coverage of Somalia is an interesting case. If it is true that the media coverage of the suffering population of Somalia didn't actually have a bearing on the US political decision to intervene, this does not mean that the media coverage did not get the United States out of Somalia. Indeed, the media images of the US soldiers killed in Somalia had an enormous bearing on the American public opinion and, consequently, on the US decision to withdraw its forces from that country. What the case of Somalia might suggest is that the media coverage of the suffering of a country's own soldiers involved in a humanitarian crisis can exceed to a large extent the effects of showing the suffering of other peoples or populations in "far away lands". This, however, is a natural social behaviour since the media has more affinity with the society in which it exists and has, thus, to reflect the anxieties of that society in order for that society to accept it.

---

258   Expanded peacekeeping in Somalia began after the failure of UNOSOM I accompanied by the specter of 500,000 Somalis dead from famine by the fall of 1992 and hundreds of thousands more in danger of dying. Clan violence in Somalia interfered with international famine relief efforts, and President Bush sent American troops to protect relief workers in a new operation called Restore Hope. The US-led coalition approved by the Security Council in December 1992 had a mandate of protecting humanitarian operations and creating a secure environment for eventual political reconciliation. At the same time, it had the authority to use all necessary means, including military force. A joint and multinational operation, Restore Hope—called UNITAF (unified task force)—was a US-led, UN-sanctioned operation that included protection of humanitarian assistance and other peace-enforcement operations. On December 3rd, U.N. Security Resolution 794 authorized the U.S. led intervention "to use all necessary means to establish a secure environment for humanitarian relief operations in Somalia as soon as possible." The US Army participated in Operation Restore Hope in Somalia from 03 December 1992 to 4 May 1993.

259   See Kennan, George, "Somalia, Through a Glass Darkly", New York Times. 30 September, 1993 and also Nik Gowing, "Real-Time TV Coverage from War: does it make or break government policy", pp. 81-91 in J. Gow et al. (eds.), Bosnia by Television, British Film Institute, London:, 1996.

260   See Piers Robinson, Op.Cit.

Another interesting example of the media's social interest in covering an international crisis is the extent of the role played by the media to incite US intervention in Bosnia in 1995 to defend the Gorazde safe area[261]. This intervention came after the fall of the *Srebrenica* safe area[262]. According to Richard Holbrooke[263], the aim of the intervention was to prevent the fall of the Gorazde safe area to Bosnian Serb forces[264]. The idea that media in this case helped stimulate intervention is supported by the research of Barry Blechman and Tamara M.

---

261   The enclave of Gorazde, situated in central Bosnia, had a pre-offensive population of some 60-65,000 of whom some 35,000 lived in the town of the same name. The population was and is predominantly Muslim. The enclave is part of the territory of and, until the offensive, was wholly under the control of the Government of Bosnia and Herzegovina. On 6 May 1993, by Security Council resolution 824 (1993), Gorazde, along with Sarajevo, Tuzla, Zepa and Bihac, was declared a safe area "free of armed attack". In resolution 836 (1993) of 4 June 1993, the Security Council, acting under Chapter VII of the Charter of the United Nations, extended the mandate of UNPROFOR to enable it to deter attacks against the safe areas. The enclave of Gorazde, declared as a "safe area" by resolution of the Security Council, has been subjected to fierce attack by Bosnian Serb forces during the weeks up to late April 1994. The attack involved gross violations of human rights and humanitarian law and resulted in loss of control by government authorities of part of the territory of the "safe area".

262   On 11 July 1995 the Bosnian-Serb army seized the Safe Area of Srebrenica. In the days that followed, several thousand Muslims met their death in the vicinity of the enclave. When these events took place Dutch troops (Dutchbat) were stationed in this 'safe area' as part of the United Nations Protection Force operating under the auspices of the UN peace mission in Bosnia-Herzegovina. The UN intervention had prevented neither the fall of Srebrenica nor the mass murder. These shocking events stirred up considerable debate, also in the Netherlands. In this debate the question of what exactly had happened became enmeshed with the issue of the responsibility of the troops and the politicians who played a role in the events. These questions were not laid to rest by a Dutch 'debriefing report' of Dutchbat or what was intended as a closing parliamentary debate in December 1995. On the contrary, they continued to figure prominently in the press and on the political scene.

263   Ambassador Richard C. Holbrooke was confirmed by the Senate as the Permanent United States Representative to the United Nations on August 5, 1999. During his career he has been a professional diplomat, a magazine editor, an author, a Peace Corps director, the chairman of two important non-governmental organizations and an investment banker. He was the U.S. Ambassador to Germany from 1993-1994 before being appointed by President Clinton as Assistant Secretary of State for European and Canadian Affairs in 1994. During that time, he was also chief negotiator for the historic 1995 Dayton Peace Accords that ended the war in Bosnia.

264   See Richard Holbrooke, <u>To End a War</u>, Random House, New York, 1998, p.72.

Wittes which examine American media coverage of the issue covering the period between the fall of the *Srebrenica* safe area on July 11 and the US threat to use force two weeks later on July 23. The research indicated the existence of a high level of media coverage present during this period[265]. This suggests a strong and even immediate impact of the humanitarian framing effect of media coverage of an international crisis on the policy guideline towards this crisis. Yet, this wasn't exactly the case of Operation Allied Force in Kosovo in1999[266]. This was basically an act of coercive diplomacy aimed at securing Serbia's compliance with US terms and was not designed to directly alleviate the immediate humanitarian crisis within Kosovo. This is the official US policy according to a White House Press briefing on the 24 of March 1999[267]. In the Kosovo case, the media efforts to effect a change in policy via an intensive and appealing framing of the refugees situation there was apparently unsuccessful. Piers Robinson explains, "it was during this period that desperate images were transmitted back from refugee camps and a debate occurred in Washington over whether ground troops (and close air support) were required to both offer immediate protection to the Albanian Kosovars and, in the long term, to ensure their return. The debate was brought to a head in the failed attempt by Senator John McCain to force an escalation to a ground war via a congressional vote in late April. At no point did the US intervene directly on the ground in order to prevent attacks on the Albanian Kosovars. Indeed, Clinton failed to even authorise the use of ground attack helicopters, requested by NATO commander Clarke, in order to offer protection to Albanian Kosovar refugees"[268]. This is, hence, a case where media efforts to act as a social consciousness representative, in order to prompt foreign policy or military action, seems to have failed. This suggests an interesting finding. It can be said that when there is no clear foreign policy guidelines towards an international crisis, the media effect is considerable. On the other hand, where a clear foreign policy direction vis-à-vis an international crisis exists, the effect of the media's empathy framing of the humanitarian situation seems to be questionable.

---

265   See Barry Blechman and Tamara M. Wittes, "Defining Moment: The Threat and Use of Force in America Foreign Policy", *Political Science Quarterly*, vol. 114, N°1, 1999, pp.1-30.

266   On March 24, U.S. joined forces with NATO in an air strike against Serbian military targets in Kosovo. More than 38,000 U.S. and allied combat sorties waged an air campaign that lasted 79 days in an around-the-clock operation to weaken Serbian forces. Over 730 U.S. Air Force, Navy and Marine aircraft and 37,100 service members took part in Operation Allied Force—a NATO lead operation. NATO objective was to force Serbian military forces to withdrawal from Kosovo, allow over a million refugees to resettle in their homeland and bring stability to the NATO's southeastern alliance and to surrounding countries.

267   See Piers Robinson, op. cit, p.5.

268   Idem, p.5.

1.3.2.3. Economic Interests

Discussing the importance of the economic factor for the media when they decide to cover an international crisis is essential. Considerations for the number of audiences, the revenues and the resources to be dispensed for the coverage of an international crisis figure highly on the agenda of media companies and corporations. Other than the most cataclysmic events (involving a disaster with high level of deaths or political upheaval), economic and financial calculations have usually a strong say, along with other factors and realities, in whether an international crisis is to be covered or not. It also has a strong say on the emphasis of the coverage.

There is in fact enough evidence that commercial concerns of news companies govern the coverage of the coverage of international crisis. Some have declared that the lack of coverage for their crisis stems from the lack of interest of the commercial sector of these media companies. Emma Bonino comments, for instance, on the diminishing coverage of international crisis in European media. She states that "the sidelining of documentary and current affairs programs about humanitarian issues is also due to lack of interest among the owners and directors of broadcasting companies"[269]. This, however, doesn't apply to some news organisations like the ARD and the ZDF[270], which have quite a number of correspondents all over the world. They still broadcast comprehensive news and documentary coverage covering most of the world, even if some programs are considered low-audience programmes by the commercial sections of these organisations.

However, commercial realities still have a strong impact on the editorial decision to cover an international crisis or not and to what degree this international crisis should be covered. Garrick Utley argues, in this respect, that marketplace realities often constrain editorial instinct and journalistic ethics to cover foreign news items[271]. This is sort of the conventional view of news coverage. According to this view ratings and audiences will increase with the coverage of domestic affaires. This, nevertheless, is not a proven view. In fact, some writers argue quite the opposite, mainly that good coverage of an international issue can produce good profit for the media company[272]. This is quite comprehensible since covering an international crisis can generate important ratings for the news company if its well-done, if the crisis is of a global interest, and if the company has the exclusivity

---

269   See Emma Bonino, "Bringing Humanitarian News Into Prime Time", <u>International Herald Tribune</u>, 28 June 1996.

270   *Allgemeiine Deutsche Rundfunkanstalten (ARD)* and *Zweites Deutsches Fernsehen* (ZDF) are public broadcasting televisions in German.

271   See Garrick Utley, "The Shrinking of Foreign News", <u>Foreign Affairs</u>, *vol.* 76, N°2, March/April 1997, pp. 2-10.

272   See John Pilger, "The Truth is Out", <u>Broadcast</u>, 10 May 1996, p. 20.

on the issue. The case of the CNN coverage of the Gulf War in 1991 and Al-Jazeera exclusivity in Afghanistan at the time of the Talibans is a very good proof of this. In both these cases, coverage of the crisis meant enormous revenues. Indeed, the number of audiences of these two media companies was unprecedented. They were not merely the only source of information for the audiences worldwide, but they also received revenues from the broadcast of their coverage by other news and media companies.

Yet, the fact remains that not all news companies can afford to send reporters to conflict areas if the conflict area is far and if there is no genuine national interest in covering it. To compensate for the lack of their own reporters and correspondents, newspapers, radio and television often use the services of trans-national news agencies such as Reuters, the Associated Press, and Worldwide Television News (WTN). These agencies would provide the pictures, videos and even the words for a fixed annual rate. This would satisfy the commercial section of these newspapers, radio and television stations since the rates are fixed and, thus, there would be no additional expenses to be considered in the budget. This arrangement also satisfies the journalists who are provided with a constant coverage material for their audience. This, however, has definitely a negative effect on the objectivity of the coverage since all the information is provided by one source.

This aspect of dependency on trans-national news agencies for foreign news coverage is illustrated in the study of Jan Servaes dealing with the European press coverage of the Grenada crisis (Table 14),

Table 14: Sources for articles on Grenada in six European newspapers, by percent

Source	LM %	NZZ %	Times %	FAZ %	NRC %	EP %	Total %
Staff member or correspondent	43	39	75	57	43	60	54
Agency							
U.S.	11	27	5	21	5	8	12
European	14	43	7	11	4	10	10
Caribbean	5	10	2	3	1	3	4
Combined	8	7	2	8	45	13	43
Subtotal	38	58	16	42	55	34	39
Unspecified	19	3	9	1	2	6	7
Total	100	100	100	100	100	100	100
n =	(89)	(88)	(127)	(67)	(80)	(84)	(535)

*LM = Le Monde; NZZ = Neue Zurcher Zeitung; FAZ = Frankfurter Allgemeine Zeitung; NRC = NRC-Handelsblad; EP = El Pais

*Source: Jan Servaes, European Press Coverage of the Grenada Crisis, op. cit., p. 37.

Although 54 % of the articles on the crisis were written by individual editorial staff members or correspondents, 39% of these originated from a news agency with one third of those articles combining different agency reports. In addition, a preference is noted for U.S. agencies over European ones. However, Servaes indicates that most of the coverage was provided by each paper's staff. It was 75 %for the *Times*, 60 % for *El Pais,* and 57 % for the *Frankfurter Allgemeine Zeitung.* For their part, the *Neue Zurcher Zeitung* and the *NRC-Handelsblad* used foreign sources (mainly news agencies) most frequently (58% and 55 % respectively).

Jan Servaes also mentions an interesting discovery. He argues that newspapers often obtained secondary information from an agency "with which they have some linguistic, journalistic, and certainly also ideological affinity"[273]. According to the outcome of his study, the *Neue Zurcher Zeitung* and the *Frankfurter Allgemeine Zeitung* used U.S. agencies, *Le Monde* and the *Times* used European agencies, while the *NRC-Handelsblad* and *El Pais* had no clear preference[274].

It can be said that economic factors largely affects the choice and extent of coverage of an international crisis or conflict. While some argue that domestic news items are more economically viable for the media organisation than international news, it has been proven that good coverage of an international crisis can generate even greater income for the media organisation. However, and in order to cover the crisis with less costs, newspapers, radio and TV often depend for their foreign news coverage on trans-national news agencies. It can be said, that other factors such as national interests and geographic proximity taken aside, commercial realities determine the coverage of international crisis in the media.

1.3.2.4. Political Interests

Political interests are very important to consider when discussing the media coverage of international crisis. Usually, political interests in the conflict or the crisis determine the emphasis on its coverage by the media. It, thus, can be a good explanation of why some media focus on certain international crisis and conflicts more than others.

This difference in the media's focus on the international crisis is well explained in the study of Jan Servaes. He explains that of all the six European newspapers in his study, the *Times* was the one to pay the most attention to the crisis events in

---

273   See Jan Servaes, European Press Coverage of the Grenada Crisis, <u>op. cit.</u>, p.37.
274   Idem.

Grenada[275]. According to him, the *Times* published the largest number of articles. It also made most frequent use of its own news sources, and scored higher on all

---

275   The tiny (110 thousand) Caribbean island of Grenada had stuck in Washington's craw for four years, including close to three years of Ronald Reagan's first term. Here, within a few miles of US territory, was a socialist government that not only declined to participate in the "neo-liberal" free trade economy on US terms, but had friendly relations with Cuba. It was especially embarrassing to someone who had announced the "Reagan Doctrine" of "rolling back Communism." The island had been one of the United Kingdom's several Caribbean possessions. But in 1967 Britain had granted it internal self-government and Grenada secured its full independence in 1974. Universal adult suffrage had been instituted in 1951 and a populist trade union leader, Eric Gairy, won five of seven general elections from then until 1979. Although seen as their champion by the large black majority, Gairy's rule was marked by fraud, brutality, mismanagement, and links to Duvalier's Haiti and Pinochet's Chile. Grenada's economic elite controlled an opposition party, the Grenada National Party (GNP). It won two elections and was in power twice (1957-61 and 1962-67). It was especially galling to the elite that Gairy used the additional power granted by Britain in 1967 to institute a land reform program that expropriated his political opponents' estates and turned them into land grants to workers. His rule was marked by buffoonery, patronage and corruption. It was also true that the opposition was corrupt when it was in power. The corruption was of little interest to the US because both administrations gave uncritical support for American foreign policy in the Caribbean. That changed when the radical New Jewel Movement took power. A revolution in March, 1979 was led by charismatic Maurice Bishop, a London educated lawyer, and his New Jewel Movement (NJM). His party, the People's Revolutionary Government (PRG), sought to pull Grenada out of its colonial legacy of dependency. During the four years it was in power, against great odds, it initiated low cost housing projects, free medical and dental treatment, and free primary and secondary education. It provided thousands of government jobs, a ministry of women's affairs (with paid maternity leave, day care etc.), and a substantial involvement of the people in decision-making through unions, zonal councils and the like—but no elections. Some of its programs received the help of Castro's Cuba, especially with educational and medical programs and with infrastructure development. Washington immediately sought a way to replace Bishop's rule with a government acceptable to the US and to the several transnational corporations interested in opportunities for trade and investment that the island offered. Those purposes would become clear when the US invaded in late 1983. Personnel from the United States Agency for International Development (USAID) arrived in Grenada at almost the same time as the troops. One of the remarkable aspects of the US invasion was that it followed the overthrow of the man the White House wanted gone: Maurice Bishop, confidant and friend of Castro's. The invasion was announced as a way "to restore order." The revolt against Bishop merely provided the sought-for pretext for the US to take charge.

measures than all the other European newspapers in his study. Servaes explains this by the fact that Britain had the closest historical, political, and economical ties with Grenada. He argues that Britain had been a colonial power in the Caribbean region for 300 years and that Grenada achieved independence in 1974, a governor-general representing the Queen (though without real power) was placed on the island. Thus, for Servaes, politically and economically, Grenada is part of the British Commonwealth. The British government reconsidered its economic and political ties after Bishop's 1979 takeover[276]. Certainly, ancient historical ties such as a previous colonial tie or a previous alliance can explain the emphasis of one media over an international crisis over another. Yet, these internal politics are not the only determinants of the coverage emphasis. Sometimes, it's the context of the internationals that determines the emphasis of the coverage.

Indeed, the context of international relations between states is an important factor to consider. In this respect, Servaes explains that, in addition to these historical, political, and economic ties between Grenada and Britain, the British media emphasis can be explained by the UK's policy of cooperation with the United States. In fact, Servaes argues, that the U.S. foreign policy had found an ally in the Thatcher government, which was illustrated by the political and military cooperation in the Falkland conflict[277]. However, when it came to the invasion of Grenada, the British government was unhappy with the fact that the Americans didn't inform them of their plans to invade the island[278]. Servaes explains, in this respect, that a White Paper published by the British Foreign Office after the Grenada crisis confirmed that "top officials in Washington were giving unreliable advice to Britain right up to the moment when President Reagan decided to send in his invasion forces"[279]. Servaes goes further saying that "the British felt slighted not only as an ally but also, according to *The Economist*, because of "America's

---

276   Jan Servaes, European Press Coverage of the Grenada Crisis, op. cit.,p.33

277   The Falkland Islands are a group of islands in the south Atlantic. The two main islands, East Falkland and West Falkland, lie 300 miles [480 km] east of the Argentina coast. About 200 smaller islands form a total land area of approximately 4,700 square miles (12,200 square km). The capital and only town is (Port) Stanley. Argentina has claimed the islands since about 1920. Britain had occupied and administered the islands since 1833 and had consistently rejected Argentina's claims. Argentina invaded and took control of the islands in April 1982. During the war, the British captured about 10,000 Argentine prisoners, all of whom were released afterwards. Argentina sustained 655 men killed, while Britain lost 236. Argentina's ignominious defeat severely discredited the military government and led to the restoration of civilian rule in Argentina in 1983.

278   Idem.

279   Idem.

offence against the rule of law; the insult to the Queen; the danger the American action clearly posed to British citizens; the precedent set for similar impetuous action elsewhere in the world"[280]. Thus, relations between states determine sometimes the attention given to an international crisis and the emphasis and direction of that attention. This is quite logical, politically speaking. Since states rarely want to jeopardize their international relations by emphasising the negative role of other states in an international crisis via their media apparatus.

As far as the Dutch newspaper *The NRC-Handelsblad* coverage of the Grenada crisis is concerned, Servaes explains that the Dutch had a political interest in Grenada, in spite of the fact that they had no direct involvement their. Servaes argues that "in addition to a long tradition of siding with the underdog in international matters, the Netherlands had experienced their own "Grenada" in 1982, when leaders of the recently independent colony of Surinam were murdered during a military coup. However, the Netherlands did not intervene militarily but used other methods of pressure and sanctions"[281]. Consequently, *The NRC-Handelsblad* had the most front-page articles and pictures (See table 15).

Table 15: Attributes of articles on Grenada in six European newspapers, by percent

Article	LM %	NZZ %	Times %	FAZ %	NRC %	EP %	Total %
Placement							
On page 1	17	16	26	25	28	12	24
On page 2	0	56	0	41	3	16	18
Length							
Long	21	18	31	27	35	43	29
Medium	61	48	65	64	64	56	60
Short	18	34	5	9	1	1	11
Use of primary sources	43	39	79	57	43	60	54
Includes opinion							
Feature	66	92	44	22	36	19	48
Editorial	7	2	19	19	9	29	14
Combined	0	0	0	16	0	6	3
With illustrations	2	9	18	7	35	20	16
n =	(89)	(88)	(127)	(67)	(80)	(84)	(535)
*LM = Le Monde; NZZ = Neue Zurcher Zeitung; FAZ = Frankfurter Allgemeine Zeitung; NRC = NRC-Handelsblad; EP = El Pais							

*Source: Jan Servaes, "European Press Coverage of the Grenada Crisis", op. cit., p. 32.

---

280   Idem.
281   Idem.

As far as *El Pais* is concerned, Servaes explains that the Spanish newspaper's coverage of the invasion of Grenada can be understood against a colonial background. He argues that after the death of Franco and the restoration of democracy in Spain in 1975, the Spanish foreign policy's emphasis was on Latin America. He explains that according to this new direction of the Spanish foreign policy, the Spanish government has continuously expressed different attitudes or political solutions from those of the U.S., on this issue. Servaes argues that such differing political attitudes voiced by the Spanish government were voiced through *El Pais*'s press coverage of Grenada. In fact, the overage of *El Pais* of the Grenada crisis was second only to that of *The Times*. It had, according to Servaes's study, the largest number of long articles on Grenada and even published the most opinion articles. Servaes states that "except for front-page articles, *El Pais* scored higher than the mean for all six papers on every variable"[282]. This is quite understandable since the Spanish's political interest at the time was to regain its natural political influence of Latin America. To do that, it had to voice its disagreement with the U.S. policy in Grenada.

As far as the other three newspapers are concerned, the fact that their countries had no direct political interest in Grenada was reflected in their media's coverage of the crisis there. Servaes explains, "France, West Germany, and Switzerland had less involvement with the Grenadian crisis. As a result, *Le Monde,* the *Frankfurter Allgemeine Zeitung* and the *Neue Zurcher Zeitung* had many fewer articles"[283]. This is apparent in table 15 above.

Thus, it can be said that political interests often govern the coverage and emphasis on a certain international crisis over others. These political interests can be understood against a colonial background at certain times. In addition, it can be explained by certain alliances or spheres of influence. It also should be viewed in the context of international relations between states. Yet, these factors are not the only ones governing the way an international crisis is presented and the way in which it is emphasised. Usually, other factors should be considered such as national tendencies and vital interests of states in a crisis.

1.3.3. National Tendencies and the Coverage of International Crises

It is essential in any research concerning the coverage of an international crisis to consider two main divisions of national tendencies. While one of those

---

282   op. cit., p.34.
283   Idem.

divisions of tendencies is the competence of the state, the other is the competence of the public. These two divisions of national tendencies are national interests of states which is of the competence of the state apparatus and national sympathies which relates to the public feeling of the majority of the state's citizens. These national tendencies often tend to manifest themselves via the coverage of an international crisis by the national media.

1.3.3.1. National Sympathies

National sympathies can be divided into three main categories: Religious Affinities, Ethnic Affinities and Social Affinities. Each of these sub categories can manifest itself through the coverage of an international crisis, even if, sometimes, certain affinities are more emphasized than others.

1.3.3.1.1. Religious Affinities

Religious affinities between countries and states are sometimes very apparent when trying to comprehend why the media of a certain country displays a different coverage of an international conflict than the majority of other world countries. Although most of the time the coverage of the international crisis or conflict might not directly mention religion and shared religious factors, the difference positions that this country might take vis-à-vis the crisis can be easily referred to as being due to religious affinities.

The possibility of measuring the impact of religious affinities is much greater during domestic media's coverage of an international crisis or conflict. In fact, the sharing of the same or of close religious convictions can provide a good explanation to some of the domestic media's stands vis-à-vis an international crisis or conflict contrasted with the mainstream media position of the majority of other world countries concerning the same subject.

A very good example of this can be seen in the coverage of the Greek media of the Kosovo crisis and the NATO air-strikes in 1999. Indeed, out of the other NATO members, the Greek media's coverage of the crisis in Kosovo is quite unique. The reasons for which the Greek media's coverage of the Kosovo crisis is interesting are many. First, it was expected that, being a NATO member, the Greek media would adopt a supportive or at least less antagonistic position concerning the NATO action in Kosovo. This, however, was not the case. Second, the Greek media apparently perceived the NATO action against Serbia according to the context of its own environment and not according to the mainstream journalistic trend of support for the action in the majority of the world countries' media. Finally, unlike the media in other NATO countries, the Greek media did not back up its government's position vis-à-vis the crisis.

This, however, does by no means indicate that the Greek government was supportive of the NATO action. On the contrary, evidence suggests that the Greek government continued to call for a diplomatic solution to the crisis[284]. Nevertheless, the different media in Greece often adopted a strong pro-Serb attitude. This fact drew the criticism of a number of journalists who accused the Greek media of "misinformation" and "bias"[285]. The criticism, however, wasn't one-sided. For its part, the Greek media often accused Western countries of being "cruel" and "unjust" towards the Serb population[286]. This is quite natural, since the two sides didn't actually see the issue from the same angel. For the Western countries, it was necessary to contain the Kosovo crisis and prevent a possible spell-over of the effects to the rest of Europe. For the Greeks, the Serbs represented much more than a problem trigger in the Balkans.

Aside from the long-term animosity with Turkey and the fact that Kosovo itself had a Greek minority living in it, the religious affinities between the two orthodox countries seems to provide a good explanation of this animosity of the Greek media towards the NATO action in Kosovo. Indeed, some of the rightwing Greek newspapers went even as far as clearly stating this religious affinity with the Serbs. For instance, the Greek newspaper *Apogevmatini* claimed that the Kosovo Albanians "rape women" and "burn churches". Furthermore, the Greek communist newspaper *Rizospstis* went as far as calling the Greek Defence Minister at the time "NATO's goon"[287]. These might, however, be interpreted as extreme stands. Yet, the fact remains that religious solidarity with the Serbian orthodox one of the main reasons behind this position of the Greek media.

Naturally, the other argument should be mentioned concerning the coverage of Kosovo. This argument stipulates that throughout the events of the conflict in ex-Yugoslavia, there was an accusation that an intense propaganda campaign is being launched against the Serbs by the majority of Western media and that this campaign is orchestrated by the United States. Indeed, supporters of such a view explain that the" deionisation" of Serbs by the world media is an intended objective of the United States.

Notwithstanding, quite a number of evidence suggests that the Serbian media itself was adopting a deionisation trend of other countries and of Muslims

---

284   See www. Primeminister.gr/speeches/199904.c.htm

285   See www. Guardian.co.uk/archive/o.4273.3666657.00.htm.

286   See www.access.online.bg/bn/hotpoints/kosovO99/greece.htm.

287   See Margarita Kondopoulou, "The Greek Media and the Kosovo Crisis", <u>Conflict & Communication Online</u>, Vol. 1, No. 2, 2002,Online document with pagination found at www.cco.regener-online.de.

throughout the very beginnings of the Balkan wars. There was notably a clear distinction in Serb media between the image of Greece and Turkey.

As far as Turkey is concerned, the image is generally that of a country suffering from an economic crisis, growing violence in political life, dictatorship and backwardness. All of these factors suggested, as far as the Serbian media is concerned, the basis for the rise of Islamic fundamentalism and for an aggressive foreign policy. For example, an article in *Politika* on 6 February described a very difficult "exam" the Turkish Prime Minister will have to pass, together with the whole nation[288]. This exam is that of "politics, economy, Kurds and Islam" according to the author, the danger is that "Muslim redeemers" could become winners.

In fact, Serb media often referred to the rise of Islamic fundamentalism. for instance, On 17 December, *Politika* states that "step by step, the fundamentalists are conquering terrain in Turkey. They find points of support in the Army, too". *Politika* continues, "Can Ankara, with *fes and fereja*, enter the European Union?" Or, can it do that with backward people who think they can escape the risk of AIDS just because they are "protected by Allah"?. Another commentary in Politika (9 February) says that Europe, "out of fear of fundamentalism, offers its hand to Turkey, pushing it to the frontline of the battle with that movement, and in return makes possible higher involvement of Turkey in European affairs". The text ends with a question: "Will Europe, for the sake of its comfort, let Islam to this side of Bosphorus, as it did six centuries ago?".

This clear criticism of Turkey by the Serb media was even more emphasized during the Balkan conflicts. Contrary to the support given to Greek military cooperation with other Balkan countries, Turkish military cooperation with other Balkan countries was generally condemned in the Serbian press. For instance, *Vecernje novosti*, (7 February) commented on the motion in the Turkish Parliament to pass a law legalizing military aid to Bosnian muslims[289], *Tanjug*[290]'s journalist revealed to the readers of all dailies on 20 March that "Since Turkey has been already secretly sending weapons to the Muslims in Bosnia, this formal denial of embargo is aimed at producing propaganda effects within domestic public, which is extremely anti-Serb oriented. It is also expected that the example of Ankara will be followed by other Islamic countries and that they will increase military deliveries to Muslims in Bosnia". Thus, religious sentiments were quite apparent in the Serbian media vis-à-vis Turkey especially in times of conflicts in the Balkans. This, however, was not the case of the Serb coverage of Greece where there was always a favorable image of the

---

288   Plolitika is a Serbian newspaper with an internet edition found on
      http://www.politika.co.yu/2003/0402/indexdan.htm
289   Belgrade based newspaper found at www.douklia.net/ck/novosti.html
290   Tanjug is a Serb News Agency.

Greek people and its government. For example, *Tanjug's* correspondent (on 10 February) gives what he calls a brief description of the meeting" (of Yugoslav and Greek foreign ministers) concerning the crisis in the Balkans. He says, "deep friendship, harmony in views on all important questions on the Balkans and on the territory of former Yugoslavia, as well as determination of Greece and FR Yugoslavia to contribute to a peaceful solution of the crisis…". There is clearly a difference in the perception of the Greek and the Turks in the Serbian media.

The religious affinities are very important when trying to understand the reaction of some media to other countries or group of countries especially during an international crisis. However, other types of affinities might be more apparent or emphasized than religious ones simply because it is politically incorrect to clearly state that religion plays a strong role in position taking or decision making in international relations.

1.3.3.1.2. Ethnic Affinities

Another important consideration, when discussing the importance of national tendencies' impact on media coverage of international crisis, is that of ethnic affinities. Indeed, ethnicity and ethnic belonging to a group has always been one of the most important causes of conflict and wars. After the fall of the Berlin Wall, the majority of world conflicts have changed in nature. Instead of inter-state conflicts, the majority of conflicts today are characterized by being intra-state ones, usually caused by ethnic cleavage and antagonism.

Many studies have discussed the effect that ethnicity might have on society and the political future or decisions of states. For instance, Donald L. Horowitz explains that ethnicity is a powerful force in the politics of many states and that it has strong effects on prospects for democracy[291]. Others have pointed out the importance of ethnicity in other aspects such as economic development or the distribution of public wealth [292]. Indeed, due to the importance of ethnicity in internal and external relations, there are numerous studies that attempt to explain and even predict ethnic related relations within or outside the state's boundaries.

The complications of the sense of belonging to an ethnic group and the resulting behaviour are quite interesting. Donald L. Horowitz, for instance, explains the complexity of the behaviour of an ethnic group. He says" members of ethnic groups seem to partake of all of these tendencies to cleave, compare, specify inventories of putative collective qualities, seek a favourable evaluation, manifest

---

291   See Donald L. Horowitz, "Democracy in Divided Societies", <u>Journal of Democracy</u>, vol.4, N°4, 1993,pp.18–38.

292   See William Easterly, and Ross Levine, "Africa's Growth Tragedy: Policies and Ethnic Divisions", <u>Quarterly Journal of Economics</u>, vol. 112, N°4, 1997, pp.1203–50.

ingroup bias, exaggerate contrasts with outgroups, and sacrifice for collective interests. Ethnic groups also seem to carry matters further. They appear frequently to
engender more loyalty from their members than competing group-types and to
engage in severe conflict with other ethnic groups"[293]. Others, such as Marilynn
B. Brewer and Norman Miller, explain the importance of the sense of similarity
that belonging to an ethnic group implies. This sense of similarity an individual
has makes him or her think they have characteristics that are representative of the
social category that the ethnic group embraces[294]. This could explain the degree
of affinities that members of an ethnic group have to each other and to other
similar members of the group. It usually results in a preference to suppress one's
individual identity to the benefit of that of the ethnic group as a whole.

Ethnicity plays a major role in social behaviour. According to Donald L.
Horowitz, it is one of the most powerful affiliations that exist. He argues, "ethnicity
is a powerful affiliation, both because similarity is valued and because genetic (or
putatively genetic) origins and early socialization are potent sources of similarity or,
in any case, of cues that signal similarity: appearance, customs, gestures, language,
clothing, tastes, and habits"[295]. Indeed, people usually tend to be more comfortable
and to identify more with those with whom they perceive common characteristics.
However, other studies indicate that the degree of affinity between group members
depends actually on the degree of similarity. Accordingly, the greater the felt similarity within a group the greater the degree of the in-group bias is[296]. The degree of
bias within an ethnic group depends therefore on the degree of similarity within
this group but in-group bias can be noted even with one similarity.

It is important at this point to examine the behaviour of the state vis-à-vis an
outside war that involves a minority of its ethnicity. According to David Carment
et al. there are two major schools of thought explaining state behaviour vis-à-vis an
outside ethnical conflict. These are the Effective Ties School and the
Instrumentalist School[297]. The distinction between the two is interesting. For The
Effective Ties School argues that a state decides to intervene in an outside ethnic

---

293   See Donald L. Horowitz, "Structure and Strategy in Ethnic Conflict", Paper
       prepared for the Annual World Bank Conference on Development Economics,
       Washington, D.C., April 20–21, 1998, p.15.
294   See Marilynn B. Brewer and Norman Miller, Intergroup Relations, Open
       University Press, Buckingham, 1996, p.22.
295   See Donald L. Horowitz, op. cit., p. 16.
296   See Marilynn B. Brewer, "In-Group Bias in the Minimal Intergroup Situation: A
       Cognitive-Motivational Analysis", Psychological Bulletin, vol. 86, N°2, 1979, p.318
297   See David Carment, et al., "Domestic Determinants of Ethnic Intervention: A
       Typology", A paper prepared for the 2001 Annual Meeting of the American
       Political Science Association, Francisco, CA.,Aug.29-Sept.2,2001, p. 4.

conflict, where a some of its ethnicity is involved, out of strong ethnic allegiances. Although this school has proven its relevance in some events, it certainly did not in others. David Carment et al. explain that this was the case with the Serb intervention to protect Serb populations in different parts of the ex-Yugoslavia but did not apply to countries like China and Russia who did not intervene for their ethnic group in other situations[298]. For the Instrumentalist School, the state would intervene in an ethnic conflict not out of mere ethnic allegiances but for a need to gain access to resources or to create division or for "a rally behind the flag" effect when they are faced with defeat or with a dangerous internal situation.

This, however, does not provide a satisfactory explanation as to the refraining of some leaders or states to use this opportunist approach whenever it suits them. It seems, thus, that intervention in ethnic conflicts depends on many considerations. Certainly, direct military intervention would suggest that there is a real state interest or an imminent threat to the state's security. On the other hand, it could be argued that some countries are more able than others to control their ethnical sympathy for the profit of their other interests. This, for instance, can be a good explanation as to why the Serbs intervened heavily and the Russians and Chinese did not when a part of their ethnicity was threatened. The interpretation can be actually very simple. The Serbs had part of their ethnicity distributed all over the ex-Yugoslavia and to prevent a chain reaction of events it was necessary for them to show support for their ethnicity. Furthermore, Serbs numbers, as an ethnicity, are small compared to the Chinese or Russian ethnicities. China and Russia, on the other hand, have the great majority of their ethnicity within the boundaries of the state. Furthermore, the number of the ethnicity in each state was not threatened by the loss of a small part of this ethnicity outside the state. This, naturally, is added to the fact that both China and Russia did not have vital interests in intervening. If they did, protecting their prosecuted ethnicity would have been an excellent pretext for intervention.

In many cases the ethnic references in the domestic media precedes and even encourages the conflict. This was certainly the case in ex-Yugoslavia. Indeed, the media in there used ethnicity as a weapon serving political interests of certain groups. To do that the factor of fear was used as a trigger of ethnic affinities. This element is probably the main emotion poisoning and disturbing ethnic relations. They see fear as that of domination of the other ethnic group, extinction by the other ethnic group, fear for ones life and property and fear of becoming once more a victim. Fear, consequently, leads to another human emotion which is hate[299]. Spreading such fears was done via different means such as education and popular

---

298   Idem.
299   See David Lake & Donald Rothchild, "Containing Fear: the Origin and Management of Ethnic Conflict"", <u>International Security</u>, vol. 21, 1996, pp. 41-75

culture but was mainly done through the domestic media. Through this logic the threatening ethnicity is usually dehumanised and demonetised.

One of these methods used by the media is delibarate exaggeration of events. One good example of this are Serb media charges of rape committed by Albanians against Serbs in Kososvo in the 1980s. In this respect, Anthony Oberschall explains that at that time "the public was fed exaggerations and total fabrications that fit the crisis frame"[300]. This was quite contrary to the actual records. Oberschall argues that in this period social studies indicated that "rape and attempted rape in Kosovo were lower than in Central Serbia, in the *Vojvodina*[301], and in all Yugoslavia, and rapes tended to be within, not across, nationality[302]. Indeed, exaggeration combined with an emphasis on the ethnicity of the perpetrators of the criminal act would certainly produce a more effective reaction, as far as ethnic animosity is concerned.

Another type of fear stressed by ethnic agitators in the media is that of extinction. As far as the Serbs are concerned, this fear is referenced to their casualties in World War II. For instance, Serbs usually claim that around 700,000 Serbs were killed in the *Jasenovac* camp[303] alone. This figure is, however, reduced into 100,000

---

300   See Anthony Oberschall, "The Manipulation of Ethnicity: from Ethnic Cooperation to Violence and War in Yugoslavia", <u>Online research paper with pagination in Pdf. Form</u>, p.6.

301   Territory of the Republic of Serbia north of Sava and Danube rivers is called Vojvodina.

Vojvodina's area totals 21506 km². Through Vojvodina flow three large navigable rivers: Danube, Sava and Tisa, which divide its territory into three areas: Srem, Banat and Backa. Banat and Backa are predominantly plain areas, apart from a part of Banat where sides of Carpathian mountains extend, while in Srem extends a low mountain Fruska Gora. Vojvodina has a continental climate and it is located in the temperate zone.

It is mainly an agricultural region.

302   Idem.

303   From August 1941 to April 1945, hundreds of thousands of Serbs, Jews, and Romas, as well as anti-fascists of many nationalities, were murdered at the death camp known as Jasenovac. Estimates of the total numbers of men, women and children killed there range from 300,000 to 700,000. And yet, despite the scale of the crimes committed there, most of the world has never heard of Jasenovac. Following the Nazi invasion and dismemberment of Yugoslavia in April 1941, the "Independent State of Croatia" was established as a pro-Nazi government. It was dedicated to a clerical-fascist ideology influenced both by Nazism and extreme Roman Catholic fanaticism. On coming to power, the Ustashe Party dictatorship in Croatia quickly commenced on a systematic policy of racial extermination of all Serbs, Jews and Romas living within its borders. Jasenovac was actually a complex of five major and three smaller "special" camps spread out over 240 square kilometres (150 square miles) in south-central Croatia.

dead, of whom only half were Serbs[304]. For their parts, Croats made similar exaggerations for the *Bleiburg massacres*[305]. Clearly, everyone used exaggeration in figures of previous victims to prepare his camp for a pre-emptive strike on the other ethnicity so that the mistakes of the past are not repeated. This attitude is noticeable now in the media coverage of international crisis or conflict. The media in many occasions of conflict tends to report on the previous historical conflicts in the region and emphasis the casualties. This can always be said to have been done unintentionally. Notwithstanding, the fact remains that this kind of emphasis by the media on the casualties in previous conflicts constitutes sort of an alert message to ethnicities that they should be sure that such past mistakes should not reoccur. The result is that everyone tends to take measures to protect himself better than it did in the past and for that sometimes striking first and striking hard the other ethnicity is the ultimate result.

Thus, ethnic affinities in media coverage are quite important. The fact that ethnic groups tend to identify with similar groups is a good explanation of why some domestic media take the defence of a certain part of an international conflict or crisis. This mobilisation of the domestic public opinion in some countries might serve a state's interest by legitimising internally its interventionist policy towards an international crisis or conflict. However, sometimes the trans-border ethnic affinity might not be enough to lead to an interventionist policy by a state or a group of states simply because there is no vital national interest for that state to intervene. Additionally, it should be noted that the domestic media's role in inflaming ethnic animosity and in the building up to the ethnic conflict and to the crisis is a very important one.

1.3.3.1.3. Social Affinities

Social affinities can have a considerable impact on the domestic media's coverage of the international crisis or conflict. Social affinities referred to in this case are cross-border ones and not inner-state ones. Indeed, recently such affinities between societies in different countries have shown an impressive ability to affect the public opinion, the governmental decision and the domestic media's orientations vis-à-vis certain international crisis and issues.

Unlike the religious or the ethnic affinities between societies of different countries, social affinities can be said to be much less limited by race, gender or religion. They are universal to all mankind. Such solidarity between societies all over the world in times of disaster and crisis underlines the effectiveness of the new concept of "humanity" in international relations. Social solidarity between

---

304   See Branimir Aanzulovic, <u>Heavenly Serbia</u>, New York University Press, New York, 1999, pp. 100-104.

305   See Anthony Oberschall, <u>op. cit.</u>, p.6.

societies in different countries and regions have produced through lengthily efforts and co-operation a multitude of laws and agreements to jointly face universal disasters as a single universal society.

The present global social responses to disasters, for instance, are indeed remarkable. These are in fact the expression of the international commitment to assist and protect civilians in disaster or conflict areas. In this respect, the International Humanitarian Law was an enormous breakthrough. It is largely constituted by four Geneva Conventions and two attendant protocols. This law places the emphasis on the need for a humanitarian conduct of international affaires. For example, it sets out the entitlements of all civilian non-combatants in conflict to be treated humanely in all circumstances. Legally, a state is committed in front of the international community to protect and assist those in need. Furthermore, states have emphasized the need to work humanely with issues through joint declarations. For instance, the Universal Declaration of Human Rights stipulates the right of those affected by natural disasters to food, water and shelter. Humanitarian responses to other specific problems were also supported legally through conventions. For instance, the 1951 Refugee Conventions define the obligation of states and warring parties to provide refugees with humanitarian assistance, or allow it to be provided to all those in need.

Indeed, at present and for hundreds of millions of people, humanitarian assistance by societies and countries from all over the world offers a vital lifeline. During a disaster or a crisis, such assistance is the expression of solidarity and humanity between societies. However, despite such efforts in disaster time, assistance does not always reach those in need of it in time. Indeed, thousands of humans around the globe still have nutritional and basic needs insufficiency.

Another event that constitutes an excellent proof of these shared affinities between societies all over the world is the humanitarian response to human tragedies during crisis and conflict times. Indeed, the effect of the global social response to human tragedies in wartime is remarkable. These efforts are highly coordinated and organised generally by non-governmental organisations and the new social movements[306]. Massive worldwide demonstrations and social protests have recently become an effective instrument in pressuring the political establishments in many democratic countries to adopt human attitudes and certainly a humanitarian interventionist policy towards many conflicts around the world. Perhaps, the first good example of this is the social protests concerning the Vietnam war which did not only have an impact on the United States action but also influenced the political positions of other world countries vis-à-vis that war.

---

306   For further information on the effect of the new social movement please refer to pp.46-49.

Domestic media is not isolated from the effects of such declared domestic social solidarity with a political or humanitarian cause in a faraway country or area. It cannot, thus, be indifferent to these public social solidarity sentiments, if not for ethical reasons then for financial and distribution capacity ones. Unlike domestic media in authoritarian countries, which usually echoes, the position of the government, domestic media in democratic countries usually tend to echo the position of those social protestations. By doing that, domestic media can be a useful means in both affecting the government's position towards the crisis or conflict and in launching a call for humanitarian aide and contributions from the citizens of the concerned country.

However, universal social solidarity is not equal vis-à-vis all conflicts and crisis. Indeed, some crisis and conflict gain more social solidarity and expression of social affinities than others. For instance, the conflict in Bosnia in the 1990's and that of Rwanda both took place almost at the same time. In both conflicts, there was an ongoing human tragedy and in both ethnic cleansing and genocide took place at a large scale and, in particular in the Rwandan case. Yet, expressions of world wide social solidarity was much more in favour of the Bosnian case than that of the Rwandan one. In fact, the reasons for this is lack of interest in the case of Rwanda and too much interest in the case of Bosnia. Interest in this case refers to state interest and, by consequence, to the media's interest.

Unlike Bosnia, the Rwandan case was not focused upon by the media. Following this logic, it can be said that there is an effective correlation between domestic media's coverage, especially in democratic countries, and the degree of declared social solidarity towards an international crisis or conflict. In a reversed scenario, lack of focus of the domestic media in democratic countries concerning an international crisis would be reflected by a diminution of the degree of the domestic social solidarity vis-à-vis the humanitarian tragedy dimensions of that crisis. In some cases, however, and especially in democratic countries the domestic social solidarity can first take place without the instigation of the domestic media. In this case, most media would follow suit and re-adjust their coverage in accordance with the declared public interest.

Social affinities are, thus, quite important in the domestic media's coverage of an international crisis. Social protests have indeed become an effective actor in the domestic political life and decision making process of many countries. Sometimes social protests expressing fear of engagement of one's own government in war and the refutation of the humanitarian impact on the adversary parties civilian population might have a great bearing on altering the state's foreign policy approach towards the issue. In this respect, the role of the domestic media is very important. It usually points the attention towards the humanitarian urgency in some international crisis and, thus, helps in creating domestic social affinities concerning this crisis. On the other hand, if the domestic media perceives that the social affinities towards an international crisis are growing up even without it (the media) focusing attention on that crisis, then it is most likely that the domestic media would re-adopt its coverage to follow suit with the domestic social affinities of its audience.

1.3.3.2. National Interests

A very important consideration to be discussed, as far as coverage of international crisis and conflicts is concerned, is that of national interests. Logically speaking, anything with a national interest would be important for the media to cover. Yet, it is useful to learn how far does this national interests factor affect the media coverage of the international crisis.

It is important to note, when discussing the issue of national interests that states deal with facts and not emotions. Thus, unless a vital state interest is threatened,such as national security, the reaction of states to a "humanitarian" crisis covered with images of human tragedy would hardly be effective. This is further complicated by the nature of conflicts today. Indeed, nowadays the great majority of such conflicts are at a sub-state level and, thus, would have no direct influence on the inter-state relations. This, in turn, makes these conflicts less interesting as national interest spots.

Often it is the change of national interests that determines the states reaction to the international crisis and not the media coverage of that crisis, no matter how emotional it is. A good example of this can be seen in the change of the U.S. policy in the Balkans and their crisis management of the situation in Bosnia. In fact, the Clinton administration's Presidential Decision Directive No. 25 dated 5 May 1994 clearly stated the limits of U.S. national interest beyond which it is highly unlikely that the U.S. will ever commit itself, certainly militarily and on the ground[307]. These stated interests governed the U.S. policy in Bosnia, even with the ongoing emotive TV coverage of the events there. Tara Sonenshine explains that later on, the change of U.S. national interests led to an interventionist approach and to the Dayton Peace Accords leading to the settlement of the Bosnian crisis[308]. Thus, it wasn't the media coverage of the crisis in Bosnia that led to the U.S. foreign policy change but rather that of an internal reassessment of national interests of the United States.

National interests are certainly not stable. They are in constant change. New threats and interests are perceived constantly. For instance, Samuel Huntingtons's

---

307 See "PDD N° ",25, 5 May 1994. Online Document.

308 See Tara Sonenshine, "Clinton Makes Foreign Policy and Electoral Positive", International Herald Tribune, 15 May 1996.

theory established that the real threat to international security stems not from ethnic fault lines[309]. For instance, National Security Adviser Anthony Lake defines
the new security challenges as being "extreme nationalists and tribalists, terrorists,
organised criminals, coup plotters, rogue states and all those who would return
newly freed societies to the intolerant ways of the past"[310]. Thus, the national
interests and threats to these interests are in constant changing. They change and
they adapt to circumstances. It can be argued also that sometimes belligerents in a
conflict might use this lack of interest in their conflict to commit more atrocities.
Their understanding of the lack of international interest in their conflict would
give them the cover and even incite them to go further in their actions.

It can be said that the challenge for the journalist's nowadays is to bring the
international conflict or crisis and its humanitarian dimensions, in particular, to
the attention of governments. Naturally, this is far from being an easy task.
Indeed, its not enough to bring a crisis or a conflict to the attention of the government for that government to adopt an interventionist or a proactive attitude
towards that crisis. In the calculations of states, national interests take precedence
over humanitarian concerns. In this respect, some journalists call for the adoption
of what they label as "journalism of attachment". Martin Bell, the BBC's former
foreign affairs correspondent, is one of those. He states "the Bosnia war, has left
me with the conviction that a foreign policy based only on considerations of
national interest, and not at all of principle, is not only immoral but ineffi-
cient"[311]. Yet, what if emphasis was put in the media on all international crisis
and conflicts. It is quite impossible to imagine that a state would commit itself to
resolving or intervening in all the international crises that happen worldwide.
Douglas Hurd[312] confirms this impossibility of acting in every international crisis. Answering Marin Bell's statement, he explains" Martin Bell's principle cannot
surely be that we should intervene against horrors only when they are televised?…Bosnia is far from unique. I can think of eight civil wars raging at this
moment, with others simmering. Britain cannot be expected, even with allies, to
intervene each time"[313]. This raises another question. If a state cant intervene or

---

309   See Samuel Huntington, "The Clash of Civilizations", <u>Foreign Affairs</u> Vol. 72, No.
       3, Summer 1993, pp. 22-49.
310   See Speech by National Security Adviser Anthony Lake to the Council on Foreign
       Relations, Washington, DC, 14 September 1994. <u>online document</u>.
311   See "BBC Man Attacks Neutral War Reports",<u>The Guardian</u>, 23 November 1996.
312   Lord Hurd served as Foreign Secretary from 1989-1995. He was Minister of State
       in the Briitish Foreign Office and the Home Office and served as Secretary of State
       for Northern Ireland from 1984-85 and as Home Secretary from 1985-89.
313   See Douglas Hurd, "Why Foreign Policy Cannot Be Dictated by Blind Emotion",
       <u>The Standard</u>, 16 July 1996.

pay enough attention to all conflicts and crisis in the world even if they are highly emphasised in the media, then what is the criteria that states use to define their reaction to an international crisis. Surely, vital national interests take precedence in such choices.

Another pretext for governments with the power to intervene in a crisis not to do so is the principle of "sovereignty" in international law. Indeed, its is often used as a pretext for not acting when its convenient for governments to do so and when there is no national vital interest for them in the crisis. Martin Bell terms such state reactions as the "nothing can be done club". He complains against those who adopt such a negative attitude saying "it is in the interests of all our children—theirs as well as ours—that they do not prevail" he wrote"[314]. However, this perception of matters can easily be labelled as an idealist one. Indeed, Martin Bell calls for a moral reaction to international conflicts and not one that is based solely on state calculations. He states, "the case for intervention is not to help one side against another, but the weak against the strong, the armed against the unarmed; to take the side of the everyday victims of war who, until now, have had no protection. It is really a question, finally, of whether we care"[315]. Again here is the choice between state calculations, which are usually realistic, and humanitarian ones, which are based on morality and doing the right thing.

Having said all that, it is useful, at this stage, to discuss some of the national interests a state may consider when reacting to an international crisis. These can largely be grouped under three main categories. They are the geographic proximity factor, economic interests and national security interests.

1.3.3.2.1. Geographic Proximity

When discussing the issue of national interests of states, the question of geographic proximity is an essential one. Indeed, the geographic location of countries, their proximity to other countries, and the borders they share with each other is one of the most important variables in studying international relations and, in particular, in the study of international conflicts.

The theoretical debate concerning the importance of closeness in determining the nature of relationships is an on-going one. For instance, Kenneth E. Boulding contemplates on the ideas of "behaviour space", "loss-of-strength gradient" and "critical boundary"[316]. If such ideas are applicable at the level of states, it is not the less applicable on the individual human level. For, individuals tend to interact more with those to whom they are closest.

---

314   See Martin Bell, In Harm's Way, op. cit., p.273.
315   Ibid., p.133.
316   See Kenneth E. Boulding, Conflict and Defence, Harper and Row, New York, 1962.

Indeed, the concept of proximity has grown to become an essential one in the analysis of international relations. Benjamin A. Most and Harvey Starr conclude that the diffusion of certain phenomena could only be studied by looking at units that were "relevant" to one another. They explain that such relevance could be indicated by geographical proximity[317]. On the other hand, the term proximity itself can be operationalized through borders. In fact, borders are considered as important indicators of proximity since they were strongly related to both the opportunity and willingness of state actors. This idea is supported by Harvey Starr and Harvey Most[318]. They also support the idea that borders create the opportunity for interaction between states[319]. The limitations of this opportunity to interact depend on the number of countries with which any single state has interaction opportunities. However, this opportunity to interact is conditioned by certain circumstances. For example, James P. Wesley explains that the length of a common border between two states is a better measure of "geographic opportunity" than simply the number of borders[320]. This could, however, be explained by the fact that long borders means more efforts to protect and entertain them.

Another importance of borders is that related to its influence on the willingness of decision makers to opt for political options. They do that by acting as indicators of areas of great importance or salience. Militarily speaking, for instance, the closeness of other states allows them greater ease of interaction and the ability to bring military capabilities to affect the strategic balance. Consequently, any activity border areas are particularly worrisome and would create uncertainty. This idea, that changes in bordering areas would create uncertainty because of their proximity, is supported by Manus I. Midlarsky[321]. In this respect, different types of borders might have different impacts on both opportunity and willingness. Hence, borders are classified in terms of homeland borders and those generated by colonial territories. Such a differentiation gives an idea of whether all territory is seen as equally important, or whether homeland territory generates greater willingness than more

317   See Benjamin A. Most and Harvey Starr, "Diffusion, Reinforcement, Geopolitics, and the Spread of War", <u>American Political Science Review</u>, N° 74, December 1980, pp. 932-946.

318   See Harvey Starr and Benjamin A. Most, "The Substance and Study of Borders in International Relations Research", <u>International Studies Quarterly</u>, N° 20 December 1976, pp. 581-620.

319   Ibid.

320   See James P. Wesley, "Frequency of Wars and Geographical Opportunity", <u>Journal of Conflict Resolution</u>, vol. 6, N° 4, pp.387-389.

321   See Manus I. Midlarsky, "Mathematical Models of Instability and a Theory of Diffusion", <u>International Studies Quarterly</u>, N° 14, 1970, pp.60-84.

distantly held colonial or imperial territories. In fact, what is important is the notion of homeland border. In other words, what is important is the proximity of homeland border to *any* homeland territory of another state.

Another important notion relating to the element of geographic proximity is that of territorial contiguity. Some researchers consider territorial continuity as a major determinant of whether or not a country will go to war with another country. One of those researchers that support this idea is John Vasquez who explains that territorial contiguity is the "source of conflict most likely to result in war"[322]. However, perhaps simple contiguity may not be the critical factor. Other researchers argue, however, that, in addition to the element of territorial continuity, the nature of the border between two countries affects the probability that states will go to war. Douglas Lemke, for instance, argues that borders which coincide with natural frontiers or that traverse uninhabited regions are seen as having little value or are less likely to provoke wars than dissimilar borders and border areas[323]. The nature of borders as an important element in the examination of international conflicts is, thus, well supported by many researchers.

However, the opposite of this theory is not completely wrong. Indeed, sometimes highly permeable and salient borders can produce qualitatively distinct behaviour. A very good example of this is the ease of interaction and salience of border areas in northwestern Europe. As far as these borders are concerned, integration rather than disintegration is the key word. The borders in this area most likely contributed to a movement from high levels of conflict to high levels of cooperation. Relations between states with highly permeable and salient borders have shown a tendency toward interdependence/integration, making military conflict less likely and agreement more likely. This idea is argued for by James E., Dougherty andRobert L. Pfaltzgraff[324].

In the case of conflict, the element of geographic proximity takes on a more important value for the neighbouring countries and sometimes for world powers which might have vital interests in the region as a whole. The coverage of media in this respect is quite essential as a means to serve the interests of the neighbours and the world powers. It is essential because the media can spotlight a conflict area and, thus, prepare the world public for future actions taken by the interested neighbours of or world powers vis-à-vis this conflict. An excellent example of this

---

322   See John Vasquez, The War Puzzle, Cambridge University Press, Cambridge, 1993, p. 307.

323   See Douglas Lemke, "The Tyranny of Distance: Redefining Relevant Dyads", International Interactions, *vol.*17, N°1, 1995, pp. 113-126.

324   See James E., Dougherty and Robert L. Pfaltzgraff, Contending Theories of International Relations, (3 rd ed), Harper and Row, New York, 1990, p.435.

relation between the geographic proximity factor, national interests and media coverage can be seen in the coverage of the conflicts in the former Yugoslavia.

The power of television images to condition geopolitics was evident throughout the evolution of U.S. foreign policy towards Bosnia and Kosovo. Indeed, it can be said that the internal conflicts in the former Yugoslavia, which began in 1991, posed no classic strategic interests of the neighbouring or world powers, such as oil resources or balance of power. This can explain the initial reaction of the U.S. and NATO to the conflicts there as being an internal and 'humanitarian" crisis" and not a strategic one. With the continuation of the ethnic cleansing, however, the fear of a spell over to the neighbouring regions and the inability of the UN and the European Union to end the conflict transformed the crisis in Bosnia from a "humanitarian" one to a strategic one. In this case, the geographic proximity of European countries to the conflict area threatened the stability of the continent and helped bring the media coverage of the conflict in Bosnia to the top of the priority list. The emphasis of the media on the humanitarian tragedies in Bosnia helped to shape the public opinion and to prepare it for an active interventionist policy of the United States in the region. The same media emphasis, however, did not take place concerning other conflicts where ethnic cleansing was even worst than the one in Bosnia. All other interests of world powers being equal (no threat to energy resources, no threat to balance of power...etc.) the only element that remains as the most evident in explaining an interventionist and a non-interventionist attitude towards and international crisis is that of geographic proximity.

The same argument can be applied to the case of the conflicts in Kosovo in 1998 and 1999 where the credibility of NATO as a security institution in Europe was challenged. Again, Kosovo represented a point where ethnic cleansing can spell to other areas of the European continent and, thus, threaten the continent's stability.

The element of geographic proximity is, indeed, an essential one in explaining why some crisis or conflicts get more media attention and coverage than others. Borders are important determinants of states' interests and any disturbance that is close to those borders would raise the interest of those states and of their media as well.

1.3.3.2.2. Economic Interests

National economic interests of states are one of the most important determinants of the foreign policy vis-à-vis international crisis and conflicts. Indeed, states would have a more pro-active foreign policy in areas in which they perceive a vital economic interest either to gain or at stake. The interest of the state in the crisis for economic reasons also stimulates the interest of the media in that crisis. Thus, there is sort of a cause and effect relationship between economic interests and media interest in the international crisis. This fact can be sustained through concrete examples and comparisons of states' reactions to different international crisis and conflicts all over the world. Two good examples that can illustrate the different reactions of states and, consequently, of the media to an international crisis are those of the 1990's Gulf War and other crisis that happened in the same span of time in Africa.

By excellence, the Gulf War in the beginnings of the 1990's[325] is the representation of the importance of guarding national economic interests in times of an international crisis. The Gulf War of the 1990's was the first major world conflict in the post-Cold War era. As such there were different explanations underlying the international community's acute interest in the crisis.

In fact many reasons underlie the Iraqi invasion of Kuwait in 1990. First of all, Iraq has always been disputing the leadership of the Arab world, mainly with Egypt. Part of the leadership qualifiers is achieving Arab unity even if it was by military means. This quest for leadership can also explain the Iran-Iraq war ten years earlier, which resulted in hundreds of thousands of deaths in both camps. Indeed, by attacking Iran, Iraq could claim that it was defending the Eastern port of the Arab world against Iranian expansion especially after the Islamic Revolution there in 1979. That in part explains his disastrous invasion of Iran ten years before. It is worth mentioning in this respect, that containing the Iranian revolution was also an objective of the Western powers. For that end, armament to Iraq was easily provided as well as financial support from the oil rich Gulf countries.

Second, this eight-year war with Iran resulted in a high debt for Iraq, due to the enormous war effort involved. As such, Iraq regarded the reluctances of rich

---

325 International conflict was triggered by Iraq's invasion of Kuwait in August 1990. Though justified by S. Hussein, the Iraqi leader, on grounds that Kuwait was illegally taking oil from an Iraqi field, the invasion was presumed to be principally motivated by desire to acquire Kuwait's own rich oil fields. The U.S. and its NATO allies, supported by a coalition of Arab nations, began massing troops in Saudi Arabia that month; when a U.N. Security Council deadline for Iraq's withdrawal was ignored, a massive U.S.-led air offensive against Iraq began (Jan. 16/17, 1991). S. Hussein, the Iraqi leader, responded by pumping millions of gallons of Kuwaiti oil into the gulf. A powerful ground offensive (Feb. 24-28) achieved victory almost immediately. Estimates for Iraqi military deaths range from 8,000 to 100,000; the Allies lost about 300 troops. Iraq subsequently faced widespread popular uprisings, which he managed to quell. A U.N.-sanctioned trade embargo remained in effect, pending destruction of Iraq's chemical-and nuclear-weapons research facilities, through the decade.

Gulf States to help rebuild the Iraqi post-war economy as an act of ungratefulness. Iraq particularly demanded the cancellation of its debt to Kuwait which did not only refuse but even angered Iraq more by increasing its quota production of the OPEC[326]. This, however, does not in itself justify an invasion of another country by any international norm. Yet, combined with the previous Iraqi grievance, it constituted for Iraq a valid reason of the invasion.

One final pretext used by Iraq for the invasion of Kuwait is the claim that this country is actually a province of Iraq and that it was detached from it unjustly by the imperial powers in the beginning of the century. This view is, somehow, supported by Robert F. Helms & Robert H. Dorff who argue that" the boundaries of every country in the Middle East from the Mediterranean to India have been defined in one way or another by imperial powers...and that those boundaries have generally followed imperial rather than indigenous interests"[327]. They even explain that Britain (the imperial power in Iraq at the time) was heavily supportive of making this country one of the strongest and most viable ones in the Middle East. They state that "it is ironic that Iraq's incorporation of the oil-rich province of Mosul, an area inhabited largely by Kurds and previously under the Turkish governor of Diyarbakir, was insisted upon in 1926 by the British, who wanted an Iraqi state to be militarily and economically viable, and whose arbitrary boundaries the Iraqis can thank for their oil reserves"[328]. Indeed, over the years and because of these oil reserves, Iraq has become one of the richest and strongest countries of the region. George Lenczowski explains that Iraq along with Saudi Arabia constitute the two major pipelines of the Middle East with the Iranian system strategically limited to a gas pipeline which links it to some of the former Soviet Union countries[329]. This indicates the importance of the oil resources in this area of the world. It also indicates its importance to the world powers as being one of the major energy sources in the world. Controlling the energy resources is one of the most important bases of a state's power.

The world power's response to the crisis caused by the Iraqi invasion of Kuwait was, thus, both immediate and decisive. After all, it is an area, which produces a huge amount of the world's oil, and any political instability there would translate into a major world energy problem. In this respect, Robert F. Helms & Robert H. Dorff explain that" the United States responded to Iraqi

---

326   Organisation of Petrol Exporting Countries.

327   See Robert F. Helms & Robert H. Dorff, The Persian Gulf Crisis: Power in the Post-Cold War World, Praeger, Westport, CT, 1993, p. 98.

328   Idem.

329   See George Lenczowski, "Major Pipelines in the Middle East: Problems and Prospects", Middle East Policy, Vol.3. N°. 4, 1995, p.40.

aggression, however, and it did so because of a combination of interests. Most concrete is the fact that over half of the world's trillion barrels of oil reserves is located in the Persian Gulf. To focus only on oil, however, and to treat it as a commodity that one might or might not choose to buy, instead of a resource whose possession has extremely important international implications, is to trivialize what was at stake in the Persian Gulf"330. There was evidently a vital economic interest for the United States in the Gulf area. When that vital interest was threatened by the Iraqi invasion of Kuwait, the United State's response was bound to be immediate and decisive. Other major countries in the world also followed suit in joining the United State's coalition to liberate Kuwait. This can by no means be said to have been done to foster international law provisions and the United Nations' decisions since many other violations of the international law, states' sovereignty and illegal occupation have been taken place prior, during, and after the Iraqi invasion of the oil rich state of Kuwait. Indeed, it should be born in mind in this respect that the United States, had made strong commitments to protect its vital interests in the region. Such commitments go as far back as the Carter Doctrine in 1980331.

Naturally other reasons can always be added to explain this prompt reaction of the United States to the crisis in the Gulf, in the beginning of the 1990's. One explanation can be that the demise of the Soviet Union has rendered the UN more active. Indeed, if the Soviet Union were still there when Iraq invaded Kuwait, it would object to any action against its ally. With the fall of the Soviet Union, the United States was free to apply its own vision on the world or what is known as The New World Order. It could, with the fall of the Soviet rival, become the policeman of the world and it could, thus, pursue its strategic policies and interests quite freely. One of those objectives of the United States was the resolution of the Arab-Israeli conflict. Indeed, by projecting its power in the region against Iraq and its vivid objection to peace with Israel, the United States was able to impose peace treaties between some of the Arab countries and Israel. Without a massive projection of power and presence in the region, something like the

---

330   See Robert F. Helms & Robert H. Dorff, op. cit., p.99.

331   The Carter Doctrine was issued in the State of the Union Address on January 23 1980 by President Jimmy Carter. Responding to the Soviet Invasion of Afghanistan that had recently taken place, the President stated that" *an attempt by an outside force to gain control of the Persian Gulf region will be regarded as an assault on the vital interests of the United States of America, and such an assault will be repelled by any means necessary, including military force"*. This policy thus warned the Soviets away from Iran, which had just had a revolution, and at the time was holding hostages in the United States Embassy, and Iraq.

Madrid Peace Conference[332] would have hardly taken place, at least within a foreseeable future.

This last idea concerning the post-Cold War era is quite important. It is important because the end of the Cold War brought about new concepts of state power. The traditional state military power was proved to be insufficient to sustain a country's domination. The case of the Soviet Union is one of the best examples of this. The concentration on gathering and building military might on the expense of economic welfare and development, due to the arms race of the Cold War with the United States, have greatly contributed to the collapse of the Soviet Union.

State intervention in conflicts was also transformed in the post Cold-War era. Indeed, its not only that the majority of the world conflicts has changed from an inter-state to an Intra-state one in the post-Cold War, but also the criteria for intervention vis-à-vis these new conflicts and crises changed as well. Instead of intervening for ideological support or balance of power reasons, for the interest of one party over the other, the new doctrine of intervention seems to follow the direction of vital national interests of states and, in particular, economic ones.

In this respect, there seems to be a tacit agreement on intervention between the two rivals of the Cold War. For, since the end of the Cold War neither the United States nor Russia have intervened militarily in response to a real or perceived threat from one another. Even with the intervention in the Gulf in the beginning of the 1990's, the United States did not stress the fact that the situation there constituted a direct threat to its national security, a reason that would have been a good pretext for intervention in the Cold War era. As far as Russia is concerned, its intervention in Chechnya was a response to a vital threat to Russia's own economic well-being as a state.

---

332   After the defeat of Iraq during the Gulf War of January-February 1991, the United States and the Soviet Union co-convened an international peace conference in Madrid, Spain, to discuss a diplomatic end to the Arab-Israeli conflict. They called for the conference to initiate two parallel negotiating tracks: a bilateral track that involved specific talks between Israel and the Arab parties, and a multilateral track that involved many delegations discussing region-wide issues. The conference opened on 30 October 1991, and included delegations from Israel, Syria, Lebanon, and Egypt and a joint Jordanian-Palestinian delegation, as well as observers from other nations and organizations. The conference lasted until 1 November and was immediately followed by bilateral talks in Madrid between Israel and each of the Syrian, Lebanese, and Jordanian-Palestinian delegations. Israel agreed to meet with the Palestinians separately from the Jordanians. The multilateral talks commenced in January 1992 in Moscow.

Economic motivations have become very significant in the post-Cold War intervention policy of both the United States and Russia. For one the vast reserves of Saudi Arabian and Kuwaiti oil was a major motivation of the U.S. organization and conduct of Operation Desert Shield/Storm[333] and for the other, securing oil pipelines by securing Chechnya and the Caspian sea huge reserves was a good enough reason for military occupation. Indeed, in both cases, the energy lobby has become more influential than ideological or traditional political ones.

The economic interests underlying an interventionist policy have become very important in the post-Cold War era. The New World Order suggests a new organization of world affairs based on a mono-polar system led by one super-power; the United States. It also suggests that economic power is as important as military one. To preserve vital national economic interests, states adopt some-times interventionist policies that go as far as direct military intervention. It is understood, that the declared reason for the intervention can rarely be clearly stated by the interventionists. Usually it is covered by other pretexts that would justify it in the eyes of the domestic and the world's public opinion. The cases of the Gulf War of the early 1990's and the Chechnya war are very good examples of the importance of economic interests in shaping a state's foreign policy. It can always be argued, however, that other interventions took place in the post-Cold War era without any important economic stakes involved. This might be true to

---

333   On the morning of August 2, 1990 the mechanized infantry, armor, and tank units of the Iraqi Republican Guard invaded Kuwait and seized control of that country. The invasion triggered a United States response, Operation DESERT SHIELD, to deter any invasion of Kuwait's oil rich neighbor, Saudi Arabia. On August 7, deployment of U.S. forces began. United Nations Security Council Resolutions 660 and 662 condemned Iraq's invasion and annexation and called for the immediate and unconditional withdrawal of Iraqi forces. On August 20 President Bush signed National Security Directive 45, "U.S. Policy in Response to the Iraqi Invasion of Kuwait," outlining U.S. objectives—which included the "immediate, complete, and unconditional withdrawal of all Iraqi forces from Kuwait," and the "restoration of Kuwait's legitimate government to replace the puppet regime installed by Iraq." A U.N. ultimatum, Security Council Resolution 678, followed on November 29, 1990. It stipulated that if Iraqi dictator Saddam Hussein did not remove his troops from Kuwait by January 15, 1991 a U.S.-led coalition was authorized to drive them out. Early in the morning of January 17, Baghdad time, the U.S.-led coalition launched air attacks against Iraqi targets. On February 24, coalition ground forces begin their attack. On February 27, Kuwait City was declared liberated, and with allied forces having driven well into Iraq, President Bush and his advisers decided to halt the war. A cease-fire took effect at 8:00 the following morning.

some extent. Yet, in states' calculations of interests there is bound to be some sort of an economic interest involved even if such an interest is shadowed or hidden by other more obvious reasons such as humanitarian or political ones. For instance, the intervention in Bosnia and Kosovo, in addition to the other obvious reasons justifying it, can always be said to have been done to preserve a unified Europe. A stable Europe is beneficial for the economic situation in the world and is better as a market. Moreover, the U.S. intervention in Somalia can always be said to have been done out of humanitarian concerns. Yet, it can also be said to have been done to have a footstep in the Horn of Africa, which is a very important area economically and strategically speaking, since it controls the access to the Red Sea. Thus, vital economic interests can sometimes shadow other interests and can sometimes be shadowed themselves by other more obvious reasons. But, whether on top of the list or hidden, economic interests always figure highly on a state's calculations of national interests.

1.3.3.2.3. Security Interests.

To begin with, the term security itself implies many meanings. In fact, the definitions found in dictionaries of the term security often usually imply a feeling of being free from fear or a sense of safety, involving both physical and psychological security. Security interests are one of the most important determinants of the coverage of an international crisis. State's security interests have always been an essential element in the calculations of politicians and leaders along with economic and social ones. Any disturbance or possible threat to these security interests of a state, group of states, or, sometimes, of an ally would immediately raise the interest of this concerned state or group of states.

One of the most important components of any state's national security interests is the concept of the state's national security. This concept, however, did not always refer to the same meaning as it does today. It developed with the development of the political philosophy over the last decades. Helga Haftendorn argues that national security became a major concern in the seventeenth century, exactly with the birth of the nation state[334]. Other researchers indicate that the term national security became well known in the twentieth century, particularly after World War II[335]. Yet, the security of a state is not only to be preserved within its own borders, it is also to be guaranteed vis-à-vis its international environment.

---

334   See Helga Haftendorn, "The Security Puzzle: Theory-Building and Discipline-Building in International Security", <u>International Studies Quarterly</u>, N° 35, March 1991), pp. 5-6.

335   See Robert Mandel, <u>The Changing Face of National Security: A Conceptual Analysis</u>, Greenwood Press, Westport, CT., 1994, p. 15.

Thus, a state's security can be said to be composed of two dimensions: national and international security.

However, it is actually difficult to separate the two concepts of national and international security of a state. In addition, the concept of national security seems to have adopted and incorporated quite a number of modern developments and concepts. A number of researchers are of this opinion. For instance, Edward A. Kolodziej argues that there is a need to enlarge the concept of national security to face the diversity of challenges in today's world[336]. Such new realms of national security may include a wider range of international problems such as sub-national and trans-national threats, the AIDS epidemic, drug trafficking, international debt and economic recession, exponential population growth, and environmental pollution.

Some believe that security means the preservation or the creation of favourable conditions for a state both internally and externally. A number of these views see national values as the main objective of this preservation. Frank Trager, for example, regards national security objectives as the creation of national and international political conditions that are favourable to the protection or the extension of vital national values of state[337]. Similarly, Arnold Wolfers sees national security as "the absence of threats to acquired values" and "subjectively" as "the absence of fear that such values will be attacked"[338]. If the security is about preserving national values then it is also about allowing no interference with such values, especially a perceived outside threat. This threat can be a direct threat to the security of a state or a threat to an area, where this state has vital interests.

In the time of an international crisis, this threat to the security interests of a state or of a group of states is quite evident. The reaction to this international conflict often depends on the perceived threat itself. The time of reaction, its degree and its objectives and its means are also determined by the perception of the threat an international crisis can produce. Thus, some international crisis and conflicts might simply go unnoticed precisely because of their unthreatening nature to the world powers or to the world political order.

---

336   See Edward A. Kolodziej, "Renaissance in Security Studies? Caveat Lector!, International Studies Quarterly, N°36, December 1992, pp.421-438.

337   Frank Trager, "Introduction to the Study of National Security", in Frank Trager and Philip Kronenberg, eds., National Security and American Society, University Press of Kansas, Manhattan, KS: 1973, pp. 35-36.

338   See Arnold Wolfers, Discord and Collaboration, Johns Hopkins University Press, Baltimore, 1962, p. 150.

1.4. The Effect of International Political Tendencies: The "Dominos Syndrome" in Media Coverage of International Crises

The coverage of international crisis by the media reveals an interesting phenomenon. The media tend to follow suit in their coverage of an international crisis. They tend to fall in line just like dominos in there concern for a certain international crisis. It is enough for one media to show interest for an international crisis in some part of the world, for the other media to imitate it in that interest. Yet, the question is why does such a phenomenon exist in the first place and why is it discriminatory, as far as the international crisis covered are concerned. Two reasons can actually be the cause of such a behaviour of the media vis-à-vis an international crisis. These are the impact of the international political tendencies and what some researchers refer to as the "critical incident" in journalism.

The multitude of international political conditions can concentrate attention on a particular international crisis and not another. Usually, the build up of the environment for this focus takes place much earlier than the date of the outbreak of the crisis itself. This build up would usually start by political manoeuvres of countries that are interested in the region, country or area where the crisis would usually take place. With this reasoning, the idea that some international crises are actually fabricated from the start is quite understandable. States have vital interests and to preserve those interests, intervention on variable levels is sometimes used.

To bring a certain crisis to the surface, different levels have to be active whether separately or with conjunction with each other. The first of these levels is the level of the interested states. Those would usually start by voicing certain positions in their foreign policy statements that would indicate the beginning of a crisis. With the progression of time, such statements or political hints would grow stronger into more direct and aggressive ones. They might also take more solid acts whether political, economic or, in some cases, manoeuvring of military troops.

The second level where the build up to the international crisis takes place is the international institutions level. The international political community would naturally be forced to more and more discussions about voiced political positions of its members. In this case, some meetings might be dedicated to a discussion of the apparent disaccord between the member states concerning the issue or issues at hand. In some cases, resolutions from these international institutions might be taken concerning theses disagreements. This can be looked upon, somehow, as an international lobbying by the concerned states for the fabrication of an international crisis.

The third level, where this build up can take place, is that of the media. The role of the media, in this respect is quite essential. According to what has previously discussed in this research, the media has usually its own political agenda. This agenda is most of the time related to the political agenda of its own state or group of states. According to this logic, the media itself can draw more and more attention to the political or economic concerns of its government. It can, furthermore, create the bases for a moral justification of the possible crisis that might take place. This gradual build up can, thereafter, result in a more favourable public opinion for the political decisions taken. On an international level, the trans-national media would have more or less the same vocation, although in its case the effects are much more stronger. In the trans-national media's case, the effects are on the international public opinion as well as on the international politician decision-making. It can be always argued that the media focused on a number of international crises prior to their outbreak. This is quite true. Yet, the evidence of a crisis such as the Gulf War of 1990 compared to the Chechnya war suggests that the international crisis that have a prior build up get more media attention than others which did not have a strong international of build-up.

Logically speaking, if a state is strong, then its arguments are usually taken more attentively than other states. According to this logic, the media would usually pay more attention to political statements, for example, from a country like the United States concerning a possible conflict in the Caribbean than the statements of the President of Niger concerning its relations with its neighbours. Although, two international crises might be taking place exactly at the same time and in the same conditions, the international media would concentrate more attention to the one in which the United States is involved. Consequently, media attention would be drown to one international crisis and sometimes completely ignore the existence of others. There are of course financial calculations of the media concerning such a situation. For if the one media did not pay enough attention to the international crisis all the other media are interested in, then this media would certainly loose a considerable part of its audience or of its readers for the profit of other media who provide those "clientele" with the information needed.

The other element, which may have a bearing on this domino effect of an international crisis, is what some researchers call the "critical incident" in journalism[339]. Some events in the history of journalistic practice can be labelled as critical incident events. Some good examples of these are the Kennedy assassination, the Watergate scandal and the Vietnam War. In critical incidents, new rules and conventions of the journalistic practice as focused upon while discussing a general topic of interest. For instance, the Kennedy assassination took place at a time where the professionalisation

---

339   See Barbie Zelizer, "CNN, the Gulf War, and Journalistic Practice", Journal of Communications, vol.42.,N°1, 1992, p.66.

of journalists was at its peak and where the "legitimisation of television news was questionable"[340]. Yet, the incident itself does not separately constitute a critical incident in journalistic practice. For this incident to become one, two features have to exist. These are technological innovation and the archetypal figures.

As far as technological innovation is concerned, the journalists are offered, through technology, an opportunity to experiment with new means to fulfil their professional goals. For example, journalists during the Vietnam war had the chance to combine words with pictures in their war reporting on television. The assassination of Kennedy and the killing of his presumed assassin Lee Harvey Oswald[341] gave the public its first live televised experience of a major event. Technological innovations are, thus, a major element of the constitution of a critical incident event.

The other element in this equation is that of archetypal figures. These are journalists or individuals who are successful in using this technological innovation in the further development of a critical incident reporting. They are personalities who are connected to the coverage of this critical incident. For instance, the Kennedy assassination produced the Walter Cronkites and Dan Rathers[342], who's

---

340   Idem.

341   Oswald was accused of assassinating President John F. Kennedy on 22 November 1963. Oswald was a drifter with a murky past; he had been dishonourably discharged from the U.S. Marines and then defected to Russia in 1959, only to be refused citizenship there and sent back to the United States. Oswald allegedly shot Kennedy with a sniper's rifle from the sixth floor of the Texas School Book Depository as the president's motorcade travelled through Dallas. Oswald was arrested hours later in a movie theatre, after also shooting and killing police officer J.D. Tippet. Oswald was never tried: two days later he himself was shot to death at Dallas police headquarters by nightclub owner Jack Ruby. In 1964 a special commission headed by Chief Justice Earl Warren decided that Oswald, acting alone, had shot and killed the president.

342   Walter Cronkites and Dan Rathers were two of the most famous news anchors of the CBS news network. It was in 1963 that the network anchors as we define them today were born: a man who is at once an authoritative reporter, a cool news reader and the nation's emotional proxy at history's events. All these elements converged in Walter Cronkite. Cronkite's evening news was the first to expand from 15 minutes to a half-hour (over the objections of CBS's affiliates), the first in which the anchor assumed the powers (and title) of managing editor and the first to unfold in a "newsroom-studio" in which the anchor sat at a horseshoe desk while nameless writers and editors clattered at typewriters on the periphery of the image. (The idea for this "Front Page" set was Hewitt's.) The Kennedy assassination did the rest. For the first time, network news offered four days' blanket coverage of a news event, with the anchor at the eye of the harrowing storm. To this day, the moment when Cronkite, after announcing the president's death, took off his glasses and ever-so-slightly lost it, remains the cathartic peak of the story for the millions who were watching.

reporting of the story was referenced as exemplary television journalism. In addition, the Watergate scandal was associated with Bob Woodwards and Carl Bernsteins[343], who were both regarded as exemplar investigative journalists.

As far as the coverage of international crisis is concerned, the CNN coverage of the Gulf War of the 1990's can equally be regarded as a critical incident in journalism. Indeed, the potentials of the Gulf War as a journalistic story were tremendous compared to other international crisis. It was a crisis that happened shortly after the end of the Cold War. It involved an agitated area of the world and it concerned one of the world's biggest energy reserves. In addition, it was the first time such a coalition of states are involved in an act of war. W. Boot explains that the Gulf War was "the biggest news story in decades"[344]. Indeed, both features of the critical incident where involved in this crisis. There was the technological innovation used successfully by the CNN in its live coverage from the heart of the place where war events where taking place and there was also the archetype. Peter Arnette[345] who's name is associated with the famous phrase" Peter Arentte.... Live from Baghdad". Thus, the Gulf War as an international crisis was bound to attract journalist's interest all over the world. The importance of

---

343   Bob Woodward is a graduate of Yale and served five years as a communications officer in the United States Navy. He joined the Washington Post in 1971, a year before Watergate, with only one year of news reporting experience. As a result of Woodward and Bernstein's Watergate coverage, the Washington Post won the Pulitzer Prize for public service in 1973. Those two reporters went on to co-author two books about Watergate, "All the President's Men" and "The Final Days." Those books were No. 1 non-fiction best sellers, as were most of the books Woodward has written since. With Scott Armstrong, he wrote "The Brethren: Inside the Supreme Court." And on his own he has written "Wired: The Short Life and Fast Times of John Belushi"; "Veil: The Secret Wars of the CIA"; "The Commanders," which was a book about the Gulf War; "The Agenda: Inside the Clinton White House"; and last year, "The Choice," which was about the presidential campaign of 1996. Bob Woodward continues at the Washington Post, where he is assistant managing editor in charge of investigations and he continues to write prolifically.

344   Boot, W., "Covering the Gulf War: The Press Stands Alone", Columbia Journalism Review, (1991, March/April), p. 23.

345   Associated Press correspondent Arnett was made a pariah by U.S. military authorities in Saigon because of his vividly blunt reports from the combat zone. He became controversial again as a CNN reporter covering the opening days of Desert Storm and as an interviewer of Saddam Hussein; he was denounced on the floor of congress and accused by several members of playing Josef Goebbels to Saddam's Hitler. One of his most important convictions is that there's no thrill comparable to covering a war, and that he's good at it.

the event combined with the technological innovations and the journalistic figure were all destined to make practically all other world media follow the coverage of the Gulf War like dominos.

For the media to adopt a domino's reaction in the coverage of a certain international crisis and not others, some conditions have to be achieved. These are the particular characteristics that the international crisis has both in international political terms and in journalistic practice terms that, in turn, would render this international crisis more interesting than others for coverage. In international political terms, the prior political build up to the international crisis is a determining factor in spotlighting that crisis. In this respect, the number and international influence in political and economic terms of the countries involved is of an utmost importance in distinguishing an international crisis. Parallel to the political build up to the crisis, there is also a media build up due mostly to the fact that the media has its own political agenda that correlates to a large extent with that of the state's or the political establishments agendas. Additionally, the media's need to follow suit because of financial considerations and the need to keep its audience also has a bearing on the production of this domino's effect in the media coverage of an international crisis. As far as the journalistic practice is concerned, the fact that some international crises constitute a critical incident in journalism is very important. Coupled with new technological innovations in media coverage and the personality of the journalists involved in this" new type of coverage'", the critical incident characteristic of an international crisis would also contribute to the production of this domino's effect in the coverage of certain international crisis.

The relationship between the media national and international politics is quite interesting. The importance of media stems from the position it occupies in national and international cultural, social, economic and political fabrics. This position has certainly been reinforced over the last hundred years in passing by different eras of the world's history: from the 19th century intellectual and partisan media to the growing power and influence of the trans-national media, passing by the technological innovations in media broadcasting and outlets of the beginnings of the 20th century and Global wars and post-Cold War media tendencies.

The relationship between the national or domestic media and the political establishment in a given country is also an important aspect to discuss. Indeed, political manifestations of national tendencies are a normal and certainly an expected behavior of the national media. The media would do that specifically because of its integrated Agenda-Setting function and it can do it by using different frames to expose these political tendencies. The media has also a role of surveillance of the governmental establishment. Thus, role of the media as the "fourth estate" can, sometimes, and even in the most democratic of societies by the state's national interests and sovereignty. As with national politics, the national or domestic media can also influence and be influenced by international politics. Naturally, the degree of the effect that the national media can produce or be subjected to, as far as the international political tendencies are concerned, depends on the place of the national media's state in the international scene.

The national media has, furthermore, a role of interaction with the non-state actors. The national media's relation with the Civil Society and the NGO's is very important, especially in transmitting the pulse of the new social movements. The media can, thus, not be indifferent to the tendencies of such non-state actors. It cannot also be indifferent to the public opinion, which helps the media to better perform its surveillance function of the governmental establishment, in the state where it operates.

The influence of Trans-National Media Corporations TNMCs and the Trans-National Media Agencies TNNA's has been duly demonstrated. Their structure, extension and trans-national nature provide such a media with a great ability to influence the course of things. It can do that, mainly, by repetition, by the dependence on the flow of information it provides, by the political ordination and manipulation of national media and of the state in host countries, and by pre-choosing the foreign news items to be presented in the national media. Indeed, the influence of trans-national media is also cultural and social oriented. The Anglo-Americanisation fo the world culture via the trans-national media information and entertainment diffusion contributes to a theory of neo-cultural and ideological imperialism. In addition, dependency on foreign news proved to be more evident between colonised and colonising imperial power, which in turn suggests a centre and periphery information flow behaviour in the media.

During an international crisis, the role of the media stems out to be quite essential as an actor of this crisis. To be an actor in an international crisis, the media has to be able to perform a number of roles. First, the media has to be able to use the enormous technological innovations that took place in the last few decades, to better transmit the international crisis or conflict from no matter which part of the world this crisis or conflict takes place. Second, the media has to cover correctly the international crisis or conflict situation, by avoid dramatisa-tion and having a full understanding of the historical and political roots of the crisis. Third, the media has to be objective in its coverage, although this can, sometimes, be difficult to do since different parties to a crisis have different points of view to convey. Finally, the media has to be conscience about the impact of its own emphasis or lack of emphasis on an international crisis and whether such a behaviour would result in resolving, aggravating or ignoring the crisis.

To understand the different roles of the media during an international crisis, it is important to understand the media's motives and interests. To have that under-standing of the media's motives, it is essential to take the level of analysis to its basic from. That is to say that journalists are the basic components of the media and as such their interests can be regarded simply as human ones. As such, journalists have a journalistic instinct of being morally responsible and of transmitting their own understanding of the crisis to their audience. They also have a social interest in being a part of, reflecting and serving the society thy live in and its values. As far as the media apparatus as a whole is concerned, it has an economic and a political interest during an international crisis. Indeed, with considerations, like ratings, economic situation, resources and competition into consideration, the economic factors can have a considerable bearing on whether an international crisis is covered or not and on the extent and conduct of such coverage. Finally, the media has a political interest in an international crisis. It can, most of the time, echo the state's position towards that crisis. Yet, when there are no clear foreign policy guidelines concerning this international crisis, the media's coverage impact would be more considerable.

Apart from the media's own interests and roles in an international crisis, other elements can also highly affect the coverage of an international crisis or conflict. Religious, ethnic and social affinities with one side or the conflict or another can be, sometimes, quite noticeable in the media's coverage of an international crisis. The media, being part of the society it lives in, cannot but echo the tendencies of such affinities in its coverage. In addition, the state's own national interests often have an enormous impact on the media's coverage or handling of an international crisis or conflict. Factors, such as geographic proximity of the conflict area, the vital economic interests involved, and perceived threats to national security, figure highly on the list of a state's priorities when determining its reaction to an international crisis. In this respect, it has been shown, that even with intense media coverage of an international humanitarian situation, conflict or crisis, the reaction of states can be minimal or non-existent if no national interests where at jeopardy. It can also, be argued, by this logic, that some international crisis get more emphasis than others, simply because of the prior political build-up to these crisis and because of the importance of the countries involved. Such a crisis often tends to produce a domino's reaction where the majority of the world's media fall in line in focusing on this crisis.

Part Two:

International Crises, Media and Public Opinion: Case Study of the French and American National Media Coverage of the Conflicts in Bosnia-Herzegovina (15/10/1991-21/11/1995) and Chechnya (1/11/1991-31/8/1996).

2.1. Historical Background of The Two Conflicts

Comparing media coverage of the crisis of Bosnia-Herzegovina (15/10/1991[346]–21/11/1995[347]) and Chechnya (1/11/1991[348]–31/8/1996[349]) constitutes a good comparative case study that can help understand the attitudes, motives, and impact of media coverage of international crises and conflicts in general on public opinion. The reasons underlying the choice of those two crises for comparison purposes are various. Both crisis share a number of characteristics yet diverge in a number of particularities. They both involved a repeated quest for independence or at least self-government after a long period of "foreign" domination and a long process of forced social, cultural, and political mixing within the federations people of these regions were placed within. Indeed, both Bosnia-Herzegovina and Chechnya were part of a "forced union" and both demanded separation from their respective central dominant powers following the implosion n or collapse of these central power (the Soviet Union for Chechnya and the Belgrade rule for Bosnia-Herzegovina). These two crises also shared the fact that the great majority of the population of the two concerned regions of conflict are of Muslim confession. In addition, both crises have caused international political and media reactions but to quite different degrees. Moreover, the time span of the two crises is almost similar. Finally, they both took place in the immediate post-Cold War era.

Nonetheless, the two crises differ with regards to certain facts. They differ first in their geographic location and, consequently, in their regional context and implications for regional powers and other world countries. They also differ in the nature of the conflict involved. In the case of Bosnia-Herzegovina, the conflict is predominantly ethno-religious, while in Chechnya's case, it was more of an anti-colonial domination strive for independence from a long lasting foreign rule with the religious dimension element being added to the conflict later on.

Two countries and two printed media outlets are chosen to make this comparison of media coverage of these two conflicts. The two countries are France and the United States and the two printed media outlets are *Le Monde* and *The New York*

---

346   Date of the declaration of sovereignty of the Bosnia-Herzegovina parliament.

347   Date of the signature of the Dayton Accords.

348   Date of the auto-proclamation of independence of Chechnya by the Chechen President Dudaev.

349   Date of the signature of the Khassaviourt Accord.

Times. The choice of national media coverage comparison between the United States and France stems from a number of considerations and one that is related to their respective national media's adherence to the two countries' respective national interests in the two crises. Accordingly, it is first interesting to see the impact of geographic proximity on the national interests and media coverage of the two countries, France being more geographically close to the Balkans than the United States is and both France and the U.S. being geographically far from Chechnya. Moreover, both countries are world political philosophy leaders and have, on certain occasions, extremely diverged in their foreign policy philosophy vis-à-vis various international affaires. It is, hence, interesting to note the effect of such a difference of foreign policy mentality and philosophy on the national interests' pursuit of both countries in the two crises. The choice of printed media is done for practicality reasons due to referencing facility compared to audiovisual media outlets. The choice of two newspapers to represent printed media is done due to the fact that newspapers are daily editions of information. They are more frequent and more circulated than other forms of printed media. They, therefore, have much more impact due to frequency and the facility of access to their information on public opinion. The two newspapers chosen for the comparison are both highly established and considered newspapers in their respective countries. They are also world renowned ones. *The New York Times*, in addition to being a very credible national media outlet of the United States is also renowned for having a worldwide audience. The same applies for *Le Monde*, who although being more European than worldwide, is nevertheless a newspaper that also has its worldwide audience.

2.1.1. Bosnia-Herzegovina

In order to fully understand the dimensions and complications of both crises, it is important to have an idea about the events leading to and resulting from each. For its part, the crisis of 1991-1995 in Bosnia-Herzegovina is, and contrary to the common beliefs, not the first crisis in this region. Indeed its origins go far back in the troubled history of the Balkans (See Explanatory Note I below). In this respect, Pierre du Bois explains that "the question of the Balkans has been a part of the field of international relations since the XIX century. Indeed, this region of the world has a history of violent conflicts and transitions that always created a new political geography in Europe. This region (South-Eastern Europe and more familiarly known as 'the Balkans) proves the fact that the destination is much more than geography"[350].

---

350   See Pierre du Bois, *"La Question des Balkans"*, <u>Relations Internationales</u>, N° 103, Fall 2000, p.271.

For their part, Tuathail and Dalby explain, in this respect, that geography is not a given but an "earth writing" that reflects relations of power and identity amongst nations[351]. Thus, the location and ethnic composition of the Balkans constitute some sort of a battlefield upon which interests of various regional powers were always tested. Indeed, Du Bois goes on to say "The fate of the region interests the highest rank of European powers. The struggles conducted by Christian nations of the Ottoman Empire to obtain autonomy and independence have been echoing at the cabinets of those who tend to support them, to instigate them or to fight them according each cabinet's own interests involved"[352]. What du Bois seems to suggest is that the geography of a region also dictates this regions fate. Some writers, on the other hand, claim that those struggles in this region (the Balkans) are simply a characteristic of the region itself. For instance, Charles Vogel claims that the conflicts are an expression of the "foundations of the half-barbarism that characterises Eastern Europe"[353]. Whatever the causes are, the facts of the multiplication of conflicts in this region are there to speak for themselves.

Indeed, the historical list of conflicts in the Balkans is quite a long one. It includes the Crimean War (1853-1856), the issue of the Rumanian Principalities (1857-1859), the insurrection of the Bosnia-Herzegovina Christians in 1862 and 1875, the uprising of the Bulgarians in 1876, the war of Serbia, backed by Russia, against the Ottoman Empire in 1876 and the war declared by Russia against the Ottoman Empire in 1877. Moreover, in the same year that the Treaty of Berlin was being prepared, a conflict explodes between Montenegro and Albania concerning access to the sea (1878-1881).

The seemingly constant result of such a troublesome nature of the Balkans is that events in that region always had an enormous interest for the European public opinion[354]. It is, however, understandable that the European public opinion should be quite interested in the events in this region since many European powers have their own national interests and affinities with one part of the conflict or the another. It is, hence, quite understandable that European public opinion is more sensitive to developments in Balkans because events in this area have previously resulted in major wars between the European powers themselves. In this respect, Francis Charmes in 1912, referring to a previous crisis in the region, explains that" the current crisis is not only that of the Balkans, it is also that of

---

351　See Ó Tuathail G and S Dalby, <u>Rethinking Geopolitics</u>, Routledge, London,1998

352　See Pierre du Bois, <u>op.cit.</u>

353　See Charles Vogel, <u>L'Europe orientale depuis le Traité de Berlin</u>, C. Reinwald, Paris, 1881, p.6.

354　See Pierre du Bois, <u>op.cit</u>, p. 272.

Europe"[355]. This is also the opinion of Pierre du Bois who states that the European powers are very sensitive to the provocation of the conflicts in the Balkans, which in turn could threaten the peace in Europe as a whole[356]. Thus, it can be said that any conflict in the Balkans is bound to draw the attention and possible reaction of the European countries, in particular, and to result in a very sensitive public opinion towards that issue, due to the history of conflicts in this region and its previous tragic outcomes on the scale of the whole European continent. This can also lead to another conclusion which is that fear amongst all other factors is the most capable mobilizing factor for action on the part of governments and for attention and sensitivity to the issue on the part of the public opinion of those governments.

The conflicts in the Balkans also resulted in other innovations in political activism that would have more of a role later on in the history and fate of many nations. For, it is in the Balkans that conflicts produced terrorism as a means of achieving political objectives of different nationalists and political factions. Indeed, the beginning of the twentieth century witnessed the birth of a number of terrorist organisations in this region such as the Macedonian Revolutionary Organisation[357], which was fighting the Turkish presence in the Balkans, the Black Hand[358] in Serbia with the assassination of King Alexander and Queen Draga in 1903[359] and the Young Bosnians with the assassination of Ferdinand-François in

---

355　See Francis Charmes, «Chronique de la Quinzaine», Revue des Deux Mondes, 1st of novembre 1912, p.237.

356　See Pierre du Bois, op. cit., p.273.

357　In 1893, the Internal Macedonian Revolutionary Organisation (IMRO) was founded to promote independence. In 1912/13, the Balkan Wars drove the Turks out of the area, and it was carved up between Serbia and Greece, with Bulgaria retaining only a small part. Vardar Macedonia became part of the new 'Kingdom of Serbs, Croats and Slovenes' in 1918 ('Yugoslavia' from 1929). This caused much anti-Serbian resentment locally during the inter-war period, when the IMRO was also used as a terrorist organisation against Belgrade by Bulgaria, which again occupied the area under German direction during World War

358　Ten men met on May 9, 1911 to form *Ujedinjenje ili Smrt* (Union or Death), also known as The Black Hand. By 1914, there were several hundred members, perhaps as many as 2500. Many members were Serbian army officers. The professed goal of the group was the creation of a Greater Serbia, by use of violence, if necessary. The Black Hand trained guerillas and saboteurs and arranged political murders. The Black Hand was organized at the grassroots level in 3 to 5-member cells.

359　On June 10, 1903, King Alexander and Queen Draga of Serbia were murdered in the royal palace at Belgrade by a band of officers of the Serbian Army. The assassination was followed by shocking indignities to the bodies of the dead and by the murder of two brothers of the Queen and of two ministers.

Sarajevo on the 28th of June 1914[360]. Many consider this last event as the trigger of the World War I in the sense that it was used by Germany and the Austria-Hungary Empire as a pretext to settle old scores with Serbia. Thus, the Balkans can also be considered the birthplace of modern political terrorism, as well as being the region of conflicts that it is. This terrorism to achieve political objectives can also be said to be the "ancestor" of the modern ethnic cleansing, where the objective is not simply to remove an opposing political figure but to remove an entire different ethnicity in order to change the demographic variables and, thereafter, obtain a stronger position in any future negotiations about the fate of the disputed region.

Explanatory Note I
The Bosnian Crisis of 1908-1909.

The annexation of Bosnia and Herzegovina by Austria-Hungary in October, 1908, led to a controversy between the Dual Monarchy and Turkey in addition to a threat of an all out war in Europe over the issue. For, according to article 25 of the Treaty of Berlin of 1878, Austria-Hungary was permitted to occupy and administer Bosnia and Herzegovina. This type of arrangement resulted from an understanding between Russia and the Dual Monarchy on the eve of the Russo-Turkish War of 1877-1878 and it also came as a result of the support given by England and Germany to the Austro-Hungarian claims at the Congress of Berlin. As such, the protests of the Serbian representatives at the Congress were in vain.

The 1908-1909 Bosnian crisis was, thus, a consequence of Serbia's attempts to stand against the full integration and occupation of Bosnia-Herzegovina by the Austria-Hungary empire and its desire to have an access through Bosnia-Herzegovina to the Adriatic Sea. As such, popular feelings in Serbia were high on the issue. Indeed, the pressure was to incite the Serbian representatives and leaders to oppose the annexation of Bosnia-Herzegovina by the Austria-Hungary Empire. On her, part Russia tried to submit a proposal to resolve the crisis and prevent the threat of war. Yet, the refusal of the main powers involved at the time, especially the strong rejection of Germany and Austria-Hungary, led to a dismissal of the Russian attempt to defuse the crisis.

---

360   See Vladimir Didijer, « *La route de Sarajevo* », Gallimard, Paris, 1969, p. 222. The Black Hand also had under its wings satellite organizations in the Balkans. They undertook anti-Austrian propaganda and organized spies and saboteurs to operate within the empire's provinces. Satellite groups were formed in Slovinia, Bosnia, Herzegovina and Istria. The Bosnian group went under the name *Mlada Bosna*— Young Bosnia. the guilt for the assassination of the Archduke had settled loosely on Serbia in general. Tensions between Serbia and Austria eventually drew in the other European powers and escalated into world war.

At the end, the crisis was defused in a manner that was unsatisfactory to Serbia and Russia mainly due to the enormous pressure made by Germany. Accordingly, Serbia was forced to recognize the status quo created in Bosnia-Herzegovina in a declaration sent to Vienna on March 31, 1909. It recognizes that the situation created in Bosnia-Herzegovina does not involve any injury to the rights of Serbia. In addition, it declared its will to conform to the decision, which the powers were going to take concerning article 25 of the Treaty of Vienna. Moreover, and in accordance with the advice of the powers, Serbia agreed to give up the tone of opposition and protest which began on October of the previous year. Serbia also agreed to modify the line of its political conduct vis-à-vis Austria-Hungary. Militarily, and In conformity with this declaration, Serbia declared its commitment to bring back its army, in the matter of organization, distribution, and of state of activity, to the situation existing in the spring of 1908. It also disbanded the volunteer troops and committed itself to the prevention of the formation of such irregular troops on its territory in the future.

In 1919 and with the Treaty of Versailles, the new order in Europe resulted in a new order in the Balkans[361]. It was a time where old Empires disappeared leaving place for "the Great Romania", the "Great Greece" and the" Great Serbia". It was the time where all the Slaves of the South were assembled in the Kingdom of the Serbs, the Croats and the Slovenians. But even then peace wasn't completely obtained in the region. The examples are many. They include, for instance, the war between Turkey and Greece in 1923, the result of which was the expulsion of Greece from Asia Minor, and the War between Greece and Bulgaria in 1925. It was also a time where terrorism was back in great force in the region. Here again the

---

361   The treaty created new borders, which recognised new states, this was to take into account of minority nationalistic identities. The nationalistic issues were addressed, as it was these issues that ignited World War 1. Most of the grievances centred on eastern Europe and the Balkans that were part of the Austro-Hungarian Empire. These ethnic groups resented the imperial hold that was held by Vienna, and as Germany's ally the Allies broke up the Austro-Hungarian Empire into separate states. They created Hungary as a separate state, and then merged the Czech lands, Slovakia and the German speaking areas of the Sudetenland, and created the new state of Czechoslovakia. In the Balkans they created the new state of Yugoslavia, which consisted of Slovenia, Croatia, Bosnia-Herzegovina (which were all part of the Austro-Hungarian Empire), the independent state of Serbia and Montenegro. The effects of the treaty would be felt 70 years on when the new state, with its political and religious differences, ignite into a bloody civil war.

examples are many. For instance, the bloody assassination attempt against King Boris[362] in Sofia in 1925, the fight of the Macedonian Revolutionary Organisation against the Serbian domination of Macedonia and the Croatian *Oustachis* movement fighting for the independence of Croatia and backed by Italy, Germany and Hungary are good examples of the continuation of the use of terrorism to achieve political objectives. Some writers also explain that such terrorist movements developed their contacts in the 1930s and were able to hit no matter when and no matter where in Europe with the continuous backing of European powers such as Germany, Hungary and Italy[363]. It should be mentioned, in this respect, that there was an attempt in 1934 to calm the region via an entente between the interested countries based on observing mutual commitments. However, the Balkan's Entente which involved Romania, Greece, Turkey and Yugoslavia did not include Bulgaria, which didn't recognize any of the borders of the four mentioned states.

During the Second World War, the fate of the Balkans was to be distributed under the zones of influence of the major powers, mainly Germany and Italy. During the war, Greece was occupied while Yugoslavia was dissected and the Independent State of Croatia was backed. The alliances between European powers were quite interesting in this period. For instance, Romania in 1940, is allied to Germany and Bulgaria enters, in 1941, the Tripartite Alliance. After the Second World War, the fate of the Balkans was that it became a playing ground for the British and the Soviets (1945-1950). This was quite evident in Greece (1946-1949) where a civil war opposing the communists supported by Albania, Bulgaria and Yugoslavia to loyalists supported by Britain and the United States took place. The Balkans, during the Cold War, similar to most of the rest of world regions and countries, was divided between the Eastern and Western spheres of influence.

---

362   (1894-1943), king of Bulgaria from 1918 to 1943, who during the last five years of his reign headed a thinly veiled royal dictatorship. he was the object of terrorist conspiracies; two attempts were made on his life within a few days in April 1925. His marriage to Princess Giovanna of Italy (1930) temporarily cemented Italian relations; but during the late 1930s he passed more into the German orbit and sought rapprochement with Yugoslavia. After the establishment of a military dictatorship in Bulgaria (1934), he worked gradually to reassert his power; by November 1935 he had successfully installed Georgi Kyoseivanov, a personal favourite, as prime minister. From 1938 until his death he was dictator in all but name. After Bulgaria's adhesion to the Axis pact (March 1941), Boris maintained a modicum of independence; even after Bulgaria's entry into World War II on the side of the Axis and after participating in the invasion of Yugoslavia and Greece, he was able to resist declaring war against Russia. He died shortly after a stormy interview with Adolf Hitler. Whether his death was caused by heart attack or by assassination is uncertain.

363   See Pierre du Bois, op. cit., p. 274.

The intentions were that an assembled central state in the Balkans would help preserve the calm of the region. But, the composition and structure of this cementing state (Yugoslavia)[364] was a unique one, indeed. Yugoslavia, in fact, was an entity that was created in the aftermath of World War I. This took place mainly through the merger of the predominantly Catholic regions of Slovenia and Croatia with the Eastern Orthodox Kingdoms of Serbia and Montenegro. For its part, Bosnia in this equation was ethnically and religiously divided among Catholic Croats, Orthodox Serbs and Muslim Slavs. Adding to this complexity of the composition of this artificial political entity was the region of Kosovo in the south with its largely Albanian Muslim population and its historical significance to the Serbs of Belgrade.

Up to the outbreak of the World War II, it can be said that this multiple ethnic and religious entity held together fairly well. However, with the German and Italian invasion and brutal occupation of 1941, the old ethnic divisions were re-projected in a civil war. In this division, the Croats allied themselves with the Axis powers[365] against the Serbs. After the end of the war, Joseph Broz Tito[366], reunited Yugoslavia with an iron fist, imprisoning nationalists from all sides and mixing up ethnicities, religions and languages in order to dissolve them into one united entity. However, this entity, which was cemented together firmly by Tito, held together precisely and simply because of his existence. Consequently, the unity he built was bound to collapse after his death in 1980. This was the prediction of most observers. But Yugoslavia, contrary to all predictions, held together for a decade after Tito's death. It seems, however, that it only managed to do so because the Soviet Bloc was still intact and not because the observers were totally mistaken about its fate after the death of Tito. There is one more interesting fact to specify about the economy of former Yugoslavia. Contrary to what might be thought about such a state, its economy was not a state-controlled one. In fact, former-Yugoslavia constitution of 1974 established eight state-controlled economies and not a unique centralized one in Belgrade. There was a state-controlled economy in each republic and in each

---

364   The word Yugoslavia literally means the "Slaves of the South".
365   Albania, Bulgaria, Finland, Germany, Hungary, Italy, Japan, Romania, Thailand.
366   Original name (JOSIP BROZ(, Yugoslav revolutionary and statesman. He was secretary-general (later president) of the Communist Party (League of Communists) of Yugoslavia (1939-80), supreme commander of the Yugoslav Partisans (1941-45) and the Yugoslav People's Army (1945-80), and marshal (1943-80), premier (1945-53), and president (1953-80) of Yugoslavia. Tito was the chief architect of the "second Yugoslavia," a socialist federation that lasted from World War II until 1991. He was the first Communist leader in power to defy Soviet hegemony, a backer of independent roads to socialism (sometimes referred to as "national communism"), and a promoter of the policy of nonalignment between the two hostile blocs in the Cold War.

autonomous province of the former-Yugoslavia[367]. In addition, and at the micro-economic level, the governments of each republic within the former-Yugoslavia was free to "interfere in the activities of enterprises and banks"[368].

With the collapse of the Soviet Union in the beginning of the 1990's, ethnic and religious sentiments resurfaced in practically all of the former Eastern European and other ex-Communist Block countries. Thus, and in 1991, the Serbian politician Slobodan Milosovic[369] gained power in Yugoslavia mainly through inciting senti-ments of Serb nationalism. Consequently, other nations in the entity such as Slovenia (Slovenian War of Independence 1991)[370] and Croatia (Croatian War of Independence (1991-1995)[371] soon sought independence from what they per-ceived as a country controlled mainly by the Serbs. In addition, Serbs in southern and western Croatia sought to create their own new nation and achieve their inde-pendence from the power of Belgrade in what was known as the *Krajina* Rebellion (1991-1995)[372]. For its part, Bosnia's turn came in 1992 (See Map 1).

---

367 See James Ridgeway and Jasminka Udovi?ki, Burn This House: The Making and Unmaking of Yugoslavia, Duke University Press, Durham, NC, 1997, p. 82.

368 Idem.

369 A native of the Serbian town of Pozarevac, Slobodan Milosevic was born August 29, 1941, to an orthodox priest and a teacher. He graduated from Belgrade University with a degree in law and climbed the political ladder as a communist technocrat. Milosevic has headed both Yugoslavia's state-run gas extraction com-pany and the country's state-run bank, the United Bank of Belgrade. He served as leader of the Belgrade Communist Party from 1978-'82, and was named head of the Serbian Communist Party in 1987. Milosevic attained international stature in the 1980s during his country's ethnic conflicts. He was handed over to the United Nations International War Crimes Tribunal in La Hague for atrocities committed during his leadership. Milosevic's overwhelming popularity among his people has been attributed to his devotion to Serbian unification. Revered as a saviour by some, he is called the "Butcher of the Balkans" by others.

370 Slovenia's war against the Serbian-dominated Yugoslav Army was short and victo-rious. This was due in part to Yugoslav President Slobodan Milosevic's realization that his main worry was the war in neighbouring Croatia.

371 Croatia fought both the Yugoslav/Serbian Army and Serb rebels in the *Krajina* region

372 Croatia's Serb minority attempted to form a separate nation during the Croatian War of Independence from Yugoslavia. The Serb rebels succeeded in driving the Croatian mili-tary out of the Krajina region bordering Bosnia. However, in May of 1995, the Croatian Army launched an effective offensive (Operation Storm), which forced an end to the *Krajina Republic*. As a result of this action, most *Krajina* Serbs fled into Serbia in a form of "ethnic cleansing." The Yugoslav/Serb Army aided the *Krajina* rebels. Many of these Serb. refugees settled in the *Voyvodina* region of northern Serbia, but some of them moved to the Serb province of Kosovo, which erupted into war in 1998. During the Bosnian War, airplanes from Krajina bombed Muslim held Bihac in Bosnia. Following this, NATO warplanes bombed the Serb airfield at *Udbina* in *Krajin*a.

Map 1: Bosnia and Herzegovina

Source: World Atlas Online at http://www.freegk.com/worldatlas/bosnia.php

The Bosnian civil war of 1991-1995 was a complicated case in this state of civil wars and ethnic conflicts, which were multiplying almost all over the world at the time. The case of the Bosnian conflict was different though. For whereas many other interethnic conflicts went totally unnoticed, the ones in the Balkans not only involved those who were physically fighting in that region but also it involved also a conflict of interests between various regional and world powers Indeed, its complication stemmed from the fact that it involved a number of parties and ethnicities with alliances formed between some against the others. It involved Croatia, Serbia, the Bosnian Muslims, the UN and NATO. On the 15th of October 1991, Bosnia declared independence from ex-Yugoslavia. Almost immediately, the Bosnian Serb population rebelled against the Muslim and Croatian portions of the new nation. Parts of the war saw the Muslims and Croatians cooperate against their common foe, but from 1993-1994, Bosnia saw a three-way war when the Muslims and Croats battled each other as well as fighting the Serbs.

Bosnia soon, moreover, became the battlefield to settle old scores between Serbs and Croats. Troops from Serbia/Yugoslavia and the rebel *Krajina* area entered Bosnia to aid the Bosnian Serbs, while the Croatian Army aided the Bosnian Croat forces. Sometimes, the atrocities committed by one side or the other resulted in an immediate international reaction. For instance, on February 5th 1994, Serb artillery hit a marketplace in Sarajevo, causing severe civilian casualties. The event was highly dramatised and consequently, resulted in an increased American pressure on the Muslims and Croats to stop fighting each other and unite against the Serbs. On February 23rd, both sides signed a cease-fire, which soon led to the formation of the Muslim/Croat Bosnian Federation. In April 1994, NATO forces began selected, limited bombing of Serb positions around the capital Sarajevo in an attempt to force the Serbs to the peace table.

On the 28th of August 1995, Serb mortars caused 37 civilian deaths in Sarajevo. As a result, major NATO (Operation Deliberate Force[373]) air-strikes against the Serbs began on August the 30th and continued until a bombing pause on September 14th of the same year. In these strikes, the U.S. airpower contributed 65.9% of the NATO air sorties. Consequently, the Bosnian Serbs agreed to end the fighting and participate in peace negotiations. The resulting American forced peace treaty was known as The General Framework Agreement for Peace In Bosnia and Herzegovina, more commonly known as the Dayton Peace Accords (See Explanatory Note II).

---

373 After the fall of the eastern Bosnian "safe areas," in July 1995, the international community agreed to steps to extend NATO air power. NATO extended its threat of air strikes against Bosnian Serbs if they attacked any of the remaining "safe areas" in Bosnia. "Safe areas" include Gorazde, Tuzla, Bihac and Sarajevo. Serb forces wasted no time testing the world's will and launched attacks against the "safe areas" of Zepa, Bihac and Sarajevo. To complicate things even further, Croatian forces entered the fighting in early August. NATO launched a sustained air strike campaign (Operation Deliberate Force) beginning on August 30, 1995, against Bosnian Serb military targets in response to a Bosnian Serb mortar attack on civilians in Sarajevo. Air strikes were conducted on eleven days during the period 29 August through 14 September 1995. Of the total of 3515 sorties flown, 2470 were penetrating sorties, which included attacks on 48 target complexes [consisting of 338 individual targets within target complexes]. Of the 1026 bombs dropped, precision munitions numbered 708 and non-precision munitions 318.

Explanatory Note II
The 1995 Dayton Peace Accords and their Aftermath

The 1995 General Framework Agreement for Peace in Bosnia and Herzegovina (the Dayton Accords) ended the 1991-95 war and created the independent state of Bosnia and Herzegovina. The agreement also created two multiethnic constituent entities within the state: The Federation of Bosnia and Herzegovina (the Federation) and the *Republika Srpska* (RS). The Federation, which has a post-war Bosnian Muslim (*Bosniak*) and Croat majority, occupies 51 percent of the territory; the RS, which has a post-war Bosnian Serb majority, occupies 49 percent. The Constitution (Annex 4 of the Dayton Accords) establishes a state-wide government with a bicameral legislature, a three-member presidency (consisting of a *Bosniak*, a Serb, and a Croat), a council of ministers, a constitutional court, and a central bank. The Accords also provided for the Office of the High Representative (OHR) to oversee implementation of civilian provisions. The High Representative also has the power to impose legislation and remove officials who obstruct the implementation of the Dayton Accords. The entities maintain separate armies, but under the Constitution, these are under the ultimate control of the presidency of Bosnia and Herzegovina. Multiethnic parties committed to building on the foundation established at Dayton, such as the Social Democratic Party (SDP), made inroads against the support for the nationalist, ethnically based parties in the November elections, resulting in a state House of Representatives almost evenly divided between the two groups. In the RS, the ethnically based Serb Democratic Party (SDS) maintained its dominant position, while the nationalist Croatian Democratic Union of Bosnia and Herzegovina (HDZ) remained strong in Croat-majority municipalities. The Party of Democratic Action (SDA) remained the largest nationalist *Bosniak* party. Although formally independent, the judiciary remains subject to influence by political parties and the executive branch and is unable to prosecute complex or even simple crimes fairly and effectively.

One of the two entities that make up Bosnia and Herzegovina, the Federation of Bosnia and Herzegovina, was established in March 1994 and transformed the government structure of the Bosnian territories under *Bosniak* and Croatian control. The President of the Federation appoints the Prime Minister subject to parliamentary approval. The Federation Parliament is bicameral. Federation structures continue to be implemented only gradually. Major steps were the creation of canton governments, the unification of Sarajevo under Federation control in spring 1996, and the 1996, 1998, and 2000 elections of the Federation Parliament. However, serious ethnic and political rivalries continue to divide Croats and Bosniaks. Furthermore, parallel *Bosniak* and Croat government structures continued to exist in practice.

The *Republika Srpska* of Bosnia and Herzegovina is the other entity that makes up Bosnia and Herzegovina. In 1997-98, most of the RS political and administrative agencies moved from Pale, a stronghold of former Bosnian Serb leader and indicted war criminal Radovan Karadzic, to Banja Luka. The President and Vice President were elected in November for four-year terms. The RS National Assembly is unicameral and elected on a proportional basis. The November general elections in the *Republika Srpska* were relatively free and fair, and resulted in the nationalist parties, led by the SDS, increasing their strength at the expense of the pro-Dayton moderates.

The Constitution gives the Government of each entity and the individual cantons within the Federation responsibility for law enforcement in accordance with internationally recognized standards. The Stabilization Force (SFOR), led by NATO, continued to implement the military aspects of the Dayton Accords and to attempt to create a secure environment for implementation of the non-military aspects of the settlement, such as: Civilian reconstruction, the return of refugees and displaced persons, elections, and freedom of movement of the civilian population. The International Police Task Force (IPTF), which was established by the U. N. under Annex 11 of the Dayton Accords, monitors, advises, and trains the local police.

Interestingly enough, The Dayton Accords have a fundamental contradiction. They attempt to preserve the territorial integrity of Bosnia while dividing it at the same time in two distinct ethnic entities: the Bosnia-Herzegovina Federation (Muslim-Croat Federation) with 51% of the territory of Bosnia and the Bosnian Serb Republic with 49% of the territory The results of ethnic cleansing there are, in fact, established and the logic of partition is reinforced with the establishment of a demarcation line between the two entities. The Dayton Accords are an interesting peace restoring and keeping attempt because they place NATO with its stationed troupes there before the United Nations and its supposedly universal peacekeeping mandate (See Map 2).

Map 2: Bosnia (The Dayton Distribution (21 December 1999)

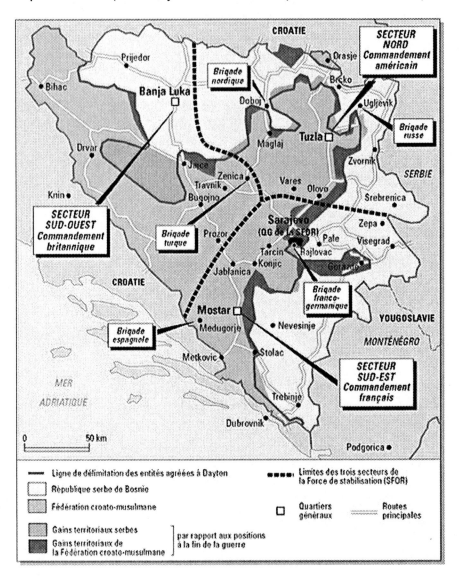

Source: Philippe Rekacewicz, Le Monde-Diplomatique, January 1999.

2.1.2. Chechnya

For its part, the case of the crisis of Chechnya (1/11/1991-31/8/1996) is of a slightly different nature from that of Bosnia-Herzegovina. Although many consider that the beginning of the crisis was In December of 1994 when Russian troops entered Chechnya to prevent Chechnya's efforts to secede from the Russian Federation, the crisis itself actually started three years earlier with the aforementioned Chechen declaration of independence. With the Russian troops entry in Chechnya on December 1994, fighting continued in Chechnya for almost two years until, finally, a peace agreement was reached between Moscow and the Chechen leaders on the 31st of August 1996. The agreement stipulated that resolving Chechnya's call for independence is to be postponed for five years. The conflict in Chechnya resulted in a number of tragedies: thousands of civilians and military casualties and around half a million displaced persons. Estimates vary of the total number of casualties caused by the war. Russian former Interior Minister Kulikov claimed that fewer than 20,000 civilians were killed while the then Secretary of the National Security Council Alexander Lebed[374] asserted that 80,000 to 100,000 had been killed and 240,000 had been injured. Chechen spokesmen claim that the true numbers are even higher. Moreover, human rights groups estimate that over 4,300 soldiers from the Federal Russian forces were killed in Chechnya. As for the displaced populations, international organizations estimate that up to 500,000 people have fled Chechnya during the war (1994-1996).

Similar to the Bosnian crisis, the crisis in Chechnya is not without historical origins. The origins of the conflict are complex. In fact, relations between Russia and the people of Chechnya have long been contentious. Four wars have already taken place over Chechnya already. Yet, the last two are more caused by vital economic interests due to the geography and geology of Chechnya than anything

---

374   Lt. Gen. Alexander Ivanovich Lebed (ret.) traded his military uniform for a politician's suit on May 30, 1995, resigning his position as the commander of the 14th Russian Army based in Moldova. By the beginning of the summer, he was one of the most popular politicians in Russia. 45-year-old Lebed is a charismatic figure whose dry wit and brusque, no-nonsense style sets him apart from most of the familiar faces of Moscow's political elite. Lebed has participated in most of the former Soviet Union's and Russia's military conflicts for the last fifteen years. He fought in Afghanistan in 1981-82. He was part of the forces that quelled unrest in the Caucasus: after the anti-Armenian pogrom in Sumgait in the autumn of 1988, the crackdown in Tbilisi in April 1989, and the occupation of Baku in January 1990. During the 1991 coup, Lebed was sent with his troops from Tula to occupy Moscow. He helped to prevent an attack on Yeltsin's headquarters in the White House of Russia.

else. The nature of Chechnya can hence be said to have had an enormous effect on the conflicts arising over it, especially the recent ones. For this mountainous region has important oil deposits, as well as natural gas, limestone, gypsum, sulphur, and other minerals. Its mineral waters have made it a spa centre. Agriculture is concentrated in the Terek and Sunzha river valleys. Oil, petrochemicals, oil-field equipment, foods, wines, and fruit are produced. Other than the economic incitation, the rise of ethnic nationalism and religious fundamentalism worldwide had also a bearing on the outbreak of conflict over in that region. Indeed, if Russia was to allow such ethnic and religious separatist tendencies, it would have to accept the secession of other regions in the Federation that are not just predominately Muslim but also, by coincidence or curse, rich in energy resources such as Tatarstan[375]. For its part, the population in that region of the Caucasus, concentrated in the foothills, is predominantly Chechen, with a sizable Russian minority. The Chechen, like the neighbouring *Ingush Republic*[376], are Sunni Muslim, and speak a Caucasian language (See Map 3).

---

375   *Tatarstan (Tamapcmдн, Tatarstan Respublikası)* is an autonomous republic of the Russian Federation, in the Privolzhsky District. It is located in the centre of the East European Plain, approximately 700 km east of Moscow. It has an area of 67,800 km2 and a population of 3.779 million (census 2002) of whom 48.5% are Tartars. It lies between the Volga River and its tributary, the Kama River, and extends east to the Ural mountains. Its capital is the city of Kazan (Qazan), the only other major city is Naberezhnye Chelny (Yar allı). The state has existed from the 9th century as Volga Bulgaria or Great Bolgaria. The Volga Bulgars were converted to Islam by missionaries from Baghdad around 925. After the area was conquered by the Mongols of the Golden Horde under Batu Khan in the 1230s, they were named *Tartars* by their conquerors. In the 15th century their land became part of the Kazan Khanate. It was conquered by the troops of Tsar Ivan IV the Terrible in the 1550s, with Kazan being taken in 1552.

376   The Ingush Republic (3,210 sq km) lies within the Russian Federation, in the N Caucasus. The capital is Nazran. Ingushetia comprises roughly the western fifth of the former Chechen-Ingush Republic. The republic of Georgia lies to the south, across the Caucasus, and North Ossetia-Alania lies to the north and west. Farming, cattle raising, and horticulture are key occupations. The Ingush are Sunni Muslims and speak a Caucasian language. The Ingush migrated from the Caucasus Mts. into the plains from the 16th cent. Long grouped with the Chechens, they were granted autonomy as the Ingush Region in 1924 but joined in the Chechen-Ingush Autonomous Region in 1934. Many Ingush, along with Chechens, were deported into Central Asia in 1944 after collaborating with invading German forces during World War II; in 1956 the deportees were repatriated. After Chechnya declared independence (1991), Ingushetia gained de facto separate status as a republic in 1992. Also in 1992, violence in Ingush-dominated sections of neighboring North Ossetia-Alania drove many refugees into Ingushetia.

Map 3: Chechnya within its regional context.

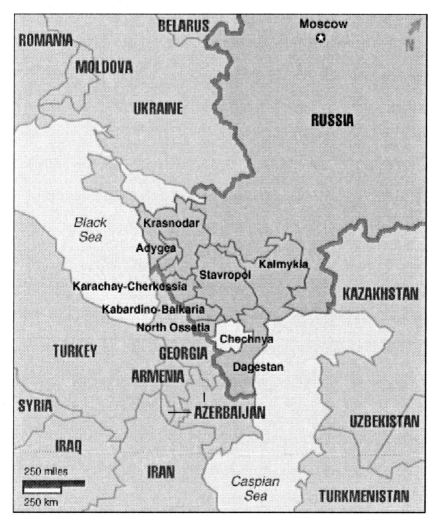

Source: Website of the Chechen Republic Online, at http://www.amina.com/maps/

The origins of the conflict can be actually dated back to the 17th century, and later to the 19th century with the Russian expansion in the Caucasus and the annexation of Chechnya. Chechens have never willingly accepted Russian rule the call for independence from Russian rule was often backed by actions. Recognized as a distinct people since the 17th century, Chechens were the most active opponents of Russia's conquest (1818–1917) of the Caucasus. They fought bitterly during an unsuccessful 1850s rebellion led by Imam Shamyl[377]. The Bolsheviks seized the region in 1918 but were dislodged in 1919 by counterrevolutionary forces under the leadership of General Anton Ivanovich Denikin[378].It is interesting to learn that the Chechens declared their sovereignty, during the Russian Civil War (1917-20). Similar to the recent reaction of Moscow, they were ruthlessly suppressed by the Red Army in 1920. After Soviet rule was re-established, the area was included in 1921 in the Mountain People's Republic. The Chechen Autonomous Region was created in 1922, and in 1934 it became part of the Chechen-Ingush Region, made a republic in 1936. After Chechen and *Ingush* units collaborated with the invading Germans during World War II, many residents were deported in 1944 to Central Asia. Deportees, however, were repatriated in 1956, and the republic was re-established in 1957. Hence, similar to the Balkans, conflicts are not strange to that oil rich area of the world. They are multiple and ancient in their origins[379]. This time, however, and also similar to the Balkans, they not only involved Russian and Chechen fighters but drew the interests of other regional and world powers, such as the United states, due to the strategic reserves of energy in the region and its geographic location (See Map 4).

---

377   In the 1830s, Czar Nicholas ordered his generals to invade the Caucasus, but the Russian armies met with fierce resistance from Chechen and Daghestani forces united under the leadership of Imam Shamyl, a brilliant military tactician and Muslim religious leader. After waging a hard-fought guerrilla war, Shamyl, known to his Russian foes as "The Lion of Daghestan" because of his courage, finally was forced to concede defeat in 1859 and the Chechens came under rule from Moscow.

378   General Anton Ivanovich Denikin (1872–1947) was the son of a serf, he rose from the ranks. After the Bolshevik Revolution in Nov., 1917 (Oct., 1917, O.S.) he joined General Kornilov, whom he succeeded (1918) as commander of the anti-Bolshevik forces in the south. He gained control of a large part of S Russia, but failed (1919) to capture Moscow. He was driven back by the Soviet army, and his forces were demoralized. In 1920 he resigned his command to General Piotr Nikolayevich Wrangel. Denikin lived in France until 1946, when he moved to the United States, where he died.

379   The Caucasus is the theatre of multiple regional and internal armed conflicts. It represents a strategic energy region. A multitude of ethno-linguistic families compose the region of northern Caucasus.

Map 4: Conflicts in the Caucasus.

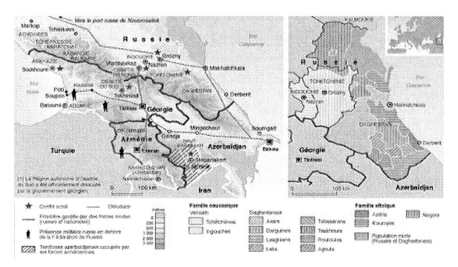

Source: **Philippe Rekacewicz, _Le Monde Diplomatique_, January 2000.**

Indeed, the need for preserving Chechnya under Russian rule, not simply for Russia but also for regional and world powers, primarily stems from economic factors. Being located on the north slope of the Caucasus Mountains (within 100 kilometres of the Caspian Sea), the preservation of control over Chechnya is vital to Russia, economically speaking, and for two reasons. First, access routes to both the Black Sea and the Caspian Sea go from the centre of the Russian federation through Chechnya. Second, vital Russian oil and gas pipeline connections with Kazakstan and Azerbaijan also run through Chechnya (See Map 5).

Map 5: Oil Rings Around Grozny

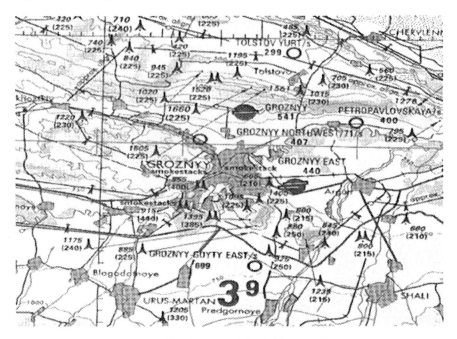

Source: Chechen Republic Online, <u>op.cit</u>.

Once again, but this time without actual realisation of its tempting strategic interest to the rest of the world, Chechnya attempts to obtain its independence in 1991. The Russian Federation's Republic of Chechnya of the northern Caucasus declared itself fully independent from the Russian Federation on the 1st of November 1991 under the leadership of Dzhokar Dudayev[380]. The following

---

380   Until his death in April 1996, Dzhokar Dudayev was the leader of the breakaway Russian republic of Chechnya. Dudayev was born in 1944, the year his family was deported from the Chechen-Ingush Autonomous Republic to Kazakhstan on the orders of Soviet leader Joseph Stalin. Of the 800,000 Chechens sent away because of Stalin's fears that the historically defiant people would collaborate with invading Nazi forces during World War II, almost a quarter of a million died in transit. Dudayev spent his childhood in northern Kazakhstan and attended Soviet military schools in his teens, took a Russian wife, and graduated from the Yuri Gagarin Air Force Academy in 1974. From 1987 to 1990, he commanded a division of Soviet bombers based in Estonia. In 1990, his division withdrawn from Estonia, Dudayev retired from the Soviet Air Force and settled in Grozny, the Chechen capital, where he became the leader of the National Congress of the Chechen People, a nationalist opposition party. Dudayev, who had sworn to fight the Russians to the death, was killed by a Russian rocket around Apr 21, 1996 during a period of intensified airstrikes against Chechen strongholds.

declaration of *full independence* launched in 1993 by the Chechen government of Dudayev led to civil war there. It also resulted in several failed Russian-backed attempts in 1993 and 1994 to overthrow Dudayev. In the summer of 1994, the Russian Government intensified its charges against the government of President Dudayev, accusing it of repressing political dissent, of corruption, and of involvement in international criminal activities. For its part, the Chechnian opposition launched a major offensive on 26 November 1994 with the covert support of "volunteers" from several elite regular Russian army units. Russian military officials initially denied any official involvement in the conflict. However and once again, this Russian guided operation failed to unseat Dudayev. Consequently and by December 1994, Russian military forces started working actively to overthrow the Dudayev regime.

During the presidency of Boris Yeltsin and on the 10th of December 1994, three divisions of Russian armour, pro-Russian Chechen infantry, and internal security troops—a force including units detailed from the regular armed forces—invaded Chechnya. The Russian objective was a quick victory leading to pacification and the reestablishment of a pro-Russian government. Nevertheless, the result obtained was a long series of military operations bungled by the Russians and stymied by the traditionally rugged guerrilla forces of the Chechen separatists. The intensive bombing of Grozny, the Chechen capital, along with the other atrocities committed during this campaign led to limited protests concerning massive human rights violations.

However, although Russian forces levelled the Chechen capital city of Grozny and other population centres during a long and bloody campaign of urban warfare, Chechen forces held extensive territory elsewhere in the republic from 1995 to 1996. Indeed, the Chechen fighters often conducted spectacular operations to voice their cause. For example, two major hostage-taking incidents—one at *Budennovsk* in southern Russia in June 1995 and one at the Dagestani border town of *Pervomayskoye* in January 1996—led to the embarrassment of unsuccessful Russian military missions to release the prisoners. The Pervomayskoye incident alone led to the complete destruction of the town and numerous civilian casualties.

Attempts to reach a peaceful settlement often stagnated. On the 30th of July 1995, the Government along with the forces loyal to president Dudayev signed a military protocol calling for a cease-fire, the disarming of rebel formations, the withdrawal of most federal troops, and the exchange of prisoners. Implementation of the protocol was slow and came to a halt in autumn of the same year, following the assassination attempt on General Romanov, the former commander of the Federal Russian forces in Chechnya. The May 1996 cease-fire agreement lowered the intensity of the conflict for several weeks. Immediately after Yeltsin's victory, however, the Federal Russian forces unleashed an offensive that caused scores of civilian casualties, as they had in March 1996. In July 1996 Russian forces began a new assault on villages described as harbouring guerrilla forces, and Russia again seemed to lack a unified policy toward Chechnya. In subsequent weeks, Alexander Lebed took over the negotiations and in August 1996 he signed an agreement with Chechen commander Aslan Maskhadov[381] that called for an end to hostilities, full exchange of prisoners, and joint administration by a coalition government. The agreement stated that Chechnya's political status would be decided within 5 years. Despite Yeltsin's dismissal of Lebed, the peace process continued during the fall and, in November, the two sides reached another agreement that called for the withdrawal of Federal Russian forces by the end of the year and the holding of elections in January 1997. During the same year, and on the 12th of May 1997, President Boris Yeltsin and Chechen President Aslan Maskhadov signed a peace agreement on in which both sides agreed to settle their dispute by peaceful means.

In the earlier 1996 agreement, the two sides agreed to resolve Chechnya's political status prior to 2001, but fundamental differences remained on that question with Chechnya asserting that it has earned the right to full independence and Russia insisting that Chechnya will remain a part of the Federation. During 1998 no progress was reported on resolving differences between the two sides, particularly on the question of Chechnya's independence. Continued kidnappings and instability in Chechnya, where the Federal Government exercises virtually no authority, exacerbated tensions between federal and republican authorities.

It should be mentioned, in this respect, that the exact routes for new pipelines from Central Asia and the Caspian basin are a matter of fierce dispute between regional and world powers (see Map 6). Over 20 major Western oil companies; their Russian, Azeri and Kazakh partners; and the governments of Russia, Azerbaijan, Kazakhstan, Georgia, Turkey, Iran, Greece, and Bulgaria are variously advocating up to 10 alternative routes. For technical reasons, new pipelines must avoid the rugged Caucasus mountains between the Caspian and Black seas. The choice of routes is complicated politically by conflicts in Chechnya to the north, and in Azerbaijan, Armenia, and Turkey to the south.

---

381   From 1992 to 1996, Maskhadov served in the Chechen Armed Forces. In December 1993 he was promoted to chief of staff. He served as prime minister in the Chechen coalition government from October 1996 until January 1997. Maskhadov also became one of the chief negotiators in talks with federal officials. He was actively involved in talks held in Grozny in the summer of 1995, signing an agreement on military issues for the Chechen side. He also took part in the negotiations with federal representatives in Nazran in June 1996 and in Novye Atagi from June 28 to July 4, 1996. On Aug. 31, 1996, following talks with former Russian Security Council Secretary Aleksander Lebed, he signed the Khasavyurt agreements, effectively ending the conflict with Russian troops. This was followed by an agreement on the principles governing relations between the Russian Federation and the Chechen Republic, signed by Maskhadov outside Moscow on Nov. 23, 1996, with Russian Prime Minister Victor Chernomyrdin.

Map 6: Routes of Petrol

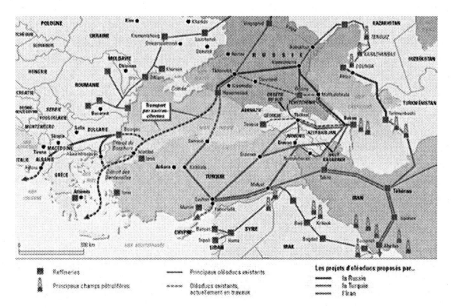

Source: Philippe Rekacewicz, Transport and Geo-strategy in Southern Russia,
Le Monde Diplomatique, june 1998.

It is important to stress, in this respect, that it was in the benefit of Russia to actively seek to pacify the area in order to better serve its vital economic and strategic interests. For even if economic interests did not exist, a successful secession of Chechnya would have tempted other ethnically or religiously different regions in the Russian Federation to do the same. It's also worth mentioning to note that both sides of the conflict seemed to have realized the importance of the economic benefits to be gained with a peace settlement. Indeed, the peace agreement paved the way for the July 1997 tripartite agreement between Azerbaijan, Chechnya, and Russia on early oil exports from Azerbaijan. However, while the deal allowed necessary repairs to begin on the existing oil pipeline, it did not settle the issues of regional security and pipeline tariffs. Chechnya and the Russian transport company, *Transneft,* have also clashed in the past over the issue of tariffs and war reparations from Russia. Russia has offered to provide economic aid to Chechnya on the condition that Chechnya secures the safety of the northern route for early oil production, which passes through its borders.

The result was that deadlocks over negotiations prompted Russia to announce that it intends to construct another pipeline that would bypass Chechnya. One of these proposed alternative pipelines would use the northern route, but will also add a new segment that supposedly would pass along the Chechen border in the southern Russian Federation's republic of Dagestan, and then go on towards the Stavropol region, ending at Terskoye in North Ossetia. Former Russian Fuel and Energy Minister Generalov stated in November 1998 that a lack of funding could cause this project to be shelved. In October 1998, Russia made another proposal to build a new pipeline from Baku, Azerbaijan via Dagestan to Novorosissk in Russia, but the proposal was rejected by SOCAR (The Azerbaijan State Oil Company) What adds to the complication of securing such an energy route is that Dagestan has security concerns of its own, including the rise of rival factions. In May 1998, the seat of the government in Makhachkala was stormed by a rival gang. The failed coup resulted in accusations attributed to the chairman of the Dagestan Supreme Council that the United States had supported the coup attempt as a means of discouraging interest in a Baku-Novorosissk route for the Main Export Pipeline (MEP) of the Azerbaijan International Oil Consortium (AIOC)[382].

In addition to securing energy supplies flow and routing, guarding, guarding against the spread of secessionist attempts, and the rise of Islamic fundamentalism, the Chechnya crisis also presented a domestic political challenge to Russia highlighted by the internal division within the Russian government and society over addressing this crisis. Indeed, the Chechnya crisis revealed a serious division

---

382   The first international PSA in Azerbaijan was signed with a 12-company consortium called the Azerbaijan International Operating Company (AIOC), and was termed the "Contract of the Century." The PSA (Production Sharing Agreements are based on one common concept: they provide for the exploration and development of selected oil fields, allow for the sharing of the proceeds by the participants, and each PSA must be approved separately by the Azerbaijan Parliament. Parties to the PSA are consortia of international oil companies headquartered in many different countries, notably the United States, the United Kingdom, Turkey, Saudi Arabia, Norway, Japan, and Russia, and are always in partnership with SOCAR, the Azerbaijan State Oil Company. This contract forms the foundation for the Government of Azerbaijan's policy of attracting foreign investment to the country and serves as a model for subsequent oil/gas PSAs. The AIOC (which includes Amoco, Exxon, Lukoil, and Pennzoil) undertook a 30-year commitment to explore and produce three significant offshore oil fields. Once the PSA was ratified, the AIOC participants/shareholders signed a joint operations agreement and set up an operating company. With investment of over US$1 billion to date, the AIOC project has just yielded the first of the nearly 600 million tons of crude oil expected over its contract life. Sale of the crude should generate about US$80 billion, with peak production of 35-40 million tons yearly by 2010. The main export pipeline should be built by 2004 or 2005, and cost recovery is expected by the year 2007 or 2008.

in Russia's government over the application of military doctrine vis-à-vis separatist attempts in the various regions of the Russian Federation. With numerous declarations of sovereignty having emerged from ethnic republics and regions in 1991 and 1992, the 1993 military doctrine had stipulated that the military could be used against separatist groups within the Federation, providing, therefore, a theoretical justification for the Chechnya action. Many military authorities argued that such a campaign was foolhardy, given military budget cuts that made proper training and equipping of troops impossible. Nevertheless, the "war party" of officials and advisers surrounding former President Yeltsin failed to foresee the media storm that resulted from a bloody military struggle within the federation and the various international protests that accompanied it.

Consequently, it can be said that comparing and contrasting the crisis of Bosnia with that of Chechnya reveals some interesting facts. In comparison, both involved a strive for independence from the central rule of another ethnicity and, indeed, another religion. Both regions have a long history of conflicts within which regional powers' interests were accentuated to different degrees whether historically or at present. The stability and pacification of both regions represents a strategic goal for a number of regional and world leading powers. In both, a civil war took place, which eventually drew the direct intervention of the outside ruling central power. In both atrocities were committed. Moreover, in both the majority of the populations are of Muslim confession. Finally, control of both regions involves economic, security and political advantages for either the central ruling powers, the regional powers, and geographically distant ones.

In contrast, Chechnya was an area that was mainly inhabited by one ethnicity, unlike Bosnia-Herzegovina. The solution for the Bosnian crisis came through an international pressure of an outside superpower (The United States) while the peace agreements in Chechnya were merely the product of the two conflicting parties. Furthermore, the stability in Chechnya concerned directly the Russian Federation, mainly because it was regarded as an internal Russian affaire by the rest of the world, while that of Bosnia concerned directly a number of European countries, the United States, Russia, the UN, and NATO. Indeed, there was direct involvement of only Russian forces in Chechnya, while a complex mosaic of forces intervened in Bosnia. Added to this and from the point of view of the international law, the Russian state was still enact throughout the Chechnya crisis which meant that, theoretically, it still had sovereignty over all its "territories" which provided the excellent pretext of "internal matter" for the rest of the world countries not to show interest in the matter, while, in the Bosnian case, the whole ex-Yugoslav republic exploded into various entities, which meant that the central State did not have any more legal jurisdiction over its former territories. Finally, it is worth-mentioning that the crisis in Bosnia was, by far, much more advocated on the international scene and, for various political and economic international considerations relating to the states interested or involved, than that of Chechnya.

It is, hence, interesting to compare the media coverage of both crises in the French and American printed media (*Le Monde* and *The New York Times*). Indeed, the effect of elements, such as national interests including economic and political ones, can constitute an interesting explanation of the conduct of the French and the U.S. national media during the coverage of both crises. Other elements such as geographic proximity, historical, and social ties and factors are also important to analyse.

2.2. National Interests of France and the United States in Both Regions

In order to better comprehend the French and the United States' media coverage of the crisis in Bosnia and Chechnya, it is essential to consider the French and American national interests involved in the two crises. For as demonstrated in the previous part of this book, the national interests of states play a vital role in determining the nature of the national media's coverage of a given international crisis or conflict. Generally speaking, the national interests of France and the United States can be grouped under five main categories; namely cultural, economic, political, regional and internal social ones. However, for a better understanding of such national interests, it is useful to have an idea about the major factors that affected and shaped the two countries' foreign policy orientations. In other words, it is useful to see what the foreign policy philosophy and doctrine of each of these two countries is, the reasons underlying its conception, and how it developed and mutated over the years.

In order to understand French political positions, it is essential to examine some of the factors that give France the status and prestige of a major world power. For it is in understanding these factors that sometimes an explanation of political positions towards various affaires of a given state are better comprehended and, indeed, adequately anchored.

Frances's sense of its own greatness and its position as a major world actor can be easily understood. Historically speaking, France exerted hegemony over Europe on two occasions during the reigns of Louis XIV and Napoleon. Military might, however, was not the sole reason behind this greatness of France. It is also, as Philip Kramer puts it, that "during much of the modern period, Paris has been the great cultural capital of Europe"[383]. Thus, these two historic facts add to France's sense of its own greatness and role on the world scene.

Another historical factor that might have had a bearing on shaping the current French political orientations seems to be that of France's history of alliances and relations with other countries in Europe. In this respect, Philip Kramer explains that before 1648 and after 1870, France was passing through periods of dangerous isolation. This is what made France seek allies against the Hapsburgs[384] and then the Germans[385]. Philip Kramer, however, explains that France's desire to appear as a major world leader is actually a means by which it can mask its own sense of lack of security compared to its neighbours. He states, "France's fundamental insecurity has often been masked in the rhetoric of grandeur or mistaken for a desire for grandeur. For example, the British erroneously construed France's hard-line diplomacy after World War I as a desire to dominate the continent; in reality, it was based on a pessimistic (and accurate) assessment of France's weakness compared with the latent strength of Germany"[386]. This is quite interesting to note. It is sort of a psychological warfare explanation of political positions taken by states. If a state realizes its own weakness, it might opt to take a strong position that would give the impression that it is a strong state and, thus, increase its own sense of security.

This attitude seems, however, related to France's lack of confidence in its own alliances based on its past experience with such alliances. Indeed, the experience that France had after 1870[387], proved how precious allies can be, while its experience

---

383 See Philip Kramer, Does France Still Count? The French Role in the New Europe, Praeger Publishers, Westport, CT, 994, p. 25.

384 The royal Habsburg Family of Europe, one of the oldest and most prominent dynasties from the 15th to the 20th centuries, was named after the family castle of Habsburg, or Habichtsburg ("Hawk's Castle"), which was built in the year 1020 on the Aare River in what is now the Swiss canton of Aargau by Bishop Werner of Strasbourg.

385 Ibid, p. 28

386 Idem.

387 Franco-German War, also called Franco-Prussian War (July 19, 1870-May 10, 1871), war in which a coalition of German states led by Prussia defeated France. The war marked the end of French hegemony in continental Europe and resulted in the creation of a unified Germany. Prussia's defeat of Austria in the Seven Weeks' War in 1866 had confirmed Prussian leadership of the German states and threatened France's position as the dominant power in Europe. The immediate cause of the Franco-German War, however, was the candidacy of Prince Leopold of Hohenzollern-Sigmaringen (who was related to the Prussian royal house) for the Spanish throne, which had been left vacant when Queen Isabella II had been deposed in 1868.

after1918 showed how unstable relying on them was. After World War I, the United States and Britain refused to enter an official military pact with France. Then again, the United States sabotaged the French occupation of the Ruhr in 1923[388]. This situation of not being able to rely on allies also continued in the post war era with the United States' position on the Suez Canal Operation of 1956, and its lack of support on the Algerian issue. Indeed, the need for foreign policy decision-making autonomy has grown to become so inherent to French political tendencies. For instance, Georgette Elgey explains, for instance, that the real reason behind the French National Assembly's initial refusal of the European Defence Community Treaty in 1954 was not only France's fear of German rearmament but also its fear of eliminating the autonomy of the French army[389]. Thus, France can be said to have learned that the best strategy is to always preserve its autonomy, or at least appear to preserve it.

The development of France's political philosophy and tendencies is quite interesting. In addition to major events and surprises that marked its political history, the philosophy and directions of France's foreign policy can be said to have always been marked by its most prominent leaders. In the past, these were personalities such as Napoleon and Louis XIV and, in the recent decades, they were personalities such as Charles de Gaulle and François Mitterrand.

For De Gaulle, the reality of the Cold War was accepted, although he was fairly convinced that it was a transient phenomenon. De Gaulle believed that the normal political status of the world is when it is composed of nation states. Philip Kramer explains that De Gaulle believed that it is "unnatural" for states to "suppress national interest in the name of ideology"[390]. Other writers suggest that De Gaulle even anticipated and helped in the breakdown of the Eastern Bloc and

---

388   In 1923 the German government was unable to pay the reparations required under the terms of the Treaty of Versailles. The French and Belgian governments responded by sending in troops to the Ruhr, the main centre of Germany's coal, iron and steel production. The occupation of the Ruhr led to a collapse of the German economy. There was massive inflation and large increase in unemployment. Germany was now unable to pay any reparations. Charles G. Dawes, an American banker, was asked by the Allied Reparations Committee to investigate the problem. His report, published in April, 1924, proposed a plan for instituting annual payments of reparations on a fixed scale. He also recommended the reorganization of the German State Bank and increased foreign loans. Gustav Stresemann, the German chancellor called off the passive resistance and began paying reparations again. The French and Belgian troops withdrew from the Ruhr in 1925.

389   Georgette Elgey, « _La République des Tourments, 1954-1959_ », Paris:, Fayard, 1992, pp.165-259.

390   See Philip Kramer, op. cit., p.29.

that he anticipated, in particular, the German reunification[391]. Thus, De Gaulle marked the French foreign policy philosophy by his own convictions. Indeed, the "Gaullist France" is still and will remain forever a synonym of a nation-state's independence in foreign policy decision-making.

As far as major world powers are concerned, it can be said that De Gaulle showed little or no trust towards the United States. This was not without logical foundation, however. In fact, De Gaulle's mistrust of the United States stemmed out of his own conviction that the United States saw him as an antagonist and wanted to remove him from the leadership of France during the war. It also stemmed from his rejection of the United State's President Franklin Roosevelt's vision of the post-war Europe, which represented future United States' dominance over the continent. Another reason for the mistrust was what Philip Kramer explains as "the fact that the British put themselves under U.S. leadership persuaded him that the UK had become an American Trojan horse in Europe"[392]. Indeed, the De Gaullist vision of an independent and sovereign France even led to a mistrust of the structure of NATO, which for him was a synonym of American dominance and French inferiority. For him, remaining part of the North Atlantic Alliance was logical but not being part of the integrated military command. De Gaulle believed that this way France would be able to decide on its own when to engage in a conflict and when not to. Another issue that De Gaulle thought would give France more autonomy in its decision was that of acquiring nuclear weapons.

As far as France's European policy is concerned, the De Gaulle vision saw the key in a strong relation with Germany. For him, such a relationship would be the driving force for political cooperation in Europe. This was the reason behind his pushing for the Fouchet Plan in 1961[393]. Again France was relatively isolated, which added to its conception of allies as being not reliable in times of need.

For his part, the political tendencies of François Mitterrand were kind of different from those of De Gaulle. In fact, it can be said that Mitterrand's decisions

---

391   See François Cornut-Gentille and Stéphane Rozès, "*La Réunification vue de L'Hexagone: les Français engourdis*", in *L'Etat de l'opinion 1991*, Paris, Seuil, 1991, pp.75-91.

392   See Philip Kramer, op. cit.

393   Generally speaking, the Fouchet Plan was proposed by De Gaulle in 1961. The aim was to implement cooperation, including security, by intergovernmental means. The plan was vetoed by the Dutch and Belgians, who disliked France's disregard for federalism and feared de Gaulle's desire to establish a European political identity that would be opposed to the United States. The plan stressed closer bilateral ties with Germany, especially in the security field. The Elysées Treaty of 1963, however, managed to embody these ties but with a preamble inserted by the Bundestag which emphasized that nothing in the Elysées Treaty should be seen as denying the primacy of NATO.

during the Cold War and prior to the reunification of Germany stemmed mostly out of his own assessment of the Soviet threat as well as the status of Germany. Mitterrand's vision of the Soviet Union can be considered to be much more negative than any of his predecessors. Mitterrand, for instance, did not minimize the invasion of Afghanistan, like former French president Valery Giscard d'Estaing[394] did. Moreover, he didn't minimize the importance of the declaration of martial law in Poland. In fact, as Philip Kramer puts it, Mitterand's reaction regarding these two issues was very close to that of the United State's President Ronald Reagan[395]. Thus, fear of the Soviet threat at the time led to positions that are very much aligned with those of the United States. It has to be remembered, however, that the Regan years were those were the highest peaks of the Cold War occurred. As such, France's political stands can be understood as being sort of a self-protection policy under the umbrella of a superpower.

It can be said that Mitterrand's policies presupposed a world in which some fundamentals remain. According to this logic, the Cold War would continue and having a strong alliance with the United States would remain imperative. Similarly, the European construction would continue and France would increase its cooperation with NATO while remaining independent from the integrated military command. Those sort of taken for granted fundamentals would, however, be highly changed with the events of 1989-1991 (end of the Cold War, German re-unification, the Gulf War, and the break-up of the Soviet Union as well as the events that shacked Europe (the disintegration of Yugoslavia).

It is, thus, useful to examine the different French national interests in the two crises based on this background of French history and political philosophy. Such a background can help better understand the French positions vis-à-vis the two crises, as well as the French national interests involved in both. France, have always had good reasons to add to its sense of its own grandeur and to give it a status of a major world power. It dominated Europe on two occasions in history and not only militarily but culturally as well. It also realizes the importance of being able and ready to act solely in case of need, and in showing that it can be independent in its positions. France's foreign policy can also be said to have been marked by the political philosophies and convictions of its most prominent leaders. Taking all these elements into consideration can, therefore, be quite useful in providing a better understanding of the French foreign policy tendencies and positions. It can also help better understand the reaction of the French public opinion to the two crises under discussion.

---

394   President of France 1974-1981;
395   See Philip Kramer, op. cit., p.30.

The same reasoning can be applied to better understand the determinants of and general foreign policy philosophy and doctrine of the United States. Understanding the national interests of the United States would, hence, be easier if examined against its own awareness of its prestigious position amongst the other world state and how this awareness works as a driving force behind its foreign policy tendencies. These interests can also be better understood by examining the impact of prominent political leaders in shaping its foreign political philosophy.

An important notion that is generally thought to be a recent one but that has existed under different forms in previous periods of the United States' history, is its awareness of its prestigious position amongst other world countries. From this self-sensed asset, the United States has an inherent belief, which has been fed by inherited folklore and media principally, that's its "leadership" is not simply useful but that it is necessary for the well functioning and the well being of the rest of the world. It might seem subjective to make such an assertion. Yet, enough evidence, supporting such a claim, does exist. Indeed, one can easily see it in some of the most known facts concerning the United States. For instance, the United States never stopped to claim that it was the defender of democracy and freedom throughout the world. Almost every new intervention of the United States' military in another country or region was conducted under the banner of brining liberty and democracy to the country or region in question. It should be said, however, that this belief is not simply that of politicians but it is one which is so common and integrated in the collective mentality of the United States because it is constantly fed by the media, notably that of the cinema and television productions. What proves the consistency of such beliefs is that the slogan did not fundamentally change, throughout the history of the United States. It was valid during the confrontation with the Soviet Union where the United States considered itself the leader of democratic and liberal states against the communists and their schemes to dominate the world. It was even more true after the disintegration of the Soviet bloc where the United States designated a New World Order, of which it will be the guardian, or the "Policeman of the World", as it was commonly referred to sometimes. It is only fair to mention, however, that there are some facts that may, in a theoretical sense, justify such an inherent belief. It cannot be denied that the United States was the first country in the world to have a democratic constitution. It cannot also be denied that its intervention in World War II was quite decisive to stop the Nazi threat and expansion. It is also true that until now, the so-called "American Dream" incites many people, and not just from less developed countries, to immigrate to the United States. It is evident, nonetheless, that the United States' national interests are and have been pursued relying on pure *realpolitik* directives and have had, on many occasions, nothing much to do with the advocated liberty and democracy delivery slogan. What is important here, therefore, is not to discuss whether such a belief is just or not but rather to see its reflection on the United States' foreign policy directions and tendencies.

To understand the United States' sense of its own "grandeur", some glances through its history and the bases of this country's "state ideology" are necessary Some writers date back the real origin of this state ideology or vision of the United States and its role as far back as Columbus and Vasco da Gama. In a superb book on the origins of the United States' state ideology and foreign policy, Walter Lafeber begins by quoting a certain William Steward, the U.S. Secretary of State under Abraham Lincoln, as saying that the most important secular event in the history of the human race[396]." He then goes on to explain "Steward might well have been correct. Americans, however, have viewed their secular, or more earthly, successes (such as making money) as part of a higher purpose. This view goes back to the origins of their country. Portuguese explorer Vasco da Gama needed few words to explain why a new world was discovered in the late fifteenth century: "We come in search of Christians and spices." Mission and money or, as some historians prefer to phrase it, idealism and self-interest have for nearly five hundred years been the reasons Americans have given for their successes. From their beginnings, they have justified developing a continent and then much of the globe simply by saying they were spreading the principles of civilization as well as making profit. They have had no problem seeing their prosperity—indeed, their rise from a sparsely settled continent to the world's superpower—as part of a Higher Purpose or, as it was known during much of their history, a Manifest Destiny"[397]. The reasoning of the importance of those first symbols in shaping the mentality and ideology of the state including its own awareness of its place in the world can be also seen in the consideration of Columbus, for instance, as an important symbol to help understand the U.S.'s foreign policy foundations because he defied the norms of existing rules. For Walter Lafeber, "Columbus is also a useful symbol and starting point in American foreign policy for another reason: he founded empires by going westward. Again, nature, perhaps even the supernatural, seemed to be guiding Americans"[398] Columbus and Da Gama are more than historical figures, they are, indeed, symbols that helped shape the mentality of national identity and collective national mentality of Americans. This driving force in the society seems to have continued to be social and economic. Social and economic satisfaction at home seems to be also a pillar of foreign policy in the United States. This desire to feel self satisfied with the mission abroad seems to be a reflection of the inherent image of the "Sacred American Mission to the World". Karl Von Vorys explains" The purpose of American foreign policy is easily defined: to advance the interests

---

396 See Walter Lafeber, The American Age: United States Foreign Policy at Home and Abroad since 1750, Norton., New York, 1994, p. *
397 Idem.
398 Ibid., p.6.

of the United States beyond its borders. Its conduct, however, poses an exasperating challenge. For it needs to meet two sets of criteria simultaneously: it must be effective abroad and popular at home: two sets of criteria that are likely to clash.... The domestic environment of foreign policy making was not much more complicated. Americans believed in limited government; their principal concerns were economic and social. They worked very hard to make a living, a good living; they worshiped God and took pride in their honour"[399]. Hence, what is considered now as a "need for American leadership" is something that lies at the heart of the mentality of the United States history. It was shaped by the historic circumstances of its creation and its rapid ascendancy to the top of the world list of countries. The logic seems of this belief seems to be, in addition to the media feeding and maintaining factor, based also on the evidence of the achievements of the United States over the last five hundred years. It is logical for a U.S. citizen, who could become a politician later on, to assume that since the country started from practically nothing and achieved all the progress it achieved in this short period of time, then this country must be special and must be correct. It is even more than special, it is sort of "blessed" and it has as a mission to lead the rest of the world and make them as well enjoy, for their own good, the benefits brought to them by this miraculous country. Indeed, the idea is simple. What has been done is supernatural, or more exactly, miraculous. Miraculous and supernatural are both notions that relate to and are explained by something that seems to be a central backbone, along with the social and economic backbones of the collective mentality of the United States' society and culture. This third backbone is the importance of religious belief. Karl Von Vorys mentions earlier (see footnote N°397) that Americans" worked hard to make a living, a good living. They worshiped God and took pride in their honour". Here again, the miraculous and the supernaturalism of "the good American" has always been the central theme of the majority of the cinematographic and television productions in the U.S. It is interesting to remark that there is a religious tradition that is so specific to the United States'. This religious tradition is called Thanksgiving. It originally relates to the miraculous achievements of the first settlers that came to the United States. As its name indicates, it is a tradition through which God is thanked for what he gave. It is thanking God for the miracle of achievement not only because of the first settlers and their miraculous survival but, indeed, for what the United States is now.

Such as prominent political personalities inspired and helped shape the very foundation of the collective society's mentality in the United States, they also, similar to the case of France, contributed to shaping the foreign policy philosophy and state

---

399   See Karl Von Vorys, <u>American Foreign Policy: Consensus at Home, Leadership Abroad</u>, Praeger Publishers, Westport, CT., 1997, p.17.

ideology of the United States. Indeed, there are a number of U.S. Presidents, whose', decisions and personal political philosophy can be said to have shaped the United States' foreign policy conduct and aims. The influence of presidents' leadership on public policy seems to be, however, dependent on the personal convictions and vision of individual presidents and not one that is common to all. In some occasions, the activism of a certain president towards one issue or another supersedes the agenda-setting priorites.of his own political party. Steven A. Shull, analysed, for example, the role of presidential leadership on the issue of civil rights in the United States. He states" In policy implementation, individual presidents again show much greater ranges than does party, particularly on program actions (cases resolved) and to a greater extent on expenditures"[400]. Concerning the issue of U.S. foreign policy and national interests, it can be said that such presidents include Abraham Lincoln, Woodrow Wilson, Franklin D. Roosevelt, Harry Truman, and Bill Clint on (because his presidency period is that in which the two crisis took place). The criteria for their choice is a genuine change they introduced to the political philosophy of the United States and not because of their continuation of already existing policies, policies with no genuine philosophical rational, or the hardening or softening of policies of previous administrations. There are, indeed, many presidents whose actions might be more spectacular but that did not, genuinely, enrich or radically alter the foreign policy philosophy or state ideology of the United States.

The 16th President of the United States Abraham Lincoln's (1809–1865) attempts to find a solution to the slavery in the United States represents a good case where the personality of the political leader and hi personal convictions had an enormous bearing on shaping the political philosophy of the country he rules. Lincoln's own personal position towards slavery continued to be reflected in the political positions he assumed up to that of presidency. It was his election as President that triggered the secession of the South and the ensuing Civil War that followed[401]. The election of Lincoln ended the South's illusions of having control over U.S. foreign policy and, more importantly, that it will "no longer hope to obtain fresh hand for slavery"[402]. On the 22nd of September1862, Lincoln signed the preliminary Proclamation of Emancipation, which was a Presidential order abolishing slavery in the Confederate States of America to be effective on the 1st of January 1863. There is an argument, however, that in spite of Lincoln's personal conviction of the necessity to free the slaves, the Proclamation of Emancipation

---

400   See Steven A. Shull, <u>American Civil Rights Policy from Truman to Clinton: The Role of Presidential Leadership</u>., M. E. Sharpe, Armonk, NY.,2000, p. 248.

401   See The Columbia Encyclopaedia (6th Edition) at
      <u>http://www.bartleby.com/65/li/LincolnA.html</u>

402   See Walter Lafeber, <u>op. cit.,</u> p. 132.

"was chiefly a declaration of policy, which, it was hoped, would serve as an opening wedge in depleting the South's great manpower reserve in slaves and, equally important, would enhance the Union cause in the eyes of Europeans, especially the British"[403]. The idea seemed to have worked, as far a drawing outside support is concerned, since "powerful British liberals favoured the North's battle to end slavery, especially after Lincoln's Emancipation Proclamation"[404]. Nonetheless and although slavery and not only of the people with a black skin colour did continue and continues to exist in our present day, under different forms, the efforts and actions of President Lincoln taken against it are memorable and did not start a radical change of mentality in the United States alone but also provided an example to be followed by other emancipator world forces.

Woodrow Wilson (1856–1924), the 28th President of the United States was also one of the political figures that marked both the domestic and foreign political philosophy of his country. As far as foreign policy is concerned, President Woodrow Wilson's name is associated with the famous Fourteen Points[405] presented to the U.S. Congress on the 8th of January 1918. The Fourteen Points "idealistic" were "idealistic in tone and primarily a peace program, which had certain very practical uses as an instrument for propaganda. It was intended to reach the people and the liberal leaders of the Central Powers as a seductive appeal for peace"[406] it can be considered that the Fourteen Points were a containment attempt of the Bolshevik Revolution and, in a sense, an earlier spark of the Cold War, since they offered a "detailed vision of a

---

403   See The Columbia Encyclopaedia (6th Edition), op. cit.

404   See Walter Lafeber, op. cit., p. 150.

405   Generally speaking the points can be summarized in: 1-Open covenants of peace, openly arrived at, after which there shall be no private international understandings of any kind.", 2-"Absolute freedom of navigation upon the seas...alike in peace and in war.", 3-A worldwide open door: "The removal, so far as possible, of all economic barriers and the establishment of an equality of trade conditions among all the nations.", 4-Reduction of armaments., 5-adjustment of all colonial claims," with the people in colonial areas having "equal weight" in deciding their fate with the colonial powers., 6-"The evacuation of all Russian territory and such a settlement of all questions affecting Russia as will secure the best and freest cooperation of the other nations in the world, 7-preservation of Belgian sovereignty; 8-settlement of the Alsace-Lorraine question; 9-redrawing of Italian frontiers according to nationalities; 10-the division of Austria-Hungary in conformance to its nationalities; 11-the redrawing of Balkan boundaries with reference to historically established allegiance and nationalities; 12-Turkish control only of their own peoples and freedom of navigation through the Dardanelles; 13-the establishment of an independent Poland with access to the sea. The last point 14 was a provision for "a general association of nations...under specific covenants." The League of Nations grew out of the last point.

406   See The Columbia Encyclopaedia (6th Edition), op. cit

Wilsonian post-war I world. But it was specially shaped to answer Lenin's demands for revolution and an end to the war without territorial annexations on either side".[407]. Although the points were a subject of debate and the following Treaty of Versailles of 1919[408] represented a compromise or defeat of many of them, it remains that they brought about a new vision of international relations and helped create later on the League of Nations whose Covenant was already included in the Treaty of Versailles. If President Wilson is to be classified amongst the two major political beliefs, he would be classified in the Idealist one as opposed to the Realist school of thought and his Fourteen Points and role in creating the League of Nations can be said to be one of the major credits to the idealist school of international affaires.

Franklin D. Roosevelt (1882–1945) the 32nd President of the United States is well known for his leadership during World War II and his outspoken criticism of the Axis countries. He also extended diplomatic recognition to the USSR in 1933 and was the instigator of a new trend in U.S. Foreign Policy. This new trend is that of "hemispheric solidarity". It was translated by a U.S. emphasis on ameliorating relations with Latin America and the signature of quite a number of trade agreements with a lot of countries in that continent.

For his part, the name of the 33rd President of the United States Harry Truman (1884–1972) is associated with one of the most important doctrines in the political history of the United States; the Truman Doctrine. The Truman Doctrine started to be formulated with the announcement, in December 1947, of an economic and military aid program to Turkey and Greece. The program of Truman was mainly aimed at containing the Communist threat. Later on; three more steps were taken to fully implement this doctrine: The adoption of the Marshal Plan (The European Recovery Program)[409] for the reconstruction of Europe in 1947,

---

407　See Walter Lafeber, op. cit., p. 309.

408　The most important treaty signed at Versailles (in the Hall of Mirrors) was that of 1919. It was the chief among the five peace treaties that terminated World War I. The other four (for which see separate articles) were Saint-Germain, for Austria; Trianon, for Hungary; Neuilly, for Bulgaria; and Sèvres, for Turkey. Signed on June 28, 1919, by Germany on the one hand and by the Allies (save Russia) on the other, the Treaty of Versailles embodied the results of the long and often bitter negotiations of the Paris Peace Conference of 1919.

409　The European Recovery Program was a project instituted at the Paris Economic Conference (July, 1947) to foster economic recovery in certain European countries after World War II. The Marshall Plan took form when U.S. Secretary of State George C. Marshall urged (June 5, 1947) that European countries decide on their economic needs so that material and financial aid from the United States could be integrated on a broad scale. In Apr., 1948, President Truman signed the act establishing the Economic Cooperation Administration (ECA) to administer the program. The ECA functioned until 1951, when its activities were transferred to the Mutual Security Agency. Over $12 billion was dispersed (1948–51) under the program.

the Point Four Program[410] for aiding underdeveloped countries and the creation of NATO[411] in 1949. The Truman Doctrine announced the triggering of the Cold War with the Soviet Union. It should not be forgotten, nonetheless, that President

---

410   U.S. foreign aid project aimed at providing technological skills, knowledge, and equipment to poor nations throughout the world. The program also encouraged the flow of private investment capital to these nations. The project received its name from the fourth point of a program set forth in President Truman's 1949 inaugural address. In the Cold War the U.S. government used The Point Four program to win support from uncommitted nations.

411   Established under the North Atlantic Treaty (Apr. 4, 1949) by Belgium, Canada, Denmark, France, Great Britain, Iceland, Italy, Luxembourg, the Netherlands, Norway, Portugal, and the United States. Greece and Turkey entered the alliance in 1952, West Germany (now Germany) entered in 1955, and Spain joined in 1982. In 1999, the Czech Republic, Hungary, and Poland joined, bringing the membership to 19. NATO maintains headquarters in Brussels, Belgium. Considering an armed attack on any member an attack against all, the treaty provided for collective self-defence in accordance with Article 51 of the United Nations Charter. In the 1990s, with the collapse of the Soviet Union and the Warsaw Treaty Organization, NATO's role in world affairs changed, and U.S. forces in Europe were gradually reduced. Many East European nations sought NATO membership as a counterbalance to Russian power, but they, along with other European and Asian nations (including Russia), initially were offered only membership in the more limited Partnership for Peace, formed in 1994. Twenty-seven countries now belong to the partnership, which engages in joint military exercises with NATO. NATO is not required to defend Partnership for Peace nations from attack. In 2002, NATO and Russia established the NATO-Russia Council, through which Russia participates in NATO discussions on many non-defence issues. In 2002, NATO and Russia established the NATO-Russia Council, through which Russia participates in NATO discussions on many non-defence issues. The same year, Bulgaria, Estonia, Latvia, Lithuania, Romania, Slovakia, and Slovenia were invited to join NATO. NATO air forces were used under UN auspices in punitive attacks on Serb forces in Bosnia in 1994 and 1995, and the alliance's forces were subsequently used for peacekeeping operations in Bosnia. NATO again launched air attacks in Mar.–June, 1999, this time on Yugoslavia (now Serbia and Montenegro) following the breakdown of negotiations over Kosovo. Aug., 2003, NATO assumed command of the international security force in the Kabul area in Afghanistan, and in October a NATO rapid-response force was established. The membership of many NATO nations in the increasingly integrated European Union (EU) has led to tensions within NATO between the United States and those EU nations, particularly France and Germany, who want to develop an EU defence force, which necessarily would not include non-EU members of NATO.

Truman authorised the first nuclear attack in human history against the Japanese cities of Hiroshima and Nagasaki. The issue of the first use of "nuclear diplomacy" is, in fact, the other thing that Harry Truman is remembered for. The current debate on that tragic nuclear strike decision revolves around the question whether president Truman's did calculate the advantages and disadvantages for the use of the nuclear bombs against Japan or whether he simply "did not intervene to halt long-contemplated operations has been debated for decades"[412].

The two-term presidency of Bill Clinton (1993-2000) was characterized, as far as foreign policy is concerned, in being the subject, especially in the first term of this presidency, of the consequences of the fall of the Soviet Bloc and the consequent multiplication of intrastate conflicts throughout the world. In 1994, President Clinton sent U.S. forces to Haiti to restore Jean Bertrand Aristide to power. In the same year, he ordered the withdrawal of the U.S. troops from Somalia following domestic public opinion's outrage at the images of U.S. casualties there. He also was involved in bringing a settlement to the conflicts in former Yugoslavia, to promoting the peace negotiations in the Middle East, and, to restoring relations with Vietnam, the former enemy, in 1995. His presidency, hence, seems to have been confronted with one essential dilemma; which is to project American post-Cold War leadership in conflict resolution and, at the same time, to promote the image of the United States as a "peacemaker" and not just the "policeman" of the world. The Clinton Administration was much more at ease in handling world affaires than any of the other administrations in the United States history. Indeed, the immediate post Cold-War world inherited by the Clinton Administration was a safe one for the United States and the conflicts that existed in the rest of the world did not seriously threaten U.S. national security. In this respect, William G. Hyland argues "No other modern American president inherited a stronger, safer international position than Bill Clinton. The Cold War was over. The nation was at peace. Its principal enemy had collapsed. The United States was the world's only genuine superpower. The major threats that had haunted American policy for nearly fifty years had either disappeared or were rapidly receding. To be sure, there were problems abroad and threats to national security, but they were manageable"[413]. This can explain the initial hesitation in dealing with a crisis like that of Bosnia, for instance. This initial hesitation, however, can be explained by another notion. For when the Cold War and the Soviet threat existed, there was a clear-cut line of foreign policy principals that

---

412 See John Lewis Gaddis, Cold War Statesmen Confront the Bomb: Nuclear Diplomacy since 1945, Oxford University Press, Oxford, 1999, p. 1.

413 See William G. Hyland, Clinton's World: Remaking American Foreign Policy, Praeger, Westport, CT., 1999, p. 1.

helped formulate and take decisions more rapidly. For decades, rivalry with the Soviet Union was actually the main rais*on d'être* of the U.S. foreign policy. Larry Berman and Emily O. Goldman explain, "Assessments of Bill Clinton's handling of foreign policy must first be placed in their appropriate international context, that of the dramatically altered world environment that emerged in the wake of the Cold War. The most distinctive characteristic of the post-Cold War era and the one that separates it from the recent past is the absence of a threat as a central organizing principle. While controversy existed during the Cold War over the nature of the Soviet threat, the mere presence of an overarching strategic imperative or compass provided an anchor for U.S. foreign policy and imposed a set of priorities that (for better or worse) defined the parameters within which U.S. leaders acted in the world and resorted to force in the defence of national interests"[414]. To better explain this idea, a comparison can be made between a state and an alliance. A state's foreign policy needs a reason to exist exactly like an alliance does. NATO was quick to realise this and to redefine its purposes of existence after the demise of its rival, the Warsaw Pact. In this, it is an exception. If it hadn't done so, it would most probably have had no more reason to exist since for an alliance and for a state structure, the reason to exist is also the purpose. If the purpose is clear, then there would be no difficulty in setting the strategies and polices to reach this purpose. If its not, then it would be very difficult to have a clear policy or "road" in mind to get to that purpose. The same can be said about the U.S. foreign policy in the immediate post Cold War period. The reason for its apparent hesitation in addressing world conflicts such as Bosnia is, in fact, the lack of general guidelines and purpose. Yet, like NATO, the U.S. also managed to redefine the purpose of its foreign policy. In the aftermath of the tragic events of September 2001, the new rais*on d'être* became the fight against terrorism.

The United States national interests can, thus, be better understood by examining the state ideology foundations and the role of certain U.S. leaderships in shaping and formulating the guidelines for its foreign policy. The U.S.'s inherent belief in its own "goodness" and the "need" for its leadership for the betterment of the world can seems to be a collective societal belief that is fed both by media and inherited tradition, namely the importance of religion, and the "unusual" historic achievements of the United States in a relatively short period of its creation. On different periods of its history, the foreign policy and national interests of the United States was shaped by the personality of the president in office. From the

---

414   See Larry Berman and Emily O. Goldman, "Clinton's Foreign policy at Midterm" in Colin Campbell and, Bert A. Rockman, <u>The Clinton Presidency: First Appraisals</u>, Chatham House Publishers, Chatham, NJ., 1996, pp. 290-324, p.292.

slaves' emancipation beliefs of Abraham Lincoln, to Bill Clinton's prudent interventionist and hesitant foreign policy and passing by Truman's anti Communist and containment strategies, the national interests of the United States expressed in its foreign policy seem to be highly affected by the domestic and international conditions prevailing at the time. It is, nonetheless, a foreign policy that proved its pragmatic adaptability to the changes in the United States national interests and to the changes in the world's political environment.

2.2.1. Cultural Interests

The French and American cultural interests in both crises constitute an important, yet, not decisive portion of their respective nation interests in the twp crises. The reason behind this importance is the fact that the cultural interests of a given country are not the same everywhere. The difference in the cultural interests that a country has in a certain region compared to its cultural interests in another region of the world is not simply a matter of arbitrary choice. In fact, it usually depends on issues such as geographic proximity, shared history and heritage, and a sense of belonging to a similar cultural group. In this respect, examining a given country's efforts to strongly its cultural ties with the region it has interests in is a fairly good method of measuring the importance of the region itself to that country.

It should also be kept in mind that preserving and promoting cultural ties with a certain region is not done without a good rationale. It would normally be a part of a country's efforts to either preserve some sort of influence on this region or expand its influence to it. Such a situation is apparent regarding the relationship between ancient colonial powers, for instance, and their former colonies. Indeed, the cultural influence of colonial powers on their ex-colonies can easily be identified. Many of the previously colonized countries still use their colonizer's language as their official language, they have mostly a very similar system of education to that of the ex-colonial power, and their taught national values are quite in harmony with their ex-colonial power's values.

This type of reasoning points back to the notion treated in part one of this book concerning the dependence of national media on the international one. Yet, in this case, it would be better to call it a "cultural centre and periphery" relationship between world countries. It is different from the concept of cultural colonialism in that, whereas cultural imperialism can be attributed to one superpower, which has the power to diffuse its culture across practically all existing borders, the "cultural centre and periphery" hypothesis suggests that each country that is able to and has an interest in a certain region would deploy efforts to strengthen its cultural ties with that region.

On the other hand, and to carry such reasoning even further, it can be said that countries would usually compete for spheres of cultural influence. This competition would, however, be dependent on relations between competing countries themselves and not simply on the good-well desire to diffuse culture for the sake of culture itself. Thus, in this sense, countries that are disputing influence on a certain region can be expected to compete in their cultural influence on that region. Similarly, other countries might sacrifice their cultural competition over a certain region for the benefit of preserving other more important interests or relations they bilaterally maintain. It is important, however, to note that not all countries see great value in promoting their cultural interests. For, normally, the importance of cultural interests to a country also depends on the importance the country itself gives to its own culture.

In France's case, the value given to culture is quite evident. David L. Looseley explains, for instance, "France's tradition of state involvement in the arts and heritage is a long one and is inseparable from the idea of a national culture. In medieval times, the preservation of Europe's cultural heritage was largely the business of the Church. Gradually, however, with the disintegration of Charlemagne's empire, national cultures began to emerge and, in France, high culture was endowed with a political rather than religious purpose"[415]. This opinion is also shared by David Wachtel who gives the example of the cancellation of Paris Expo 89 saying, "The cancellation of Expo '89 was, however, a serious symbolic blow to France's socialist government"[416]. Wachtel goes further in making the distinction between the importance of culture to France compared to other countries. He states, "In many countries, cancellation of a cultural event, no matter how large, would have few grave repercussions. Not so in France. The death of Expo '89 marked the beginning of a major challenge to the government and a symbolic end to an ideological commitment that the Socialist party was no longer able to manage"[417]. This idea of the importance of culture and the strength of its connection to politics in France might seem to be a little excessive. It is, however, not a sudden preoccupation of France. Indeed, the importance of culture in this country developed over a long period of time and through various stages.

---

415   See David L. Looseley, <u>The Politics of Fun: Cultural Policy and Debate in Contemporary France</u>, Berg Publishers Ltd. Oxford, 1995, p. 11.

416   See David Wachtel, <u>Cultural Policy and Socialist France</u>, Greenwood Press, New York, 1987, p.1.

417   Ibid, p.2.

To begin with, it is important to know that the task of preserving Europe's culture was mainly the occupation of the church in medieval times. With the rise of different national cultures in Europe, the one in France was different. It was different because it had more of a political rather than a religious objective. Different French monarchs voiced their support of culture by collecting art works and distributing favours to artists. In this context, the concept of Royal Patronage was meant to benefit the state in enhancing the national prestige and developing a unified single national culture that can, eventually, be projected outside the country.

The French Revolution changed matters to a certain degree because with it came a weakening of the traditional guarding institutions of culture (the monarchy, the nobility and the Church). With the French Revolution, cultural treasures, monuments and arts became the property of the whole nation and became one of the major responsibilities of the state. Indeed, Revolutionary discourse emphasized that the French nation was one and indivisible and that it is one that has no place for elites, minorities, or sectional interests. Moreover, the cultural heritage became the emblem of that unity. To crystallize this importance of culture in France, museums such as the *Louvre* were opened and institutions such as the *Ecole nationale des beaux-arts*[418] *(National* School of Fine Arts) and the *Institut de France*[419] (Institute of France) were established.

As far as the United States is concerned, the promotion of its culture to the rest of the world has often been regarded differently from that of France, and indeed, the cultural promotion efforts of many other nations. The reason is, not simply in the content but also in the method of promotion as well for the United States' cultural promotion efforts have always had one principal default. This major default of the American cultural "marketing" efforts is the worldwide negatively perceived military and economic strength, and hegemony of the United States. What started being regarded as an aspiration to live the "American Dream" ended up being regarded as "cultural imperialism". One other important default of the American cultural promotion efforts is that American culture is mostly referred to in "economic terms". For while other world countries might be seen as promoting their culture, the culture promotion of the United States has mostly been looked at as an attempt for an imposed "Americanisation' and as "products" that are exported to other countries and that try to impose on local or cultural

---

418   The successor to the royal academies of the seventeenth century, the *Beaux-Arts* school is located in the premises of the convent of the *Petits Augustins* since 1816.

419   A unique institution in its originality, traditions and work, the *Institut de France*, (The protector of arts, literature and science), created in 1795, is the union of Five Academies: Besides sponsorship and humanitarian action, the *Institut de France* promotes other French cultural foundations.

values of these countries[420]. Although it has a few defenders who attempt to attribute to cultural Americanisation "a positive sense of democratisation and economic promotion"[421]. Some would, nonetheless, explain the rejection of American culture diffusion in host countries as being simply a gap of generations. This, for instance, is an argument of John Dean and Jean-Paul Gabilliet in explaining European popular attitude towards the diffusion of American culture in Europe. They state" When Europeans argue that they see America as a threat and a contrast to things dear to their hearts, what do they mean? It is never the case that they speak on behalf of all Europeans; indeed, for every European who has called for the rejection of American culture, another has welcomed it as a source of renewal and rejuvenation. Often it is a matter of generations clashing in Europe, of older generations rising in the defence of European culture as they see it, and younger generations defiantly adopting American cultural forms. Often it is also a matter of time before European views of American culture change from rejection to acceptance"[422]. Many more, nonetheless, would argue that cultural Americanisation reflects a negative image of American imperialism and hegemony[423]. Heide Fehrenbach and Uta G. Poiger state, however, that most analysis on this issue would understand "Americanisation as describing the transfer of goods and symbols from the United States to other countries and focus on how societies abroad have taken up and, in the process, transformed these influences"[424]. The difference of "age" for the two cultures should, however, be always kept in mind. For while French culture goes back a long way in history, American culture is relatively new. Some even argue that the American culture is in a sense a continuity of the European one; yet, they stop short of labelling America as "Europe's Offshore". John Dean and Jean-Paul Gabilliet, for example, state "Psychologically, America has always been Europe's "significant other", helping Europeans to define their sense of self by offering contrasts and counterpoints. Clearly, as a national culture, America stands within a larger framework of Western civilization. There are much continuity across the Atlantic in terms of

---

420   See Heide Fehrenbach and Uta G. Poiger, Transactions, Transgressions, Transformations: American Culture in Western Europe and Japan, Berghahn Books, New York, 2000, p. xiii.

421   See for instance Herbert I. Schiller, Mass Communications and American Empire, Westview Press, Boulder, 1992.

422   See John Dean and Jean-Paul Gabilliet, European Readings of American Popular Culture, Greenwood Press, Westport, CT., 1996, pp. xxv-xxvi

423   See Peter Gann and L. H. Duignan, The Rebirth of the West: The Americanization of the Democratic World, 1945-1958, Blackwell, Cambridge, MA., 1992.

424   See Heide Fehrenbach and Uta G. Poiger, op. cit., p. xiv

cultural standards, aesthetic appreciation, and communities of taste. Yet at the same time America is not merely an offshoot of Europe in the sense that Iceland is. America is a cosmopolitan blend of many cultural repertoires, the result of a blithe bricolage that endlessly changes the context and content of culture as Europeans know it. Thus, not only has American culture developed into something that is predominantly contrapuntal to European views of culture, but also, retroactively, it has worked to instill a sense of Europeanness into Europeans"[425]. If there are general characteristics to the American culture, these would, hence, be that it is a new one, that it has aspects of many cultures, precisely because the United States is frequently regarded as the "melting pot", and that the instruments and forms of its diffusion are quite controversial.

Indeed, to conduct an effective cultural policy, a good philosophy of diffusion and effective instruments have to be put in place. It is, hence, important to understand the difference of philosophies and tools used by the two countries to promote their culture. For its part, the instruments employed by France to conduct its cultural policy are extraordinary. The cultural policy of France has been strongly anchored with the creation of instruments that serve France's promotion of its cultural interests worldwide. Some writers go as far as calling the modern cultural policy of France as the "cultural shinning" or le *Rayonnement Culturel*[426]. For France, the pursuit of cultural objectives is distinguished by a particular philosophy and is done through the instruments of language and cultural cooperation with other countries.

As far as the French philosophy in pursuing its cultural objectives is concerned, it can be said that there are two main currents underlying the French foreign cultural policy. The first of the two currents is that which calls for less state intervention in the cultural policies of France while the other is that which still believes in the unconditional strength of France as a dominant country and which, by consequence, supports the state's monopoly of France's foreign cultural policy.

According to Martin Bulard, partisans of the first line of thought believe that the foreign cultural activates of France should be left to the market to decide. In this sense, the cultural policy would be a by-product of the economic policy of France and highly dependant on economic developments[427]. On the other hand, partisans of the legacy of France and believers in its leadership see foreign cultural policy as an instrument that, if combined with certain foreign policy positions of the French state, can raise the status of France as a world leader on the international scene and

---

425   See John Dean and Jean-Paul Gabilliet, op. cit., p. xxv.
426   See Martine Bulard, "*Hors des Frontières, la France à la Recherche d'une Ambition Culturelle*", Le Monde Diplomatique, June 2001, pp. 8-9.
427   Idem.

consequently raise interest in French culture. For instance, Jacuqes Rigaud, explains that the bases of France's cultural policy should be "an instrument of fighting against influence on the international scale and should use new technologies to do so"[428]. This vision of France as the representative of such concepts as "liberty", "equality", and "fraternity" as well as being a supporter of the Third-World causes was fairly expressed by the late French President François Mitterrand at the conference of Cancun in 1981 when he said "salutations to those who we imprison, that we persecute and that we torture…who want to live free…to all of you the France says have courage…freedom will conquer"[429]. Thus, the other vision of the French cultural policy saw it as a means of reinforcing the image of France, particularly amongst Third-World countries, as a defender of human rights and justice and, also, as a means guarding against the manipulation of the world culture by one country, namely the United States.

Yet, it can be said that that idea of the French cultural objectives and policy was particular to the post-colonialism period and the general atmosphere of support to the causes of the Third-World. Some writers, such as Martin Bulard, suggest that the change of international realities have proven the point of those who think of the cultural policy of France as one that should be dependent on the economic realities and on political ambitions. He explains, for instance, that the cultural policy budget of France hasn't changed for the last fifteen years (around nine billion French francs a year). He also explains that even the French Ministry of Foreign Affaires has to take into consideration the evaluation of cultural centres according to their revenues[430]. Hence, the first perspective of the promotion of French cultural interests and cultural ties is subjected to more or less economic capabilities.

Nevertheless, evidence of the priority given to foreign cultural policies, which are contrary to the aforementioned view of economic capabilities are quite abundant. Indeed, the current world challenges such as globalisation and the monopolarity of the world political system engage France more than ever to affirm its difference and its defence of the principal of multi-polarity of the world political system. Such a notion is well expressed by the former French Minister of Foreign Affaires Hubert Vedrin who explains that there is a necessity to build good bases for a "restructuring of the foreign policy" that refuses "the diminishing of the role of states" and that aims at a "controlled and progressive evolution of sovereignty" that would "contests the hegemonic will of the United States and defends another

---

428   See Jacques Rigaud, "*Les Relations Culturelles Extérieures*", Report to the Ministry of Foreign Affaires, Documentation Française, Paris, 1979.

429   See quoted from Martin Bulard, op. cit.

430   Idem.

regulation of international relations"[431]. For his part, the former French Prime Minster Lionel Jospin explains, during a visit to Brazil on the 8th of April 2001, that globalisation doesn't signify "uniformity" and that "the world is too complex not to be treated in different manners"[432]. Thus, for France, taking distinguished political positions can help with the expansion of its cultural influence in rallying other nations behind it. Peoples of such nations, would according to this reasoning, would naturally be tempted to seek to apprehend more about the culture of such a country which takes such bold political stands. On the other hand, promoting its culture worldwide would help France politically by increasing its weight on the international scene. To pursue its cultural objectives, France has two main instruments. The first one is spreading the usage of its language and the second is to promote its culture through its active cultural and development cooperation programs located worldwide.

As far as diffusing French as a means of realising cultural objectives is concerned, it can be said that France has realised excellent results in this field. According the French Ministry of Foreign Affaires' statistics, French is spoken by 181 million persons around the world and 82,5 millions are currently learning the language. Evidently the distribution of French language speakers is not the same everywhere (See Table 16 below).

This result did not come without considerable efforts from the French government. Indeed, France's action concerning the teaching of French worldwide includes a certain number of agents and institutions that work together in a complementary manner in a network supervised by the French Ministry of Foreign Affaires. Furthermore, this network works closely with other networks of partners to assist in the promotion of French worldwide.

These networks are quite impressive and complex. The networks under the supervision of the Ministry of Foreign Affaires have, for instance, over 800 specialised agents (essentially attached to the educational cooperation, cooperation attachés for French teaching…etc.), 150 cultural centres, 220 Alliance Française centres and 267 establishments for French language teaching that follow the Agency for French Teaching to Foreigners AEFE (*Agence pour l'Enseignement du Français à l'Etranger*) which has around 160000 students of whom two thirds are foreigners and which usually works closely with national French teaching establishments.

Yet for this task, the Ministry of Foreign Affaires is not alone. It has several partners working to reach the same objective. Those include over 900 000 French professors worldwide (notably the teaching associations and the Federation of

---

431   See Hubert Védrin, *"Réformer la Politique étrangère française»*, _Le Monde Diplomatique_, December 2000.

432   Quoted from the article of Martin Bulard, <u>op. cit.</u>

French Professors FIPF), the institutions of the Francophonie (a community of 55 countries and governments, Intergovernmental Agency of the Francophonie and the University Agency of the Francophonie), other French ministries such as the Ministry of National Education and the Ministry of culture and Communications, and other institutions working for the spreading of the French language worldwide.

Table 16: Distribution of French Speakers and French Learners

Region	Number of French Speakers	Number of French Learners
Sub Saharan Africa	39 413 000	20 705 000
The Maghreb Countries	34 380 000	8 720 000
Indian Ocean	4 307 000	3 133 500
North America	11 873 000	4 500 000
The Caribbean	2 622 000	2 987 300
Far East	402 000	441 000
Near and Middle East	1 823 000	2 400 000
Central and Oriental Europe	4 105 500	3 117 000
Western Europe	70 183 000	16 450 000
Oceania	444 000	17 000
Total	181 000 000	82 500 000

Source: French Ministry of Foreign Affaires website.

It should be mentioned, in this respect, that France's policy in the diffusion of the French language has shown a very good ability to adapt to new emerging conditions and environments. Indeed, with the new innovations in communications technology and the emerging new society of information technology, the linguistic diversity becomes an essential element of the cultural diversity. Moreover, the new political realities and integration into regional and economic groups and geographic zones (ALENA, MERCOSUR, ASEAN, European Union...etc), call for a modification of the linguistic policies in order to be able to adapt to the new realities and to be able to compete. Hence, the French cultural policy can be said to have used effectively two elements in its favour. The first one is that of new technological developments in communications and language teaching materials and the second is that of the realities of the "global village".

As far as the use of new innovations in the service of French language diffusion is concerned, the examples of the success of the French cultural policy are quite abundant. For instance, the introduction of an obligatory second foreign language in secondary education has proven to cause an important increase in the number of students choosing to study French. In Spain, according to the French Ministry of Foreign Affaires, this method has resulted in a spectacular increase in the number of students studying French, (1300000 in the academic year 1999-2000). The number is four times more than it was four years ago[433]. Indeed, this decision to introduce another living language besides French in order to attract more students is not without a good logic. According to Martin Bulard, diversifying the approaches would diversify the public and consequently help to attract new audiences, especially amongst the youth[434]. This approach of diversifying the languages besides French is evident also in the current policy of French broadcasting companies such as Radio France International which started to diffuse its programs in other world languages. It was also voiced during the Summit of the Francophonie in Beirut in 2001 where France's emphasis was on a new policy that consists in promoting the French language while respecting at the same time other languages and cultures. This point of view is also shared by Erlends Calabuig, the director of foreign language antennas in *Radio France Internationale,* who explains that "the voice of France is not necessarily in the French language…it is a vision of the culture of the world[435.] Hence, the French policy in diffusing French to larger new audiences has adapted fairly well to the concept of respect for cultural and linguistic identity. This method is quite intelligent since it eliminates the perception of French as an imposed hegemonic language and, hence, facilitates its acceptance.

This, however, wasn't the only concept brought about by the new political and economic world realities. France also works to promote the usage of the French language within the various international organisations. For instance, France works on promoting the teaching of French amongst the employees of the European Union. In fact, special linguistic programs adapted to professional use of European Union employees are being held in the various capitals of the EU member states, as well as in the capitals of candidate countries, for this purpose. In 1999-2000, around 1800 European Union's employees benefited from such

---

433   See French Ministry of Foreign Affaires Website.
434   See Martin Bulard, Op.Cit.
435   Quoted from the article of Martin Bulard, Idem.

linguistic training. Moreover, prestigious French institutes, such as the National School of Administration (ENA), organize a number of training sessions for employees of the European Union, as well as officials of other countries, combined with courses of public administration, which aim at perfecting the French language of the participants.

As far as the usage of new innovations in communications technology and the teaching of foreign languages is concerned, France has also used these new advantages to the benefit of the diffusion of its language worldwide. For example, the French Ministry of Foreign Affaires has developed in cooperation with The International Center of Pedagogical Studies a website on the Internet in July 2000 aiming at providing a data base necessary for the usage of French language professors.[436] Another example of the good usage of the new technology is the various new technological instruments provided by France to the institutions of the European Union (electronic spelling correctors, interactive linguistic games, grammar correctors...etc.) aiming to facilitate and encourage the use of French within these institutions. Moreover and far as distant learning technologies are concerned, the programs of TV5[437] are also a good example of how such new technology can be used in diffusing one's language. Thus, France can be said to have conducted very well so far its linguistic conquest of other world countries. Yet, to conduct a successful cultural policy and to achieve the cultural goals desired, cultural influence has to be effected.

This influence, for France, can be said to have been achieved through a combination of the concept of cultural influence with that of cooperation and development aid and carried out through a network of cultural missions, attachés, and institutions worldwide. Indeed, the battles over images and winning opinions have become of an enormous importance these days. Consequently, without an instrument of influence over the decision-makers and the opinions in other countries, diplomatic efforts alone would not be able to win many causes.

In this respect, the network of cultural agents employed by France is quite impressive. Working within international organizations or French public foreign establishments, there is around 7000 cultural agents deployed outside of France. Added to this figure are around 5000 locally recruited employees, 600 agents based in Paris, and the 6000 professors and agents of the French Agency for the Teaching of the French Language AEPA[438]. It is worth mentioning, in this context, that the choice of such cultural agents is not arbitrary. In fact, they come

---

436   The website created is found at the <u>address http://www.franc-parler.org</u>
437   TV5 is one of the instruments of the organisation of French Speaking Countries (Francophonie).
438   Source: statistics of the French Ministry of Foreign Affaires.

from different backgrounds (artistic, cultural, public service, medicine, law, statisticians, professors, diplomats… etc.).

As far as development aid is concerned, France's usage of this instrument to draw a more favourable image, especially amongst Third-World countries, is remarkable. Indeed, the French diplomacy concerning development aid seems to be one that aims at defending global moral political principals such as fighting poverty, social inequalities and world heritage. France has also taken active steps to alleviate the heavy burden of the debt of the worlds least developed countries. Indeed, the concept of development for France has also cultural connotations. For instance, France works actively to conclude scientific partnerships with world countries, especially those members of the European Union. It also has over 60 archaeological missions and 28 research centres and institutes working around the world in addition to receiving over 195000 foreign students to continue their study in France.

Concerning France's specialized cultural establishments, the French Ministry of Foreign Affaires relies heavily on the General Department for International Cooperation and Development DGICD (*la Direction Générale de la Coopération Internationale et du Développement*). The principal aim of the DGCID is to coordinate the efforts of the various French establishment (See Graphic 1 for an idea on the fields of activity of the DGCID).

Graphic 1: Distribution of the Sectors of Activity of the DGCID

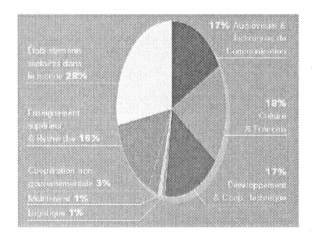

Source: Website of the DGCID.

To consolidate these efforts in order to better achieve the desired objectives, the DGCID works within three main axes. The first axe is to coordinate the efforts of the various concerned French ministries through the Inter-ministerial Committee for International Cooperation CICD, which is headed by the French Prime Minister. Together with the French Treasury, the DGCID heads the secretariat of this committee, which principally elaborates development strategies for countries and orients the public aid for development. The second axe through which the DGCID conducts its objectives is that of the French civil society and through building, developing, maintaining continuous cooperation and coordinating its efforts with those of all concerned non-governmental organisations. The third axe of DGCID action is that of working with international organisations such as the European, though which France can coordinate aid efforts and even influence the orientation of such international aid.

Nevertheless, if the geographical distribution of the DGCID action is taken into consideration, it would reveal that the distribution of the efforts is not equal to all regions of the world (see Graphic 2).

Graphic 2: Distribution of the DGCID by Geographical Sectors.

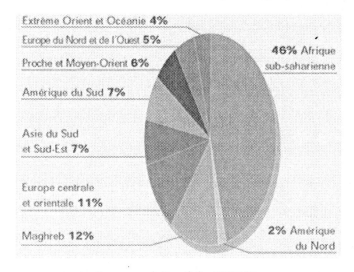

Source: website of the DGCID.

France, hence, holds high the conduction of its cultural policy and the achievement of its cultural interests. From the enormous efforts deployed by the French government and explained earlier, it can be deducted that France's cultural interests figure high on its foreign policy agenda. These cultural promotion efforts are combined with its diplomatic and development efforts to achieve the maximum desired effect. It is interesting to note, nonetheless, from the above chart that Sub-Saharan Africa gets the lion share of the French governments development aid and cultural attention (47%) while North America gets the least attention with only 2%. This of course can be always explained by economic factors. It can be said, for instance, that Sub-Saharan Africa is in much more need of aid than North America. Yet, it can also be more solidly explained by spheres of influence, geographic proximity, and former colonial ties. For instance, the Maghreb countries get 12% share, while those of South America get 7% although the economic status of most of the countries in South America is much worst than those of the Maghreb countries. This fact can mainly be explained by ex-colonial ties and geographic proximity.

For its part, the United States cultural policy presents a number of differences from the cultural diffusion philosophy and cultural diffusion instruments employed by France. As mentioned above, the American foreign cultural policy is quite a recent event compared to the French one. Indeed, it was only in 1938 that the United States President Franklin D. Roosevelt and Secretary of State Collin Hull decided to establish a division of cultural relations in the U.S. Department of State[439]. Prior to this date, American foreign cultural policy "had been occasional, incidental, and restricted in large part to the eminently 'practical'"[440]. André Kaspi and Randolph Wieck explain that one of the major disadvantages to the cultural relations policy of the United States is the fact that unlike other world powers it had no significant colonial history. They state "Lacking colonial ties like those of England or France, the United States had never filled the role of a mother country. For much of America's history it had been a cultural importer taking ideas from extraneous contributors for its own needs, combining these contributions with native genius"[441].

Examples of American emphasis on cultural foreign policy promotion are particularly scarce prior to the Kennedy Administration. In 1900, the United States took in 1400 Cuban teachers for a summer course at Harvard University. In addition, and in the aftermath of World War I, the Belgian-American Education Foundation was established promoting exchange programs between Belgians and Americans. In 1936, the United States participated in a Conference for the Maintenance of Peace in Buenos Aires, where it proposed the establishment of Convention for the Promotion of Inter-American Cultural Relations,

---

439   See André Kaspi and Randolph Wieck, Ignorance Abroad: American Educational and Cultural Foreign Policy and the Office of Assistant Secretary of State, Praeger Publishers, Westport, CT., 1992, p. 5.
440   Idem.
441   Idem.

which was later, ratified by the US Senate on the 29th of June 1936. The aim of this convention was to exchange graduate students and teachers. Yet, what was unusual about it was that "the United States government had never before committed itself to a policy of financial support for an international cultural exchange program".[442] Other than this convention and during the Eighth International Conference of American States held in Lima (Peru) in 1938, the United States along with the other participating countries declared that they intend to increase "the interchange of scientific, technical, cultural, and educational knowledge and skills among their peoples"[443]. Moreover, the Interdepartmental Committee on Cooperation with the American Republics, which later became known as Interdepartmental Committee on Scientific and Cultural Cooperation and whose specialty is that of technical assistance, was created in May 1938[444].

It should be noted here that, initially, the reasons behind the American cultural foreign policy had more to do with propaganda and counter propaganda. In this respect, André Kaspi and Randolph Wieck, quoting the first chief of the Cultural Division of the United States Department of State Ben M. Cherrington, state "When Hitler and Mussolini's exploitation of education as instruments of national policy was at its height…our Government was determined to demonstrate to the world the basic difference between the methods of democracy and those of a "Ministry of Enlightenment and Propaganda." There was to be established in the Department of State an organization that would be a true representative of our American tradition of intellectual freedom and educational integrity"[445]. In this sense, the United States cultural foreign policy" aimed at promoting an image of the United States as a land of intellectual freedom and integrity"[446]. There were two guidelines to achieve this aim of the newly created cultural division. The first one was that "the educational relations activities of the United States [should] be reciprocal and there must be no imposition of one people's culture upon another"[447]. The second was that "the exchange of educational interests [should] involve the participation of people and institutions concerned with those interests in the respective countries, that is, the program should stem from established centres of education and culture and should be educational rather than propagandistic"[448].

---

442   Ibid. pp. 5-6
443   Ibid., p. 6.
444   See Charles A. Thomson and Walter H. C. Laves, <u>Cultural Relations and U. S. Foreign Policy</u>, Indiana University Press, Bloomington, 1963, 36.
445   See André Kaspi and Randolph Wieck, <u>op. cit.</u>, p. 8
446   Idem.
447   Idem.
448   Ibid., p. 9.

As in the case of France, personalities marked significant changes in American cultural foreign policy. Indeed, for the United States the momentum given to cultural foreign policy by President John F. Kennedy is quite interesting to note. For what was different with the Kennedy Administration is that "John Kennedy took on the responsibility of providing a new political orientation for the United States"[449]. Nonetheless, although policy" innovation" marked the Kennedy Presidency, "evidence indicates that the president was above all else sensitive to the rivalry with the Soviet Union, to the cultural combat which, in the developing countries, pitted the United States against the Communist world"[450]. The innovation in foreign cultural policy brought about by the Presidency of John F. Kennedy was both in the philosophy of the foreign cultural policy itself as well, as in the creation of new cultural promotion instruments. In 1961-1962, Kennedy created the post of Assistant Secretary of State for Educational and Cultural Affairs to be held by Philip Coombs. Yet, some argue that this innovation was not effective because neither the tools used by Philip Combs for this post nor the briefness of his stay in office were adequate[451]. Nonetheless, Kennedy, on the 27th of February 1961, created another instrument of cultural foreign policy (U.S. Advisory Commission on Educational Exchange). Kennedy's view of cultural foreign policy "expressed his faith in creating an educational and cultural policy as a key to aiding developing countries"[452]: Kennedy states on the same day "As our own history demonstrates so well, education is in the long run the chief means by which a young nation can develop its economy, its political and social institutions and individual freedom and opportunity. There is no better way of helping the new nations of Latin America, Africa, and Asia in their present pursuit of freedom and better living conditions than by assisting them to develop their human resources through education. Likewise there is no better way to strengthen our bond of understanding and friendship with older nations than through educational and cultural interchange"[453]. Nonetheless, and once again, the view of such policies, no matter how noble they were intended to be, cannot be detached from the notion of the East-Went competition over spheres of influence in the world.

The instruments used by the United States for the conduct of its cultural foreign policy are many. The most important of these instruments is one that works within the U.S. Department of State: Bureau of Educational and Cultural Affairs (ECA). The mission of the State Department's Bureau of Educational and Cultural Affairs is to assist in the development of friendly, sympathetic and peaceful relations

---

449   Ibid., p. xiv.
450   Ibid., p. xv.
451   Ibid., p. 2.
452   Ibid., p. 28
453   Idem.

between the U.S. and other countries through fostering mutual understanding. The ECA does this through a wide range of international exchange and training programs, as authorized by the Mutual Educational and Cultural Exchange Act of 1961. The ECA also works in close cooperation with U.S. Embassies overseas to promote personal, professional and institutional ties between private citizens and organizations in the United States and abroad, as well as through presenting U.S. history art, and culture in all of its diversity to audiences overseas. The direction of the ECA is entrusted to the one who occupies the post of the Special Assistant Secretary of State. This post was created in 1958 after the signing of a cultural agreement with the Soviet Union in the same year[454]. Nonetheless, the ECA did not actually start to work effectively except in 1960 due to previous numerous reorganizations of the office[455].

Several sub-instruments work in coordination with the ECA. The Fulbright Program provides, for instance, grants for graduate students, scholars, professionals, teachers and Administrators. The Fulbright Program was established in 1946 under legislation introduced by former Senator J. William Fulbright of Arkansas. Since its inception more than fifty years ago 255,000 "Fulbrighters," 96,400 from the United States and 158,600 from other countries, have participated in the Program. The Fulbright Program awards approximately 4,500 new grants annually[456]. In addition to the Fulbright Program, the Office of English Language Programs creates and implements high quality, targeted English language programs in specific regions and countries of the world. All programs are administered through the local American Embassy or Consulate[457]. The Office has a staff of Regional English Language Officers (RELOs), program specialists, and support staff based in Washington and overseas. The Office of English Language Programs provides professional teacher training programs worldwide to promote further understanding of American language, society, culture, values and policies[458]. Founded in 1978 in honour of the late Senator and Vice-president, the Hubert H. Humphrey Fellowship Program brings accomplished mid-level professionals from designated countries in Africa, Asia, Latin America, the Caribbean, the Middle East, and Eurasia to the United States for a year of study and professional experience. The program encourages a variety of U.S. and foreign partnerships worldwide. Fellowships are awarded competitively to candidates with a commitment to public

---

454   Ibid., p. 18.
455   Ibid. p. 22.
456   See Website of the Fulbright Program found at
      http://exchanges.state.gov/education/fulbright/.
457   See Website of the Office of English Language Programs found at
      http://exchanges.state.gov/education/engteaching/.
458   Idem.

service in both the public and private sectors, specifically in the fields of natural resources and environmental management, public policy analysis and administration, law and human rights, finance and banking, economic development, agricultural development/economics, human resource management, urban and regional planning, public health policy and management, technology policy and management, educational planning, communications/journalism, and drug abuse epidemiology, education, and treatment and prevention[459]. In addition, the U.S. Department of State's educational partnership programs encourage educational reform, economic development, civil society, and mutual understanding through cooperation between U.S. colleges and universities and foreign post-secondary institutions. Partnerships may focus on disciplines in the social, political and economic sciences; public administration; the humanities; business; economics; law; journalism and communications; public health policy and administration; library science; and educational administration. The programs are administered by the Humphrey Fellowships and Institutional Linkages Branch of the Office of Global Educational Programs. Since 1982, more than 700 awards have been made across the U.S. in support of partnerships with educational institutions overseas[460]. Moreover, The International Visitor Program brings participants to the U.S. to meet and confer with professional counterparts and to experience firsthand the U.S. and its institutions. The International Visitor Program operates under authority of the Mutual Educational and Cultural Exchange Act of 1961 (The Fulbright-Hays Act). The emphasis of the program is to increase mutual understanding through communication at the personal and professional levels. More than 200 current and former Heads of State, 1,500 cabinet-level ministers, and many other distinguished world leaders in government and the private sector have participated in the International Visitor Program[461]. There is also a relatively new innovation. This is the Ambassador's Fund for Cultural Preservation, established by Congress for the fiscal year 2001 and which aims at assisting less developed countries in preserving their cultural heritage and demonstrating U.S. respect for other cultures. Finally, The Office of Citizen Exchanges manages professional, youth, and cultural programs through grants with non-profit American institutions, including community organizations, professional associations, and universities. This partnership benefits thousands of Americans and foreign visitors taking part in exchanges at the grassroots level, both in the U.S. and abroad. Thematic categories for grants include civil society, NGO development, civic education, media development, judicial

---

459   See website of Hubert H. Humphrey Fellowship Program found at
      http://exchanges.state.gov/education/hhh/
460   See Website of the partnership programs found at
      http://exchanges.state.gov/education/partnership/
461   See Website of the Program found at http://exchanges.state.gov/education/ivp/

training, intellectual property rights, and public administration among other themes. The office has three geographic divisions—Europe/Eurasia; Near East, South Asia and Africa; and Western Hemisphere and East Asia. Yet, in spite of these numerous cultural promotion policy instruments, the foreign cultural policy of the United States seems to be hindered by two main obstacles. The first one is that of the United States' image as an imperialist power and the second is what some writers explain as the lack of understanding of the real value of investing in culture rather than relying on the language of arms in the United States. André Kaspi and Randolph Wieck state, in this respect, "People-to-people exchanges embody a slow yet inexorable force for good—difficult for politicians elected at two-, four-, or six-year intervals to discern—that dwarfs delivery of arms, bank loans, or an ambassador's smile. *And* these exchanges are cheap! For the price of a Stealth bomber or two, the gamut of ECA programs could operate for several years. These programs make up a sort of foreign policy whose benefits, come to fruition, could effect change more swiftly and with greater impact for good than all the smart bombs a Stealth could ever drop. Considering what we pay for a Stealth—or any recent bomber—we behave foolishly in ignoring the force we could harness in ECA. Simply put, we are wasting our money. We could get a more substantial return on our investment. But huge defence contracts and kickbacks are a great short-term temptation: they're wonderful income enhancers"[462].

It can be said, thus, that usually cultural interests and development efforts are directed more to those countries, where there is a possible sphere of influence, whether political, economic, ex-colonial, or whether the concerned country is geographically close to the sphere of influence of the interested country. This is particularly true in the case of the relationship between an ex-colonial power and its former colonies.

The previously mentioned notes in this section indicate that there is a clear difference between the philosophies and instruments used by France and the United States because both countries do not weigh the value of their respective cultures and their promotion equally. Accordingly, France holds a great deal of interest for the proper projection of its culture throughout the world. Its *"Rayonnement Culturel"* philosophy is clearly opposed to the "Americanisation" policy of the United States. For one thing, the *"Rayonnement Culturel"* of France is quite inherent to the French way of thinking and was not merely invented for political competition circumstances at a recent period of its history. Furthermore, historic inherited image of a country often affects the reception and acceptance of its culture. France, for its part, was the one who transmitted the concepts of "liberty", "equality", and" brotherhood" to the entire world. Its numerous pro-developing

---

462   See André Kaspi and Randolph Wieck, op. cit., p. 1.

countries political positions are deemed to facilitate the reception and adoption of its culture worldwide. On the other hand, the "Americanisation policy" of the United States is often met by rejection from host countries. The argument that the rejection to Americanisation, in all its forms whether in cultural promotion activates or "cultural-economic products", such as MacDonald's, is simply a matter of generations' gap does not hold today. Indeed, most of the anti-globalisation and anti-Americanisation supporters and activists nowadays belong to the young generations. Moreover, the value that the United States holds for the language of culture as a means of communication with other nations is not significant compared to its concentration on the accumulation of and projection of its might.

2.2.2. Economic Interests

As far as the coverage of an international crisis is concerned, the importance of national economic interests has been amply demonstrated in the first parts of this research. Indeed, the various economic national interests of a given country in an international crisis have an enormous influence on the coverage of this international crisis or conflict; the example of the coverage of the Gulf War of 1991 compared to the media's disregard of conflicts that went unnoticed in Africa, is a clear-cut example of conflict coverage discrimination due mainly to discrepancies in economic interests involved in these conflicts. In the case of France and the United States, national economic interests are also essential in the consideration of their respective reactions to the crisis in Bosnia compared to their respective reactions to that of Chechnya. To fully appreciate the importance of economic interests' impact on both the French and the United States' foreign policy, it is useful to have some general indicators on the economic status of both countries in the world. Such an understanding of the economic status of each of the two countries would facilitate understanding the importance of their respective economic interests in both crises.

For its part, France occupies a major status in world economy. It produces 4% of the world GDP, placing it fourth in a list where only the United States, Japan and Germany precede it. France, in this respect, holds alone 6% of the commercial exchanges of the world. In certain areas, such as agricultural products and services, it is only second to the United States, and in other areas, such as industrial products, it occupies the fourth place.

Moreover, according to the French State Secretariat for Foreign Trade consulted in November 2003, The French exportations represent 21% of its GDP putting it in a place that is inferior to that of Germany (24%) but ahead of Japan (10%) or the United States (9%). Indeed, the overall stock of France's Foreign Direct Investments amounted to US$166,6 billion. The direct foreign investments in France for the same year amounted to $125 billion[463]. The period covering the entirety of the duration of the two crises of Bosnia and Chechnya is extremely important as far a economic indicators for France are concerned. For between 1990-1996, France was the third major investor after the United States and the United Kingdom. Indeed, the status of the French economy is very much expressed by the balance of payments between France and other world countries (See Table 17).

Table 17: France's Exterior Commerce balance 1995-1996 (Excluding Military Material & Including manufactured gold)

	Imports CAF			Exports FAB			Balance		Rate of Coverage	
	1995	1996	Variation	1995	1996	Variation	1995	1996	1995	1996
A. Classification by Products										
1. Agricultural Products, Forestry and Fishing.	55,3	54,3	-1,9	75,4	78,5	4,1	20,1	24,2	136,3	144,7
2. Agricultural Industry and agro-alimentation products	107,6	107,4	- 0,2	134,4	135,7	1,0	26,7	28,3	124,8	126,4
Agro-Alimentary Products	163,0	161,7	- 0,8	209,8	214,2	2,1	46,8	52,5	128,7	132,5
3. Energy products	93,7	115,7	23,5	33,0	36,7	11,1	-60,7	- 79,0	35,2	31,7
4.Primary Mineral materials	7,3	7,0	- 4,2	1,6	1,5	- 1,3	- 5,7	- 5,4	21,4	22,1
5. metals and products for metal works.	130,4	120,3	- 7,7	122,2	121,0	- 0,9	- 8,2	0,7	93,7	100,6
6.Half-Products non metallic.	230,2	223,7	- 2,8	222,3	222,3	0,0	- 7,9	- 1,4	96,6	99,4
7.Items for profession equipments	340,8	359,2	5,4	389,8	409,8	5,1	49,1	50,6	114,4	114,1
8. House hold Equipment	34,8	33,7	- 3,4	25,4	26,8	5,3	- 9,4	- 6,9	73,0	79,5
9. Automobile maintenance équipement	83,1	92,7	11,5	83,6	92,9	11,1	0,5	0,1	100,5	100,1
10.Spare parts & utilitarian material of ground transport	78,2	75,5	- 3,5	98,4	100,4	2,0	20,2	24,9	125,9	133,0
11.Items of common consumption	225,1	230,0	2,2	211,1	221,7	5,1	- 14,0	- 8,3	93,8	96,4
Civil Industry	1 129,9	1 142,1	1,1	1 154,3	1 196,4	3,6	24,4	54,3	102,2	104,8
1é. Divers	5,8	4,2	- 26,9	8,5	7,1	- 16,4	2,7	2,9	146,9	167,9
Total (Excluding military material)	1 392,4	1 423,7	2,3	1 405,6	1 454,4	3,5	13,2	30,7	101,0	102,2
Military material (in FAB-FAB data)	3,7	4,0	9,9	10,8	18,6	71,3	7,2	14,5	294,7	459,3
B. Clasification by geographic Zones										
European Union (EU) of which:	889,7	895,4	0,6	904,8	927,2	2,5	15,1	31,8	101,7	103,6
Germany	257,7	247,4	- 4,0	251,2	251,8	0,3	- 6,5	4,4	97,5	101,8
Denmark	12,4	12,5	1,1	12,7	13,2	4,0	0,4	0,7	102,9	105,9
Spain	90,0	98,2	9,1	103,6	115,6	11,6	13,6	17,4	115,2	117,7
Greece	3,1	3,0	- 2,7	10,8	11,6	7,3	7,8	8,6	352,6	389,0
Ireland	17,7	19,5	10,4	7,3	7,4	2,3	- 10,4	- 12,1	41,0	38,0
Italy	139,8	144,4	3,3	137,5	135,3	- 1,5	- 2,4	- 9,1	98,3	93,7

---

463   See Official website of the French Ministry of Foreign Affaires found at
      http://www.france.diplomatie.fr/france/fr/politiq/11_2.html

Netherlands	75,8	74,1	- 2,3	66,9	66,8	- 0,2	- 8,9	- 7,3	88,3	90,1
Portugal	15,7	16,4	4,8	20,0	20,0	0,2	4,3	3,6	127,2	121,7
United kingdom	110,5	118,6	7,3	131,9	137,6	4,3	21,4	19,0	119,3	116,0
UEBl	124,3	119,7	- 3,7	122,2	124,1	1,5	- 2,1	4,4	98,3	103,7
OCDE outside the EU	238,9	242,9	1,7	203,3	214,4	5,4	- 35,5	- 28,5	85,1	88,3
United States of America	110,6	114,8	3,8	83,7	88,5	5,7	- 26,8	- 26,3	75,7	77,1
Japan	48,8	45,9	- 6,0	28,0	27,4	- 2,0	- 20,9	- 18,5	57,3	59,7
Switzerland	35,4	35,0	- 1,2	55,0	56,6	2,8	19,6	21,6	155,5	161,8
Asian Countries with rapidly developing economies.	79,3	87,2	10.0	87,0	83,4	- 4,2	7,7	- 3,8	109,7	95,6
Middle East	28,7	30.5	6,5	36,1	34,9	- 3,3	7,4	4,3	125,9	114,2
Africa	57,4	61,5	7,1	80,1	82,5	3,0	22,7	21,0	139,5	134,1
Eastern Countries	39,3	46,5	18,3	35,9	47,5	32,1	- 3,3	1,0	91,5	102,2
Rest of the World	59.2	59,7	0.9	58,4	64,6	10,6	- 0,8	4,9	98,7	108,1

- CAB/ FAB. Net Figure
- Figures are in billions of francs.
- Variations are in percentage.

Source: French Central Bank, "Annual Report of 1996", Official Website of the French Central Bank, document in pdf form, p.190.

A very important indicator of these worldwide investments and economic presence is the existence of French companies and affiliates in the world. In this respect, the number of French companies implanted worldwide is quite impressive (See Table 18 Below). According to the French Ministry of Foreign Affaires, this number amounts to 16000 companies employing around 2,6 million people.

Table 18: Stocks of Foreign Direct Investments compared to GDP

Country	On the 31 of December 2000		On the 31 of December 2001		Stocks/PIB
	Stocks of Foreign Direct Investments	Stocks/GDP	Stocks of Foreign Direct Investments	Stocks/GDP	Ratios in%
1.United States	1628,5	15,4	1841,7	16,1	9
2.United Kingdom	977,2	64,2	1027,1	62,9	3
3.Germany	514.0	25,3	573,4	27,7	7
4.BLEU^	519,0	193,5	562,0	203,6	1
5. France	478,3	33,7	555,4	38,0	4
6.Netherlands	330,7	82,2	373,4	87,1	2
7.Japan	299,2	6,2	343,0	7, 8	10
8.Canada	243,7	32,0	276,6	35,7	5
9. Spain	177,1	29,1	215,4	33,1	6
10.Italy	193,7	16,6	205,9	17,0	8

- Amounts are in billions of Euros.
- Ratios are in percentage.
- Belgium-Luxemburg Economic Union.

Source: French Central Bank Report, "Stocks of Foreign Direct Investments on the 31 December 2001", Official website of the French Central Bank, Document in pdf. Form with pagination, p.6

The geographic distribution of these companies and this economic existence is, nonetheless, not equal, however. On the top of the list of French investments abroad, there is the United States (1100 companies with 224000 employees), the United kingdom (1200 companies and 221000 employees), Spain (1000 companies and 218000 employees). Generally speaking, the European Union countries have the lion share of the French Foreign investments. In developing countries, Brazil occupies comes on top of the list of countries where French companies exist. However, the French existence in South America and in Africa did not very much develop during this period (1990-1996). On the other hand and during the same period French foreign investments increased in Asian emerging countries by 60% and by 57% in Eastern Europe and the ex-USSR countries[464]. The same trend seemed to exist in later years. In 2001, for instance, French foreign investments in the European Union countries represented the lion share of total French foreign investments with 40,9%. The French investments in the EU countries were second only to North America (23, 6%). For its part, South America had 9,6%, Eastern European countries and the Commonwealth of the Newly Independent States had 8,2%, Africa had 8,2, % Asia had 7,6%, and the Near and Middle East countries had only 2% of French foreign investments[465]. A detailed classification of the distribution of these investments is depicted in Table 19 below.

---

464   See Website of the French Ministry of Foreign Affaires.
465   See Central Bank of France Website

Table 19: Geographical Distribution of French Foreign Investments Worldwide as of 31 December 2001

Country	Proper Capital	Loans	Real Estate Investments	Total	Share
United States	94236	45007	885	140129	25,2
Belgium	63858	16956	1938	82752	14,9
United kingdom	45645	24788	421	70854	12, 8
Netherlands	29333	9963	320	39616	7,1
Canada	35847	2271	124	38242	6,9
Germany	18287	12298	713	31298	5,6
Switzerland	9900	10045	718	20663	3,7
Italy	11115	5913	157	17185	3,1
Spain	10901	3853	509	15263	2,7
Luxemburg	5036	4551	276	9863	1, 8
Japan	8685	241	0	8906	1,6
Poland	7554	1176	13	8744	1,6
Brazil	7066	1309	14	8389	1,5
Argentina	4886	652	15	5553	1,0
Sweden	2925	1818	29	4772	0,9
Irland	899	3268	5	4172	0,7
Singapour	3031	489	10	3510	0,6
Denmark	1149	1212	33	2394	0,4
Australia	1533	774	68	2375	0,4
China	1882	339	12	2233	0,4
Portugal	1439	624	90	2153	0,4
Czech Republic	1509	347	4	1861	0,3
Venzuela	41	1606	-	1647	0,3
Mexico	1038	504	16	1556	0,3
Morroco	1318	88	82	1488	0,3
Norway	780	852	14	1445	0,3
Hongary	1043	283	14	1339	0,2
Hong Kong	793	456	0	1249	0,2
Bermuda	789	455	0	1245	0,2
Gabon	342	822	-	1164	0,2
Turkey	851	130	15	996	0,2
South Korea	931	49	0	980	0,2
Austria	469	511	-	977	0,2
Kenya	813	102	0	915	0,2
Greece	557	109	39	701	0,1
Chlli	686	11	0	698	0,1
Roumania	564	110	4	679	0,1
Other countries	10948	32805	587	17539	3,0
Total	388653	159607	7105	555364	100,0

- Amounts are in billions of Euros.
- Ratios are in percentage

Source: French Central Bank, «*Le stock des investissements directs français à l'étranger au 31 décembre 2001* », Official Website of the french Central Bank, Document in Pdf. form with pagination, p.15.

According to the French Central Bank, French foreign direct investments have been increasing substantially since 1993 to reach € 388,7 billion at the end of

2001 against € 347,6 billion at the end of the year 2000[466] (See Graphic 3 below). Thus, the French investments abroad can be said to be a solid constituent of the strength of the French economy and, hence, are an important economic interest to take into consideration.

Graphic 3

Stocks of French Foreign Investments
From 31/12/1993-31/12/1994

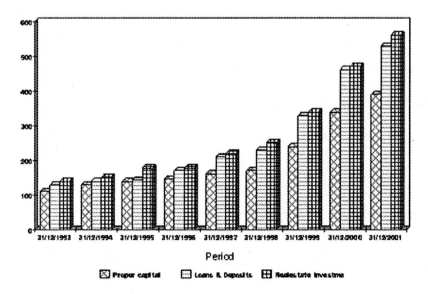

Period

◻ Proper capital   ◻ Loans & Deposits   ⊞ Realestate Investme

Source: French Central Bank Report," Stocks of Foreign Direct Investments on the 31 December 2001", Official website of the French Central Bank, Document in df. Form with pagination, p.7

The importance of foreign investments in France has also to be taken into consideration as being a pillar of the strength of the French economy and domestic social stability. According to recent figures, foreign companies amount to 10000 foreign financed companies mainly in the sectors of telecommunications, electronics, hotels and other commerce and services. Moreover, the principal

---

466   See French Central Bank »Le stock des investissements directs français à l'étranger au 31 décembre 2001 », official Website of the French Central Bank, Document in pdf. form, p.7.

investors in France are the United States followed by the United Kingdom, the Netherlands, Germany and Belgium. These, foreign investments in France, other than the immediate financial benefits they represent for the French economy, they also represent a social benefit for the French government, mainly in reducing the unemployment rate.

Table 20: Distribution of the Origin of Foreign Direct Investments in France by Country as of 31 December 2001.

Country	Proper capital	Loans	Real Estate Investments	Total	Share
Netherlands	40226	23803	2604	66674	20,3
United Kingdom	22349	23925	4872	51146	15,6
United States	34122	12193	1361	47676	14,5
Belgium	13747	24609	1613	39969	12,2
Germany	21420	10226	5676	37323	11,4
Switzerland	11è84	4088	5239	21111	6,4
Luxemburg	9809	3121	900	13831	4,2
Italy	9600	1348	2680	13826	4,1
Sweden	3865	1645	558	6068	1, 8
Spain	2448	2754	85	5287	1,6
Japan	1954	2459	818	5031	1,6
Irland	280	2992	143	3415	1,0
Denmark	2102	148	388	2538	0, 8
Finalnd	1792	223	76	2091	0,6
Norweg	953	652	132	1737	0,6
Canda	555	685	77	1297	0,4
Austria	507	322	95	924	0,3
United Arab Emirates	50	694	60	803	0,2
Portugal	88	487	23	578	0,2
Hong Kong	49	382	131	562	0,2
Russia	396	21	32	449	0,1
Saoudie Arabia	60	67	314	441	0,1
Australia	4	226	47	276	0,1
Other Countries	1514	2328	1150	4988	1,9
Total	179714	119354	28874	327943	100,0

- Amounts in millions of Euros.
- Shares are in %
- Accounting value.

Source: French Central Bank, «*Le stock des investissements directs étrangers en France au 31 décembre 2001*», Official Website of the French Central Bank, Document in Pdf. Form with pagination, p.12

Having all those economic indications in mind, the economic interests of France would certainly have a high priority in its foreign policy calculations and directions. Indeed, France has to be conscience of and sensitive to its economic interests worldwide in the conduct of its international relations. It has to be conscious first of its own economic investments in various regions, of the investments and economic benefits that certain regions have in France, and in the prospects for economic interests that some regions or countries present, or are likely to present in the future. Taking all this into consideration, it is, thus, useful to discuss now the French economic interests in the regions where the two crises took place.

For its part, Russia has always presented huge economic interests for various countries. For France, such a fact is not one to be ignored. According to an information report presented to the French National Assembly, this reality is quite evident. The report mentions that "Russia is not a country in transition like others. It offers uncommon perspectives compared to the rest of the Eastern Countries. According to Antoine Kuruneri-Millet, a specialist on Russian Commercial Law, the exceptional natural and humane resources make this region the biggest zone of economic development of the planet. This is also an opinion shared by the representatives of French and foreign companies working in Russia and interviewed in Moscow"[467]. The report goes on to state "The existence of French companies in Russia goes back in history to the Soviet era and even to the 19th century. The progress accomplished since the end of the Communist era and particularly since the accession to power of Vladimir Poutine have convinced the big groups to invest this new market and are now all present in the Russian Federation"[468] Yet, this opinion is not shared by everyone. Pascal Chaigneau, for instance, explains the situation of the Russian economy after the collapse of the Soviet Union. He states "In one year, the Russian exports fell from 63 to 51 billion dollars. Imports were divided by two: Today France sells more to Tunisia than to Russia..... The Russian economy has become today a Mafiosi one According to analysts, between 45 and 50% of the Russian economy is controlled by mafia networks. Additionally, it should be known that worst conditions will come still because, if Russia has inflation and even flirts with hyper-inflation, it still doesn't know unemployment[469]". Other opinions also contest the status of the Russian economy. Thierry Garcin, for his part, explains the degrading conditions of the inhabitants of the Russian Federations. He states, commenting on the failure of economic reforms in Russia," The discontentment does not stop growing: penury (rationing of coffee, of soap, of sugar, of alcohol, depriving paradoxically the state of taxes); rare housing (20% of Soviets lived in comminatory apartments), abandon of the retired, rise of organised criminality and of teenage delinquency, soar disaffection for work (high absenteeism, lost working days,

---

467 See Hervé Manton (Deputy), « l'implantation des entreprises françaises en Russie », Information Report N° 955 Presented to the French National Assembly, 1st July, 2003.

468 Idem.

469 Pascal Chaigneau, Les Grands Enjeux du Monde Contemporain, Ellipses, Paris,1996, p.20.

double or triple profession, loss of initiative). Forty to a hundred million people out of a population of two hundred eighty five million were considered by the State Committee for Work and Social Problems as being "poor", the average of salaries being two hundred francs at the end of the eighties[470]". The Russian economy might have, indeed, passed through a black period of its history. Nevertheless, the future prospects of investments in and with the Russian Federation cannot be denied, especially with the worldwide interest in the petrol and gas resources of the Caspian Basin.

The French economic presence and interest in the Russian Federation remain, hence, evident and can be easily indicated by facts and figures. Indeed, France occupies the 8th place of foreign investors in the Russian Federation, after the United States, the Netherlands, Cyprus, Germany, the United Kingdom, Japan, and Switzerland, and the 4th on the level of the European Union[471]. The amount of French Foreign Direct Investments in the Russian Federation in 2001 were € 46 million. This figure places the Russian Federation in the 50th position of countries receiving French Foreign Direct Investments. This represents a promotion in the status of the Russian Federation as a destination of French Foreign Direct Investments since the Russian Federation occupied the 194th position amongst world countries receiving French FDI's in 1999[472]. However, the stock of foreign investments also includes portfolio investments in addition to FDI's. Accordingly, the stocks of French investments (FDI &Portfolio) in the Russian Federation amounted to 649 million Euros in 2001 placing the Russian Federation at the 28th position of countries receiving French foreign investments[473]. In 2003, this figure amounted to € 3,7 billion[474]. As far as exports are concerned, France's share of the Russian market is 4,1% placing the Russian Federation as the 27th client of France worldwide, and the 2nd amongst Central and East European countries after Poland and before the Czech Republic, Hungary, and Romania. However, compared to Germany's market share (12, 9%) or the United States (7,9%), the position of France concerning its shares of the Russian market is the 8th amongst world countries after Germany, the United States, China and

---

470　See Thierry Garcin, _les Grands Questions Internationales depuis la chute du mur de Berlin_, Economica, Paris, 2001,p.37.

471　This fact is according to the Russian Federation Committee of State Statistics. Website found at http://www.gks.ru/eng/

472　French Economic Mission in Moscow. Website Found at http://www.dree.org/russie/infopays.asp

473　See French Economic Mission in Moscow, op. cit.

474　See Hervé Manton (Deputy), « _l'implantation des entreprises françaises en Russie_ » op. cit.

Italy[475]. Notwithstanding and concerning the flux of French FDI destined to the Russian Federation, it should be said that the amount of this FDI fell down from € 74 million to € 64 million in 2000. Indeed, it should be mentioned that the stock of French FDI destined to the Russian Federation is in constant regression since 1999 and that their level today is twice less than they were in 1997[476]. In addition to French FDI and portfolio investments, the presence of French companies operating in Russia is also important to mention. Those companies' number is currently around 400 companies, especially the big companies such as Total, Auchan, Renault and Michelin[477]. The domains of interest for the French companies in the Russian economy are many. As far as energy industry and energy-derived products' sectors are concerned, it is important to notice that the Russian Federation, other than the United States and OPEC, disposes of 45% of the world reserve of petrol. Indeed, Russia has become the first producer of petrol worldwide and before Saudi Arabia. It is interesting to notice, in this respect, that the French company Total was present in Russia since 1995 and in the year 2000, it became the first Western importer of Russian petrol[478]. As far as industry is concerned, the French automobile industry seems to be the most promising one. The French Renault occupies the 3rd place of foreign cars imported in Russia with 400000 cars sold in 2002. Equally, the French mark *Michelin* is the first importer of tires in Russia[479]. In the pharmaceutical products sector, the French companies are the number one providers in Russia occupying, in this field, the first place before Germany and India[480]. In the agro-alimentary industry, French companies and their subsidiaries' share is 10% in 2003[481]. As far as commercial services are concerned, 24 branches of French companies operate in Russia such as *Société General, BNP-Paribas, Credit Lyonnais,* which contribute to the financing various sectors of the Russian economy[482].

On the other hand and as far as the Russian investments in France are concerned, it should be mentioned that these investments are certainly not negligible. According to the French Central Bank statistics shown in table 26 above, the share of Russia in Foreign Direct Investments destined to France as of the 31st of December 2001 is 0.1%. The total of Russian FDIs in France amounted, accordingly, to € 449 million

---

475   Idem.

476   See French Economic Mission, op. cit.

477   See Hervé Manton, op. cit.

478   Idem.

479   See French Economic Mission in Moscow, op. cit.

480   See Hervé Manton, op. cit.

481   See Les Echos, 13 June 2003.

482   See Hervé Manton, op. cit.

of which € 32 million represented investments in Real Estate, € 21 million in loans, and € 396 million in proper capital FDI investments.

The economic environment in the ex-Yugoslavia was not at all as promising as it was in Russia. In fact, the major contributor to the economy in this region is the agricultural sector, which represents 22% of the GNP[483]. In the year 2000, the total value of exports reached 1723 million dollars (15% more than in 1999 and 40% less than in 1998) while imports were valued at US $ 3711 million (12,6% more than in 1999 but 23,5% less than in 1998) Moreover, inflation reached 115,3% in 2000. The GDP of 2000 was only 40% of that of 1990 and 40% of that of 1996[484].Another problem that has to do with the Yugoslav economy is the amount of the exterior debt. It is estimated that this amount was US$13,5 billion in the year 2000[485]. The conditions of war and the embargo imposed on ex-Yugoslavia by the United Nations since the 31st of May 1992 have rendered the flux of foreign investments in the region quite hazardous. In this respect, and according to the United Nations Conference on Trade and Development (UNCTAD), the stock of FDI destined for the main regions of the former Yugoslavia (Serbia & Montenegro, Bosnia-Herzegovina, Croatia is quite insignificant compared to the investments in the Russian Federation (See Table 21 below & Graphic 4).

Table 21: Total Stock of FDI Flows in the main ex-Yugoslavia Successor States compared to that of the Russian Federation.

Year	Serbia & Montenegro	Croatia	Bosnia- Herzegovina	The Russian Federation
1995	329	478	20	5465
1997	740	550, 7	1,0	4865,0
1998	113	1013,6	54,6	2761,3
1999	112	1635,2	148,8	3309,0
2000	25	1126.8	131,5	2714,0
2001	165	1442.1	164,0	2540,0
Total	1462	6232,2	519,9	21654,3

- Amounts in millions of $ dollars.
- The figures of the French Economic Mission in Belgrade, however, puts the amount of flow of FDI in 2001 at 164 million $.

Source: UNCTAD document "Foreign Direct Investment inflows, in individual countries, website of UNCTAD.

---

483   Se French Economic Mission in Serbia & Montenegro, Website found at http://www.france.org.yu.
484   Idem. Note: These figures are for the Serbia and Montenegro.
485   Idem.

Indeed, the total amount of FDIs destined to the three main ex-Yugoslav successor republics over the period 1995-2001 amounts to US$ 6234,1 million, which is less than half of the FDI destined to the Russian Federation over the same period of time (US$ 21654,3 million).

Graphic 4

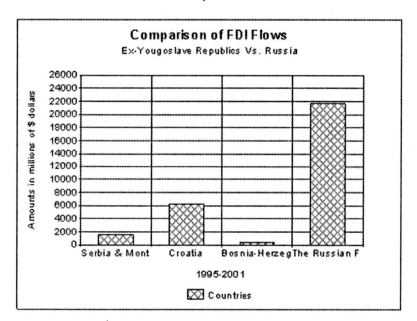

For its part, the total of French FDI investments in these republics of the ex-Yugoslavia is quite modest. Statistics on their amount indicate a modest some of € 40 million in 2002. This modest investment is moreover not a sudden economic rediscovery of the benefits of investments in this region. In fact, it is merely attributed to the continuation of the presence of a number of French companies that used to operate in Serbia and Montenegro before 1990 and continued their existence afterwards[486]. The number of French companies working there is also modest. They include companies that existed before such as *Société Génerale*, *AlCATEL* and *BULL*. They also include representative offices of French companies such as Air France and ALSTOM[487]. It Should be noted, in this

---

486   See French Economic Mission in Belgrade, « *Investissements directs étrangers et présence française en RFY* », 18 October 2002, p.3.
487   Idem.

respect, that the major investors in Serbia and Montenegro are Italy, Greece, and Germany[488]. As far as commercial exchange is concerned, France exported merchandise with the value of € 73 million in 2001 and € 95 million in 2002 to the ex-Yugoslav republic. This increase made France progress from the 11th to the 6th position as a worldwide supplier of the republic and in the 3rd position amongst European Union member states. As far as market share is concerned, France had 2, 97% of the ex-Yugoslav republic market in 2002. For its par, Serbia and Montenegro progressed in 2002 to become the 88th client of France from its former position as the 95th client in 2001. French imports from the ex Yugoslav republic passed from € 29 million in 2001 to € 35 million in 2002 with Serbia and Montenegro providing for 0,02 of the French market needs of imports[489]. For its part, the case of Croatia is not different from that of Serbia and Montenegro. The principal investors in this republic are Austria (24,68%) and Germany (21,95%). The United States investments are mostly portfolio ones ((16,87%) while that of France never passed the barrier of 1, % of the share of FDI stock with US$ 92.5 million only from 1993-2003[490]. As for French companies' presence in this republic, their number doesn't exceed 30. They include amongst others companies such as *Renault, Peugeot, Citroën, l'Oréal, Danone, Publicis, Rhodia.* and representative offices such as *(Strafor-Steelcase, Air-France, AFP...etc[491].* The figures for Bosnia-Herzegovina not being available, the share of that republic of French investments and trade should not be expected to exceed any of the other two ex-Yugoslav ones.

It seems, thus, that the Russian Federation represented to France much more in terms of present and future economic interests than the agrarian based former Yugoslavia economy. The comparison of the amounts of French FDI stocks and portfolio investments, in addition to the commercial exchange balance and the implantation of French companies in the two cases reveals that France has much more economic interests to consider in its relations with the Russian Federation than in its relations to former Yugoslavia and its successor republics.

As far as it is concerned, the United States' economic might is a well-known fact. It is the world's leading economic power. Moreover, this economic might did not cease to increase (See Table 22 below for indicators of the economic might of the United States). The United States' economy is also a very diversified one. For

---

488   Ibid., p.2.

489   See French Economic Mission in Belgrade, « Les échanges bilatéraux entre la France et la RFY au cours du premier semestre 2002 », 1 Octobre 2002, p.1.

490   See French Economic Mission in Zagreb, « *Investissements Directs Etrangers et présence française en Croatie (1 er semestre 2003)* », 16 October 2003, p.1

491   Ibid, p. 2.

instance, the manufacturing sector of the economy accounted for 17% of the United States' GDP in 2001 while services accounted for 80%. Indeed, if it was not for oil needs, the United States' economy would have been self-sufficient in almost all raw materials[492].

Table 22: United States' Economic Indicators 1997-2001

Indicator	Period				
	1997	1998	1999	2000	2001
GDP at market prices (US$ bn)	8,318.4	8,781.5	9,268.6	9,872.9	10,208.1
Real GDP growth (%)	4.4	4.3	4.1	4.1	1.2
Consumer price inflation (av; %)	2.3	1.6	2.2	3.4	2.8
Population (m)	272.5	275.7	278.9	281.8	284.4
Exports of goods fob (US$ bn)	681.7	672.4	686.9	774.9	723.8
Imports of goods fob (US$ bn)	-876.4	-917.1	-1,030.0	-1,224.4	-1,147.5
Current-account balance (US$ bn)	-140.5	-217.4	-324.4	-444.7	-417.4
Foreign-exchange reserves excl gold ($ bn; year-end)	58.9	70.7	60.5	56.6	57.6
Nominal effective exchange rate (1995=100)	113.8	119.3	116.4	121.1	130.8

Source: **Economist Intelligence Unit, Economist Website at www.economist.com**

In 2001, for example, the United States' GDP amounted to US $10, 2 trillion which was almost three times that of Japan, five times that of Germany, and seven times that of the UK[493]. To have a better idea about the United States' economy compared to other world economies see Table 23 and Graphic 5 below.

Table 23: Comparative Economic Indicators between the United States' and other Major World Economies in 2001.

Indicator	Country				
	United States	Japan	UK	Canada	Mexico
GDP (US$ bn)	10,208.1	4,147.8	1,424.1	699.5	621.0
GDP per head (US$)	35,900.0	32,775.8	23,831.8	22,733.7	6,186.8
Consumer price inflation (av; %)	2.8	-0.7	1.2	2.6	6.4
Current-account balance (US$ bn) (a)	-417.4	87.8	-23.5	18.9	-17.5
Current-account balance (% of GDP)	-4.1	2.1	-1.6	2.7	-2.8
Exports of goods fob (US$ bn)	723.8	383.3	275.3	266.6	158.5
Imports of goods fob (US$ bn)	1,147.5	313.0	322.9	226.7	168.3
(a) IMF data, which may differ slightly from national sources.					

Source: **Economist Intelligence Unit, op. cit.**

---

492 See The Economist's Country Profile found at
      http://www.economist.com/countries/USA
493 Idem.

Graphic 5

United States' Vs Other World Powers

GDP Comparison in 2001

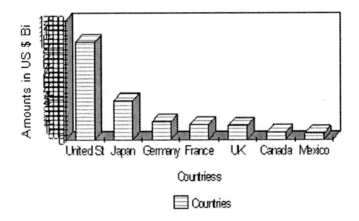

The place of foreign trade and foreign direct investments is certainly not less, in the United States' economy than it is for France's economy. Indeed, the realisation of the importance of inward and outward FDI and its share of the GDP is a worldwide economic phenomenon. The increase in the importance of FDIs is the rise in their amounts worldwide. Indeed, the flows of FDI witnessed a worldwide increase of 17% in 1997 and another 10% amounting to US$ 440 billion in 1998[494]. The FDI operations were embodied in the operations of 50,000 parent and 450,000 affiliates that operated worldwide in the same year[495]. The share of the operations of these affiliates in the world GDP also increased from 2% in 1982 to 6% in 1998[496].

As far as the United States' FDI is concerned, the first remark on this FDI's importance to the United States' economy can be seen in the nature of the relationship between foreign trade and FDI for the United States as compared to France. In

---

494   See, "World Investment Report: Trends and Determinants", <u>UNCTAD,</u> Geneva, 1998.

495   Idem.

496   See Lionel Fontagné and Michaël Pajot, "Foreign Trade and FDI Stocks in British, US and French Industries: Complements or Substitutes? ", Online document with pagination in pdf form found at <u>http://team.univ-paris1.fr/trombi/fontagne/papers/ichapterpain.pdf</u>, p.2.

the case of France, there is no evidence that there is a complementary relationship between outward FDIs and exports. On the other hand, inward FDIs in France's case have a complementary relationship with inward trade, which means that countries, which trade more with France invest more in France than others[497]. The case of the United States is different. As far as outward FDIs are concerned, there is a "one to one" complementary relationship with the United States trade. For instance, in the industry sector, for every US$ 1 invested abroad there is a US$ 1 of exports. As far as the United States' inward FDI, there is no evidence on it having a complementary relationship with U.S. exports. This means that "the huge US market attracts foreign investors and there is low chance that foreign countries invest in the US in order to ship products back home"[498]. The growth of inward and outward FDI flows and stocks and their growing share in the country's 'GDP over the 1990 and up to 2002 is quite remarkable (See Table 24 below).

Table 24: United States' Inward & Outward FDI Flows, Stocks, and Percentage of GDP.

FDI Flows	Year					
	1985-1995	1998	1999	2000	2001	2002
Inward	44,434	174,434	283,376	314,007	143,978	30,030
Outward	42,571	131,004	209,391	142,626	103,764	119,741
FDI Stocks	Year					
	1980	1990	1995	2000	2001	2002
Inward	83 046	394 911	535 553	1 214 254	1 321 063	1 351 093
Outward	215 375	430 521	699 015	1 293 431	1 381 674	1 501 415
FDI Stocks as % of DGP	Year					
	1980	1990	1995	2000	2001	2002
Inward	3.0	6.9	-*	12.4	13.1	12.9
Outward	7.8	7.5	-	13.2	13.7	14.4
* Data for 1995 was not available.						

Source: UNCTAD Division on Investment, Technology and Enterprise Development

More than it was the case of France, the United States' economic interests in Europe, where the Balkan region is, are quite vital for its economy. Indeed, the United States' relationship with the European Union as a whole has bypassed the importance and volume of economic relations between members of the EU themselves. An interesting fact-sheet published by the European Union on the occasion of the EU-US Summit held in Washington, on the 25th of June 2003, mentions some interesting facts about the extent of this strong economic relationship between the EU and the United States. The fact-sheet states" The

---

497   Ibid., p.17
498   Ibid., p.19

economies of the European Union and of the United States are becoming more intertwined and interdependent. Particularly over the last decade, this far-reaching and powerful momentum has driven our economies ever further towards the creation of an open and integrated transatlantic marketplace. Businesses on both sides of the Atlantic now invest and produce overseas much more than they export from their national borders"[499]. This vital transatlantic economic relationship is manifested in a number of significant economic indicators. The European Union and the United States are, by far, the world's international trade leaders. Together they accounted in 2002 for 37% of the world merchandise trade and in 45% of the world's trade in services. Furthermore, together the EU and the United States are the most important source and destination of FDIs. In 2000, the two accounted for 54% of the total world FDI inflows and 67% of the worlds FDI outflows[500]. As far as the bilateral economic exchanges in trade between the two, it is interesting to note that the EU and the United States are in fact each other's single largest trading partners and each other's most important destination and source of FDI. The volume of these trade exchanges has not ceased to increase over the years, especially in trade in services. For example, in 1988, total bilateral trade in services between the two represented 33% of each other's single exterior trade volume (goods and services). In 2000, Trade in services between the US and the EU amounted to 36% of total trade between the two, and in 2001, this ratio increased to 39% of total trade of the EU, and 35 % of total trade of the US[501]. As far as trade in goods in concerned, it its interesting to note that the EU and the United States each accounted in 2002 for 21% of each other's trade in goods. Indeed, the bilateral cross-border trade in goods and services (exports and imports) between the two was around € 650 billion in 2002 (€ 412 billion in trade of goods and € 238 billion in trade of services)[502]. This strategic transatlantic economic relationship between he United States and the European Union is also manifested in the status of the investment relationship between he two. Indeed, the EU and the US have "the world's most important bilateral investment relationship" and, in fact, "each other's most important source and destination for FDI"[503]. There are of course some interesting figures that support this statement and, indeed, the growing importance of this strategic economic relationship. As

---

499   See "EU-US Bilateral Economic Relations", European Union, Washington, 25 June 2003, online document with pagination in pdf form found at http://europa.eu.int/comm/external_relations/us/sum06_03/eco.pdf, p.1

500   Idem.

501   Idem.

502   Idem.

503   Idem.

far as FDI flows are concerned, it is interesting to note that in the 1990s, almost three quarters of the foreign investment in the United States (US$659 billion) originated from Europe. Later on, the United States, between 1998-2001, was the destination of 52% of the EU's outward FDI flows. In the same period, the US was the source of 61% of inward FDI flows in the EU[504]. As for FDI stocks as an indicator of the importance of this strategic economic relationship, the EU fact sheet gives some valuable indictors on the importance of these FDI stocks, the complementarily, and the increase in importance of this bilateral investment ties, over the past decade. The paper states" By 2001, cross investment stocks between the EU and the U.S. reached (on a historical cost basis) € 1500 billion— by far the largest investment relationship in the world. EU investment in the U.S., on a historical-cost basis, reached €870 billion, and the U.S. investment position in the EU grew to €628 billion. Therefore the U.S. is by far the largest investor in the EU (accounting for 62% of total EU liabilities), while the EU is by far the biggest investor in the U.S. (accounting for 61% of total U.S. FDI stock by 2001). At the same time the bulk (46%) of U.S. investment assets abroad is located in the EU, and 50% of EU FDI stock is located in the U.S. Bilateral direct investment stocks have also been growing very quickly over the past decade, almost tripling between 1997 and 2001"[505].

It is interesting to note, however, that the distribution of the United States' FDI flows towards Europe is not equal. For instance, the United States' assets in the United Kingdom is greater than its assets in Asia, Africa, and the Middle East combined. Moreover, during the 1990s, the United States' investments in the United Kingdom amounted to US$175 billion, which is 50% higher than its total investments in the entire Asia Pacific region[506]. This fact, however, could suggest a geographic distribution of investments based on political relationships and alliances with countries. The third indicator of these strong economic ties between the United States and the European Union has to do with employment opportunities and affiliate and parent companies localisation in both. Indeed, for many European companies, the United States' market is that which represents the highest earnings in the world. For their part, the United States' affiliate companies' earnings from working in Europe increased five fold in the 1990s to reach US$26 billion[507]. Affiliate companies also represent employment. Directly, United States' affiliates employed around 4.1 million persons in Europe in 2000 and, indirectly, backed through U.S. investments the employment of 6 million in

---

504   Ibid., p.2
505   Idem.
506   Idem.
507   Ibid., p.3

the same year[508]. For their part, and in the same year, European companies' affiliates in the United States' employed 4,4 million and, indirectly, supported by European investment the employment of another 7 million United States' citizens[509]. Hence, the United States' economic ties with the European Union is a highly strategic one and one that has not ceased to increase in volume and importance all through the past decade. It can be said, thus, that for the United States, the European region is placed high on its list of priorities of national economic interests. Europe is a viable economic partner that if strong economically can substitute the need for other economic blocs with which the United States does not share any ideological or cultural binds, like china for instance, as economic partners. This is a view of the economic interests of the United States' with Europe as one economic bloc and more importantly as a stable one. It is useful at this stage to discuss the economic interests of the United States in the Balkans only as compared to its economic interests in the Russian Federation.

As far as Bosnia is concerned, the United States exports to the country represented US$ 59 millions in 1996, US$103 million in 1997, US$ 40 millions in 1998, US$ 44 millions in 1999[510], US$44.13 million in 2000, US$ 43.1 million in 2001, and US$ 31.67 million in 2002. On the other hand, the United States' imports from Bosnia amounted to US$ 10 million in 1996, US$ 8 millions in 1997, US$ 7 million in1998, US$ 15 in 1999[511], and US$17.81 millions in 2000, US$11.88 million in 2001, and US$ 15.53 million in 2002[512] (for a detailed data of the U.S. Trade Relations with some of the successor states of the ex-Yugoslavia see Table 25 below). For its part, Serbia and Montenegro received US$ 30.05 millions worth of United States' exports in 2000, US$ 55.19 millions in 2001, and US$ 78.13 million in 2002. Serbia and Montenegro exported $US 2.27 millions' worth of good to the United States in 2000, US$ 5.89 million in 2001, and US$9.57 millions' worth in 2002[513]. The top foreign investors in the country in 2001 were the United States and Austria followed by France[514]. As for Croatia, the United States exported US$ 89.86 millions worth to Croatia in 2000,

508   Idem.
509   Idem.
510   See the United States' International Trade Administration Website found at http://www.ita.doc.gov/
511   Idem.
512   See Central and Eastern Europe Business Information Centre (CEEBIC), United States Department of Commerce website found at http://www.mac.doc.gov/ceebic/countryr/bosniah.htm
513   Idem.
514   See Serbian Investment and Export Promotion Agency

US$ 109.54 millions in 2001, and US $ 78.15 millions in 2002. On the other hand, the Croatian exports to the United States amounted to US$ 140.99 million in 2000, US$ 139.02 million in 2001, and US$ 145.62 million in 2002[515]. The top foreign inventors in Croatia, furthermore, were Germany and Austria. The United States only came in the third place with US$ 1,189 millions in 2001.[516]

Table 25: United States' Trade Relations with Bosnia-Herzegovina, Serbia and Montenegro, and Croatia (1996-2001) in millions of US$.

Country	Bosnia - Herzegovina		Serbia and Montenegro		Croatia	
Year	US Exports	US Imports	US Exports	US Imports	US Exports	US Imports
1996	59	10	46	8	106	71
1997	103	8	49	10	139	83
1998	40	7	74	13	97	73
1999	44	15	59	5	108	110
2000	44,13	17,81	30,05	2,27	89,86	140,99
2001	43,1	11,88	55,19	5,89	109,54	139, 02
2002	31,67	15,53	78,13	9,57	78,15	145,62
Total	364,9	85, 22	391,37	53,73	727,55	762,63
Total US exports for the three countries	1483, 82			Total US Imports		901,58

For its part, the United States economic relationship with the Russian Federation is much more voluminous. The huge energy prospects of the Russian Federation is perhaps the number one reason explaining the importance of the United States economic interests in this country. Indeed, in 2002, the Russian Federation occupied the number one place in the world oil and gas producing countries with over.6 million barrels of oil and 598 billion cubic meters of natural gas produced per day[517]. What is interesting to note at this point is that "ever since U.S. energy companies entered Russia in the early 1990s, they have been urging the Russian government to create a basis for concluding Production Sharing Agreements (PSA's) that would allow companies to undertake long-term, risky investments in Russia's more remote and technically difficult oil fields"[518]. Those economic interests of the United States in Russia are manifested in a number of economic indicators such as bilateral trade and the flows and stocks of FDI status between he two countries.

---

515   See Central and Eastern Europe Business Information Centre, op. cit.
516   See Croatian National Bank Webite.
517   See United States Department of Commerce report on the U.S. Oil and Gas Mission to Russia page found at http://www.osec.doc.gov/obl/russiamission2003/
518   Idem.

The difference in the trade volume between the United States' economic relations with the Russian Federation and its relations with the ex-Yugoslavia successor states is enormous. In 1996, the United States exported to Russia US$ 3346 millions worth of goods and services (more than double the volume of its exports to the Croatia, Bosnia, and Serbia-Montenegro combined over the period 1996-2002), US$ 3365 million in 1997, US$ 3553 million in 1998, US$ 2060 million in 1999, US$ 2092 million in 2000, US$ 2716 millions in 2001, and US$ 2399 millions in 2002[519]. On the other hand, the United States imported US$ 3577 millions worth from Russia in 1996, US$ 4319 million in 1997, US$ 5747 million in 1998, US$5921 million in 1999, US$7659 million in 2000, US$6264 million in 2001, and US$ 6825 million in 2002. The total of U.S. export to the Russian Federation during the period 1996-2002 amounts to US$ 19 billions and 531 millions. The to total of imports from the Russian Federation for the same period was higher and amounted to US$ 40 billion and 312 millions. Indeed, A report of the Business Information Services for the newly Independent States on US-Russian bilateral trade mentions "Russia is the U.S.' leading trading partner in the NIS, capturing nearly 80 percent of our trade with the NIS countries. Russia also provides more products to the United States than all Central and Eastern European countries combined" yet that wit all this, Russia only accounts "for less than 1 percent of total U.S. trade worldwide"[520]. Nonetheless, The difference between the economic trade interests of the United States in the Russian Federation as opposed to the successor states of the ex-Yugoslavia republics is quite evident. (See graphic 6).

---

519   See The United States' International Trade Administration Website, op. cit.
520   see the Business Information Services for the Newly Independent States Website found at http://www.bisnis.doc.gov/bisnis/bisnis.cfm

Graphic 6

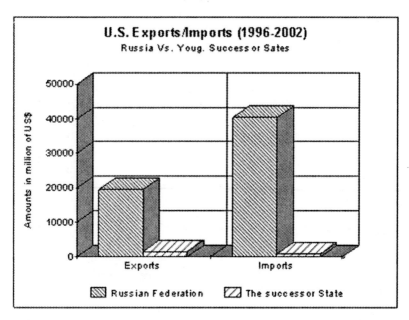

U.S. Exports/Imports (1996-2002)
Russia Vs. Youg. Successor Sates

Amounts in million of US$

Russian Federation   The successor State

Another indicator of the United States economic interests in Russia as opposed to the successor states of the ex-Yugoslavia has to do with the number of U.S. affiliate companies in the two regions. The difference between the two regions as far as the U.S. affiliate companies are concerned its quite evident, as it was the case in the evident difference in the U.S. trade interests with the two. In 2000, for example, the number of U.S. affiliate companies working in Russia amounted to 119 affiliates, with a total of US$ 6212 million of assets. On the other hand, in the same year, there was 2 affiliates in Bosnia-Herzegovina, 4 in Croatia, and only one in Serbia and Montenegro[521]. As for the U.S. FDI, available records of the United States Bureau of Economic Analysis (BEA) indicate that the total of U.S. FDI flows to the whole of Eastern Europe (Albania, Armenia, Azerbaijan, Belarus, Bulgaria, Czech Republic, Estonia, Georgia, Hungary, Kazakhstan, Kyrgyzstan, Latvia, Lithuania, Moldova, Poland, Romania, Russia, Slovakia, Tajikistan, Turkmenistan, Ukraine, and Uzbekistan) was quite insignificant compared to the U.S. FDI flows to the European Union, the Asia Pacific Region, or the for example, Canada alone(See Table 26 below).

---

521   See United States Bureau of Economic Analysis at <u>www.bea.gov.</u>

Table 26: U.S. Direct Investment Abroad Capital Outflows by Selected Regions (1994-2002) by millions of US$.

Region	Year								
	1994	1995	1996	1997	1998	1999	2000	2001	2002
Canada	6047	8602	7181	7642	7832	22824	16899	15510	12893
Latin America & Some Western Hemisphere countries	17710	16040	18138	21539	16699	44658	23212	26152	8610
Africa	762	352	1678	3436	3075	596	716	1120	861
Middle East	709	879	467	619	2092	1000	1375	1585	1837
Asia & the Pacific Region	13437	14342	15363	13733	14715	30831	22449	14680	28779
European Union	29762	48835	36182	46910	75771	97815	70625	39625	55553
Eastern Europe	1444	1112	1508	1330	1797	3315	-717	107	2116

As indicated in the table above, the U.S. FDI flows into the entire region of Eastern Europe is quite insignificant compared even to Canada alone. Moreover, Africa, for instance, received more U.S. FDI in 1997 and 1998 more than double the amount of FDI destined to Eastern Europe. Russia itself is the destination is of modest portion of this U.S. FDI. In 1999, for example, it received US$ 296 million of U.S. FDI flow out of the US$ 3315 millions destined for the whole of Eastern Europe[522]. The geographic distribution of these FDI flows indicates a number of conclusions concerning the basis of their geographic distribution. The first of those conclusions is that FDI flows are related, other than to the economic favourable conditions, legislations and opportunities, to the political stability of the region. This is evident from the case of the Middle East, for example, which received less than all of the other regions. Political instability can also justify the low FDI flow in Africa and, to some extent, Russia as well. The second of those conclusions is that geographic proximity is an important determinant of foreign investment flows. This can be seen in the case of Canada and Latin America. The third conclusion that can be made is that cultural and political affinities considerably count as a determinant of FDI flows. This is shown in the case of the European Union. Other than the drops in flows in 1996 and 2001 (See Graphic 7 below), the U.S. FDI flows to the European Union continued to surge making the EU, by a huge margin, the number one destination of U.S. investments worldwide. The EU is geographically not close to the United States as Latin America but it is stable, democratic, and culturally close to the United States.

---

522   Idem.

Graphic 7

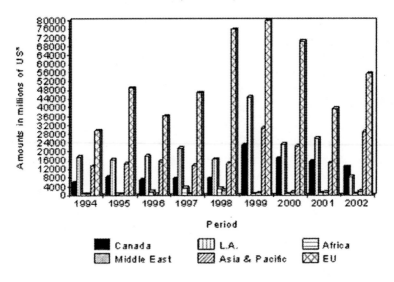

U.S. FDI Outflows by Selected Regions
(1994-2002)

Concerning on the economic interests that France and the United States each have in the crisis in Bosnia and that of Chechnya, it is important to first note that economic interests are not only calculated at present, but as a possible future prospect as well. Indeed, a country that conduct its foreign policy wisely would always guard against risking its economic interests in the future in a certain region and not simply at the present time. For both France and the United States, it is certain from the aforementioned comparisons and evidence that their economic interests with Russia, and the future prospects of those interests especially concerning energy exploitations, is much higher than their economic interests or the future prospects of these economic interests in the Balkans. Nonetheless, for both, lack of stability in the Balkans threatened their long-term economic interests. It risked those of France because of its economic interests with the rest of Europe and not simply with the Balkans. It threatened much more the long-term economic interests of the United States. Indeed, the number one economic partner for the United States is the European Union and any lack of stability caused by the contamination of the Balkans' conflict of the rest of the continent would have threatened to deprive Washington of its most precious and viable economic partner.

2.2.3. Political Interests.

Vis-à-vis the crisis in both Bosnia and Chechnya, both France and the United States had to take into consideration their respective national political interests. The estimation of the national political interests of both countries depends on various considerations such as their position as a major regional and world powers, their security needs, their relations with other major regional and world powers interested in both crisis, and their status as major world powers with a desire to project their importance on the international scene.

As far as it its concerned, it can be said that the Treaty of Maastricht[523] constituted an important objective of the majority of French politicians. Indeed, the success of France with this treaty is the realisation of a desired vision of European integration that would help prevent further conflicts in the European, contain Germany, and create an economic block capable of rivalling with other major powers, notably with the economic might of the United States. With the success of reaching the Treaty of Maastricht, French politicians can be said to have regained confidence in France's role as a major and active European and world actor. This success also meant that a coherent Europe would be more able to assume its role as a major actor on the international scene. However, this French ambition to be the instigator of the creation of a new world power which, might dispute the post-Cold War supremacy of the United States, was soon to be tested with the disintegration of former Yugoslavia, and especially with the turbulent events of the crisis in Bosnia (15/10/1991-21/11/1995). Two facts to highlight the importance of the crisis in Bosnia for France should be mentioned. The first

---

523 The Treaty on European Union (TEU), or Maastricht Treaty, is a key axis for the achievement of the European Union. It modifies the Treaty of Paris, the Treaties of Rome and the Single European Act, and officially establishes the name European Union in substitution of the European Community. This Treaty was signed on February the 7th,1992 in the Dutch city of Maastricht and entered in force on November the 1st,1993, giving a new dimension to the process of the European integration. If there is a fundamental point for which the TEU is remembered, it is for starting the process towards monetary union, The Treaty also included two intergovernmental pillars: Common Foreign & Security Policy (CFSP): it permits the undertaking of common actions in the area of Foreign Policy, the European Council who defines their general principles. Justice and Home Affairs (JHA): it handles subjects of vital importance for every one of the member states such as terrorism, drugs trafficking, customs, judicial cooperation, illegal immigration, internal crime or asylum policy. Europol, keystone for a future European Police force, was created within the ambit of the JHA.

one is that the region where the conflict was taking place was as far as two hours flight from Paris. Thus, the element of geographic proximity is important in this case. The second fact that indicates the level of French political interest in the settlement of the crisis is that the signature of the Dayton Accords took place in Paris on the 14th of December 1995. Another important fact, which is not directly related to this case but would help understand more the importance of the stability inn the Balkans for France is the signature of the Rambouillet Accords on the 6-19 of February, 1999, concerning the Kosovo conflict. Indeed, the Contact group (Foreign Affaires Ministers of the United States, Germany, France, the United Kingdom, Italy and Russia) decided to impose a diplomatic solution on the two conflicting parties of the Kosovo crisis. The Conference of Rambouillet took place on the 6th of February 1999. The negotiations conducted in Rambouillet are followed by the Conference of Paris on the Kosovo crisis, on the 15th of March 1999. The choice of France as a venue for all these diplomatic negotiations and manoeuvres highlights, hence, the political importance France holds for the Balkans.

Indeed, the disintegration of Yugoslavia and the ensuing conflicts can be said to have reinforced the French conviction that its autonomy is the best strategy to guarantee its security and also that the European Community needed a European military instrument to guarantee the collective security of the continent. In the summer of 1991, and when the fighting started in Slovenia and then Croatia, the need for effective security provisions in the Maastricht Treaty seemed to be more necessary than ever.

The conflict in the Balkans, however, not only interested European states but had the advantage of also drawing the interest of geographically distant non-European powers. Hall Gardner explains the conflictual nature of the conflicts in the former Yugoslavia on the international scene. He states" The fact that Yugoslavia was at the geo-strategic crossroads between the interests of the United States, Germany (and Europe), Russia, Turkey, Ukraine, the Middle Eastern states, and Iran should have indicated that the present conflict could have been defused only by a truly concerted approach from the outset"[524]. Gardner goes on to describe the state of international support for various parties of the former Yugoslavia conflicts. He states" American interests were directly involved due to the NATO membership of Greece and Turkey. Russian interests were involved because of historical links to Serbia. Germany had historical influence in Croatia, while Turkey, Iran, and Saudi Arabia had interests to support in Bosnia. At the same time, these international linkages tended to be conflictual and contradictory.

---

524   See Hall Gardner, <u>Dangerous Crossroads: Europe, Russia, and the Future of NATO</u>, Praeger Publishers, Westport, CT, 1997, p. 75.

For example, Greece supported Serbia, while Turkey supported Bosnia. As the conflict escalated, a partial rift developed within the EU itself: Germany took a pro-Croatian tilt; while the UK and France sought intermediate ground between Croatia and Serbia. Russia supported Serbia, but did not necessarily support Bosnian Serbs. The United States backed Bosnian Moslems, but attempted to bring Bosnian Moslems and Croatians into an alliance (despite their own bitter animosities) against Bosnian Serbs backed by Serbia"[525]. Parallel to the escalation of the conflict in former Yugoslavia, there was a trial of various aspects of collective security approaches for the European continent. Such approaches are represented in the fact that notions such as concerted diplomacy (the formation of the Contact Group in April 1994) and war preventive diplomacy (the UN Preventive Deployment Force UNPREDEP) in the Former Yugoslav Republic of Macedonia were soon to be tested in former Yugoslavia.

The least that can be said about the crisis in Bosnia is that it helped to spotlight major differences of points of view between the sole winner of the Cold War (the United States) and Europe. Richard N. Haass states in this respect "The break-up of Yugoslavia presented a different kind of challenge-more a source (and a reflection) of transatlantic friction than a successful experience. In Europe but "out-of-area" from NATO's perspective, Bosnia was a venue where for years the United States and Europe were unable to concert either their diplomacy or the use of military force. (The American inclination to avoid entanglement and hand responsibility for Bosnia to a Europe that proved unable and unwilling to take it on only made matters worse)[526]". This discordance of view between the United States and Europe on managing the conflict in Bosnia is also supported by Michael Brenner and Jonathan Dean who explain these differences by the historical experiences of both Europe and the United States more than by the element of geographic proximity. They state "European governments have priority scales that are not exactly the same as Washington's: they weigh factors in the equation differently or disagree over the means for achieving agreed objectives. They also have strikingly different styles of conflict management, as was most apparent in Bosnia and the Gulf. Are they a matter of geography or philosophy? Both—with philosophical differences emerging from a different historical experience, itself function of geography"[527]. Yet, this difference in philosophy they present is somewhat unjust. For where Europeans have a "reflex" to "avoid confrontation"

---

525   Idem.

526   See Richard N. Haass, <u>Transatlantic Tensions: The United States, Europe, and Problem Countries</u>, The Brookings Institution, Washington, DC., 1999, p. 2.

527   See Michael Brenner and Jonathan Dean, <u>Terms of Engagement: The United States and the European Security Identity</u>, Praeger., Westport, CT., 1998, pp. 11-12.

because of "their highlighted sense of danger to themselves of its escalation", Americans, on the other hand, "do not experience the feelings of vulnerability with the same intensity" vis-à-vis conflicts in the Balkans and the Middle East[528]. Furthermore, their explanation goes on to claim that "the U.S foreign policy elite also is more comfortable handling crises and playing power games than allies who have not borne the responsibility of providing for their own security for the past two generations. Again, attitudes are rooted in a history correlated with geography"[529]. Subjectivity is, indeed, easily found in this explanation of the difference of approach between the United States and Europe to conflict management. For avoiding confrontation is not always a sign of weakness or an easy escape. Avoidance of confrontation for fear over ones security, moreover, is a quite legitimate reaction. Furthermore, it can be said that the strategy of confrontation would, in most cases, lead to more conflicts even if this was not an immediate result, while avoiding confrontation allows more for a chance to reach a peaceful solution that avoids more and more escalation. Nonetheless, it cannot be denied that in some cases deterrence is sometimes the only effective prevention for the escalation of or the initiation of violence. There is another point to be taken into consideration in criticizing the statement of Michael Brenner and Jonathan Dean mentioned above concerning the "European reflex of avoiding confrontation". Indeed, William C. Banks and Jeffrey D. Straussman explain that the decision of sending troops and engaging in an extraterritorial war is so couched in the power of the American Congress which makes it extremely difficult to have approval for a military operation[530]. They give an example of the period of World War II, where President Franklin D. Roosevelt was so sympathetic with the plight of Europeans but that when the French appealed for American military assistance, Roosevelt's answer was that" only the Congress can make such commitments"[531]. Hence, this "pre-reflex" is not restricted only to Europeans.

The crisis is Yugoslavia and the response of France and the United States to it seems to have gone through two stages. The first one is the collapse of Yugoslavia as a state, the ensuing succession of Slovenia and Croatia and Serb attempts to establish greater Serbia. The second stage of this crisis can be said to be that of the armed conflict in Bosnia...

---

528 Ibid., p. 12.
529 Idem.
530 See William C. Banks and Jeffrey D. Straussman, "A new imperial presidency? Insights from U.S. involvement in Bosnia", <u>Political Science Quarterly</u>, Vol.114, N°2, 1999, pp. 195-217.
531 Ibid., p. 196

It should be said that it was neither in the interest of the United States nor in that of France or Europe to accept the disintegration of Yugoslavia In 1991. The disintegration was unacceptable at that time because it threatened to destabilize the whole European continent. Indeed, many of the European countries have their own secessionist movements. It also threatened to regenerate further dormant tension, which it effectively did later on. Hall Gardner explains in this respect, "The EU's overriding concern was that the secession of one state or region would cause others to follow; from this perspective, support for Slovenian and Croatian secession would risk the widening of the war into Bosnia (which it did). It could also set a precedent for secessionist movements in the USSR (which it did), plus in Czechoslovakia (idem), if not movements in France and Spain (Corsica and the Basque region), Northern Ireland, and even northern Italy. EU states also feared that secessionist movements in Yugoslavia would also influence secessionist movements in India (Kashmir). The break-up of Yugoslavia might additionally regenerate Greek, Bulgarian, and Serbian tensions over Macedonia (the site of ethnic slaughters in the late nineteenth and early twentieth centuries); hence, Greece opposed the Slovenian and Croatian secessionist movements. Another fear was the rise of Greek, Serbian, Albanian, and Turkish disputes over Kosovo province[532]". This refusal to accept the disintegration of Yugoslavia was even more pertinent to France, which helped create Yugoslavia after World War I[533]. As a whole, Europe seemed to have an idealistic wish that even if the disintegration of the Yugoslavian state is inevitable, violence could be somehow avoided. This was probably the cause of the European weak response to the crisis at its very beginnings, which mainly consisted of economic and diplomatic pressures of the European Community, like the threat of exclusion from the EC.

It seems, however, that there was a change of attitudes towards Yugoslavia before and after the Cold War. This was especially the case for the United States. Lorraine M. Lees explains, in this respect, that "during the early years of the Cold

---

532   See hall Gardner, op. cit., pp. 158-159.

533   The great powers participated in creation, maintenance, life and death of Yugoslavia, perhaps more than its nations. The victorious forces in the World War I—Great Britain, France, USA and Italy—supported the creation of Yugoslavia in 1918 by attaching the South Slav nations of defeated Austria-Hungary, namely Croats, Slovenes and Serbs, respectively Croatia, Slovenia, Bosnia and Herzegovina and Vojvodina, having in mind two basic aims: to create from the new state strong barrier against possible revival of the new German imperialism (Drang nach Osten) and to include it in cordon sanitaire against spread of bolshevism from Russia. In that way Yugoslavia became an important element of European Versailles order between the two world wars.

War, Yugoslavia was the focal point of an attempt by the United States to promote fissures within the communist world"[534]. To do that, the United States used the "wedge" strategy, which consisted as "a crucial and innovative aspect of the foreign policies of Harry S. Truman and Dwight D. Eisenhower, relied on nationalism and a combination of U.S. pressure and support to create divisions between the Soviet Union and other communist states"[535]. This presents in itself a change of the United States policy towards that country since, ironically enough, the United States was the first country in the world to recognize the Kingdom of Slaves, Croats and Slovenes (former name of Yugoslavia)[536]. The break-up of Yugoslavia came at an inappropriate time for everyone. It was at a time when the end of the Cold War was bewildering the West at the fall of Communism everywhere, and when Europe was in the middle of a public argument about its future. It was exactly at such a time when the events in Yugoslavia threatened to destabilize the whole continent along with the new World Order[537]. Attempts to prevent the disintegration of Yugoslavia were taken both on the European level as well as by the United States. For, in May 1991, the United States "made an attempt to prevent the break-up of Yugoslavia by withdrawing economic and financial aid, but promising its reinstallation"[538]. Simultaneously, "the European Community (EC) was attempting the same objective, but with the carrot before the stick-offering additional aid if Yugoslavia remained whole"[539].

The initial concrete European reaction to the start of the conflict was the attempt to reach a ceasefire and to reach a political settlement of the crisis. For Europe, the ceasefire meant that a European force can be put in place to monitor the situation which meant a success of the idea of the European Community as unified political force on the international scene.

Yet, the problem with the above logic was that hostilities were taking place precisely when the security provisions of the Maastricht Treaty were being negotiated. For its part, France believed that the positioning of an interposition force under the authority of the WEU (Western European Union), when the fighting seemed

---

534 See Lorraine M. Lees, <u>Keeping Tito Afloat: The United States, Yugoslavia, and the Cold War</u>, Pennsylvania State University Press, University Park, PA., 1997, p. xiii.

535 Idem.

536 See Stevan K. Pavlowitch, ""Who is 'Balkanizing' whom? The misunderstandings between the debris of Yugoslavia and an unprepared West", <u>Daedalus</u>, Vol.123, N°2., 1994, pp. 203-223.

537 Idem.

538 See Susan L. Woodward, "Yugoslavia: Divide and Fall", Online document found at <u>http://www.thebulletin.org/issues/1993/n93/n93Woodward.html.</u>

539 Idem.

to get worst, was the best immediate manner to deal with the situation. The French insistence on the interposition force was, however, a subject of controversy. Some saw in it a contradiction in the French policy towards the ex-Yugoslavian successor states. For instance, the *Financial Times* mentions this contradiction in the French position at the time by saying "France is seen by some as traditionally pro-Serb and opposed to German suggestions that Slovenian and Croatian independence be recognized. This is said to be through fear of a new "Teutonic bloc" emerging, and/or to discourage its Corsican separatists. Yet the continuing insistence of Mr. Roland Dumas, France's Foreign Minister, that a WEU force may eventually have to "interpose" itself in Croatia could—if carried out—greatly strengthen the Croat case for recognition. What appears overriding in the French position is its vision of Europe's defence future"[540]. Indeed, the French position on the crisis cannot be looked upon separately from its relations with and interests in Germany, in particular, and the notion of its affinities with the various parties of the conflict.

Indeed, France can seems to have tried to exchange the German desire to secure recognition for Croatia from the EC with that of Germany's support of its September 1991 proposal of the interposition force under the WEU. Eventually, the French proposal was sabotaged by the UK, which has no real interest in the region and which saw in the French proposal an attempt to strengthen the WEU at the expense of NATO. Yet, some researchers suggest that the French proposal of the interposition force was more of an effort to exhibit leadership and that France didn't actually believe that such a proposal would be implemented[541]. The evidence on the French desire to appear as the leader of the continent with this proposal, rather than being an actual belief that it would be implemented, are interesting. Some saw in the French backing of an interposition force a means of weakening the supremacy of NATO and exhibiting military supremacy over Germany, which couldn't send its own troops to the Balkans. Hall Gardner states, in this respect, "On the surface, NATO/WEU decisions taken in June-July 1992 to support a naval blockade of former Yugoslavia were "complementary." Yet France tended to push for limited intervention (including ground troops) to protect refugees from the fighting. French actions were in part taken as a means to counterbalance NATO initiatives and also to assert political-military *primacy* over Germany, which, for historical and legal reasons, was initially unable to contribute forces. Washington and London, however, had been more reluctant to intervene in what both saw as largely a continental affair, and fearing that they would be dragged into a quagmire"[542]. Even with the strong French rhetorical

---

540   See the Financial Times, August 8, 1991.
541   See Philip Kramer, op. cit., p.49.
542   See Hall Gardner, op. cit, pp. 159-160

nature of the interposition force proposal there was a well-known lack of available forces to implement this proposal. For, logically speaking, it wasn't possible to involve German forces in the interposition force, France would not send one on its own, the UK didn't have an vital interest in the issue, and the United States had no interest to participate in a WEU operation. Eventually, and with the failure of the French proposal and the lack of capacity of the EC to obtain a ceasefire or to use military force against Serbia, the handling of the first stage of the Yugoslavian crisis was delegated to the United Nations.

A UN supported ceasefire in Slovenia resulted in the end of the first phase of the conflict in the ex-Yugoslavia in early 1992. The problem, however, didn't completely disappear. The issue of the territorial dispute between Serbia and Croatia was left unsolved. This provided the opportunity for the former Serbian president Slobodan Milosevi? to turn his attention to Bosnia, which has declared its independence after a referendum supporting independence from Belgrade on the 15th of October 1991.

Unlike Croatia, with the outbreak of the fighting, Bosnia's very existence was threatened by Serbia. Again the response of Europe was insufficient. It would support the negotiations through the UN (with the UK's Lord Carrington and David Owen, as well as America's former Secretary of State Cyrus Vance as mediators). However, the Vance-Owen Plan (1992-1993)[543] was not acceptable by the United States for three main reasons. First, it seemed to legitimise the Serbian gains and overlook "ethnic cleansing". Second, the rules of engagement of the UN forces did not allow the UN forces to respond effectively to clearly hostile situations. Finally, the United States wanted a NATO instead of UN forces to be deployed under U.S. command[544]. Europe made it clear that there is no possibility of military intervention in the crisis. It should be mentioned, for instance, that France's who only entered the NATO military command in April 1993, was of the position that the whole operation should be under the UN[545]. This seems to have removed any limits on the Serbian action in Bosnia. It can be also said to have contributed to prolonging the reaching of a peaceful settlement. The issue of

---

543 UN mediators Cyrus Vance and Lord David Owen, the EC mediator, developed a plan for peace in Bosnia that would have divided the country into 10 ethnically-based provinces; three each were to be controlled by Serbian, Croatian, and Muslim governments, while Sarajevo was to be jointly administered. The plan was widely criticized, including by the Clinton Administration in January 1993, for rewarding the "ethnic cleansing" carried out by Serbian forces as part of their territorial conquests.

544 See Hall Gardner, op. cit, p.162.

545 See Nicole Gnesotto,"Lessons of Yugoslavia, ", Chaillot Paper N°14, WEU Institute for Security Studies, March 1994;,pp. 21-41.

ethnic cleansing, however, could not leave Europe without doing something or at least give the appearance that it is reacting effectively to the crisis.

As far as the Bosnian crisis is concerned, it can be said that the French political interest was in containing the conflict within Bosnia while pushing for humanitarian aid to the civilian population and waiting for the fighting to phase out. To some extent, the French position at the time can be qualified as one that was attempting to contain the damages. France had also to respond to various internal and conflicting pressures concerning the crisis in Bosnia, such as that of the elite and public reaction to the atrocities there, even if the idea of military intervention was excluded at the time.

The United States' national political interests in having a stable Balkans can be explained by a number of reasons. Stephen Biddle, commenting on the reasons underlying the United States' national interests in the Balkans saying" The United States is involved in Bosnia today because our national interests are engaged there. The Balkans lie in a critical fault zone between the industrial democracies of Europe to the west, Russia to the east, and the Persian Gulf to the south. Our European allies are among our most important trading partners; Russia owns some 6,000 strategic nuclear weapons and is politically and economically unstable; the Persian Gulf is critical to world oil prices yet remains a tinderbox. Conflict in the Balkans can thus easily spread into parts of the world with major economic and strategic importance to us. Preventing Balkan warfare from spreading is in our direct national self-interest"[546]. As far as humanitarian considerations are concerned, Stephen Biddle states" We are an idealistic people, and we want our foreign policy to reflect the better angels of our nature"[547]. Yet, humanitarian driven action is "not America's responsibility alone" and "must be balanced against other considerations"[548]. Thus, humanitarian driven action, cannot be considered as the basis for American involvement in Bosnia. Indeed, if it were the sole reason for intervention in a crisis or a conflict, there would be interventions and active involvement of the United States in all conflicts taking place in the world. What emphasizing the humanitarian tragedy of a conflict or crisis can do is to give legitimacy to involvement with domestic and world public opinion. Indeed, not all conflicts are responded to in the same manner. Even if there is involvement of troops, it depends on the importance of national interests involved. As for the crisis in Bosnia, the idea was that" containing conflict in the

---

546   See Stephen Biddle, "Role of the United States in Bosnia", online document without pagination found at
       http://www.unc.edu/depts/europe/articles/biddle_s010228.pdf.

547   Idem.

548   Idem.

Balkans is worth the modest effort "the United States is putting in "and probably couldn't be done without that American effort[549]". It is important to mention that the U.S. involvement in the Balkans was by all means modest. Indeed, in terms of volume of involvement, the United States participation in the stabilization of the Balkans, including Bosnia, was much less than other European countries. In fact, out of the 60,000 troops stationed in the Balkans, only one fifth is American. The United States have 4000 soldiers in Bosnia and 7000 in Kosovo, which makes a very insignificant percentage of the United States' 1.3 million active military personnel[550]. In addition, its total share of economic aid to the region is only around 10% of the total aid[551]. It seems, nonetheless, that for the United States, the Balkans was another field to project their leadership. Stephen Biddle describes, in this respect, what he labels as a "reasonable investment" of the United States in the Balkans. He states" American leadership remains important, and without us, our allies often find it difficult to act—but the great majority of the effort is being put out by our allies, not us"[552]. Yet, exhibiting leadership alone cannot be the sole reason for involvement. Indeed, other suggestions indicate tensions between the United States and Europe over fears of a United States attempt to establish a base of influence in the Balkans. Michael Brenner and Jonathan Dean state" The stuttering alliance dialogue on Bosnia's future was further hampered by the imputation coming from some U.S partners that Washington had the un-stated goal of carving out for itself a Balkan sphere of influence. The Clinton administration's voiced concerns for Turkey's interest in Bosnia's fate prompted those suspicions"[553]. Hence, for the United States it can be said that it was "reasonable" to have an active involvement in the Balkans because the Balkans is a strategic area geographically, because it was important to exhibit leadership in the post-Cold War era, and because it had its own ambitions of extending its sphere of influence to the area. One more reason should be kept in mind though. The United States, and the West, in general, were conscience of the negative impact of the Gulf War of 1990-1991 on Arab and Muslim public opinion, and indeed, on the world opinion a a whole. For even if Iraq was the aggressor in that conflict, the response to it was considered by many as hypocritically over-exaggerated and selective since other conflicts and aggressions were

---

549   Idem.
550   Idem.
551   See Ivo H. Daalder and Michael E. O'Hanlon, "The United States in the Balkans: There to Stay", Online document with pagination found at http://www.twq.com/autumn00/daalderohanlon.pdf., p.2.
552   See Stephen Biddle, op. cit.
553   See Michael Brenner and Jonathan Dean, op. cit., p. 16.

taken place all over the world at the same time. In this sense, it can be said that the United States' involvement in Bosnia and the Balkans in general stemmed from a desire to appease Arab and Muslim hostile public opinion. The message seems to have been that we (the United States) intervene as well to defend Muslim populations that are being brutalised and not only in the Middle East but in the heart of Europe.

For its part, the pressures that the French diplomacy had to cope up with in its handling of the crisis of Bosnia were quite diverse. First of all, there was the pressure of the French political elite and personalities such as Bernard Kouchner[554] who were pushing for a humanitarian assistance. Second, France clearly saw the need for a unified European position vis-à-vis the crisis in Bosnia and it also recognized the negative consequences of the European failure to deal with the Bosnian crisis on the prospect of the European defence capacity. Thirdly, France had a clear preference for solutions, which involve the WEU or the UN rather than those that would involve NATO. This can be interpreted as a French attempt to exercise leadership in resolving the crisis. On the other hand, there was unwillingness, especially on the part of the French President, to cut all ties with Serbia even with the well-known fact of it being the aggressor in the crisis. Internally, there was also the question of the differences of opinion that existed between Paris and the French military leaders positioned in ex-Yugoslavia. Finally, there is another fact that added to the dilemma of the French diplomacy concerning the crisis in Bosnia, which is that France had to be conscience of the importance of marinating good relations with the Moslem world. For France, reconciling all of these factors and elements was not an easy task. This is maybe why its policy towards the crisis in Bosnia seemed to be changing according to circumstances sometimes.

One good example of the apparent contradiction of the French position concerning the Bosnian crisis can be seen in the late French president resident Mitterrand's dramatic flight to Sarajevo on June 28, 1992. The visit had, in fact, different objectives. For the besieged population in Sarajevo, it signalled a message of hope and solidarity. For the French voters before the Maastricht referendum, it was meant to emphasise the fact that France and Europe would not deal passively with the dramatic events in Bosnia. On the other hand, the visit of the late French president did not mean that France was willing to support any military intervention to stop the conflict. What France managed to support at the time was the humanitarian assistance under the auspices of the United Nations. Indeed, if

---

554   Bernard Kouchner established the *Médécins du Monde* in 1980. He served as State Secretary for humanitarian Action ((1988-1992), as Minister of Health and Humanitarian Action (1992-1993), and European Socialist Deputy (1994-1997),

France wanted to support a military intervention at that stage, it would have been a feasible thing to do. The United Nations Protection Force (UNPROFOR), for instance, which was stationed there to protect the humanitarian operation, may have been used to protect the civilian population. Yet again, the UN mandate of these troops did not allow them to intervene.

The issue of the composition of the UNPROFOR[555] is yet another French contradiction regarding this crisis. Even with a lack of well to support military intervention, France provided the largest national contribution to UNPROFOR. This was probably, however, meant to send a message about France's commitment to UN peacekeeping operations. Some writers suggest, in this respect, that the fact that the British and the French forces in Bosnia under the UN were ineffective was actually beneficial to France and the UK in the sense that the presence of such troops helped delay any active military intervention which, by consequence, would have meant wagging a war against Serbia. Claire Tréan and Yves Heller explain that the French government was convinced that it is impossible to disengage completely yet it supported the UNPROFOR route because the UNPROFOR excluded the possibility of war against Serbia. They state "France did the most to get the UN to take responsibility for the Yugoslav problem, to get it to send forces and to define the completely new type of mission engaged in. But if France was the leader in all these humanitarian and political initiatives, which presumed the agreement of all parties, including the aggressor, it also constantly watched to make sure that it will not go beyond this framework, and only accepted when absolutely forced the few coercive measures adopted against Serbia, resisting as much as possible"[556]. This French stand of not fully going until the point of active military engagement was also reflected in France's insistence on the policy of the "security zones" as opposed to the U.S. choice of "lift and strike". This French policy of pushing for "security zones" was commented on by the U. S. Secretary of State at the time Warren Christopher who was quoted in *Le Monde* saying that" the French authorities had worked hard for the creation of these protected zones, an initiative by which they attempted to compensate for their renunciation of certain of the principles of the late Vance-Owen Peace Plan to which the Bosnian Moslems remain attached. The demarche of Paris is based on the conviction that the more the Bosnian Moslems were given the sense that one was ready to give them an international protection, the more they would be disposed to negotiate in Geneva"[557]. The establishment of those "security zones" wasn't, however, an easy

---

555 By May 1995, UNPROFOR operations involved 43,926 troops, with 160 killed in action. The UN role (at a cost of $1.6 billion a year).

556 See Claire Tréan and Yves Heller, <u>Le Monde</u>, Novembre 4, 1992.

557 *Le Monde*, July 29, 1993.

thing to do, even with the French lobbying for their creation. Indeed, it took the UN a long time to decide to establish such zones, which at the end, didn't have enough forces or mandate to make them secure.

The change in the French policy guidelines regarding Bosnia took place in the summer of 1993. The fact that Serb forces managed in the summer of 1993 to attack French soldiers working within the UNPROFOR and that the UN seemed incapable to provide the proper response to such an a attack along with an internal public reaction to the issue probably contributed to a more favourable position on the part of France to use active force in Bosnia. It can also be said that this change of policy coincided with the strong position of the Clinton Administration on the issue. Yet, the French position on the use of force was still somewhat ambiguous. For instance, French former Defence Minister François Léotard declared in Washington at the time, that the UN forces stationed in Bosnia had a "humanitarian mission", that they are not in "a situation of war," and that UNPROFOR was "not there to defend Sarajevo"[558]. Nevertheless, a deal between the United States and France on the issue of using force in Bosnia seemed to be finally reached on August 9, 1993. According to this deal, France managed to state its point of view in requiring NATO to take prior consent from the UN Secretary General. For some this yet seemed like another French manoeuvre to avoid using force against the Serbs and push the different parties to the negotiating table simply because the UN Secretary General seemed unlikely to authorize NATO to use force. For instance, Alain Lamassoure, the then new Minister of European Affairs, was quoted saying, in this respect "that use of force against the Bosnian Serbs by NATO under the authority of the UN could facilitate a diplomatic solution"[559]. It appears that the French objective remained the initial one concerning the crisis, which is to push for negotiations and, if these failed, to wait for the fighting to phase out in order to avoid a war against Serbia and the expanding of a fighting that might attract other European countries.

The criticism of this policy of inaction came from inside of France as well as from the outside. For instance, François Heisbourg and Pierre Lellouche explain that failing to deal effectively with the first European crisis in the post-cold war era meant a failure for the European hopes of full integration and unification. They state "what is the point of erecting heavy and complex structures like the Treaty of Maastricht, when Europeans are not even capable of acting with enough vigour to impose—if all else fails—by arms—respect for the simple principles of non-aggression and of non-expansion by force...Before even being ratified, the treaty of Maastricht, and in particular...the sections on "foreign policy and

---

558   *Le Monde,* August 2, 1993

559   *Le Monde,* August 12, 1993.

common security" are null and by-passed by History.... [At the same time] the European-American alliance gives evidence of its lack of relevance...for the real conflicts of the post Cold War in Europe"[560]. Other accusations that European countries were unable to use effective action against Serbia came from Bosnia itself. The UN arms embargo and its role in the conflict was a subject of controversy because it benefited the Serbs on the expense of Bosnians. Hall Gardner, states "On one hand, the UN was late to enter the conflict; on the other, Washington refused to support its efforts. In effect, Serbia (seizing roughly 70 percent of Bosnian territory) and Croatia (seizing 17 percent) had by 1993 entered into a condominium agreement over Bosnia, prior to the tenuous U.S. engineered Croatian-Bosnian "confederation" of March 1994 (the previous Croatian-Bosnian alliance of July 1992 had broken down in May 1993). Despite the U.S.-inspired "confederation," Bosnia had regarded Russia, France, and Britain as favouring Serbian and Croatian factions. Moreover, Bosnian Moslems still suspected Croatian intentions, due to the latter's control of access to the Adriatic and its claims to Bosnian territory, particularly Mostar, the "capital" of the Croatian-Bosnian state of Herceg-Bosna. Bosnia continued to press for an end to UN sanctions against obtaining its own arms. From late 1993 to late 1994, the issue of whether to lift the UN arms embargo to former Yugoslavia as a whole and adopt a "lift and strike" policy split allied opinion and weakened the credibility of the UN. The UN embargo was only partially effective and until 1995 was largely justified as a means to limit the conflict and protect UN forces. States that were lax on controls included Albania, Macedonia, Italy, Greece, Iran, Saudi Arabia, and Hungary. Russia has been accused of permitting at least a thousand "volunteers" to supervise pan-Serbian military operations. The United States itself was accused of overlooking large Iranian shipments of small arms to Bosnia, at least from May 1994, opening the door to closer Iranian-Bosnian ties"[561].

In addition to the UN mission in Bosnia, the establishment of the Contact Group in 1994 seems to have represented a desire to actively involve European countries in the search of s solution for the crisis. Some estimate that the Contact Group was formed to support the U.S. backed Croatian-Serbian federation and also actively involve Russia[562]. The proposals of the Contact Group, on the tripartite division of Bosnia, were rejected by Bosnian Serbs although it was accepted by

---

560   See François Heisbourg and Pierre Lellouche, *Le Monde* on June 17
561   See Hall Gardner, op. cit, p.162-163
562   See Pauline Neville-Jones, "Dayton, IFOR, and Alliance Relations in Bosnia," Survival, *vol. 38*, N°4, Winter 1996-97, pp.46-47

Turkey, Croatia and Bosnia[563]. The involvement of Russia in the Contact Group was positively felt later on when Russia managed to convince Serbian leaders in August 1994 to accept UN monitors of the blockade against Bosnian Serbs. The benefit for Serbia was a promise of the Contact group to suspend selectively the sanctions against Serbia imposed since 1992[564]. Things, however, took a sudden change of direction when the Republic Party won the legislative elections in the United States in November 1994 brining Bill Clinton to presidency. Contrary to his election promises, Clinton refused the lifting of the embargo against Serbia[565]. Indeed, the United States seemed to be a fervent supporter of maintaining the sanctions regime. David C. Morrison explains, in this respect, that in the 9th of June 1994, United States' Defence and State Departments along with the Joint Chief of Staff issued a statement emphasising that a unilateral lifting of the sanctions would compromise United States' relations with the UN, NATO, the EU and damage the partnership with Russia[566]. For its part, Russia used its veto right in the UN Security Council for the first time since the collapse of the Soviet Union to bloc UN sanctions' vote on Serbia in December 1994.

The issue of the embargo created tensions amongst European countries themselves especially the UK and France on one hand and Germany on the other. It also created blocs with Germany and the U. S. on one side and the UK and France on the other. Hall Garner explains "The turning point in the war came when tensions between the UN (plus the UK and France) and NATO (the United States plus Germany) became increasingly evident. At this point, the United States began to demand an end to the "dual key" approach, by which any military decision had to be accepted by both the UN and the NATO staff. In general, the UK and France opposed U.S. and German proposals to remove the UN total embargo on Bosnia as an action that would widen the war"[567]. The UK and France were also opposed the air-strikes because they feared for the security of their forces deployed in Bosnia and France, in particular, accused the United States of favouring the Bosnians at the expense of a peaceful settlement with the Serbs[568]. The events that

---

563　See Hall Gardner, op. cit., p. 163. The Contact Group plan granted Bosnian Serbs roughly 49 percent of former Bosnian territory and Bosnian Croat and Moslems 51 percent. Bosnian Serb rejection of the plan was explained by the fact that it did not include a right of confederation with Serbia and Montenegro, did not provide access to the sea, or define the status of Sarajevo.

564　See Hall Gardner, op. cit., p.165.

565　Idem.

566　See David C. Morrison, "How Bosnia Is Becoming a Priority," National Journal, N°. 26, 20 August 1994, pp. 34-35

567　See Hall Garner, op. cit, p.165.

568　Idem.

followed changed the position of both France and the UK concerning the use of effective force in Bosnia. This occurred when 350 UN blue helmets were taken hostage by the Bosnian Serbs on May 1995. In addition, they shut down a U. S. F-16 in a no-fly-zone. The Bosnian Serb blue helmets hostage move was aimed at bargaining against a cease of NATO air strikes. In July of the same year, Bosnian Serbs took the "safe areas" of Srebrenica, and Zepa. Some writers explain that the fall of Srebrenica simply reflects the West's and, in particular, the European inability to handle the UN hostages situation. Hall Gardner states" Western impotence as a result of the UN hostage crisis permitted the fall of *Srebrenica* in July 1995. It was reported that UN forces had failed to stop the seizure of *Srebrenica*. The French president, Jacques Chirac, reportedly ordered General Bernard Javier to cease air strikes in return for the freeing of hostages, a charge denied by Paris[569]". At the end it was the United States that imposed the solution for the Bosnian Crisis at the detriment of European powers, especially France. Hall Gardner adds" Confronted with a dangerous option involving the retreat of UN forces in the face of renewed combat, the United States engaged itself diplomatically. Washington stole the initiative away from Paris, but only after the Croatian and Bosnian alliance had regained some 20 percent of Bosnian territory by force. Now a ceasefire could be established: "greater Serbian" aspirations were on the retreat, and Belgrade was willing to negotiate. By August, NATO had obtained clear rules of engagement and guidelines for the use of force on its terms. From 28 August to 14 September 1995, NATO's Operation "Deliberate Force" began air operations that ultimately helped bring Serbia (backing the Bosnian Serbs) to the negotiating table—despite Bosnian Serb accusations that their leader Milosevic had sold out"[570]. This led to the Dayton Peace Accords of the 21st of November 1995.

Thus, it seems that there was a destabilization of three institutions in 1993 concerning the crisis in Bosnia. The first one is that of the UN ability to carry out peacekeeping operations in the post-Cold War era. The second is that of the European Union's aspiration for an effective Collective Security Policy caused by the French and, certainly European, hesitation to use effective force in Bosnia. The third is that of NATO, as a security institution, which was also undermined by the United States' hesitation to employ effective force in Bosnia as well. In a way, it can be said that at that stage of the crisis, two of the institutions that were supposed to prove more effectiveness and freedom of action after the end of the Cold War failed to do so at the early stages of the conflict in Bosnia: the UN and NATO.

The political interests of France and the United States in the crisis in Chechnya (1/11/1991-31/8/1996) have, for their part, to be considered with

---

569   Ibid., p. 169.
570   Idem.

respect to the history of both countries' bilateral relations with Russia, the integration of Russia into the European construction and other Western collective security institutions and, the relevance of Russia to the crisis in Bosnia, in particular, and to the conflicts in the Balkans in general. It is in the analysis of such factors and considerations that a better understanding of the the two countries' political interests in this crisis in Chechnya can be reached.

Historically speaking, the year 1717 is very significant in tracing the official relations between Russia and France. It is the year in which, for the first time, diplomatic relations represented in the naming of an ambassador to each other's capitals were established. Strong relations between the two countries reached their climax with the military and political alliance, which was created at the end of the 19th century. Indeed, the Franc-Russian alliance of 1892-1894 is an interesting case to discuss for a better understanding of the bilateral relations between the two countries.

The alliance between the Russian and France was a reflection of the state of international affaires during that period, in which alliances and counter alliances were quite frequent. In this respect, William Leonard Langer states that" in the pre-war European system the Franco-Russian Alliance played a role similar to that of the Austro-German Alliance of 1879. Each served as the kernel of an international group, into which other powers were drawn and around which the smaller states gravitated"[571] The system of alliances in that period included alliances such as the Dreikaiserbund Treaty[572] (1881-1878) Dual Alliance[573] (1879-1902), The Triple

---

571   See William Leonard Langer, The Franco-Russian Alliance, 1890-1894, Harvard University Press, Cambridge, 1929, p. V.

572   This treaty was otherwise known as the "The Three Emperors League" It included Germany, Russia and Austria-Hungary and was aimed at maintaining a peaceful status quo in Europe and also at preventing an alliance between Russia and Germany. The treaty broke down in 1878 when Russia entered war against Turkey in the Balkans.

573   The Dual Alliance (1879-1902). This alliance included Germany and Austria-Hungary and was concluded after the breakdown of the Dreikaiserbund and the disruption in Russo-German relations caused by the diplomatic setback suffered by Russia at the Congress of Berlin in 1878, this was Bismarck's device to bind Austria to Germany in case either was attacked by Russia. It was a purely defensive treaty. It also committed each power to be benevolently neutral in case either was attacked by another power(i.e., France). If Russia joined with France in such an eventuality, however, both Austria and Germany would act together. The treaty was secret (though it soon became generally known and was revealed by Bismarck in 1888) and remained permanent via automatic renewal after 1902.

Alliance[574] (1882-1914) the Reinsurance Treaty[575] (18871890), The Anglo-Japanese Alliance[576] (1902-1905), The Entente Cordiale[577] (1904-1911) and the Anglo-Russian Agreement[578] (1907-1921). For its part the Franco-Russian Alliance of

---

574 The Triple Alliance was sort of renewal of the Dual Alliance with the addition of Italy on the Germany and Austria-Hungary side. The alliance finally broke down when Italy left it after Austria-unilaterally attacked the Serbs at the outbreak of World War I in 1914

575 This was Bismarck's attempt to reconcile Russia with Germany after the breakdown of the Dreikaiserbund two years earlier. It also pointed up Bismarck's dilemma of remaining on good terms both with Austria and Russia at the one time

576 At this time Britain was not on friendly terms with Russia, France or Germany. Indeed, she had growing apprehensions about an apparent increasing Russian influence in the Far East as well as about the very real French advances in West Africa and the developing naval strength of Germany. Moreover, Japan (already a developing imperial power in Asia since her defeatof China in 1895) had watched with anger the menace of Russian encroachments in northern China and her seizure of the warm water port of Port Arthur in1887 which seemed directed against Japan's influence in Korea. Thus both Japan and Britain found common interest in containing Russia.

577 This was not a formal alliance exacting fixed obligations from each, but rather a "friendly Agreement" between two former enemies Britain and France to resolve their outstanding differences in Africa, North America(in Newfoundland) and Asia. The two main problems involved Egypt (Britain's sphere of interest) and Morocco, which France was seeking to bring under her control. Under the Agreement, Britain was to have a free hand in Egypt without French interference while France received a similar assurance as regards Morocco.

578 This drawing together of mutually suspicious Britain and Russia stemmed from a number of considerations—a change in the Russian foreign ministry in the direction of matching the Triple Alliance with a Triple Entente by including Britain on the side of France and Russia; the Russian desire to resolve outstanding differences with Britain over A Afghanistan, Persia and Tibet; the British desire to allay her fears of Russian encroachments on her Indian frontier. This publicly declared Agreement liquidated the long standing grievances existing between the two powers but there was no accompanying military convention or promise of diplomatic support. Yet appearances served to lend support to the notion that the "ring» around Germany, whom they all feared, was now complete. Against the firmly established Triple Alliance of Germany, Austria-Hungary and Italy (though that didn't prove to be all that firm in 1914) there stood the equally firm Franco-Russian alliance, with Britain finally declaring her interest in standing with the latter powers against Germany. In the event, the so-called Triple Entente proved the more durable in view of Italy's defection from the Triple Alliance at the crucial hour in 1914. In 1917, the Communist Government in Russia repudiated all the international engagements of the tsars, and when, in 1921, the 1907 Treaty was cancelled by agreement.

1890-1894 is an interesting case to study. Indeed, for several years the Russian policy tended towards agreement with that of France, as far as foreign policy is concerned. It was a trend that was largely encouraged by French military assistance and maintained by major loans to Russia allocated by French banks. It should be mentioned, in this respect, that Russia had been diplomatically isolated since the lapse of the Reinsurance Treaty in 1890, while Britain was still considered ass a hostile power. Moreover,.the Triple Alliance of Germany,. Austria-Hungary and Italy had been renewed. Negotiations between France and Russia formally begun in 1892 and a military convention was soon concluded which finally received the Tsar's signature in 1894. The alliance was, of course meant to be discreet but it became generally public in the following year. The dangerous implications were that Europe was now divided into two groups of opposing states, with each armed camp motivated by fear and suspicion of the other—the Triple Alliance of Germany, Austria-Hungary and Italy versus the newly formed alliance of France and Russia. According to the provisions of this alliance, Russia would come to the aid of France if France were to be attacked by Germany, or by Italy supported by Germany. Likewise, France would come to the aid of Russia if Russia were to be attacked by Germany, or by an Austria supported by Germany. In addition, mobilization by one or more members of the opposing Triple Alliance would entail immediate mobilization (i.e., readying the army for action) of both France and Russia, in such a manner as to oblige Germany to fight simultaneously on both the eastern and western fronts. The alliance was to have the same duration as the Triple alliance.

Some writers argue that the outcome of World War I left France as the sole hegemonic effective power in the European continent. René Albrecht-Carrié, explains, for instance, that "there was no question in 1919 that Germany's defeat was total, her power at the time nonexistent. But, to make matters worse, in addition two other great powers were eliminated: revolution in Russia had led to civil war and chaos in that country; the Habsburg state had simply ceased to exist. Add to this—again largely for reasons of power—the negative Italian contribution. The total result was to leave France the one effective and organized unit on the continent of Europe[579]". This resulted in a French "Obsession" with security in Europe and with containing Germany that soon alienated countries such as the United States and the UK who accused France of seeking hegemonic interests in the continent[580]. This is probably what led to the Franco-Soviet Pact of Mutual Assistance. This pact was signed in Paris on the 2nd of May 1935. Some writers indicate that the fact that this alliance was set up one year within the

---

579   See René Albrecht-Carrié, France, Europe and the Two World Wars, Harper, New York, 1961, p.10.

580   Ibid., pp10-11.

accession to power of Adolph Hitler represents a continuity of the Franco-Russian Alliance and had the same goal of containing Germany[581]. This, however, did not prevent the Soviet Union from entertaining strategic relationships with Germany at the time. In the period between the two world wars, Russia made alliances with only Germany and France. It had an alliance with Germany from 1922 to 1933, with France from 1933 to 1939, and it joined hands again with Germany in August 1939[582] Yet, this time other currents, such as economic interests and the strength of the communist trends in France at the time, played a vital role in setting up this pact between the two powers. William Evans Scott explains "The outset found the French Communists sunk in futility, a factor of utmost significance in easing the acceptance of the pact. The miscry produced by the depression and the need for leftwing unity against semi-fascist movements revived the fortunes of the Communists. They exploited the opportunity with skill and vigour and became the driving force behind the Popular Front. Ironically, the evidence of this resurgence did not appear until the pact had been signed. Here, too, there was historical continuity. The Franco-Russian alliance of 1892 was not the exclusive creation of "cabinet diplomacy"-there were currents beyond the control of the diplomats. It was buttressed, almost bought and re-bought, by staggering French investments in Russian securities. It, too, was troubled by an ideological conflict, between Tsarist orthodoxy and autocracy and the anticlerical, bourgeois, democratic Third Republic"[583]. After the end of World War II and the devastation it caused, it can be said that the period of reconstruction (1945-1952) also signalled the emergence of a new international order in Europe, with the United States and the Soviet Union emerging as the principal powers on the continent and on the level of the whole world. This was mainly a result of the decline of the European great powers and the defeat of fascism. The cold War that resulted divided the continent in an East-West spheres of influence that lasted until the collapse of the Berlin Wall. Yet, even with the divisions, some overtures occurred between France and the Soviet Union during the Cold War era. Those are largely owed to the Gaullist policy of France at the time. In this respect, John W. Young comments on the international achievements of the Fifth Republic under Gaullism. He states "the Fifth Republic alienated those who feared an authoritarian presidency, but it seemed far more successful than the Third and Fourth Republics. De Gaulle had also reduced the division brought about by the other two 'Cs', which had emerged since 1945. Algeria was the last

---

581   See William Evans Scott, <u>Alliance against Hitler: The Origins of the Franco-Soviet Pact</u>, Duke University Press, Durham, NC, 1962, p. vii.

582   Idem.

583   Ibid., pp. vii-viii.

serious problem brought by colonial issues; and the impact of Cold War divisions lessened as de Gaulle opened relations up with Russia, China and Eastern Europe, asserted French independence from NATO and developed the *force de frappe'*, an independent nuclear deterrent which helped compensate the armed forces for the loss of empire"[584].This Gaullist tradition of détente with the Soviets was followed by other French presidents such as Valéry Giscard d'Estainng whose attempt to maintain this détente in 1980 after the invasion of Afghanistan by meeting Leonid Brezhnev provoked a lot of controversy at the time[585]. The late French president Mitterrand (1981-1995), however, tried to avoid this controversy over relations with the Soviet Union especially after the invasion of Afghanistan and the rekindling of the Cold War. Wayne Northcutt explains, for instance, that "for the first three years of his presidency he had not been willing to visit the Soviet Union, partly because of the need not to appear too friendly toward the East since he had appointed four Communist ministers, and partly because of the new Cold War that followed the Soviet invasion of Afghanistan in late December 1979, and the 1980 election of Ronald Reagan. Now, however, Mitterrand believed that the time was right for a visit to the Soviet Union since the West had weathered the storm against the deployment of the Euromissiles, partially because of his own crusade for deployment. The president hoped that this visit would help to initiate an East-West dialogue on such issues as disarmament, would make France appear less dependent on the United States, and would aid France in cutting the trade deficit with the Soviet Union, $1 billion in 1982 and $0.5 billion in 1983"[586]. It can be said, hence, that the bilateral relations between France and Russia were historically of a good nature even at the time of the Cold War.

The other axe of analysis when discussing the French political interests vis-à-vis the Chechnya crisis is that which relates to the future of Russia in the European construction. Indeed, after the collapse of the Soviet Union, it was time to insert Russia in the various bodies of the European Union. This mainly took place through its insertion in Council of Europe, the Organisation of Security and Cooperation in Europe (OSCE), and the EU.

Indeed, it is a largely accepted notion, that the existence of a democratic system creates obstacles to belligerent acts and, hence helps preserve stability. This was the underlying motive behind transporting democratic values to the East after the fall of the Berlin Wall. Mark Webber states "If we are to believe the

---

584   See John W. Young, Cold War Europe, 1945-1991: A Political History, Arnold., London, 1996, p. 111.
585   Idem, p. 118.
586   See Wayne Northcutt, Mitterrand: A Political Biography, Holmes & Meier, New York, 1992, p. 163.

'democratic peace' hypothesis, stability in Europe relies, in large part, on the extension of democratic, pluralistic political systems to the east of the continent, Russia included. The spread of democratic institutions, it is argued, provides domestic obstacles to belligerent acts by governments, while the diffusion of democratic norms promotes compromise and cooperative practices among states"[587]. It should be said, however, that the attempt to encourage democratic transformation in the Communist Bloc took place when the Parliamentary Assembly of the COE (PACE) introduced in 1989 a pre-membership 'special guest status' which was to the Soviet Congress of People's Deputies in June 1989[588]. This was met by Mikhail Gorbachev's call for a 'common European home' in Strasbourg in July of the same year[589]. The Council of Europe's reaction to the events in Russia in 1993 and to the crisis in Chechnya are interesting to discuss. The events of 1993 in Russia, which opposed Boris Yeltsin to his parliamentarians were attributed in a declaration of the Vienna Summit of October 1993 to those called the "opponents of reform[590]". For its part, the Russian brutal campaign in Chechnya in 1995 didn't have an effect or a mentionable reaction on the individual European governmental level. Mark Webber states, in this respect, that "the Committee of Ministers meeting in January 1995 (one month after the launch of the Russian military campaign) issued a communiqué which not only made no mention of these events, but which congratulated Russia on 'the progress achieved in building a democratic society' and welcomed its admission into the COE 'at the earliest possible date'"[591]. Nevertheless, the events in Chechnya indicated Russia's inability to satisfy the terms of the European Convention on Human Rights (ECHR). Accordingly, the PACE decided with a large majority in February 1995 to differ examining Russia's application of admission because of its indiscriminate use of force in Chechnya and the imbalance of power which favoured the executive branch in that country[592]. Indeed the tones tone of this resolution was quite strong:

---

587   See Mark Webber, <u>Russia and Europe: Conflict or Cooperation?,</u> St. Martin's Press, New York, 2000, p. 125.
588   Ibid., p.126.
589   See R. L. Garthoff, <u>The Great Transition. American-Soviet Relations and the End of the Cold War,</u>The Brookings Institution, Washington D.C.:, 1994), p. 587.
590   See PACE Document 7000, 24 January 1994, p. A5
591   See Mark Webber, <u>Op. Cit.,</u> p.129.
592   PACE "1055 Resolution 1055 (1995)<u>1</u> on Russia's request for membership in the light of the situation in Chechnya ", 2 February, 1995. Website at http://www.coe.int/DefaultEN.asp

1. The Assembly considers that although the political conflict between Chechnya and the central authorities of the Russian Federation is an internal matter, the means employed by these authorities violate Russia's international obligations.

2. The Assembly thus unreservedly condemns the indiscriminate and disproportionate use of force by the Russian military, in particular against the civilian population, which is in violation of the 1949 Geneva Conventions and their 1977 Second Protocol as well as of the OSCE Code of Conduct on Politico-Military Aspects of Security, accepted by Russia as recently as December 1994.

3. These actions also constitute a grave violation of the Council of Europe's most elementary human rights principles, which Russia, by requesting membership of the Organisation, pledged to uphold[593].

The suspending of the Russian application for membership is further indicated in the two last provisions of this resolution:

10. The Assembly takes note of the resolution of 19 January 1995 of the European Parliament and supports the Parliament's position that the European Union should, under the present circumstances, not ratify a "partnership agreement" with Russia.

11. The Assembly decides to suspend the procedure concerning its statutory opinion on Russia's request for membership. The Assembly, in plenary session, will decide at a later date when to resume its examination of this request for membership.

The second important institution in this discussion relating to the Russian insertion attempts into the European Union's institutions is that of the Organisation of Security and Cooperation in Europe (it was known until January 1995 as the Conference on Security and Cooperation in Europe—CSCE). Indeed, since 1992, Russia sought to increase its role of the OSCE in the regional security and peace. Some writers argue that this was Moscow's intention even as early as 1989[594]. The reason is that the OSCE was regarded by Russia as a counterpart to NATO, from which Russia was excluded[595]. Out of this importance given to the organisation by Russia, the OSCE was allowed for the first time to perform a mission in Chechnya in April 1995[596] the OSCE Assistance Group in Chechnya has played a "limited" but also and "important" role in the mediation

---

593   Idem.
594   See Dov Lynch, "Russia and the Organization for Security and Cooperation in Europe" in Mark Webber, <u>Russia and Europe: Conflict or Cooperation?</u>., St. Martin's Press, New York, 2000, p. 99.
595   Ibid., p.100.
596   Idem.

of the conflict[597]. Dov Lynch, however, explains that "the Assistance Group helped to oversee negotiations between the parties after the hostage taking crisis in *Budyennovsk* in June-July 1995, and in the run-up to the *Khasavyurt* Agreement reached in August 1996"[598]

For its part, the European Union occupied a less important place than the other European institutions on the agenda of the Russian policy makers[599]. Jackie Gower argues "the EU has been perceived primarily as an economic organization and its aspirations to play a leading political and security role in the 'new Europe' have only gradually come to be recognized, let alone accepted, by the Russian authorities"[600]. As far as the position towards Chechnya is concerned, it can be said that this position was quite similar to that of the OSCE in 1995. The human rights violations accusations towards Russia resulted in a suspension of the ratification of the PCA[601] with Russia for several months[602].

The third axe of analysis in the discussion of the French political interests in the crisis in Chechnya is that which relates to the role of Russia in the Balkan conflicts. Indeed, it should be noted that both crises took place in almost the same period of time. It was logical, hence, to use the conflicts of the former Yugoslavia to demonstrate a new order of collective cooperative security between former enemies of the Cold War. Michael Andersen states, in this respect, "the settlement of the Yugoslav crisis is in many ways the key not only to peace in the region but also to the long-term development of U.S.-European-Russian relations—if not the viability and legitimacy of NATO itself."[603] The importance of having Russian support for settling the conflicts in the region is quite evident. Without this support, efforts to resolve the conflicts would have been met with

---

597 Ibid., p.114.

598 Idem.

599 See Jackie Gower, "Russia and the European Union", in Mark Webber, <u>Russia and Europe: Conflict or Cooperation?</u>., St. Martin's Press, New York, 2000, p. 99.

600 Idem.

601 The TCA (Trade and Cooperation Agreement) signed by the Soviet Union and the EC in 1989 was very similar to agreements reached by the EC with Poland and Hungary, and served only to normalize trading relations on the basis of granting most-favoured nation treatment in accordance with rules under the General Agreement on Tariffs and Trade (GATT). The PCA (The Partnership and Cooperation Agreement) marks a significant upgrading of relations from the earlier TCA. It is regarded often as the broadest and most comprehensive agreement concluded so far between Russia and any Western country or organisation.

602 See Jackie Gower, <u>àp. cit</u>, p.74.

603 See Michael Andersen, "Russia and the Former Yugoslavia ",in Mark Webber, <u>Russia and Europe: Conflict or Cooperation?</u>., St. Martin's Press, New York, 2000, p.156.

difficulties. A good example of this is the Russian obstacles in the UN Security Council in 1992 that were aimed against the U. S. proposals to deploy a preventive UN peacekeeping force in Kosovo. The inclusion of Russia in the Contact Group was mostly done in order to make it more involved in finding a peaceful settlement and to prevent its isolation[604]. Michael Anderson explains that this inclusion had very good results with regards to the efforts made to solve the Bosnian crisis. He states" In August 1994, Russian influence helped to gain Serbian leader Milosevic's acceptance of the Contact Group's latest peace endeavour. In 14 September, Serbia accepted international monitors on its borders to oversee the enforcement of the blockade on Bosnian Serbs[605]". This role was more evident in the UN hostage situation, which at the same time, helped Russia avoid the accusations of human rights abuses in Chechnya taking place at the same time. Michael Anderson argues in this respect that "Moscow indicated that it wanted to play a key role in the release of UN "blue helmets" taken hostage by Bosnian Serbs. While condemning the hostage taking, both Slobodan Milosevic and Boris Yeltsin (despite his own brutal actions in Chechnya) hoped to make political capital out of their efforts to help release UN forces taken hostage. These actions were taken as a means to gain international recognition for Russia as a "peacemaker" and put an end to sanctions placed against Serbia even if it meant some sacrifice of pan-Serbian goals"[606]. The call for more active Russian involvement in the solution of the Bosnian crisis was largely voiced in France. Indeed, on the 25th of January 1995, the French Prime Minister Alain Juppé called for more involvement of the EU and Russia in the resolution of the conflict and warned against a "catastrophe" if the United States didn't support the Russian and EU efforts in this direction[607]. However, the French Prime Minister's call for a summit in Paris which would include the leaders of Bosnia, Croatia, and Serbia and which aimed at preventing a new round of fighting that might result in the withdrawal of UN peacekeeping forces failed to materialize, largely due to American opposition[608].

The French political interests in the Bosnian crisis seem to have concentrated in a push towards the containment of the conflict so it would not have a spell over effect on the rest of the European continent and disrupt the work done in favour of a solid European construction. These interests also focused on exhibiting leadership in a post-Cold War crisis management and in pushing for a European solution to it. It also seemed to favour a European security reaction to the conflict as

604   Idem, p.164.
605   Ibid., pp. 164-165.
606   Idem, p. 168
607   Idem, p.169.
608   Idem.

apposed to an involvement of NATO and the United States. For its part, the crisis in Chechnya seems to have occupied a small place on the agenda of the European powers as a whole. The few incidents where Europe took stands condemning Russian acts in Chechnya were almost all attributed to European collective institutions and not individual governments and were limited to suspension of Russian membership applications in some institutions. Moreover, it was in the interest of France and the other European countries to involve Russia in the new post Cold War order in Europe. For France, this meant introducing a balance to the hegemony of NATO and the United States in the continent. It also meant that Russia should not be alienated by strong criticism of its policies in faraway Chechnya because its cooperation is needed in preserving the stability of the nearby Balkans.

As far as the United States is concerned, its interests in the crisis in Chechnya should also be weighed against the historical relations with Russia, its post-Cold War relations with the country and its inclusion in American led collective security institutions as well as the role of Russia in the crisis in Bosnia and the Balkans.

On the whole, an examination of the history of the relations between Russia and the United States would reveal a fluctuation of the state of these relations between the two countries marked by mainly four periods of friendship and alignment and periods of friction. These are the period prior to the 20th century and the Bolshevik Revolution in Russia, the period between the Bolshevik Revolution and World War II, the Cold War, and the Post-Cold War period.

Indeed, on the whole, relations between the two countries can be qualified as periods of protracted "periods of friendship and protracted periods of friction" but that, especially during the reign of Tsars and prior to the 20th century" the United States got along "reasonably well—at times conspicuously well—with Czarist Russia, in spite of the ideological gulf that yawned between the two great nations"[609]. The explanation given is that, at that time, there were common enemies to both countries, notably Britain, and common problems such as guaranteeing the freedom of sea traffic[610]. Other writers argue that prior to the 20th century, there were no intense relations between the two countries, except for a few scattered incidents such as the purchase of Alaska, because there was no real need to maintain such relations. Yet, in the beginning of the 20th century, new changes on the European and Asian balance of power, resulted in a greater "coincidence of strategic interests" is spite of the huge politico-ideological differences

---

609   See Thomas A. Bailey, <u>America Faces Russia: Russian-American Relations from Early Times to Our Day</u>, Cornell University Press, Ithaca, NY., 1950, p. 347.

610   Idem.

between the two countries[611]. In the time of the Tsars, other than the Consul of the United States in St. Petersburg, the contact between the two countries on the diplomatic level was rare. This continued until Russia, at the time of Tsar Alexander I, decided to recognize the United States in 1809. The recognition came after the defeat of Tsar Alexander II by Napoleon in 1807[612]. Tsar Alexander I then changed sides and instead of continuing to side with Britain, he decided to pact with France. Consequently, Alexander I was soon at war with the British who decided to blockade sea-borne supplies to Russia[613]. It is at this point that the need for the United States became evident. For after depending on British shipping for so long, Russia after this sea embargo decided to turn to the United States merchant marine as a substitute sea carrier[614]. This one of the two major diplomatic manoeuvres known between the two countries prior to the 20th century. The other major diplomatic manoeuvre between the two countries concerns the purchase of Alaska on the 30th of March 1867. On 30th March, 1867, Secretary of State William H. Seward agreed to purchase Alaska from Russia for $7 million. Russia had already established its presence in this region and offered to sell it to the United States during President James Buchanan's Administration. The conditions of the United States at the time and the civil war that was taking place, however, stalled negotiations[615]. Indeed, even though the purchase of Alaska meant an increase in the geographic size of the United State by 20%, Secretary of State William H. Seward encountered a number of difficulties in trying to convince the Congress to ratify the agreement, which was finally done but with only one vote to make the difference[616].

The second period relating to this dissection attempt of the historical state of relations between the United States and Russia is that which stretches from the Russian Revolution of 1917 until the start of the Cold War. The Bolshevik Revolution in Russia seems to have brought a dramatic chain of impacts on the relations with the United States. Indeed, the new Russian political regime's intentions to undermine the capitalist foundation was quite shocking to the

---

611   See James M. Goldgeier, "The United States And Russia", <u>Policy Review</u>, Oct-Nov 2001 Online document found at <u>www.questia.com</u>.

612   See Thomas A. Bailey, <u>op. cit.</u>, p. 13.

613   Idem.

614   Idem.

615   See the chapter entitled "The Purchase of Alaska" in Thomas A. Bailey, America Faces Russia: Russian-American Relations from Early Times to Our Day, <u>op. cit.</u>, pp. 95-108.

616   Idem.

United States, who did not even recognize the new order in Russia except in 1933, during the Presidency of Franklin Delano Roosevelt and probably only to gain a new ally against the threat of Nazi Germany[617]. The reasons advanced for the non-recognition of the new regime, according to the United States' Secretary of State at the time Bainbridge Colby, were that" the Bolshevik leaders had used force to obtain power and were maintaining their position through "savage oppression" of the Russian people".[618] In addition, there was a complaint against the new Communist regime for not honouring the international financial obligations of the predecessor state in Russia[619]. Indeed, the reaction in the United States to this dramatic turn of events in Russia was a fluctuating one. Between 1917 and 1941, "American attitudes toward Communist Russia ran through cycles of hysteria, ignorance, indifference, and wishful thinking"[620]. In the period of the Second World War, however, attitudes changed and differences were put aside[621]. This close cooperation between the two countries during World War II formed what is known as the "Grand Alliance"[622]. One of the most prominent projections of this "Grand Alliance" was a United States' decision to allocate an enormous economic aid to the Soviet Union. For, during the years of World War II, the United States sent to the Soviet Union over 17,000,000 tones of supplies with an overall value of $10 billion[623]. This aid, however, was not a direct one. For at the time there was much resistance to providing direct American aid to the Communist regime of Russia. The aid of the United States to Russia, hence, was in the form of what was known as the "Diplomacy of Lend—Lease"[624]. The Lend-Lease Act was passed in March 11, 1941 and permitted the President of the United States to "sell, transfer title to, exchange, lease, lend, or otherwise dispose of, to any [country whose defence the President deems vital to the defence of the United States] any defence article". It

---

617 See James M. Goldgeier, op. cit.,

618 See Thomas R. Maddux, Years of Estrangement: American Relations with the Soviet Union, 1933-1941, University Presses of Florida, Tallahassee, FL., 1980, p. 1

619 Idem.

620 See Thomas A. Bailey, op. cit., p. 348.

621 Idem.

622 See the chapter entitled "Franklin D. Roosevelt and the Grand Alliance, 1933-1945" in Ronald E. Powaski, The Cold War: The United States and the Soviet Union, 1917-1991, Oxford University Press, New York, 1998, pp. 35-65.

623 See George C. Herring Jr., Aid to Russia, 1941-1946: Strategy, Diplomacy, the Origins of the Cold War, Columbia University Press, New York, 1973, p. xiii.

624 Ibid., p. vii.

thus extended Cash and Carry policy[625] of the beginning of 1939, which, in its time replaced the Neutrality Act[626]. The value of the items to be lent was not supposed to exceed $1,300,000,000 in total. US President Franklin Delano Roosevelt approved US$1 billion in Lend-lease aid to the Soviet Union for the first time on October 30, 1941[627]. Evidence, however, indicates that this assistance to the Soviet Union caused more tensions between the two countries on the long run. The United States delay in assisting Russia in the first years of the war resulted in a Soviet "distrust" of the West and "at a time threatened the existence of the alliance"[628]. The settlement of the Lend-lease aid of the United States to Russia, hence, resulted in frictions between the two countries. Indeed, negotiations over the settlement of this economic aid stretched from 1946 until 1972[629]. The aid itself to Russia ended in the middle of 1947. The negotiations over the Soviet Union's settlement of the Lend-Lease aid was subject to an impasse until 1972 when the reaching of an agreement between the two countries on the issue was possible. In addition, the Lend-Lease aid was a cause of controversy that fed antagonism between American and Russian writers on the role of the United States' Lend-Lease Act in the Soviet Union's victory over the Axis countries in World War II[630].

The third period of this historical analysis of the bilateral relations between the United States and Russia is that which concerns the state of relations between the

---

625   Originally, *cash and carry* simply designates a method of making purchases where the customer pays the purchased goods immediately and takes them away himself—as opposed to having the goods delivered and paying a bill later. In that sense, most retail shops are "cash and carry". The policy of *Cash and Carry* established at the onset of World War II in 1939 revised the Neutrality Acts so any ship could come to United States ports and carry away anything they could buy. This policy aided Great Britain and France.

626   The Neutrality Act in the United States legislation underwent several changes depending on the cause and period. The *Neutrality Act* of 1935 prohibited American citizens from selling arms to belligerents in international war. It resulted from Italy's invasion of Ethiopia. The *Neutrality Act* of 1937 stated that United States citizens could not sell arms to belligerents in Civil Wars, including the government side. It resulted from the Spanish Civil War. Later in 1937, a second *Neutrality Act* forbade travel by U.S. citizens on ships of belligerents. This was aimed at the Sino-Japanese War (1937-1945).

627   See George C. Herring Jr., op. cit, p. 21.

628   Ibid., p. xiii.

629   Ibid., see Appendix entitled "Lend-Lease Settlement Negotiations, 1946-1972", pp. 295-303.

630   Ibid., p. 278.

two countries during the Cold War era. For after the end of World War II, the enthusiasm in the United States that the aid policy would smooth relations with the Soviet Union have gradually faltered, although, a few months after the end of the war, the United States provided $50 million of reconstruction supplies to the Soviet Union[631]. This, nonetheless, was mainly done "to maintain the appearance of allied cooperation, in part to secure immediate advantages[632]". The Administration of Harry Truman then, in its offer of aid in March 1946, to the Soviet Union manifested growing reluctance for assisting the Soviet Union and attached "sweeping political and economic conditions to its offer"[633]. These events can be said to have constituted the prelude to the Cold War. Nonetheless, some writers would consider that the Cold War between the United States and Russia did not start only in aftermath of World War II. This opinion is founded on the notion that the Cold War actually stretched from 1917 until 1991[634]. However, even after considering that this argument is correct, the term "Cold War" was, only, first used by Bernard Baruch[635] during a congressional debate in 1947.

In the aftermath of World War II, The United States and Britain, alarmed by the Soviet domination of Eastern Europe, feared the expansion of Soviet power and communism in Western Europe and elsewhere. For their part, the Soviets were determined to maintain control of their natural sphere of influence, Eastern Europe, and also to safeguard against a possible renewed threat from Germany. The Cold War was waged mainly on political, economic, and propaganda fronts and had only limited recourse to weapons except, of course, where the theatre of power measurement between the two countries used to crystallize in conflicts that took place far away from their borders, such as the Korean War theatre, The War of Vietnam, or the War of Afghanistan. The Cold War was at its peak in 1948–1953. This was a period that was characterized by various escalations both

---

631 Ibid., p. 238.

632 Ibid., p. 239.

633 Idem.

634 See Ronald E. Powaski, *The Cold War: The United States and the Soviet Union, 1917-1991*, op. cit.

635 Bernard Baruch (1870-1965) was a U.S. financier and adviser to presidents. In 1919 he was a member of the Supreme Economic Council at the Paris Peace Conference at Versailles and one of Wilson's advisers on the terms of peace. During World War II he served as an unofficial adviser on economic mobilization to Pres. Franklin D. Roosevelt. Later he was instrumental in setting UN policy on the international control of atomic energy.

parties initiated such as the Berlin blockade and airlift (1948–1949)[636], the formation of NATO in 1949, the victory of the communists in the Chinese Civil War (1926-1949)[637], and the Korean War (1950–1953). Another intense stage occurred was with the famous Cuban missile crisis episode (1958–1962), which resulted in an intensification of mass destruction weapons' build-up race on both sides. Later on, a period of détente in the 1970s was followed by renewed hostility. The Cold War ended with the collapse of the Soviet Union in 1991. The state of strained relations between the two camps was, nevertheless, marked with a short period of détente (1972-1973) in which agreements such as that meant to limit strategic offensive nuclear launchers (SALT I), the Anti-Ballistic Missile (AEM) Treaty, The Basic Principals Agreement, and the Agreement on the Prevention of Nuclear War were reached[638]. The end of this period of relative rapprochement between the two camps seems to have been caused by the outbreak of the Arab-Israeli war of October 1973, as well as the civil war in Angola (1975-1976).

The period that followed the collapse of the Berlin Wall was marked with intense cooperation between the two countries. This is the fourth period in this analysis of the relations between the two countries. However, the period to be considered in this examination would only be from 1990 until 1996, which is the year when both crises under discussion (Bosnia and Chechnya) ended. For after Russia's cooperation, during the Presidency of Michael Gorbachev, with the United State's of President George Bush Senior in the reunification of Germany and its cooperation in the Gulf War of the beginning of the 1990's, "it seemed at the beginning of 1992 that a future partnership between Russia and the United

---

636   the Berlin blockade and airlift (1948–1949) was an International crises that arose from an attempt by the Soviet Union to force the Allied powers (U.S., Britain, and France) to abandon their post-war jurisdictions in West Berlin. The Soviets, regarding the economic consolidation of the three Allied occupation zones in Germany in 1948 as a threat to the East German economy, blockaded all transportation routes between Berlin and West Germany. The U.S. and Britain responded by supplying the city with food and other supplies by military air transport and airlifting out West Berlin exports. An Allied embargo on exports from the Eastern bloc forced the Soviets to lift the blockade after 11 months.

637   The Chinese Civil War was a conflict in China between the Kuomintang (the Nationalist Party; KMT) and the Communist Party of China (CPC). It began with the takeover of the KMT by the right-wing General Chiang Kai-shek and purges of leftist and Communist members in 1926 and ended in 1949 with an unofficial cessation of hostilities, with the Communists controlling mainland China and the Nationalists controlling Taiwan and several Fujianese islands.

638   See James M. Goldgeier, op. cit.,

States in a post-Soviet era would be relatively easy to achieve"[639]. Indeed, the beginning and the mid-1990 can be considered as a "golden age" of rapprochement between the two countries on various levels. It should be remembered, in this respect, that Russia's economic conditions at this time were not the subject of anyone's envy. Accordingly, the Russian President Boris Yeltsin sought further rapprochement with the West and, in particular, with the United States between 1991-1993[640]. The cooperation between the two countries was at its best in this period precisely with the election of president Bill Clinton in January 1993[641]. Indeed, the image of the "Clinton-Yeltsin" couple is a very significant and a very famous one. Notwithstanding this, some have other explanations for this intense rapprochement with the Russia during the Clinton Administration (1993-2001). These reasons were more related to the internal agenda of the United State's President Clinton at the time. James M. Goldgeier states "after Bill Clinton assumed the presidency in January 1993, Yeltsin had a partner whose domestic political needs for good relations were equal to his own. Clinton's agenda (like Gorbachev's after March 1985) was focused like a laser beam on the domestic economy. And given his spending priorities in education and health care, he could not afford any renewed threat from Moscow that might lead to higher defence budgets. Even more, it seemed to many in the West that with Boris Yeltsin in power, a new world order could be forged—with a democratic, market-oriented Russia integrated with the rest of Europe (finally). Assisting Russian political and economic reform became Bill Clinton's top foreign security policy priority at the start of his presidency, as he and his top advisors proclaimed often in the first half of 1993. Signalling this, his first trip outside the country was to meet Yeltsin in Vancouver in April 1993, where he unveiled a huge assistance package for his new friend"[642]. It seems, hence, that the bilateral relations between the two countries, although characterized by antagonism at certain points in history, were also marked by various attempts of rapprochement. It appears, considering the historical evidence mentioned-above, that the United States kept in mind, throughout all the stages of this relationship, the importance of Russia's weight in the balance of international relations. For the United States, if Russia can not be won as an ally, then it is important that it remains neutral. This might explain the various "appeasement "attempts of the United States vis-à-vis Russia represented in the United States' economic and political assistance to

---

639   Idem.
640   Idem.
641   Idem.
642   Idem.

that country, from the time of the Tsars until that of the well known image of the "Clinton-Yeltsin" couple.

As far as the question of the crisis in Chechnya is concerned, the United States' political interests and involvement in this crisis is certainly based on the background of its bilateral political relations with Russia, as well as on a realization of the importance of Russia's pan-Slavic leadership in the stabilization of the Balkans. Moreover, the least that can be said about the United States' policy toward the Caucasus and Central Asia in the beginning of the 1990s is that it was a rather chaotic one. In an interesting article on the United States' policy toward the Caucasus and Central Asia in the 1990s, Fiona Hill explains "The United States policy toward the Caucasus and Central Asia over the last ten years has been marked by a distinct lack of direction. The U.S. stumbled into the region with only the vaguest idea of its geography, history, or political complexities. It has since failed to transform improvised responses to regional challenges into a coherent strategy. Bureaucratic wrangling over jurisdictions and attempts by domestic interest groups to push their own regional agendas have further undermined the rationality and unity of policy"[643]. This idea is also supported by Paula J. Dobrinsky and David B. Rivkin who argue that the United States policy vis-à-vis the crisis in Chechnya "amounts to a major strategic blunder"[644]. The reasons of this "policy blundering" are various. For one thing, it can be said that the United States was in a period where it was still absorbing the shock of the worldwide collapse of the Soviet Union and Communism, its declared enemy for so long. The United States, furthermore, had "no history of significant engagement" with these regions prior to the 1990s and they never figured in its calculations of bilateral relations with the dominant neighbouring regimes to the USSR in the region such as Turkey, Iran, and the China[645]. The real interest came with the "re-discovery" of the energy resources in the region. For if it wasn't for that, these "regions would have likely remained a marginal backwater for crafters of U.S. foreign policy"[646]. Apparently and due to this lack of experience in Central Asia and the Caucasus, the United States seems to have committed two principal

---

643   See Fiona Hill, "A Not-So-Grand Strategy: United States Policy in the Caucasus and Central Asia since 1991", *Politique étrangère*, February 2001, online document without pagination found at
http://www.brook.edu/dybdocroot/views/articles/fhill/2001politique.htm

644   See Paula J. Dobrinsky and David B. Rivkin, "U.S. Policy Toward Russia: A Brief Critique", Online document found at
http://www.watsoninstitute.org/bjwa/archive/7.1/Russia/Dobriansky.pdf, p. 3.

645   See Fiona Hill, op. cit.,

646   Idem.

mistakes in its there. The first of these mistakes is to consider the Caucasus and Central Asia as "one extended unit" in spite of the existing cultural, historical and other individual differences that characterize each one of these regions[647]. The second is that the United States did not fully take into consideration the "historical vested interests" of neighbouring powers in the region[648]. This lack of appreciation of the individual traits of the region's components was, furthermore, coupled by the fact that pressuring Russia would have probably resulted in no significance change. This was particularly the case in Chechnya. For although, there was clear evidence of the atrocities committed in Chechnya, pressuring Russia, by cutting economic assistance would not have changed Russia's behaviour in that region[649]. The consequence was that the United States "reluctance" to "issue strong condemnations of Russia's actions in Chechnya" indicated" beyond any doubt" what can be labelled as "a hypocritical double standard" applied by the United States in "in judging the behaviour of other countries"[650]. The fact that there were no real vital interests of the United States in the region can also be said to have substantially influenced this "reluctance". In fact, the first official "foray" in the region only came in 1991 "as the Bush Administration grappled with the unexpected dissolution of the USSR and diplomatic recognition "of the 15 new states that emerged from the collapse of the Soviet Union[651]. Prior to the signing of contracts between the United States oil companies and some of the countries of the region, notably with Kazakhstan and Azerbaijan (1993-1994), the parameters of the United States' foreign policy there were, to say the least, "unclear"[652] It seems, therefore, that real political interest in the conflict in Chechnya did not exist in the early 1990s. The United States' political interests in the Caucasus and Central Asia region as a whole seems not present much compared to its historical and strategic interest in "seducing" Russia, or at least, in not antagonising it. In addition, to this initial lack of vital political interests in Chechnya, the United States needed Russia's assistance for the stabilization of the Balkans. It should be kept in mind that it was in the interest of both the United States and Russia at the time to stabilize this sensitive area. The United States, in addition to its political interest in maintaining peace in the European continent, also had two of its major allies in NATO (Greece and Turkey) with their historical antagonism, involved in the conflict in the Balkans. On the other hand, Russia could not have,

---

647   See Fiona Hill, <u>op. cit.</u>
648   Idem.
649   See Paula J. Dobrinsky and David B. Rivkin, <u>op. cit.</u>, p. 4.
650   Idem.
651   See Fiona Hill, <u>op. cit.</u>
652   Idem.

for historical, internal, and strategic reasons, have been not involved considering its affinities with the Serbs[653]. Russia, in addition, seems to have understood that the United States' and the West's need for its active involvement in the Balkans would overshadow its actions in Chechnya. This was clearly seen with the episode of the hostage situation in Bosnia, when Bosnian Serbs took the UN's "blue helmets" as hostages as explained earlier. Hall Gardner states, in this respect, that Boris Yeltsin (despite his own brutal actions in Chechnya) hoped to make political capital" out of the efforts made by Russia to secure the release of the hostages[654]. By doing that the Russian President aimed at gaining "international recognition for Russia as a "peacemaker"[655].

The United States' and France's political interests in the crisis in Bosnia were much more vital and much more expressed than their respective political interests in Chechnya. For its part, France vis-à-vis the crisis in Bosnia, was interested in containing the conflict because it is taking place nearby. For France, the non-containment of the conflict would have destroyed all the efforts taken so far to reach the aspired European unity and to contain Germany. France also needed to exhibit its leadership of the European continent and on the world as a whole. Exhibiting leadership also meant projecting the ability to act without the help of the exterior "United States" and its security instrument: NATO. France, thus, favoured a European collective security solution to the conflict in Bosnia. On the other hand, the crisis in Chechnya seems to have occupied a small place on the agenda of the European powers as a whole. The incidents, where Europe took stands condemning Russian acts in Chechnya were limited to suspension of Russian membership applications in some of the European institutions. Nevertheless, it was in the interest of France and the other European countries to involve Russia in the new post Cold War order. For France, this meant introducing a counterweight to the hegemony of NATO and the United States in the continent. It also meant that Russia should not be alienated by strong criticism of its policies in faraway Chechnya because its cooperation is needed in preserving the stability of nearby Balkans.

The United States also had a vital political interest in containing conflict in Bosnia and in stabilising the Balkans as a whole, even if, practically, its involvement in the region represents an insignificant percentage of the its active military personnel. Indeed, for only one fifth of the operating multinational forces operating in the Balkans, the United States can be said to have made a reasonable investment by its involvement in the region. In addition, the United States could

---

653 See Hall Gardner, Dangerous Crossroads: Europe, Russia, and the Future of NATO, op. cit., p. 155
654 Ibid., p. 168.
655 Idem.

not have afforded to jeopardize its economic interests in Europe by allowing the destabilization of the continent. Finally, involvement in Bosnia, for the United States, in addition to exhibiting leadership, provided a golden opportunity to appease hostile Arab, Muslim, and world opinion resulting from a criticism of adopting double standards following its highly mediatised and phenomenal involvement in the Gulf Crisis of 1990-1991. This was not at all the case of its policy concerning the crisis in Chechnya. For the United States, it is important to win Russia to its side because of Russia's weight in the balance of international relations or at least not to have it" again" as a rival. The United States have historically no experience in the region and, prior to the re-discovery of energy resources, Chechnya and the rest of the Caucasus did not occupy much priority on the agenda of the United States' foreign policy. The re-discovery of "energy interests", however, meant more marginalizing of Chechnya and the human rights violations in it and more appeasement of Russia. Furthermore, there was a need for Russia's help to stabilize the Balkans; which was a region that is more important to stabilize at the time for the United States, than the newly discovered people of Chechnya.

2.2 4. Regional Interests

France and the United States both have regional interests involved in both crises. Whether in nearby Bosnia or in faraway Chechnya, the two countries can be said to have had important regional interests involved. These interests range from a desire of maintaining regional stability to a desire of gaining regional hegemony. In both crises, regional interests have a great bearing on the two countries reactions and involvement.

In the case of France and, as far as the crisis in Bosnia-Herzegovina is concerned, the first important regional interest to be discussed is that of European Collective Security, which is an issue so precious to French diplomacy. The disintegration of Yugoslavia and the ensuing conflicts in the Balkans posed a serious threat to the interest of France in having a secure and stable Europe and in having a European effective security response to anything that would jeopardize the region's stability. Such a destabilization of the regional security would have had a spell over effect that might have involved all of Europe and that might have resulted in the destruction of all the efforts and steps taken toward the construction of a unified Europe. Accordingly, the first real test to this concept of unified Europe was the conflicts in the Balkans and the disintegration of the Soviet Union.

Many writers argue that the conflicts of the Balkans and the disintegration of the Soviet Union produced considerable impact on the European countries and their regional considerations. Gilles de la Menardiere explains, for instance, "it is true today that the European continent is not directly threatened by a power as important as the Soviet Union was. But the fragmentation of the Balkans and the ex-Soviet Union, after the implosion of the Soviet Empire, presents a constant risk of an explosive and contaminating situation"[656]. Gilles de la Menardiere goes on to say that "the paradox of this situation for the Western Europeans is that the absence hegemony on the continent scale and the disappearance of a nuclear threat should have created a period of significant security, but on the contrary this produces a return to the ethnic conceptions of international relations. And this threatens to spread insecurity in Europe by a competition between rival ethnicities". For his part, Thierry Garcin explains the significance of the events of the conflicts in the Balkans and the events that followed the fall of the Berlin Wall on the European continent and on international relations. He states" If we disregard the Greek civil war, the Basque and the Northern Ireland conflicts, the war in Yugoslavia is the first in Europe since 1945. Nevertheless, in 1975, during the time of the reaching of the Entente (the Helsinki Treaty), the thirty-six members who signed it committed themselves to not changing the frontiers by force. The international upheavals of 1989-1991 decided otherwise. In addition, taking history into consideration (occupation of Spain, Ottoman Empire, protection of Christian minorities in the Near East) and in the context of Islamism, it indicated nothing less than a Moslem state in the heart of the European continent. Finally, there is an aggravating fact, which is that the Yugoslavia war was a civil and an international war at the same time"[657]. Others, such as Pascal Chaigneau, stress the regional repercussions of the conflicts in the Balkans on the European continent. He states" out of the 36,000 kilometres of frontiers existing in Europe, two thirds were created in the aftermath of the two World Wars. We are witnessing today the implosion of this frontier game. Certainly, "velvet separations" exist, for example, between the Czech Republic, historically the Bohemia Moravia, and Slovakia. But it is through the Yugoslav case that we see the perfect example of the questioning of the accords of Yalta and Versailles[658]". Some writers, for their part, explain that the mistake Europe made was not to try to prevent a disintegration of Yugoslavia even when such disintegration was predicted much earlier. Alfred Cahen, for instance, states "Already and even when Tito was alive, we were saying that Yugoslavia would explode with his death. But Tito died and Yugoslavia didn't explode immediately. And because there where other problems we were

---

656   See Gilles de la Menardiere, « Regards sur l'Imbroglio Yougoslave », in Pascal Chaigneau, Les Grands Enjeux du Monde Contemporain, Ellipses, 1996, p.97.

657   See Thierry Garcin, op. cit, p.10.

658   See Pascal Chaigneau, op. cit., p.7.

not interested in Yugoslavia. Our greatest error is not to have done any prevention: We reacted after the explosion. And restoring and even maintaining is much more difficult to manage"[659]. Thus, the conflicts in the Balkans represented by all means a serious risk to the whole of the European construction and the long desired pacification of the European continent due to a direct threat to Europe's security.

Yet, the issue of a disintegration of the Yugoslav state itself and the ensuing conflicts, with their threat for the European structure and security, was not the only realm where regional interests of countries lie. Indeed, the disintegration of the Soviet Union and Yugoslavia also presented a field where hegemonic interests of European powers resurfaced. A good example of this is the different reactions and conflicting interests of the major European powers such as Germany, France, and the UK to the above events. In this respect, Pascal Chaigneau argues, for instance, that Germany is the main winner of the consequences of the disintegration of the Soviet Union. He states "We can think that Germany is the principal beneficiary of the collapse of the Soviet Union because it has 17 million more inhabitants. But the essential is not that Germany has now 80 million inhabitants. What has fundamentally changed is its geography: Germany has radically changed its face. Germany was situated four years ago to the extreme East of an economic system—capitalism—, to the extreme East of a system of military alliances—NATO—,and to the extreme East of an economic and political integration—the European Community. Today, Germany, repositioned in its geography, became the centre of Europe"[660]. Thierry Garcin, for his part, adds "if the English and the French were supporters of maintaining Yugoslavia, the new unified Germany had a clear interest in favouring the splitting up of the Balkans with regard to its history"[661].

Indeed, it can be said that the Dayton Peace Accords were a direct result of the failure of the concept of collective security in Europe. The bombing of Bosnian Serb positions by NATO in the summer of 1995 combined with the joint Bosnian and Croat offensive produced a political and military environment which permitted the United States, represented by Richard Holbrooke, to negotiate a ceasefire in the Bosnian conflict and to eventually reach the Dayton Peace Accords on the 21st of November 1995. Thereafter, NATO sent 60,000 troops to Bosnia to guarantee the security of the area and to implement the various provisions and annexes of the Dayton Accords. This fact also indicated the failure of one of the major European powers (Germany or France being the EU's motor) to take the lead in

---

659   See Alfred Cahen, « L'Europe de la défense est-elle possible? », in Pascal Chaigneau, *Les Grands Enjeux du Monde Contemporain*, Ellipses, 1996, p40.

660   See Pascal Chaigneau, op. cit., p.7.

661   See Thierry Garcin, op. cit., p. 16.

heading and guaranteeing the collective security of the continent. Instead, the new collective security architecture in Europe was lead once again by the United States.

There seems to be two main reasons behind the failure of the concept of Collective European Security vis-à-vis the Bosnian crisis. First, the Bosnian crisis, according to the explanation of Richard Holbrooke, proved how difficult it was for the European Union to articulate a unified foreign policy and to develop an effective process to address urgent military provocations on the European continent. Indeed, to have a unified active position, the European Union is challenged with the task of coordinating and unifying its various national impulses in response to a security threat to the continent. Compared to NATO, the EU was lacking any effective security arm of its own[662]. Second, it appears that at the time the security of the European continent was somewhat dependent upon the quality of decision-making in the United States, which left Europe vulnerable to the bureaucratic interests of the United States specialised agencies such as the Pentagon, the leadership ability of American presidents in office, and the political climate in the United States. For instance, some writers explain that the Pentagon was against any U.S. involvement in the Bosnian War due to the U.S. previous experience in Vietnam[663]. This opinion is also supported by Charles Boyd who explains that, at the time, the United States' military leaders and their supporters in Congress frequently claimed that air power would not be able to end the Bosnian conflict[664]. Another factor that manipulated the United States positions on the Bosnian conflict was that of the economic costs of involvement. According to Rose Gideon, the existing concerns about budget costs at the time in the U.S. degraded military readiness for the intervention in Bosnia[665]. Indeed, all of these factors added to what Michael Cox explains about the poor personal diplomatic leadership at the time in Washington which left the European security vulnerable[666]. Thus, the European collective security immediately after the end of the Cold-War was highly dependent on the internal political arrangements and tendencies in the United States.

It should be mentioned, in this respect, that the context of the conflict in Bosnia was important not only for the affirmation of the Europeans' ability to

---

662 See Richard Holbrooke, To End a War, op. cit.

663 See Mark Danner, "The US and the Yugoslav Catastrophe", New York Review of Books, vol. 44, N° 18, 1997, pp. 56-64.

664 See Charles Boyd," Making peace with the guilty: The truth about Bosnia", Foreign Affairs, vol. 74, N° 5, 1995, pp.22-38

665 See Rose Gideon, "The Exit Strategy Delusion", Foreign Affairs, N°.77, 1998, pp. 56-67

666 See Michael Cox, US Foreign Policy after the Cold War, Pinter, London,1995.

guarantee the security of their own continent but also for the survival of NATO itself. Indeed, the dilemma facing NATO after the end of the Cold-War is the one that faces every alliance; to always have a *raison d'être*. It is the alliance that won the Cold War and was supposed to be one of the most successful alliances in history yet, it is probably one of the most successful not just because it won but rather because it continued to exist after the demise of its enemy. The conceptualisation of the alliance in its beginnings is quite interesting. According to the NATO Handbook of 2001 "the initial formulation of NATO strategy known as the "Strategic Concept for the Defence of the North Atlantic Area" was developed between October 1949 and April 1950. It set out a strategy of large-scale operations for territorial defence. In the mid-1950s the strategy of "massive retaliation" was developed. It emphasized deterrence based on the threat that NATO would respond to any aggression against its member countries by every means at its disposal, specifically including nuclear weapons. Discussions of possible changes in this strategic approach began later in the 1950s and continued until 1967 when following intensive debate within the Alliance, "massive retaliation" was replaced by the strategy of "flexible response"[667]. Indeed, one of the most important factors that added to the success of NATO and, indeed to its existence until this very day, is the fact that its conceptualisation and strategy is flexible and can adopt to new circumstances and variants.

More importantly, nonetheless, and other than a flexibility of its strategy, it had to find a new post-Cold War role in order to justify the continuity and the utility of its existence. Indeed, it seems that the functionality of this alliance was always been greater than simply providing military security for its members and deterring a possible Warsaw Pact attack on Western Europe. As a result of strong American pressure, the alliance began to reshape its role in the post-Cold War Europe as a guarantor of the existing security environment on the continent and as an outside power capable of responding to situations in other parts of the world like the Gulf War. To formalize this new role, the alliances' heads of states adopted In November 1991 a "new strategic concept" that identified instabilities resulting from economic, social and political reform in central and Eastern Europe as being the new types of threat faced by NATO and its members. The role was even enhanced in the following summer. According to Richard Ullman

---

667   See <u>NATO Handbook</u>, NATO Office of Information and Press, Brussels, 2001?
       P.43. According to this concept of "flexible response", the idea was to give NATO
       the advantages of flexibility and of creating uncertainty in the minds of any poten-
       tial aggressor about NATO's response in the case of threat to the sovereignty or
       independence of any single member. The concept was designed to ensure that
       aggression of any kind would be perceived as involving unacceptable risks". Idem.

"NATO's foreign ministers emphasized that the new role of NATO would be manage European crisis and peacekeeping in coordination with European institutions such as the OSCE (Organisation of Security and Cooperation in Europe), the European Union, the Western European Union and the United Nations[668]. It can be said, thus, that the conflict in the ex-Yugoslavia as a whole and in Bosnia, in particular, gave NATO the opportunity to re-define its new strategic objectives in the new post-Cold War era. Had NATO not been flexible and fast enough to find a new enemy, it would have had no more reason to exist. France, in such a context, was a fervent supporter of a European (Including Russian) security response to the conflict to balance NATO.

Containment is another aspect of these European regional interests of France. In particular, containment of Germany's hegemony on the continent is a high priority of France's regional interests. This aspect has been a long time tradition of French regional interests in the European continent. Paul Scott Mowrer states, for instance, "The key to all French action in Europe, now as before the war, is fear of Germany—a fear which is beyond any doubt fully justified"[669]. Paul Scott Mowrer explains this fear by the French lack of confidence in alliances because of its past experiences, which also explains France's continuous efforts for a non Balkanised Europe. He adds" As far as "Balkanized Europe" is concerned, it is France, and one might almost say France alone, which has anything like a concrete reconstruction policy; for Britain's principal interests lie elsewhere, and Italy's internal condition is too troubled to permit it the luxury.... In the second place, disappointed in the hope of having a permanent defensive alliance with Britain and the United States, thrown back, as it were, on its own resources, France is resolved to contrive whatever other defensive combinations, or barriers against German expansion, circumstances or the ingenuity of statesmen may make possible. For this reason, it is deploying at present a vigorous diplomatic activity in every country of "Balkanised Europe." Pending the reestablishment of equilibrium, it is trying to play the role of general conciliator, and to pose as everybody's friend, so that, whatever the future may bring, it will never be left entirely alone[670]". The new unified Germany with its economic and regional weight and its revisited regional influence in the ex-Yugoslavian states and the East European ones is certainly an annoying reality for French regional interests. Allison Brown states, "Though President Mitterrand says he does not fear

---

668   See Richard Ullman, The World and Yugoslavia's Wars, Council on Foreign Relations Press, New York, 1996, p.25.

669   See Paul Scott Mowrer, Balkanized Europe: A Study in Political Analysis and Reconstruction, E. P. Dutton & Company, 1921, p. 311

670   Ibid., pp 310-312.

German reunification, France doesn't want it. Reunification complicates Paris's priority of moving ahead quickly with Western European economic integration. A new fatherland of 80 million Germans would tip the balance in the European Community even further in West Germany's direction"[671]. Indeed, the reunified Germany carries much more weight with its revisited sphere of influence after the fall of the Berlin Wall in the East and the Baltic Sea States. Yet, this reunification was far from being expected by Western politicians. Allison Brown explains, for instance, that" German unification came as a complete surprise. As late as 1989 politicians and pundits were convinced that the Germans had been divided for good"[672]. The old "fears "of German hegemony were "rekindled" in France and also in the United Kingdom[673]. The fear of the hegemony of Germany in Europe after its re-unification is probably due to the fact that the only advantage that the other great powers (France and the UK) still have is their nuclear advantage. Allison Brown goes on to say, "For France and Britain, the implications are particularly potent. The two have played worried spectators in the fast-moving German drama of recent weeks, and many experts see a single Germany gradually nudging them off the centre stage of European politics. So far, Paris and London have urged a cautious approach to German reunification, but neither appears to have designed a long-term strategy to deal with the new challenge, as if they are counting on their status as Western Europe's only nuclear powers to maintain their political influence"[674]. Thus, a new unified Germany is much more threatening on a regional European level than a divided one. Other than the demographic and the economic weight of the new unified Germany, its relations with the Balkans and its influence in the East is of particular interest to other European powers such as France.

It is true, yet, that such a fear of Germany's new hegemony on the Balkans and on Eastern European states is quite understandable since it is a historically justified fact. J. F. Brown explains" In the Middle Ages, German colonialism, led eastward by the Teutonic Knights, extended its sway as far as Lithuania. The Habsburg Reich, which would eventually become Austria-Hungary, stretched deep into the Balkans, and it incorporated much of what is today Czechoslovakia, Yugoslavia, and Poland. Modern, post-1871 Germany was essentially the product of Prussian hegemony. Prussia, in turn, had its origins in that part of Europe that is today an integral part of the East—in the Electorate of Brandenburg. Before the Kingdom

671   Allison Brown, <u>Uniting Germany: Documents and Debates, 1944-1993</u>, Berghahn Books, Providence, 1994, p. 84

672   Idem, p. xvii.

673   Idem, p. 104.

674   Ibid., pp 115-116.

of Prussia unified the *kleindeutsch* part of the empire, it extended crescent like almost as far as Krakow in the south and the Niemen River in the north"[675]. Indeed, the interesting regional particularity of Germany is that it belonged to both East and West at the same time[676]. The other European power that showed interest in Eastern Europe through its foreign policy is France. J. F. Brown states, here, "In a sense France is the positive exception to a generally negative answer…. France has paid special attention to the division of Europe symbolized by the Yalta Conference, in particular to East Central Europe as such. This was especially the case under de Gaulle, but has been shown more recently by the attention, greater than in any other Western country, given in France to the Polish events of 1980-81"[677]. Yet, this never materialized into an effective policy. J. F. Brown adds" From de Gaulle to Francois Mitterrand, French leaders were cast more than ever as specialists in vision rather than policy, in words rather than deeds"[678]. Indeed, the re-unified Germany, moreover, didn't take long to show its interest in Central and Eastern Europe. Some writers argue, in this respect, that the reunification of Germany had an important effect on its foreign policy. Simon Bulmer and William E. Paterson explain, for instance that reunifying Germany had a "liberating effect on the *potential* for German diplomacy"[679]. This sometimes happened at the expense of European and international consensus. It particularly took place when Germany unilaterally recognized the independence of Croatia and Slovenia. Ralph Piotrowski states, "At the beginning of 1991 a broad consensus existed internationally that the unity of Yugoslavia had to be preserved to guarantee international stability. However, on December 19, 1991, the German government announced its decision to recognize the former Yugoslavian republics of Slovenia and Croatia. Shortly after (1992), the international community took similar action[680]". Thus, one of the important French regional interests in the crisis is to guard against the hegemonic tendencies of Germany in Central and Eastern Europe. It is not a new regional of France, however. It is one that is central to its European foreign policy due to its historical experience with Germany.

675　See J. F. Brown, <u>Eroding Empire: Western Relations with Eastern Europe</u>, The Brookings Institution, Washington, DC., 1987, pp. 129-130.

676　Idem, 131.

677　Idem, p. 189

678　Idem.

679　See Simon Bulmer and William E. Paterson, "Germany in the European Union : gentle giant or emergent leader?", <u>International Affairs</u>, Vol.72, N°1, 1996, p. 30.

680　See Ralph Piotrowski, "Recognising Croatia," <u>Paper presented at the 3 Annual Graduate Student Workshop, The Kokkalis Program</u>, Harvard University, 9-10 February 2001, p. 1.

It is also important, for France as a regional interest, to guard against the rise of nationalistic feelings and separatism in the continent. France itself has regions where nationalistic separatist sentiments are quite strong such as Corsica and the Basque region. A success of a separatist nationalistic movement in an area that is as close as Central Europe would, hence, encourage other separatist movements or regions to do the same.

On more important consideration in the regional interests of France and which this time has to do with its larger regional interests (geographically speaking) is the French consideration of its Arab and Muslim policy at the time of reacting to the crisis in Bosnia. Indeed, the French relations with the Arab and Muslim worlds go far back history. Some writers explain that these relations go as far back as the time of Charlemagne and Haroun al-Rachid who exchanged ambassadors for the first time[681]. Other writers explain that the term *Politique Arabe de la France* (Arab Policy of France) is a relatively new one[682] while that of *Politique Musulmane de la France* (is one that only appeared in the beginning of the 20th century[683]. In this respect, the Mediterranean has also been on top of the French regional interests. Rálph Piotrowski states" Napoleon used to say that "geography dictates a country's policy" and one notes that the two axes of the French foreign policy—under the monarchy, the convention, the empire and the republic—have been Europe and the Mediterranean[684]". Indeed, the French regional interest in the Mediterranean and in preventing other powers hegemony over it is well anchored in history. The alliance between Soleiman the Magnificent and Francois 1er in 1535 aimed at preventing the hegemonic penetration of outside powers such as the Habsbourgs, the Russians and also the English[685]. The episodes of the Suez Campaign in 1956 and the Algerian War of (1954-1962) had a very negative effect on Franco-Arabe relations. Yet, it did not completely damage them. A fervent advocate of a close relationship with the Arab world was Charles de Gaulle who estimated that a renewed cooperation between Europe and France with the Arab and Muslim worlds can function as a counterbalance to the hegemony of the two superpowers at the time[686]. This relation or

---

681 See Paul Balta, « *La politique arabe et musulmane de la France* », <u>Confluences Méditerranée</u>, N° 22, Summer 1997, Docmuent found onlin at e.
http://www.ifrance.com/confluences/numeros/22.htm

682 See Paul Balta, Claudine Rulleau, <u>La politique arabe de la France. De de Gaulle à Pompidou</u>, Sindbad, Paris 1973.

683 See Henry Laurens, « *La politique musulmane de la France* », <u>Monde arabe. Maghreb-Machrek</u>, N°152, April-June 1996.

684 Ibid.

685 Idem.

686 Idem.

policy towards the Arab and Muslim world is, thus, neither new nor monotonous but a historical one that is also felxible. It can be said that it depends on the tendencies of the leadership in France. Claude Cheysson explains, for instance, that France didn't have an Arab Policy since 1985 and that it was only with Jacques Chirac that France had an Arab Policy again[687]. Thus, France holds particular interests to its relations with the Arab and Muslim worlds. Although the intensity of this relation depends more on the well and tendencies of the French leadership, this does not deny the fact that France has to be particularly conscience of its image in the Arab and Muslim world in order not to damage this relationship. In this sense, it can be said that one of the regional interests of France with regards to the crisis in Bosnia is taking into consideration the religious affinities that the Arab and Muslim world have for the Muslims in this area and to their plight as well as France's interests in the Mediterranean Basin.

As far as the crisis in Chechnya is concerned, it appears that France had no tangible regional interests involved in that crisis. This seems to be due to three main reasons. First, there is the clear cut factor of geographic proximity and to quote Napoleon once more" "geography dictates a country's policy". Second. it can be assumed that since both crisis were taking place in almost the same time, France preferred involving Russia in solving its immediate next door conflict in Bosnia rather than anger Russia and loose its support and hope of integrating it as a balancing force in a European defence mechanism, with less or no dependency on the United States Third, it can be said that France has vital economic interests at stake in having a good relationship with Russia and in having stability brought to the Caucasus even by force. It is, after all, much easier to deal with one single country for energy and petrol interests than to deal with a multitude of countries.

However, some of the regional interests it had vis-à-vis the crisis in Bosnia can also apply as far as that of Chechnya is concerned yet with lesser importance. These shared regional interests between the two crises are the fear of a dissemination of separatist movements and the sensitivity of the relations with the Arab and Muslim worlds. The effect of these two factors in the Chechnya case have, nonetheless, certain particularities. In the case of guarding against contamination of the success of separatist and nationalist movements, it seems that the effect for France is higher than that of Bosnia because separatist (Chechnya) is regarded as an integral region of the Russian Federation. Here, it can be noted that France has similar regions that are considered integral parts of the French Republic, namely Corsica and the Basque region. On the other hand, however, and as far as its relations to the Arab and Muslim worlds are concerned, it can be said that the effect for France is less and

---

687   See Calude Cheysson, « *La France doit avoir une politique arabe* », <u>France-Pays arabes, Eurabia</u>, Paris, N°232, May 1997.

for two reasons. The first reason is that France is not a key player in the region who's action is liable to change the course of things. Second, that interest is less for Chechnya than it was for Bosnia in the Arab and Muslim world precisely because the conflict in Bosnia was much more mediatised than that of Chechnya. Furthermore, Bosnians were primarily stressed by the media coverage, as being Muslims while, the reference to Chechens as Muslims by the media, was quite rare.

The regional interests of France in the two crises appear to be totally different at certain points and somewhat similar at others. In the case of the crisis in Bosnia, the regional interests of France were to seek a viable European collective solution to the crisis which excludes, if possible, the hegemony of the United States and NATO and which includes Russia in the security arrangements in the continent. Another regional interest is guarding against the reunified Germany's revisited hegemony on Central and Easter Europe. The relations with the Arab world and its vision of a Euro-Mediterranean cooperation that can counterbalance the hegemony of the United States can also be said to have been taken into consideration. Finally, guarding against a dissemination of separatist temptations that the conflicts in the Balkans might produce in the European continent, particularly vis-à-vis the French regions with separatist tendencies. France, on the other hand, did not have any tangible regional interests in the Chechnya crisis. This is probably due to the factor of geographic distance from the crisis area, the need to involve Russia in stabilising the nearby Balkans, and the easiness of dealing with one country for the benefit of economic interests than with a multitude of countries. The similarities with regional interests in Bosnia had more to do with its relations with the Arab and Muslim world and with guarding against a success of a separatist movement that would rekindle or encourage French regions to do the same. These two last factors had, however, their own degrees of effect in the case of Chechnya. They were sometimes less and sometimes more than they were in the case of the crisis in Bosnia.

Even, though its modest involvement in the Balkans (20% of the military force and 10% of economic aid as mentioned in the previous section relating to political interests) is quite modest and only done to exhibit leadership, the United States is anything but disinterested in the Balkan. Indeed, its involvement, in addition to exhibiting leadership, is also done to safeguard its vital interests in this region. The United States interests in "staying involved" in the Balkans "are real and fundamental," and cannot be separated from "the need to forge a Europe that is peaceful, undivided, and democratic"[688]. In no case would the United States

---

688   See Ivo H. Daalder, "The United States, Europe, and the Balkans*, <u>The Brookings Institution</u>, December 2000, Online document with pagination found at http://www.brook.edu/dybdocroot/views/articles/daalder/useurbalkch.htm, p. 2.

have allowed the collapse or the division of Europe and not simply because of a noble sentiment but because of a strategic vision. Ivo H. Daalder and Michael E. O'Hanlon explain" For decades, the United States deployed hundreds of thousands of troops to safeguard the security of Western Europe. With the collapse of the Soviet Union, it became possible to extend the stability and security that NATO countries long enjoyed to the rest of Europe—to build a Europe that was "whole and free" (in President George Bush's words) and "undivided, peaceful, and democratic" (as President Bill Clinton has urged). That is not just a noble sentiment, but a vision with deep strategic meaning. Such a Europe is more likely to be a partner of the United States in meeting the many challenges of the global age, and much less likely to pose a threat to U.S. interests"[689]. It can also be said that it is in the interest of the United States to insist all the time that it is the one doing the Europeans job. This, however, is not at all true. Indeed, considering the little share that the United States had in the military and economic stabilization of the Balkans compared to that of the Europeans, "complaints about the United States doing too much, and the allies falling short, are not backed up by the facts"[690]. Moreover, Europeans had "dozens" of deaths amongst their troops in Bosnia in the early 1990s prior to the involvement of the United States in that region[691]. Thus, the Europeans are more actively involved in the efforts to stabilize and help the Balkans financially than the United States would want them to believe. This is quite logical since they are the first affected by the lack of stability in the Balkans and the possible spell over effect that might, if not contained, enflame the whole continent and destroy the European construction.

In spite of the continuous United States' internal political debate about the need for "burden sharing" with Europe in the Balkans, the actual centre of the discussion is not whether the United States should or shouldn't be involved there but whether such involvement actually represents the level of the national interests of the United States in this region.[692] There are, indeed, two general views in this debate. The first one is that the U.S. involvement in the region is a "peripheral one" and one that is only there to reflect "at best humanitarian concerns and possible an interest in seeing NATO succeed or at least not fail"[693]. The other view suggests that the United States involvement in the Balkans is "reflects core American interests that are inextricably tied to its continued presence in the rest

---

689   See Ivo H. Daalder and Michael E. O'Hanlon, "The United States in the Balkans: There to Stay", The Washington Quarterly, Vol. 23, N° 4, p. 158.

690   See Ivo H. Daalder, op. cit., p. 5.

691   Idem.

692   See Ivo H. Daalder, "The United States, Europe, and the Balkans", op. cit, p. 6.

693   Idem.

of Europe"[694]. It is, useful, therefore, to examine more closely these two interpretations of the United States' engagement in the Balkans.

The first interpretation of the United States involvement is that which suggests that the United States interests in the region are peripheral and humanitarian only. This interpretation is supposed to be a reflection of the low level of involvement in the Balkans. It was, furthermore, the dominant policy interpretation of the United States engagement their in the 1990s[695]. This view is backed for, instance, by statements, of U.S. policy makers at the time. For them, the conflict in the Balkans is described as a "regional dispute" compared to their national interests in other regions of the world such as Iraq. Former United States Secretary of State James Baker states, in this respect, "Unlike in the Persian Gulf, our vital national interests were not at stake. The Yugoslav conflict had the potential to be intractable, but it was nonetheless a regional dispute. Milosevic had Saddam's appetite, but Serbia didn't have Iraq's capabilities or the ability to affect America's vital interests.... The greater threat to American interests at the time lay in the increasingly dicey situation in Moscow, and we preferred to maintain our focus on that challenge, which had global ramifications for us, particularly with regard to nuclear weapons[696]". According to this logic, the United States has "little geo-strategic interest" in the Balkans and the "only appreciable interest" for it there is to "show tangible support" for its European allies[697]. Supporters of this view call, hence, for a transfer of this burden to the European allies of the United States and a redirection of the its foreign policy towards a strict adherence to the "the principle of national interest" in its engagements[698]. In fact, such an interpretation would explain the hesitation of the United States to be totally involved in the Balkans as well as its push for a transfer of the stabilization burden in the region are to the Europeans. Furthermore, this view suggests that the United States supports a more European than a U.S. responsibility in the Balkans "not because it believed Europe could do much to slide stem the slide into war" but rather because it "the Europeans desired to take the lead in a region where Europe's interest were more definitively at stake than America's"[699]. This also would explain the fact that in the early stages of the

---

694   Idem.

695   Ibid, p. 7.

696   See James A. Baker, III, <u>The Politics of Diplomacy: Revolution, War, and Peace, 1989-92</u>, G.P. Putnam, New York, 1995, p. 636.

697   See <u>James S. Robbins,</u> "The Balkans: A Time for Principled Action", Online document without pagination found at <u>http://www.objectivistcenter.org/articles/jrobbins_balkans-time-principled-action-op-ed.asp</u>

698   Idem.

699   See See Ivo H. Daalder, "The United States, Europe, and the Balkans", <u>op. cit</u>, p. 6.

conflict the United States' participation was mainly limited to the helping the victims rather than to punish the criminals. Indeed, since the start of its mandate, the previously enthusiastic about intervention in Bosnia Bill Clinton, refused to deploy any ground troops in Bosnia" under any circumstances" except for" to help enforce a peace agreement."[700]. This would render the low level of the U.S. engagement in the Balkans as more a humanitarian than a strategically driven one[701]. Nonetheless, the initial reluctance to be actively engaged in the Balkans on the part of the United States seems to have complicated its position rather than assist it. For failure to resolve the conflict in Bosnia, threatened the "viability and continuity" of NATO, caused the United States criticism on the part of its European allies, especially from France, for lack of leadership and determination on the issue, and threatened the worldwide "credibility" of the United States as the world's leading power[702]. The growing concern, which took place over a decisive solution to the crisis in Bosnia is best illustrated by the advice of Anthony Lake, the first National Security Adviser to president Bill Clinton. His view in the early 1995 was that Bosnia "is a cancer in Presidency'" of Bill Clinton and that "it had to be cut away before it metastasised"[703]. Apparently, later on, President Clinton asserted his conviction that if the United States does not lead a peacekeeping mission in Bosnia, the conflict would lead to a "wider war" that will risk to contaminate the whole European continent[704].

Thus, the United States finally overcome its hesitation and decided to intervene in Bosnia and the Balkans. Yet, the question is whether the Clinton Administration's decision to intervene in Bosnia and the Balkans was justified simply by humanitarian motives, or whether this engagement is driven by tangible regional interests. This leads to the second interpretation of the United States' involvement in stabilisation of the Balkans, namely that which explains such an engagement by "core American interests" in the region[705]. At first glance, the apparent strategic interests in the Balkans would be a need to exhibit leadership, the need to prevent a future conflict between its two major allies in southern Europe (Greece and Turkey), and the credibility of the United States itself and its

---

700   Ibid. p. 7.
701   Idem.
702   Ibid., p. 8.
703   Ibid.
704   See Ted Galen Carpenter, "The Domino Theory Reborn: Clinton's Bosnia Intervention and the "Wider War" Thesis", Cato Foreign Policy Briefing, No. 42, August 15, 1996, Online Docmuent without pagination found at C:\windows\Bureau\Bosnia Clinton domino theory. tm.
705   See Ivo H. Daalder, "The United States, Europe, and the Balkans", op. cit, p. 11.

New World Order. Nonetheless, a more thorough look would reveal that the "core" interest of the United States in the region concerns "the future of Europe" as a whole[706]. It is a view, which suggests that the United States fought the Cold War to build a whole democratic Europe. This, however, was not done for "altruistic reasons" but for two "fundamental ones"[707]. The first one is that a stable Europe would not be the source of an instability that, in the past 100 years, has "kept the U.S. engaged at great cost and sacrifice". The other fundamental reason, according to this view, is that a stable peaceful Europe would be more able to "be a faithful and full partner of the United States" in its international policies[708]. Indeed, fear of much more significant engagement might well explain the decision of the United States to end the conflicts in the Balkans. Former United States Secretary of State Warren Christopher asserts this fear of a repetition of American costly engagement to stabilize Europe in saying "Twice in this century we have had to send our soldiers to fight in wars that began in Central Europe"[709]. For his part, James Steinberg, former Director of Policy Planning at the United States' State Department, elaborated more the dangers of inaction for the United States in the Balkans by saying "Without U.S. leadership in Bosnia, we would face the imminent danger of a widening war that could embroil our allies, undermine NATO's credibility, destabilize nearby democracies, and drive a wedge between the United States and Russia"[710]. Indeed, the Clinton Administration's Balkans' Policy constitutes only one portion of its European Policy aiming at reaching this "faithful and reliable" Europe. According to Ivo H. Daalder, the European Policy of the Clinton Administration was based four major objectives: "promoting a stronger" and a "more integrated Europe (including security)"," changing the objective of NATO from the "principal collective defence" to "managing security throughout the Euro-Atlantic are", winning Russia as a "partner" in Europe and guarding against having it again as a "rival", and "finally bringing peace and stability to the Balkan region"[711]. It seems, therefore, that the United States involvement in the Balkans, in itself, is solidly based on a core element of its strategy and interests in Europe. The view that the United States' intervention in Bosnia and the Balkans stems only from peripheral and

---

706   Ibid., p.12.

707   Idem.

708   Idem.

709   See Warren Christopher, "Send Troops to Bosnia», USA Today, October 18, 1995, p. 13.

710   See James Steinberg, "Foreign Policy Myopia," Washington Times, January 19, 1996, p. A19.

711   See Ivo H. Daalder, op. cit., p. 13.

humanitarian interests, does not seem to be a strong one, even if the level of engagement in the Balkans is lower than that of other European countries. In fact, this low level of engagement in the Balkans on the part of the United States can be interpreted in two ways. The first one is that the United States needed to involve the European more in their security and, therefore, did not intervene heavily in the region. The second is that the European powers were probably more than willing to provide the largest participation in the stabilisation of the Balkans. Yet, even with this large participation, it cannot be denied that there is no unified political voice in Europe. The *Old Continent* seems to have needed the United States' unifying and mobilizing symbolic leadership of the United States, who exerted this mobilizing leadership in other conflicts and crisis before such as those of Iraq (1990-1991) and Somalia. But saying that the Europeans needed the leadership of the United States and that the United States does not need the Europeans is not a fair statement. In fact, the United States, for the conduct of its affaires in the international arena, needs a reliable partner who can support it in times of need. If this partner is divided and unstable, then it would first, not help it much in its conduct of international policies and, second, would probably force it to engage in a costly re-stabilisation action on a much larger scale.

On the other hand, the United States strategic interests in Central Asia and the Caucasus are, to say the least, much more obvious and articulated than those it has in the Balkans. The importance of this region to the United States is well expressed by Fiona Hell who states, "The Caspian Basin and the surrounding states of the Caucasus and Central Asia have crept from obscurity onto the U.S. foreign policy agenda. While the individual countries of the two regions may not be of vital interest to the United States, the countries that border them are. Four have nuclear weapons, one is an important NATO ally, and two are states that have posed direct challenges to U.S. security by their support for terrorist move-ments"[712]. Ariel Cohen, for his part, comments on this re-emergence of the Caucasus and Central Asia as a region where the interests of many countries are involved and where the competition of those countries is acute. He says, "The Caucasus has emerged as a pivotal geo-strategic region within which the interests of the U.S., Europe, Russia, Iran, Turkey, and the broader Islamic world inter-sect"[713]. The region is certainly not the subject of all this international and regional competition for no good reasons. In fact, what has been known as the Ancient Silk Road and its historical economic benefits to various countries seems,

---

712   See Fiona Hill, "The Caucasus and Central Asia", <u>Policy Brief N° 80,</u> The Brookings Institution, May 2001, p. 1.

713   See Ariel Cohen, "Ethnic Interests Threaten U.S. Interests in the Caucasus", <u>Heritage Foundation Executive Summary N° 1222</u>, 25 September 1998, p. 1.

nowadays, to have regained its economic and strategic value. What is economically interesting enough for competition over spheres of influence in this region is that "oil and gas reserves and future auxiliary investments are estimated in the hundreds of billions of dollars"[714]. In a sense, the revival of the Silk Road seems to be incarnated in the billions of dollars worth projects of pipelines that are supposed to channel "the abundant energy resources of the Caspian Sea and Kazakhstan to global markets"[715]. The estimates of these reserves are quite tempting. Even the name of Silk Road has been reused. In fact, there is a pending act in the United States' Congress called the Silk Road Strategy Act (S. 1344)[716]. The gas and oil reserves of the Caspian Basin (Caspian Sea and surrounding countries: Azerbaijan, Iran, Turkmenistan, Kazakhstan, Turkey and Georgia) are estimated at $3 trillion, those of Central Asia (Kazakhstan, Kyrgyzstan, Tajikistan, Uzbekistan, Turkmenistan, Afghanistan, Pakistan, as well as parts of India and China) are estimated at 6.6 trillion cubic meters of natural gas and 10 billion barrels of undeveloped oil reserves"[717]. Although those energy resources are important for many countries, the United States seems to be more in need of them than others. Indeed, the United States imports 60% of its energy needs with only 13% of oil imports originating from the Persian Gulf. Furthermore, its consumption of energy is quite high compared to the percentage of its population to that of the worlds. For with only about 5% of the population of the world, the United States consume around 25% of the world's oil[718] (See Map 7 for a better idea on these energy projects and routes in the region). Central Asia and the Caucasus seem then to have regained its historical strategic importance for many world countries. Yet, benefiting from this region means having it stabilized first. For without this stability, the energy vein would not function.

714　Idem.
715　Idem.
716　Idem.
717　See Catherine Baldi, "How oil Interests Play Out in US Bombing of Afghanistan", online document without pagination found at http://www.peacenowar.net/Nov%208%2001—Oil.htm.
718　Idem.

Map 7: Oil and Gas Export Infrastructure in the Caucasus and the Black Sea

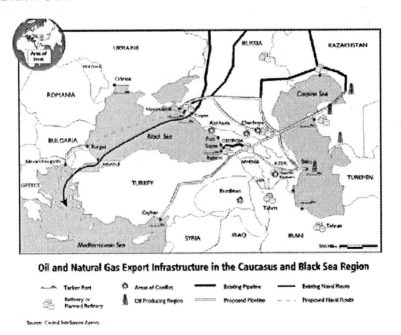

Oil and Natural Gas Export Infrastructure in the Caucasus and Black Sea Region

Source: Ariel Cohen, op. cit., p. 7. (The CIA is cited by Cohen as the primary source)

For the United States, having access to the energy resources in the region appears to be the major interest from which stems a number of other auxiliary strategic interests. In the Caucasus these "auxiliary" strategic interests seem to be preserving an independent and stable Armenia and Georgia, "keeping Iran and Islamic fundamentalism in check", and guarding against the re-emergence of Russian imperialism"[719]. To do that, the United States have to prevent the proliferation of ethnic conflicts (See Map 8 on Ethnic Groups in the Caucasus), re-enforce the authority of central governments and use its allies in the region to assist in guaranteeing the oil flow. Ariel Cohen argues that "the United States must secure its priorities by strengthening civil societies and markets within three Caucasian states, an developing an East-West coalition of Georgia and Azerbaijan" which are to be, interestingly, supported by the two strategic allies of the United States in the Middle East (Turkey and Israel)[720]. Furthermore, the

---

719　See Ariel Cohen, op. cit., p.1.
720　Idem.

routes of the pipelines have to be secured by friendly countries. In order to do that, the United States must "ensure that "American energy companies are able to establish oil and gas pipelines in a western direction to the Black Sea and the Mediterranean instead of north (to Russia) and south (to Iran)"[721]. For his part, Vladimir Radyuhin, explains how the United States is "keen to increase its influence and involvement in the region" but that its "ability for dealing with local conflicts, political instability and lack of democracy is questionable"[722]. The proliferation of local ethnic conflicts is probably the "unforeseen" backfire of the Stalinian policy of forced displacement and mixture of ethnicities. The ideal of the policy, as indeed it was the case of Tito's Yugoslavia, was to produce a new miraculous or utopian social structure where ethnicity does not have any bearing out of the mixture of different societies and ethnicities to make up an artificially and forcefully cemented national and societal mosaic. The result, however, was that such a product imploded violently as soon as the central cementing force disappeared. In the Caucasus, the matrix of ethnic conflicts renders difficult the task of its stabilisation. Between Armenia and Azerbaijan, there is the question of the Nagorno—Karabakh region. The gateway to the Caucasus, Georgia, still has to resolve the separatist Abkhazia issue, which exploded in 1993[723]. In Chechnya, the conflict is most harmful to this objective of stabilising the whole region. Indeed, Russia, in the past decade, had been "aggressively promoting" what is known as the "northern oil pipeline", which passes through Baku to Novorossiysk on the Black Sea by way of Grozny"[724]. Accordingly, this conflict seems to pose two major problems. The first one is the difficulty of providing security for this pipeline route in and around Chechnya and the second is that such a conflict is expanding to the neighbouring Muslim republic of Daghestan, which is located between the Caspian Sea and Chechnya[725]. Indeed, the first threat to the United States interests in this region is the proliferation of these ethnic conflicts. Apparently, this explains why the objective of resolving these regional ethnic conflicts has become "Job One" of the United States policy in this region[726].

---

721 Idem.

722 See Vladimir Radyuhin, "A new Big Game in Central Asia", <u>The Hindu</u>, 18, July 2003, Online Document without pagination found at http://www.cdi.org/russia/268-12.cfm.

723 See Ariel Cohen, <u>op. cit.</u>, p. 8.

724 Ibid., p. 10.

725 Idem.

726 See Fiona Hill, "A Not-So-Grand Strategy: United States Policy in the Caucasus and Central Asia since 1991", <u>op. cit.</u>

Map 8: Ethnic Groups in the Caucasus

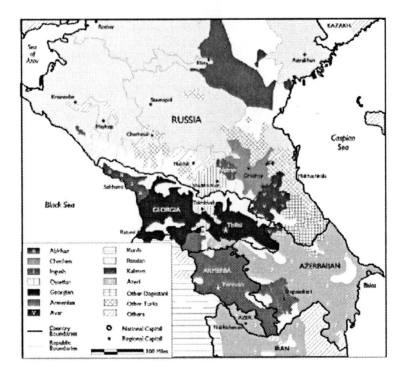

Source: Ariel Cohen, op. cit., p. 3. (The CIA is cited as the primary source)

The other interest, which the United States has to pursue in the region, is to guard against the ambitions of other regional player, especially those of Russia, Turkey, and Iran. Indeed, its seems that this region has emerged to become the new interstate competition grounds for neighbouring and world powers, such as the Middle East and Northern Asia[727]. The threat of intervention by both Turkey and Iran in the Nagorno-Karabakh war (1992-1993) is a good example of the sensitivity of this region and the risks of its "Balkanisation"[728]. Both Turkey and Iran have ethnic extensions and ambitions in the region due to the ethnic, religions, and linguistic affinities that the populations of Central Asia, for instance, respectively have with these two countries. Nonetheless, if Turkey's ambitions of pan-Touranism in the region can be contained due to its close relationship with

---

727   See Fiona Hill, "The Caucasus and Central Asia", op. cit., p. 1.
728   Idem.

the United States, and if the Iranian Pan-Chiite ambitions can be contained because of the fear of the United States, the ambitions of Russia in the region seem be the only ones that are difficult to contain for the United States. Indeed, Russian natural historical influence in the region seems to be more challenging to the United States' policy there. Central Asia and the Caucasus, due to their strategic economic importance, have become the "new focal point of rivalry" between the United States and Russia[729]. This new rivalry is well described by Fiona Hill who states that "the Caspian Basin itself has become one of the principal points of tension in U.S.-Russian relations, and the Caucasus and Central Asia are focal points for a range of issues on America's global agenda"[730]: In a sense, it can be said that against the backdrop of this rivalry, it is in the interest of Russia that the Caucasus remains an unstable area. In fact, the only existing "export routes" for the oil of the Caspian Basin pass through Russia[731]. Investors, however, which are mainly American and European ones, insist on building other "alternative" routes that pass by Turkey, Europe and Asia[732]. Fiona Hill explains the advantage for Russia in having a weak, divided and unstable Caucasus and Central Asia. She states "The internal weakness of the Caucasus and Central Asian states, combined with brutal regional wars, makes them extremely vulnerable to outside pressure—especially from Russia. Although Russia itself is weak, it is far stronger than all the states combined, and while its direct influence over their affairs has declined since the collapse of the Soviet Union, it remains the dominant economic, political, and military force"[733]. The insstability in the Caucasus and Central Asia also provides Russia with a pretext to have larger access to the West's and, in particular, the United States' badly needed economic assistance. Ariel Cohen suggests that the United States have to pressure Moscow with the threat of cutting U.S. economic assistance, if Russia continues to support separatist movements in the Caucasus[734]. He adds "influential Moscow believes hardliners believe that instability in the Caucasus enhances Russia's power in the region"[735] Hence, for the United States, containing Russia's and other major powers in the region is also a very important regional interest. Accordingly, the United States would tend not to encourage separatist movements in the region but, on the contrary, fortify the central governments in their

---

729   See Vladimir Radyuhin, op. cit.
730   See Fiona Hill, Fiona Hill, "The Caucasus and Central Asia", op. cit., p. 1
731   See Catherine Baldi, op. cit.
732   Idem.
733   See Fiona Hill, Fiona Hill, "The Caucasus and Central Asia", op. cit., p. 1
734   See Ariel Cohen, op. cit., p. 2.
735   Idem.

conflict with these separatist movements. For, at the end, it is much easier to make agreements over energy resources with a few countries than with a multitude of conflicting ethnic units.

in Bosnia, and the Balkans in general, the regional interests of France were multiple. France seems to have been keen on coming up with a viable European collective solution to the crisis, which at the same time would marginalize the hegemony of the United States and NATO and, one that will include Russia in the security arrangements in Europe. Second, France was conscious of the importance of guarding against reunified Germany's revisited hegemony on Central and Easter Europe. Thirdly, France, through a larger regional vision, needed to preserve the good relations is maintains with the Arab world and its vision of a Euro-Mediterranean cooperation that can counterbalance the hegemony of the United States. Finally, guarding against a dissemination of separatist temptations that the conflicts in the Balkans might produce in the European continent, particularly vis-à-vis the French separatist regions with tendencies for independence. However, in the case of Chechnya and the Caucasus, France is not actually a major regional player or one that has spheres of influence there. This is probably due to the factor of geographic distance from the crisis area, the need to involve Russia in stabilising the close Balkans, and the easiness of dealing with one country for the benefit of economic interests. For its part, the United States' regional interests in the Balkans and in the crisis in Bosnia were as vital as those of France, although not openly admitted. The notion that motives of the United States' engagement in the Balkans are merely humanitarian or peripheral does not hold. The mere fact that the United States did not intervene in other humanitarian tragedies worldwide renders this view obsolete. In fact, the United States need a stable and reliable Europe and also needs not to repeat past mistakes of not intervening in time in the continent and having to pay a much higher price for it later on. This engagement was, furthermore, quite affordable to the United States compared to the risks of not intervening. As far as the Caucasus and Central Asia are concerned, the United States' need to exploit the enormous energy reserves of the region underlies its other interests there. In order to be able to exploit these huge gas and oil resources of Central Asia and the Caspian Basin, the United States is interested in containing the proliferation of ethnic conflict by aiding central governments involved in these conflicts. It is also interested in containing he influence and ambitions of major regional players in there, especially those of Russia.

2.2.5. Internal Social Interests

The internal social interests of France and the United States vis-à-vis the two crises is quite interesting to discuss. These interests mainly have to do with preserving the social stability and the prevention of disturbances inside the two countries. They include the social movements activities in both countries and the larger Trans-national Social Movement Organisation effect. They also include the factor of the impact of the ethnic composition of the societies of both countries as well as the impact of trans-national ethnic ties on foreign policy.

The interaction between foreign policy and domestic policy is a well-known fact. Some writers explain that public policy is formed of two branches: domestic and foreign policy. According to this analysis, each of the two components of public policy has its own distinctive characteristics as well as those characteristics common to each[736]. The clear-cut distinction between the two components is, nevertheless, quite clear. For whereas domestic policies are "those that are implemented primarily within the territorial and jurisdictional boundaries of the state", foreign policy is that which is "implemented primarily outside the country and is directed toward the governing authorities or nationals of other states and international organizations[737]". In this sense, domestic policy can sometimes affect foreign policy, especially when there is an affinity between the domestic social group and the foreign policy issue. Frank B. Feigert et al., for instance, state, "The basic constituencies of foreign and domestic policy have also traditionally been different, although for some issues, domestic groups may be quite active on behalf of foreign policy issues that affect the domestic well-being of their members or foreign groups with which they have a strong affiliation[738]". Other researchers, however, see a clear distinction between foreign and domestic policy which doesn't allow them to interact. Alper Kaliber, argues, in this respect, "Within the realist IR theory, foreign policy is conceptualised as the conduct of serious diplomatic practices by the state elite to pursue pre-determined national objectives and interests and to ensure national security. Thereby in the conventional discourse the sphere of foreign policy refers to the external orientations and rational choices of self-interested states towards others within a contending, anarchic interstate system. Furthermore, foreign policy is represented as a bridge linking atomised and completed states with fixed, already established and stable

---

736   See Frank B. Feigert et al., Interaction, Foreign Policy and Public Policy, American Enterprise Institute, Washington, 1983, p.1.

737   Idem.

738   Idem.

identities[739]". Yet, others insist on the importance of domestic social policy impact on foreign policy decisions. Georgi Arbatov, for example, explains that this was particularly true for the Soviet Union and the end of the Cold War after which, the idea became that foreign policy is made from the "inside out." He affirms" For both historians and political scientists the end of the Cold War has invited a return to seeing foreign policy as made from the inside out. Its demise seemed to have derived from the Soviet Union's domestic situation, the impact of a particular leader, and the surprising shift in foreign policy he introduced"[740]. Many writers are now supporters of this view, namely that internal domestic conditions influence foreign policy decision-making. This view is even supported by Alper Kaliber, who after discussing the various approaches to the relationship between foreign policy and domestic policy affirms "Put in this context, my argument is that foreign policy is not only an external relationship that the state initiates toward other states in international politics, but also, it functions as one of the central means through which the state rules the society and thus there is an un-ignorable inter-twined-ness between internal and external political processes"[741]. Other writers, however, suggest that the discoveries and the findings concerning the nature of this relation between internal social and domestic factors and international policy of a state is still evolving. Amongst such writers is David Skidmore who states that "The field of international relations has long since moved beyond the traditional billiard ball model that once dominated the discipline. Few scholars today would take issue with the assertion that "domestic politics matters" when it comes to explaining foreign policy behaviour. Yet our understanding of just how societal actors influence international politics continues to evolve and expand. A growing number of studies have documented the significance of domestic forces at both the elite and mass levels of opinion[742]". Thus, there is a connection between internal social factors in a country and its foreign policy. The case of France and the United States is no exception. It is, hence, interesting to examine the impact of social movements and social pressure in both countries and the relevance of this impact on their domestic and most importantly on their foreign policy considerations.

---

739   See Alper Kaliber, "Securing Domestic Order through Securised foreign Policy: A critical Outlook to Turkey's Official Discourse on the Cyprus Issue", Online Document with pagination found at, p. 1

740   See Georgi Arbatov, Re-Viewing the Cold War: Domestic Factors and Foreign Policy in the East-West Confrontation, Praeger, Westport, CT, 2000, p. xviii

741   Ibid., p. 4

742   See David Skidmore, "Domestic Society and International Cooperation: The Impact of Protest on US Arms Control Policy", Political Science Quarterly, Vol. 114, N° 2, 1999, p. 336.

There exists, furthermore, a recent development in the extent and effect of social movements, which can be considered as a by-product of globalisation. This by-product is represented in the phenomenon of trans-national social movements. Charles Chatfield et al. identify Trans-national Social Movement Organisations (TSMO) as "those INGOs that promote institutional and policy changes in the international order. Borrowing from sociological scholarship on social movements, we refer to these associations as trans-national social movement organizations (TSMOs)[743]". This relatively new phenomenon of trans-national solidarity and coordinated action became possible due to certain factors. These include the growing democratisation, increasing global integration, converging and diffusing values, and proliferating trans-national organizations.

As far as the worldwide democratisation process is concerned, it is worth mentioning that for the last two hundred years, there actually has been a process of worldwide democratisation. Accordingly, "more people are able to participate in the political process in more societies as suffrage has gradually been extended to men without property and to others who had been disenfranchised because of their race, ethnicity, sex, or social status[744]". This idea of a massive process of democratisation is supported by the findings of Freedom House[745]. According to their survey entitled Democracy's Century, "In a very real sense, the 20th century has become the "Democratic Century.[746]" Furthermore, there were no fully democratic systems in the world in 1900, which was an era where empires and monarchies were predominant. After World War II, and in 1950, "the states with restricted democratic practices were 25 in number and accounted for just 12.4 percent of the world population[747]". Bye the close of the century, however, "electoral democracies now represent 120 of the 192 existing countries and constitute 62.5 percent of the world's population (See Graphic 8)"[748].

---

743 See Charles Chatfield et al., Transnational Social Movements and Global Politics: Solidarity beyond the State., Syracuse University Press, Syracuse, NY., 1997, p. xiii.

744 Charles Chatfield et al., op. cit., 4.

745 Freedom House is a non-profit, nonpartisan organization. Since 1978, Freedom House has published Freedom in the World, an annual comparative assessment of the state of political rights and civil liberties in 192 countries and 18 related and disputed territories. Widely used by policy-makers, journalists, and scholars, the 700-page survey is the definitive report on freedom around the globe

746 See Freedom Houses survey, "Democracy's Century: A Surevy of the Global Political Change in the 20th Century", Online Document found at http://www.freedomhouse.org/reports/century.html

747 Idem.

748 Idem.

Graphic 8

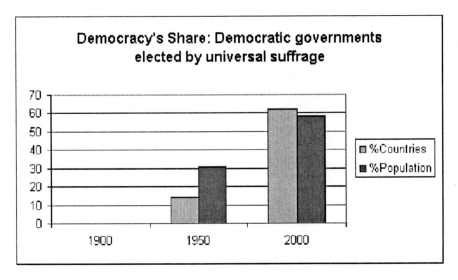

Democracy's Share: Democratic governments elected by universal suffrage

Legend: ▨ %Countries ▨ %Population

Source: Freedom House survey, «Democracy's Century: A Survey of the Global Political Change in the 20th Century", Online Document found at http://www.freedomhouse.org/reports/century.html

The other factor underlying the existence and functioning of the TSMOs is the increased global integration. This largely means that people are more and more being displaced from their original birth places and mixed in a global world population. Charles Chatfield et al. explain, in this respect, "Humans are believed to have originated in East Africa and migrated to all parts of the earth, living in relative isolation for many thousands of years. During the last few thousand years, however, human beings are becoming increasingly reintegrated. In recent decades that has been an exponential increase in social exchanges, and the human species increasingly recognizes that its members share a common fate, whatever that may be"[749]. This global integration is manifested in a number of things. These include increasing economic interdependence, the rising scale of information exchange and the appearance of "challenging world problems[750]".

The third and last of these factors explaining the existence and work of the TSMOs is that which has to do with the growing diffusion of "converging and diffusing values. This means that there is a constant increase in a global sharing of

749 See Charles Chatfield et al., op. cit., pp. 7-8.
750 Idem, p. 8

values and ideas. Some, however, would label this as a sort of hegemony mainly by the West and the United States. Yet, Charles Chatfield et al. argue that the movement of the diffusion is not uni-directed. They state, "Increasingly, values and norms are widely shared. Some people see this tendency as the diffusion of Western and particularly U.S. ideas, a kind of hegemony. But the movement is not unidirectional. Challenges to the apparent Western cultural domination are evident in the growth of ethnic and religious particularism"[751]. It is obvious, nonetheless, that the diffusion of ideas and values depends on two main vehicles. These are the power to diffuse represented by the technological advances of diffusion and the power to impose ideas. In this sense, it can be said that Charles Chatfield et al are probably mistaken in the assumption that the movement is not uni-directed. For if one considers that the ones who possesses both the power to impose, either by military or by economic superiority and a better representation of the way of life set as a model to follow for inhabitants of less favoured countries or regions, and the technological ability to diffuse in mass, the movement of diffusion is essentially uni-directed and not multi-directed as suggested above by Charles Chatfield et al.

As far as social action and movements are concerned, France is placed on the top of the list of world countries where social activism is quite vivid. Some writers even go as far as labelling social protest in France as a "national way of life". Stanley Hoffmann states, for instance, "There are few other nations where protest movements have been so frequent and so diverse in their origins, channels, and purposes, and so similar in their manifestation, as France"[752]. Stanley Hoffmann goes on to say "There are times in French history when every social group and political organization seems to be protesting against the *status quo*; in other periods, protest originates in a clearly limited sector of society or politics. If we take a long-term view of France since the collapse of the Second Empire in 1870 and establish a chart of the principal protest movements, their universality will be striking"[753]. These social movements and protests in France have for reasons issues that range from the "status of certain groups in the French Society" to issues relating to "the role of France in the and the policy to be followed by the country towards other nations[754]." Of those social protests in France and other than the French Revolution, the events of May-June

---

751 ibid., p.9.
752 See Stanley Hoffmann, <u>Decline or Renewal? France since the 1930s</u>, Viking Press, New York, 1974, p. 111.
753 Idem.
754 See Stanley Hoffmann, <u>op. cit.</u>, p. 113.

1968[755] are perhaps the strongest evidence on the ability of social movements to influence political decisions in a democratic society. Stanley Hoffmann elaborates, "The most interesting aspect of France's great crisis of May-June 1968 was neither its suddenness, nor its scope, nor its spectacular ending. It was its ambiguity. What was at stake was nothing less than a nation's capacity to change not its skin (France has done that often) but its soul[756]". Another type of social movements in France which this time has to do with its international conduct seems to be that related to what Martin Evans calls *The Memory of Resistance: French Opposition to the Algerian War*[757]. Martin Evans explains the French social resistance to the war in Algeria by the legacy of French anti-nazi in World War II. This at least was the motivation for French intellectuals. Martin Evans states" The decision to resist the Algerian war forced interviewees into an agonising confrontation. The more they learnt about the war, the more they suffered from bouts of radical self-examination, leading them to question the limits of their allegiance to the French nation and the French state. Importantly too, they reflected on how their sense of personal and national identity intersected with a myriad of other loyalties related to family, gender, class, ethnicity, religious convictions and political parties. For resisters, resolving these moral dilemmas and coming to a clear political position was a common starting point for action"[758]. The other category that showed resistance to the war came from those that participated in the war in Algeria. However, their resistance started for what Martin Evans terms as the *Reservists Rebellion of*

---

755   In May 1968, student demonstrations for education reform in France developed into a nationwide labour strike that threatened to topple the government of President Charles de Gaulle. On May 6, battles between the police and students in the Latin Quarter led to hundreds of injuries. On the evening of May 24, the worst fighting of the May crisis occurred in Paris. Police fired tear-gas grenades at students demonstrating in the streets and revolutionary students temporarily seized the Bourse (Paris Stock Exchange), raised a communist red flag over the building, and then tried to set it on fire. On May 30, President de Gaulle went on the radio and announced that he was dissolving the National Assembly and calling national elections. In the aftermath of the crisis, de Gaulle's government made a series of concessions to the protesting groups, including higher wages and improved working conditions for workers and passed a major education-reform bill intended to modernize higher education.

756   Ibid., p. 145.

757   See Martin Evans, <u>The Memory of Resistance: French Opposition to the Algerian War (1954-1962)</u>, Berg Publishers, Ltd., Oxford, 1997.

758   Ibid., p. 31

1956[759] and for purely social reasons that had to do with careers and family and not as a form of genuine opposition to colonialism.

The other axe of analysis to discuss concerning the French internal social interests is that which has to do with the composition of the French society and the effect this composition might have on foreign policy decision. Indeed, many researchers argue that the ethnic composition of a society would have an impact on the country's foreign policy tendencies[760]. Others have found that the scope of this can also extend to the level of political violence in the country[761] and even to civil wars[762].

For his part, Milton J. Yinger defines an ethnic group as a "a segment of a larger society whose members are thought, by themselves and/or others, to have a common origin and to share important segments of a common culture and who, in addition, participate in shared activities in which the common origin and culture are significant ingredients"[763]. For his part, Donald L. Horowitz defines an ethnic group saying that "Ethnic groups are defined by ascriptive differences, whether the indicium is colour, appearance, language, religion, some other indicator of common origin, or some combination thereof."[764]. The number of mono-ethnic states in the world is quite limited. Walker Connor explains, in this

---

759   In the spring of 1955, the Republican Front decided to increase the number of troops in Algeria from 200,000 to 450,000, a level which was to remain constant until the end of the war. produced strong opposition on the part of the reservists, not out of any straightforward identification with the FLN, but because many now had families and careers which they had no desire to disrupt. Ties of this nature created a moral dilemma about going to Algeria, leading to spontaneous protests up and down the country. The movement began on 11 September 1955 at Lyon station with violent confrontations between the CRS and reservists lasting many hours, as the latter refused to get into the special train taking them to Marseille. It continued in Rouen, on 7 October 1955, when reservists refused to leave the Richepanse barracks, openly flouting officers' orders. Protests of this nature were repeated with even greater intensity in the spring of 1956. The reservists' movement, allied to their subsequent war experience, was to form a powerful matrix of events. See Martin Evans, Op. Cit., p. 104.

760   See David R. Davis, & Will H. Moore, "Ties that Bind? Domestic and International Conflict Behavior in Zaire," Comparative Political Studies, 1997., Vol. 31, pp. 45-71.

761   See Edward N. Muller, & Mitchell A. Seligson, "Inequality and Insurgency," American Political Science Review, 1987, Vol. 8, pp. :425-452.

762   See Paul Collier & Anke Hoeffler, "On Economic Causes of Civil War," Oxford Economic Papers, 1998, Vol.50, pp.563-573.

763   See. Milton J. Yinger. "Ethnicity." Annual Review of Sociology, 1985, Vol. 11, p. 169.

764   See Donald L Horowitz., Ethnic Groups in Conflict, University of California Press, Berkeley, 1985, pp. 17-18

respect, that up to the 1980's, there were only 15 homogenous nation states out of the number of world states at the time.[765] According to this analysis, states have to be conscience of the impact of their foreign policy on the ethnic groups that form a part of the population of the country. Will H. Moore argues, for his part, that "ethnic ties are the most important factor determining levels of international support for a given minority group"[766]. A good example of this influence or sensitivity a country has in conducting its foreign policy with regards to the ethnic minorities that form a part of its population is the case of the United States' sanctions against Cuba. Will H. Moore states, "Although opinion polls suggest that U.S. citizens favour a normalization of relations with Cuba, Washington continues to maintain sanctions initially imposed in the 1960s. The first generation of the Cuban Diaspora supports this policy, and it is not a major issue in national elections: candidates know that U.S. voters will not withhold their votes over support for economic sanctions to Cuba. They also know that first-generation Cuban voters will tend to withhold support for candidates that refuse to endorse the sanctions[767]". This process, through which politicians try to win the favour of certain minorities in their country via foreign policy gestures that are not necessarily contrary to national interests, is called *minority foreign policy capture*[768]. Yet, there are other examples where minorities' presence in a country has failed to capture foreign policy's favourable gestures. The case of the Basque minority in France and Spain is a clear on. It can be said, thus, that capturing of a foreign policy by a minority depends largely on whether there is not a contradiction with national interests. Accordingly, it can be said that minority foreign policy capturing is of a little priority on the political agenda. Nevertheless, sensitivity of politicians in their foreign policy to the effect of certain foreign policy decisions on the domestic ethnic minority cannot be denied. Indeed, ignoring such an effect would probably lead to social tension and even violence from the part of the ethnic minority group in reaction to the foreign policy that affects their wider ethnic group and ethnic ties with similar ethnic groups outside the country. France is no exception to this rule. For in the two crises of Bosnia and Chechnya, there was ethnic ties and affinities between the majority of the population of the two regions and a large segment of the French society, namely those of Muslim confession. Indeed, Islam has become the second religion in France. The exact number of Muslims in France, however, is controversial. They range

---

765   See Walker Connor, "Beyond Reason: The Nature of the Ethnonational Bond." Ethnic and Racial Studies, 1983, Vol. 16: p. 374.

766   See Will H. Moore, "Ethnic Minorities and Foreign Policy", SAIS Review, Vol. 22, N°. 2, (Summer–Fall 2002), pp. 77-91.

767   Ibid, p. 84

768   Idem.

from 5 to 6 million people[769]. They, hence, account for almost 10% of the population. Thus, even if there was no capturing of foreign policy by this ethnic minority in France, their existence meant that France should be more careful in its foreign policy conduct towards the two crises to avoid social disturbance that this ethnic minority might cause domestically.

Public policy includes both domestic and foreign policy attributes. Accordingly, the activity of social movements can affect the foreign policy in a country. France has a very impressive tradition of social movements and activities. This can concern practically all sectors of French life, for all sorts of reasons, and serving the goals of all kinds of social groups. Trans-national social movements have a growing contamination effect on domestic social movements. A minority in a country can influence certain foreign policy directions of that country. Accordingly, foreign policy makers have to be conscience of the effect on and reaction of the domestic minority or minorities in its foreign policy decisions or actions that affect the largest ethnic group with which this minority has affinities. Politicians might sometimes try to capture the favour of the ethnic minority through their foreign policy gestures. France has 5-6 million Muslims that have affinities with the populations of the regions of both crises. Ignoring or antagonising the ethnic minority in foreign policy conduct can sometimes result in social disturbance and even violence on the part of this minority, and in a democracy it can also mean loss of useful electoral votes.

Similarly, the United States' foreign policy cannot be expected to be indifferent to the effects and variations of the components of the United States society, as shown in the example of the economic sanctions against Cuban and the Cuban Diaspora in the United States, nor to the effects of social activism or those of Trans-National civic activism.

Indeed, the internal ethnic and religious composition of the United States' society is quite unique in the world and one, which entitles it to be justly called the "melting pot". In 1999 and according to the estimates of the United States' Census Bureau on the ethnic composition of the society, 225 million (82%) were White, 35 million (13%) were Black or of African origins, 11 million (4%) were of Asian or Pacific Islander origin, and 2 million (1%) of Alaskan or Indian origin. Of those who were labelled as White, 31 million (12%) were of Hispanic origin, while 196 million (72%) classified themselves as non-Hispanic[770]. Moreover, the fastest

---

769   The number os based on estimates given by *the L'Union des Jeunes Musulmans de France* and *l'Union des Organisations Islamiques de France (UOIF)*. On their respective websites.

770   See The page on the composition of the United States society in The United States' Diplomatic Mission to Poland website found at http://www.usinfo.pl/aboutusa/society/demographics.htm

growing rate of an ethnic group in the United States is that of Hispanics with more than 9.1 % the 1990s period[771]. The religious affinities diversity of the United States' society although not as apparent as the ethnic origins one, is a constantly growing one. Religious freedom and diversity in the United States is certainly not a recent phenomenon. It is well entrenched in the Constitution of that country. This Constitution, which is considered to be the "oldest written constitution in the world", was adopted in 1789[772]. In its deliberations, the first Congress of the United States adopted what is known as the Bill of Rights, which is constituted of ten amendments. The first of these amendments stipulates, in addition to the establishing the freedom of speech and the freedom of assembly, that "Congress shall make no law regarding an establishment of religion or prohibiting the free exercise thereof"[773]. Some argue that early in the history of the United States, these religions and their variants amounted to 32[774]. The dominant religions in the United States remain Christianity and Judaism. Nonetheless, the growth ratio of other religions has been increasing rapidly. Conducted surveys indicated that those minority religions accounted for 0.8 % of the adult population (1973-1980), increasing to 1.3 % (1981-1990), and reaching 2.6 % (1990-2000)[775]. Islam, Buddhism, and Hinduism account for half of those fast growing minority religions in the United States[776].

The internal ethnic and religious fabric of the United States' society does not only seem to have an influence on its foreign policy but also on its national security. This is particularly the case with the United States' immigration legislations and its echoing of the United States foreign policy and national security interest[777]. Kenneth J. Franzblau elaborates on this triangle relationship between immigration, foreign policy, and national security and its function in the United States. He says"

---

771 Idem.

772 See "Religious Freedom in the United States of America", International Coalition for Religious Freedom, Online document without pagination found at http://www.icrf.com/wrpt/USrpt.htm.

773 Idem.

774 See Tom W. Smith, ""Classifying Protestant Denominations", Review of Religious Research, N° 31, 1990, pp. 225-245.

775 See Tom W. Smith, "Religious Diversity in America: The Emergence of Muslims, Buddhists, Hindus, and Others", The American Jewish Committee, online document without pagination found at http://www.ajc.org/InTheMedia/PublicationsPrint.asp?did=400.

776 Idem.

777 See Kenneth J. Franzblau, "Immigrations Impact on U.S. National Security and Foreign Policy", Research Paper for the US Commission on Immigration Reform, October 1997, pp. 1-48.

Immigration, foreign policy, and U.S. national security are closely intertwined. Immigration policy could be changed according to circumstances, but always with the larger goal of advancing U. S. national security. Emigration from communist enemies was promoted with the goal of destabilizing those countries; it was discouraged from repressive Cold War allies to avoid U.S. with a country's policies that forced its own people to flee"[778]. He goes on to say "The activities of immigrants also can change perceptions of national security and thus impact foreign policy. U.S. foreign policy can also unintentionally cause migratory movements; alternatively, migratory movements can affect foreign policy by creating humanitarian crises that require a response or national security threats resulting from large numbers of migrants arriving in a short period of time"[779]. Examples of such an "unintentionally caused" migratory movements are those of the Cold War era, the United States' promoted exodus from Cuba in 1994 to prevent the spread of the Cuban Revolution, "the massive resettlement of Indo-Chinese in the United States from 1975 on—a by-product of the Vietnam War" which provide a clear example on the internal social concerns that should be taken into consideration concerning foreign policy decision-making, in addition to the United States foreign policy in Central America which is also cited as "a cause for emigration"[780]. Hence, it is established that foreign policy in the United States as well as national security polices use immigration as a policy tool. On the other hand, immigration policies as a tool of national security or foreign policy needs, also tend to result—on the long run—in internal social disturbances. Nonetheless, this triangle relationship between foreign policy, national security, and immigration polices in the United States tends to be restricted to the usage effects and results of immigration polices on foreign policy and national security and does not relate to the question of the impact of the ethnic and religious components of the United States' society on the country's foreign policy. One of the interesting theories that relates to this issue is that explained by Natsu Taylor Saito[781]. He states" We have been conditioned to define ourselves in terms of citizenship, and to think of ourselves in relation to the border. With respect to human rights, we uncritically accept the distinction between "Americans" and "foreigners," and frame the struggle for justice and human decency in terms of "civil rights" for those at home and "human rights" for those overseas. This is reinforced

---

778   Ibid., p. 17.

779   Ibid., pp. 17-18

780   Ibid., pp. 18-19.

781   See Natsu Taylor Saito, "Crossing the Border: The Interdependence of Foreign Policy and Racial Justice in the United States", <u>Yale Human Rights & Development Law Journal</u>., online document in pdf formatwth pagination found at http://www.yale.edu/yhrdlj/vol01/Natsu_Taylor_Saito_YHRDLJ.pdf

by the belief that the U.S. Constitution provides significantly more protection than is afforded by international law, and that we can only take advantage of this higher level of protection by maintaining the power of the border"[782]. He continues to say that "Because these concepts are so deeply rooted in our thinking, it is easier to see the connections between foreign and domestic policy if we leave aside, for the moment, the concepts of race and citizenship, and think in terms of the identification of the "other." The distinction between "us" and "them" is, of course, one that affects all social interaction, creating complex layers of overlapping identities"[783]. The notion of "them" or "otherness" for Natsu Taylor Saito, "people of colour, people who speak languages other than English, and people from significantly different cultural traditions"[784]. Nonetheless, the suggestion is that this concept of "otherness" is an evolving one that responds to both social and political developments. One of the examples given to illustrate such an evolution is the African Americans who have been classified as "other" in the 17th and 18th century, are being enlisted recently in campaigns to restrict the rights of new immigrants in the United States[785]. Another is that White Cuban refugees who arrived to the United States in the 1960s were first regarded as "foreign". Now they are regarded as "insiders" while the new arriving immigrants from Cuba with a darker skin are considered as the "other"[786]. The problem with this classification of "us" and the "other", as Natsu Taylor Saito argues, is that "Although who is "other" can change over time, once people have been identified as outsiders, public perceptions of them often do not keep pace with advances in their legal status"[787]. His theory addresses the manners according to which the United States' foreign policy influences the treatment of the United States' society components who are regarded as the "other" because of their ethnicity, race, or national opinions and how the United States' foreign policy is influenced by the treatment of such groups that are labelled as "others"[788]. The part in Natsu Taylor Saito's arguments which is relevant to this discussion of the importance of internal social interests to foreign policy considerations, is that which relates to the "situations in which the U.S. government has exhibited a flagrant disregard for human rights and international law in our foreign policy, and the adverse effect this disregard has on racial and ethnic minorities at home"[789]. The relevance

---

782 Ibid., p. 2.
783 Ibid., pp. 2-3.
784 Ibid., p. 3.
785 Idem.
786 Idem.
787 Idem.
788 Ibid., p.4.
789 Idem.

to this discussion can be seen in the internal social responses to international crises and international humanitarian tragedies and the evolution of those responses over time. Indeed, the distinction made between "others" and "us" in the United States made it easier in the pass, especially during the 1990s, to disregard the tragedies and crises of populations around the world and to legitimise some of the United States acts that are contrary to human rights and international law norms. Natsu Taylor Saito says, in this respect, "The identification of some peoples as "other," the distinguishing of "them" from "us," is often used as an explanation of why some people control more resources, are regarded with more favour, or wield more power. In the 1980s and 1990s the distinction between "Americans" and "foreigners" seems to have taken on added significance, strengthening the notion that those who are foreign need not be treated as well as those who are American. Sometimes this is seen in American attitudes towards other nations and their peoples. Because it affects *them* and not *us*, it has apparently been acceptable to most Americans to disregard slaughter in the Balkans, to buy products made by child labour in Pakistan or prison labour in China, and to allow our government to mine Nicaraguan waters and use drug money to fund the Contras. There has been little public outcry over the government's kidnapping Mexican citizens in blatant disregard of international law, or its refusal to ratify international conventions or pay monies owed the United Nations"[790]. Although this theory is quite interesting, it seems to suggest that ethnic, racial or cultural affinities of certain groups within the society of the host country towards their larger ethnic group outside are weakened by their newly acquired nationality affinities and environment loyalties. This seems, however, to be not quite correct as an assumption at least in the United States. The period of non-reaction to these violations of international law and human rights by the society of the United States, which Natsu Taylor Saito cites as proof of indifference to the suffering of the "other, actually took place in the 1980s. The Cold War was still going on in this period. When a population is saturated by war propaganda, it has no room to think otherwise. Accordingly, minority ethnic groups of the society in question are actually unable to express their discontent with the tragedies of the larger ethnic group or groups outside the border of their host country, at least on a large scale, for two main reasons. The first one is that the overall propaganda atmosphere in the period of conflict that involves the host country results in the creation of a net that does not allow reflections, which are contrary to those set by the government's propaganda machine. The least that a contradictor to the propaganda machine in times of conflict can be accused of is that of not being a nationalist or even of being a traitor. Access to information that might disturb this collective brain washing process of the society is also very difficult in times of war or conflict. Therefore, the

---

790   Ibid., pp. 5.6

society as a whole, and not simply the minority group or groups inside this society, have no other option in times of conflict or a crisis involving their host country except to rally behind their government. The second reason is that this minority group of "others" which is defined by race, culture or ethnicity as mentioned above, is probably not willing to jeopardize its past efforts of aiming at finally being integrated and accepted in the new society. Indeed, sometimes members of the "others" minority tend to show their attachment to the host country and society, their nationalism, and their total detachment from the larger ethnic group quite excessively in order to disperse any doubt on their loyalties' priorities. This, for instance, can be seen in the case of the Drouze community in Israel. For although members of the greater ethnic group of this community are known for their resistance to French occupation of Syria, those in Israel are famous for their severity towards Palestinian Arabs that goes far beyond the severity of the Israeli army. This example seems to be in line with the example of the member of the African American community in the United States who are enlisted in campaigns to restrict the rights of new immigrants[791]. The result, however, is that often the minority group that does that ends up being not accepted totally by both the host country and by the larger ethnic group. This was the case of the Harkis[792] in France who are still neither accepted by France nor by Algeria.

Unfortunately, in most known cases foreign policy actions of the state or its engagement in a conflict that involves the larger ethnic group seems to create more discrimination against the small minority group inside, which is trying to integrate and be accepted in this new society. This is due to a false conception of a separation between foreign and domestic policy. The United States' case is unique, in this respect. Natsu Taylor Saito explains, "It is a mistake to think that we can remedy discrimination against Americans while allowing our government

---

791   Ibid., p.3

792   Harkis is the name given to France's forgotten allies—the Muslims who fought alongside the French against their fellow Algerians more than forty years ago but who have since been treated as embarrassing reminders of a lost imperial war. Following the French withdrawal, from Algeria, many Harkis who had fought against the FLN revolutionary movement in Algeria were left to face bloody reprisals in their homeland. The Evian peace accords which France and Algeria signed in March 1962 offered the Harkis only small compensation payments and did nothing to protect them against attacks from supporters of the Algerian republic. According to official estimates, 150,000 Harkis were slaughtered by republican supporters within months of the accords being signed. More than 40,000 Harkis were able to escape to France after the war, but claim they were treated shabbily once they arrived, housed in makeshift camps for decades, cut off from French communities and often unable to find anything but the most menial work.

to treat people who live in other countries or carry different passports as not deserving of full, or even basic, human rights. Taking such a position allows the basis of the discrimination to be constantly re-created at the same time that we deplore its consequences. It is like cutting off the head of a weed while fertilizing its roots. This cycle is especially problematic in the United States because our population has cultural and historic ties with so many parts of the world. We cannot expect a formal legal distinction between "citizens" and "non-citizens," or "Americans" and "foreigners" to protect the rights of racial or ethnic minorities simply because we live inside the U.S. border, particularly when prejudice and disregard move so easily across its territorial boundaries"[793].

Nonetheless, on many occasions the affinities between a minority group and the larger ethno-religious group outside seems to have bypassed the restrictions of borders and the new nationality status accorded by the host country. The minority group's affinities with the plight of the larger ethnic group outside can, in its turn, affect the foreign policy decision of a country and even be perceived as a threat to its national security. This last case is well illustrated by the example of the Japanese community in the United States during World War II. Around 120,000 Japanese Americans from the West Coast were forcefully evacuated and collectively imprisoned during World War II[794]. On many occasions, public pressure inside the United States, led mainly by the small ethnic group and other civil society activists, resulted in altering the country's foreign policy. This was the case, for example, with the public pressures against apartheid in South Africa. In this case, "public insistence" forced the United States policy makers to establish, in 1986, the Anti-Apartheid Act in spite of the veto of President Ronald Reagan[795]. This is an excellent case were internal public pressure of a minority group forces the government to change its foreign policy at the expense of its national interests. Indeed, there exists no interest for any government to have public protests even by a small group inside its borders, which criticize its action or inaction vis-à-vis international affaires. For even if the group that starts such protests is small at its outset, it would probably grow bigger with time and draw more attention to the issue by forcing domestic public opinion to, at least, question the foreign policies of its government. The degree of a government's sensitivity and resistance of its foreign polices to these internal considerations depends naturally on the vitality of its national interests involved in the international affaire in question. Examples of such protests conducted by the minority group in the host country out of sympathy with the larger ethnic group are many. For

---

793   Ibid. p. 2
794   Ibid., p. 15.
795   Ibid., p. 27

example, on the 24th of March 2000, The Serbian Cultural Association of Arizona along with other Serbian organisations organised a demonstration against the United States' and NATO's bombing of Serbia[796]. Furthermore, on the 30th of June 1999, American-Cubans staged violent protests against treatment of Cuban refugees in the United States[797]. This was followed by demonstrations of Haitian-Americans in Miami to protest against the ensuing change of treatment of refugees announced for Cuban refugees only which was regarded as a discrimination against refugees of Haitian origin[798].

Similar to the case of France, the United States has its fair share of civic activism, which can affect its foreign policy or at least slightly alter it. Of the many forms of civic activism, Anti-war activism is that which is more relevant than other types of civic activism to the discussion of internal social interests and foreign policy during an international conflict. For Instance, the widespread anti-war in Iraq protests that spread all over the world did not spare the United States. Nonetheless, in the United States' case, the most notable of those anti-war protests is of course the anti-Vietnam war ones.

What is worth mentioning as far as anti-war and other civic activism movements are concerned, is a radical change in their strategy, timing, and rapidity that took place due to the technological innovations in the communication industry. For, the difference between the anti-Vietnam protests, first Gulf War protests, and anti War on Iraq (2003) recent ones, is the growing role of Internet as a factor of mobilization for peace activists. Leander Kahney states" While the Vietnam-era anti-war movement took years to gather momentum, hundreds of thousands of protestors turned out in dozens of U.S. cities on Saturday to protest a possible war in Iraq" of 2003[799]. The high momentum of this anti-war activism was not due to the media but to internet as a means of free diffusion. He continues to explain that "The disparity of protestors is a sign the anti-war movement has gone mainstream, observers said, and it's thanks not to the media, but to hundreds of anti-war websites and mailing lists"[800]. The innovation in anti-war activism due to the use of interent is that in the anti-war protests of 2003, the protests took place prior

796　See "Protests Around the World and at Home against US/NATO in Yugoslavia", Online document without pagination found at http://www.iacenter.org/yugdemos.htm.

797　See "Cubans react in anger to treatment of refugees", Online document without pagination found at http://www.fiu.edu/~fcf/anger63099.html.

798　Idem.

799　See Leander Kahney, "Internet Stokes Anti-War Movement ", Online document without pagination found at http://www.wired.com/news/culture/0,1284,57310,00.html.

800　Idem.

to the start of the military offensive[801]. The difference here with internat is quite important. For, prior to Internet and other technology transmission innovations such as SMS messages, anti-war protests used to taqke place after the start of hostilities. With Internet and other personal transmission technologies, not only did it become much easier and fasster to gather people for a protest but also to gather them prior to the sstart of hostilities. Furthermore, this new form of Internet and other personam trnasmission technologies' mobilized activism is an indication of the power that the media have in manipulating public opinion. For when the only ssource of information for the public was the media, the public had no other source of information, and by consquence, no other alternative pictures of the situation. With the freedom of information circulation and thought transmission on the Internet, the public has more freedom to see those alternative pictures and to be less exposed to the the media as the soul source of information on a conflict or a crisis.

In order for a country to be more effective in its foreign policy conduct, it has to realize the importance of considering the link that exists between its foreign and internal social interests. If the policy makers are not conscience of the sensitivity of their internal social specificities, then this might lead to internal social disturbances or even constitute an internal threat for the country's national security. Public policy includes both domestic and foreign policy. There is a correlation between foreign policy and domestic policy especially when it comes to the minority groups in the host country. Sometimes a country's foreign policies directed against the larger ethnic group outside the borders might lead to domestic discrimination against the smaller group inside the borders. Discriminatory foreign policy can sometimes, in the case of the United States, for example, be a reflection of the domestic discrimination inside the country because its much easier to discriminate against those outside the border who are looked at as the "other". The characteristics of social activism in a country have also to be taken into consideration. For its part, France has a long tradition of social activism that includes all aspects of French daily life and international affaires and that takes all forms and on all levels. In the case of Bosnia, France also had to be conscience of the fact that it had a considerable Muslim community inside its borders. This means loss of electoral votes and social disturbances in case France's foreign policy makers were not careful enough not to antagonise this segment of the society. The case of minorities is even more stressed in the United States. It has a multitude of immigrant communities, which also have affinities with their respective larger ethnic, racial, cultural groups outside the borders of the US. Furthermore, due to the freedom of information diffusion brought about by the Internet, anti-war activism in the United States, and indeed worldwide, has gained momentum and is tending to act nowadays for war prevention rather than war lamenting as it was the case with the Vietnam anti-war rallies.

---

801   Idem.

2.3. The Coverage of the Events in the Two Crises

Both *Le Monde* and *The New York Times* exhibit a number of distinctive characteristics in their respective coverage of the crisis in Bosnia compared to their coverage of the crisis in Chechnya. To establish the existence of such distinctive characteristics, a thorough examination of the coverage of *Le Monde* and *the New York Times* of the two crises would have to take into consideration a number of aspects. Those include an examination of the texts used for the coverage of each crisis, the images that accompanied the coverage, the repetition of the occurrence of the coverage in every newspaper, the place that the two crisis occupied as part of the overall coverage of the two newspapers of more or less simultaneous other major international events, the orientations of the journalists who were most involved in covering the two crises, and, finally, the extent to which trans-national media influenced the two newspapers' coverage of the two crisis. In order to practically manage to perform such an analysis, limitations on the coverage sample to be examined are made. Thus, twenty articles and news items are chosen from each newspaper on each crisis. The articles are chosen randomly. However he choice is spread over the period of each crisis. Generally, news items or articles that were less than 300 words were not chosen. Furthermore, the choice of news items and articles is done without prior consideration to whether the article or news item is accompanied by an illustration or an image of the events of the crisis.

2.3.1. The Texts Used to Cover the Two Crises

Analysis of the texts used in the coverage of the two crises is quite important. Other than expressing opinion of events related to the crisis at hand, the texts used can sometimes imply certain ideas or connotations that would alter or shape the reader's opinion of the crisis or conflict.

Indeed, the language used in news coverage is an extremely important factor of influence of public perceptions. According to Marbury Bladen Ogle, Jr. "language is any meaningful response to a stimulus, and the term includes, therefore, gestures and facial expressions by which we may indicate our emotions, give assent or dissent, approval or disapproval"[802]. Other researchers endow language with an enormous power within a given human society and a given meaning to culture as a whole. For instance, Leonard Bloomfield states, "the division of

---

802   See Marbury Bladen Ogle, Jr., <u>Public Opinion and Political Dynamics</u>, Houghton Mifflin, Boston, 1950, p.59.

labour, and, with it, the whole working of human society, is due to language"[803]. Others go as far as to argue that the essence of governing lies with the use of language, which, if used properly, can alter public opinion and obtain public consent. Marbury Bladen Ogle, Jr. explains in this respect "the art of engineering the consent of those governed by the use of language"[804]. Consent being obtained, "language also permits the transformation of opinion to law, which in turn can be administered only through the medium of language"[805]. Gustav LeBon is also a supporter of this opinion. He explains that the function of language in a given government is sort of an art, such as that of advocates, that consists in the science of employing words.[806] Thus, language, as a concept, is quite essential in defining human behavioural attitudes. However, on a narrower point of view that excludes the verbal expression of language, the concept of language relating to this research is that of it as kind of an instrument for formulating written ideas and communicating them to the receiving public.

One of the most important factors contributing to the powerful nature of language use is that relating to the meaning of words. This different meanings of words used in language to communicate is a human science known as semantics. In fact, semantics, as a science, implies that words can have different meanings to different audiences, and different interpretations according to their context. Indeed, it is quite possible to have different interpretations for the same word used. This is due to the fact that each word goes through a different analysis process and, thus, a different meaning, evoked symbols, and connotations in the mind of the receiver. Marbury Bladen Ogle Jr. explains, in this respect, that the meaning of words is not as simple as it might appear to be but that, instead, meaning implies a complicated psychological phenomena"[807]. Moreover, there are times when the use of words and sentences is set up on purpose to refer to something entirely different from their original context. This usage of language is referred to, generally, as the pre-symbolic usage. The pre-symbolic employment of words can be divided into words bearing intentional and words bearing extensional meanings. According to semanticists' classification, extensional words are those words used to report or to describe objects or demonstrable facts or situations. Thus, it can be said that extensional references are demonstrable by reference to the discernible facts. On the other hand,

---

803   See Leonard Bloomfield, <u>Language</u>, Henry Holt and Company, New York, 1933, p. 24.

804   See Marbury Bladen Ogle, <u>op. oit</u>, p.60

805   Idem.

806   See Gustav LeBon, <u>The Crowd</u>, The Macmillan Company, New York, 1922, pp. 120-122.

807   See Marbury Bladen Ogle Jr., <u>op. cit</u>, pp. 64-65.

Intentional words are those, which are related to personal beliefs or emotional states of the user. They are, thus, by nature subjective and usually employed to suggest to the receiver the subjective view of their user towards a certain issue. Semantics also distinguish between two other uses of a language to give meaning. These are the informative connotations and the affective connotations, for instance. When an object is out of view and cannot be physically pointed out, yet, has been sufficiently described for full understanding, then the usage is that of informative connotations of words. On the other hand, affirmative connotations indicate those vague, yet, extremely powerful feelings or emotions, which can be suggested by words.

Accordingly, many of the human reactions to the received information depend on the meanings that this receiver associates with the received words. Manipulation of words, their context, and their repetition can, therefore, lead to manipulation of the meaning and, consequently, to a manipulation of the individual's perfections vis-à-vis the received information. The significance of the language used in coverage is, hence, very essential in determining its effect on the public mind. An analysis of the languages used can be done through and examination of the terminology used in the coverage as well as the repletion of certain words.

2.3.1.1. The Terminology used to Comment the Two Crises

The dictionary definition of terminology is that it refers to "special words or expressions used in relation to a particular subject or activity". Thus, it is special words related to a special profession. In journalism, this concept of terminology is not a static one. Indeed, it depends on the branch of journalism and the developments in the field. Philip Gaunt, for instance, states "In general, terminology reflects successive developments in communication structures. At the beginning of the century, at a time when mass communication was virtually limited to the printed media, the first training establishments were called schools of journalism and were largely devoted to producing recruits for the newspaper industry, which needed reporters, editors, layout people and photographers. The film industry, which can certainly be regarded as a mass medium but not perhaps as a channel for the deliberate delivery of specific messages, had its own apprentice-type training systems concentrating almost exclusively on the technical aspects of cinematography. Over the years, with the appearance of radio and television, new needs have emerged, and schools of journalism have adapted their programs to include broadcast production and broadcast news courses[808]". The choice of terminology to be used in coverage is, therefore, important. It is choosing a specific component of a

---

808   See Philip Gaunt, Making the Newsmakers: International Handbook on Journalism Training, Greenwood Press, Westport, CT, 1992, p. 11.

language to designate an act or to describe one. Yet, this choice of terminology can have an important impact on the perception of the receivers and, consequently, on their reaction to the event or action being described or told in the coverage. George Orwell, states, in this respect that "...if thought corrupts language, language can also corrupt thought. A bad usage can spread by tradition and imitation, even among people who should know better[809]".

Some writers suggest, however, that the media has sometimes to adopt terminology that is forced by the event or imposed by the government. Alex Schmid and Janny de Graaf, for instance, explain this with relevance to the media coverage of terrorism. They argue that when a journalist carries out an interview with a terrorist, there is a chance that the media would adopt in its coverage of similar future events some of the terminology this terrorist employs in this interview[810]. Yet, the media, according to Alex Schmid and Janny de Graaf, is on many occasions compelled to use the nomenclature of the government[811]. Sometimes this adoption and use of terms in news coverage is so abundant. Adam Lockyer, for example, explains that "a quick survey of the use of language in *The New York Times* suggests that it is indeed a culprit. *The New York Times* has an extensive electronic database of articles published in the newspaper since 1 January 1996. The terrifying, vague, and inaccurate term of 'Weapons of Mass Destruction' or 'WMD' has gained favour in political circles since 11 September 2001. The term also seems to have gained favour within articles published in *The New York Times*. Since 1 January 1996, there have been 3,878 articles published with the term, 1,903 (or 49.07 percent) of which were printed after 11 September 2001. Since 1 January 1996, there have been 1,122 articles printed with the more neutral and accurate term 'Nuclear, Biological and Chemical Weapons' or 'NBC', 224 (or 19.96 percent) of which were printed after 11 September 2001. A similar percentage of 22.18 can be found for the term 'Unconventional Weapons'. Therefore, these figures indicate that, since 11 September 2001, there has been an overall increase in the number of articles referring to Nuclear, Biological and Chemical weapons; however, the term 'Weapons of Mass Destruction' has by far enjoyed the greatest relative increase in popularity"[812]. Thus, the excessive use of some terminology in journalism can, in

---

809   See George Orwell, 'Politics and the English Language', in <u>The Collected Essays of George Orwell</u>, Penguin, Harmondsworth, 1968 p.167.

810   See Alex Schmid and Janny de Graaf, <u>*Violence as Communication: Insurgent Terrorism and the Western News Media*</u>, Sage Publications, London, 1982, p.88.

811   Idem, p.65.

812   See Adam Lockyer, "The Relationship between the Media and Terrorism", research paper for the <u>Strategic and Defence Studies Centre</u>, *The Australian National University, 2003*, p.5.

fact, be related to government-imposed nomenclature. Adam Lockyer, however, argues that this use of governmental nomenclature is not caused by fear of the government but rather by the perceived information superiority of the government[813]. The result of this is that the terminology used or chosen by the media soon become, according to Philip Schlesinger, the "primary definitions of social reality"[814]. This adoption and employment of certain terminology in setting such primary definitions of reality would then limit the use of contradictory terminology or opposition to those thoughts already established by the frequent usage of certain terminology. A good example of this is given by Adam Lockyer who explains that an Australian citizen who was not pleased with the Australian government's backing of the U.S. foreign policy was forced to employ the same terms used by the United States in his letter to an Australian newspaper. This displeased Australian citizen used in his letter terms such as "pre-emptive strikes", and "rouge states"[815]. Such a targeted use of terminology would make citizens fully dependent "on the official jargon of the government which makes individuals slaves to this jargon and compelled to follow the 'mindless thought grooves"[816]. Yet, this reasoning excludes the free choice of journalists in opting to use their own terminology, which in some case, might be different from that employed by the government. It remains, however, that quoting an official government source does imply repeating this source's terms.

It is interesting to fully discus, therefore, the kind of terminology used in the coverage of the two crises by the two newspapers and whether such a terminology differs from one newspaper to another, or whether it differs from the coverage of one crisis to another. It is also interesting to see whether such terminology develops all along the different stages of the crisis and whether it is affected by the context and by the different players in the crisis being covered.

The terminology of *Le Monde* concerning the crisis in Bosnia can be said to exhibit a number of characteristics. First, ever since the outset of the crisis, there seems to be an emphasis on the ethnic composition of Bosnia as a region that concerns multiple nations. *Le Monde*, for instance, uses such terms as "this multinational republic, "three Bosnias"[817], "multinational Bosnia", "an independent

---

813   Idem, p. 2.

814   See Philip Schlesinger, <u>Media, State and Nation: Political Violence and collective Identities</u>, Sage Publications, London, 1991, p. 20.

815   Ibid., p. 3.

816   See Adam Lockyer, <u>op. cit.</u>, p.5.

817   See Florence Hartmann, *"Yougoslavie Les Serbes de Bosnie-Herzégovine ont décidé de créer une huitième "République"*, <u>Le Monde</u>, 11 January 1992.

and multinational state"[818]. Part of the emphasis on this "multinational" aspect of the crisis was also manifested in an emphasis on the aspect of the "three communities"[819], "three republics"[820], "three nations"[821], "peoples"[822], and by giving statistics in a number of articles on their proportions whether in terms of land surface reference or population ratio[823]. Thus, at this point, it can be said that the first reflection of the crisis is that it concerns many nations and that it is basically that of a distribution of territory between different peoples. The second characteristic of the terminology used by *Le Monde* in its coverage of the crisis in Bosnia is that relating to warning against the possibility of the spell over effect of the crisis to the rest of the continent. *Le Monde* employed terms such as "the risks of derailing are multiple[824]", "risk of the extension of the conflict"[825], "the waive of hatred[826]", "the Balkans' Storm"[827], "a conflict taken place on Europeans soil"[828]. Here the emphasis of the terminology seems to be on the fact that the conflict can contaminate the whole European continent. It also gives subtle references to the historical tragic consequences of the outcome of past conflicts in the Balkans. The

---

818   See Florence Hartmann, *"Tandis que des rassemblements pour la paix avaient lieu dans toute la République Le leader de la communauté serbe prône l'éclatement de la Bosnie-Herzégovine en trois Etats "*, Le Monde, 7 March 1993.

819   See for instance Yves Heller, "Accord à Genève sur l'éclatement de la Bosnie-Herzégovine La présidence bosniaque a accepté" provisoirement "la création d'une" Union "de trois Républiques", Le Monde, 1 August 1993.

820   See Florence Hartmann, *Le Monde*, 7th March 1992, op. cit.

821   See Florence Hartmann, *Le Monde*, 11 January, op. cit.

822   See Yves Heller, "Le sort des Républiques de l'ex-Yougoslavie La Bosnie-Herzégovine se prononcera par référendum sur son indépendance Une poudrière ethnique menacée d'explosion", *Le Monde*, 19 January 1992. See also his article in *Le Monde* on the 1st August 1993, op. cit.

823   See, for example, Florence Hartmann, *Le Monde*, 11 January 1992, op. cit. and that of 7th March 1992, op. cit. See also Alain Debove, "En permettant la sécession des Serbes et des Croates de la future Union Le nouveau plan de paix ouvre la voie à l'éclatement de la Bosnie Herzégovine ", *Le Monde*, 18 septembre, 1993 and Yves Heller, *"Bosnie: Un puzzle mal assemblé"*, *Le Monde*, 30 July 1994.

824   See Florence Hartmann, *Le Monde*, 11 January, op. cit,

825   See Florence Hartmann, *"YOUGOSLAVIE Tandis que lord Carrington tente d'obtenir un nouveau cessez-le-feu La Croatie met en garde contre l'extension de la guerre à la Bosnie-Herzégovine "*, *Le Monde*, 15 November, 1991.

826   See Yves Heller, *Le Monde*, 19 January 1992 op. cit.

827   See Michel Tatu, "BOSNIE L'improbable "tempête des Balkans", *Le Monde*, 14 August 1992.

828   Idem.

third characteristic that can be noted in the terminology used in the coverage of *Le Monde* of this crisis are numerous references to an international, including essentially, a European solution to the crisis. In the sample of *Le Monde* articles concerning the crisis in Bosnia, terms such as "to prevent an inadmissible situation in Europe"[829], "for Europe, the danger is decisive"[830], "an Islamic state in the heart of Europe"[831], "Americans, Europeans and Russians are confronted today-one in front of the other-and all together facing Serbs and Muslims in a situation that is out of their hands"[832], "subcontractor of the UN",[833] "to put in place a military UN"[834], "it is time to "politicise" NATO but, parallel, to "militarise" the UN."[835]. Furthermore, *Le Monde* mentioned testimonies of atrocities committed against the Muslims in Bosnia but would, on many occasions, also reminded that atrocities were made against Serbs as well. For instance, in one article, and prior to citing the numerous testimonies of Serb aggressive action in Bosnia, *Le Monde* reminded its readers that "naturally, such testimonies should not make us forget that serious aggressions are committed in the regions and the camps—totalling twenty, according to the Serbs-that are held by Croats and Muslims"[836]. Moreover, a number of terms that that were used by authorities, or fighting parties, were used again in the terminology of journalists covering the conflict. For instance, *Le Monde* quoted the Croat Minister of Defence at the time Mr. Gojko Susak saying the phrase "zones of war" then repeated it in the same article.[837]. The same thing was noted with another famous expression, which is that of the so-called UN "safe zones"[838]. In addition, *Le Monde's* journalists quoted the former UN Security General's description of the war in Bosnia in deliberations held

---

830   Idem.

831   Idem.

832   See Yves Heller, "BOSNIE Un puzzle mal assemblé", *Le Monde*, 30 August 1994.

833   See Michel Tatu, "Armer l'ONU Les échecs des Nations unies en Somalie comme en Bosnie soulignent la nécessité d'un renforcement des structures de l'organisation ", *Le Monde*, 22 July 1993.

834   Idem.

835   Idem.

836   See Alain Debove, "La querelle entre M. Boutros-Ghali et le Conseil de sécurité sur la Bosnie-Herzégovine Le secrétaire général de l'ONU juge excessive la part prise par la crise yougoslave ", *Le Monde*, 26 July 1992.

837   See Florence Hartmann, *Le Monde*, 15 November, 1991, op. cit.

838   See Remy Ourdan, "Le massacre de Tuzla entraîne de nouveaux raids de l'OTAN Les artilleurs serbes ont ouvert le feu sur deux cafés de la ville bosniaque, faisant soixante et onze morts. Tandis que deux cents «casques bleus» étaient pris en otage à Sarajevo, les Occidentaux répliquaient par de nouvelles frappes aériennes, ", *Le Monde*, 27 May 1995.

with the UN Security Council on the Bosnian War as the "war of the rich"[839]. The same term "war of the rich" was used by *Le Monde* later to comment on the need and result of a hasty military intervention in Bosnia[840].

For its part, *The New York Times'* terminology in its coverage of the crisis in Bosnia presents a number of characteristics that sometimes present similarities with the terminology used by *Le Monde*. Unlike, *Le Monde*, however, *The New York Times'* terminology reveals a treatment of the situation as a clear-cut aggressor-victim situation. According to this formula, Serbs were systematically and almost always designated as the aggressor and those who *The New York Times* referred to often as Muslims, Muslim Slavs, or Muslim Bosnians as the victims. In addition, unlike *Le Monde*, references in the terminology for the complexity of the ethnic composition in the crisis were rare. Furthermore, the reference for the quest of independence of the victims who should not live under the oppressions of the designated oppressors was often made. For instance, *The New York Times* resumed the causes of the crisis in Bosnia for its readers as follows: "The violence in Bosnia and Herzegovina had been sparked by a series of Serbian attacks mounted since late February, when the republic's Muslim Slavs, and Croats in a referendum overwhelmingly approved independence"[841]. Diabolising terminology to designate Serbs was frequently used and stressed by *The New York Times*. Serbs' best military units in *The New York Times* coverage were led by "a gangster known as Arkan who is wanted for bank robbery in Western Europe" and who led forces "that have been condemned by international human rights organizations for atrocities and widespread looting"[842]. Furthermore, *The New York Times* speaks of a "gang of nationalist Serbs" driving Muslims away from their homes[843], "a savage Serbian campaign"[844], "Serbs began a third wave of ethnic cleansing in July"[845], and "Serbian militias accused of being the main instigators

---

839   See Bassir Afsane, *"La querelle entre M. Boutros-Ghali et le Conseil de sécurité sur la Bosnie-Herzégovine Le secrétaire général de l'ONU juge excessive la part prise par la crise yougoslave" Le Monde*, 26 July 1992.

840   See Michel Tatu, <u>*Le Monde*</u>, 14 August 1992, <u>op. cit.</u>

841   See Chuck Sudetic, "Serbs Attack Muslim Slavs and Croats in Bosnia", <u>The New York Times</u>, 4th April, 1992, p. 3.

842   Idem.

843   See Chuck Sudetic, "Serb Gang Expels 566 Muslims From Their Homes", <u>The New York Times</u>, September 3rd, 1994, p. 2.

844   See John Kifner, "Refugees Forced Out in Systematic Drive of Ethnic Hatred", <u>The New York Times</u>, 27 March 1994, p. 16.

845   See Chuck Sudetic, "Serb Gang Expels 566 Muslims From Their Homes", <u>op. cit.</u>

in the fighting"[846]. When *The New York Times* refers to the ethnic composition of the region, it usually does this by stating that Serbs reclaim more than their right in territory, and that the other two "supposed victim communities" simply reclaim their independence because of fear of living in a state dominated by Serbs. For Instance, *The New York Times* states "Serbs who amount to 38% of the republic's 4,3 million people.... The Muslim Slavs and Croats, who account for 44 and 17 percent of the population respectively, are pushing for the republic to become independent because they fear being left in a Serb-dominated state"[847], "featuring the kind of brutality often associated with the Serbian forces"[848], "loyalty to this country has been at the heart of the Bosnian war since nationalist Serbs backed by the Yugoslav Army started it in April 1992.... Militarily unprepared to withstand the Serbian onslaught, desperate Bosnian officers scraped to gather an army of local crime gangs, Muslim officers who had deserted the pro-Serbian Yugoslav Army and men desperate to defend their homes"[849], and "the republic's 1,9 million Muslim Slavs, 1,4 million Eastern Orthodox Serbs and 750,000 Roman Catholic Croats live in an intricate patchwork that would be impossible to unravel without violence. Muslim Slavs and many Croats seek independence because they oppose being left in Serb dominated rump in Yugoslavia"[850]. Another characteristic about the terminology of *The New York Times'* coverage of the crisis in Bosnia is that it recited more stories about the human suffering in Bosnia in a more dramatic manner than *Le Monde*[851]. The terminology of *The New York Times* also reveals a description that is more "detached" than that of *Le Monde*. This is, however, probably due to the geographic distance element. For while *Le Monde* was describing events that happen on European soil and that are close to France, *The New York Times* was describing events that are taking place in a "far away country". This gave *The New York Times* more liberty in its descriptions of events precisely because it was more detached than *Le Monde*. Indeed, the geographic distance element is quite influential in a crisis coverage. When a crisis or a conflict is close and affects people that are close

---

846   See Paul Lewis, "U.N. Rules Out A Force to Halt Bosnia Fighting", <u>The New York Times</u>, 12 May 1992, p. A1.

847   See Chuck Sudetic, "Serbs Attack Muslim Slavs and Croats in Bosnia", <u>op. cit.</u>

848   See John F. Burns, "Bosnia Fights New War Against Croats", <u>The New York Times</u>, 20 April 1993,p. A10.

849   See Chuck Sudetic, "Bosnia Prepares to Offer Pardons to Draft Dodgers", <u>The New York Times</u>, 13 July 1993, p. A3.

850   See Chuck Sudetic, "Ethnic Clashes Increase in Bosnia As Europe Recognition Vote Nears", <u>The New York Times</u>, 6 April, 1992, p. 12.

851   See for instance the article of John F. Burns, "Bosnia's Elderly Fall to a New Enemy: Cold", <u>The New York</u> Times, 6 January 1993, p. A1.

both in culture and history, it is more difficult to admit atrocities committed. People, by nature, tend to deny their own defaults and emphasize others'. *The New York Times* was describing events in another continent. It was, therefore, more easy to emphasize the atrocities committed and to be more radical in taking sides. Similar to the case of *Le Monde*, there is at least one instance in *The New York Times'* sample of articles on the crisis in Bosnia where an expression of a source (in this case a political U.S. figure) was re-employed by the journalists in their coverage. One of the sections in a New York Times article on Bosnia is entitled "No More "Wait and See". The phrase was originally that of Warren Christopher, the former U.S. Secretary of State, who was quoted by Alain Juppé, the former French Foreign Minister in an interview with *The New York Times*. Mr. Juppé was quoted saying" he said just wait and see. Well, a wait-and-see policy is no longer possible for moral and political reasons"[852].

As far as the coverage of Chechnya is concerned, it can be said that the terminology used by *Le Monde* in its coverage was a bit different from that used in the case of Bosnia. The first characteristic of this terminology is the frequent usage of terms referring to Chechnya itself as a no-law zone, or an area of total anarchy, and to the Chechens as a people so coherent with the culture of war. For instance *Le Monde* mentions terms and phrases such as "The Chechens, whose name was used since the time of Pouchkine to frighten little children and this name is accompanied, often, today by the word mafia"[853], "in reality, even if all the Chechens living outside Chechnya are not thieves[854]", "Chechens are famous for another speciality (arms traffic)"[855], "this anarchy can easily be explained"[856], "the accumulation of arms in the heart of an ethnically explosive region calls for the foreign powers to be careful"[857], "the democratic anarchy that is manifested in the Chechen Republic since the proclamation of its independence"[858], "like the Chechens of rigid mountains"[859], "became "displaced persons having nothing

---

852   See Elaine Sciolino, "U.S. Rejects Plea to Act in Bosnia", <u>The New York Times</u>, 25 January 1994, p. A8

853   See Sophie Shihab, "Anarchie en Tchétchénie Un an après la proclamation de son indépendance, la remuante République du Caucase, livrée à tous les trafics, va à vau-l'eau ", <u>Le Monde,</u> 25 October 1992.

854   Idem.

855   Idem.

856   Idem.

857   Idem.

858   See Sophie Shihab, *"Russie: en Tchétchénie" indépendante "Les chars du président tirent devant le Parlement",* <u>Le Monde,</u> 6 June 1993.

859   See Maudet Jean Babtiste, *"Europe : Djokhar Doudaev, le général tchétchène qui défie l'" empire russe,* <u>Le Monde,</u> 15 September 1994.

more to loose and feeding on a will for vengeance that is growing in the ranks of the resistants".[860]. The image of the Chechen people was often that of a people with "warrior traditions"[861] and as one that has as a main characteristic "mystical-warrior traditions"[862]. The second characteristic of the terminology used in the coverage of the crisis in Chechnya by Le Monde seems to reflect an emphasis on a certain personification of the conflict, as well as an emphasis on labelling it as an internal quarrel. Indeed, on many occasions, the emphasis was on the personality of the Chechen President Doudaev and his power struggle with the Russian President and with the opposition inside Chechnya. An examination of the terminology employed by Le Monde reveals the use of terms and expressions to describe President Doudaev as a "little man"[863], "the little general"[864], "the little president"[865], "no doubt suffering of megalomania eventually doubled by a certain paranoia"[866], "champion of the revolution of little peoples"[867], "implacable rebel, like the Chechen mountains, rigid and sure of himself like a Soviet general, Doudaev the wolf will not retreat in the face of the Russian bear"[868], "Djokhar Doudaev is profiting from the divisions in the opposition to stay in power"[869], "each time he reacts in calling wolf strongly"[870], "the rebel regime of Doudaev"[871]. Other than Doudaev being a "little president" of a "little republic", the opposition to the Chechen president is described as "the pro-Moscow" opposition. The democratic opposition—that is to say, the intelligentsia, regrouped in the Daimakh movement"[872], and "the democratic forces"[873]. Similarly, as in the case of the

860   See Sophie Shihab, "La fuite en avant du Kremlin en Tchétchénie ", Le Monde, 11 February 1995.

861   Naudet jean Baptiste, "Les guerriers de Tchétchénie fourbissent leurs armes", Le Monde, 11 September 1994.

862   See Sophie Shihab, Le Monde, 11 February 1995, op. cit.

863   See Maudet Jean Babtiste, Le Monde, 15 Septembre 1994. op. cit.

864   See Jan Krauze, "A la suite des pressions de la Russie Le président Djokhar Doudaïev a décrété la mobilisation générale en Tchétchénie ", Le Monde, 13 August 1994.

865   See Maudet Jean Babtiste, Le Monde, 15 Séptembre 1994. op. cit

866   Idem.

867   Idem.

868   Idem.

869   See "Tchétchènie: Le retour de Rouslan Khasboulatov l'ancien rebelle de la" Maison Blanche ", Le Monde, 16 August 1994.

870   See Jan Krauze, Le Monde, 13 August 1994, op. cit.

871   See Sohpie Shihab, "Boris Eltsine a annoncé la publication d'un statut pour la Tchétchénie ", Le Monde, 30 May 1996.

872   See Sophie Shihab, Le Monde, 25 October 1992, op. cit.

873   See Jean-Baptiste Naudet, "Après un an de guerre en Tchétchénie, Moscou renonce à négocier avec les indépendantistes ", Le Monde, 29 December 1995.

Bosnia crisis coverage, sometimes journalists would tend to use terms that are stereotyping like "the solitaire wolf" for the Chechens or even an expression quoted by President Yeltsin ("do not sleep Cossack") repeated later in the same article in the full version as a quotation of Alexandre Pouchkine[874] "do not sleep Cossack, in the darkness of the night. Beyond the river, the Chechen rods".[875]

The New York Times was quite similar in its terminology used to cover the crisis in Chechnya and even more than *Le Monde* in diabolising the Chechens and their region, its lack of reference or dramatization of human casualties, and in describing the conflict as more of a "Russian internal affaire". *The New York Times* referred to Chechnya and the Chechens in terms such as "despite the presence of tens of thousands of Russian soldiers, the region has become completely lawless"[876], "the Chechen, who have been defeated on the ground and pushed back into the far mountains, have only the threat of more terrorism, like the attack rebels staged on the Russian town of Budyonnovsk, to wield to negotiations[877]", "fierce and heavy armed Chechens"[878], "suspicions of heavy casualties during the Russian effort to recapture the city from the rebels"[879], "the separatists seized major buildings and held dozens of Russian soldiers under siege"[880], "cast the Chechen underdogs in a nasty new role", "the Chechen attack may be the first of such terrorist acts on Russian soil"[881], "the rebellious republic of Chechnya"[882], "fearing terrorist reprisals by Chechens[883]", and "Chechnya, a republic of fiercely independent Muslim". What is interesting in this "diabolising" of the Chechens and their region is that *The New York Times* in one of the articles openly admitted that such demonization is directed against the Chechens by the Russian authorities, criticized it, in spite of the fact that, probably without realizing, *The New*

---

874   Alexandre Pouchkine) is a Russian writer (1799–1837).

875   See Jan Krauze, *Le Monde*, 13 August 1994, op. cit.

876   See Michael Specter, "After Lull, War Revives in Chechnya's Ruins", <u>The New York Times</u>, 26 November 1995, p. 1.

877   See Alexandra Stanley, "Chechnya: New Hope", <u>The New York Times</u>, 23 June 1995, p. A10

878   Idem.

879   See "Death Toll in Battles in Chechnya Put at 600", <u>The New York Times</u>, 26 December 1995, p. A9.

880   Idem.

881   See Michael Specter, "No Way Out On Chechnya ", <u>The New York Times</u>, June 18,1995, p. 10.

882   See Alexandra Stanley, "Russian General Halts His Tanks As Qualms Over Rebellion Grow", <u>The New York Time</u>, 17 December, 1994, p. 1.

883   See Alexandra Stanley, "Strains of Chechnya War Setting Russians on Edge", <u>The New York Time</u>, 29 Januaray, 1995, p. p. 1.

York Times was participating in this Russian diabolising campaign of the Chechens. *The New York Times* states" The Chechens are a bunch of born hoodlums and religious fanatics. Their criminal clans are running an island of banditry within the Russian Federation. Their gross national product is stolen goods. What's more, they were on the side of the Nazis in World War II. That's what Moocow wants the world to believe[884]". One more interesting fact about the terminology used by *The New York Times* in the Chechnya coverage is that on many occasions Chechnya's right to independence was referred to as a "bid for independence". Unlike the case with the civilian casualties in Bosnia, there was rare dramatisation of the civilian tragedy in Chechnya. Furthermore, often and prior to speaking of Chechen civilian losses, the losses of the Russian Army are cited. *The New York Times* states, for instance, "The Russians say they have lost 1,200 men in the fighting. Russian human rights commission said last month that as many a 24,000 civilians had been killed in Grozny alone"[885]. In an article that appeared one month before that, *The New York Times*, in a fully dedicated article to the number of civilian casualties, already questioned not the figure of Russian casualties, but that of the 24,000 civilian ones by saying "but the figure-so high that the researcher who came up with it likened the Chechen conflict to the massacre of Polish civilians during World War II-was questioned even by the head of the Human Rights Commission, Sergei A. Kovalyov"[886]. Moreover, similar to *Le Monde*, there was a personification and a personalisation of the conflict as if it only involved President Yeltsin, Chechen President Doudaev, and his opponents. Yet, one thing that *The New York Times* was different in is that although it described the Russian action in Chechnya as a "military operation", an "Offensive", and a "Russian campaign", on four occasions, it reminded its readers that Russian forces invaded Chechnya. Finally, *The New York Times*, in at least one article re-used adjectives "miscalculations, and offensive) employed by a high ranking U.S. Official commenting a new Russian operation in Chechnya[887].

The terminology used by the two newspapers reveal a number of similarities and some differences as well in their coverage of the two crises. The two newspapers were similar in referring in more negative terms to Serbs and Chechens. *Le*

---

884   See William afire, "Whom to Root for in Chechnya", <u>The New York Times</u>, 19 December 1994, p. A19.

885   See "Russia Pounds Rebel Positions Outside Capital of Chechnya", <u>The New York Times</u>, 21 March, 1995, p. A8.

886   See Alexandra Stanley, "24,000 Dead in Chechnya, Rights Group Tells Yeltsin", <u>The New York Times</u>, 22 February 1995, p. A8

887   See Steven green house, "U.S. Sharply Rebukes Russia For Its Offensive in Chechnya", <u>The New York Times,</u> 12 April 1995, p. A16.

Monde was less intense in this in the case of the Serbs but more in the case of the Chechens. *The New York Times* was more intense in doing that in the case of the Serbs than in that of the Chechens. What is ironic in this is that in the case of Chechnya is that, if applied, the logic adopted in the coverage of Bosnia, would suggest that it is the Russians who should be labelled as the "aggressors". Moreover, while the Bosnian Muslim's quest for independence is natural and legitimate, that of the Chechens is not considered to be the same. One more indication of this is the frequent dramatisation of civilian casualties in the case of Bosnia by both newspapers (the New York Times more) than in the case of Chechnya (*Le Monde* slightly more). The second characteristics is that while *Le Monde* used more "coloured" terminology to describe the roots and course of the events in Bosnia, and less "coloured" ones in Chechnya, the terminology of *The New York Times* seems to be a rigid aggressor-victim clear cut one especially in the case of Bosnia but less in the case of Chechnya. Finally, there was evidence that both newspapers and in the coverage of both crisis re-used terms employed by their sources.

2.3.1.2. The Repetition of the Terms or Adjectives used to describe the Two Crises

The repetition of certain words and expressions can have a tremendous effect on the human mind's memory and, subsequently, on his decision-making process. Hence, it is important to examine the effect of repetition on the human mind in general prior to an analysis of the repetition of terms and objectives in the coverage of the two crises by the two newspapers concerned. One of the ways to help proceed in such an analysis is to proceed on three levels of analysis. The first one is examining the repetition of certain terms and adjectives describing Serb or Russian actions in the course of the two crises. The second is an examination of the repetition of significant terms and adjectives describing each crisis events in general. The third is to examine the repetition of specific terms and adjectives in describing the two crises, the description given to the parties to each crisis, and the designation or labelling of the "origin" of the "supposed" victims in the two crisis.

As far as the first level of analysis is concerned, it is helpful to discuss the differences and similarities, if any, between the coverage of the two newspapers vis-à-vis the two crises at hand. Table 27 compares the usage of certain terms and adjectives to describe the actions of Serbs or Russians in the two crises. This comparison of the usage of terms and adjectives reveals a number of similarities and diversions relating to the repetition of terms and adjectives used by the two newspapers.

Le Monde mentioned the word "genocide" once in its coverage of the two crises, yet, with a special sense. In the case of Bosnia, the word was used to describe acts committed against Serbs in World War II[888]. In the case of the crisis is Chechnya, the word "Genocide" was used in quoting the Russian President Yeltsin saying "we can not negotiate with Doudaev, who organised the genocide of his own people[889]". The sample of the New York articles had no mention of the word "genocide". On the other hand, *The New York Times* mentioned ethnic cleansing 10 times in the case of Bosnia against only 4 times for *Le Monde*. Moreover, the term "concentration camps" was mentioned 2 times by *The New York Times* in the case of Bosnia against no mention of the term for *Le Monde*. In the case of the coverage of Chechnya, there was no mention of "genocide", "ethnic cleansing", or "concentration camps" by either of the two newspapers. Moreover, *Le Monde* repeated, in the case of Bosnia, the terms "Massacre/Massacres" 6 times, "Crime/Crimes" 5 times, "Aggression/Acts of Aggression" 5 times, "Violations of Human Rights/Ceasefires/Accords" 6 times, "Violent/violence" 12 times. Respectively, the same terms and adjectives were repeated by *Le Monde*, in the case of Chechnya, 3, 0, 1, 3, and 6 times. As for *The New York Times*, the coverage of Bosnia reveals the repetition of the terms "Massacre/Massacres" 0 times, "Crime/Crimes" 2 times, "Aggression/Acts of Aggression" 5 times, "Violations of Human Rights/Ceasefires/Accords" 5 times, "Violent/violence" 16 times. Respectively, the same terms and adjectives were repeated by *The New York Times*, in the case of Chechnya, 0, 3, 0, 1, and 0 times. The two newspapers seem to repeat more negative terms and adjectives in their description of Serb acts in Bosnia compared to the action of Russians in Chechnya. The repetition of the New York Time of these negative terms and adjectives seems to be more intense in the case of Bosnia than the repetition of *Le Monde*. However, *Le Monde* was slightly higher than *The New York Times* in its repetition of negative terms and adjectives describing Russian acts in Chechnya.

---

888   See Florence Hartmann, *"Yougoslavie Les Serbes de Bosnie-Herzégovine ont décidé de créer une huitième "République "*, *Le Monde*, 11 January 1992.

889   See Sophie Shihab, "M. Eltsine réaffirme son refus de négocier avec le président tchétchène", *Le Monde*, 20 January 1995.

Table 27: Occurrence of certain adjectives/terms used to describe Serb or Russian military acts in both crises.

Word/ Expression	Le Monde		The New York Times	
	Bosnia	Chechnya	Bosnia	Chechnya
	N° of Occur.	N° of Occur..	N° of Occur.	N° of Occur.
Genocide	1 ♦	1 ♠	0	0
Ethnic Cleansing	4	0 •	10	0
Concentration Camps	0	0	2	0
Massacre/ Massacres	6	3	0	0
Crime/ Crimes/Criminal	5	0	2	3
Aggression/ Acts of Aggression	5	1	5	0
Terror/ Terrorism/ Terrorist/ terrorise	1	5	7	0
Victims/ Victims	5	7	2	0
Murder/ including organised murder	2	0	2	2
Torture	0	0	0	0
Violation/ of Human Rights included./ of accords/ of ceasefires	6	3	5	1
Violant// Violence	12	6	16	0
Atrocities/	1	0	5	1
Brutal/ Brutality	0	0	2	2

♦ The word genocide was used once in the sample of articles to describe acts against Serbs during World War II.

♠ The word genocide was used in quoting of President Boris Yeltsin accusing Chechen President Doudaev of "genocide against his own people"

• word "cleaning" was used between practices as a quote from a Russian declaration to clean a city of Chechen fighters.

The other axe of analysis is that of the use of certain terms and adjectives to describe events in the two crises and warring parties in general. According to Table 28 below, *Le Monde* repeated the word "Crisis" in describing events in Bosnia 17 times against 11 times only for Chechnya. The word "war" (alone) was used by *Le Monde* 39 times to describe the events in Bosnia against 43 times used in the case of Chechnya. The term "civil war" was used by *Le Monde* 10 times against 2 times only in the case of Chechnya. Similarly, the word "conflict (alone)" was repeated 22 times by *Le Monde* in the case of Bosnia against 12 times only in the case of

Chechnya. In addition, *Le Monde* mentioned the terms "War of Liberation" 2 times, compared to no mention of this term in the case of Chechnya. No mention of the term "War of Independence" was found for *Le Monde* coverage of any of the two crises. However, the term "right to independence" was mentioned once in the case of Chechnya. "Self-determination" was found in none of the sample articles of coverage of *Le Monde* of the two crises. Nonetheless, the term "independence" was mentioned 22 times in the case of Chechnya against 17 times in the case of Bosnia. Similarly "Autonomy" was cited 5 times in the case of Chechnya and only 3 times in that of Bosnia. As far as the geographic limitation description of the crisis is concerned, *Le Monde* used the terms "local conflict" and "internal ethnic conflict" once to describe the crisis in Chechnya while these terms were not mentioned as far as Bosnia was concerned. Concerning the reference to the fighting parties in the two crisis, *Le Monde* repeated the term "belligerents" 13 times in the case of Bosnia against one time only in the case of Chechnya. However, the term "separatists" was used more by *Le Monde* to describe fighters in Chechnya (4 times) against only one time to describe those of Bosnia. Moreover, "combatants" was mentioned by *Le Monde* 16 times to describe fighters in Chechnya against only two times to describe those of Bosnia.

For its part, *The New York Times* used the term "crisis" 3 times to describe events in Chechnya against 2 times for Bosnia. Similar to *Le Monde*, *The New York Times* used "war" more to describe events in Chechnya (31 times) than to describe events in Bosnia (24 times). The term "civil war" was mentioned once in the case of Chechnya by *The New York Times* against 3 times in the case of Bosnia. *The New York Times* did not mention "war of independence or "right to independence" in its coverage of any of the two crises. Also similar to Le Monde, the term "independence" was mentioned more for Bosnia (17 time) than for Chechnya (11 times). *The New York Times* used the term "conflict» much lass than *Le Monde* in describing events in Bosnia (4 times), and Chechnya (3 times). Moreover, *The New York Times* used the term "Chechen war" 6 times against only 2 times for "Bosnian war". *Le Monde* didn't designate the conflict in these terms in either of the two cases. Finally, the term "fighting/combats" was used more by *The New York Times* to describe events in Bosnia (35 times) and Chechnya (25 times) against 17 times each in the case of *Le Monde*. In general, the repletion of terms and adjectives by the two newspapers can be interpreted as representing the situation in Chechnya as more of that of "war" than a crisis or even a "civil war". This can also be deducted from the lesser mention of the term" independence" or "liberation" in the case of Chechnya as compared to Bosnia and the apparent more mention of the term" fighting/combats" in Chechnya's case as well. The significance is that the world "war" automatically suggests to the receiver that warring parties are equal.

Table 28: Occurrence of Certain Adjectives/Term used to Describe Crisis Events in General.

Word/ Expression	*Le Monde*		The New York Times	
	Bosnia	Chechnya	Bosnia	Chechnya
	N° of Occur.	N° of Occur.	N° of Occur.	N° of Occur..
Crisis including Chechen or Bosnian crisis	17	11	2	3
War (Alone)	39	43	24	31
Civil War	10	2	3	1
War of Aggression	2	3	1	0
War of Liberation	2	0	0	0
War of Independence	0	0	0	0
Right to Independence	0	1	0	0
Independence	17	22	17	11
Self Determination	0	0	0	1
Autonomy	3	5	1	1
Conflict (alone)	22	12	4	3
Bosnian/ Chechen Conflict	4	0	1	2
Bosnian/ Chechen War	0	0	2	6
Balkan/ Caucasus War	0	0	2	0
Yugoslav/ Caucasus Conflict	3	0	0	0
Local Conflict	0	1	0	0
Internal Ethnic Conflict	0	1	0	0
Combats/ Fighting	17	17	38	25
Belligerents	13	1	0	0
Separatists	1	4	0	3
Combatants/ Fighters	2	16	1	7
Nationalists				
Rivals	0	2	2	0
Warring Sides/ Parties	0	1	3	0
Factions	0	2	1	0

The third axes of analysis, as far as the repetition of terms and adjectives in the two newspapers coverage is concerned, is that related to the repetition of special terms, the designation of the warring sides, and the designation of the ethnic or religious origin of the "supposed "victims in the two crisis (See Table 29 below).

The discrepancy in the repetition of special adjectives to describe the situation of the two crises is quite evident. In general, both newspapers used more tragic adjectives to describe the events in Bosnia than in Chechnya. The word "siege" and its derivations were used 13 times to describe events in Bosnia by *The New York Times* and 5 times by *Le Monde*. But there was no mention of the word-by *Le Monde* and this word was only mentioned two times by *The New York Times* in the case of Chechnya. The same with "nightmare" which was mentioned three times by *Le Monde* in the case of Bosnia and one time by *The New York Times*, but neither of the two newspapers mentioned the same word for Chechnya. The same thing can be said about the word "catastrophe". This word was mentioned once by both *Le Monde* and *The New York Times* for Bosnia but was not mentioned at all for Chechnya. The word "death" and its derivations were mentioned, however, equally by *The New York Times* (24 times) for both Chechnya and Bosnia). The same word and its derivations was mentioned more by *Le Monde* (26 times) in the case of Chechnya than in the case of Bosnia (10 times)

Other than those special terms and adjectives, the designation of the warring sides is another important indication of the repetition effect. The words describing warring parties have been arranged starting with the term that invokes notions such as order, discipline and professionalism in the receiver's mind and gradually descending to terms that invoke less "noble" notions in the receiver's mind. Accordingly, for Bosnia the words are Army, Militia, and Guerrillas. There was more mention of the Bosnian forces as an army for *Le Monde* (7 times) and *The New York Times* (17 times) than for the Serbs, or the Croatians whose forces were not described even once as being an army. Bosnian forces were labelled as militia by *Le Monde* 5 times while the Serbs were called militias 7 times. *The New York Times* labelled Bosnian forces as militia only once, 6 times for Serbs, and 4 times for Croatians. Finally, "guerrillas" was only used by *The New York Times* (6 times) to designate Serb forces.

The designation of Chechen forces was even more degrading than the designation of Serbs. For while both newspapers, generally referred to the Russian forces as an army, troops, and soldiers, the Chechens were referred to as rebels, bandits, militants and even criminals. The labelling, however, of Chechen forces in this manner was more noticeable in *The New York Times* than *Le Monde*. As far as the designation of ethnic or religious origins of Bosnians and Chechens are concerned, discrepancies were also found. Bosnians were referred to as "Muslims" (alone) by *Le Monde* (96 times), and by *The New York Times* (55 times). Chechens on the other hand were identified as Muslims only once by *Le Monde* and 3 times by *The New York Times*. Moreover, *The New York Times* used the term "Muslim Slavs" 19 times against no usage of the term by *Le Monde*. Moreover, both newspapers identified Chechens simply as" Chechens" (194 times by *Le Monde* and 73 times by *The New York Times*). Finally, Chechens were only referred to as being a "people" only 4 times by *Le Monde* and 2 times by *The New York Times*.

Table 29: Occurrence of Certain Special Adjectives/Terms to describe the events, the warring sides, and the labelling of the ethnic or religious origin of the "supposed "victims.

Type of Terms	Term or Adjective		Le Monde		The New York TImes	
			Bosnia	Chechnya	Bosnia	Chechnya
Terms used to describe total situation of particular cities or whole region of crisis	Siege		5	0	13	2
	Suffering		2	2	1	0
	Nightmare		3	0	1	0
	Catastrophe		1	0	1	0
	Death/ Deaths/ Dead		10	26	24	24
Terms used to describe military units in the Bosnia Crisis	Army	Bosnian	7	N/A	17	N/A
		Croat	0	N/A	0	N/A
		Serb	3	N/A	7	N/A
	Militia	Bosnian	5	N/A	1	N/A
		Croat	0	N/A	4	N/A
		Serb	7	N/A	6	N/A
	Guerrillas	Bosnian	0	N/A	0	N/A
		Croat	0	N/A	0	N/A
		Serb	0	N/A	6	N/A
Terms used to describe military fighting units in the Chechnya Crisis	Army	Russian	N/A	19	N/A	14
		Chechen	N/A	0	N/A	0
	Troops	Russian	N/A	20	N/A	29
		Chechen	N/A	1	N/A	1
	Forces	Russian	N/A	21	N/A	10
		Chechen	N/A	13	N/A	1
	Soldiers	Russian	N/A	15	N/A	13
		Chechen	N/A	0	N/A	3
	Guerrillas	Russian	N/A	0	N/A	0
		Chechen	N/A	0	N/A	2
	Resistance	Russian	N/A	0	N/A	0
		Chechen	N/A	8	N/A	4
	Militants	Russian	N/A	0	N/A	0
		Chechen	N/A	0	N/A	4
	Rebels	Russian	N/A	0	N/A	0
		Chechen	N/A	5	N/A	32
	Bandits	Russian	N/A	0	N/A	0
		Chechen	N/A	3	N/A	4
	Criminals	Russian	N/A	0	N/A	0
		Chechen	N/A	0	N/A	2
	Terrorists	Russian	N/A	0	N/A	0
		Chechen	N/A	4	N/A	1
	Underdogs	Russian	N/A	0	N/A	0
		Chechen	N/A	0	N/A	2
Designation of "supposed victims" in both crisis	Bosnian Muslims		0	N/A	3	N/A
	Muslim Slavs		0	N/A	19	N/A
	Muslims (Alone)		96	N/A	55	N/A
	Chechens		N/A	94	N/A	73
	Chechen People		N/A	4	N/A	2
	Muslims		N/A	1	N/A	3

The repetition of certain terms and adjectives to describe events, actors, and situations in an international crisis or conflict has an enormous effect on the audience's perception of the crisis. The repetition of the terms and adjectives in the coverage of the crisis in Chechnya and the crisis in Bosnia reveals a number of findings. The first one is that negative terms and adjectives were more repeated and associated with Serb actions by both newspapers than with Russian actions in Chechnya in general. Yet, while *Le Monde* seems more critical of Russian actions in Chechnya, the opposite is true for *The New York Times* and its coverage of Bosnia. The second finding is that the situation of Chechnya was more associated to a war of equal sides situation by repetition of certain terms to describe it as such, than it was the case of Bosnia. The third finding is that the repetition of negative degrading terms designating Serb and Chechen forces involved was much more frequent than the same designation for their rivals. In the case of Chechens, the degrading designation of their forces was much more obvious. Finally, repetition revealed that Bosnians are more "Muslims" or "Muslim Slavs" than Chechens who were quite rarely identified as Muslims or even as a separate ethnicity. This last fact is interesting if it is taken in consideration with the Muslim public opinion. It also reveals some sort of hypocrisy.

2.3.2. The Images Used

In addition to words, images can be said to be another important constituent of the language of human communication. It too can engage the human mind in a process of interpretation and opinion formation. Ron Burnett states, in this respect, "The idea of the image implicates the mind in a representational process defined and measured through reflection and linearity. In part, this is a question of power— the subjective power to control "sight" and to locate the "seen" discursively, within or as a part of the everyday language we use. It is also about efforts to drive the process of seeing into an anatomical and physical sphere, however metaphorical that might finally end up being, and thus to anchor vision in the "real" world of human thought, perception, experience, and practice"[890]. Thus, images are an important means of conveying feelings and suggestions to the viewer. Yet, images are not usually supposed to give an unlimited scope of vision. Indeed, images used can be looked upon as windows that frame and mediate the possibilities of vision. This implies the existence of a boundary between the perceiver and the perceived. Robert D. Romanyshyn explains that the window limitations "the self becomes an

---

890   See Ron Burnett, Cultures of Vision: Images, Media, and the Imaginary, Indiana University Press, Bloomington, 1995, p.4.

observing *subject*, a *spectator*, as against a world which becomes a *spectacle*, an *object* of vision"[891]. Thus, there are limitations on the boundaries an image can have for a human perception. Other researchers also suggest that formulating perceptions in a human mind depends on the interaction of many elements most of which are already inherent to the individual. For instance, Gerald Edelman explains that parts of the human brain receive input only from other parts of the brain, and that they give outputs to other parts without intervention from the outside world. The brain, according to Edelman, might be said to be in touch more with itself than with anything else."[892] This can also be said to be the opinion of Jonathan Crary who states, "Once the objects of vision are coextensive with one's own body, vision becomes dislocated and depositioned onto a single immanent plane. The bipolar set-up vanishes...subjective vision is found to be distinctly temporal, an unfolding of processes within the body, thus undoing notions of a direct correspondence between perception and object."[893] The significance of images is, thus, that it is a part, though an important one, in the formulation of opinions over issues. It is an essential part of communicating messages. In news coverage, such a tool is usually chosen and used effectively to enhance the messages transmitted by the coverage. Studying the role of the images used can be done by analysing the types of images used in the coverage and the number of occurrences of those images.

2.3.2.1. Types of Images Used

Words backed by images or vice versa is a much more effective combination than words alone or images alone. The effectiveness of such a combination can be explained by the fact that an image that reinforces the message of the news transmitted would leave less room for the receiver's mind to create its own "images" about the news received. It is also easier for the receiver's mind to accept the already provided image than to be troubled by creating an image out of the received words. This is why the use of images (audiovisual, photos, caricatures, maps, illustrations...etc) is quite effective in altering public opinion. Indeed, the images used are immediately imprinted in the receiver's mind reinforcing, therefore, the coverage's message. It would be interesting, hence, to see, what kind of images the two newspapers used to reinforce their news messages concerning the

---

891   See Robert D. Romanyshyn, <u>Technology as Symptom and Dream</u>, Routledge, New York, 1989, p.42.

892   See Gerald M. Edelman, <u>Bright Air, Brilliant Fire: On the Matter of Mind</u>, Basic Books, New York, 1992, pp. 18-19.

893   See Jonathan Crary, <u>Modernizing Vision, Vision and Visuality</u>, ed. Hal Foster, Bay Press, Seattle: 1988, p 35.

two crisis, and whether the usage and type of these images does or does not form a part of the overall attitude of the two newspapers towards the coverage of the crisis in Bosnia and Chechnya. What will also be taken into consideration are the commentaries that accompany the images used in coverage, since commentaries guide the viewer of the image to the desired interpretation of visual backup tool.

The images used by *The New York Times* for the coverage of the crisis of Bosnia seem to have some common characteristics. In addition to the fact that they were almost all photos, they seem to follow the general line of the coverage attitude of the newspaper; namely the demonization of Serbs, the victimisation of Bosnian Muslims, and the dramatisation of events. Examples of such common characteristics within the images of the sample articles and news items are many. In one of the articles, the image was of Serbian artillery stationed around Sarajevo accompanied by the phrase "Despite a deadline, Serb artillery stayed in place around Sarajevo"[894]. Another image published by *The New York Times* showed an old man in Sarajevo sitting beside his wife who died of cold with a comment that says "An elderly grieved in Sarajevo as the body of his wife was bound in a blanket. She was one of 10 people in two days to die of the cold in an unheated home for the elderly on the battle-turn outskirts of the city"[895]. The same article had two more illustrations of this tragedy. One of these is an image of dead bodies placed side by side on a truck with a comment saying "The bodies of the victims of the bitter Bosnian winter; who died in an unheated home for the elderly near Sarajevo, being loaded aboard a truck by French soldiers of the United Nations force in the city"[896]. There was also a map in the same article. It was composed of two parts. The upper part showed Bosnia-Herzegovina and Sarajevo and the second was a map indicating the location of the elderly home in question with a comment saying "Death knocks often at a home for the elderly in Sarajevo"[897]. In another article, an image of U. N convoy of refugees was accompanied by a comment "A U. N. convoy of refugees from the eastern Bosnian enclave of Srebrenica arrived here last night",[898] and a map indicating the small Bosnian Muslim controlled enslaves surrounded by Serb and Croat controlled areas in Bosnia[899]. In

---

894   See Roger Cohen, "A NATO Deadline in Bosnia Passes Without Attack", <u>The New York Times</u>, 5 September 1995, p. A1.

895   See Johan F. Burns, "Bosnia's Elderly Fall to a New Enemy: Cold", <u>The New York Times</u>, 6 January, 1993, p. A1.

896   Idem.

897   Idem.

898   See John F. Burns, "Bosnia Fights a New War Against Croat", <u>The New York Times</u>, 20 April 1993, p. A10.

899   Idem.

another article, an image of a miserable man amidst ruins and carrying a sack on his shoulders was accompanied by a comment that explained "Residents of Sarajevo are having to make do with what can be scrounged from the ruins of their city. A man seeking to repair his own house filled with ceiling tiles from the rubble of a gutted Croatian Church"[900]. *The New York Times* included another image in another article showing the body of a dead woman and accompanied by a comment that goes "A woman was shot and killed yesterday in Sarajevo, Yugoslavia, where snipers opened fire on thousands of peace demonstrators"[901]. Finally another image showed a family of Bosnian Muslims with a desperate look in their eyes accompanied by a comment that explains "Nazif Beganovic, left, and his family were evacuated to Croatia from Banja Luka, were Serbs are driving out Muslims and Croats"[902].The same article also included the photo of an old Bosnian Muslim woman with a comment that says" Every Bosnian refugee at a camp in Gacinci, Croatia, seems to have a memory that brings tears. For Ifeta Kubaras, 58, it is the farm she built near Banja Luka with her husband, slain by Serbian neighbours"[903].

The New York Times' images included in its article and news items about the crisis in Chechnya were also consistent with its general attitude towards this crisis, namely, dehumanising the region and its inhabitants and referring more humanly to Russian actions. The examples of such images within the selected sample of articles are abundant. In one article, an image of the devastated Chechen capital was accompanied by a comment that explains" Much of Grozny' remains an extremely dangerous military zone"[904]. The same article included another larger size photograph of a Russian soldier playing piano in Grozny with a comment that explains" In Grozny, the ruined capital of the secessionist Chechen republic, a Russian soldier plays a piano that has been left behind in a central park".[905] Another article included an image of a young Russian soldier cleaning up rubble in Chechnya with a comment saying "Russia is hoping to end visible resistance in Chechnya before world leaders meet in May. In Grozny, the

---

900   See Chuck Sudetic, "Serbs' Militia Still Blocks UN. Evacuation of Muslims", <u>The New York Times</u>, 10 March 1993, A8

901   See Chuck Sudetic, "Ethnic Clashes Increase in Bosnia as Europe Recognition Vote Nears", The New York Times, 6 April 1992, p. A12.

902   See John Kifner, "Refugees Forced Out in Systematic Drive of Ethnic Hatred", <u>The New York Times</u>, 27 March 1994, p. 2.

903   Ibid., p. 16.

904   See Steven Erlanger, "A Famous Victory", The New York Times, 10 February 1995, p. A8.

905   Idem.

Chechen capital, Russian servicemen had to clean up old Russian rubbles scattered around a bank"[906]. In another article, an image of Shamil Basayev, the Chechen leader who led the commando incursion in Budyonnvsk with a comment underneath that explains" Shamil Basayev, left, the Chechen rebel who led the commando attack in the southern Russian city of Budyonnvsk, surveying the situation at the hospital where his fighters were holding hundreds of hostages"[907]. Whenever Chechnya is referred to in the comments explaining the images, it is always either the secessionist, separatist, the rebel republic, or Chechnya region in Russia. For instance, an image in one of *The New York Times* articles showed a Russian soldier trying to warm himself at a fire in Grozny with a comment that explains, "A Russian soldier warmed himself up at a fire in the ruins of Grozny, the capital of the separatist area of Chechnya. Russian troops attacked rebel forces yesterday south and east of the capital".[908] It also seems to stress the *bravery of Russian soldiers*. An example is an image of one article in *The New York Times* that shows a young Russian soldier at a checkpoint in Chechnya with an explanation saying "A young Russian conscript from Astrakhan manned his post at a checkpoint in the Russian countryside"[909]. The same article included another image of Russian soldiers with a comment that explains" Russian military said it finally captured Shali and Argun"[910]. Another article showed a map of Chechnya with a comment saying "Russian troops took back a police station from rebels in Argun".[911] In another article, there was an image of a Russian mother sitting in the hospital besides her son, a wounded soldier in Chechnya, with a comment saying "Russia's war in Chechnya has cost thousands of lives and left the country a bundle of nerves, with paranoid rumours of plot sweeping the nation. At a hospital in Moscow, Valentina Svietova sat by her son, Sergei, an army soldier paralysed by injuries he suffered in Chechnya"[912]. Even the instances were images of Chechen civilians suffering were included in articles, the photographs and the

---

906   See Steven Erlanger, "Dissent on Chechnya: Word to the West", <u>The New York Times</u>, 14 April, 1995, p. A6.

907   See Steven Erlanger, "Moocow Accepts Chechnya Talks", <u>The New York Times</u>, 19 June 1995, p. A6.

908   See "Russia Pounds Rebel Positions Outside Capital of Chechnya", <u>The New York Times</u>, 21 May 1995, p. A8.

909   See Steven Elanger, "Russia Sees Long Fight in Chechnya", <u>The New York Times</u>, 24 March 1995, p.A 6.

910   Idem.

911   See Alexandra Stanley, "Russian Assault Recaptures Police Station in Chechnya", <u>The New York Times,</u> 22 August 1995, p. A3.

912   See Alexandra Stanley, "Strains of Chechnya War Setting Russians on Edge", <u>The New York Times,</u> 29 January 1995, p. A12.

comments were far less dramatic than the ones used for the coverage of the crisis of Bosnia. For example, in one of the articles, an image of a woman walking in the ruins of Grozny was accompanied by a comment saying "A woman walk by the ruins of the presidential palace in Grozny, Chechnya's' capital. After a lull, war has returned to the secessionist republic"[913]. The same article included another image of a Chechen getting water from a public tap with a comment that explain "War is again battering the Chechnya region in Russia, and people in the capital get water from outdoor taps"[914]. *The New York Times*, in another article, published an image of a nurse with a comment saying "Evetlana Dmitriyeva, a nurse, fear that Chechen civilian will suffer"[915].

For its part, none of the sample articles of *Le Monde* for the coverage of the crisis of Bosnia and Chechnya included any photos relating to the conflict. Instead, the images used in *Le Monde* sample articles on Bosnia were one of two forms. They were either caricatures or maps. Nonetheless, the effect of a good caricature on public opinion and, indeed, on the political state apparatus, is much more effective sometimes than the use of photos or even audiovisual material. The reason is that a caricature is, by nature, a satirical depiction of reality, which has a number of assets that make it very powerful in modelling public opinion. It is a very intelligent and safe way of social and political criticism. Indeed, a caricature is followed daily by a majority of people, some of whom even buying the newspaper because of the talents of the caricatures' artists, precisely because it camouflages political and social criticism in humour and satire. As such, the author of the caricature can disseminate almost any type of criticism or depiction of reality in humour precisely because the caricature is, after all, a comic brake to many readers and, most importantly, because it leaves a huge space to its interpretations. It is, thus, a very viable and effective tool of the printed media and certainly a legally safer one since it gives room for dismissing, in cases of need, the caricature as being mere humour. It is not by pure accident, then, that *Le Monde* opts for the use of caricatures to accompany its coverage of the Bosnia and Chechnya events, and indeed in the majority of its news coverage. it is also fair to say that the use of a caricature in coverage adds more to objectivity than the use of photographs does. The reason is that the caricature, unlike the photograph, leaves much more room for the imagination of the reader who can always dismiss the caricature as nothing more than humour. On the other hand, photographs leave

---

913   See Michael Specter, "After Lull, War Revives in Chechnya's Ruins", <u>The New York Times</u>, 26 November 1995, p. 12.

914   Ibid., p. 1.

915   See Alexandra Stanley, "In the Provinces, Russians Back Drive on Chechnya", <u>The New York Times</u>, 29 December 1995, p. 12.

no room for free construction of imagination. A photograph usually leaves little or no free choice for the reader or the receiver than to connect this presented photograph with the words used by the media.

Le Monde's caricatures were somewhat supportive of its coverage attitude of the conflict in Bosnia, yet, to a much more less degree than the directness of association found between the coverage of the New Your Times of the conflict and the photographs and maps it used. For instance, in one of the articles warning against the spread of the conflict and the European inaction entitled "The Improbable Tempest of the Balkans", the caricature used showed soldiers fighting each other with a man in a suit, supposed to represent Europe, saying" Through down your weapons. You are not surrounded"[916]. In another article, which criticises the inaction of Western and mostly European powers to put an end to the conflict in Bosnia, the caricature in *Le Monde* showed a pile of corpses under a window with a man standing in the window and saying "No. Although I would swear I heard cries"[917]. The same issue of *Le Monde* which also included on the same page an article on the atrocities in Bosnia entitled" Testimonies of a Nightmare" did not include, however, any photograph or even a more expressive caricature of these atrocities[918]. In another article where *Le Monde* continue to criticise the inaction of the West and especially the inefficacity of the peacekeeping forces in Bosnia, the caricature used showed two soldiers, with no identification of their appurtenance, loading a dead body in a truck with a man representing the peacekeepers telling them to do it "Gently"[919]. In one of the articles, *Le Monde* used a caricature that subtly indicated the Serb extremists' policy of ethnic cleansing. The caricature concerning the signing of an accord in Geneva on Bosnia showed former Serbian President Milosovic drawing a map with people behind him whispering, "He is preparing the new map of Serb-Herzegovina"[920]. In addition, *Le Monde* caricatures supported the vision of the conflict as one where the interests of international and regional powers are involved. For example, in an article entitled "Bosnia: A

916   See Michel Tatu, "*Bosnie: L'Improbable "tempête des Balkans"*, <u>Le Monde,</u> 14 August 1992, p. 1.

917   See Asfane Bassir, "*L'adoption par le Conseil de sécurité des résolutions autorisant le recours à la force en Bosnie Les Occidentaux espèrent intimider les Serbes avant la conférence de Londres*", <u>Le Monde</u>, 15 August 1992, p. 1.

918   See Alain Debove, "*Témoignages sur un cauchemar*", <u>Le Monde</u>, 15 August 1992, p. 1.

919   See Claire Tréan and Yves Heller, "*Le Conflit yougoslave: Impuissance et fatalisme*", <u>Le Monde</u>, 3 Novembre 1992, p. 4.

920   See Yves Heller, "*Accord à Genève sur l'éclatement de la Bosnie-Herzégovine La présidence bosniaque a accepté" provisoirement "la création d'une" Union "de trois Républiques*", <u>Le Monde</u>, 1 August 1993, p. p.5.

Badly Assembled Puzzle", *Le Monde* used a caricature showing a round table with the map of Bosnia-Herzegovina in the middle of the table. The caricature showed five empty chairs representing the Contact Group on Bosnia with a pair of scissors in front of every chair[921]. Finally, the caricatures used by *Le Monde* also expressed its reserve on the NATO strikes against the Serbs and its hegemony over Europe. In an article, for instance, the caricature used was that of a NATO jet bombarding, while the Serb on the ground is gathering the missiles and saying" This is good timing. We are in need of ammunitions"[922].

The caricatures used by *Le Monde* in its coverage of the events in Chechnya were quite few. The ones found, however, credit more objectivity to *Le Monde* because they indicate that the conflict is disregarded because of the strategic U.S.-Russian post Cold War ties, yet at the same time, indicate that the conflict in Chechnya is not only internal but one which is happening in a far away land. In one of the articles, for instance, the caricatures used shows former U.S. President Bill Clinton joking with former Russian President Yeltsin saying "There is no reactor in Chechnya?"[923]. In another article, the caricature showed former U.S. Secretary of State Warren Christopher raising a toast and saying "The war in Chechnya will not affect our relations" and answered with a reversed phrase attributed to the former Russian Minister of Foreign Affaires saying "Our relations will not affect the war in Chechnya"[924]. Finally, depiction of Chechen civilian victims of the conflict was not found in the sample of *Le Monde* articles and its caricatures. Nonetheless, a depiction of the excessive use of force by Russian troops in Chechnya was found in one of the articles which has a caricature showing a Russian tank shooting with a comment saying" The truce is over: You did not vote Yeltsin"[925].

---

921 See Yves Heller, "*Bosnie : Un puzzle mal assemblé*", *Le Monde*, 30 July 1994, p. p.5.

922 See Remy Ourdan, "*Le massacre de Tuzla entraîne de nouveaux raids de l'OTAN Les artilleurs serbes ont ouvert le feu sur deux cafés de la ville bosniaque, faisant soixante et onze morts. Tandis que deux cents «casques bleus» étaient pris en otage à Sarajevo, les Occidentaux répliquaient par de nouvelles frappes aériennes*", *Le Monde*, 27 May 1995. p. 2.

923 See Sophie Shihab, "*Bill Clinton et Boris Eltsine ont constaté leurs divergences à Moscou Concession symbolique sur la coopération nucléaire avec l'Iran et promesse d'un vague cessez-le-feu en Tchétchénie sont les seuls résultats tangibles de cette rencontre*", *Le Monde*, 12 May 1995. p. 2.

924 See Sophie Shihab, "*M. Eltsine réaffirme son refus de négocier avec le président tchétchène*", *Le Monde*, 20 January 1995, p. 2.

925 See Sophie Shihab, "*M. Eltsine réélu, les bombardements reprennent en Tchétchénie*", *Le Monde*, 11 July 1996, p. 2.

2.3.2.2. Number of Occurrences

In addition to the type and nature of images used, a fairly good indication of the importance of a crisis to the media and the importance that this media indicates in return to its receivers vis-à-vis this crisis or conflict can be measured by a quantitive comparison of the usage of visual illustrations and images pertinent to the events of one crisis as opposed to another. More images and illustrations can better help carry the coverage message of the media to the public. In the case of the images and illustrations used by the two newspapers in their respective coverage of the crisis in Bosnia and the crisis in Chechnya, it can be said that discrepancies in the quantity of images and illustrations were evident.

For its part, *The New York Times*, in its coverage of Bosnia used twenty photos and ten illustrations (mostly maps). This is an average of one photo for each article published. On the other hand, for its coverage of the events in Chechnya, *The New York Times* used a total of sixteen photos and only five illustrations. For its part, *Le Monde's* sample of articles on Chechnya and Bosnia had no photos what so ever of the events of the two crises. In its coverage, *Le Monde* indicates a clear-cut preference for the use of other types of images and illustrations such as caricatures and maps. Yet, this usage is much more less than that of *The New York Times* for both crises but like *The New York Times*, more frequent for the coverage of the crisis of Bosnia than for that of Chechnya. The difference in the frequency of usage of images and illustrations between *Le Monde* and *The New York Times* is quite obvious. For its coverage of Bosnia, *Le Monde* used six maps and seven caricatures. This is close to a ratio of one caricature for every three articles and one map for every four. The images of the Chechnya coverage are even scarcer. The sample of *Le Monde* articles on Chechnya included only one map and three caricatures. This is close to a ratio of one map per twenty articles and one caricature per seven articles.

2.3.3. The Repetition of the Occurrence of the Coverage.

The repetition of the occurrence of coverage of the two crises can be measured on two levels of analysis. The first one is that of the number of occurrences of articles or news items relating to the two crises in the two newspapers and the second is the measurement of the volume of words allocated to the coverage of each crisis based on the sample of articles from the two newspapers.

As far as the first axe of analysis is concerned, it can be said that apparent discrepancies were depicted in the number of articles or news items dedicated to the coverage of the two crises between the two newspapers and between the two crises within each newspaper. The examination basis in this case is the occurrence of certain relative words in either the title or the body of the article or the news item. As far as *Le Monde* is concerned, the total number of articles and news items concerning the crisis is Bosnia with the words "Bosnia", "Bosnian", "Sarajevo", "Balkans" or "Balkanian" in the title amounts to 3476. This number is compared to 590 articles and news items of *Le Monde* with the words "Chechnya", "Chechen", "Grozny", "Caucasus", "Caucasian" in the title. (See Table 30 below) As far as the news items and articles of *Le Monde* containing reference to the two crises (including the title), discrepancies between the quantity of articles and news items relating to each of the two crises is also noted. In this case, the articles and news items of *Le Monde* containing the same words amount to 11586 in the case of Bosnia against only 3044 in the case of the crisis in Chechnya.

Table 30: Quantitive Statistics of the Occurrence of coverage

Type of Occurrence	Le Monde				The New York Times			
	Bosnia		Chechnya		Bosnia		Chechnya	
N° of News Items & articles the word appeared in title coverage of an article or a news item.	Word	N° of Occur.	Word	N° of Occur.	Word	N° of Occur.	Word	N° of Occur.
	Bosnia	2281	Chechnya	292	Bosnia	1274	Chehcnya	121
	Bosnian	336	Chechen	100	Bosnian	434	Chechen	129
	Sarajevo	775	Grozny	110	Sarajevo	404	Grozny	18
	Balkans	79	Caucasus	86	Balkans	152	Caucasus	74
	Balkanian	5	Caucasian	2	Balkanian	0	Caucasian	0
	Total	3476	Total	590	Total	2264	Total	342
N° of News Items & articles the word appeared in text coverage of the whole article or the news item.	Word	N° of Occur.	Word	N° of Occur.	Word	N° of Occur.	Word	N° of Occur
	Bosnia	5294	Chechnya	1116	Bosnia	6785	Chechnya	920
	Bosnian	2324	Chechen	656	Bosnian	4250	Chechen	621
	Sarajevo	3108	Grozny	513	Sarajevo	3317	Grozny	307
	Balkans	712	Caucasus	724	Balkans	1675	Caucasus	556
	Balkanian	148	Russia and Caucasian	35	Balkanian	0	Russia and Caucasian	990
	Total	11586	Total	3044	Total	16027	Total	2507

The result of an analysis of the occurrence of coverage of the two crises in *The New York Times* indicates that the articles and news items with the words Bosnia, Bosnian, Sarajevo, Balkans, Balkanian in their title amount to 2264, which is less than the total of the same search criteria for *Le Monde*. As far as the crisis in Chechnya is concerned, the total number of news items and articles in *The New*

York Times having either of the words, Chechnya, Chechen, Grozny, Caucasus, Caucasian is 342 which is, again, less than the total of news items and articles published in *Le Monde* within the same search criteria. However, the search reveals that the total of news items and articles published in *The New York Times* and having either of the words Bosnia, Bosnian, Sarajevo, Balkans, Balkanian in the whole article and news item (including the title) is 16027, which is higher than the search results *for Le Monde*. Yet, the number of news items and articles in *The New York Times* having either of the words Chechnya, Chechen, Grozny, Caucasus, Russia and Caucasian in the whole title including the title is less than that of *Le Monde* and amounts to 2507.

The discrepancy between the occurrences of coverage between the two newspapers is obvious. Nonetheless, a greater discrepancy exists between the ratio of coverage between the two crises. Indeed, the total number of *Le Monde* and *The New York Times'* articles and news items having Bosnia, Bosnian, Sarajevo, Balkan and Balkanian, for instance, is 5740. On the other hand the total number of articles and news items published by the two newspapers having the words Chechnya, Chechen, Grozny, Caucasus and Russia/Caucasian in their title is 932. This is almost a 1 to 6 ratio. This means that for one article or news item published in the two newspapers about Chechnya, six news items and articles are published about Bosnia.

The second level of this quantitive analysis of the occurrence of coverage is the one relating to the volume of words used in the coverage by the two newspapers. It is interesting to note that differences also exist in the volume or size of coverage of the two crises within the same newspaper and between he two newspapers vis-à-vis the same crisis. For, the total number of words in *Le Monde* articles and news items used in the coverage of the crisis in Bosnia is 28274 against a total of 19921 words for *The New York Times*. On the other hand, the word count of articles and news items dedicated to the coverage of the crisis in Chechnya was significantly less for the two newspapers, although *Le Monde* used more words than *The New York Times* in this case as well. In covering Chechnya, *Le Monde* used 22751 words against only 17979 for *The New York Times* (See Graphic 9 below).

Graphic 9

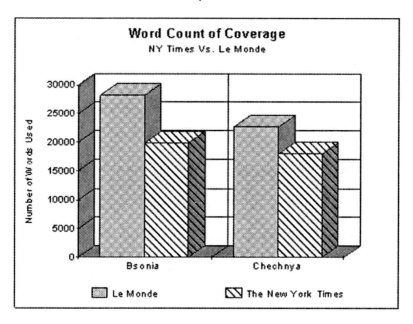

Word Count of Coverage
NY Times Vs. Le Monde

An analysis of the occurrence of coverage of the two crises can be done by comparing the total number of articles and news items published by the two newspapers on these two events. It can also be measured by the volume or "size" of each crisis's coverage within the concerned newspaper. The two newspapers published more articles and new items concerning the crisis in Bosnia than the crisis in Chechnya. For each article or news item published by the two newspapers on Chechnya, six news items and articles were published on Bosnia. *Le Monde* published more articles and news items on Bosnia and Chechnya than *The New York Times*. A significant difference in the volume or "size" of the coverage between the two crises was also found. The volume of coverage for Bosnia was higher in the two newspapers than the total number of words for the coverage of Chechnya, although Le Monde allocated slightly more words to cover the two crises than *The New York Times*.

2.3.4. The Place of the Two Events as Part of The Coverage

The placement of a news item or an article gives an idea of its priority to the media outlet and, hence, reflects its importance to the audience. The audience gives naturally more importance to news items, articles, and stories that are presented in a more attractive manner. A news item or an article, for instance, which is not really important can be given a lot of importance by the news media outlet, in a newspaper for example, by giving it a sensational title and placing it in front of other news items or stories. The audience, or the reader, would normally be more intrigued to follow this news item or story, which this media outlet places in a more noticeable area than the other news items because first; this news item or article catches the audience's eye before the others do, and, second, because the audience would tend to think that the news item or the article must be important to be placed in front of the other news items.

The placement of news gives, hence, a fairly good idea about the importance that the news media outlet gives to this news and also about the effect that this news media outlet wants to create in the audience through the priority it gives to the placement of this news. Accordingly, an examination of the place occupied by the news items and articles published by the two newspapers regarding the crisis in Bosnia and Chechnya would give a good idea about the perceived importance of each of these two crises first to the newspaper as compared to other news this news paper is covering simultaneously, and, consequently, to the newspaper audience. Accordingly, estimating the place of the coverage of each of the two crisis within the two newspapers can be done by analysing the placement of the news items and articles relating to each crisis within the newspaper concerned and by examining the priority given to these two crises compared to other major international crises and conflicts which took place within more or less the same period of time.

2.3.4.1. The Placement of the Coverage of Each Crisis within the French and the U.S. National Printed Media

As mentioned above, the physical placement of news largely indicates its importance to both the news media outlet and to the receiving audience. Placement of news can also have another significance. If a news item is relevant to the editorial line of the newspaper concerning a certain crisis or conflict, it usually would take a priority placement. If, on the other hand, this news item were a bit contradictory to this general attitude towards the crisis or conflict, it would usually not have a priority placement. This hypothesis is in a certain manner relevant to the journalistic claim of "objectivity". Indeed, it can be said that simply publishing a different opinion means that "objectivity" is attained. Yet, the question is in the priority of placing the exposure of this different opinion. If this different opinion or view of events is published but in a less prestigious place than the favourable news items, then objectivity has the appearance of being attained but, in fact, is not. It can be said then, that in addition to reflecting the importance of the international crisis or conflict to the media outlet, the placement of undesirable news also reflects the objectivity level of this media outlet.

Out of the sample articles of the New York Time on Bosnia, six were placed in the front page against four in the case of Chechnya. The rest of the articles in *The New York Times* about the two crises were placed in the international section of the newspaper, except for one editorial article found about Chechnya. Yet, even in the placement within the international section of *The New York Times* discrepancies were found. Two of the articles on Bosnia were placed in page 3, one in 2, and one in page 5 against only one article about Chechnya placed on page 1. Three of the articles and news items on Bosnia were placed on page A3 against only one in the case of Chechnya. One article about each crisis was published in page A6. The rest of the articles and news items on Bosnia were published in pages A8 (2), A 10 (1), and one each for A 12, A14, and page 16. On the other hand, for Chechnya, the rest of the articles were published on page A 7 (1 article), A8 (5 articles), A 10(2 articles), A 12 (1 article), A 14 (1 article), A 16 (1 article) and A 19 (1 article). Neither in the front page number neither of articles nor in the placement in international section of *The New York Times* is there equality between the placements of coverage of the two crises. The same thing can be said about the placements of *Le Monde's* articles on the two crises. For its coverage of Bosnia, *Le Monde* placed nine of its articles on the front page against only one in the case of its articles on Chechnya. The priority of placements for articles on Bosnia was also seen in the distribution of placements between articles covering the two crises on the interior pages of the French daily. Four articles of *Le Monde* on Bosnia were placed on page 2 of the newspapers, six articles on page 3, and one on page 5. Against this order of placement, *Le Monde* published six articles on Chechnya on page 2, four articles on page 3, three articles on page 4, four articles on page 5, one article on page 20, and one on page 26. Thus, for *Le Monde* as well priority of placement was given to the conflict in Bosnia.

It is interesting, though, to examine at this stage the hypothesis concerning the relationship between the placement of news items and the objectivity of the media. A comparison between the front-page articles of both newspapers seems to be an appropriate tool to measure the relevance of placement to objectivity and the attitude of the newspaper in question towards the crisis in general. As far as *The New York Times'* six front page articles about Bosnia are concerned, two of these articles stressed the plight of the Bosnian Muslims and the atrocities of Serbs[926], one was a criticism of the lack of action of the U.N.[927], one concerned a U.S. official stand

---

926   See John F. Burns, "Bosnia's Elderly Fall to a New Enemy: Cold: Bosnia Now Faces the Cruelest Enemy of the Siege: Winter's Cold", The New York Times, 6 January 1993. and John Kiefner, "Refugees Forced Out in Systematic Drive of Ethnic Hatred: Serbian Violence Rising in North Bosnia", The New York Times, 27 March, 1994.

927   See Paul Lewis, "U.N. Rules Out A Force to Halt Bosnia Fighting: U.N. Chief Rules Out Role For Peace Force in Bosnia", The New York Times, 14 May 1992.

toward the crisis[928], one praised a success of NATO in the crisis[929], and one related to two U.S. envoys killed in Bosnia[930]. The result of the same analysis applied to the New York Time four front-page articles on Chechnya is one article on the psychological effect of the war in Chechnya on the Russians[931], one article about the "war culture" of Chechnya[932], one article about the effect of the Budyonnvsk hostages' situation on Russian policy in Chechnya[933], and one about Russian soldiers[934]. The same applies to Le Monde's front-page articles on both crises. The nine front-page articles and news items on the conflict in Bosnia-Herzegovina published by Le Monde were one on the risk of the spread of the conflict in the Balkans[935], four on the impuissance of the United Nations and Western powers to deal with the conflict[936], two on the risks of implosion of Bosnia[937], one

---

928   See Elaine Scioling, "U.S. Rejects Plea to Act in Bosnia", The New York Times, 25 January, 1994.

929   See Roger Cohen, "A NATO Deadline Passes in Bosnia Without Attack", ", The New York Times, 5, September, 1995

930   See Tim Weiner, ".S. Vows to Carry On Work Of 3 Envoys Killed in Bosnia", The New York Times, 22 August 1995.

931   See Alexandra Stanley "Strains of Chechnya War Setting Russians on Edge", The New York Times, 29 January 1996.

932   See Michael Specter, "After Lull, War Revives in Chechnya's Ruins", The New York Times, 26 November 1995.

933   See Steven Erlanger, "Moscow Accepts Chechnya Talks: Cease-Fire Declared in New Effort to Free Hostages Moscow Accepts Talks in Chechnya to End Hostage Crisis", The New York Times, 19 July 1995.

934   See Alexandra Stanley, "Russian General Halts His Tanks As Qualms Over Rebellion Grow:Russian General Halts Tanks in Chechnya, ", The New York Times, December 17, 1994.

935   See Michel Tatu, "Bosnie: L'Improbable "tempête des Balkans", op.cit

936   See Asfane Bassir, "L'adoption par le Conseil de sécurité des résolutions autorisant le recours à la force en Bosnie Les Occidentaux espèrent intimider les Serbes avant la conférence de Londres", op. cit. and Alain Debove, "L'adoption par le Conseil de Sécurité des résolutions autorisant le recours à la force en Bosnie Témoignages sur un cauchemar", op. cit., Also seeClaire Tréan & Yves Heller "Le Conflit Yougoslave : impuissance et Fatalisme", op. cit., and Michel Tatut, "Armer l'ONU Les échecs des Nations unies en Somalie comme en Bosnie soulignent la nécessité d'un renforcement des structures de l'organisation", op. cit.

937   See Yves Heller, "Yougoslavie : Tandis que lord Carrington tente d'obtenir un nouveau cessez-le-feu La Croatie met en garde contre l'extension de la guerre à la Bosnie-Herzégovine ", op. cit. and Alain Debove, "En permettant la sécession des Serbes et des Croates de la future Union Le nouveau plan de paix ouvre la voie à l'éclatement de la Bosnie-Herzégovine", op. cit.

on the various international interests and dimensions of the crisis.[938], and one on the signature of a peace accord concerning the conflict[939]. As far as the one article published by *Le Monde* on the first page is concerned, it was one that described Chechnya as an anarchist mafia run region[940].

An examination of the priority of placement of coverage between the two newspapers reveals that both gave much more priority placements to their coverage of the crisis in Bosnia as opposed to their coverage of the events in Chechnya. Furthermore, the front-page articles of both *The New York Times* and *Le Monde* all had this priority placement because they seem to reflect the general attitude of the newspaper cornering the conflict in question.

2.3.4.2. The Other Major International Crises and Conflicts Covered Simultaneously with the Coverage of the two Crises

Understanding the importance given to the coverage of a given international crisis or conflict can be done through a comparison with the coverage received by other international crises and conflicts that took place in the more or less same period of time. Accordingly, it is necessary to examine the occurrence of coverage of other major international conflicts and crises in the two newspapers. The conflicts and crisis chosen for the comparison are those of Rwanda, The Gulf War & Iraq, Somalia, Congo (Zaire), and Haiti. For practical reasons the search conducted on these crises and conflicts is limited by two criteria. The search in the database of the two newspapers concerned was done to cover the period of 1991–1996.for all cries and conflicts concerned, regardless of each crisis's respective period. They all, however, took place in the beginning of the 1990s and continued, with different chronological extensions, until the end of the decade. The period of search, nonetheless, only included the coverage from 1991-1996. The second criterion of the search was that it only concerned articles and news items that include the name of the region where the crisis or conflict took place in their title. After this search was done, a comparison with the estimated number of victims in each conflict and crisis was conducted taking into consideration the importance of geographic proximity, direct involvement in the conflict, and historical ties to the respective regions for both France and the United States (See Table 31 below).

---

938   See Yves Heller, *"'Bosnie : Un puzzle mal assemblé'*, op. cit.

939   Yves Heller, *"Accord à Genève sur l'éclatement de la Bosnie-Herzégovine La présidence bosniaque a accepté" provisoirement "la création d'une" Union "de trois Républiques"*, op. cit.

940   See Sophie Shihab, *"Anarchie en Tchétchénie Un an après la proclamation de son indépendance, la remuante République du Caucase, livrée à tous les trafics, va à vau-l'eau"*, op.cit.

Table 31: Coverage of Other Major Conflict and Crisis by *Le Monde* & *The New York Times* Compared to Estimates of Victims and Certain National Interest.

Crisis or Conflict	Le Monde				The New York Times.				Estimates of Civilian Victims*
	N° of Occur.	Direct Involv.	Geo. Proxm..	Historic ties.	N° of Occur.	Direct Involv.	Geo. Prox.	Historic ties.	
Bosnia (1991-1995)	2281	X	X	X	1274	X	N	N	250,000
Chechnya (1994-1996)	292	N	N	N	121	N	N	N	+104,000
Rwanda	697	X	N	X	284	N	N	N	700,000-1700,000
Iraq & Gulf (1990-1999)	816	X	N	N	1483	X	N	N	1000,000-1500,000
Somalia (1992-1999)	575	N	N	N	808	X	N	N	500,000
Congo (Zaire) 1992-1994	187	N	N	X	16	N	N	N	+7000
Haiti (1991-1994)	541	X	N	X	716	X	X	N	5000

*Source for Estimates of Victims: 1-Bosnia Herzegovina: U.S. State Dept. Report (*Bosnia and Herzegovina Country Report on Human Rights Practices for 1996*) found at http://www.state.gov/www/global/human_rights/1996_hrp_report/bosniahe.html, 2- Chechnya (94-96) figure from Time of Dec. 1999 (4000 Russian soldiers and + 100,000 civilians) found at http://users.erols.com/mwhite28/warstat5.htm#Chechnya, 3- Rwanda according to the website: Death Tolls for the Major Wars and Atrocities of the Twentieth Century found at http://users.erols.com/mwhite28/warstat2.htm#Rwanda, 4- Iraq & Gulf: Ramsey Clark found at Death Tolls for the Major Wars and Atrocities of the Twentieth Century, op. cit. (Death toll includes 750,000 children death), 5-Somalia: War Annual 8 (1997) found at http://users.erols.com/mwhite28/warstat3.htm#Somalia, 6- Congo: Amnesty International http://www.amnesty.org, 6-,Haiti: Death Tolls for the Major Wars and Atrocities of the Twentieth Century op. cit. *N=No, X=Yes.

The results of this comparison are interesting. The priority of coverage for *Le Monde* according to this comparison was Bosnia followed by Iraq, Rwanda, Somalia, Haiti, Chechnya, and Congo (Zaire). For *The New York Times*, the priority of the occurrence of coverage seems to be Iraq, Bosnia, Somalia, Haiti, Rwanda, Chechnya, and Congo (Zaire). If coverage depends on the humanitarian tragedy represented by victims, the priority should have been Rwanda, Iraq, Somalia, Bosnia, Chechnya, Congo (Zaire), and finally Haiti. Yet, this humanitarian motives do not seem to be the priority of media coverage. Other elements and factors seem to determine the priority of coverage. *Le Monde* covered Bosnia more because it is close, because France was directly involved, and because France has historical ties with the region. It covered Iraq more than Rwanda again because France was directly involved in the conflict and because of French interests in the region. Rwanda occupied the third place on the priority list because France was involved in the crisis and because of historical ties to Rwanda. For its part, *The New York Times* covered Bosnia and Iraq more also because it was directly involved in the conflict and because of its vital interests in the region. It covered Somalia more than Rwanda because it was directly involved in the country for public relations purposes. It covered Haiti more than Rwanda, Chechnya or Congo (Zaire) because it was also directly involved in the crisis and because of Haiti's geographic proximity to the United States.

For both newspapers, the coverage of Bosnia took priority over coverage of other international conflicts, except for the New York Time which dedicated more coverage to Iraq and the Gulf War than to Bosnia. Chechnya was fifth on the priority list of *Le Monde* and sixth on the list of *The New York Times* amongst the seven crisis and conflicts in the comparison. Priority of coverage cannot be explained by the scale of humanitarian tragedy. It can be, however, explained by other factors such a geographic proximity, direct involvement and interest, and historical ties.

2.3.5. The Journalists Covering the Two Crises

The first notion that comes to mind when discussing the issue of the journalists involved in the coverage of the two crises is that of "objectivity". It is, indeed, imperative to clarify some of the concepts and values relating to this basic, yet, more and more contested, notion of journalistic ethics, in order to better understand the conduct of the journalists involved in the coverage of the crisis in Bosnia and in that of Chechnya.

The origins of journalistic objectivity go far back in the history of media and journalism. The event that affected journalism the most in the 1830s was probably the introduction of what was known as the Penny Press, which had the advantage of appealing to the readers because of their low prices and the innovative distribution techniques they used. Indeed, the Penny Press was a revolution in media, both in concept and in scale. It should be kept in mind that in the early 1800s, the majority of existing newspapers were weeklies. At that time, only two types of newspapers were circulated: all commercial and all political ones. The political papers, or what was known as the "party press," received their funding from their respective political parties. In return, these political parties had the upper hand and openly dictated what would be published in the newspaper. The major disadvantage, for both the producers and receivers of these newspapers, was that both commercial and political newspapers were quite expensive. Because of their high cost, the majority of people could not buy them on the street. To be able to get a newspaper, a full year subscription was required. The result was that only the most fortunate would be able to afford a newspaper at the time. Consequently, since the audience was mainly the most fortunate in society, news focused on politics, business and the comings and goings of ships in ports. The radical change came in the 1830s (closer to the 1870s and 1880s in Canada). The introduction of the concept of the Penny Press revolutionized the way news was produced, distributed, and consumed. For, with the Penny Press, instead of relying on subscriptions and political funding for revenue, the penny papers started to rely on advertising. They were, hence, able to offer their version of news to the public for as little as one penny (the price was around 6 before) and to distribute, by the process, more copies.

Another rather important innovation for journalism brought about by the Penny Press was, however, the new tradition of separating the stories based on facts from editorials. This tendency developed with time to place the news on the front-page, while opinions were placed farther back in the newspaper. The Penny Press, thus, lessened substantially the grip of politicians on journalists, separated facts from editorials, and contributed to more access to information. This can be said to have contributed to the devolvement of the concept of journalistic objectivity. Nonetheless, it brought in one of the weapons with which the media is criticized sometimes i.e. advertising.

Further developments also helped shape the concept of journalistic objectivity. Kevin Stoker explains, in this respect "the introduction of the telegraph, press associations, and professionalization of journalists influenced the development of objectivity as a guiding norm for news coverage"[941]. For his part, M. Schudson explains that at the beginning of the 1890s, journalists started taking pride in their devotion to facts. He adds that they "believed that facts of themselves, once revealed, would lead to right thought and right action"[942]. This devotion kept developing at a fast pace during the late 1800s. H. Stensaas, for instance, explains that, by the late 1800s, one third of the news stories in a sample of metropolitan newspapers in the United States adhered to the tenets of objectivity[943]. In those years, the development of the concept was also the result of the efforts of certain personalities. A good example of this would be the management of Carr Van Anda of *The New York Times* in 1904. In this respect, W. Irwin, explains that Van Anda used an empirical and a scientific approach to gathering news stories and facts. According to him, Van Anda believed that too much literary quality, humour included, blurred the reader's "reliability of what he was reading"[944]. For his part, B. Fine, explains that Van Anda was a strong supporter of the idea that journalists shouldn't be allowed to give their own opinions or to take sides in their stories. He asserts that journalists "may state the facts, but inferences are to be left to the editorial page or to the understanding of the reader"[945]. Thus, it can be said that during this period technical innovations in the form and distribution of the press along with the influential personalities of certain journalistic figures helped to give birth and later shape the concept of journalistic objectivity.

---

941   See Kevin Stoker, "Existential Objectivity: Freeing Journalists to Be Ethical", Journal of Mass Media Ethics, Vol. 10, 1995, p.6.

942   See M. Schudson, Origins of the Ideal of Objectivity in the Profession, Garland, New York, 1990, p. 25.

943   See H. Stensaas, "Development of the objectivity ethic in U.S. daily newspapers", Journal of Mass Media Ethics, vol.2, N°1, 1986-1987, pp. 50-60.

944   See W. Irwin, The making of a reporter, Putnam, New York, 1942, p. 114.

945   See B. Fine, A giant of the press: Carr Van Anda, Acme Books, Oakland, CA, 1968, pp. 74-75.

It should be said, nonetheless, that when it was time to start discussing the definition of the concept of journalistic objectivity between the 1920s and 1930s, there was two notable directions. The first of those lines of thought was based on theory, while the other was based on pragmatism. For Walter Lippmann, who represented the first line of thought, reporters were considered as people who use objective realities to interpret news[946]. The other line of thought, represented by Nelson Crawford believed that the basic role of journalism is to disseminate objective facts[947]. Hence for Lippmann's school, the journalists' role in life is that they are essentially people who reshape the pure or absolute truth with their own interpretations, while the school of Crawford advocated that journalists are there to transmit their harness of objective facts. Both concepts seem, however, to be an understanding of journalists as being similar to "machines" that gather facts and redistribute them, with or without these "machine's" chosen flavour. This analogy seems, hence, to ignore the various factors that interact and shape human behaviour.

As far as the journalists' quest to be objective is concerned, Nelson Crawford believed that journalists couldn't be totally objective even if they try so hard to be so because they will always be influenced by their own interests, interpretations and philosophies, unless they are "guided by some definite standard"[948]. For him, to do that, there is a need to create organizations that set the norms and "specific rules as to what sort of news must be printed"[949]. For his part, Lippmann thinks that objectivity should free journalism from the" hidden control "and "subserviency to the whims of the system"[950]. So for Nelson Crawford, objectivity can only be established by making organizations and setting rules while Lippmann believes that it's the journalists themselves that should be free to make their judgement of the facts and not simply to uncover them.

Crawford and Lippmann were not the only ones to defend their view of the concept of journalistic objectify. Other researchers participated in the controversy over the definition of journalistic objectivity and its relation to public relations. For instance, M. Schudson believes that the observing of objectivity by journalists in their work would help protect them from the influence of the agents of public relations[951]. He states, in this respect, that "public relations threatened the very

---

946 See Walter Lippmann, "Two revolutions in the American press", <u>Yale Review</u>, 1931, N° 20, pp.437-440.

947 See Nelson Crawford, <u>The Ethics of Journalism</u>, MI: Scholarly Press, St. Claire Shores, 1924.

948 Ibid., p.101.

949 Idem.

950 See Walter Lippmann, "Two revolutions in the American press", <u>op. cit.</u> p. 440.

951 See M. Schudson, Origins of the Ideal of Objectivity in the Profession, <u>op. cit.</u>

idea of fair reporting"[952]. Some writers suggest that this threat to objectivity coming from public relations agents and practitioners intensified in the aftermath of World War I. Frank I. Cobb, for example, explains that most newspapers in the period that followed the end of World War I were transformed into tools for the public relations agents and for advocates of propaganda[953]. He explains that the newspapers in the period that followed World War I have been transformed into mere tools of propagandists, that these newspapers only scan the surface and fail to reach "the heart of things," and that a reporter of those newspapers rarely "gets under the skin of great events"[954]. For Lippmann, reporting was compared to "the beam of a searchlight that moves restlessly about, bringing one episode and then another out of darkness into vision"[955]. Obviously, the definition of Lippmann of a good reporter is that this reporter should always be on the search for evidence, reasons and interpretation guided by his obligation to be a good journalist. However, other researchers such as C. Argyris and D. Schon, explain that this ideal case is rarely applied. They argue that there is quite a contradiction between what news editors say and what is applied namely because of the imposed conditions of having to be competitive and to protect one's interests[956]. Another criticism of Lippmann's idea of journalistic objectivity comes from R. Streckfuss who argues that the perception Lippmann has of journalistic objectivity was part of a larger cultural movement of scientific naturalism and that the sense of this definition of objectivity has been transformed by time into an idea suggesting that reporters should keep their own opinions out of their reports and stories[957].

Indeed, the notion of objectivity in journalistic practice is not a static one. It has evolved and has managed to adapt to different variants affecting the journalistic environment over the years. In this respect, Meenakshi Gigi Durham explains that "journalistic objectivity has always been a slippery notion; its definition has varied over the years and continue to be the focus of considerable debate"[958]. Other researchers such as K. Stoker, emphasize that the constructions of journalism have

---

952 Idem, p. 252.

953 See Frank I. Cobb, "The press and public opinion", The New Republic, December 31, 1919, pp. 144-147.

954 Idem, p.147.

955 See Walter Lippmann, Public Opinion, op. cit, p.229.

956 See C. Argyris and D. Schon, Theory in practice: Increasing Professional Effectiveness, Jossey-Bass. San Francisco, 1974.

957 See R. Streckfuss, "Objectivity in journalism: A search and a reassessment", Journalism Quarterly, N°67, 1990, pp.973-983.

958 See Meenakshi Gigi Durham, "On the Relevance of Standpoint Epistemology to the Practice of Journalism: The Case for "Strong Objectivity", Communication Theory, vol. 8, N° 2, 1998, p.118.

changed over the last century in response to existing economic, moral and social climates at the time[959]. Originally, it can be said that the synonymous of journalistic objectivity was the notion of impartiality. In this respect, M. Schudson argues that "objectivity was understood as an ideal counter to the reality of a reporter's own subjectivity"[960]. Other researchers claim that this notion (objectivity) is simply a tactic used by the news media organizations to achieve economic goals. In this respect, E. Oginanova and J. Endersby state, "objectivity is a successful tactic used by the news media for maximising their audiences"[961]. According to this interpretation, the news media organizations would use journalists as political centrists in order to increase their market of audiences. Noam Chomsky is also close to this point of view. He argues that the intentions of journalists and their integrity are usually subject to strong pressures. He states" what is at issue is not the integrity of those who seek the facts but rather the choice of topics and the highlighting of issues, the range of opinion permitted expression, the questioned premises that guide reporting and commentary and the general framework imposed for the presentation of a certain view of the world"[962]. Edward E. Herman and Noam Chomsky further elaborate on the notion of journalistic objectivity as becoming more and more of a tactic aimed at increasing audiences and minimizing costs. They declare, "Another reason for the heavy weight given to official sources is that the mass media claim to be "objective" dispensers of the news: partly to maintain the image of objectivity, but also to protect themselves from criticism of bias and the threat of libel suits; they need material that can be presumptinaly accurate. This is also partly a matter of cost: taking information from sources that may be presumed credible reduces investigative expense, whereas material from sources that are not *prima facia* credible, or that will elicit criticism and threats, requires careful checking and costly research"[963]. These last views are quite logical. Indeed, it is more plausible to draw more interest and credibility to a seemingly objective rather than a subjective presentation of news. According to this reasoning, claiming objectivity would certainly have positive effects in expanding the base of the receiving audience and, consequently, the market share of the news organization concerned.

---

959   See K. Stoker," Existential Objectivity": Freeing Journalists to be Ethical, Journal of Mass Media Ethics, vol.10, N°1, 1995, pp.5-23.

960   See M. Schudson, op. cit, p.268.

961   See E. Oginanova and J. Endersby, "Objectivity Revisited; a Spatial Model for Political Economy and Mass Communication", Journalism and Mass Communication Monographs, N°159, October 1996, p.23.

962   See Noam Chomsky, Necessary Illusion: Thought Control in Democratic Society, South End Press, Boston, 1989, p.12.

963   See Edward E. Herman and Noam Chomsky, Manufacturing Consent: The Political Economy of Mass Media, Pantheon Books, New York, 2002, p. 19.

The evolution of the notion of objectivity in journalistic practice has also generated, in the process, the introduction of new interpretations, notions and values. In this respect, Meenakshi Gigi Durham explains that, in the process of its evolution, the notion of journalistic objectivity has moved away from focusing on "neutrality" towards a focus on concepts such as "fairness", "accuracy" and "balance". However, Durham continues to say that "these concepts still involve a separation of the reporter's view from the views being presented"[964]. These values or concepts are considered, for example, by the American Society of Newspaper Editors as being highly pertinent to the notion of journalistic objectivity. The Society's 1995 report identifies the concepts of "balance", "fairness", "accuracy", "authenticity", and" wholeness" as the main values of journalism[965]. The last of these listed values (wholesome) is synonymous to another concept resulting from the evolution of the notion of journalistic objectivity, which is that of pluralism. R.D. Barney explains that this concept means that journalists are supposed to do two things at the same time. They have to be objective and to be pluralist by introducing a multiplicity of viewpoints into their presented work[966]. Hence, such new concepts or values can be said to add to the journalists' quest of being objective. Indeed, considering the above-mentioned values, objectivity can be understood as being about having the right balance in what is being presented to the public.

Nevertheless, the contestation of the notion of objectivity in journalistic practice as a "myth" and an "ideal" which is difficult to reach is quite evident amongst researchers. M. Schuldson, for instance, explains, "objectivity might be a professional idea, but it is one that seems to disintegrate as soon as it was formulated. It becomes an ideal in journalism, precisely when the impossibility of presenting the news was widely accepted. Criticism of the "myth" of objectivity has been a contrapuntal accompaniment to the enunciation of objectivity as an ideal from the beginning"[967]. Indeed, other debates have emerged with the evolution of the notion of journalistic objectivity, namely concerning whether, nowadays, journalists should be simple observers or regulators of the society to which they belong.

The issue of passing judgements is the first of such controversial notions relating to objectivity. Indeed, the American Society of Newspaper Editors' 1995 report also adds "judgement" to journalists concepts associated the actual meaning of the notion of journalistic objectivity. The report asks journalists to "act as the regulator

---

964   See Meenakshi Gigi Durham, op. cit, p.119.
965   See the report of the American Society of Newspaper Editors, "Reconsidering Journalism Values", 1995, Online document found at www. Asne.org.
966   See R.D. Barney, "The Journalist and a Pluralistic Society: An Ethical Approach", in D. Elliott (Ed.), Responsible Journalism, CA. Sage, Beverly Hills, 1986, pp.60-80.
967   See M. Schuldosn, op. cit, p. 269.

of the other journalistic values by selecting, shaping and bringing definition to what is important, interesting and meaningful in a community"[968]. Hence, journalists are asked to make choices by selecting what they present and by giving it their own interpretation. Yet, even with their personal interpretation and judgements, journalists are still requested to seek the "truth". In this respect, E.B. Lambeth says "the obligation to tell the truth goes to the very heart of journalistic function"[969]. Meenakshi Gigi Durham is, however, of the opinion that there might be not a single truth but a "multiple, layered and conflicting truths concerning a single issue and that such truths or versions of the truth might be dependent on one's social location[970]. What Durham seems to be trying to say is that the "truth" can be different things to different people and that it depends on the position of the one who is viewing it. In other words, journalists don't all see the same truth because everyone can be looking at the issue from his or her own different angle.

Another consequence of the evolution of the notion of objectivity is that which has come to be known as "civic" or "public" journalism. According to J. Rosen, journalism is a theory and a practice that recognizes the overriding importance of improving public life"[971]. The key to the distinction, as far as public journalism is concerned, seems to be the choice journalists make of whether to be passive observers or active participants in their society. Again the controversy on public journalism and objectivity exists here as well. For his part, J. Rosen goes as far as saying that the concept of public journalism negates the idea of "impartiality"[972]. Yet, others see public journalism as a sort of middle ground for journalists. A. Charity, for instance, states "journalists do more than furnish us with facts. They frame and narrate the story of our common life.... Without relinquishing their stance as observers and critics, they can try to nourish a particular understanding of American society"[973]. The point here seems to be that journalists can achieve both goals. They can be objective and can also be active members working for the amelioration of their society.

Thus, it can be said that the notion of journalistic objectivity is not a static one. It has developed with time and managed to adapt to different variations that interact and affect the journalistic environment. Indeed, it has developed from the notion of journalistic objectivity as being synonymous of impartiality and the

---

968   See the 1995 report of the American Society of Newspaper Editors, op. cit.
969   See E.B. Lambeth, Committed Journalism: An Ethic for the Profession (2nd ed.), Indian University Press, Bloomington, 1996, p.37.
970   See Meenakshi Gigi Durham, op. cit, p. 120.
971   See J. Rosen, "Beyond Objectivity", Nieman Reports, vol.47, N°7, 1993, p.53.
972   Idem.
973   See A. Charity, Doing Public Journalism, Guilford, New York, 1995, pp.146-147.

presentation of value-free facts to that where an acknowledgement of the journalist's personal convictions' effect on objectivity due to the recognition that a journalist can be both an observer and a regulator of the society he or she belongs to.

It is interesting at this point to apply these notions of journalistic objectivity to *The New York Times* and *Le Monde's* journalists that covered the crisis in Bosnia and Chechnya. The issue, of course, is certainly not to accuse any of them of lack of objectivity. Such an accusation is not easy to be made since the definition of objectivity itself is quite vague and since no two journalists can be said to have gone through the same exact circumstances, when covering an event or to have had the same factors that interacted to shape their personality and view of matters. Accordingly, the analysis relating to the journalist involved in the coverage would attempt to establish at least a vague hypothetical image of their political orientations and personal involvement since, due to the lapse of time, it is quite difficult to gather more solid information concerning them. There is, however, an interesting fact that is worthy of mentioning concerning the journalists involved of the coverage of the two crises. This fact concerned the diversity of journalists allocated for the coverage of each crisis by the two newspapers. The difference between the the two newspaper and, indeed, between the two cries is evident. Based on the sample of twenty articles for each crisis and from each newspaper, the number of different journalists covering the crisis in Bosnia, in the case of *The New York Times* was eight against four only in the case of Chechnya. Surprisingly, the number of different journalists of *Le Monde* covering Bosnia was also eight against five in the case of Chechnya.

The political orientation or political affinities of the journalists involved in the coverage of the two crises is an important aspect to discuss in order to better understand the nature of their news coverage. In other words, the personal political subjectivity of each journalist is bound to have its mark on the conduct of his or her profession. It is hypothetical, yet, logical to assume that a person's environment is the principal factor that influences this person's beliefs and, consequently, acts. Environment is, nevertheless, a word that can involve quite a number of notions. Indeed, many things can be considered to be an environment such a society, family, geographic location, political party, a country's overall political atmosphere...etc. For practical purposes, analysis of the journalists involved in coverage would only include two from each newspaper and for each crisis. They are chosen because they wrote or reported the highest news items and articles compared to the others in the sample of articles. It is interesting to examine these journalists' personal attitudes towards the conflicts they covered and whether they, other than simply writing articles, get personally attached to the subjects they cover.

For *The New York Times*, the journalists or reporters that provided more news than others, within he sample of articles, are Chuck Sudetic (eight articles), and

John F. Burns (four articles) for Bosnia and Alexandra Stanley (seven articles) and Steven Erlanger (six articles) for Chechnya. As far as *Le Monde* is concerned, the journalists are Florence Hartman (Four articles) and Remy Ourdan (four articles)[974] in the case of Bosnia and Sophie Shihab (eleven articles) and Jean Baptise Naudet (four articles) for Chechnya.

Amongst *The New York Times* journalists and reporters, Chuck Sudetic and John F. Burns are the two that contributed more articles on the conflict in Bosnia than others. For his part, Chuck Sudetic did not only cover the war of Bosnia for *The New York Times* but he also ended up writing a book about it called *Blood and Vengeance: One Family's Story of the War in Bosnia*[975]. He is quoted saying that, as a reporter, war was a great opportunity for him but that as a human being, he was horrified[976]. Chuck Sudetic, however, and because of his Croatian origins was accused of bias in his coverage of the conflict in Bosnia[977]. For his part, the other New York Times journalist, John F. Burns, have had an impressive carrier in war reporting. In his four decades in journalism, Burns has gone down many roads, in many parts of the world. Along the way, he's been honoured with two Pulitzer Prizes for his work in war zones (in 1997 for reporting on the rise of the Taliban in Afghanistan and in 1993 for his coverage of the siege of Sarajevo) and two George Polk Awards (one as part of a team reporting on Africa in 1979 at the height of apartheid and one in 1996 for his Afghan coverage[978]. When asked why journalists risk their lives to cover a story, he says" "Journalists want to know; we are incessantly curious people....There is a compulsion to bear witness, to tell the story of the afflicted. But we can't tell that story if we don't go down that road"[979]. Unlike the two New York Times' correspondents on Bosnia, the newspapers' correspondents for Chechnya (Alexandra Stanley and Steven Erlanger) do not seem to have the same prestigious status of the ones covering Bosnia. Nothing was found to indicate these two journalists' personal view or involvement in the conflict in Chechnya, which they covered unlike Chuck Sudetic and John F. Burns who both either published books or received prizes for their coverage of events in the Bosnia conflict.

---

974   Note: Yves Heller also had four articles on Bosnia in *Le Monde*. The choice of the two others, hence, does not render their choice arbitrary since all three had an equal number of articles. Choice was left to be determined by pure alphabetical order of first names.

975   See Covering War, found at http://www.wpr.org/book/990131a.htm

976   Idem.

977   See http://www.balkan-archive.org.yu/kosta/licnosti/sudetic.html

978   See "International Press Freedom Awards 2003", CPJ (Committee to Protect Journalists) at http://www.cpj.org/awards03/burns.html

979   Idem.

As far as *Le Monde's* journalists are concerned, the two that covered most the crisis of Bosnia, amongst the sample of articles, are Florence Hartman and Remy Ourdan. For her part, Florence Hartman seems to have been much more involved and attached to the conflict of Bosnia she covered than just being a detached transmitter of facts. She participated in debates and even in realising theatre plays on the conflict such as "Requiem for Srebrenica"[980]. Moreover, Florence Hartman testified in the trial of the former Serb President Slobodan Milosevic in the International Criminal Tribunal for Former Yugoslavia in the Hague presenting herself as an "an objective reporter during all the wars of Yugoslavia"[981]. For his part; Rémy Ourdan, the other journalist who covered Bosnia the must within the sample articles, is a very experienced war reporter who also showed his continuous involvement and interest in the conflicts he covered. He is responsible for the French edition of a book called *Crimes of War: What The Public Should know*. This book is a collection of various journalists' coverage articles during conflicts that took place all over the world[982]. This book was published on the eve of the fiftieth anniversary (in August 1999) of the Geneva Conventions, with the aim of encouraging public knowledge of the principles of conduct in war. The measuring tools of this book's judgements on what is a war crime are the grave breaches, or serious war crimes, delineated in the four Geneva Conventions of 1949 and the First Additional Protocol of 1977. To provide a broader overview of contemporary conflict, the editors asked reporters and one historian to take a fresh and critical look at recent conflicts and examine them in the light of the crimes of war. These ten case studies offer insights into the dynamics of crimes in nine wars and can be read as a book within a book. Complementing the case studies are three experts' overviews of the applicable law: "Categories of War Crimes" by Steven Ratner, "Crimes against Humanity" by Cherif Bassiouni, and "Genocide" by Diane Orentlicher[983]. The book is conceived as a handbook for reporters to distinguish war crimes in times of conflict which are recognized by applicable international law[984].

Le Monde's other two journalists chosen for their coverage of Chechnya are Sophie Shihab and Jean Baptise Naudet. For her part, Sophie Shihab was not only a simple journalist covering the conflict in Chechnya but someone who has

---

980   See http://www.fluctuat.net/theatre/paris99/chroniq/srebr.htm
981   See « *Procès Milosevic : la parole est aux « insiders »*, *Le Courrier des Balkans*, 7 November 2002, found at http://www.balkans.eu.org/article1641.html
982   See http://www.ridi.org/adi/colloques/2002cdg.pdf
983   See Crimes of War Project page, Website of The Humanitarian Assistance Training Inventory found at http://www.reliefweb.int/
984   Idem.

proven attachment and personal involvement in the conflict. She is described as one of the "rare French journalists that can explain the history of the Chechen Republic since the proclamation of its independence in 1991"[985], "one who does not hesitate to enter secretly the Chechen territory disguised as a Chechen woman in spite of the growing rigidity of border controls"[986], and one "who is engaged and loyal to a people (the Chechens) whose destiny is subject to diplomatic arrangements"[987]. Other than by her writing for Le Monde on Chechnya, Sophie Shihab indicates strongly her attachment to the Chechen people with other writings such as her article Réponse Á Un Anti-Tchétchène[988], and in writing the preface of a book produced by a Chechen support committee called Tchétchénie, dix clés pour comprendre[989]. Similar to the two previously mentioned New York Times journalists covering Chechnya, nothing was found to indicate that the other Le Monde journalist covering Chechnya, Jean Baptise Naudet, was particularly personally involved or active towards the conflict of Chechnya.

This examination of the journalists' covering the two crisis reveals a number of interesting facts. Except for Sophie Shihab, the two newspapers seem to send their most experienced and qualified journalists to cover certain international crises that are considered to be more important than others. It seems also that a number of journalists, due to their coverage of certain conflicts, become attached to the peoples of these regions. This attachment can be seen more in their work and writings outside the newspaper in question more than within their articles. Whether this growing attachment to certain causes is journalistic bias or a normal human reaction remains a subject of discussion. For, if journalists are supposed to be totally objective, then logically they are also supposed to be totally detached. Some might argue here that the editorial executive pen would work as a regulator in the sense that it would limit a journalist's attachment to one party of an international conflict or another. Though this argument might be true in certain cases, it is doubtful that it is true for all cases. From the above discussed cases of involved journalists and their articles, it can be seen that none of those journalists who became attached to the conflict they covered, or to a one party in this conflict or another, exhibited excessive bias in his articles. Instead, they all expressed their personal attachments outside of their respective media outlet's channels.

---

985   See Philippe Mangeot, *"Cap au pire (Sophie Shihab)"*, April 2004, found at http://www.vacarme.eu.org/

986   Idem.

987   Idem.

988   See Sophie Shihab, «*Reponse A Un Anti-Tchéchene*», <u>Politique Internationale</u>, N° 98, Winter 2002-2003.

989   See Website of *Comité Tchéchénie* ar http://www.comite-tchetchenie.org/

This does not all mean that there were no traces of their personal attachments in their conflict or crisis reporting or, indeed, that their articles were totally objective. Before being what their profession makes them, journalists are, and above all, susceptible human beings.

2.3.6. The Effects of Trans-National Media Coverage

The effects of trans-national media on the coverage of the two crises by *The New York Times* and *Le Monde* is an important element in the attempt to understand the two newspapers' respective coverage. Understanding this influence of trans-national media on the coverage of the two crises can be analysed by examining the sourcing effect of trans-national media on the coverage and by examining the effect of such sourcing on the orientations of these two media outlets.

2.3.6.1. Trans-national Media as a Source of Crisis Coverage

Trans-national media can constitute an important source of information for various local or national media outlets. This is particularly true during an international crisis or conflict where not all national or local media have the possibility of having their own correspondents in the crisis area. In the case of *The New York Times* and *le Monde*, examining the degree of reliance on trans-national media for the coverage of the two international crises is, hence, important. It is also interesting to see if there is more dependence on trans-national media for sourcing purposes from one international crisis to another and from one newspaper to another. The analysis of the number of times each newspaper used trans-national media sourcing, within their respective sample articles, for the two crises reveals some interesting findings (See Table 32 below).

Table 32: Trans-national Sourcing Occurrences for *The New York Times* & *Le Monde* in their Coverage of the Two Crisis.

Transnational Media Source	Le Monde		The New York Times	
	Bosnia	Chechnya	Bosnia	Chechnya
Agence France Presse (AFP)	1	7	0	1
Reuters	0	1	1	4
Associated Press (AP)	0	0	1	5
Itar-Tass	0	7	0	8
Interfax	1	3	0	3
Total	2	18	2	23

The table above reveals some interesting findings. The first of these findings is that both newspapers used more trans-national sourcing in the case of Chechnya than in the case of Bosnia. For Bosnia, the total for trans-national media sources was only 2 for each one of the two newspapers. On the other hand, in *Le Monde*, there were a total of 18 citations of trans-national sources against a total of 23 for *The New York Times* in the case of the coverage of Chechnya. The second finding is that national media tends to usually prefer, if they have to, sources from a trans-national media that is either linguistically close or politically close. Even with a sample articles as many as twenty for each crisis, this fact is quite evident. *Le Monde*, for instance, used 7 sources from *Agence France Presse* (AFP) in the case of Chechnya against only one from the Associated Press. Similarly, *The New York Times* used 5 from the Associated Press and 4 from Reuters in the coverage of Chechnya against only one from Agence France Press. The third finding is that both newspapers, in the case of Chechnya, often cited Russian semi-official trans-national media sources. *The New York Times* cited a total of eleven sources from Itar-Tass and Interfax combined against 10 citations for *Le Monde*.

The result of the analysis of the dependence of the two newspapers on trans-national media sources in the coverage of an international crisis or conflict is quite interesting. Both newspapers were more dependent on trans-nationals sourcing in the case of Chechnya than in the case of Bosnia. This might suggest that lack of interest in an international crisis can lead to more dependence on trans-national media sourcing. Both newspapers also seemed to prefer trans-national media sourcing from organisations with which they have more linguistic or political affinities than others. Moreover, both newspapers often-cited trans-national media sources in the case of Chechnya that are more or less affiliated with the Russian authorities.

2.3.6.2. The Effect of Orienting National Media

Trans-national media can, through sourcing, have an effect on the orientation of coverage of the national media vis-à-vis an international crisis or conflict. This can take place through the dissemination of certain terms to describe the crisis that will eventually be adopted by the national media outlets and, henceforth, taken for granted as being the most correct terms to use. The second is that trans-national media sourcing can orient national media outlets to adopt a certain attitude towards the crisis in question through the effective use of news dissemination and framing. It is, therefore, useful to see the instances, within the chosen sample articles, where this trans-national media orienting effect took place and to which extent if it did.

Due to the poor number of trans-national media sourcing citations by the two newspapers in the case of the coverage of Bosnia, the examples of trans-national media orientation will only be taken from the sample articles relating to the coverage of the crisis in Chechnya.

As far as *Le Monde* is concerned, various examples can be given of the influence of trans-national media sourcing on its coverage of the crisis in Chechnya. In an article that was sourced by three trans-national media organisations (AFP, Reuters, Itar-Tass) acts of violence were referred to simply as "incidents", President Yeltsin was referred to as "confronted with the threat of the disintegration of Russia", and as someone who is "weakened by the nationalist rededications", Tatarstan and Chechnya were referred to as the "separatist republics", and the situation in Chechnya was referred to as an "explosive situation"[990]. In another article *Le Monde* mentions that foreign media agencies including the AFP reported that" small groups of Chechen fighters captured a growing number of Russian soldiers who do not hesitate to surrender. This is no doubt why aviation is used"[991] to bombard the city in question which, the article and its sources does not fail to remind that the city (Grozny) has "lots of women, children, and old people, most of which are Russian"[992]. In another article, *Le Monde* says, "The AFP correspondents, have signalled, Monday morning, the restart of bombardments. The Russian armed forces have lost "hundreds" of men since they entered the city (Grozny)"[993]. The instances above where the AFP was quoted as a source seem to be slightly adding to the image of Chechnya as a "war culture zone" and to the emphasis of Russian suffering in trying to pacify the "secessionist republic". Yet, though the reports of the AFP can be looked upon as not having that much of an effect on orienting *Le Monde*, sourcing from the Russian Itar-Tass and Interfax were. It should be said, however, that in many cases, *Le Monde* would warn its readers on the susceptibility of the source usually with the use of quotation marks or by reminding its readers that Itar-Tass and Interfax are close to Russian authorities. The problem, nonetheless, is that continued repetition would make the reader subconsciously disregard these warnings. Similarly, quotation marks' usage can sometimes suggest emphasis and not doubt. Examples of such warnings by *Le Monde* are abundant, within the sample of its

---

990   See "Russie : sur fond de combats en Tchétchénie Le traité de la Fédération a été signé ", Le Monde, 2 April, 1992.

991   See Sophie Shihab, "M. Eltsine réaffirme son refus de négocier avec le président tchétchène ", le Monde, 20 January 1995.

992   Idem.

993   See Jan Krauze, "*Les forces russes subiraient de lourdes pertes dans Grozny*", Le Monde, 3 January 1995.

articles on Chechnya. For instance, in one of the articles *Le Monde* uses quotation marks to warn its readers against the subjectivity of the source. It states" the Itar-Tass agency affirmed, on Wednesday, that the Russian forces have "resumed their operations against the separatists in Gekhi"[994]. In another article, Le Monde also used quotation marks for terms and news from Itar-Tass. It states" during this time, an "explosive situation", according to the Itar-Tass agency developed in Grozny"[995]. In another article, *Le Monde* quotes the Interfax agency, yet again, warns its readers through the use of quotation marks. *Le Monde* conveying the supposed justifications of the renowned General Lebed concerning the action in Chechnya of a Russian general that was close to him by saying "He justified the action of his former subordinate by "throwing all responsibility of the events on the chiefs of Chechen armed formations", according to the Interfax agency. The general says nonetheless," that he still favours a pacific solution to the conflict in Chechnya" where, he does not, however, have the intention to go "prior to July 17"[996]. Within all the sample articles on Chechnya, *Le Monde* referred to Itar-Tass as a "Russian "news agency only once[997].

For its part, *The New York Times* also tends to reflect more or less the same characteristics of trans-national media sourcing and citations in its coverage of the crisis of Chechnya. Similar to *Le Monde*, various examples of these trans-national media sourcing characteristics and effects can be found within *The New York Times'* sample articles on Chechnya. There appears, however, to be one difference between *The New York Times* and *Le Monde* as far as warning their respective readers against "suspected" trans-national sourcing is concerned. For while, *Le Monde* seems to tend to use quotation marks to mark the news it employed from the news agencies it seems to consider doubtful, *The New York Times* tends to use such quotation marks less. Yet, in its case, *The New York Times'* references to the doubtfulness of the objectivity on the source were, within the sample articles, expressed more directly[998]. The Itar-Tass agency is referred to on one article as the "semi-official news agency. This designation of Itar-Tass as being "semi-official" was

---

994   See Sophie Shihab, "*M. Eltsine réélu, les bombardements reprennent en Tchétchénie*", *Le Monde*, 11 July 1996.

995   See "*Russie : sur fond de combats en Tchétchénie Le traité de la Fédération a été signé*", *Le Monde*, op. cit.

996   See Sophie Shibah, "*M. Eltsine réélu, les bombardements reprennent en Tchétchénie*", *Le Monde*, op. cit.

997   See "Russie : sur fond de combats en Tchétchénie Le traité de la Fédération a été signé", *Le Monde*, op. cit.

998   See Steven Erlanger, "Dissent on Chechnya: Word to the West", The New York Times, 14 April 1995.

repeated in another article where *The New York Times* states "The semi-official news agency Itar-Tass announced with fanfare that Russian soldiers had crossed the *Sunzha River* and taken the *Minutka* roundabout"[999]. In the same article, *The New York Times* makes the distinction between the degrees of objectivity of transnational media sources. It states". In fact according to Western reporters and other objective news agencies, like Interfax, the Russian army has not taken Grozny or even encircled it"[1000]. There was a kind of irony in this particular article, however. For instead of projecting the suffering of Chechen civilians, as it was the case of Bosnian civilians, the article included a photo of a Russian soldier playing piano in Grozny provided by Reuters[1001]. Indeed, explaining that the Itar-Tass and Interfax might be less objective because they have Russian affinities does give more objectivity credit to well-known international agencies. In fact, the use of an "image of objectivity" because the agency is a world-leading one, can have a negative impact. If a news agency is pre-supposed to be objective simply because its "Western" or because it's a world leading one, anything coming from this agency can be taken for granted by both journalists and audiences even if it is not truly objective. A good example of this is one of the news items on Chechnya within the sample pertaining to *The New York Times* that is attributed to the Associated Press as a source, although bits and pieces of the news there were sometimes referred to Interfax or Itar-Tass. In this article, Chechens were referred to as "rebels" and "separatists", Russian attack on Grozny was called "Russian effort to recapture the city from the rebels", and there was an emphasis on Russian casualties[1002]. In another news item attributed to Reuters as a main source this time, Chechens were also referred to as "rebels", there was an emphasis on Russian casualties, and Russian action was described as" Russian forces, which are trying to crush resistance after moving into the territory to end a bid for independence, took Grozny in February after fighting that devastated the city"[1003]. The similarities of description between the news items attributed to the Associated Press and those attributed to Reuters might suggest a sort of a "unified "vision of certain international crisis diffused by such transnational media agencies.

The effect of trans-national media sourcing can be more apparent in certain international crises than in others. The dependence on trans-national media

---

999   See Steven Erlanger, "A Famous Victory", The New York Times, op. cit.

1000 Idem.

1001 Idem.

1002 See "Death Toll in Battles in Chechnya Put at 600", The New York Times, 25 December 1995.

1003 See "Russia Pounds Rebel Positions Outside Capital of Chechnya", The New York Times, 21 March 1995.

sourcing seems to reflect the importance of the crisis to the media outlet in question. Both *The New York Times* and *Le Monde* used more trans-national media sources in the case of Chechnya than in the case of Bosnia. Both newspapers seemed to warn their readers against the susceptibility of the objectivity of the trans-national media source, especially when news was taken from Itar-Tass or Interfax. *The New York Times* would directly warn its readers by designating Itar-Tass or Interfax as semi-official or Russian and by reminding that there are degrees of objectivity for news agencies' sources. *Le Monde* seems to designate the sources when it comes to Itar-Tass or Interfax as more "Russian" as well but it tends to use quotation marks to warn its readers when its quoting these two agencies. Yet, quotation marks can sometimes be interpreted as an emphasis rather than a warning and sometimes readers would not pay much attention to the designation of the source, or simply would not understand the difference. The result is that even if the newspaper in question places a net on the information it receives from a "subjective" agency, the majority of the information provided by this "subjective" agency would slip through this net and certain terms would even be later adopted by the journalists themselves as the best designation of the protagonists or the events. Moreover, except for mentioning the name of the leading news agency providing the news, non of the two newspapers actually seems, within their respective articles dedicated to Chechnya, to have suggested that the information supplied by those world leading trans-national agencies is questionable. The news provided by world leading trans-national media agencies is pre-assumed by both journalists and audiences to be unquestionable. Precisely because of this assumption, the world leading trans-national media agencies' sourcing of national media seems to be much more influential on orienting national media than the pre-assumed "subjective" trans-national media sources. In at least two of the news items attributed to Reuters and the Associated Press on Chechnya in *The New York Times*, for instance, the same pattern of describing and framing the protagonists and events was found.

2.4. The Two Crises and the Effect on the French & American Public Opinion

Prior to discussing the various parts comprising this section of the research, an overview of public opinion tendencies in the United States and in France vis-à-vis the two crises in Bosnia and Chechnya seems necessary. It goes without saying, however, that public opinion tendencies in these two countries towards the two conflicts in question are surely not the result of just the coverage of *The New York Times* and *Le Monde*. These tendencies or attitudes are the results of many factors, the most important of, which is, however, attributed to the different forms and outlets of media coverage of these two crises. The analysis of public opinion in the two countries would examine two main notions. First, it is important to know if public opinion was equally measured in the two countries towards the two crises, or whether there was an interest and preference of measuring public opinion tendencies toward one crisis and not the other one. Indeed, this interest in knowing and measuring domestic public opinion reflects not only the interest of the crisis or conflict itself to the media but, indeed, to the government or political establishment as well. Second, it would be useful to see if public opinion towards a crisis, if measured, remained stable and didn't change throughout the duration of the crisis or conflict, and how did this public opinion change.

Public opinion polls on Bosnia in the United States seem to be quite abundant. A simple search request on the Internet would reveal the numerous opinion polls conducted on Bosnia in the United States[1004]. Some opinion polls were conducted by specialised institutions, such as the United States Information Agency, but most were done by media outlets, including media giants such as Mirror/CNN. The same result seems to be true in the case of France, concerning public opinion on the crisis in Bosnia. Here again, the examples of a simple Internet search can, although much less than in the case of the United States, be found[1005]. The first conclusion that can be derived from such interest in measuring domestic opinion

---

1004   See for instance The California Poll 95-04 found at http://socrates.berkeley.edu:7503/sdadata/calpolls/cal9504/Doc/cbook001.html, and Rachal N. Louis,." U.S. Strategy in Bosnia: Are We Really Committed?", 1997, found at http://www.globalsecurity.org/military/library/report/1997/Rachal.htm, and Kurt Holden, "Public Opinion: American Public Would Intervene in Bosnia, But Not Unilaterally", Washington Report on Middle East Affaires, July/August 1993, found at http://www.washington-report.org/Washington-Report_org/www/backissues/0793/9307034.htm, and Alexander E.R. Woodcock & James E. Heath, "Q-Analysis of Inter-Ethnic Relationships can Support Information Operations", found at http://www.dodccrp.org/1999CCRTS/pdf_files/track_3/woodc.pdf

1005   See for instance *"Bosnie : la question qui tue—La France doit-elle entrer en guerre en Bosnie, et si oui, pour quels objectifs. Sinon, pourquoi?*, Réseau Voltaire Pour la Liberté D'Expression, found at http://www.reseauvoltaire.net/imprimer6839.html, and "Europinion n°6—*Octobre 1995*
Résultats des sondages "suivi continu" de l'opinion européenne (juillet à octobre 1995)", Opinion Publique, found at http://europa.eu.int/comm/public_opinion/archives/europinion_cts/eo6/eo6_fr.htm.

towards the crisis in Bosnia reveals, hence, the importance of the crisis in Bosnia itself to both countries' media and governments.

The availability of opinion polls on the conflict in Bosnia in the two countries also reflects the public opinion debate on the issue. It should be noted that a debate on an issue means that this issue is presented as being crucial or problematic, and also as one that affects the greater public" itself. This can be done off course by concentration on this issue. In the case of the United States, public opinion polls on Bosnia not only reflected the public interest in the crisis but also how this opinion changed. An opinion poll, for example, shows that 46,1% of those included in this poll approve President Clinton's handling of the Bosnia issue against 41,1% who don't approve, that 51, 9% believe that the United States has a moral obligation in Bosnia against 41,4%, and that 55% agree that if the U.S. and other NATO allies do not intervene in Bosnia there will be a bigger war against 37,9% who disagree[1006]. However, on the question of weather intervention in Bosnia is worth American lives, 38.5% answered that it is worth American lives against 53,6% who considered that it wasn't worth American lives[1007]. In a very interesting article on public opinion in the United States and its policy towards Bosnia, Kurt Holden explains that one of the major mistakes of former U.S. President Lyndon Johnson was that he realised the importance of opinion polls regarding American foreign policy, especially the U.S. involvement in Vietnam, but that he used the opinion polls as to justify the hardening of his policies and not to explain those policies. Holden, further explains" Wise presidents use polls to determine when their policies need further explaining. Foolish presidents use polls to justify those policies. Only leaders without a political compass use polls to determine where to go"[1008]. One of the key issues in public opinion in the United States on Bosnia, according to the article of Kurt Holden was not if force should be used or not against the Serbs, but whether the U.S. should intervene alone or alongside NATO and European allies or within the auspices of the United Nations. Reference is made to eleven opinion polls conducted on Bosnia. In six of these eleven polls the question was whether the U.S. military should be sent to Bosnia[1009]. To this question, 47% reacted negatively, and 43 % were supportive of such an opinion. In the other five polls, the same question of sending troops was asked but this time as part of a U.N. operation. Interestingly enough, support for

---

1006   Sse The California Poll 95-0, <u>op. cit.</u>
1007   Idem.
1008   See Kurt Holden, "Public Opinion: American Public Would Intervene in Bosnia, But Not Unilaterally", <u>op. cit.</u>
1009   Idem.

this option averaged 60-68%[1010]. Other results of these polls are quite interesting to mention. On whether the U.N. should set a deadline for the Serbs to withdraw from Bosnia or face a "deadly military attack", 76% said that it should[1011]. Moreover, 68% of the respondents seemed to agree with the statement "Since the war in Bosnia is a war of aggression by Serbia, the U.N. principal of collective security obliges U.N. members to help defend the Bosnian government"[1012]. The other section of public opinion polls on Bosnia related to moral responsibility. In this respect, 67% of the poll respondents said that "ethnic cleansing is a form of genocide and that the U.S. should take strong steps to stop it[1013]. On the other hand, 53% agreed with the statement that" the U.S. has no real interests in Bosnia and that the U.S. should focus on programs at home"[1014]. The opinion poll on Bosnia conforms to a large degree with the attitude of *The New York Times* coverage of the issue. Notions such as "War of aggression", "ethnic cleansing", bigger war", "Serbs" as aggressor are very similar to the terms and coverage attitude of *The New York Times* of Bosnia. Yet, it is again important to mention that *The New York Times* is a media outlet amongst many others and that it is surely not the only factor in these opinion polls tendencies towards Bosnia. Its should also be kept in mind that the questions posed in an opinion poll can sometimes be constructed and presented in a way that leads to certain desired results. Nonetheless, the striking similarity between *The New York Times'* coverage and public opinion attitude is quite significant. One explanation of the abundance of public opinion polls on Bosnia is that public opinion was one of the foundations the U.S. policy towards Bosnia was built upon. This idea also provides an explanation of the hesitation of the United States' policy on Bosnia, in addition, to the explanation relating such a hesitation to the state of "foreign policy void", that occurred with the sudden absence of the Soviet Union as the anchor, the containment of which, represented clear guidelines for U.S. foreign policy. The other explanation of hesitation says that the U.S. policy on Bosnia was an "evolutionary" one. Rachal N. Louis explains, "The U.S. pursued a vacillating policy that was "evolutionary" in nature, influenced by world and public opinion, and key tragic events on the ground"[1015]. If the policy can be an evolutionary one, and, indeed, it is since policy is also a synonym of pragmatism, then public opinion can also be evolutionary. If it is not, then it can be made evolutionary. It can be modeled according to the needs of policy makers. Rachal

---

1010   Idem.
1011   Idem.
1012   Idem.
1013   Idem.
1014   Idem.
1015   See Rachal N. Louis,." U.S. Strategy in Bosnia: Are We Really Committed?", op. cit.

N. Louis gives an example of such a change in public opinion, especially through a dramatization of an event, by saying "Although slow, evolution towards military commitment ultimately occurred as situations moved from one set of events to another. It was not until the 5 February 1994 Sarajevo mortar massacre, during which 68 civilians were killed, that U.S. public opinion was swayed to support the commitment of American military forces to limited participation with NATO"[1016]. This is similar to the effect of showing the bodies of dead American soldiers in Somalia on public opinion in the United States. In both cases, public opinion changed drastically due to a dramatization of an event by the media. In both cases the U.S. had no strictly immediate vital interests involved in the two regions. This suggests that in the absence of immediate vital national interests, public opinion shifts occur more rapidly and drastically than if national interests were involved. After all, if a citizen sees one of his countries soldiers dead in a place where this soldier is sent to defend the country's national interests, this soldier would more likely be considered as doing a duty that is vital to the society as a whole, and also to the respondent citizen answering the opinion poll's questions. On the other hand, if the same soldier is dead in a place where the country has no vital national interests, his death would be considered as an unnecessary waste of life. This is probably why the shift in public opinion is faster vis-à-vis involvement in a region where national interests are not threatened.

The case of French public opinion on Bosnia seems to be similar to that of the United States', except that it was more pushing to act in the conflict. Indeed, the controversy over the French role in the Bosnia conflict was not only caused by media coverage but through the engagement of many French intellectuals and philosophers, such as Bernard Henri Lévy, in the debate. Gavin Bowd explains," Rocard's (Michel Rocard, French Prime Minister at the time) shrinking electoral base was further affected by the media event of Bernard Henri-Lévy's 'List for Sarajevo'[1017]. This 'philosopher' who rarely writes books, and who placed himself in an unelectable fourteenth position on his List, proposed the lifting of the arms

---

1016 Idem.

1017 On the 15th of May 1994, Bernard Henri Lévy speaking to the French television station France 2 defends the Bosnian cause and comments on his film *Bosna!*. In the debate he announces the creation of a Sarajevo List backed by intellectuals and which would present its candidature for the European Parliamentary elections in June of the same year. The mediatisation of this call was enormous. The list finally gets 1.56% of votes in the elections. During the same period of media "saturation" over the initiative, a genocide was, ironically, taking place in Rwanda accompanied by media silence.

embargo on Bosnia. He would, as Régis Debray[1018] pointed out, fight in Paris until the last Bosnian. Lévy's 'public debate' on Bosnia was an event reminiscent of the Cultural Revolution he so despised: invited speakers who contradicted the message of the banners in the hall—'Arms for Bosnia!'—were catcalled by Lévy's intellectual cohorts. Nevertheless, the List managed to shake the campaign out of its torpor. It also displayed the excitability of Rocard who, taken by surprise, fell in behind Lévy's proposals for Bosnia, thus deepening his rift with Mitterrand"[1019]. The roar that took place in French public opinion on Bosnia, especially this Sarajevo List Initiative was only a mere reflection of the media's focus on this crisis. *The New York Times* commented on this roar caused by the initiative of Bernard Henri Lévy by saying that "the press has accorded this initiative a coverage which is close to saturation"[1020]. This media concentration on this Bosnian cause initiative took place at the same time when "in a great media silence, genocide took place in Rwanda"[1021].

General speaking, European public opinion was, in its great majority, against not doing anything concerning the situation in Bosnia. An opinion poll conducted between the 1st and 8th of February 1994, indicated that four out of five European citizens (83%) were against letting things" as they go now" in the Bosnia conflict[1022]. In the same poll, the French were most enthusiastic to "fight when

---

1018   Régis Debray (1940-) is a French journalist and government official. He went to Cuba, taught philosophy at the Univ. of Havana, and, after lengthy conversations with Fidel Castro, wrote *Revolution in the Revolution?* (1967), a handbook on guerrilla warfare that offered a philosophical justification for the use of violence. In Apr., 1967, Debray was captured in Bolivia while accompanying a guerrilla force under Ernesto "Che" Guevara. Tried by a military tribunal, he first insisted that he had accompanied the guerrillas only as a journalist, but then abandoned his defence after learning of the capture and death of Guevara. He was sentenced (1967) to 30 years in prison. Such notables as Charles de Gaulle, Pope Paul VI, André Malraux, and Jean-Paul Sartre petitioned for his release, and he was pardoned in Dec., 1970. He sought refuge in Chile, where he wrote *The Chilean Revolution* (1972) after interviews with Salvador Allende. Later he became an adviser on foreign affairs to François Mitterrand and from the mid-1980s to the mid-1990s held a number of official posts in the French president's office.

1019   See Gavin Bowd, "'C'est la lutte initiale': Steps in the Realignment of the French Left", <u>New Left Review</u>, vol. a., N° 206, 1994, p. 83, pp. 71-85

1020   See Serge Halimi, "*Réseaux*", <u>*Le Monde Diplomatique*</u>, February 1995, p.15.

1021   Idem.

1022   *See* 'Europinion n°1—April 1995 *Results of "Continuous Tracking" surveys of the European Union (January to April 1994)*", Eurobarometer surveys, found at <u>http://europa.eu.int/comm/public_opinion/</u>

necessary" as a measure to take against letting things in Bosnia as they are with 90% of the French respondents in favour[1023]. Furthermore, on launching air strikes, the French scored 53% in favour[1024]. However, in an opinion poll that was conducted on behalf of the French Army Information Service on the 8 and 9th of January of the same year (1994), which included 957 respondents, results were a bit different, especially concerning the question of air strikes. This opinion poll showed that 47% of the French people wished for an intensification of the U.N. military action in Bosnia against 34% who believed that only humanitarian aid should be pursued without interfering in the fighting[1025]. The poll also indicated that 12% opted for a rapid withdrawal of former Yugoslavia for next spring[1026]. The French were also at 53% against air strikes that would present risks for ground troops. This concern about the ground troops of the UN is understandable since France had a lot of soldiers within these UN forces. Moreover, 62% considered it useful to have UN forces in former Yugoslavia and 85 % declared that they are very concerned about the events in that region[1027]. This opinion poll indicates two things. It shows a slight change of attitudes between the first and second opinion poll (where the French are 53% with air strikes) and indicates that public opinion is certainly not a static one. It changes with new developments and new events and can sway so radically from one end of the scale to the other in certain cases. Moreover, the importance given to both the UN and the humanitarian aid as opposed to direct intervention, the absence of "Serb demonization", the emphasis on the "European problem" is similar to the positions of the of the French politicians and, more importantly, to the French media coverage attitudes of events. Again, however, the factor of the types of questions asked in an opinion poll and its influence on the results is not to be ignored.

2.4.1. The Orientation of the Public Mind

The orientation of public opinion is an interesting media attribute. The media can do this by focusing the public's attention on certain issues. It can, thus, focus the public's attention to what is important to the media itself. In other words, the media has the incredible ability to shape public opinion to suit its own agenda. Yet, this ability to orient the public attitudes towards issues is not without certain limitations.

1023 Idem.

1024 Idem.

1025 See "*Le conflit en Bosnie-Herzégovine Les Français hostiles à un retrait des "casques bleus", selon un sondage* ", *Le Monde*, 14 January 1994.

1026 Idem.

1027 Idem.

One of the most important examples of this power of the media to orient the public mind is its power, for instance, to influence the public's opinion of political figures. Shanto Iyengar and Donald R. Kinder explain that by focusing on certain issues and not others, television news and other media influence the principals by which politicians and governments are judged[1028]. For the media to be able to do that, it employs priming. Basically, the priming is focusing the attention of the public on selective issues since by nature the public is unable to pay attention to all events. Thus, priming can simply be identified as the means of selecting, for the public, what to pay attention to. Psychological, this tool has an enormous effect on the public's judgement. Amos Tversky and Daniel Kahneman explain, in this respect, that usually citizens of a country when taking a decision about a public issue, rely upon little bits of information that are particularly salient rather than engage in a comprehensive analysis based on their already stored information about the issue[1029]. Hence, priming effect is quite important in orienting the public's opinion towards certain issues.

Indeed, the examples proving the extent of the media priming in controlling the public's attitudes are many. For instance, Lars Willnat and Jian-Hua Zhu in their study of the newspaper coverage and public opinion in Hong Kong mention the case of the last British governor of Hong Kong who's proposals to broaden public participation in the election of the legislative council of the region were greatly influenced by the newspapers' coverage of the issue. Lars Willnat and Jian-Hua Zhu explain that according to the numerous opinion polls conducted, the governor's over all performance was highly primed by the pattern of the coverage in three major Hong Kong newspapers of his proposals[1030]. Another example of the ability of media coverage to orient the public opinion is given by Shanto Iyengar and Adam Simon concerning news coverage of the Gulf War of 1991. According to them, intense television coverage had, as a result, a high salience of the Gulf War on the public agenda, which, in turn, made the war the most important problem facing the United States. Interestingly enough, those amongst the public who were most exposed to television coverage of the crisis, which emphasized military options in its framing

---

1028 See Shanto Iyengar and Donald R. Kinder, News That Matters!, Television and American Opinion, University of Chicago Press, Chicago, 1989, p.63.

1029 See Amos Tversky and Daniel Kahneman, "Availability: A heuristic for judging frequency and probability", Cognitive Psychology, N°5, 1973, pp.207-232.

1030 See Lars Willnat and Jian-Hua Zhu, "Newpaper coverage and public opinion in Hong Kong: A time-series analysis of media priming", Political Communication, N°13, 1996, pp. 231-246.

of the war, were mostly opting for a military rather than a diplomatic solution to the crisis[1031]. As far as internal political orientations are concerned, the priming effect of media coverage has also its proven record. For instance, Hans-Bernd Brosius and Hans Mathias Kepplinger, mention the influence of the media priming on the choice of political parties in Germany in the 1986 elections. They explain that the news coverage of two issues at the time affected the preference for the Christian Democrats as the winning party. These are the energy supply and the situation in East Germany. For its part, the preference for the SPD was affected by the priming of three issues (East-West relations, environmental protection, and pensions). The patterns found, according to Hans-Bernd Brosius and Hans Mathias Kepplinger, indicated that salient issues on the media agenda were strongly linked with shifts in political partisanship in Germany during 1986[1032]. Thus, the media can focus the public's attention on certain aspects of an issue and, by doing so, alter or model the public's attitude towards the issue as a whole.

The media has come to be the primary source of information for the public on almost all aspects of their lives. The public's attention or attached importance to an issue largely depends, thus, on the importance given to this issue by the media coverage. In this context, every outlet of the media can induce the priming of the issues it wants according to its nature. Thus, a newspaper can focus on a story by placing it on the first page or giving it an attractive headline. For its part, television can do that by offering the story as a lead story in its news coverage and by allocating more coverage time for it than its other news items. The effect of the repetition of such a behaviour concerning a certain issue on a daily and continuous basis results in an orientation of the public mind on the importance of the issue covered. Walter Lippmann describes this power of the media to set the agenda to what the public should see. He explains" The news media are a primary source of those pictures in our heads about the larger world of public affairs, a world that for most citizens is "out of reach, out of sight, out of mind"[1033]. Accordingly, what is important to the media becomes important to the public and in doing that it is the media that

---

1031   See Shanto Iyengar and Adam Simon, "News coverage of the Gulf crisis and public opinion: A study of agenda-setting, priming and framing" in *Do the media govern? Politicians, voters, and reporters in America*, eds., Shanto Iyengar and Richard Reeves (Sage, Thousand Oaks, CA, 1997), pp.248-257.

1032   See Hans-Bernd Brosius and Hans Mathias Kepplinger, "Beyond agenda setting: The influence of partianship and television reporting on the electorate's voting intentions", <u>Journalism Quarterly</u>, N°69, 1992, pp.893-901.

1033   See Walter Lippmann, <u>op. cit</u>, p.29.

sets the agenda of the public opinion. This is seen in the case study of the coverage of the crisis of Bosnia compared to that of Chechnya where excessive priming was noted in Bosnia's case, making it a highly important issue on the agenda of the public.

This power of the media to orient the public opinion cannot be done by simply focusing the public's attention to certain topics. In order to orient, the media has also to influence the perspectives and points of view of the public toward the issue. This can be done by considering the items on public opinion agenda as objects. These objects are the public issues and can be other issues as well, such as the private life of a political candidate for instance. Each object has numerous characteristics or attributes that describe it. The media can choose to give attention to some of these attributes of this object and ignore others. The attitude of the pubic opinion has been proven to follow the same pattern of media coverage presentation and focus on these attributes. For example, Maxwell McCombs et al. have found that the voters descriptions of the three major party leaders in Navarro (Spain) in the 1996 general elections corresponded highly to the media's presentation of the three candidates[1034]. Lee Becker and Maxwell McCombs reached similar results concerning the United States' national elections of 1976. The study indicates that the public presented similar attributes to the eleven candidates of the Democratic Party in the city of New York that corresponded to the sketches made of these candidates by Newsweek[1035]. Similar findings were found by Pu-tsung King who found that the voters' descriptions of the three candidates for the post of mayor of Taipei corresponded to the images of these men found in the newspapers and in television[1036]. Therefore, media coverage can shape the public's view of issues simply by focusing on certain aspects and ignoring others.

Nevertheless, this ability of the media to orient the public opinion on issues is not without limitations. Indeed, the public, especially in democratic societies, can always relay on their ability to determine and analyse the relevance of objects and attributes and to form their own opinions that can go in a totally opposite direction than that of the media's public opinion agenda. The media is more

---

1034 See Maxwell McCombs et al., "Setting the agenda of attributes in the 1996 Spanish general election", Journal of Communication, vol.50, N° 2, 2000, pp. 77-92.

1035 See Lee Becker and Maxwell McCombs,"The role of the press in determining voter reactions to presidential primaries", Human Communication Research, N°4, 1978, pp.301-307.

1036 See Pu-tsung King, "The press, candidate images, and voter perceptions" in Communication and Democracy, eds. Maxwell McCombs, Donald Shaw and David Weaver, Lawrence Erlbaum Associates, Mahwah, NJ:, 1997, pp.29-40.

capable to orient public opinion only if the public themselves consider the news items or stories presented as relevant. There is, however, a basic physiological characteristic that helps the media's orientation effort. Indeed, there is a basic human need for orientation, especially if he or she finds himself in a new environment or a new situation.

The degree of this need for orientation is not the same for everyone. Some individuals need more orientation than others. This need to be oriented can be said to be dependent on two elements. These are relevance and uncertainty. For its part, relevance can be simply regarded as the initial defining condition that determines the level of need for orientation for each individual. In other words, if an individual feels that a topic is not relevant to him or her then the degree of need for orientation would be low. Uncertainty, for its part, basically means that if the individual feels that he or she has sufficient knowledge and understanding of a certain issue, then his need for orientation on that issue would be low. Thus, this individual wouldn't be paying too much attention to the media's focus on the issue.

2.4.2. Making and Unmaking the Existence of a Crisis

With its coverage, the media has the ability of making and de-making the existence of an international crisis. This astonishing ability that the media has can be said to be a natural consequence of the priorities and determinants of its agenda-setting.

Yet, the question is how does this media create or un-create a crisis?. Naturally, two arguments can be advanced to negate the concept that the media actually has the power to create and un-create an international crisis. The first one is that the media can hardly be able alone to create an international crisis. The second is that a crisis is by definition an unexpected radical change in the natural order of events. The argument against those two conditions is that the media, even if unable to create or control the existence of such an unexpected event, can set its agenda in a manner that would focus the attention on the existence of one international crisis, while at the same time ignoring others as if they do not exist. This is done simply because, most usually, the media's own agenda runs in the same line as that of other agendas. In the preface to their interesting work "manufacturing consent", Edward S. Herman and Noam Chomsky explain this concordance of agendas to focus on an event and ignore others. They state" There are important actors who do take positive initiatives to define and shape the news and to keep the media in line. It is a "guided market system" that we describe here, with the guidance provided by the government, the leaders of the corporate community, the top media owners and executives, the assorted individuals and groups who are assigned or allowed to take constructive initiatives. These initiatives are suffi-ciently small in number to be able to act jointly on occasion, to do sellers in markets with few rivals. In most cases, however, media leaders do similar things because they see the world through the same lenses, are subject to simi-lar constraints and incentives, and thus feature stories or maintain silence together in tacit collective action and leader-follower behaviour"[1037]. Thus, it can be said that this focus on one crisis as compared to others is not without a valid reason for the media. Indeed, as Edward S. Herman and Noam Chomsky put it, there are "worthy" and "worthy" news and victims to the media[1038]. Basically, the idea is that the media has its own criteria for judging the rele-vance of an event (economical, political, religious, cultural...etc) and that the focus on one event and the ignoring of another is a consequence of such rele-vance. Edward S. Herman and Noam Chomsky give the example of the cover-age of the murder of Popielusko, a Polish priest, compared to that of other religious people murdered in Latin America (Table 33 below). The example indicates that the United States' media coverage of the Polish priest's murder was more than that of all the other victims despite the fact that amongst those other victims there were American nationals. The reason given is that the Polish priest was a Solidarity Movement activist and that his murder would support the case of the United States against communism at the time of the Cold War and, further, justify the arms race.

1037   See Edward S. Herman and Noam Chomsky, op. cit, p.Ix.
1038   Ibid, see the chapter of the book entitled "Worthy and Unworthy Victims", pp.37-86

Table 33: Mass Media Coverage of Worthy and Unworthy Victims Case of a Murdered Polish Priest Versus One Hundred Murdered Religious in Latin America.

Victims	New York Times								Times & Newsweek				CBS News			
	Articles*		Columns Inches		Front Page Articles		Editorials		Articles*		Columns		N° of News Programs*		N° of evening news programs	
	N°	% of row 1	N°	% of row 1	N°	% of row 1	N°	% of row 1	N°	% of row 1	N°	% of row 1	N°	% of row 1	N°	% of row 1
1. Jersy, Popielusko, Murdered on Oct. 10, 1984.	78	(100)	1183.0	(100)	10	(100)	3	(100)	16	(100)	313.0	(100)	46	(100)	23	(100)
2. 72 religious victims in Latin America 1964-78 ▶	8	(10.3)	117.5	(9.9)	1	(10)	---	---	---	---	16	(5.1)	--- •	---	--	---
3. 23 religious murdered in Guatemala Jan. 1980-Feb.1989.	7	(9.0)	66.5	(5.6)	---	---	---	---	2	(12.5)	34.0	(10.9)	2	(4.3)	2	(8.7)
4. Oscar Romero, murdered Mar.18, 1980.	16	(20.5)	219.0	(18.5)	4	(40)	---	---	3	(18.8)	86.5	(27.6)	13	(28.3)	4	(17.4)
5. 4 U.S. religious women murdered in El Salvador, Dec. 2, 1980	26	(33.3)	201.5	(17.0)	3	(30)	---	---	5	(31.2)	111.0	(35.5)	22	(26.3)	10	(43.5)
6.Total of lines 2-5	57	(73.1)	604.5	(51.1)	8	(80)	---	---	10	(62.5)	247.5	(79.1)	37	(80.4)	16	(69.6)

* The media coverage is for an 18-month period from the time of the first report of the victim's disappearance or murder.
▶ Listed in Penny Lernoux, Cry of the People, Doubleday, New York, 1980,pp. 464-465.
• The CBS News Index begins in 1975.

Source: Edward S. Herman and Noam Chomsky, <u>Manufacturing Consent: The Political Economy of Mass Media</u>, Pantheon Books, New York, 2002, pp.40-41.

The contradictions of the media labelling of what is a crisis are quite interesting. Generally speaking, if the media is to emphasise a crisis, it has to support the hypothesis of its relevance to the concerned public. If the public is convinced that the crisis is relevant to its security, economical, or cultural life then the concern for the events involved in the crisis would be evident. If, on the other hand, the public is convinced that the events are not relevant to it, then the impact of the events of the crisis wouldn't be of much interest to be followed. Considering the fact that the task of informing the public is carried out by the media, the media's ability to create relevance or irrelevance of issues to the public is quite impressive. Indeed, this ability of the media to emphasise relevance or irrelevance of an international crisis has often been indicated by a number of contradictions. A good example of these would be a comparison between the media coverage of the shooting down by the Soviet Union in September 1983 of the Korean KAL007 plane compared to the Israeli shooting down of a Libyan plane in February 1973. The U.S. media, for instance, emphasized the crisis of the shooting down of the

Korean airliner at the time that served former President Regan's arms race plans. Indeed, the crisis was quite useful to focus upon by the U.S. media. In this respect, Bernard Gwertzman, states that "worldwide criticism of the Soviet handling of the crisis has strengthened the United States' position in its relations with Moscow"[1039]. The crisis of the shooting down of the Libyan airliner, however, didn't cause much condemnation or criticism by the media. This lack of interest is best expressed by *The New York Times* in its editorial at the time. It states, "No useful purpose is served by an acrimonious debate over the assignment of blame for the downing of a Libyan airliner in the Sinai Peninsula last week"[1040]. It can be logically assumed that the Soviets would not intentionally shoot a civilian plane if they knew it was one. Yet, this fact was totally obscured by the media coverage, which in turn, supports the arguments of the previous section of this research, mainly that some traits of an event can be chosen to be under the focus of the media while others are ignored to better manipulate public opinion. Noam Chomsky also supports this view, of the media focusing on what it sees as being useful to focus upon. He explains that the media presented picture of Iraq as the source of evil, in the Gulf War of 1991, overlooked the fact that there is democratic opposition in that country, composed of quite a number of intellectuals, who have been asking for the United States' support for there cause for a long time[1041]. Thus, creating relevance or finding a "useful purpose" for coverage is an important factor in the media's ability to focus the public's attention on a crisis.

Yet, building up the case for the relevance of the events taking place to the public alone is usually not enough to emphasize the crisis. Indeed, it is always useful to emphasize the negative human consequences of events for the great majority of the public in order to draw upon the public's emotional and humanitarian concerns. During, the Gulf Crisis (1990-1991), for instance, the majority of the American public were convinced that it was up to the United States to prevent human rights violations and prevent atrocities in the region and that as such, the United States was acting simply out of moral convictions[1042]. This is a clear contradiction in the sense that there were more atrocities committed elsewhere in the world at the same time but with no response from the neither the international community nor the United States. It can also be argued that the United State's itself has often preached and disregarded international law for its own interests. Indeed, the fact that the public of such a country is convinced that it is

---

1039　See Bernard Gwertzman, New York Times, August 31, 1984.

1040　See The New York Times editorial, March 1, 1973.

1041　See Noam Chomsky, Media Control: The Spectacular Achievements of Propaganda, Seven Stories Press, New York, 2002, pp. 53-55.

1042　Idem, p.53.

doing the right thing out of pure moral responsibility and justice reflects the power of the media coverage to create relevance based on basic human emotional and humanitarian instincts.

Moreover, repetition of the use of negative traits in the description of events helps to focus the public's attention on one crisis while ignoring others. By doing that, all interested parties (the media, the economic sector, the politicians…etc.) can be said to have achieved their goal from focusing on one crisis in which there are involved. In this respect, Edward S. Herman and Noam Chomsky give the example (See Table 34) of the news coverage use of the word "genocide" in four different conflicts or crisis (The Serbs and Kosovo 1998-1999, Indonesia and East Timor 1990-1999, Iraq and the Kurds 1990-1999, Turkey and the Kurds 1990-1999, and the Sanctions on Iraq 1990-1999).

Table 34: Mainstream Media: Usage of "Genocide" for Kosovo, East Timor, Turkey and Iraq

Countries/ Dates	N° of times word applied to Serbs, Turks, ..etc.	N° of eds/op-eds doing the same	News Articles	Front Page
Serbs/Kosovo 1998-1999	220	59	118	41
Indonesia/East Timor1990-1999	33	7	17	4
Turkey/Kurds 1990-1999	14	2	8	1
Iraq/Kurds 1990-1999	132	51	66	24
Iraq Sanctions 1990-1999	18	1	10	1
?Mainstream media used in this tabulation, based on a Nexus database search, were the *Los Angeles Times, The New York Times, Washington Post, Newsweek* and *Time*.				

Source: Edward S. Herman and Noam Chomsky, <u>op. cit</u>, p.XXi

As the table above clearly shows, the two countries against whom the word genocide was used the most were Serbia and Iraq. While the same event (genocide) was taking place even with more vigour in other places, the political, economical and media interests deemed that only Iraq and Serbia should be most accused of genocide. As far as Serbia is concerned, the United States conducted operations with NATO against the country, which, thus, makes it an enemy state. The same argument can be applied to Iraq. On the other hand, both Turkey and Indonesia are considered friendly states and both receive both military and economic aid from the United States and are, moreover, a good market for its products. It can be said, that the media's behaviour in the coverage of these four crises constitutes simply the expression of the voice of the United States' government regarding these conflicts. Edward S. Herman and Noam Chomsky's above view of the U.S. media behaviour, however, would reduce the media to a simple tool of the government's propaganda machine. But, the media is more than simply a tool of the government's propaganda machine and a simple servant of its purposes, particularly in democratic political systems.

The ability to create or dismiss a crisis is, thus, an important characteristic that the media has. The media can emphasize a crisis by paying more attention to it and by ignoring others. By doing that, the media focuses the attention of the public on the crisis and in doing that creates relevance to the public. Relevance is created either by insisting on the risks the public has in the crisis or by emphasizing certain negative aspects of the events or the parties to the events in order to draw on the public's emotional and humanitarian reaction.

2.4.3. Public Opinion's Effect on Domestic Politics

Public opinion is an important determinant in the decision making process in almost all political systems whether democratic or authoritarian, although its effects are much more apparent and effective in democratic political systems. Even the most authoritarian of governing systems realize the importance of observing public opinion at least, if not wanting to respond to its exigencies. The ability of public opinion in sanctioning the government in democratic societies has recently been demonstrated in Spain through the sanction vote against the Conservative actual government of the country, in the aftermath of the terrorist attacks of the 11th of March 2004 in Madrid. It is, therefore, essential to examine the role that this domestic public opinion can play in determining, shaping or altering domestic politics in general and in doing that vis-à-vis international conflicts or crises, in particular. In this discussion of the relationship between public opinion and domestic policy, it is important to distinguish between the different kinds of public opinion, the different measuring frameworks involved, and the interaction between public opinion and domestic politics.

It should be said that researchers have come to distinguish between at least three types of public opinion. These are mass opinion, majority opinion, and effective public opinion. As far as mass public opinion is concerned, James B. Lemert states that it can be thought of "as the views of people about some psychological object they have in common. Their views toward the object may or may not be the same, but presumably they all know enough about the object to have an opinion about it. The object may be a consumer product, a composer's music—or a million other things that have nothing to do with a public affairs issue object. An issue object is the subject of a public controversy"[1043]. In order to understand fully this type of public opinion, it is important to identify the key

---

1043 See James B. Lemert, "Effective Public Opinion", in J. David Kennamer's, Public Opinion, the Press and Public Policy, Praeger Publishers, Westport, CT., 1992, pp. 43-44.

word involved which is that of a "mass". According to H. Blumer, a mass can be identified as being a group of people who by coincidence are doing or thinking the same thing about the same subject and at more or less the same time[1044]. Thus, the word mass, in this respect, regroups a number of characteristics. The first one of these characteristics is that it happens by coincidence. In other words, that people happen to be doing the same thing at almost the same time. For instance, a group of people might be reading one newspaper, while others might be watching a reportage on television at roughly the same time. This means that each group didn't have coordination between its members to read the newspaper or watch the television reportage. The other characteristic pertinent to members of a mass is that its members are thinking about something essentially without the knowledge that others might be thinking about the same thing at the same time. The final trait about members of a mass is that its members are usually, as James B. Lemert remarks "disengaged and separated from the political system"[1045]. Thus, the concern of a mass is primarily more attentive to non-political issues and debates. For instance, those members of a society that are not interested in voting for candidates in an election campaign can be said to pertain to the segment of mass public opinion. Thus, those people who don't turnout in elections to vote on a political issue or to make their political choice are members of mass public opinion. Indeed, members of such a segment are more interested in consumer oriented non-political objects of daily life. Abstention from voting is a common and well-known behaviour of this mass public opinion. James B. Lemert explains, in this respect, that this is probably the result of the overall consumer-oriented system. He states, "The marketing system makes it far easier for people to participate as consumers than the political system does for them to participate as citizens.... The general mass media also make it easier for citizens to act as consumers than the news media do for citizens to act as political participants"[1046]. It can be said that the usefulness of such type of public opinion for decision makers is that it can serve as a measurement of public interest vis-à-vis certain issues. Indeed, if the voting turnout on the issue at hand is low, then the mass's interest for the issue can be said to be weak. On the other hand, if the turnout of the voting on the public issue is high, then the interest of this issue to the public can be said to be strong. Accordingly, politicians can determine the degree of importance they would attach to the issue concerned and even modify

---

1044   See H. Blumer, "The mass, the public, and public opinion". In A. M. Lee (Ed.), <u>New outline of the principles of sociology</u>, Barnes and Noble, New York, 1946, pp. 185-193,

1045   See James B. Lemert, <u>op. cit</u>, p.44.

1046   Ibid, p.45.

their position concerning this issue if they perceive a need to do so. Its is indeed important for politicians to realize the importance of not antagonizing this mass public opinion. If this mass public opinion is disinterested in politics and voting and, hence, often sees no benefit or point in voting, it does not mean that this mass public opinion will not respond if provoked, especially if governmental policies endanger its interests. The example of the massive sanction vote during the French regional elections of April 2004 against the government of Prime Minister Jean-Pierre Rafarain and his Right party, is a clear illustration of the ability mass public opinion to respond when provoked.

The other type of public opinion is that which is known as the majority opinion. Roughly speaking, majority public opinion can be said to be that of the majority of those participating in voting about the choice of a certain candidate in elections or a solution to a public problem. Thus, the choice of the majority in a given interrogation might be labelled as the majority public opinion. Yet, such choice is also not an entirely adequate expression of public opinion. The reason is that it ignores the opinion of those who did not take part in the voting or the inquiry, which, if included, might have changed the result. In general, politicians can be said to be aware of such a deficiency in majority public opinion. Therefore, for a better determination of the public opinion on policy issues, what is important to decision makers in democratic societies in particular is that which is known as effective public opinion.

Effective public opinion is that which reaches the decision makers and politicians and which assists in determining the public opinions to certain matters and also that which helps those decision makers and politicians to reach to this public opinion[1047]. Effective public opinion can be perceived or can reach policy decision makers by one of two frameworks or outlets. These are the elections framework and the influence framework.

In the elections framework, the information that reaches the candidates can be said to belong to one of three categories. The first one is that of the voting outcome. Thus, candidates can determine whether they have a large percentage or not of votes and can, consequently, work on improving their popularity if they had a sufficient but a weak percentage for example. It can also help them to determine the popularity of a measure or a policy decision they made, if the voting is not to elect them as candidates for a political position. The second notion politicians can get out of this voting framework is the percentage of the turnout. Logically, the higher the turnout the higher the interest is for the issue and vice versa. They can, thus, determine the importance of the issue for the public. Finally, politicians can

---

1047 See James B. Lemert, op. cit, pp.41-42.

use what is known as exit poll interviews to predict the outcome of the voting. Exit poll interviews are those done with voters exiting a polling post.

Unlike the elections framework, which has the particularity of occurring only on polling or voting days, the influence framework can be said to have the advantage of being rather a continuous one. Furthermore, input reaching policy makers and politicians through the influence framework can reach them in a variety of forms. It can also change over the concerned period of time. One means of evaluating public opinion vis-à-vis an elected candidate and that fall within the influence frameworks is, for instance, to analyse the incoming mail addressed to this political figure within his or her constituency. In this sense, it can be said that even the number of letters received can be quite expressive of public opinion. A high number of received letters indicates high expectations and confidence of the electors or the citizens and vice versa. Furthermore, the subjects of the letters received can be analysed and grouped and compared to establish a set of public opinion's priorities and a sense of public opinions wishes regarding these issues.

What is important here is to discuss the effect that journalist practice can have on public opinion and whether it has the ability to affect this public opinion towards certain issues. In this respect, it can be said that journalists can affect public opinion by doing or failing to do certain things. They can withhold information that can mobilize public opinion, they can ignore the issues, they can label the issue or problem as being that of others in a far away place, and to imply that the problem at hand originated from the choice of the majority.

Indeed, the media can withhold information that, otherwise, could change the public opinion's tendencies towards a given issue. This is what James B. Lemert calls Mobilizing Information. He explains that this refers to any kind of information, which would make the public act[1048]. This mobilizing information can be divided into three categories. First of all there is the Locational Mobilizing Information. This type regroups such items as dates, times and places mentioned in the media outlets' coverage. The rule to identify a locational information is that it should at least include two elements, namely time and place. A good example of such type of information is a table in a newspaper including times and places of cultural events or television programs. Another sub-category of mobilizing information is what is known as the Identificational Mobilizing Information. Basically Identificational Mobilizing Information is all information that is descriptive and that allows the recognition and identification of objects or persons. An example of identificational information would be, for instance, a description given in the media of a consumer product (such as its commercial name, components...etc.) or

---

1048 See chapter 6 in James B. Lemert, <u>Does mass communication change public opinion after all? A new approach to effects analysis</u>, Nelson-Hall, Chicago, 1981.

the description of a criminal pursued by the police. The third sub-category of mobilizing information in media is what is known as the Tactical Mobilizing Information. For its part, this type of information includes either explicit or implicit models of behaviour. In other words, it is that which describes a mode of action of an event either implicitly or explicitly. Implicitly, for instance, the media can give a description of how a bank robbery took place successfully. Explicitly, the media can, for example, give advices on how to testify before the police in a case. This type of information (Tactical Mobilizing Information) is usually left out of news about politics and controversial political decisions and provided in other less serious or "safe" kind of news[1049]. Yet, this is quite logical considering the journalist's quest to be objective in their work. Providing information, for instance, about the home address of a politician prior to a decision on a controversial political issue would probably label journalists as siding with one part over the other. Indeed, such information (home address for instance) would result in a scenario according to which the politician might be bombarded with protesters or letters to make him or her change his political decision, or even worst it can put his or her life in danger in certain extreme controversial cases. The withholding of such information in political related journalism can also be explained by the fact that journalists do not usually wish to antagonize the politicians, who can sometimes be a valuable source for their political news stories and political decisions. Other journalists might withhold such information simply because they might consider it as unnecessary details and that it would occupy unnecessary space in the newspaper, or unnecessary time as far as broadcasted programs are concerned. In an interesting study, the public was shown to prefer to be provided by mobilizing information concerning political, as well as concerning consumer news stories. According to this study, interviewers presented the examined sample with two versions of the same political and consumer story. One half of the sample was presented with a version of the version in the newspaper that included mobilizing information while the other half was provided with a version of the story that didn't have mobilizing information in it. The study showed that, even with the fact that the concept of mobilizing news was not explained to the sample of readers examined, the majority of the sample noticed the difference between the two versions of the stories presented. Furthermore, a majority of the sample stated that they wanted their newspaper to produce the version with the mobilizing news[1050]. Thus, the public actually needs

---

1049 See J. B. Lemert, Mitzman B. N., Seither M. A., Cook R. H., & O'Neil R. M., "Journalists and mobilizing information", <u>Journalism Quarterly,</u> N° 54, 1977, pp. 721-726.

1050 See James B. Lemert, <u>Criticizing the Media: Empirical approaches,</u> CA: Sage, Newbury Park, 1989, pp. 111-114

to be provided with this withheld mobilizing information. Perhaps, if provided with such information, the outcome of public opinion towards certain issues might change or be altered.

The other manner in which the media can affect the outcome of public opinion is simply by ignoring some issues and stories. It is, logically, impossible to form an opinion about something if this something is not known. Indeed, many researchers indicate that there are quite a number of stories that are usually left out of coverage by the media, simply to avoid controversy over the issue. For instance, Warren Breed explains that the most improbable news story that might be excluded from coverage in a local newspaper is that about a politico-economic issue that would have, otherwise, been highly controversial if the newspaper's readers were to know about it[1051]. To him, the overall result of the study was that politico-economic matters were areas where the private industries were given special political advantages at the expense of the public. Other researchers such as M. Hirsh found out that the news media in Chicago, for instance, ignored a major Federal Trade Commission administrative law trial of Sears for consumer fraud. The reason was that Chicago is considered as the world headquarters for the company, which employed nearly 30,000 people there[1052]. Thus, one mean of affecting public opinion for the media is simply to overlook the coverage of the issue. In the example provided by M. Hirsh above, this was apparently done for economic reasons, but it can also be done for other reasons as well.

Another way through which the media can affect public opinion is by giving the impression that the issue is happening in a far away place or that it is other people's problem. This tendency is often known amongst journalistic circles as "Afghanistanism"[1053]. In short, what is meant by afghanistanism is that journalists would sometimes write about an issue or a story as if it happened in a place far away while at the same time ignoring a similar story that happened in their area or community. The utility of displacing the problems and issues to other places and ignoring their existence in one's own community or country is that the problems wouldn't raise much concern as if they were said to be taking place within the media's community or the country. As such, public opinion concerning these problems wouldn't be the same as if such issues or problems were taking

---

1051   See Warren Breed, "Mass Communication and Sociocultural Integration", <u>Social Forces</u>, N° 37, 1958, pp.109-116.

1052   See M. Hirsh, "The sins of Sears are not news in Chicago", <u>Columbia Journalism Review</u>, N° 5, 1976, pp. 29-30.

1053   See James B. Lemert, "Effective Public Opinion", in J. David Kennamer's, <u>Public Opinion, the Press and Public Policy, op. cit</u>, p. 52.

place inside the country itself. A good example of such behaviour is one relating to environmental problems, for instance.

With all this in perspective, the question becomes how would the media serve as a connection between public opinion and the policy decision makers, especially in democratic systems of government. Indeed, some writers claim that this has become one of the most important dilemmas facing policy makers and the media in democratic societies. David Pritchard, for example states, "As societies become more and more complex, the distance between citizens and government grows. This phenomenon poses difficult problems in political systems with representative forms of government. In a system in which policymakers are increasingly distant from citizens"[1054]. Indeed, an effective link between citizens and their elected representatives or the policy makers in their country is one of the pillars of a democratic system. For its part, the government's actions or inactions are what can be labelled as the public policy. Thomas. R. Dye, for instance, defines public policy as simply "what governments choose or not choose to do"[1055]. Ideally, in a democratic system public opinion would act as sort of an observer and a regulator of the government's actions or inactions. The media in such an ideal situation would be the connection between this regulator (public opinion) and policy makers. This is, however, the ideal but not the real actual situation. Indeed, the reason behind such a weak role of the media as a link between public opinion and policy makers is the fact that there are different agendas involved in the equation. A stronger link is, however, found between policy makers' agendas and the media's agendas. In this respect, David Pritchard states, "it is difficult to document the direct link between citizens and policymakers envisioned by classical democratic theory. Instead, there is considerable evidence of a direct link between the agendas of the news media and the behaviour of policymakers"[1056]. Others, such as Robert Entman, argue that news medias agendas are used by the policy makers as a surrogate for the agendas of the public[1057]. Thus, the conflict of agendas between the public, the media, and the policy makers can be considered to be the cause of this weakness of the linkage, which the media should ideally be attentive, to between the public and the policy makers in democratic political systems in particular.

1054   See David Pritchard, "The News Media and Public Policy Agendas", in J. David Kennamer's, Public Opinion, the Press and Public Policy, op. cit, p. 103.

1055   See Thomas R. Dye, Understanding public policy (6th ed.), Prentice-Hall, Englewood Cliffs, NJ: 1984,p.2.

1056   See David Pritchard, op. cit, p.105.

1057   See Robert Entman, Democracy without citizens: Media and the decay of American politics, op. cit.

However, blaming the media solely for such a linkage weakness is not totally fair. In fact, a large potion of the blame goes also to the policy agendas of the policymakers. Policy agendas are, according to David Pritchard, simply "lists of issues to which policymakers pay attention"[1058]. In this hierarchy, some issues get more attention than others. According to this logic, it can be assumed that the issues that don't figure in the first place in such agendas would hardly get the attention of policymakers. It can also be said that here is where the lobbying is more effective. Different interests would work to forward certain in the hierarchy of the issues on the policy agenda at the expense of others and placing, therefore, the issues of interest to these lobbying parties on the policy agenda. Some researchers, such as Stephen Hilgartner and Charles L. Bosk argue, however, that it is much more harder to place an issue on the policy agenda in the first place than to improve an issue's place on that agenda[1059]. The difficulty here to place an issue on the policy agenda of policymakers may also be caused by the fact that there are generally two types of policy agendas. The first one is called the symbolic agenda. For Murray Edelman, symbolic policy agendas are those agendas, which contain issues that need apparent yet not substantive action from policymakers[1060]. The second type of policy agendas is that which is called the action agenda. According to David Pritchard, action agendas "are those lists of issues that require substantive action that includes the allocation or reallocation of government resources to address a perceived problem"[1061]. Thus, the issues that can be on a symbolic policy agenda can hardly be the same as those on an action one and vice versa. Indeed, this is quite common in political action of any government who might opt to conduct symbolic activity to give the impression that it is actively addressing a problem to appease or elude public opinion. This, according to F. Cook et al., for instance, is a common practice of policymakers[1062]. Hence, for an issue to be acted upon, it should be placed first on the action and not on the symbolic policy agenda of policymakers. Here all factors of the equation interact and the result of their interaction can be an action or a non-action on the part of policymakers. Indeed, each actor has his own interests, the media, the public, and the policymakers. If the public needs to see an action on a problem

---

1058   See David Pritchard, op. cit, p.103.

1059   See Stephen Hilgartner and Charles L. Bosk, "The rise and fall of social problems: A public arenas model", American Journal of Sociology, N° 94, 1988, pp. 53-78.

1060   See Murray Edelman, The symbolic uses of politics, University of Illinois Press, Urbana, 1964.

1061   See David Pritchard, Op. Cit, p.106.

1062   See F. Cook et al., "Media and agenda setting: Effects on the public, interest group leaders, policy makers, and policy", Public Opinion Quarterly, N°47,1983, pp.16-35.

concerning it, then it can pressure the policymakers to put this problem on their action policy agenda. Yet, the public cannot pressure the policymakers to do that if it wasn't informed properly of the problem by the media. According to this logic, it can be argued that the agendas of the media and the policymakers have much more of probability of being in harmony with one another than for the public agenda to be in harmony with any of these two. Another reason for this is that the public's agenda is a chaotic one and is subject to the information the public receives. For example, if the public were informed of a threatening environmental problem, it would put this problem on the top of its agenda and pressure the policymakers to act. If the public is not informed, the problem would not figure in the first place on the public agenda and, thus, there would be no pressure on the policymakers to act.

2.4.4. Domestic Public Opinion's Effect on the State's World Image

An important concept has come to being in the post-Cold War era. This new concept is that of the image of a country in what has come to be known as the World Opinion. This new concept is a consequence of a number of the post-Cold War characteristics, such as the emergence of a New World Order, the re-rise of nationalism, and the change in the determinants of development.

Indeed, numerous voices, especially the international media, declared the emergence of a New World Order after the events of 1989-1991[1063]. What was called new order, nevertheless, was also referred to as "new world disorder", especially after the crisis and conflicts in the Balkans[1064]. Some believe that the world order during the Cold War was more of a social construction were ideologies compete with each other. This is the position of M.J. Shapiro who states that the world order during the Cold War was sort of a "system of intelligibility for the separation of the world into kinds of space"[1065]. However, despite the different points of view on the new situation, the emerging system, according to Frank

---

1063　See Unger David C., "Ferment in the Think Tanks: Learning to Live with No Global Threat", The New York Times, January 1991.

1064　See Ron Hinckley, "World Public Opinion and the Persian Gulf Crisis", Proceedings of the American Association for Public Opinion Research, Phoenix, May 1991,pp. 16-19.

1065　See M. J. Shapiro,"Textualizing Global Politics" In International/Intertextual Relations: Postmodern Readings of World Politics, eds. J. Der Derian and M. J. Shapiro. D.C. Heath, Lexington, MA:, 1989, p.13.

Louis Rusciano and John Crothers Pollock exhibits certain "primary features". They state, "First of all such features assume a *consensus*, real or perceived which exists regarding acceptable behaviour in international affairs. Second, they assume leaders may invoke the sanction of *international isolation,* in various ways, to punish nations that violate this consensus. Both features relate directly to the concept of "world opinion." Consensus implies that nations generally share opinions about proper behaviour in the international sphere, while the threat of isolation implies that these nations are willing to act upon this consensus to punish errant countries or leaders"[1066]. Thus, the collapse of the Cold-War ideological competition system gave way for a new concept, even if perceived, of the importance of not violating the new acceptable behaviour of nations and of the importance of observing the "world opinion".

The second characteristic of the post Cold-War era is the re-emergence of nationalism. The primary explanation to this re-emergence of nationalisms is that such strong nationalist sentiments already existed under the Soviet controlled regions but that because the whole system was centralized, such sentiments were suppressed by the centre. Once this centre disappeared, the nationalist feelings were free to emerge. However, it should be said that most of the existing nationalistic movements existed before the Soviet control. Moreover, some researchers indicate that the Soviet regime itself used to encourage nationalistic movements to serve its purposes sometimes[1067]. It can also be argued that nationalism always and will always play an essential role in the construction of states and no matter under the ideology of which authority these states might be. Furthermore, the reconstruction of national and social identity was done with a new set of denominators in the post-Cold War era.

It can be said that during the ideological division of the Cold War, definitions relying on economic development for establishing the development hierarchy amongst nations provided an alternative definition, according to Frank Louis Rusciano and Bosah Ebo, of "national development" and "national identity[1068]." The division of nations into first, second and third worlds depended largely on the economic activity and richness of the nation concerned. Eugene Rostow

---

1066 See Frank Louis Rusciano and John Crothers Pollock, "World Opinion During Times of Crisis" In <u>World Opinion and the Emerging International Order </u>by Bosah Ebo et al., Praeger Publishers, Westport, CT., 1998, p.29.

1067 See Liah Greenfield, "Nationalism and Class Struggle: Two Forces or One"?, <u>Survey</u>, N° 29, 1985, pp.153-174.

1068 Frank Louis Rusciano and Bosah Ebo, "National Consciousness, International Image, and the Construction of Identity" in <u>World Opinion and the Emerging International Order </u>by Bosah Ebo et al., Praeger Publishers, Westport, CT., 1998, p.60.

explains, for instance, that the notion of development for the "First World" nations was established according to economic measures such as the GNP (Gross National Product)[1069].

According to this purely economical definition, the Third World occupied the last position on the world hierarchy of development. Nevertheless, this Third World was also the subject of competition between the Liberal and the Communist interpretations of development. This competition led to another result, which is the search for national identity. In this respect, Yael Tamir explains, "Aspiring to national self-determination is…bound up with the desire to see communal space not only as an arena for cooperation for the purpose of securing one's interests, but as a place for expressing one's identity"[1070]. For their part, Frank Louis Rusciano and Bosah Ebo, state "national self-determination, or the claiming of a common culture leading to national identity, presents citizens with considerations of economic viability"[1071]. However, Liah Greenfeld explains, "National identity is, fundamentally, a matter of dignity. It gives people reasons to be proud"[1072]. Thus, it can be said that the collapse of the Cold War competitive ideologies' system permitted the re-emergence of nationalism, and that this re-emergence of nationalism is, in its turn, resulted in a definition of national identity and national pride that is not purely based on economic measurements.

Indeed, the new elements constructing national identity appeared to be in conflict since the end of the Cold War. Some claim that this status of conflict between nations for the definition of their national identity can be even labelled as "resentment". Frank Louis Rusciano and Bosah Ebo, for instance, remark, "As resentment rises among nations, the tangible and intangible aspects of their national identity become issues in the struggle for status. The tangible aspects include the exact borders of the nation, its economic condition, and the peoples over which it has legitimate authority. The intangible aspects include a shared historical memory, a common cultural heritage, and a common ethnicity"[1073]. One of the important components of national identity is a desire to export national values and to gain a good place in the hierarchy of nations with respect to the World Opinion. Harry Pross explains, in this respect, that "national dreams and dangerous myths" that constitute national identity have to be communicated to

---

1069   See Eugene Rostow, The Stages of Economic Growth: A Non-Communist Manifesto, Cambridge University Press, London, 1971.

1070   See Tamir Yael. "The Right to National Self-Determination", Social Research, N°58, 1991, p. 587.

1071   See Frank Louis Rusciano and Bosah Ebo, op.cit., p.61.

1072   See Liah Greenfeld, Nationalism: Five Roads to Modernity, Harvard University Press, Cambridge, 1992, p. 487.

1073   See Frank Louis Rusciano and Bosah Ebo, op. cit., p.63.

others[1074]. It is, therefore, also important to communicate a good image of the national identity to the other world nations.

In the post Cold-War era, national identity began to acquire more its definition through a relationship with the surrounding environment. Carol Gillian explains, in this respect, that similar to relations between individuals, national identity has come to be defined "in the context of a relationship"[1075]. Thus, national identity has come to be the recognition of one's nations by other world nations. To provide a sense of dignity for citizens, national identity has to represent a high "social value" and acquire the respect of other nations. However, the process of acquiring such a respect includes the interaction of different factors. In this respect, Frank Louis Rusciano and Bosah Ebo explain that "this respect must necessarily arise out of a process by which citizens' perceptions of their country are reconciled with other nations' images of it. Hence, national identity grows out of an interactive process, a negotiation between national consciousness and international image that is conducted in world forums such as the United Nations and global media outlets"[1076] (See Diagram 2 below).

Diagram 2: The Construction of National Identity.

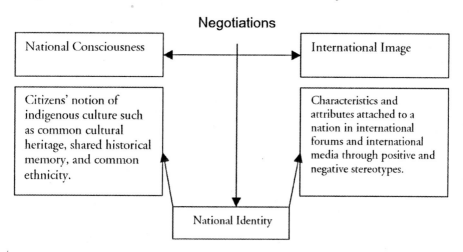

Source: **Frank Louis Rusciano and Bosah Ebo, op. cit., p.64.**

1074 See Harry Pross, "On German Identity", <u>Media, Culture, and Society</u>, N°13, 1991, p.342.

1075 See Carol Gilligan, <u>In a Different Voice: Psychological Theory and Women's Development,</u> Harvard University Press, Cambridge, 1992, p.160.

1076 See Frank Louis Rusciano and Bosah Ebo, <u>op. cit.,</u> p.64.

Thus, a nation's international image is constituted through a process of interaction with its world environment. The image of objects inside the societies themselves are, as Rusciano Frank Louis explains, defined by public opinion, reputation and the individuals associated with them[1077]. On the international larger scene, it is the world opinion and the international reputation of the nation that determines the nation's higher moral status. Disregarding the growing importance of this projection of good image of the nation is not at all in the interest of any state particularly due to this "consensus" of world opinion and, even more importantly, due to the damage a negative image of a country can have on its interests. One of the interesting examples of the growing importance of a state's world image especially in democratic systems is the events that followed the publishing in the U.S. printed press of American and British occupation force' abuses of prisoners in Iraq in April 2004. This was a sharp blow to the U.S. and the U.K's world image since the beautiful banners of liberators bringing democracy and human rights to Iraq all became obsolete; not that these banners were already false in the first place. The scandal in the U.S. has taken enormous proportions forcing apologies from the highest U.S. legislative institutions as well as from political leaders, and forcing U.S. leaders to engage in a media campaign and interviews aiming at repairing the damage to the United States' world image[1078].

A case study has been conducted to examine the impact of media coverage of an international crisis or conflict on public opinion. During this case study, it was important, not merely to see the difference in media attitudes towards vis-à-vis certain international crisis, but also to understand the justifications and reasons behind these attitudes, how these attitudes are manifested in media coverage, and what the impact of this coverage was on public opinion. Therefore, the case study in this part is much more than being a simple comparison of two countries' printed media coverage of two international crises. Other than the comparison of coverage, there is an examination of national interests and their impact on national media coverage, an examination of the impact of trans-national media on national media coverage, and an examination of the impact on domestic public opinion. It also relates such a case study to the media's ability and mechanisms employed to affect public opinion, how can this public opinion be identified, how can it influence policy decision makers, how can the state's image be important to the pursuit of its interests.

1077 See Frank Louis Rusciano, Isolation and Paradox: Defining "The Public" in Modern Political Analysis, Greenwood Press, Westport, CT., 1989, pp. 79-110.

1078 See "Bush condemns abuse of Iraqi prisoners", at http://uk.news.yahoo.com/040505/325/esvxv.html

A country's world image is important to this country's leaders and can be sometimes affected by the decision they make vis-à-vis certain international issues. Indeed, a political leader can do a lot of good to his country's world image because of a certain positions that he or she adopt, especially during a controversial international issue. This, for example is the case of the French leadership's anti-war on Iraq (2003) position, which reflected a highly positive image of France to the rest of the world nations. Similarly, domestic public opinion's tendencies and manifestations towards an international crisis or conflict can also reflect a positive or a negative image of this country to other world nations. For instance, the intensity and scale of ant-war demonstrations in a certain country can also reflect a positive or a negative image of this country to the rest of the world, if not to leaderships, then at least to the inhabitants of the regions where the conflict takes, is taking, or will take place.

The choice of the crisis of Bosnia-Herzegovina (15/10/1991-21/11/1995) and the crisis of Chechnya (1/11/1991-31/8/1996) for this case study stems from a number of similarities in the nature and duration of these two international conflicts. The choice of the United States and France for national media and national interests comparison purposes essentially stems from the fact that these two countries, first, represent two distinct state ideologies in their conduct and reactions to international affaires, and, second, from the fact that they are both long established democracies. Furthermore, it was interesting to see the effect of geographic proximity on both countries national and media reactions vis-à-vis the two crises.

To better appreciate national media coverage attitudes towards an international crisis or conflict it is essential to consider the respective national interests of countries involved in this crisis or conflict. Moreover, the national interests and foreign policy positions of both France and the United States are better understood if they are examined against the background of their respective state ideology and general foreign policy guidelines and philosophy. Accordingly, France's sense of its own grandeur, hegemonic history, lack of confidence in alliances, importance of autonomous decision-making, and prominent political figures all interact to shape a general foreign policy philosophy and guidelines for the conduct of its foreign policy. Similarly, the united States' own inherent sense of its "goodness" and "the need for its leadership" due to historic and media related influences, its *realpolitik* pursuit of its interests under beautiful, yet, repeated slogans, and the influence of certain of its presidents on state ideology and foreign policy philosophy all interact to form general philosophical guidelines for the conduct of its foreign policy. For their part, national interests of France and the United States in the crisis of Bosnia and in that of Chechnya can be grouped under five main categories: cultural, economic, political, regional, and internal social interests.

France seems to give much more importance to its foreign cultural interests than the United States does. It is assisted in this task by a long cultural hegemonic history, recent pro-Third World political positions, and an impressive network of institutions and instruments aimed at French cultural diffusion and promotion. In this, France's concept of cultural shinning and respect for cultural diversity fundamentally differs from the philosophy of imposed Americanisation worldwide. Indeed, the interest that the U.S. has in promoting its own culture is a fairly recent one. Moreover although adequate instruments have been set up to promote American culture, the foreign policy of that country seems to be the essential barrier inhibiting the acceptance of American culture in host countries, since a culture of a country is often associated with its policies. As such, foreign cultural promotion efforts of the United States are quite often regarded as a form of cultural imperialism that are, even worst, hiding economic imperialist connotations, since American culture exportation is represented by products (MacDonald's, Cinema,...etc). Both the Untied States and France seem, however, to have stronger cultural ties with those countries in which they have vital interests, or with those countries that are geographically close. In France's case, relations to former colonies seem to play a major role in determining the allocation of its foreign development aid as well as the strengths of its cultural ties. The same thing can be said, theoretically; about the U. S. and Japan if Japan is to be considered as a *de facto* colony of the U.S.

As far as national economic interests of both countries are concerned, it is evident that both the United States and France have much more present and future prospects of economic interests to be considered in their relation with the Russian Federation than in their relation with the ex-Yugoslavia successor republics. Nonetheless, the stability of the European continent is also vital for the economies of both countries.

Both countries seem to have had much more political interests involved in the crisis of Bosnia than they did in that of Chechnya. For both, exerting regional and world leadership in the post-Cold War world was important. While France was more interested in stabilising the newly constructed European bloc, the U.S. was mainly interested in stabilizing a continent, which is its most reliable partner, economically, politically, culturally, and ideologically. Furthermore, France aimed at containing a geographically close conflict through its leadership exhibition initiatives and preferably through the use of a European security organ that limits the hegemony of the U.S. and NATO over the European continent. France's political interests in the conflicts in the Balkans in general can be seen in the numerous French political and diplomatic manoeuvres directed towards finding as solution to the conflicts there in addition to the high number of French soldiers sent for pacification purposes to the region. The United States' political interests in the Balkans weighed against its past costly experience in European wars made it quite reasonable and feasible investment for the U.S. to take the lead in imposing a peace settlement to the conflict in Bosnia. Both countries, on the other had little or no political interests in the Chechnya conflict. Moreover, the importance of both countries' respective political interests with Russia seem to have been much more valued than any critical political stands concerning the issue of the Chechnya crisis. For France, inserting Russia into the European construction and its various institutions in the post-Cold War period meant introducing a counterweight to the United States and NATO's hegemony over Europe. It also meant having Russia's precious assistance in solving the more urgent nearby Balkan's conflict due to Russia's affinities and influence on the Serbs. For its part, the U.S. had no clear foreign policy line concerning central Asia and the Caucasus because it had no previous experience in the region and because it never dealt with individual countries in there. Moreover, it was quite important for the United States to have a neutral Russia than to have it as an antagonist once again.

Both the United States and France had much more articulated regional interests in the crisis of Bosnia. For France, it was important to experiment with a European collective security organ that would possibly include Russia as a counterweight to the U.S. and NATO, to guard against a renewal of a re-unified Germany's hegemony, to guard against independence and nationalistic tendencies that can contaminate certain regions in the French Republic, and, finally, to take into consideration its Mediterranean and Arab and Muslim relations in dealing with the crisis. For the United States, its regional interests in the Balkans are also vital and based on core regional interests of the United States in spite of the attempts to deny the existence of such vital interests and to dismiss the U.S. involvement in the region as simply peripheral. Furthermore, the United States seems to have wanted to guard against a repetition of the errors resulting from the "appeasement policy" and to take action now, at this relatively early stage of the conflict, than to suffer much more costly involvement to stabilize a war ravaged Europe. As far as Chechnya is concerned, France has no articulated vital regional interests in that region of the world other than the energy related ones. The same conclusion applies for the United States but with a U.S. articulated intention to dispute Russia's and other regional powers' hegemony in Central Asia and the Caucasus (U.S. strong ties with Armenia and Georgia), to guard against the proliferation of ethnic conflicts, and to support regional central governments against separatist movements. Guarding against the success and the proliferation of separatist tendencies in Central Asia and the Caucasus is, however, a regional interest of both the U.S. and France since it is much more easier to deal with a small number of countries for energy resource's routes and exploitation reasons than to deal with a much larger multitude of authorities and small newly born republics.

Public policy is constituted of domestic and foreign policy. The interaction between foreign and domestic policy makes the consideration of internal social interests concerning foreign policy reactions to an international crisis or conflict a wise policy conduct. Internal social forces in a society represented by ethno-religious minority groups, national social movements, or the extended effects of trans-national social movements have all proved their effect on foreign policy options and decisions. France and the United States are no exception to this rule. In addition to ethno-religious minority groups and affinities in host countries, anti-war activism have been given a new mobilizing instrument represented in the use of new technological innovations in personal and widely spread free information diffusion and transmission gadgets, such as SMS messages, and in the Internat. Accordingly, anti-war or pacifist protests that previously took a lot of time and efforts to be organized and only took place during the international conflict are now being organised and called for much more quickly and, most importantly, are taking place prior to the start of hostilities. Technological innovations have helped transform these protests into preventive ones.

A good dissection of the two newspapers' coverage of the two crises would take into consideration an analysis of the texts used in coverage in terms of the terminology used and the repetition of certain terms and adjectives, as well as an analysis of the types and frequency of the images used. It will also take into consideration the frequency of coverage in terms of articles and news items published and in terms of their volume in words, the priority of the placement of coverage allocated to each crisis, the journalists involved in coverage, and the effect of trans-national media on the two newspaper' coverage of the two crises.

As far as the texts used in the coverage of the two crises is concerned, they can be adequately analysed by examining the terminology used and the repetition of certain terms and adjective in coverage. Research indicates that the two newspapers' shared a number of general characteristics in their terminology but differed in others. The first shared characteristic is that they both used more negative terminology that dehumanised both Serbs and Chechens. *Le Monde* was less intense in this in the case of the Serbs but more in the case of the Chechens. *The New York Times* was more intense in doing this in the case of the Serbs than in that of the Chechens The second is the frequent dramatisation of civilian casualties in the case of Bosnia by both newspapers as opposed to that of Chechnya. There was evidence that both newspapers, and in their coverage of both crises, re-used terms employed by their sources. The general difference between the terminologies of the two newspapers is that one adopted in its coverage a rigid clear-cut aggressor-victim terminology (the New York Times), while the other (*Le Monde*) opted for a more coloured terminology.

As far as each newspaper's coverage attitude is concerned, it has been proven that each of the two newspapers' coverage attitude conformed to their respective country's national interests involved in and positions cornering the crisis being covered. Dehumanisation of the Serbs, victimisation of Muslims, and excessive dramatisation of events characterised *The New York Times*' coverage of Bosnia. On the other hand, dehumanisation of Chechnya and its inhabitants and humanising the Russian forces action characterized its coverage of Chechnya. Insisting on the dangers of the spread of the conflict for Europe, indicating the U.N's failure to deal with the crisis, and projecting a more balanced designation of aggressors and victims in the conflict characterised *Le Monde*'s coverage attitude of the Bosnia conflict. On the other hand, dehumanisation of Chechnya and its inhabitants, limiting the conflict to a power struggle within Chechnya, and dismissing the conflict as an internal Russian issue characterised *Le Monde*'s coverage attitude of Chechnya.

The second axe of analysis in analysing coverage texts is that relating to the repetition of certain terms and adjectives by the two newspapers in their coverage. The repetition of certain terms and adjectives to describe events, actors, and situations in an international crisis or conflict has an enormous effect on the audience's perception of the crisis. The repetition of the terms and adjectives in the coverage of the crisis in Chechnya and the crisis in Bosnia reveals a number of findings. The first one is that negative terms and adjectives were more repeated and associated with Serb actions by both newspapers than with Russian actions in Chechnya in general. Yet, while *Le Monde* seems more critical of Russian actions in Chechnya, the opposite is true for *The New York Times* and its coverage of Bosnia. The second finding is that the situation of Chechnya was more associated to a war of equal sides situation by repetition of certain terms to describe it as such, than it was the case of Bosnia. The third finding is that the repetition of negative degrading terms designating Serb and Chechen forces involved was much more frequent than the same designation for their rivals. In the case of Chechens, the degrading designation of their forces was much more obvious. Finally, repetition revealed that Bosnians are more "Muslims" or "Muslim Slavs" than Chechens who were quite rarely identified as Muslims or even as a separate ethnicity. This last fact is interesting if it is taken in consideration with the Muslim public opinion. It also reveals some sort of hypocrisy.

The images used in printed media coverage are important to discuss because these images (photographs, illustrations, maps, caricatures,...etc) reinforce the coverage message and leave little or no room to alternative interpretations in the audience's mind, especially if these images are accompanied by adequate commentaries. While *The New York Times* opted for the use of photographs, *Le Monde* indicates a clear preference for the use of caricatures. For its part, the New York Times' images strongly reinforced its general attitude of coverage of the Bosnia conflict (demonization of Serbs, victimisation of Muslims, dramatisation of events) and of the coverage of Chechnya (dehumanisation of the region and its inhabitants and humanising the action of the Russian troops). *Le Monde*, on the other hand, was much less direct in the connection between its coverage content and the caricatures used. This does not mean that the images of *Le Monde* didn't back its coverage attitudes of the two crises. Yet, by opting for the use of caricatures instead of photos, *Le Monde* leaves more freedom of imagination for its readers and, thus, can be said to have opted for more objectivity in its coverage. On the quantitive side of analysis, discrepancies in the frequency of the occurrence of these images were found between the two newspapers in general and in the coverage of each of the two crises in particular. *The New York Times* used much more images in its coverage of the two crises than *Le Monde* did (a rate of one photograph for each article in the case of Bosnia against a rate of one caricature for every four articles for *Le Monde*). Moreover, both newspapers used much more images in their coverage of the crisis of Bosnia than they did for that of Chechnya.

More discrepancies were found concerning the occurrence of coverage. Indeed, the frequency of the concurrence of coverage and its volume (in words) reveals that priority of coverage was clearly given by the two newspapers to the Bosnia conflict. In terms of the number of articles and news items published with a word in their title definitively indicating reference to the two crises, *The New York Times* published a total of 2264 articles on Bosnia against 342 articles only on Chechnya (a ratio of almost seven articles to one), while *Le Monde* published 3476 articles on Bosnia against only 590 articles on Chechnya (a ratio of approximately six articles to one). In terms of the number of articles and news items with a clear reference to one of the two crises in their content but not in their title, *The New York Times* published 16027 articles and news items on Bosnia against only 2507 on Chechnya (a ratio of approximately six to one), while *Le Monde* published 11586 articles and news items on Bosnia against only 3044 on Chechnya (a ratio of approximately four to one). Although *Le Monde* published slightly more news items and articles on Chechnya than *The New York Times*, the two newspapers generally published six to seven articles and news items on Bosnia against every article and news item they published on Chechnya. Moreover, *Le Monde* published more direct coverage articles and news items on Bosnia (3476) than *The New York Times* did (2264) due to geographic proximity and the immediacy of French national interests involved. Discrepancies were also found in the volume of the articles and news items published by the two newspapers. Based on the sample articles examined, the two newspapers' volume of words of their coverage of Bosnia (*Le Monde* used 28274 against a total of 19921 words for *The New York Times*) was significantly more than for their coverage of the crisis of Chechnya (*Le Monde* used 22751 words against only 17979 for *The New York Times*).

The priority of placement of a news item reflects its importance to the media outlet and, consequently, to the audience. Both newspapers gave much more priority placement to news items and articles on Bosnia than on Chechnya. Moreover, higher priority placement is given to articles and news items supporting the general coverage attitude of each newspaper. In this respect, *Le Monde* published 9 front-page articles and news items on Bosnia against only one on Chechnya, while *The New York Times* published 6 front-page articles and news items on Bosnia against four for Chechnya. All front-page articles and news items published by the two newspapers and on the two crises seem to support their respective general coverage attitude towards the two crises. Finally, it has been proven from a comparison of the frequency of coverage between the coverage of the two crises and that of other international conflicts and crises, which took place in more or less the same period of time, that the scale of humanitarian tragedy does not determine priority coverage. Indeed, priority coverage is more driven by concrete factors such as geographic proximity, direct involvement, and historical or ex-colonial ties rather than by mere humanitarian concerns. For the media, humanitarian concerns in an international conflict or crisis coverage seem to be nothing more than peripheral.

To fully understand the coverage attitudes towards the two crises, it is important to discuss the role and attitudes of the journalists involved in this coverage. However, discussing the role and attitudes of the journalists involved cannot be done without discussing the developments in the notion of journalistic objectivity. Objectivity, as a notion, benefited from the innovations in the forms and in the concept of journalism itself. These innovations were essentially brought about by innovations in the forms of the media available to the public and by the growing facility of its accessibility to this public. It also developed due to the contributions of certain prominent journalists and researchers. In this respect, there seems to be two schools of thought concerning journalistic objectivity. These two schools are represented by Walter Lippmann and Nelson Crawford. For his part, Lippmann believes journalists should shape their own interpretations of the facts they have, while Crawford believes that journalists should only disseminate objective facts. Both schools, however, seem to disregard the various factors which, in their interaction, shape human behaviour. Crawford, furthermore, thinks that institutions should be set up to monitor and preserve journalistic objectivity, while Lippmann believes in freeing journalists from the domination of such institutions.

What is important to know is that the controversy over this notion of journal-istic objectivity is an ongoing one. Indeed, some researchers consider this notion as being simply a media tactic to increase audiences, while others dismiss journal-istic objectivity as being simply a "myth" and an "ideal". The controversy, how-ever, seem to be centred around the issue of whether journalists should be observers or regulators of their society, or whether they are able to be both at the same time. It also seems to stem out of the fact that truth can mean different things to different people.

Based on the sample of articles and news items, the first interesting finding about the journalists covering the two crises is the difference in the number of journalists covering one crisis as opposed to the other. It is, indeed, interesting to note that the differences in the volume and in the priority of coverage may stem from discrepancies in the number and even "quality" of journalists sent to cover the two crises. As far as the number is concerned, journalists covering Bosnia (8 different journalists) for the two newspapers was exactly double the ones covering the conflict in Chechnya (4 different journalists). Moreover, an analysis of the journalists involved reveals that some of them were influenced by their environ-ment such as Chuck Suedic of *The New York Times*, who was accused of impar-tiality due to his Croatian origins. It also reveals that some journalists get personally attached to the conflict they cover. Some end up testifying in courts on war crimes (Florence Hartman of *Le Monde* in Bosnia), some write about the atrocities they witnessed (John F. Burns of *The New York Times* in Bosnia), and some write and defend on various forums the cause of one people in the conflict they cover (Sophie Shihab for *Le Monde* in Chechnya). Furthermore, except for Sophie Shihab of *Le Monde*, it seems that there is a tendency to send the best qualified and most reliable journalists to cover one international crisis or conflict but not another.

Having less or no journalists to cover an international crisis or conflict can also well explain why trans-national media sourcing influences national media. Indeed, if not for priority related reasons, most domestic or independent small media outlets are financially unable to dispatch their own correspondents to the crisis or conflict area in order to obtain a first hand look at events there. They usually end up, therefore, publishing news, which they are totally unable to ver-ify. In this respect, the case study in this research reveals that relied much more on trans-national media sourcing in the case of Chechnya but not in that of Bosnia. Moreover, it seems that both newspapers preferred sourcing from trans-national news dispensers that are linguistically and politically closer to them. *Le Monde* indicated a clear preference for AFP as a source, while *The New York Times* pre-ferred using Reuters and the Associated Press for sourcing purposes. Finally, both newspapers relied heavily on semi-official Russian agencies (Itar-Tass and

Interfax) for their news items on Chechnya. Trans-national media sourcing can influence national media in two ways. It can disseminate certain terms that will end up being adopted by the national media and taken for granted as being the most appropriate to use. It can also do this by selecting to disseminate certain facts or news and not others and, most importantly, by the original framing given to this disseminated news. These two effects were proven to be true in the case of the two newspapers' coverage of the crisis in Chechnya. *Le Monde*, however, and in the case of suspected trans-national media sourcing, warned its readers more, either through the use of quotation marks or directly though indicating that the certain sources are doubtful, more than the New York Time did. It is important to remind, nonetheless, that pre-supposing that a trans-national media source is more objective because its bigger or because its 'Western" is dangerous. Indeed, evidence found after comparing *The New York Times'* sourcing from Reuters and the Associated Press in certain articles suggests that these two agencies seem to offer a "unified" vision of the things. As such, it is also likely that they did that because they project a unified vision of the world.

The importance of an international crisis or conflict to a country can be indicated by the frequency of opinion polls conducted to sense public opinion tendencies towards this crisis. The examination of the cases of Bosnia and Chechnya indicates that frequent opinion polls were conducted in the United States and in France in the case of Bosnia, but that none were found for that of Chechnya. This, however, is not surprising since for the public of both countries the conflict of Bosnia is presented as a problem of general interest because of intensive media coverage and effective framing, while Chechnya simply does not exist. Indeed, no questions can be posed about a subject that does not exist in the first place. In both countries, public opinion in the United States and in France conformed to the media coverage tendencies and attitudes of the two crises. In addition, it appears that public opinion did not remain static but that it changed radically sometimes, precisely when there were some sort of media coverage concentration or dramatisation of an event in the crisis. Another interesting finding is that public opinion can change radically from one end of the scale to the other much more easily when there is no immediate vital national interests involved in this international crisis or conflict, especially after a media dramatisation of certain events. The example of the rapid radical change in the American public opinion at the images of dead U.S. soldiers in Somalia compared to the less or no change in American public opinion tendencies at the images of dead U.S. soldiers dragged on the streets of the city of Falluja in Iraq in 2004 seems to provide a solid proof of this relationship between the speed of public opinion changes and the existence or not of vital national interests.

The importance of studying and understanding media coverage attitudes vis-à-vis international crises and conflicts is due to the extraordinary ability of this social actor to orient the public mind. One of the reasons behind this ability is that the media is the primary source of information for the public in almost all aspects of this public's daily life. Due to this advantage, the media can focus public opinion on certain issues or traits of issues and not others through the use of priming and salience. Accordingly, what is important to the media becomes an important issue on the public's agenda. Hence, the media, due to this dependency on it as a primary source of information, is endowed with an enormous ability to orient the public and make this public perceive issues through the lenses of this media's frames. It can also do that by withholding or publishing Mobilizing Information (Locational, Identificational, and Tactical). Finally, the media can always use a tool called the Afghanitisation of issues in the sense that it may choose to focus on negative issues and stories in faraway countries but ignore them at home. Not all people, however, have the same need for media orientation. In fact, the need for orientation depends on how relevant the issue is to the individual in question and on how uncertain this individual is about his own knowledge of the issue presented by the media.

As far as international crises' coverage is concerned, the media can make or unmake the existence of an international crisis or conflict by choosing to focus on this crisis, while ignoring others. To create an international crisis in the public's mind or to negate the existence of one, the media can either choose to stress relevance or irrelevance of this crisis to the general public. Moreover, repetition of the use of negative traits in the description of one crisis's events, while ignoring the same traits in others helps focus public opinion on the urgency of certain international crises and not others. This is how the media creates relevance of a given international crisis or conflict to the public. One of the most effective manners of this relevance creating ability, as far as media coverage of international crises and conflicts is concerned, is by creating relevance that draws on universal and basic human emotional and humanitarian concerns.

Understanding public opinion mechanisms and functions is important because of the growing weight of public opinion in democratic societies as a regulator of public policy (domestic and foreign policy). There are, however, not one but many categories of public opinion. Indeed, researchers distinguish between at least three types of public opinion. These are mass public opinion, majority public opinion, and effective public opinion. For its part, mass public opinion generally designates that segment of society whose members are more interested in consumer-oriented non-political issues of daily life. Members of this segment are those who do not vote in elections or are those commonly designated as *the silent majority*. Mass public opinion is important because it helps measure public interest in issues (abstention level) and is also dangerous to provoke for politicians. Majority public opinion, on the other hand, is the opinion of those who participate in voting on choices of policies or politicians. This type of public opinion is not reliable, however, because it excludes the opinion of those who did not take part in the voting. What politicians rely on to sense public opinion towards issues is what is known as effective public opinion. This type of public opinion is that which actually reaches politicians. Effective public opinion towards issues can be measured through the elections framework (voting outcome on elections or policies, ratio of abstention, exit poll interviews) and through the influence framework (the number and nature of received mail on issues for instance). While the elections framework is a public opinion measurement tool whose usage is limited to election periods, the influence framework is a continuous one.

Domestic public opinion tendencies are increasingly becoming an important factor affecting a country's image in the eyes of the rest of the world. Due to the collapse of the Cold War system of competing ideologies and the distancing of the development measurements of a state from purely economically defined criteria to one which is more based on national characteristics, a national interest is becoming more and more important in international affaires. This new national interest is the image a country reflects of itself to the rest of the world. The preservation of this image is important because there has developed a sort of consensus on acceptable behaviour amongst world countries, which defines a countries moral status amongst other world nations mainly through its relations with other world nations, as well as its dealings with its own citizens. This growing importance can provoke seduction campaigns on the highest level in the political establishment of a given country in order to improve its damaged world image. On the other hand, it can gain certain countries higher moral status in the eyes of the world opinion due to these countries political leadership's stands. This, for instance, can be said about the French leadership's opposition vis-à-vis the war on Iraq of 2003, which won France the admiration of the majority of world nations. Similar to the ability of politicians to modify or influence the world image of their country, public opinion manifestations and polls concerning international affaires, such as an international crisis or conflict, can also influence this country's world image. Indeed, a negative national public opinion poll on participating in an "un justified or an unfair war", for instance, can give a positive image about the whole country to other world countries.

Part Three:

Coverage of International Crises between Interests and Objectivity

3.1. Media Coverage of International Crises as a Political Tool.

Media coverage of international crises has the merit of being considered as a double-edged political tool. It can be beneficial to the political and strategic national interests of a country interested in and by an international crisis if this media coverage was supportive of the country's objectives involved. On the other hand, media coverage can damage the pursuit of a country's national interests if this coverage did not support the policy of this country towards the international crisis in question. Thus, using this media coverage wisely is an important tactic, which the political organization in the interested country should master. Yet, if the usage of this media coverage tactic is to be more effective, the political establishment in this country should be able to neutralise certain currents and factors working against its control of over media coverage. Such currents and notions include journalistic objectivity, the media's own sense of the necessity of observing public opinion's tendencies, and the media's own interests in the coverage such as its financial interests.

In order to fully discuss the means through which the media can become either a valuable political tool or a liability for the governing political organisation of a country, it is essential to discuss the means depending on which over or under exposure of an international crisis can serve national interests, the independence between the media and the governing political organization's interests, and the mutual surveillance between the media and the political establishment in democratic systems of government.

Some of the important issues to be discussed at this point and which seem to have a strong relationship to the coverage of an international crisis, national interests, and public opinion orientation are concepts such as "war culture","peace culture", "escalation-oriented coverage', "de-escalation oriented coverage" and propaganda. It is, indeed, important to have an idea about such concepts and notions relating to media coverage of an international crisis or conflict and also to the sociological factors affecting public opinion prior to proceeding further in this research.

Certain researchers argue that one of the most important legacies of the Cold War for Western media and Western societies is the instillation of what is called a "war culture". In this respect, Wilhelm Kempf states "Due to the Cold War, war discourse has become the dominant discourse in Western media and popular culture. We live in a deeply militarised culture in which for instance many ordinary metaphors have their roots in war and popular culture is full of war material. Consuming war as a natural part of everyday entertainment, the "war logic" has become a naturalized way of outlining social reality and international life. As the previous "classical" war with clear phases—like preparations, fight and demilitarisation—was replaced with continuous arms race and low intensity warfare during the Cold War, both, the military and the civilian population had to be maintained in military preparedness for decades, and a permanent atmosphere of crisis was created"[1079]. Similar references to this "war culture" can also be found in the writings of Noam Chomsky who explains that efforts are done sometimes so that the population wouldn't be overcome with what he calls the "sickly inhibitions" which are objections to the use of violence. He states" it is very dangerous for a population to be overcome by those sickly inhibitions, as Goebbels understood, because then there is a limit to foreign adventures. It is necessary, as the Washington Post put it rather proudly during the Gulf War hysteria, to instil in people respect for "martial values". That's important. If you want to have a violent society that uses force around the world to achieve the ends of its own domestic elite, it's necessary to have a proper appreciation of the martial virtues and none of those sickly inhibitions about using violence"[1080]. For his part, Agner Fog elaborates on how a peace oriented culture can be pushed in the war direction or what is known as the "regal" direction (See Explanatory Note 3). He says "A culture can be pushed in the regal direction not only by war, but also by the threat of war. If people perceive the likelihood of being involved in a war as high, then they will feel the need for a strong political leadership, and the culture will drift in the regal direction"[1081]. These directions, of course would be following the necessities of the national interest or the environment at the time.

1079 See Wilhelm Kempf, "De-escalation-oriented conflict coverage? The Northern Ireland and Israeli-Palestinian peace processes in the German press", Paper presented at the IAMCR Scientific Conference at Leipzig (Germany)/Online Publication with pagination., July 26-31, 1999, p.1

1080 See Noam Chomsky, Media Control: The spectacular Achievements of Propaganda, Seven Stories Press, New York, 2002, p.34.

1081 See Agner Fog, "Mass Media and Democracy Crisis", Online Publication with pagination, p. 12.

Explanatory Note III
Cultural r/k Theory

The cultural r/k theory is a theory of how cultures adapt to peaceful or belligerent environments. The Zeitgeist, or spirit of a society will, according to this theory, adapt to the environment in which a society finds itself. A belligerent neighbour state that threatens the nation or social group will give rise to a kind of psychological armament in the citizens who see their nation or tribe as threatened. The solidarity and feeling of group identity will be strengthened. It has been discovered that these social psychological reactions give rise to a whole series of emergent cultural phenomena. The political structure will be more hierarchical because people feel the need for a strong leader. The ideology will go in the direction of saying that individuals exist for the sake of the society, rather than vice versa. Religious life will be stricter. Discipline will be harsh and the tolerance for deviants will go down. Sexual morals will also be stricter, and the birth-rate will go up. Interestingly, it has been found that these cultural changes are also reflected in the artistic production. Architecture, pictorial art, fiction, and even music becomes more formalistic, embellished and perfectionist so as to achieve a cognitive congruence between the art and the social system where political and religious leaders have a grandiose and majestic status.

A culture that exhibits these characteristics is called *regal*. The opposite tendencies are called *kalyptic*. A kalyptic culture is typified by peacefulness, tolerance and individualism. You may imagine a continuous scale going from the extremely regal to the extremely kalyptic, where most cultures and their individual members fluctuate somewhere around the middle of this scale. A culture can be pushed in the regal direction not only by war, but also by the threat of war. If people perceive the likelihood of being involved in a war as high, then they will feel the need for a strong political leadership, and the culture will drift in the regal direction. Other dangers that are perceived as threatening to the social order and to the nation as a whole can have a regal influence. This effect has been exploited by despots throughout history who have created witch-hunts and fictitious enemies in order to boost social solidarity and thereby consolidate their dwindling power. The regalization (i.e. regal development) not only makes a social group better armed to resist violent attacks, but also more likely to *initiate* a violent conflict, even against other enemies than those who caused the regalization.

> A culture will drift in the kalyptic direction in the absence of any serious threat to the nation and to the social order. People will not accept a tyrannical rule when nothing legitimizes the call for a strong leadership and nothing justifies the requirement that people make great sacrifices for the sake of their nation. The concept of regality has a noteworthy resemblance with the concept of authoritarianism. The latter concept has been widely used in social psychology for half a century despite the fact that it is strongly criticized for being vaguely defined and politically biased. The cultural r/k theory may thus be seen as providing an alternative to the theory of authoritarianism, and a model that is based on evolutionary psychology, social psychology and cultural adaptation rather than on implicit accusations of psychopathology.

Source: Agner Forg, op. cit., pp 11-12.

Others such as Wilhelm Kempf, have attempted to explain the difference between "war culture" and "peace culture". He states, "war culture is *a* competitive environment in which conflicts are dealt with in the framework of a win-lose model according to which any of the conflict parties can achieve their goals only on the expense of their opponents. War culture is conflict oriented. It is based on dualistic thinking, which constructs an antagonism between "us" und "them", between in-group and out group, between "good" and "evil".[1082]." On the other hand, "Peace culture" is "a cooperative environment in which conflicts can be dealt with in the framework of a win-win model that aims at a resolution of the conflict which serves the needs of all parties involved. Peace culture is solution oriented. It is based on diversified thinking which deconstructs the antagonism"[1083]. At the time of a conflict or a conflict perception the transformation of a culture from a peaceful to a war one or vice versa can also be noticeable in the discourse used (See Table 35 below).

1082 See Wilhelm Kempf, "De-escalation-oriented conflict coverage? The Northern Ireland and Israeli-Palestinian peace processes in the German press", op. cit., pp. 1-2.
1083 Ibid., p.2.

Table 35: Distortion of conflict perception during the process of escalation.

Level of conflict escalation	Cooperation	Egoism	Competition	Struggle	War
Conceptualisation of the Conflict	Win-win orientation	Bias towards win-lose orientation; win-win still possible	Win-win orientation controlled by rules of fairness	Win-lose orientation; employing strategies of threat	Win-lose turns into zero-sum orientation (to win becomes a super-goal and to win means not to be the loser); designation of force as the appropriate means to conflict resolution; emphasis on military values & rejection of peaceful alternatives.
Evaluation of rights and goals	Mutual respect for all sides' rights and needs and accentuation of common interests.	Focus on "our rights and needs (including common interests); their rights and needs get out if sight.	Focus on "our rights and needs common interests get out of sight.	Idealisation of "our" rights and needs & deionisation of their intentions.	Idealisation of "our" rights and needs; deionisation of» their "intentions" and denial of common interests
Evaluation of actions	Taking all sides' benefit into account.	Focus on "our "benefit (also from mutual relationship)	Focus on "our" benefit.	Justification of "our» action and condemnation of "their "behaviour.	Justification of "our» action and condemnation of "their "behaviour
Emotional Involvement	Mutual trust and empathy..	Ambivalence between perceived threat to "our "goal achievement and trust in "their " readiness for cooperation.	Accentuation of threat to "our" gaol achievement; trust gets lost.	The opponent is mistrusted and emphasis on " our" strength and "their " dangerousness create a balance between threats to "our" goals and values and confidence to win the struggle.	Not only enemy but also neutral third party who try to mediate in the conflict are mistrusted; focus on "their viciousness and dangerousness is counterbalances by accentuation of "our" strength reinterpretation of small losses as wins; win-lose is gradual transformed into lose-lose.
Identification suggestions	All-sided	Self-centred	Dualistic	Antagonistic	Polarized.

Source: Wilhelm Kempf," De-escalation-oriented conflict coverage? The Northern Ireland and Israeli-Palestinian peace processes in the German press", <u>op. cit.</u>, p. 3.

When a country is involved directly in a conflict or when it perceives that it will soon be due to its national interests, then it would be imperative to use all means possible to prepare for this conflict, engage in it, and win it. Thus, if the international crisis is of vital importance to a certain country then it is in the interest of this country to be prepared for any eventuality and to have a population that is psychologically ready for the possibility of armed conflict and ready to be supportive of it as well. But this would all fall into the scope of official propaganda and not objective journalistic media coverage or news reporting. The question, therefore, is whether the media's role in the coverage of an international crisis, to borrow Noam Chomsky's expression, is to "instil in the population respect for the martial values" especially if the political leadership opts for direct involvement in this crisis or conflict due to the vitality of the national interests involved.

Researchers such as Wilhelm Kempf have identified two types of discourse that can be said to be media discourse in the coverage of an international crisis or conflict (See Table 36 below). As far the coverage of the Gulf War[1084] of the beginnings of the 1990s and the one in Bosnia-Herzegovina[1085], kempf is of the view that the American and the European mainstream media largely used war discourse in their coverage of these two crisis. This is similar to the findings of the case study in this research. Indeed, the systematic emphasis on Serbs as the aggressors, on the acts of war, on warning against the danger for Europe and the risk of the spell over effect of the conflict was quite evident in the Bosnia coverage sample articles of both *The New York Times* and *Le Monde*.

1084 See Wilhelm Kempf, "News media and conflict escalation—a comparative study of the Gulf War coverage in American and European media". In: Nohrstedt, S.A., Ottosen, R. (Eds.). Journalis in the New World Order. Volume I. Gulf War, National News Discourses and Globalization. 1999.

1085 See Wilhelm Kempf, "Escalating and deescalating aspects in the coverage of the Bosnia conflict". In: Kempf, W., Luostarinen, H. (Eds). Journalism in the New World Order. Volume II. Studying War and the Media, 2000.

Table 36: War discourse vs. peace discourse

	War Discourse	Peace Discourse
Main questions	Who is the aggressor ? How can he be stopped?.	What are the issues? How can they be transformed?.
Identification suggestions	Polarized. -Humanizes "our" political and military leaders & dehumanizes " their "political and military leaders. -Humanizes "our" soldiers and dehumanizes "their" soldiers. -"Humanizes» "our" victims & dehumanizes " their" victims. -Humanizes "our" civil population for its loyalty and sacrifice & disregards or dehumanizes "their" civil population for its nationalism. -Humanizes "their" anti-war opposition & disregards or dehumanizes "our" anti-war opposition.	All-sided. -Keeps aloof from identifying with political or military leaders on both sides. -Keeps aloof from identifying with military personnel on all sides. -Humanizes or at least respects victims of war on any side. -Humanizes or at least respects members of the civil society and keeps aloof from identification with supporters of war on any side. -Humanizes or at least respects those who strive for a peaceful conflict resolution on any side.
Truth Orientation	Truth is only raw material & referential levels are humanized. -Tells stories about "our" heroism, "their atrocities". -Explains the conflict context as an unsolvable antagonism. -Tells stories about the roots of antagonism and "our" victories. -Bases "our" values on political, historical or ethnic myths.	Follows unconditional standards of truth & makes contradictions visible. -Tells also stories about "their" suffering and "our" evil. -Explores possibilities for the transformation oft eh conflict. -Tells stories about successful cooperation and the overcoming of antagonism. -Deconstructs mythical interpretations and searches for common values.
Motivation Logic.	Designates warfare as a wall against destruction and/or as a bridge into a brighter future.	Points at the price of victory, on the damage to culture, economy and social relations etc. and explores the perspectives for peace and reconciliation.
Conflict coverage.	Escalation oriented with respect to. - Conceptualization of the conflict. - Evaluation or rights and goals. -Evaluation of actions. -Emotional involvement.	De-escalation oriented, with respect to. - Conceptualization of the conflict. - Evaluation or rights and goals. -Evaluation of actions. -Emotional involvement.

Source: Wilhelm Kempf," De-escalation-oriented conflict coverage? The Northern Ireland and Israeli-Palestinian peace processes in the German press", op. cit., p. 6.

Noam Chomsky is also of a similar opinion. He explains how this "war discourse" functioned in the coverage of the Gulf War of the 1990s. He states, "the decision to use violence is very serious one. In a functioning democratic society— I don't mean one with democratic forms, but I stress "functioning"—that decision would only be taken after a lot of public discussion of the issues, and consideration of the alternatives, and weighing of the consequences. Then after appropriate public debate, maybe a decision would be made to resort to violence. Well, that never happened in the case of the Gulf War-and it was the fault of the

American media that it never happened[1086]". Noam Chomsky goes on to say "By refusing to allow the discussion and debate—and even the information—that would be the bases for some decision-making about the need for war in a democratic society, the media set the stage for what turned out to be, predictably, a very destructive and murderous conflict. People don't wont a war unless you absolutely have to have one, but the media would not present the possibility that there were alternatives—so therefore we went to war very much in the manner of totalitarian society. That's really the main point about the media and the Gulf War, in my view"[1087]. As far as the crisis in Bosnia is concerned, Noam Chomsky is of the view that there has been what he termed as "class bias" in the media coverage of that crisis[1088]. There exists then two types of discourse that can characterizes coverage of an international crisis; a war and a peace oriented discourse. There is also two types of media coverage that can be built upon such a distinction. There is the escalation type of coverage and there is the de-escalation one (See Table 36 below). According to such reasoning, the coverage of the crisis of Bosnia by the two newspapers, as seen in the case study of this research, can be easily classified as an escalation type of coverage due to the national interests involved for both countries while, on the other hand, the coverage of the crisis in Chechnya is a de-escalation type pf coverage since the national interests of both the United States and France with Russia were much more important to preserve. This is apparently the reason behind labelling the Chechnya conflict as an internal Russian affaire.

1086 See Noam Chomsky, <u>Understanding Power</u>, The New Press, New York, 2002, p.165.
1087 Ibid.,p.166
1088 Ibid., p.171.

Table 37: Escalation-vs. de-escalation-oriented coverage

	Escalation oriented coverage	De-escalation oriented coverage
Conceptualisation of the conflict.	Logic of war. - Emphasizes antagonism. - Zero-sum or at least win-lose orientation (arguments are interpreted as "giving in"). - Emphasis on military values. -Designation of force as an appropriate means. - Rejection of peaceful alternatives.	Logic of peace. - Emphasizes all-sidedness or at least avoidance of splitting the protagonists into two camps. -Win-win orientation and /or query of win-lose and/or presentation of structures for possible cooperation. -Query or at least distance to militarism or military values. -Emphasis on negative effects of force and/or query of its appropriateness. -Demands for peaceful alternatives.
Evaluation or rights and goals.	Antagonistic. - Idealisation of " our" rights and goals. - Denial of "their "rights and deionisation of " their" intentions. -denial of common interests.	Balanced. -Realistic and self-critical assessment of "our" rights. -Respect for "their" rights and unbiased description of "their" intentions. -Emphasis on common interests and description fo the benefit that both sides could gain from ending the war.
Evaluation of actions	Confrontative. - Justification of " our" action and underlining of "our" correctness. - Condemnation of "their" behaviour. -Possibilities for cooperation are denied and /or cooperation between conflict parties is not taken serious. - The role of third parties is interpreted rather as executing (moral, economic or military) pressure (win-lose) than as mediating (win-win).	Cooperative. - Realistic and self-critical assessment of "our" actions. - Unbiased assessment of "their" behavior. - Emphasis on cooperative behavior - The role of third parties is interpreted as mediating (win-win) rather than executing (moral, economic or military) pressure (win-lose).
Emotional involvement	Destructive: - Focus on "their" viciousness and dangerousness & accentuation of "our" strength create a balance between threat and confidence, which promotes "our" willingness for war. - Not only the enemy but also neutral third parties who try to mediate in the conflict are mistrusted. - Focus on "their" atrocities and "our" correctness converts indignation with the war into indignation with the enema. - Deionisation of "their" intentions and justification of "our" behaviour jeopardize empathy with "their" situation: if the behave well, they have nothing to fear. - Denial of possibilities for cooperation avoids rebuilding of trust.	Constructive: - While unbiased assessment of "their" intentions & behaviour reduces the threat "we" experience, emphasis on the price of victory promotes "our" willingness for peace. - Respect for "their" rights and unbiased assessment of "their" behaviour reduce mistrust. - Empathy with both sides victims, emphasis on both sides causalities and unbiased evaluation of both sides behaviour redirects the indignation against the war. - Empathy for "their" situation opens a new perspective: if together we find a solution that takes all sides' needs into account, reconciliation will become possible. - Emphasis on cooperative experiences (also from the past) rebuilds trust.

Source: Wilhelm Kempf," De-escalation-oriented conflict coverage? The Northern Ireland and Israeli-Palestinian peace processes in the German press", <u>op. cit.</u>, p. 8

A criticism, however, which can be made to the above models of behaviour would probably be that they exhibit the characteristics of a propaganda behaviour, especially the models explaining war culture discourse and escalation type of coverage. Nonetheless, it is a criticism that is apparently becoming more and more difficult to guard against, as far as the media is concerned. In this respect, Edward S. Herman and Noam Chomsky explain in their suburb work Manufacturing Consent that the media's selective bias and coverage of war, in particular, is nothing more than the performance of propaganda behaviour[1089]. It should be noted, however, that Noam Chomsky seems to be a fervent advocate of applying the propaganda model on mass media and, in particular, on American media. In another book, he explains that the alternative conception to the media, ideally, being a counterweight to the government in the United States is the propaganda model. Noam Chomsky goes further to explain this model by saying, "The alternative conception is that the media will present a picture of the world which defends and inculcates the economic, social, and political agendas of the privileged groups that dominate the domestic economy, and who therefore also largely control the economy. According to this "Propaganda Model", the media serve their societal purpose by things like the way they select topics, distribute their concerns, frame issues, filter information, focus their analyses, through emphasis, tone, and a whole range of other techniques like that"[1090]. Noam Chomsky, however, argues that this Propaganda Model is not an absolute and unchanging certainty. He goes on to say "Now, I should point out that none of this should suggest that the media will always agree with state policy at any given moment. Because control over the government shifts back and forth between various elite groupings in our society, whichever segment of the business community happens to control the government at a particular time reflects only part of the elite political spectrum, within which there are sometimes tactical disagreements. What the "Propaganda Model" in fact predicts is that this entire range of elite perspectives will be reflected in the media—its just there will be essentially nothing that goes beyond it"[1091]. Other researchers have attempted to interpret propaganda behaviour as being a consequence of the hostile conflict marked history of a society. According to this view distorted views of the conflict would emerge to become an inherent part of societal beliefs giving rise to a self-glorifying image and a conviction of the justness of the societies' cause. In cases of war or threats of war, such beliefs are crystallized and highly activated in patriotic discourse that gives right only to the justness of ones cause. In this respect, Wilhelm Kempf explains that such beliefs "are part of the psychological infrastructure, which helps society members to cope with the burdens of war, and that they result from

1089 See Edward S. Herman and Noam Chomsky, <u>Manufacturing Consent: The Political Economy of the Mass Media,</u> Pantheon Books, New York, 2002.
1090 See Noam Chomsky, Understanding Power, <u>op.cit</u>, p. 15.
1091 Idem.

a long history of experience with concrete conflicts at a high level of escalation and can be understood as a generalized interpretation of such conflicts"[1092]. He adds, "Once, these beliefs have emerged in a society, they provide a framework that interprets literally every interaction with the opponent as another scene in the big drama of "good" vs. "evil". And once an event has been interpreted in this way, it seemingly gives proof to the stereotypes and prejudices that created this interpretation"[1093]. Such stereotyping was evident as a as one of the findings of the case study in this research concerning Serbs and Chechens. Indeed, there was a systematic diabolising of both Serbs and Chechens in the coverage of both *Le Monde* and *The New York Times* of the Chechnya and Bosnia crises. Furthermore, the two newspapers tended to personalize the Chechnya crisis in general Doudaev (the Wolf) Vs. Yeltsin (the Bear). This has also been proven true during the Gulf War (1990-1991) media coverage, where personification of good and evil were represented by "Bush" versus "Saddam" with "Bush" as naturally being the representation of good "Saddam" as the personification of evil. In this respect, Lise Garon explains, "On the media side, however, there are signs that the Gulf War patterns of international news still hold. After villain Saddam lost the war, new lords of darkness appeared on the screens for our entertainment: the Serbs and the Algerian fundamentalists among others. International broadcasting remains more dramatic and spectacular than objective"[1094]. Other researchers also pointed to this personification of a conflict and gave one of the most Important examples of this (The Gulf War of the 1990s coverage)[1095]. Some researchers suggest that the media should not simply be considered as a mere victim to the whims of the war propaganda machine but as actors that can produce their own propaganda machine. Lise Garon, explains, for instances, "There is no doubt, of course, that war propaganda can control information efficiently and the recent advances in satellite technology may have caught the media organizationally unprepared to face an unprecedented competitive situation. However, are the media totally innocent?. A complementary hypothesis to these two explanations will be proposed as an answer: all actors, and not only the state, create their own legitimising ideology and their own seductive propaganda. War propaganda, for

---

1092   See Wilhelm Kempf, "De-escalation-oriented conflict coverage? The Northern Ireland and Israeli-Palestinian peace processes in the German press", op. cit., p. 4.

1093   Idem.

1094   See Lise Garon, "A Case Study in Functional Subjectivity in Media Coverage, The Gulf War on TV", Canadian Journal of Communications, Vol.21, N°3, 1996. (Online Publication Without Pagination).

1095   See Frederick Fico et al., "Fairness and balance of newspaper coverage of U.S. in the Gulf War", Newspaper Research Journal, vol.15, N°1, pp.30-43.

instance, is well known as a form of communication that deforms reality to entice, frighten, or persuade. Similarly, should we not consider the media as actors (not only witnesses) of the public sphere who generate their own propaganda (functional subjectivity) through the news stories they produce about the war while they seek to camouflage the shortcomings in information in order to attract or maintain their audience?"[1096]. The notion of the existence of what amount to a media's proper propaganda machine is not without support amongst researchers. Some, however, prefer to give it refer to it in other terms such as the "privatisation of propaganda[1097]". In fact, this view suggests that the privatisation of propaganda began when the traditional function of war propaganda has been delegated in recent conflicts to PR—Agencies. Wilhelm Kempf argues, in this respect, "The role of PR-agencies, finally, became so massive, and filters used to sort out virtual PR-reality from real facts were so few, that it became extremely difficult to assess the situation without knowing what the PR firms had transmitted"[1098]. For his part, Noam Chomsky comments on the role of such agencies during the crisis in Somalia, for instance. He explains" By the time of the November 1992 Presidential elections here, It was clear that Somalia could provide some good photo op's—if we send thirty thousand Marines in when the famine is declining and the fighting is calming down, we'll get really nice shots of Marine colonels handing out cookies to starving children; that'll look good, it'll be a real shot in the arm for the Pentagon budget. And in fact, it was even described that way by people like Colin Powell (then Chairman of the Joint Chiefs of Staff) and others—they were saying well, you know, it'll look good for the pentagon[1099]". PR—agencies and work was also detected in the coverage of other crisis such as the Gulf War of 1991 and the Bosnia-Herzegovina one[1100]. The privatisation of propaganda is an interesting concept presented by Wilhelm Kempf. It is interesting because, according to it, subjective judgements are emphasized by journalists in their coverage of war for various personal and "war culture" related reasons. He states" Based on the assumption that reporters must not remain detached or neutral in the face of modern evils like genocide in Bosnia, journalists have deliberately thrown away professional standards of truth and replaced them by the rules of propaganda. The coverage of the Bosnia and Kosovo conflicts is full of examples, how journalists served their moral impetus

---

1096　See Lise Garon, Op.Cit.

1097　See Wilhelm Kempf, De-escalation-oriented conflict coverage? The Northern Ireland and Israeli-Palestinian peace processes in the German press", op. cit., p. 5.

1098　Idem.

1099　See Noam Chomsky, Understanding Power, op. cit., p.164.

1100　See Wilhelm Kempf, op.cit. p.5.

by means of information control and fabrication of news. Journalists suppressed news stories which didn't fit into the enemy image. Journalists faked empirical evidence and—maybe even more symptomatic—journalists openly justified the forgery by claiming that it served the goal of opening the eyes of the public"[1101]. According to this assumption, the journalists own views and judgements are being emphasized while other views are suppressed due to personal wishes. But this is not simply due to personal wishes. In fact, this would seem like a very simplified explanation. What is questionable is the ability of a journalist to stress his personal view of the issues. Journalists as individuals can not do that. They don't have the means to stress and diffuse their opinions by themselves. They are part of a bigger organization and this organization is sometimes part of another one that is even bigger. The resulting multitude and complexity of interests would, thus, make it very difficult for a journalist to stress his own view particularly if such a view is harmful to this higher body of interests. The case of the dismissal of the most famous and influential war reporters, Peter Arnett, from his news company during the coverage of the United State's war on Iraq of 2003 because of his declared criticism of the American policy in, is a clear example of the difficulty of imagining that a single journalist can have a propaganda behaviour by himself. It is the bigger media organization, which employs him, with all its filters, that may have a propaganda behaviour. With the existence of higher hierarchical filters on his reporting, a journalist would be simply a piece in this media's private propaganda machine. It is, in fact, quite beneficial for the media to have its own propaganda behaviour during the coverage of a conflict or a crisis because it would satisfy its audience and would obtain information from military sources as well. And most of all it would appear patriotic. In this respect, Lise Garon explains "while television did yield to military propaganda, it was not completely victimized; the choices it made, between reinforcing and neutralizing propaganda, coincided with cultural proximity to the Western public and spectacular footage. Thus, one actual social function of media subjectivity comes to light: to attract and maintain an audience"[1102]. Thus, it would seem to be that it is in the interest of the media not to contradict too much the official war propaganda machine at the time of the coverage of an international crisis or a conflict.

The use of media coverage of an international crisis for political and strategic purposes is not a new notion. Cultural studies have explained the important the notion of risk for human beings and their behaviour. A society can be directed in either the *regal* or the *kalyptic* direction. This would largely depend on the past history of conflicts and the environment in which this society exists. War culture

---

1101 Idem.

1102 See Lise Garon, op.cit.,

is the product of a history and an environment of conflict where conflict and war values become inherent in societal behaviour. Some studies have indicated that because of the past conflicts and the Cold War experience the coverage of international crisis in American and Europeans media seems to adopt a war discourse where polarization is emphasized. Furthermore, a number of researchers have advanced that the media is subjected largely to a propaganda model where the opinion of the elite is always advanced and where other opinions are systematically suppressed due to the filtering net of the media propaganda machine. This also suggests polarization of points of view and a propaganda behaviour. Others have suggested that the introduction of PR—agencies in the recent conflicts and crisis have caused a sort of privatisation of propaganda where each journalist defends and stresses his point of view of the crisis and a conflict as part of an inherent societal propaganda behaviour that can be found in every individual that lives within a culture of war. Others have indicated that journalists, as individuals, are not capable of this privatisation of propaganda because they have to follow the direction of the bigger organisation that employs them and diffuses their work and which, in its turn, is subjected to a multitude of complex interests.

3.1.1. The Over-Exposure and Under-Exposure of a Crisis for National Interests

National interests of a certain country can determine whether an international crisis is more beneficial being over or under exposed. The choice to under expose an international crisis might occur to lessen public interest in that crisis and may also be done to support the inaction of the government vis-à-vis this international crisis. On the other hand, over exposure of the international crisis might be done to justify the action taken by the government of a certain country or, in some cases, a group of countries to address this international crisis.

In both cases, domestic public opinion and, in a larger sense, the world opinion seems to be the key target of under exposing or over exposing an international crisis. in this respect, perhaps the best description that can be given to applying the rule of national interests on media coverage is Edward S. Herman and Noam Chomsky's expression "worthy and unworthy victims"[1103] where the coverage of an international event or crisis in which victims are involved is presented according to its relevance to the national interests of the state. Accordingly, one victim in

---

1103   See the chapter "worthy and unworthy victims" in Edward S. Herman and Noam Chomsky, Manufacturing consent, the political economy of mass media, op. cit., pp.37-67.

certain international conflicts or crisis might receive, and do receive, much more coverage than a hundred other victims in another international conflict. It would be useful, thus, to examine in detail the reasons that make the coverage an international crisis extremely linked and dependent on the national interests involved.

The use of media coverage to justify political stands vis-à-vis an international crisis seems to be an established practice. Such an ability of the media to focus its coverage on a certain international crisis and to cause, by consequence, the adoption of certain political positions, or even military action, is labelled by some researchers as "the media driven intervention". Piers Robinson, for instance, explains that such a phenomenon is a well-known one. He states" It is widely asserted that news media coverage of suffering people, often and erroneously referred to as the "CNN effect[1104]" plays a pivotal role in causing military intervention during humanitarian crisis. Interventions in Northern Iraq 1991 and Somalia 1992-93 are widely cited as evidence for media driven intervention. More recently, the plight of Kosovar Albanians and Operation Allied Force against Serbia have forced the issue of 'humanitarian intervention and the media to the forefront of debate."[1105]. Yet, Piers Robinson also argues that the media can only cause such an effect when there is no concrete government policy concerning the crisis. He goes on to say "media coverage can drive policy when there exists policy uncertainty, and critical and empathising media coverage. Alternatively, when there exists policy certainty, not even critical and empathy framed coverage can force a policy change[1106]". Other researchers have the same notion. N. Gowing, for instance, argues that media influence on foreign policy occurs when there is policy uncertainty and extensive and critically framed media coverage[1107]. For his part, Martin Shaw explains how in the case of the Kurdish refugees' crisis media coverage incited western leaders to take action and to criticize their inaction. He states, "The graphic portrayal of human tragedy and the victims' belief in Western leaders was skilfully juxtaposed with the responsibility and the diplomatic evasions of those same leaders'[1108]. In other words, not only the content of the news but also the priority of their placement within the media

---

1104 The term "CNN effect" is commonly understood as the media driven foreign policy ability.

1105 See Piers Robinson, "The News Media and Intervention: critical media coverage, policy uncertainty and air power intervention during humanitarian crisis", op. cit.

1106 Idem.

1107 See Nik Gowing, Real-Time Television Coverage of Armed Conflicts and Diplomatic Crises: Does it Pressure or Distort Foreign Policy Decisions, The Joan Shorenstein Barone Center on the Press, Politics and Public Policy, Harvard, 1994, p. 38.

1108 See Marin Shaw, Civil Society and Media in Global Crises, op. cit, p. 88.

outlet is an influential tool in altering public opinion. This was the case with the priority placement and empathy framing of the Bosnia crisis compared to the crisis in Chechnya. Indeed, the exaggerated dramatisation of events, the images used, as well as the titles of news articles examined in the second part of this book all point to the exaggerated empathy framing of the Bosnia crisis compared to the crisis in Chechnya, which for its part, was more described as events taking place in a far away country, with no or very little dramatisation, and with a much less priority placement in the two newspapers (*Le Monde* and The New York Time).

To incite for action or inaction, the media has to first focus on the crisis. In order to note the focus of the media on a particular international crisis, there has to be what Piers Robinson identifies as "extensive and critically framed coverage". Extensive and critically framed coverage is characterized by "front page news stories and headline TV news persisting for several days that both empathises with suffering people (empathy framing) and criticises (either explicitly or implicitly) government inaction"[1109]. Thus, media focus on an international crisis can, if there is no clear policy line, affect the direction of foreign policy towards this crisis. It can also be said that effective framing of the coverage of the crisis can incite public opinion to pressure the government to act vis-à-vis this crisis. However, these explanations all suggest that the media would act alone in focusing on one crisis and not another. It would, thus, lead to the conclusion that the media's own agenda functions, first, separately from the influence of the political establishment's agenda and, second, that sometimes the media's agenda can model the political establishment's one. This leads to the issue of whether it is in the interest of the media to focus on an international crisis that the political establishments agenda has no interest in.

The question is to understand how focusing or not focusing on an international crisis can serve national interests. As far as the first possibility is concerned, which is focusing on an international crisis to serve national interests, some researchers suggest that, at the time of an international crisis, the agendas of the media and the political establishment would go in parallel. This is the view, for instance, of Noam Chomsky who places such a focus of the media under the auspices of official propaganda, however. He states, commenting on the media reaction to the September 11 2001 terrorist attacks, "it is entirely normal for the major media, and the intellectual classes generally, to line up in support of power at a time of crisis and try to mobilize the population for the same case. That was true with almost hysterical intensity, at the time of the bombing of Serbia. The Gulf War was not at all unusual"[1110]. Others such as Lance W. Bennett, are also some-

---

1109 See Piers Robinson, op. cit, p. 3.
1110 See Noam Chomsky, 9-11, Seven Stories Press, New York, 2002, p.30.

what supportive of Chomsky's idea, at least in the United States. He explains that the content of the media in the United States seems to reflect the agendas of the elites of the country and its decision makers. In the case that there is consensus between the agendas of the elites, then the media reports would normally reflect such a consensus and would avoid criticism of the policies taken. On the other hand, if such a consensus did not exist, then the media reports would normally reflect critical coverage and reporting[1111]. Hence, If there is elite consensus, then the media focus can be extremely effective in orienting public opinion.

This is done through intensive framing, usually empathy, and sometimes done in a manner that would intensify the options for military action. For instance, Maxwell McCombs argues that, as far as the intensive coverage of the Gulf Crisis in the United States and its effect on the public mind is concerned, "extensive television coverage resulted in the high salience of the war on the public agenda as the most important problem facing the country, a traditional first-level agenda-setting effect"[1112]. He goes on to say that "members of the public who reported higher levels of exposure to television news, which emphasized military options in its framing of the war, favoured a military rather than a diplomatic solution in the Persian Gulf"[1113]. Extensive carefully framed coverage, when it takes place, can help reinforce the political establishment's position on certain issues or justify its action towards these issues.

Noam Chomsky gives an interesting comparison of the carefully selective coverage of the media of certain events over others to serve national interests. He offers a comparison between the media focus in the United States on the release of the Cuban prisoner Armando Valladares in may 1986 and that of the media ignoring completely the release of what he called "the surviving members of The Human Rights Group in El Salvador" one month after Valladeres was released due to the good relations between the U. S and El Salvador at that time[1114]. He also gives, in a section of his book called "Selective Perception" other examples such as ignoring the massacres in East Timor because of the good relations of the United States with the Indonesian government[1115]. This attitude of the media is more applicable sometimes where there are crises resulting in atrocities and humanitarian tragedies. Some like Edward S. Herman and Noam Chomsky explain that the victims of such tragedies or atrocities would be "worthy" to men-

---

1111 See Lance, Bennett, W., "Toward a Theory of Press State Relations in the United States", Journal of Communication., *N°*,40, 1990, pp. 103-125.

1112 Maxwell McCombs, The Agenda-Setting Role of the Mass Media in the Shaping of Public Opinion, op. cit., p.13.

1113 Ibid, p.14.

1114 See Noam Chomsky, Media Control, op. cit, pp.46-49.

1115 Ibid., p.51.

tion in the eyes of the media if these crimes were done by enemy states. If, on the other hand, the crimes where done by friendly states, then the victims are "unworthy" to be mentioned. They explain that "the victims of enemy states will be "worthy" and will be subject to more intense and indignant coverage than those victimized by the United states or its clients, who are implicitly "unworthy". They give an example that "a 1984 victim of the Polish Communists, Priest Jerzy Popiluszko, not only received far more coverage than Archbishop Oscar Romero, murdered in the U.S. client state El Salvador in 1990; he was given more coverage than the aggregate of one hundred religious victims killed in U. S. client states, although eight of those victims were U. S citizens. This bias is particularly advantageous to U. S. policy makers, for focusing on victims of enemy states shows those states to be wicked and deserving of U.S. hostilities; while ignoring U.S. and client state victims allows ongoing U.S. policies to proceed more easily, unburdened by the interference of concern over the politically inconvenient victims".[1116] The high emphasis indicated in the case study on the victims of the Bosnia conflict compared to the media disregard of the victims of the Chechnya conflict can only be explained by such a notion of "worthy" victims of Bosnia because there are interests for both the United States and France in the region and the implicitly "unworthy" victims of Chechnya because both countries needed to preserve good relations with the Russian Federation.

Yet, quantitive over exposure of a crisis is usually not enough to achieve the desired results. In order be more productive, effective framing is usually sued to reinforce the quantitive side of the coverage. The level of public concern over the issues can also be a reflection of the framing of the coverage of an international crisis. In the U.K., this was true in the last decade of the 20th century. Stuart N. Soroka explains, in this respect, that there is notable correspondence between public concern over international issues in the U.K. (1990-2000) and the pattern of the Times coverage of these issues[1117]. Additionally, some words can be used to describe an event or an action, while in other occasions the same event would be described differently. Edward S. Herman and Noam Chomsky give the example of the use of the word genocide to describe actions taken by client and unfriendly states to the United States. As Table 38 (used also in the second section of this research to illustrate the ability of the media to create a crisis or disregard it's existence), the use of certain words in the coverage can also be part of the over or under exposure of a crisis and can very well serve the political establishments guidelines of foreign policy mainly through controlling the public perceptions.

1116 See Edward S. Herman and Noam Chomsky, Manufacturing Consent, op. cit, p. xx.

1117 See Stuart N. Soroka, 'Media, public opinion, and foreign policy'. Paper presented to the American Political Science Association, San Francisco, 2001.

Table 38: Mainstream Media? Usage of "Genocide" for Kosovo, East Timor, Turkey and Iraq

Countries/ Dates	N° of times word applied to Serbs, Turks, .etc.	N° of eds/op-eds doing the same	News Articles	Front Page
Serbs/Kosovo 1998-1999	220	59	118	41
Indonesia/East Timor1990-1999	33	7	17	4
Turkey/Kurds 1990-1999	14	2	8	1
Iraq/Kurds 1990-1999	132	51	66	24
Iraq Sanctions 1990-1999	18	1	10	1
•Mainstream media used in this tabulation, based on a Nexus database search, were the *Los Angeles Times, the New York Times, Washington Post, Newsweek and Time*.				

Source: Edward S. Herman and Noam Chomsky, op. cit, p.Xxi

As illustrated by the table above, the word genocide has been used much more in describing what "enemy" states are doing and much less in describing the same thing done by "client" or friendly states. The same thing was noted in the case study with the use of the words "genocide" and "ethnic cleansing" in reporting the Bosnia conflict and not in the Chechnya one.

Thus, the national interests of a country can sometimes determine the over exposure of a crisis or a conflict and its framing in a manner that would serve national interests both inside the country, mainly through achieving consensus on the foreign policy amongst the population, or outside the country, mainly through justifying intervention and action taken by the political establishment towards the crisis. A good example of this careful framing and exposure of the crisis according to national interests can be seen in the coverage of TV5 of the Gulf War of the beginning of the 1990s as compared to that of American national media, for instance. In this respect, Lise Garon explains, "TV5 showed the official American viewpoint less often than any of the other networks (in 23% of stories versus 43% at the other networks). Furthermore, it portrayed censorship (in 26% of the stories, compared to 6% for the other networks) and Iraqi civilians more often (in 30% of the stories, compared to 23% for CBV, 18% for CBC, and 12% for CNN), thus implicitly responding to reproaches from its Arab audience that it patronized coalition's victims"[1118]. This, however, wasn't done without a reason. It was done to be more competitive and, in particular, done because of the existence of France's own foreign policy guidelines and the existence, internally, of a large Arab and Muslim community in France. Lise Garon states" three reasons may explain why TV5 (French '*Antenne 2*' was caught up more tightly than the three other networks in that old dilemma the media always faced in wartime,

---

1118 See Lise Garon, "A Case Study in Functional Subjectivity in Media Coverage, The Gulf War on TV", op.cit.,

torn between their patriotic duty and the public's right to know. First, one must keep in mind that France was a minor power in the coalition. France is also a country that is struggling to maintain its power and influence worldwide, particularly where its former colonies and the Arab world are concerned. Besides, French television was trying to captivate a heterogeneous audience comprised, on the one hand, of 3 million French Muslims and the pacifist far left, and, on the other hand, of nationalist opinion that would not have hesitated to criticize *Antenne 2* for any lack of patriotism in wartime; the coalition's military propaganda was also France's, and to oppose the coalition's propaganda might have meant opposing the nation's interests. TV5 was facing yet another problem: as an international network and a competitor of CNN, it was represented in the pools (by journalists and affiliates), but with its more modest resources, TV5 needed to find a way to distinguish itself from its competitor"[1119]. Another example of the different coverage and framing due to national interests and particularities of the country was that of the Canadian media coverage of the Gulf War. In this respect, Lise garon explains, "The more balanced and neutral Canadian coverage contrasted with that of CNN. The Canadian networks used official information the least (in less than 30% of the stories, compared to 40% for CNN and over 50% for TV5), created original news the most (in close to 70% of the stories, compared to less than 60% for CNN and grossly 40% for TV5), and provided interpretation of the conflict the most often (in 62% of the stories for CBC and 58% for CBV, compared to 30% for CNN and 18% for TV5). Our data disclose more frequent appearances of Bush (in almost 35% of the stories for CBV and 25% for CBC, compared to less than 20% for CNN and TV5) and Hussein (40% and over for both networks, compared to less than 25% for CNN and TV5) on Canadian screens than on the competing networks. Finally, the Canadian networks showed Iraqi civilians more often (in 18% of the stories for CBC and in 23% for CBV) than CNN (12%), which helped to balance the information they broadcast"[1120]. Again this was due to the particularities of Canada vis-à-vis the conflict in the Gulf at that time. Lise Garon goes on to say "The greater creativity and better information balance of the Canadian networks should not be explained by a stricter sense of ethics but rather by Canadian networks' scarcer competitive resources and Canada's particular situation…Canada's absence from the journalistic pools probably shielded it somewhat from the coalition propaganda. The Canadian networks thus found no better strategy to improve their competitive position than a more critical attitude. Furthermore, the country's involvement in the war was only symbolic: issuing official statements and sending

1119 Idem.
1120 Idem.

a few troops and some equipment to Qatar. The Canadian networks' more criti-cal attitude did not put them at risk of accusations of failing to do their patriotic duty; Canada was not really at war. Moreover, the Canadian networks had all the more liberty as Canadian nationalism was at a low point following the failure of constitutional negotiations at Meech Lake. One can easily imagine the indiffer-ence, or even the guffaws, with which Canadians would have greeted a patriotic show at CBV or CBC. Under these circumstances, the public's right to know was a better positioning strategy than the patriotic duty"[1121]. Thus, particularities or national interests of countries could determine the nature and the focus of their coverage of an international crisis. It can determine whether a crisis or a conflict should be over focused upon or not and can determine the degree of this focus-ing. This logic assumes, however, that the media simply adopts and follows the directives of the political establishment as far as foreign policy is concerned, sim-ply out of patriotic duty and for a "rallying behind the flag effect". The question is whether the media can alone decide to focus on an international crisis or lead to intervention, or inaction by its coverage and, whether such an attitude would be more beneficial to the media itself than simply following the "higher" political agenda of the country's elite.

If the media is endowed with the power to direct foreign policy by its cover-age, then most probably this power is limited and only effective when it is con-tradictory to the national interests of the state involved. In this respect, Piers Robinson states, "The media influence occurs when there exists policy uncer-tainty and critical and empathising media coverage. With regard to the scope of media impact on policy, it appears that media coverage can trigger air power intervention during humanitarian crisis but not the deployment of ground troops. Claims regarding a media driven foreign policy are therefore not without substance"[1122]. His case studies included those of the intervention in Somalia 1992-1993, Bosnia (fall of the *Srebrenica* 'safe area' on July 11 and the US threat to use force two weeks later on July 23rd and Operation Allied Force in Kosovo in 1999. His findings indicate a difference between these two cases and demonstrate that media alone would not induce a significant change in foreign policy, if there were clear guidelines for that policy made already. Furthermore, it indicates that for the obvious case where the media could have used intensive coverage and effective framing to cause a change in the policy, it didn't but rather followed the political establishment. In the case for Somalia, for instance, Piers Robinson

---

1121 Idem.
1122 See Piers Robinson, "The News Media and Intervention: critical media coverage, policy uncertainty and air power intervention during humanitarian crisis", op. cit., p. 9.

states "Critical framing and policy uncertainty preceded intervention in Bosnia but in the apparently easy case of intervention in Somalia the media actually tended to follow executive decisions and, indeed, help build support for them rather than cause policy[1123]". In other cases, such as Kosovo, where there were a clearly adopted policy line, intensive coverage did not produce substantive results. Piers Robinson explants, "Despite critical and empathy framed media coverage within the newspapers, the US did not prevent the attacks on, and expulsion of, the Albanian Kosovar population. Instead the Clinton administration stayed with an air campaign that was aimed at applying pressure on Milosevic rather than offering direct protection to suffering people."[1124]. However, the same didn't apply to the Bosnia case where the policy was uncertain. Piers Robinson explains "The hypothesis that media influence occurs when policy is uncertain and framing is critical was supported by the Bosnia case study in which critical media coverage helped cause policy-makers, uncertain of whether to intervene"[1125] Thus, the media focus impact is limited by the existence or not of a concrete foreign policy towards the crisis or conflict itself.

Apparently, it is also not in the interest of the media to focus on a crisis in which there is national political interest involved. Indeed, the media has to consider a number of factors before doing that. It has to consider that it is in its best interest to have a smoothly functioning relationship with the political establishment because it needs the political establishment for a number of things like official sources on issues and technical facilities such as licences and franchises. It also needs to consider the fact that it has to be competitive and if it does not follow the line of other more powerful media in focusing or not on a certain crisis, then it would loose its ability to compete. Furthermore, the media would usually be careful not to be labelled as unpatriotic in focusing on an international crisis and in framing it in a way that is contradictory to the declared, and well-implanted interests of the country in the minds of its audience.

The over-exposure or under-exposure of an international crisis can be done to serve the national interests of a country. The media extensive coverage of an international crisis accompanied with appropriate and effective framing can assist the political establishment in reinforcing its positions both internally with its domestic public opinion and externally with the world's public opinion. This would allow the political establishment more freedom and more support in its action and more easiness in advancing their justifications. An international crisis can also be ignored for national interests. If there is no interest for the country in the

---

1123 Ibid., p.8.
1124 Idem.
1125 Idem.

crisis, then there would be no need to focus on it because focusing on it would make it seem like a national problem and would place it, thus, high, on the public agenda. It seems that it is not in the ability or the best interest of the media to focus on an international crisis if there were no national interests involved. Moreover, the media's coverage seems capable to trigger a change in foreign policy only if the politicians themselves were not certain of the action to take. In such a case, they would be compelled to satisfy the public protest resulting from the media's intensive coverage and framing, especially empathy framing. This is particularly true in humanitarian crisis and humanitarian intervention. The media, also, has to consider the fact that it needs to be competitive and for that it needs to have a good relationship with the political establishment and with the public in not appearing as being unpatriotic.

3.1.2. The Interdependence between the Media and the Political Machine's Interests

In order to better understand how the media coverage of an international crisis can be an effective political tool and, consequently, serve vital national interests, it is essential to discuss the interdependence that exists between the agendas and interests of the political and the media machines. Indeed, on many occasions the concordance between the interests of the two parties is quite noticeable and beneficial for the interests of both. On other occasions, the lack of common interests results in a divergence in both machine's attitudes vis-à-vis the international crisis. In order to better understand this interdependent and complex relations between the media and the political machine, it is useful to start with a discussion of the relationship between the media and the various interest groups within any given society (political, economic, social...etc) prior to developing the discussion the relationship between these two institutions during an international crisis.

To start with, it is important to discuss the nature of the apparent hostility climate that is usually noticeable between the media and the political establishment especially in democratic societies. Indeed, it is not unusual to encounter mutual accusations of "bias" or "discrimination" coming from the media or the political establishment. For instance, loosing politicians in election times tend sometimes to justify their failure by the media bias towards them. Some writers call this perception of the media as the "hostile media attitude"[1126]. Similarly, the media can,

---

1126 See R. Giner-Sorolla and S. Chaiken, "The causes of hostile media judgements", <u>Journal of Experimental Social Psychology</u>, N°*30*, 1994, 165-180 pp.

for its part, always accuse the political establishment of being biased against it, namely in showing preferences in its allocation of information to certain media organisations and outlets in the country.

These apparent hostilities between the two institutions should not, however, be taken as a portrayal of the real state of relations between them. Indeed, this relation can be characterized more as one in which the interests of one side are related to the other and one, according to which, none can survive without the other. In this respect, the existence of interest groups institutions working at a higher level in both institutions whose interests are entangled is a good proof of the interdependence that exists between the media and the political machines. Certain writers, in this respect, stress the fact that highly placed interest groups in the political and the economic establishments usually consider the media as much more favourable to their goals than similar groups of interest that are lower in the hierarchy[1127]. Thus, it can be said that the apparent antagonism between the media and the political establishment is one that is found on the lower and possibly outer-shell levels of the hierarchy of both institutions and not a deeply routed and genuine one.

One important manifestation of this interdependence that exists between the media and the political machine's interests is that which can be seen in what Michael Karlberg and Robert A. Hackett identify as the "source-media" relations. They explain that there "is much research indicating that information subsidies, power imbalances, and structural advantages create such substantial source bias in the news that bureaucratic institutions and political elites become the "primary definers" of mass-mediated public issues"[1128]. This is also somewhat true for Edward S. Herman and Noam Chomsky who argue "The mass media are drawn into a symbolic relationship with powerful sources of information by economic necessity and reciprocity of interest. The media need a steady reliable flow of the raw material of news. They have daily news demands and imperative news schedules that they must meet. They cannot afford to have reporters and cameras at all places where important stories may break. Economics dictates that they concentrate their resources where significant news often occurs, where important rumours and leaks abound, and where regular press conferences are held"[1129].

1127 See G. A. Donahue et al., "Media evaluations and group power". In A. Arno & W. Dissanayake (Eds.), The news media in national and international conflict, (pp. 203-215), Boulder, CO: Westview, 1984,

1128 See Michael Karlberg and Robert A. Hackett, "Cancelling each other out? Interest group perceptions of the mass media", Canadian Journal of Communication (Online publication without pagination), Vol. 21, N° 4, 1996.

1129 See Edward S. Herman and Noam Chomsky, Manufacturing Consent, op. cit., pp. 18-19.

According to this view, economic necessities seem to be the underlying factor of this source based relationship between the media and the political machine. Yet, it can also be said that it is the considerable weight given to official sources by the media, or, indeed, the media official sources, have always the advantage of being more credible than others. In this respect, Mark Fishman explains, "News-workers are predisposed to treat bureaucratic accounts as factual because news personnel participate in upholding a normative order of authorised knowers in the society. Reporters operate with the attitude that officials ought to know what it is their job to know…In particular, a news-worker will recognize an official's claim to knowledge not merely as a claim but as a credible, component piece of knowledge. This amounts to a moral division of labour: officials have and give the facts; reporters merely get them".[1130]. This view suggests that the relationship between the two institutions is a relationship of convenience where it is convenient for the media, in order to guard its economic interests, to have a good relationship with the political establishment because it is this establishment that is either the source or the subject of the media's news.

However, it can be said that such a relationship is an unequal one. It is unequal because it suggests that there is no media freedom in choosing its sources which means that the media has a dependency relationship with the political establishment. Consequently, since there is dependence then there is bias as well. Nonetheless, this logic is not totally true since there is a mutual dependency relationship between the two institutions. In democratic societies, if the media is bias, it does not mean that it is biased only because such bias would serve the interests of the political or economic establishment's agenda. Indeed, media bias can as well save its own agenda sometimes.

Indeed, the interest of such as media-source relationship for the political establishment is rather different from that of the media. For its part, the political establishment needs the media as an effective social control and mobilization actor. In this respect, R. Ericson et al, explain that the political establishment often perceive the media as a very effective agent of social change, social control and of political pressure[1131]. As a social control agent, the media can be said to serve the purposes of the political establishment. Edward S. Herman and Noam Chomsky explain, in this respect "Because of their services, continuous contact on the beat, and mutual dependency, the powerful can use personal relationships, threats, and rewards to further influence and coerce the media. The media may

---

1130 See Mark Fishman, <u>Manufacturing the News</u>, University of Texas Press, Austin, 1980, p.143.

1131 See R. Ericson et al., <u>Negotiating control: A study of news sources</u>, University of Toronto Press. Toronto, 1989.

feel obligated to carry extremely dubious stories and more criticism in order not to offend their sources and disturb a close relationship"[1132]. This last assumption is quite logical. If the media wants to preserve a good relationship with their sources in the political establishment it has to present some concessions in return, even if such concessions meant a lack of objectivity. This lack of objectivity can also be carried out through a pressure on the media to deny the right to discuss issues to controversial parties. Edward S. Herman and Noam Chomsky explain in this respect that "powerful sources may also use their prestige and importance to the media to deny critics access to the media"[1133]. Edward S. Herman and Noam Chomsky further present a number of cases in which such denial of access to critics of the political establishment in the United States occurred. Yet, their line of thought places the media in a position from which it would appear nothing more than a mere propaganda machine for the political establishment[1134].

The media-source convenient arrangement is, however, not the only consequence of this dependency relationship of the media on the political establishment. For the media also needs to have good ties with the government even without the need for sources and for purely practical and legal facilities. Indeed, it needs to maintain good ties with the political establishment for such technical and legal facilities such as providing licences and franchises. To counter-balance such a need for the government and to have an effective lobbying corps, the media usually tends to employ ex-government officials. Edward S. Herman and Noam Chomsky explain, for instance, that fifteen of the ninety-five outside directors of ten of the media giants in the United States in 1986 are former government officials (See Table 38).

1132 Edward S. Herman and Noam Chomsky, Manufacturing Consent, op. cit., p. 22.
1133 Idem.
1134 Idem.

Table 39: Affiliations of the Outside Directors of Ten Large Media Companies (Or Their Parents) in 1986°.

Primary Affiliations	Number	Percent
Corporate Executive	39	41.1
Lawyer	8	8.4
Retired (Former Corporate executive or banker)	13 (9)	13.7 (9.5)
Banker	8	8.4
Consultant	4	4.2
Non-profit organization	15	15. 8
Other	8	8.4
Total	95	100.0
Other Relationships		
Other Directorships (Bank Directorships)		255 (36)
Former Government Officials		15
Member of Council on Foreign Relations		20
° **Dow Jones & Co.; Washington Post; New York times; Time, Inc; CBS; Time-Mirror; Capital Cities; General Electric; Gannett; and Knight-Rider.**		

Source: Edward S. Herman and Noam Chomsky, Manufacturing Consent, op. cit., p.11.

Another technical dependency in the media relation with the political establishment has to do with economic needs. Being part of the market system, the media companies are after all companies that have to depend on the economic polices of the political establishment. They, thus, need facilities is such issues as labour laws, taxes and interest rates. This too makes this dependency relationship between the media and the government govern the point of view in which most issues are looked at.

At the time of an international crisis, this relationship between the media and the political establishment is further accentuated since at the time of such a crisis, the national interests would be strongly dictating the conduct of both the political establishment and the media. Indeed, a number of methods stem out of this media-source relationship emphasising the interdependence between the two institutions, especially during the coverage of an international crisis or conflict.

The first of these methods is that of bombarding the media with facts and news items in order to manipulate the media and make it follow an agenda that is convenient to that of the political establishment. Stephen L. Vaughan explains, in this respect, that such a method goes as far back in history as World War I and the Committee on Public Information which found out that "one of the best means of controlling news was to bombard the news channels with "facts" or what amounts to be "an official information"[1135]. Some writers explain that the reason behind this ability of the political establishment to bombard the media with such news items and information is the media's source dependency relationship with the political establishment. For instance, Mark Hertsguard argues that such a method was used by the Reagan administration to manipulate the press. He argues that such powerful sources within the political establishment can take advantage regularly of the media routines and its dependency on their news items in order to manipulate them into following a special line of thought or a special agenda that is convenient to the interests of the political establishment[1136]. Edward S. Herman and Noam Chomsky further present examples of the use of such a method in crisis coverage. They explain that part of this manipulation or "management process" consists of "inundating the media with stories, which serve sometimes to foist a particular line and frame on the media (e.g. Nicaragua as illicitly supplying arms to the Salvadorian rebels), and at other times to help chase unwanted stories off the front page or out of the media altogether (the alleged delivery of the MIGs to Nicaragua during the week of the 1984 Nicaraguan elections)"[1137]. Indeed, both the media and the political establishment's interests can be said to have been served using such a method. For its part, the political establishment is served by supplying the stories that would support its interests and the media would have served its interests by having a continuous flow of stories about the crisis or conflict and, thus, ensuring its competitively and economic survival.

Another method that belongs to this source-media relationship between the media and the political machines and that is, particularly applied, at the time of the coverage of an international crisis is that of using experts' views on the crisis. According to Edward S. Herman and Noam Chomsky such experts can be defined as being those "highly respectable unofficial sources that give dissident views with great authority"[1138]. Indeed, the existence of experts' opinions at the time of an international crisis is highly important. It gives more credibility for the media and projects the views of an "independent" voice that is not identified as being part of the government's voice for the political establishment. In this respect, Henry Kissinger explains, "In this age of experts, the constituency of the expert is those who have a vested interest in commonly held opinions elaborating

---

1135 See Stephen L. Vaughan, Holding Fast the Inner Lines, Chapel Hill University of North Carolina Press, North Carolina, 1980, p.194.

1136 See Mark Hertsguard, "How Reagan Seduced Us: Inside the President's Propaganda Factory", Village Press, September 18, 1984.

1137 See Edward S. Herman and Noam Chomsky, op. cit. p.23.

1138 Idem.

and defining its consensus at high level has, after all, made him an expert"[1139]. Thus, the existence of experts helps create consensus for the political establishment and helps the media to appear as credible and consequently draw more audiences to it and increase, by the process its capabilities to compete and increase the market share of audiences.

The problem with using experts for the political establishment, however, is that sometimes they can present dissident views that are contrary to this establishment's interests. According to Edward S. Herman, such a problem has been solved by what he termed as "co-opting" the experts. This means placing them on the payroll of the government through different means, such as funding their research, employing them as consultants or by organizing think tanks to employ them and help disseminate their messages. By doing that, the political establishment can ensure that the bias in the news items and in the supply of opinions is structured and that the supply of experts will be in the direction that would be determined by the government and the market[1140]. The media as well has an interest of creating its own supply of experts. It can do that by continuously focusing on them and, by the process, making them appear as very credible commentators on the crisis. In this respect, Edward S. Herman and Noam Chomsky explain that the media itself provides experts who "regularly echo the official view"[1141]. They go on to say" John Barron and Claire Sterling are household names as authorities on the KGB and terrorism because the *Reader's Digest* has funded, published, and publicized their work…. By giving purveyors of the preferred view a great deal of exposure, the media confer status and make them the obvious candidates for opinions and analysis"[1142]. The point here seems to be that the concordance between the media and the political establishment's interests as far as using experts comment the events of an international crisis or conflict is concerned, is that experts disseminate the needed messages, can disseminate these messages while being considered by the audience as "neutral" observers, and can disseminate such messages while being considered authorities in the subject, due to the recurrent use of their comments and opinions by the media. It is a process that starts with the selection of experts to use and ends in excessive-focusing on them to give them more credibility in the eyes of the public.

1139　See Henry Kissinger, <u>American Foreign Policy</u>, Norton, New York, 1969, p.28.
1140　See Edward S. Herman, "The Institutionalisation of Bias in Economics", <u>Media, culture and Society</u>, July 1982, pp. 275-291.
1141　See Edward S. Herman and Noam Chomsky, Manufacturing Consent, <u>op. cit.</u>, p.45.
1142　Idem.

The interests of the media and the political machines seem to be highly inter-dependent in spite of the occasionally apparent animosity between the two. This interdependence of interests is found in the concordance of interests between various interest groups that are placed at the higher hierarchical levels of both institutions. The milestone of this interdependence of interests appears to be fairly represented in the media-source relationship between the two. The preservation of such a relationship seems to be quite important for both establishments. For the media this relationship allows it to have a continuous flow of information that would keep it spinning and for the political establishment this flow of information it supplies would allow it to use the media as a an agent of social control and to manipulate it to its ends.

Two important methods seem to stem out of this media-source relationship between the two machines. These methods are used quite often at the time of an international crisis. They consist in the bombardment or the withholding of information from the media and the use of selected experts as "neutral" and credible sources of opinion on the international crisis or conflict by both machines to disseminate the desired messages.

3.1.3. The Mutual Surveillance between the Media and the Political Machine

There exists, especially in democratic systems of government, a function of mutual surveillance between the media and the political machines. This mutual surveillance can be looked upon as an indication of the well functioning of the democratic system but it also can considered as an indication that each of these two machines surveys the other in order to better preserve its own interests.

The notion of mutual surveillance indicates a certain degree of equality between the two parties who are supposed to survey each other. While the status of the political establishment is very much established and recognized as the highest in any state, that of the media is still a bit hazy and largely depends on the nature of the political establishment itself.

Thus, in order to have the ability to survey the political establishment, the media has to be recognized as being at least an almost equal partner to this establishment. In democratic systems of government, this status has very much developed over the years. Indeed, the limit to which the power of the media has come to reach nowadays is quite impressive. It has come to a point where some writers would even label it as not simply just the "fourth estate" but even as something that amounts to a "shadow government". William L. Rivers, for instance, explains that in the United States the media has become a "shadow government". He states, "There is another side to Washington—another government. The Other Government—the Washington news corps—has come to consciousness of its power and is gradually moving into larger, more official, less eccentric structures…they have acquired the authority and sometimes even the power of a shadow government. The Washington press corps has certainly acquired the trappings of power. Privileged as no other citizens are, the correspondents are listed in the Congressional Directory; they receive advance copies of governmental speeches and announcements; they are frequently shown documents forbidden even to high officials; and they meet and work in special quarters set aside for them in all major government buildings, including the White House. Fantastic quantities of government time and money are devoted to their needs, their desires, and their whims. Some White House correspondents talk with the president more often than his own party leaders in the House and in the Senate, and there are Capitol correspondents who see more of the congressional leaders than do most other congressmen"[1143]. Another reason explaining why the media today amounts to an equal of a political establishment and why it is given the status and the privilege to perform a surveillance of the political establishment is the media's economic weight. This factor is, indeed, quite impressive and is one which allows the media the privilege of being an equal to a government, or even to a group of governments, if measurements of power where top be only based on economic weight (see the example of Table 39 below).

1143   See William L. Rivers, "The Media as Shadow Government" in Maxwell McCombs Agenda Setting: Readings on Media, Public Opinion, and Policymaking, Lawrence Erlbaum Associates, Hillsdale, 1991, pp.153-154.

Table 40: Wealth of the Control Groups of Twenty-Four Large Media Corporations (or Their Parent Company), February 1986.

Company	Controlling Family or Group	Percentage of Voting Stock held by Control group (%)	Value of Controlling Stock Interest ($ Millions)
Advance Publications	Newhouse family	Closely Held	2.200p
Capital Cities	Officers and directors (ODs)	20.7 (Warren Buffet, 17. 8)	711p
CBS	ODs	20.6 ▲	551 p
Cox communications	Cox Family	36	1.900f
Dow Jones & Co.	Bancroft-Cox families	54	1.500 f
Gannett	ODs	1.9	95p
General Electric	ODs	Under 1	171p
Hearst	Hearst family	33	1.500 f
Knight-Rider	Knight and Rider Families	18	447p
McGraw-Hill	McGraw Family	c.20	450f
News Corp.	Murdoch Family	49	300f
New York Times	Sulzberger Family	80	450f
Reader's Digest	Wallace estate managed by trustees; no personal beneficiaries	NA	NA
Scripps-Howard	Scripps heirs	NA	1.400f
Storer	ODs	8.4	143p
Taft	ODs	4. 8	37p
Time, Inc.	ODs	10.7 (Luce 4.6, temple 3.2)	406p
Times- Mirror	Chandlers	35	1.200 p
Triangle	Annenbergs	Closely held	1.600 f
Tribune Co.	McCormick heirs	16.6	273p
Turner Broadcasting	Turner	80	222p
U. S. News and World Report	Zuckerman	Closely held	176▶
Washington Post	Graham family	50 +	350f
Westinghouse	ODs	Under 1	42p

P: Means taken from proxy statements and computed from stock values as of February 1986.
F: Means taken from Forbes magazine's annual estimate of wealth holdings of the very rich.
▲ These holdings include William Paley's 8.1 percent and a 12.2 percent holding of Laurence Tisch trhough an investment by Loews. Later in the year, Loews increased its investment to 24.9 percent, and Laurence Tisch soon thereafter became acting chief executive officer.
▶ This is the price paid by Zuckerman when he bought U.S. News in 1984.

Source: Edward S. Herman and Noam Chomsky, Manufacturing Consent, op. cit., pp 9-10.

The above table gives a fairly good idea about the economic might of some of the big media companies in the world. This economic might combined with the weight of the media as a social mobilization agent gives it the status of a body that can survey in its turn the political establishment especially in democratic societies. Such a function of surveillance has actually been established a very long time ago. In this respect and in democratic societies, Walter Lippmann, "There are two processes of justice, the one official, the other popular. They are carried on side by side, the one in the courts of law, the other in the press, over the radio, on the screen, at public meetings"1144. This is particularly true because the public

---

1144 See Walter Lippmann, Public Opinion, op. cit.

depends on the media to a very large extent for getting information on its daily life and on the government policies and activities. William L. Rivers, argues here that not only the ordinary person would depend for his daily information on the media but also the government and its members. He elaborates, "In our daily lives, we trace a path from home to work and back. Without the news media, we would know almost nothing beyond our own sphere of activity. The public's knowledge of national government depends not on direct experience and observation, but on the news media; and it is the media that set the agenda for public discussion and decision. To a large degree, the employees of the government—including the president himself-must also depend on the reports of the news media for information about some of their most important concerns. In government, as elsewhere, each worker is circumscribed, and his sphere is small"[1145]. Thus, the media, in democratic societies, appears to be practicing, to a fairly good degree, its role of surveillance of the political establishment. It does this because it is essential for the media to survive and be competitive in democratic societies where market laws govern and where people tend to be attracted to news media outlets which they perceive to be more objective and, indeed, daring in its criticism of the government, than other media outlets. For If a media outlets neglects such a function, the public would probably turn to other information outlets, including concurrent media outlets, for its daily doze of information on its government's policies and activities.

On the other hand and for the political establishment, the daily media survey is essential for a safer conduct of its work. Indeed, the filter that the media provides everyday for governmental policies and actions is always examined by members of the political establishment. This is quite necessary since ignoring media criticism on certain policies and issues can result in more criticism and in the media focusing more on such policies, which could result in a social mobilization against such policies.

Yet, the question is how would the government in democratic societies ensure that it too could survey the media and ensure that this media's conduct is not harmful to its policies and decisions. In democratic societies, and in addition to using economic facilities and the sources supply of information as a means of control over the media, organising directed protests against media coverage can also be used by politicians. These protests are what Edward S. Herman and Noam Chomsky call "flak". According to them, "Flak refers to negative responses to a media statement or program. It may take the form of letters, telegrams, phone calls, petitions, lawsuits, speeches…and other modes of complaint, threat, and

---

1145 See William L. Rivers, "The Media as Shadow Government", op. cit., p.154.

punitive action. It may be organized centrally or locally, or it may consist of the entirely independent actions of individuals"[1146]. These protests can be quite harmful to the media if they were organized and focused. In order to have large organization and concentration of such protests, a powerful body must be the instigator. Edward S. Herman and Noam Chomsky affirm, in this respect, that such a powerful body is mostly the political and economic establishment. They state, "If a flak is produced on a large scale, or by individuals or groups with substantial resources, it can be both uncomfortable and costly to the media. Positions have to be defended within the organization and without, sometimes before legislatures and possibly even in courts". They continue to say that "the ability to produce flak, and especially flak that is costly and threatening is related to power"[1147]. Thus, powerful agents in the political and economic establishments can use their ability to mobilize protests against the media conduct in order to get this media back on the right track if, for one reason or another, it deviated from the reasonably permitted track.

At the time of an international crisis, such a mutual surveillance between the media and the political establishment is more acute. William L. Rivers, for instance, gives a good example of the importance of such surveillance during an international crisis or conflict. He explains, "John Kennedy admitted that he acquired new information from *The New York Times* about his own secret sponsorship of the Bay of Pigs invasion. Eleven days before the invasion that the CIA had been shepherding so carefully, the editors of the Times informed Kennedy that their correspondent, Tad Szulc, had discovered the secret and that a detailed news report was imminent. Kennedy persuaded the publisher to postpone publication until after the landing in Cuba. But, during the discussions with the Times editors, the president picked up new information about the mounting of the invasion Afterward, in regret at the fiasco, Kennedy said to Turner Catledge, the executive editor of the *Times*, "If you had printed more about the operation, you would have saved us from a colossal mistake"[1148]. This is a good example of how much importance is to be given to this mutual surveillance between the two because at the time of an international crisis, the interests involved are enormous, for both institutions.

Generally speaking, the interests of both the media and the political establishment would be highly at risk at the time of an international conflict or crisis. For the political establishment, the necessity would be the preservation of the national interests and having popular support for the government's position

---

1146 See Edward S. Herman and Noam Chomsky, Manufacturing Consent, op. cit, p. 26.
1147 Idem.
1148 See William L. Rivers, op. cit, p.155.

regarding such a crisis. For the media, the interest would be also to appear as preserving the national interests and to preserve its competitive status in the market through a balance in which there is a projection of its surveillance of the government's actions vis-à-vis this crisis and, at the same time, a preservation of good ties with this government for the supply of information and for economic and technical facilities.

The mutual surveillance between the media and the political establishment is quite interesting. Although the political establishment remains the most important and the highest authority in any given country, the media has over the years came close to rival with this privileged status of the political establishment, especially in democratic societies. The media's growing importance stems from the natural need pf both the public and the political establishment to be informed of issues on daily bases, and from its enormous economic weight. Furthermore, the media can rely on these two factors as the bases justifying its surveillance of the political establishment. For its part, the political establishment surveys the media to ensure that it doesn't harm its interests or that it doesn't deviate too much from the government's line of conduct. The political establishment can always use pressures such as flaks, economic facilities, or access to sources to get the media back on track if needed. At the time of an international crisis, the interests of both the media and the political establishment are accentuated and, thus, the degree of mutual surveillance is significantly higher.

3.2. The Influence of Media Coverage of International Crises on Public Opinion

It is important at this stage of the research to discuss the influence that the media coverage of an international crisis can have on domestic public opinion. This influence is important because public opinion can legitimise the action or inaction of the governing political establishment vis-à-vis the international crisis in question, because of the dependence of the public on the media coverage of an international crisis for the formation of its opinion, convictions and actions, and also because the media's ability to shape public opinion in its coverage of an international crisis is not without limitations.

3.2.1. Public Opinion as a Source of Legitimacy for the Political Establishment

In many cases, the main function of the media coverage of an international crisis consists in legitimising the position and action, including direct military involvement, of the political establishment towards the international crisis or conflict in question. On the other hand, and when needed, the media can also legitimise inaction concerning this international crisis or conflict.

To begin with, however, it is important to discuss the nature of this public opinion. For, indeed, the term "public opinion" has come to be the source of an ongoing debate amongst scholars because it represents quite a number of ambiguities, symbols, and uncertainties. For their part, Anne-Marie Gingras and Jean-Pierre Carrier explain, in this respect, "Public opinion may be seen as superficial and fluctuating, or it may be conceived of as deep-seated and slow to change. It may relate to public mood and irrational feelings, or to a more structured or reasoned collective opinion. It can be captured by polls but also manipulated by them. It can be viewed simply as an artefact of polls, having no reality outside of polling data"[1149]. As such, the definitions of the term are as multiple as opinions are. For instance, Harwood L. Childs presents up to fifty definitions of the term "public opinion" in his work[1150]. Yet, some scholars insist that as far as democratic societies are concerned, the ideal as an essence of the term "public opinion" remains constant. This ideal for democratic societies is what Anne-Marie Gingras and Jean-Pierre Carrier explain as the process by which "the people can govern themselves through rational thinking"[1151]. However, they insist, that for this ideal to be realized, the public have first to be informed. They state, "The democratic aspiration for "government by consent" is necessarily premised on the existence of informed public opinion; in this sense, popular wisdom is synonymous with rational thinking"[1152]. Hence, the importance of public opinion in a democratic society is that it is the translation of the very essence of democracy itself. In other words, if democracy is the people's control of their own destiny then public opinion can be understood as the outcome of these peoples' thoughts and opinions concerning their destiny. This, nonetheless, can always be labelled as the

---

1149 See Anne-Marie Gingras and Jean-Pierre Carrier, "Public Opinion : Construction and Persuasion ", Canadian Journal of Communications (On-line Publication), vol.21, N°4, 1996.

1150 See Harwood L. Childs, Public opinion: Nature, formation and role, D. Van Nostrand, Princeton, 1965.

1151 See Anne-Marie Gingras and Jean-Pierre Carrier, op. cit.

1152 Idem.

ideal situation where the well-informed people would have accurate information, think objectively and correctly, and consequently adopt an objective and accurate opinion. Yet it is precisely due to the fact that this people, audience, or public relies on the accuracy and objectivity of the information provided to it and over which it has no control that public opinion can be manipulated.

It is important to stress here that public opinion has always been at the heart of practically all political system, politicians, and leaders and not simply in democratic ones. in democratic systems and societies, however, its activeness is much more appreciated and much more effective. In this respect, Murray Eldman argues that in a democratic society the aspiration is that the will of the people or what he calls "the most cherished common political hope" would finally be realized[1153]. There are, indeed, two main schools of thought that discuss this role of public opinion within the political systems. These are the liberal positivist and the critical theory schools of thought. Each one of these two schools of thought or perspectives on public opinion has its fervent advocates.

Jerry L. Yeric and John R. Todd are, for instance advocates of the liberal positivist school of thought on public opinion. For them, public opinion is the dominant opinion concerning an issue of public interest[1154]. According to this school of thought, public opinion in a society refers to the opinion of the majority. Furthermore, adepts of this school believe that public opinion can be captured and measured through polls and similar techniques that can measure quantity. The other school of thought, the critical theory school, believes, on the other hand, that public opinion is a utopian ideal that is used to legitimise the political establishment's actions. One of the most prominent advocates of this school of thought is Patrick Champagne who believes that public opinion is a myth[1155]. Another supporter of this view can be also found in the person of Claude-Danièle Échaudemaison who explains that public opinion is simply the "breaking result of the diffusion of public speeches by the political class and the media"[1156]. Contrary to the liberal positivist school of thought, adepts of the critical theory

---

1153 See Murray Eldman, <u>Political language: Words that succeed and policies that fail</u>, Academic Press, New York, 1977, p.40.

1154 See Jerry L. Yeric and John R. Todd, <u>Public opinion: The visible politics</u>, F. E. Peacock. Itasca, IL, 1989.

1155 See Patrick Champagne, 1990, « *Faire l'opinion* », In <u>*Le nouveau jeu politique*</u>, Minuit, Paris, 1990, pp. 87-124. Patrick Champagne believes that polls are actually part of the political game and that while researchers tend to analyse the outcome of these polls they themselves become integrated into this political establishment's manoeuvres.

1156 See Claude-Danièle Échaudemaison (Ed.), <u>*Dictionnaire d'économie et de sciences sociales.*</u>, Nathan. Paris, 1989. p.210.

school are advocates of the idea that public opinion is not simply the sum of individuals' opinions in a society. but, it is the sum of the opinions of social actors who have certain interest in supporting their plans or linking them to the people's opinion. An important pillar for the adepts of the critical theory school, in their disagreement with the advocates of the liberal activist school of thought, can be found in the article of Pierre Bourdieu "Public Opinion does not exist" (*L'opinion publique n'existe pas*)[1157]. Bourdieu is a supporter of the notion that polls are unable to reflect the thinking of the people for a number of reasons. He explains that the use of polls implies the use of leading questions that actually reflect the thinking of the political establishment. These leading questions result, because of the way they are constructed and posed, in desired answers and, thus, in a certain manipulation of public opinion. Furthermore, the same answer in a poll is always interpreted in a certain manner, although there might be different reasons for this answer, such as the individual's belonging to a political class or thought, the individual's ignorance of the subject being asked about, or the individual's fondness of this subject. This seems to be quite understandable as an argument of the critical theory school. Indeed, polls are not the sole and unique measurement of public opinion. The other means of measuring public opinion is that of social movements, lobbying or protests...etc. These popular manifestations, which are sometimes quite spontaneous, constitute an excellent rival to the use of polls in the measurement of public opinion.

Noam Chomsky's idea of the usage of public opinion by the political establishment seems somewhat close to that of the adepts of the critical theory. He distinguishes between two types of democratic societies and two resulting types of public opinion meanings and uses. According to Chomsky, the first type of democratic conceptions is that, where the public participate in an effective way in the running of their own affairs and where "the means of information are open and free"[1158]. The other conception of democracy, according to Chomsky, is that where the public "must be barred from managing their own affairs and the means of information must be kept narrowly and rigidly controlled"[1159]. Thus, it seems that the relationship between public opinion and the political establishment is a two fold one depending on the conception of democracy used. In one there is active and real participation of the public in the making of their own destiny because its objectively well informed about the issues, while in the other it is simply mislead

---

1157 See Pierre Bourdieu, « L'opinion publique n'existe pas », <u>*Les Temps Modernes,*</u> N°*318*, 1973, pp. 1292-1309.

1158 See Noam Chomsky, Media Control: The Spectacular Achievement of Propaganda, <u>op. cit</u>, pp. 9-10.

1159 Idem.

and used by the political establishment because it is kept in ignorance or because the information provided to this public is selected and diffused to result in a desired effect serving the interests of the leading political elite.

Yet, the question is how can a democratic society accommodate two so distinct conceptions at the same time. The answer to this question maybe found in what some researchers label as the "doublethink" and "doubletalk" behaviours of politicians. Anne-Marie Gingras and Jean-Pierre Carrier explain, in this respect, that "doublethink" is "holding two contradictory opinions simultaneously, being aware of it, and believing in both"[1160]. For his part, George Orwell's idea of "doublethink" is that it's the belief in two contradictory things at the same time. He explains "To know and not to know, to be conscious of complete truthfulness while telling carefully constructed lies, to hold simultaneously two opinions which cancelled out, knowing to be contradictory and believing in both of them…to believe that democracy was impossible and that the Party was the guardian of democracy"[1161]. Hence, people, according to Orwell, can hold two completely distinct views about an issue. This is maybe why rational political thought accompanies emotions. Furthermore, this cognitive process (doublethink) is quite common amongst politicians. Daniel Green, for instance, explains that such a cognitive process is quite common in free democratic societies such as the United States of America[1162]. In political sociology, therefore, the psychological process according to which a politician can be having two different and distinct thoughts about an issue does exist, especially in democratic societies. Indeed, It is logical to assume that such a cognitive process does exist, since the politician would be joining two his rational thinking to his human emotions. Usually, however, it is the rationale that takes the upper hand.

Supposing the existence of double thinking suggests the existence of another cognitive behaviour that is simply called "doubletalk". Anne-Marie Gingras and Jean-Pierre Carrier explain that at the opposite of doublethink, doubletalk is not a cognitive process but a process referring to contradictions and ambiguities in political discourse. Thus, doubletalk is intentional and not unconscious such as doublethink[1163]. Other researchers have a different name for doubletalk. Kathleen Jamieson, for instance, calls it "double-message"[1164]. Others, such as David

---

1160 See Anne-Marie Gingras and Jean-Pierre Carrier, op. cit.

1161 See George Orwell, Nineteen eighty four (critical introduction and annotation by Bernard Crick), Clarendon Press, Oxford, 1950, p. 186.

1162 See Daniel Green, Shaping political consciousness: The language of politics in America from McKinley to Reagan, Cornell University Press, Ithaca, 1987.

1163 See Anne-Marie Gingras and Jean-Pierre Carrier, op. cit.

1164 See Kathleen Jamieson, Dirty politics: Deception, distraction and democracy, Oxford University Press, New York, 1992.

Kertzer, refer to it as the "joining of opposites"[1165]. Hence, it is common, for political purposes, to use doubletalk as a means of reaching objectives. In fact, such a behaviour is part of the political persuasion techniques and is often used to delude public opinion and direct it. In this respect, Kathleen Jamieson explains, "Masters of persuasion use dual codes either to mystify one audience while seducing another or to convey meanings that for varying reasons could not be made explicit"[1166]. This view is also shared by Murray Edelman who explains the importance of political discourse in maintaining public support saying, "Political language can win or maintain public support or acquiescence in the face of other actions that violate moral qualms and typically does so by denying the premises on which such actions are based while retaining traces of the premises"[1167]. It is, thus, common to use such doubletalk to persuade the public of a certain action or a certain position of the political establishment especially in democratic societies.

Indeed, it is important to win public support for the political decision or action in democratic societies because doing so would give the impression that the essence of democracy itself is being respected. The idea is that since, in democracies, public opinion is the representation of the voice of the people in their own democracy, winning public opinion would provide more legitimacy for the political establishment. In this respect, Jean Padioleau explains that since the people are supposed to be the ultimate and supreme authority within a democratic society, public opinion is a "fundamental belief in the symbolic universe of liberal societies"[1168]. This is quite understandable as a proof of the importance of supportive public opinion in democratic societies and systems of government, since the ideal of democracy suggests that nothing could be done without the will of the majority. Thus, proving that the majority opinion is supportive of the political establishment's positions and policies would certainly increase the legitimacy of the policies and positions of such an establishment. It would, furthermore, give momentum and justifications to political decisions and actions.

This idea of mobilizing public opinion to support the political establishment's projects is well explained by Noam Chomsky. He gives the example of the mobilization of the United State's population and its transformation from a pacifist to

---

1165 See David I. Kertzer, Ritual, politics and power, Yale University Press. New Haven, 1988, pp. 69-70.

1166 See Kathleen Jamieson, op. cit, p. 84.

1167 See Murray Edelman, Constructing the political spectacle, University of Chicago Press, Chicago, 1988, pp. 115-116.

1168 See Jean Padioleau, « De l'opinion publique à la communication politique ». In Jean Padioleau (Ed.), L'opinion publique: examen critique, nouvelles directions, (pp. 13-60), Paris: Mouton,1980, p.27.

a pro-war one in t World War I during the presidency of Woodrow Wilson. Noam Chomsky states, "Woodrow Wilson was elected President in 1916 on the platform "Peace Without Victory". That was right in the middle of World War I. The population was extremely pacifistic and saw no reason to become involved in a European war. The Wilson administration was actually committed to war and had to do something about it. They established a government propaganda commission, called the Creel Commission, which succeeded, within six months, in turning a pacifist population into a hysterical, war-mongering population which wanted to destroy everything German, tear the Germans limb from limb, go to war and save the world"[1169]. The criticism which, however, can be made to Noam Chomsky's aforementioned statement about mobilising supportive public opinion for the political establishment's projects and actions is the fact that it is more focused on the effect of a clear-cut organized propaganda campaign in affecting public opinion and not on the effect that the media can have in similar situations. Indeed, propaganda campaigns have their deficiencies, especially nowadays. For since it is considered to be too direct and coming straight from regime, it can be simply pre-perceived as being misleading and, consequently, be rejected by the public which, is almost always and in under all forms of political regimes, suspicious of direct governmental propaganda campaigns. Furthermore, direct propaganda would particularly be less effective nowadays due to the innovations in communication technologies which simply means that people can always turn to other outlets of information anytime and are no longer obliged to solely receive what the political regime in their countries diffuses.

To gain legitimacy for its policies, the political establishment often resorts to an effective strategy. If the public perceives the political establishment's interests as being its own, then it would naturally be supportive of these interests and, consequently, the political establishment would draw on this supportive public opinion as a source of legitimacy. In this respect, Anne-Marie Gingras and Jean-Pierre Carrier explain that there is a kind of hierarchy or hegemony of ideas leading or controlling public opinion. They state, "Dominant social actors try to *create public opinion* that is favourable to their economic interests, thus associating domination with a leadership of ideas. These social actors use very specific strategies: they promote their special interests by presenting them as public interest and as the ideal way to solve public policy problems"[1170]. Thus, public opinion seems to fall under the hegemony of certain elite social actors. Promoting these social actors' interests would be more effective if such interests are also being supported by a wide public opinion. This is why some researchers think of public opinion as a

---

1169   See Noam Chomsky, Media Control, op. cit., pp.11-12.
1170   See Anne-Marie Gingras and Jean-Pierre Carrier, op. cit.

tool and not as a reflection of public thoughts and wishes. Murray Edelman, for instance, explains that public opinion "refers to a method of influencing popular demands, not necessarily of reflecting them"[1171]. The idea, however, that people would be more supportive of something if they had the impression that it's the opinion of the majority is not new. It is known as the "bandwagon effect". The study of alliance behaviour on the level of states reveals that a "bandwagon" behaviour can eb said to have taken place when a group of weak countries decide that it is in their best interest to ally to a powerful state. The other alliance behaviour on the state level takes place when the group of small and weak countries decide to form an alliance amongst themselves to balance that of the powerful state[1172]. What takes place on the individual level and as far as public opinion formation is concerned, if, indeed, the logic of state alliances is to be applied, is a bandwagon behaviour. The idea is that people would usually rally behind what they perceive as being the strongest to protect their interests. Thus, believing that a political policy or position is supported by the majority would bring more support to these policies and positions. Some researchers prefer to label this opinion hegemony of social actors on public opinion as the "elite opinion". Noam Chomsky is one of those. He argues that in the second perception of democratic societies or what he calls the "spectator democracy", the elite would be those imposing their opinion on the wider public and those presenting this opinion as the best to serve the general interest. By presenting this opinion as the general interest, the elite can then elude or control public opinion entirely and, thus, gain more legitimacy in its actions[1173]. Other writers such as Stuart Hall prefer to use the term "primary definers" to describe those public opinion leading elites or hegemonic social actors. For him, primary definers are those social actors who would define the events, and then impose their opinion concerning these events when its time for the public to debate and make its opinion on such events. For him such social actors are normally those who are governing or who are having an economic interest, and are usually part of the elite circles[1174]. The basic idea here seems to be that, in order to legitimise the interests of the elite (political, economic, social elite…etc.), these interests should be presented as the interests of the greater all and certainly as not the interests of an elite. In order to present

---

1171   Murray Eldman, Political language, op. cit., p.55.
1172   James E., Doughert and Robert L. Pfaltzgraff, Jr., Contending Theories of International Relations, Longman,Newyork, 1996.,p.402.
1173   See Noam Chomsky, Media Control, op. cit., pp. 14-15.
1174   See Stuart Hall et all., Policing the crisis: Mugging, the state, and law and order, Macmillan, London, 1978.p.59.

these interests and, consequently, promote them, there must be some sort of hegemony or leading opinion that can direct or lead the rest of public opinion.

During an international crisis, the political establishment can be said to be more in need of a supportive public opinion, whether this political establishment opts for action or inaction vis-à-vis this crisis or conflict. Here, the need for hegemonic social actors to lead the public opinion in the direction the political establishment wants is quite crucial. As far as taking action is concerned, it is important for the political establishment to convince the public that the interests of everyone are in jeopardy. In this respect, Noam Chomsky explains," it is also necessary to whip up the population in support of foreign adventures. Usually, the population is pacifist just like they were during the First World War. The public sees no reason to get involved in foreign adventures, killing and torture. So you have to whip them up. And to whip them up, you have to frighten them"[1175]. This statement is quite logical since it explains the mobilizing role of fear and its impact on public opinion. Indeed, fear can be said a very effective motivation tool for action. People have natural fears, like fears for their life or their economic situation and if they perceive that these are threatened they would be supportive of an action or an intervention in an international crisis. In fact, examining various international conflicts and crisis would reveal that the use of fear as a mobilizing factor for intervention is much more effective than the use of humanitarian concerns as a mobilizing factor. Similarly, if the political establishment sees no interest in acting vis-à-vis an international crisis, then the hegemonic opinion actors would suggest to the public that not intervening is in the better interest of the greater public. Generally and to eliminate the existence of the perception of a problem in the mind of the public, the international crisis would not be focused upon. If it is, then it would be presented as somebody else's problem and in a manner that would suggest that taking an action would harm the general interest.

The political establishment can, hence, use public opinion as sort of a legitimising means for its policies and actions. The best method to do this is not by direct propaganda, since the public can be doubtful and, hence, reject aggressive and direct propaganda campaigns, and since much more outlets other than those of the government can be sued to get different information. To obtain consent and legitimacy from the public, interests and projects have to be presented as those primarily bearing interest to the public itself. They have to be presented, furthermore, as being those of the greater public and not of an elite. When people believe that the policy is what they want it to be then they would be more supportive of this policy and the political establishment can have the necessary

---

1175 See Noam Chomsky, op. cit., p. 30.

legitimacy for the pursuit of its projects. To influence public opinion and obtain this legitimacy, elite opinion or opinion definers play a central role. They do that in leading public opinion and imposing their own opinion in a manner that would make it be adopted by the wider public, which, consequently, would provide legitimacy for their actions. During an international crisis, this issue of securing supportive public opinion for the political establishment's action or inaction becomes more urgent. Fear is usually used to mobilize public opinion in support of an involvement in a crisis by convincing the public that its basic interests are at risk. On the other hand, ignoring the crisis or presenting inaction as the best means of maintaining the greater public interest can be used if the political establishment needs to legitimise its inaction vis-à-vis the international crisis or conflict at hand.

3.2.2. The Dependence of Public Opinion on Media Coverage

It is natural to assume that for people to form their own opinion on a particular issue, they have to be amply informed on that issue. Indeed, the need to be informed is inherent to human behaviour. In the current age of speed, being informed faster, more comprehensively and more precisely about daily issues is a must in order to be able to conduct day to day life, take the necessary decisions, and form opinions.

This need to be informed seems to become much higher at the time of an international crisis. It would be even much more higher when the country, where the coverage of the crisis is performed is linked somehow to the proceedings or outcome of such a crisis due to its national interests. It should be always remembered that, globally, public opinion could be understood as being the opinion of a group of individuals, which together form this public. The basic level of reaction to the crisis then is that of the individual.

As mentioned in the previous section, fear seems to be key element of the individual's reaction here. It can be fear for property, life, social disorder...etc. It is, thus, this fear that would make this individual seek more knowledge about the crisis that he or she is facing in order to be better prepared for any outcome and at all times. Indeed, it is this constant fear that creates a constant dependency on the news information all along the proceedings of this international crisis or conflict. In this respect, the need to be informed seems to go in parallel with the actual proceedings of the international crisis in the sense that the degree of the need to be informed corresponds to the degree of intensification of the crisis or conflict itself. If this crisis is still at its beginnings, then the level of individual fear is still low and the dependence on the media coverage of this international crisis can be said to be still at a low level. On the other hand, if the crisis is at its climax, then the level of individual fear can be said to become higher, consequently, creating a higher degree of dependency on the media coverage of this crisis. Thus, as far as the coverage of an international crisis is concerned, it can be said that this urge to be informed or the natural curiosity of human beings due to fear for one's survival or property, can be justly considered as a form of dependence on this international crisis coverage. For the public, the more information acquired, the more accurate and just the opinion would be and the more their own sense of fear is confused.

This, however, is the case when there is no other factors such as religious, national, or social affinities involved and which can limit this dependence on the coverage and even reject the information transmitted by the media is labelling it, sometimes, as being subjective, especially if this coverage contradicts with the inherent collective affinities of the public with one party or another in this international crisis or conflict. Other individual elements can also affect the degree of the dependence of the public on the media coverage of an international crisis such as the different individual nature of each member of the public such as the difference in intelligence, personality, interests, and the degree of reliance on personal efforts to acquire information ed such as one's own research on the issue, for instance.

During an international crisis, the media's most important desire would be to be more competitive than the other media covering this crisis. In order to do so, it has to first create the interest, within the public, and then to keep that public tuned in for more information by giving the impression that its news coverage is more accurate and objective than other media. In this respect, Lise Garon explains, "The media must reconstruct reality in ways which will allow them to survive and become influential among the social actors. This process may imply considerable distortions of reality and variable dosages of subjectivity and objectivity. In extreme cases, such as wartime, objectivity may still be present but reduced to a ritual ornament of media discourse, at the expense of the informative function. In fact, capturing the public eye belongs to a more general category that has little to do with objectivity: influence. In order to capture the public eye, each medium may try to convince the audience that its programs are the most entertaining, that it always tells the whole truth, that its editorial standpoint always provides new and deep insights into actuality, that it is useful and even essential to society, and so on. In order to reproduce such an image efficiently, the media do not have to be objective but they do have to look so. The media's power is essentially nothing but influence over its public (in the sense of persuading it to tune in)"[1176]. Maxwell McCombs explains, in this respect, that the public

---

1176 See Lise Garon, "A Case Study in Functional Subjectivity in Media Coverage, The Gulf War on TV", <u>op. cit.</u>

agenda, for instance, is always formed of those things that are presented as a problem. He states, "The public agenda-the focus of the public mind-is commonly assessed by public opinion polls that ask some variation of the long-standing Gallup poll question "what is the most important problem facing this country today?"[1177]. For his part, Noam Chomsky comments on the media's ability to create the interest of the public and elude it. He distinguishes between a minority of few intellectuals who are to lead the society and the rest of the population, which he caught Walter Lippmann in calling them the "bewildered herd". Chomsky states, "The rest of the bewildered herd basically just have to be distracted. Turn their attention to something else. Keep them out of trouble. Make sure that they remain at most spectators of action, occasionally lending their weight to one or another of the real leaders"[1178]. He goes on to say that such a strategy has long been instilled in what he termed as "spectator democracies"[1179] Chomsky continues to insist, "The this point of view has been developed by lots of other people. In fact, it's pretty conventional. For example, the leading theologian and foreign policy critic Reinhold Niebuhr, sometimes called "the theologian of the establishment", the guru of George Kennan and the Kennedy intellectuals, put it that rationality is a very narrowly restricted skill. Only a small number of people have it. Most people are guided by just emotion and impulse. Those of us who have rationality have to create "the necessary illusions" and emotionally potent "oversimplifications" to keep the naïve simpletons more or less on course"[1180]. The idea is that there are a few people who are supposed to direct the majority for this majority's own good because this majority is two ignorant to know what is good for it and what is not. In order to do this, this majority has to be first interested in the event they are being informed about and their attention on the diffused information or (pictures of their world) should be constantly maintained. Maintaining this majority's interest can simply be done through presenting the outcome of this event they are told about as something that is very much related to their daily life or to what Chomsky calls "the public good". A criticism that can be made to Chomsky's ideas, however, is that he supposes the existence of a propaganda machine in democracies which has a similar function

---

1177 See Maxwell McCombs, "The Agenda-Setting Role of the Mass media in the Shaping of the Public Opinion", op.cit.,p.2.

1178 See Noam Chomsky, Media Control, op. cit., p.19.

1179 For Chomsky, there are two types of democracies. The first one is one where the people have actually the means and the power to govern their own destiny and the second which he calls the "spectator democracy" is one in which they are only allowed to be spectators of action and eluded by the governing minority.

1180 See Noam Chomsky, Media Control, op. cit., pp19-20.

to that of a totalitarian regime and which directs the media. Chomsky himself emphasizes the similarities between the two systems of government. He continues, "The logic is clear. Propaganda is to a democracy what the bludgeon is to a totalitarian state. That's wise and good because, again, the common interests elude the bewildered herd. They can't figure them out"[1181]. This view, of course, can be contended. Other researches, for instance, suggest that the media too can have its own functioning propaganda machine essentially for capturing more audiences. Lise Garon, in this respect, argues, "There is no doubt, of course, that war propaganda can control information efficiently and the recent advances in satellite technology may have caught the media organizationally unprepared to face an unprecedented competitive situation. However, are the media totally innocent? A complementary hypothesis to these two explanations will be proposed as an answer: all actors, and not only the state, create their own legitimising ideology and their own seductive propaganda. War propaganda, for instance, is well known as a form of communication that deforms reality to entice, frighten, or persuade. Similarly, should we not consider the media as actors (not only witnesses) of the public sphere who generate their own propaganda (functional subjectivity) through the news stories they produce about the war while they seek to camouflage the shortcomings in information in order to attract or maintain their audience?[1182]. This appears to be a more logical supposition. For if the purpose of propaganda is to focus attention on a specific idea or notion in order to mobilize, the media can also use its own strategies to attract and maintain the attention of the public for various reasons that are mostly economic benefit related ones. Thus, presenting the crisis in an emotional and sensational way would make the public more attracted to it since most people are easily manipulated by playing on their emotions. Emotional mobilization, for instance, has been noted in *The New York Times* and *Le Monde*'s coverage of the tragic events of the Bosnia crisis.

Other researchers, however, argue that there are two types of manipulations the media can do to form, shape, and maintain audiences and opinions. Jürgen Habermas, for instance, argues in his theory that the mass media is controlled by economic and political forces that have an interest in manipulating the public. The manipulation is twofold in this theory. The political manipulation is something like directing opinions and public relations work. In this kind of manipulation, the media not only transmits the debates but also help create and mould them. On the other hand, economic manipulation uses the designed psychological methods of advertisement. It does so by selecting and identifying the themes and subjects that the audiences are predisposed to accept and interact with

---

1181 Ibid. pp 20-21.
1182 See Lise Garon, op. cit.

more.[1183] This view of economic controls conditioning media coverage is also supported by Charles Baker who explains that since most media outlets get most or all of their income from advertisement or sponsoring, the media has to satisfy those sources of income, which are not necessarily in line with the best interests of the audiences themselves or of their wishes[1184]. The media, therefore, has to create the interest for a public, in order for this public, to be following its supply of information. If not for political reasons, the interest can be created for purely financial ones. For instance, presenting an international crisis event in a sensational manner would result in more audiences and more ratings, which, consequently, would direct advertisers to the concerned media outlet because the audiences that are tuned to this media outlet are higher in number than those tuned to other media outlets who present les sensational crisis coverage to the audiences. For advertisers, more audiences mean more marketing for their products. For the media, more advertisers mean more financial profit.

A good example of this ability to create the interest and capture the public's attention during an international crisis is found in the study conducted by Shanto Iyengar and Adam Simon on the coverage of the Gulf Crisis (1990-1991) coverage and its impact on public opinion in the United States. According to them, 70% of the American public were following the news coverage of the crisis "very closely", while 80% stated that they stayed up" very late "to get the latest information on the events of the crisis[1185]. The benefits of the media were also substantial during the coverage of this crisis. For instance, according to Dominique Wolton, the ratings of the French networks TF1 and *Antenne 2* during the coverage of the Gulf Crisis (1990-1991) increased substantially, in January and February, altogether from 29% to an average of 33.8%, and occasionally with peaks reaching up to 40%[1186]. As for the ratings of the most privileged news coverage carrier in this crisis (CNN), the ratings were enormous. In this respect, Lance W. Bennett and David L. Paletz explain that the ratings of CNN increased ten times during the period of coverage from January the 15th

1183　See Anger Fog, "Mass Media and Democracy Crisis", <u>Online Publication.</u>
1184　See Charles Baker, <u>Advertising and a Democratic Press</u>, University Press, Princeton, 1994.
1185　See Shanto Iyengar and Adam Simon, "News coverage of the gulf crisis and public opinion: A study of agenda-setting, priming, and framing". In W. Lance Bennett & David L. Paletz (Eds.), <u>Taken by storm: The media, public opinion, and U.S. foreign policy in the Gulf War</u> (pp. 167-185). Chicago & London: University of Chicago Press, 1994, p. 167.
1186　See Dominique Wolton, <u>*War game/L'information et la guerre*</u>, Flammarion, Paris, 1991.

until the 21st of 1991[1187] only Thus, during an international crisis the media can increase its profits and market share by capturing and maintaining the attention of the audience and attracting even more audiences to its coverage.

Amongst all emotions used for creating interest in the coverage of an international crisis, fear seems to be the best one to use in order to capture the audiences' attention. The creation of fear can be explained better as a means of manipulation in society when it is explained against what is known as the sociology of deviance. Basically, what this means is that society would usually define certain things as dangerous and deviant for the society as a whole. The notion of dangerous and deviant can be accordingly constructed. Society can reject unwanted behaviour by labelling it as dangerous. Consequently, anyone with the power to define what is dangerous would have an enormous influence on the society as a whole and an ability to manipulate it[1188]. If fear is used as an element of mobilisation by the official war propaganda of states then, supposedly, it can be also used by the media's propaganda machine as well. Again fear appears to be the best means to attract the attention of the public and make it follow the international crisis coverage closely. Noam Chomsky, for instance, explains, "It is also necessary to whip up the population in support of foreign adventures. Usually, the population is pacifist, just like they were during the First World War. The public sees no reason to get involved in foreign adventures, killing and torturing. So you have to whip them up. And to whip them up you have to frighten them"[1189]. The notion of creating fear as an element of attracting interest and mobilizing the public is mentioned by Lise Garon, who comments on the coverage of the Gulf War (1990-1991) saying, "The theme of prisoners of war, for one, furthered allied military propaganda in trying to conquer public opinion: the spectacle of "evil Saddam" martyring "good Americans" could only create fear and loathing in the collective American imagination"[1190]. This is what Noam Chomsky calls selective perceptions. According to him it is basically the idea that the media would take a single information about an atrocity or a crime committed, for instance, and concentrate on it in a way that would make it the centre of the attention of the moment, while at the same time, other more serious atrocities are committed elsewhere and ignored[1191]. He also argues that the presentation of Saddam Hussein, at the time

---

1187 See Lance W. Bennett and David L. Paletz (Eds.), <u>Taken by storm: The media, public opinion, and U.S. foreign policy in the Gulf War,</u> University of Chicago Press, Chicago & London, 1994.

1188 See N. Ben-Yehuda, <u>The Politics and Morality of Deviance,</u> SUNY Press, Albany, 1990.

1189 See Noam Chomsky, Media Control, <u>op. cit.,</u> p. 106.

1190 See Lise Garon, <u>op. cit.</u>

1191 See Noam Chomsky, Media Control, <u>op. cit.,</u> pp 46-52.

as the evil monster that should be taken care of for the safety of all, is not much different than the official propaganda used in World War I. Noam Chomsky states, "This is not all that different from what the Creel Commission did when it turned a pacifistic population into raving hysterics who wanted to destroy everything German to save ourselves from Huns who were tearing the arms off Belgian babies. The techniques are maybe more sophisticated, with television and lots of money going into it, put its pretty traditional"[1192]. Another example of such selective perceptions can be seen in the media portrayal of the civilian hostages during the Gulf Crisis (1990-1991) also to harness the factor of fear in audiences. In this respect, Lise Garon explains, "As the coalition's civilians, they were usually seen to be furious with Saddam Hussein or worried about their friends or relatives on the front, crying out in horror over President Hussein's barbarity. Such a spectacle undoubtedly helped fan the flames of enmity between Iraq and the United States and thus projected a favourable image of the coalition actions to the public[1193]".This feeding of fear also results in another notion that further contributes to this dependence on international crisis coverage. It is the creation in a society of an atmosphere of war or what Noam Chomsky calls "martial rituals". It is an atmosphere that would incite the public to be more dependent on the news coverage because the whole environment in which this audience lives its marked by manifestations of this atmosphere. For instance, during the Gulf War coverage, Daniel C. Hallin and Todd. Gitlin noted the existence of what they called "the culture of war" in the United States. It is the idea that ordinary Americans found themselves participating in their everyday life in the war atmosphere with flags and slogans everywhere[1194]. Thus, the existence of this war culture also serves the media's purpose of having more audiences tuned to its news stories about the conflict or the crisis. The media, also, seems to be principal creator of this war or "regal" culture in society.

The dependence of public opinion on media coverage of an international crisis is an interesting phenomenon. It reveals the ability of the media to maintain an audience tuned to its coverage. Some writers suggest that the media applies the official war propaganda in its coverage of the crisis, while other suggests that the media has a propaganda machine of its own. This is more logical to assume. Since the media has also its own agenda. In many cases, however, the agendas of the

---

1192 Ibid. p.64.

1193 See Lise Garon, op. cit.

1194 Daniel C. Hallin and Todd. Gitlin, "The Gulf War as popular culture and television drama". In W. Lance Bennett & David L. Paletz (Eds.), Taken by storm: The media, public opinion, and U.S. foreign policy in the Gulf War, University of Chicago Press, Chicago & London, 1994, pp. 149-163,

media, the political, and the economic establishments would concord vis-à-vis an international crisis. In this case, the official war propaganda and the media's own propaganda machine would both be moulded, due to shared interests, in one and only propaganda machine.

To be competitive in the market, the media has to find an audience. It can do that by creating the interest and in presenting or framing this interest in a way that would preserve the audience and increase its number as well. The best means of creating an interest in the public is to play with the notion of fear. If this basic human emotion is harnessed effectively, it can translate into higher ratings due to increased need for information and news coverage of the international crisis or conflict.

3.2.3. Public Opinion's Orientations: Limitations, and Strengths of Media Influence

The media orientation ability of public opinion is certainly not an absolute and unviable reality. Though the media is extremely influential in forming, modelling, and directing public opinion. This ability of the media is, nonetheless, not without limitations. It is important, hence, to examine at this point the strengths and weaknesses of the media's influence on public opinion, as far as its coverage of an international crisis or conflict is concerned.

Media influence on public opinion is a well-established fact. The first factor adding to this ability of the media to influence the public has to do with one of one of the media's principal functions, namely its ability to select the information upon which the public sets his daily agenda of public affaires and, to a certain degree, even of private affaires relating to each individual in this public. In this respect, Maxwell McCombs elaborates, "The power of the news media to set a nation's agenda, to focus public attention on a few key public issues, is an immense and well-documented influence. Not only do people acquire factual information about public affairs from the news media, readers and viewers also learn how much importance to attach to a topic on the basis of the emphasis placed on it in the news"[1195]. The media can, according to this logic, be considered like a window through which the public is presented its daily public affaires agenda each time this window opens. Walter Lippmann explains, for his part, that the media gives us the chance to explore the larger public affairs world that is "out of reach, out of sight, out of mind"[1196].

1195 See Maxwell McCombs, "Agenda—Setting Role of the Mass Media in the Shaping of the Public Mind", op. cit., p.1.

1196 See Walter Lippmann, Public Opinion, op. cit, p.29. In particular the chapter entitled "The world Outside and the Pictures in Our Heads".

This is similar to the view of Agner Fog, who also emphasizes the manipulation that this sole window the public has on the world can cause. He argues, "The media excesses do more than this; they shape people's worldview. The intense focus on everything that is dangerous makes people believe that the world is more dangerous than it really is. And most of the time we are afraid of the wrong things. A bizarre and unusual sex crime can get full media coverage even if it takes place on the opposite side of the Earth, while other trivial, but much more relevant, dangers like traffic accidents, smoking, and unhealthy life style are considered much less newsworthy"[1197]. This is close to the view of Maxwell McCombs who states, "What we know about the world is largely based on what the media decide to tell us. More specifically, the result of this mediated view of the world is that the priorities of the media strongly influence the priorities of the public. Elements prominent on the media agenda become prominent in the public mind"[1198]. Niklas Luthmann, in this respect, advances a theory of social systems, which places communications as a fundamental process in any social system. According to his theory, communication is formed of a triple selection process in which there is selection of information by the sender, selective attention at the receiver's end, and the selected effect of the information received[1199]. The examples of the influence of mass media selectivity on the public mind are, indeed, well illustrated by Niklas Luthmann. He gives the examples of the Gulf War (1990-1991) and immigrant crimes as events demonstrating this media selectivity and its ability to influence the public mind. As for the selection criteria the mass media uses. He found that these are mostly surprising news, topicality, conflicts, quantitative data, local relevance, scandals, norm violations in relation to individual actors and moral judgments[1200]. One basic functional characteristic of the media is its ability to select the information presented to the public. The mere fact of being able to select the information presented means that the media has ability to decide what the daily agenda of the public mind is and, hence, gives the media an enormous importance within a society in deciding what is important to this society and what is not. There are, however, certain criteria for such a selection. In this respect, some researchers argue that such criteria are mainly shaped by sociological related factors such mainly what is called the risk sociology, and what is known as the sociology of deviance.

A number of researchers have already identified the importance held by risks, fears, and risk assessment reactions in a society and the impact of their inflation.

1197   See Agner Fog, Mass Media and Democracy Crisis, op. cit., p.2.
1198   Ibid., p.2.
1199   See Niklas Luhmann, _Soziale Systeme: Grundriss einer allgemeinen Theorie,_/M: Suhrkamp, Frankfurt, 1984,.
1200   See Niklas Luhmann, _The Reality of the Mass Media_, Polity Press, Cambridge: 2000.

The anthropologist Mary Douglas, for instance, in her work Parity and Danger, conducted studies on tribal communities and societies in which mass media does not exist. According to her, the issues or events that mostly disrupt and disturb more are those that actually disturb the habitual order of nature[1201]. Other researchers, for their part, have identified four types of an individual's reaction to perceived risks and dangers. According to Psychologist Karl Dake, for instance, these are the hierarchical, individualist, egalitarian, and fatalist. The reactions to risks vary according to the category. Hierarchical oriented individuals are usually more concerned with risks connected to crimes and social deviance behaviour in their society. The second category (individualists) is usually fearful of any economic related risk. On the other hand, egalitarians fear anything that could threaten the environment, which are mostly technological risks. As far as fatalists are concerned, it was shown that they do not give fear of risks and dangers much attention[1202]. Further studies in this field found that sometimes exaggeration of risks can be done deliberately. At least this was true for Mary Douglas and N. Wildavsky concerning environmental movements[1203]. Their study indicates that environment protection organisations sometimes invent fictive risks to consolidate their own organisations[1204]. If an event disturbs the natural order,or to put it more precisely the usual order of things, then this event would have more attention allocated to it because of this sociology of risk inherent to humans. Consequently, focusing on such risks would also attract the attention of people. The result is that the entity that points to such risks would enjoy high standing in any social system. Yet, this does not mean that danger or risk stories are the only types of information which can catch the attention of the public. Indeed, Some researchers argue that anything that is relative to the survival of a human being is bound to catch the attention of people but that, then again, it would only catch their attention because such topics are vital to them.

Agner Fog, for instance, argues, "Some of the most important survival factors for primeval man were food, danger, sex, and children. It is deeply ingrained in

---

1201 See Mary Douglas, Purity and Danger, Routledge, London,1966.

1202 See Karl Dake, "Orienting Dispositions in the Perception of Risk", Journal of Cross-Cultural Psychology, Vol. 22, pp. 61-82.

1203 See Mary Douglas and A. Wildavsky, Risk and Culture: An essay on the Selection of Technical and Environmental Dangers, University of California Press, California, 1982.

1204 See notably the work of B.B. Johnson, "The Environmentalist Movement and Grid/Group Analysis' in B.B. Johnson, & V.T. Covello (Eds.), The Social and Cultural Construction of Risk.
Dordrecht: D. Reidel, 1987, pp.147-175.

every human being that these topics catch our attention wherever we meet them. For example, it has always been of vital importance to collect knowledge about everything that is dangerous. Therefore, we listen attentively when the TV tells about disasters, and we always buy the newspaper when the front page tells about dangerous criminals"[1205]. In fact there exists a name to such topics, which, if selected by the media, would help catch more audiences and increase the ratings. These topics that catch the attention the most are called *buttons*. In this respect, B. Brodie explains that, in order for a news item to sell well, it has to push the right button[1206]. This effect of catching attention in pushing the right buttons, which attract people the most because in these topics people perceive danger or risk threatening the natural course of their daily life, may well be explained by the behavioural trait of human society.

This behavioural trait is what is known as the sociology of deviance. It is a discipline that suggests how the society defines certain norms or behaviours as being dangerous or deviant. According to reasoning, which is well represented well by the work of N. Ben-Yehuda[1207], the sociology of deviance suggests that the ones who have the ability to define dangers and risks in a society will, consequently, have a high status in the hierarchy of this society. Accordingly, pushing the danger button seems to have the most immense effects on the behaviour of a society. This is very similar to the view of Noam Chomsky, although in the context of a "propaganda model" controlling the media choices quoted earlier in a previous section of this part. He explains that" it is also necessary to whip up the population in support of foreign adventures. Usually, the population is pacifist just like they were during the First World War. The public sees no reason to get involved in foreign adventures, killing and torture. So you have to whip them up. And to whip them up, you have to frighten them[1208]". Agner Fog explains, for instance, that the pushing this danger button can have an immense reaction in a society and even cause what he termed as a "moral panic". He states, "When the danger button is pushed hard and persistently, the result may be a moral panic"[1209]. According to Fog, moral panic can be defined as the exaggeration of fear in a society[1210]. This is close to the cultural r/k theory of the transformation of societies from pacifist to regal or vice versa depending on the environment and perceived threat.

1205   See Agner Fog, "Mass Media and Democracy Crisis", op. cit., p.10.

1206   See R. Brodie, Virus of the mind: The new science of the meme, Integral press, Seattle, 1996.

1207   See N. Ben-Yhuda, The *Politics and Morality of Devianc*e, op. cit,

1208   See Noam Chomsky, Media Control, op. cit., p.30.

1209   See Agner Fog, "Mass Media and Democracy Crisis", op. cit., p.11.

1210   Ibid., p.4.

Some researchers explain his by the fact that such an ability to define danger in a society has been part of professions like those of priests, lawyers and psychiatrists, for instance, whose members have always had a special monopoly in defining what is deviant and what is in society. This notion is what P. Jenkins calls "the issue ownership"[1211]. Further studies have indicated that in today's societies various groups constantly compete to have this status of being able to define what is dangerous, risky, or what poses social problems to a society. This atmosphere of competition for setting the public's agenda of social concerns is what J. Best, for instance, calls "social problems' marketplace[1212]. Being one of the most influential social actors, the media is one of the most influential members of such a group of competitors. In this respect, Agner Fog explains, "There is an unusually fierce competition between sources when it comes to informing about risks. Various interest groups, politicians and experts seek to promote each their agenda on which dangers to fear. The media inevitably play a key role in this conflict because their choice of sources influences the definition and framing of risks. The politicians have to take a stance to whatever problem the media place high on the agenda. This is a fundamental democratic problem. The media's decision on who is allowed to define a risk problem, or whether the risk is mentioned at all, is not controlled in a democratic way"[1213]. This is certainly not an unusual assumption since the media has many advantages to its benefit. It has the advantages, for example, of having the broadest diffusion platform through its various outlets whether printed, electronic or audio-visual amongst other "risk pointers and definers" in human society.

If the definition of social risks and dangers is a market of competition, in which different social actors compete for a higher status, then the competition in this market must have profit as an objective for such competitors or otherwise there would be no point in competing. Some researchers argue that the bases of selection of these dangers and risks and the process, of inflating them disproportionably sometimes, is caused by a competition for more financial profit. Noam Chomsky explains, for example, that the media's choices are limited by the realities of the market in which media companies and enterprises exist. He argues, "Larger media outlets" have "some crucial features in common. First of all, the Agenda-Setting institutions are big corporations; in fact, they're mega corporations, which are highly profitable and for the most part they're even linked into bigger conglomerates. And they, like other corporations, have a product to sell

1211 See P. Jenkins, Intimate Enemies: Moral panics in contemporary Great Britain, Aldine de Gruytes, New York, 1992.

1212 See J. Best, <u>Threatened Children</u>, University of Chicago Press, Chicago, 1990.

1213 See Agner Fog, "Mass Media and Deomcracy Crisis", <u>op. cit.</u>, p. 8.

and a market that they want to sell it to; the product is audiences and the market is advertisers. So the economic structure of a newspaper is that it sells readers to other businesses"[1214]. For his part, Agner Fog also explains that market values dominate the selection mechanism in the media. He insists, "The most evident selection criterion is, of course, that the newspapers need a new sensation on the front page every day to boost their sales, and preferably something with sex and violence"[1215]. He adds, "The relentless economic competition forces the media to concentrate on those topics that immediately catch our attention and make us buy today's newspaper or stay tuned on the TV channel through the commercial breaks. Serious quality media that do not mesmerize their audience with psychological means get fewer customers and thus less revenue from advertisements. The reduced income forces them to cut down the journalist staff whereby the quality is reduced and more readers or viewers fall away. This vicious circle continues until the medium goes bankrupt or changes its policy"[1216]. Thus this selection mechanism is very much subjected to the economic realities in which the media as a market player exists. Accordingly, it is more beneficial for the media to select the news items that would allow them to have higher ratings because otherwise they would simply drop out of business. This is the view of the media as business entities that have economic interests such as benefit production for their owners or shareholders, and even salaries for their employees. This could, in a certain way, soften the harshness of any moral criticisms over the media news items' selection mechanism. Furthermore, it can also be said, that if the media adopts such a mechanism of news selection, then it is simply because the selection criteria is already established by inherent human behaviour and psychology. Hence, the media can be said to be only giving the public what this public psychologically and subconsciously already reclaims.

Nonetheless, this selection ability of the media is not enough on its own to explain the media's enormous ability to affect public opinion and tendencies. Indeed, after selection, comes the process of presentation. In fact, it is even more important that this selected news item be presented in an attractive manner as well to the audiences in order to produce the desired effect. In this context, framing ass explained in the first part of this book, is one of the key elements of the presentation ability of the media. Agner Fig explains, in this respect, the need to place an attractive frame on the message being diffused by the media. He states," The psychological appeal in the media lies not only in the choice of topics but also in the way they are framed. A message is more appealing when it is focused

---

1214 See Noam Chomsky, <u>Understanding Power</u>, The New Press, New York, 2002, p.14.
1215 See Agner Fog, <u>op. cit.</u>, p. 1.
1216 Ibid., p.10.

on a real person that people can identify with. Therefore, the media prefer to give a story a personal angle rather than discussing abstract principles. Thus, political debates are often presented as personal conflicts between politicians rather than as discussions about ideologies. The personality, private life, and media appeal of a politician thus becomes more important than his ideological stance".[1217] Such a personalisation framing was found, as indicated in the previous case study part, in the coverage of *Le Monde* and *The New York Times* of the Chechnya conflict where the conflict itself was mostly reduced to a personal dispute between Boris Yeltsin and General Doudaev. Such a technique was also particularly true in the coverage of the Gulf War crisis (1990-1991) where the conflict was personalized in "Bush" versus" Saddam". For his part, Noam Chomsky explains hat this is part a larger framework influence imposed by higher and stronger bodies in the hierarchy, particularly as far as the American media is concerned. He states, "There are various layers and components to the American media-the National Enquirer that you pick up in the supermarket is not the same as the Washington Post, for example. But if you want to talk about presentation of news and information, the basic structure is that these are what are sometimes called "agenda-setting" media: there are a number of major media outlets that end up setting a basic framework that other smaller media units more or less have to adapt to. The larger media have the essential resources and other smaller media scattered country pretty much have to take the framework, which the major outlets present and adapt to it-because if the newspaper in Pittsburgh or Slat Lake City want to know about Angola, say, very few of them are going to be able to send their own correspondents and have their own analysts and so on"[1218]. The media, thus, and in addition to selecting the news items has to frame them in a way that would also be attractive to the audiences which is liable to attract and, consequently, maintain their attention. Framing can, hence, be compared to packaging of products (news items). The media in such a process chooses the right frame to associate to the news item. This of course is done with sufficient knowledge and understanding of the effect of each frame on the public mind. And although there is controversy over an agreed definition of such frames, the main idea is that they are a window or an attractive packaging through which the public is presented the desired view to adopt[1219]. These frames have been discussed in the first part of this book.

1217 See Agner Fog, op. cit., p.11.

1218 See Noam Chomsky, Understanding Power, op. cit., p.14.

1219 See the section entitled "National Political Tendencies and Media Manifestations" in part one of this work. The identified frames in this section are the Conflict Frame, the Human Interest Frame, the Economic Consequences Frame, the Morality Frame and the Responsibility Frame.

With this authority to select, the ability to appropriately frame, and the advantage of broad diffusion, the media is endowed with a considerable influence in orienting the public mind. In this respect, Maxwell McCombs states, "The agenda-setting influence of the news media is not limited to this initial step of focusing public attention on a particular topic. The media also influence the next step in the communication process, our understanding and perspective on the topics in the news"[1220]. Other researchers argue that public opinion can be associated with ideological hegemony because of its importance to influential social actors. Anne-Marie Gingras and Jean-Pierre Carrie explain, in this respect, "Public opinion is even associated with ideological hegemony, an expression coined by Antonio Gramsci meaning "the supremacy a given social group obtained by virtue of its ability to be both 'dominant' and "leading". Hegemony implies that persuasion plays a major role in the governance of a society, founded on the consent of groups that are subjectively constituted"[1221]. It should be noted here that this idea of ideological hegemony is quite similar to Noam Chomsky's notion of elite public opinion where the enlightened few impose their opinion and disseminate it through the various media outlets to the majority[1222]. At first look, it would seem, hence, that there is no limit to the media's influence in its orientation ability of public opinion.

Yet, there are, in fact, limitations on this influence of the media on public opinion. Indeed, the idea, which is central to this assumption is that not all individuals in a society think the same and not all rely on the media to the same degree in order to form their opinions about public issues. In fact, the need for orientation varies from one individual to another and depends on the intellectual abilities of this individual and on the relevance of the subject presented by the media to that individual. In this respect, Maxwell McCombs argues, "Although the influence of the media agenda can be substantial, it alone does not determine the public agenda. Information and cues about object and attribute salience provided by the news media are far from the only determinants of the public agenda. This substantial influence of the news media has no way overturned or nullified the basic assumption of democracy that the people at large have sufficient wisdom to determine the course of their nation, their state, and their local communities. In particular, the people are quite able to determine the basic relevance—to themselves and

---

1220 See Maxwell McCombs, the Agenda-Setting Role of the Mass Media in the Shaping of Public Opinion, op. cit., p.5.

1221 See Anne-Marie Gingras and Jean-Pierre," Public Opinion: Construction and Persuasion", op. cit.

1222 See Noam Chomsky, Understanding Power, Op. Cit., in particular the chapter entitled "the Media and Elite Opinion" pp. 18-24.

to the larger public arena—of the topics and attributes advanced by the news media. The media set the agenda only when citizens perceive their news stories as relevant"[1223]. This relevance depends, first of all, on each individual. Maxwell McCombs continues to say, "Because it is a psychological trait, the degree of need for orientation varies greatly from one individual to another. For some individuals in any situation, there is a high need for orientation. For other individuals, there is little or no need for orientation at all. They just aren't interested. Need for orientation is defined by two components: relevance and uncertainty. Relevance is the initial defining condition that determines the level of need for orientation for each individual. If a topic is perceived as irrelevant—or very low in relevance—then the need for orientation is low. Individuals in this situation pay little or no attention to news media reports and, at most, demonstrate weak agenda-setting effects. For individuals among whom the relevance of a topic is high, their degree of uncertainty about the topic determines the level of need for orientation. If this uncertainty is low, that is, they feel that they basically understand the topic, then the need for orientation is moderate"[1224]. Thus, the need for orientation varies from one person to another because it is basically a psychological trait and because it depends on elements such as the individual's intellectual capacity, the individual's own need for orientation, and his own perception of the issue presented in the media.

The media has an influential ability to influence the public mind. This ability is stems from three basic media functional characteristics: its ability to select, to frame, and to diffuse the information to the public. Human behaviour studies and sociological analysis suggests that humans react more to issues that disturb their natural and usual course of life. Danger and risk seem to be the most useful buttons the media can push for more audiences. Sometimes exaggeration of fear or a "moral panic" instigator can be used to capture the audiences attention and increase the number of these audiences. The social actor that has the ability to determine what is deviant or not in a society would also have a high status in the hierarchy of the social system. The selection mechanism of information and news seems to follow the lead of the market and seems to respond to economic realities, such as competition to attract more audiences. The media's ability to present those selected news items and information in an attractive package can further influence public opinion. The presentation itself can be also called the framing of the news items and information. Framing is the window through which the public would see the set for it by the media. Framing as well follows market realities and demands. In this sense, it can be looked upon as attractive packaging for selling

---

1223 See Maxwell McCombs, the Agenda-Setting Role of the Mass Media in the Shaping of Public Opinion, op. cit., p. 8.
1224 Ibid., p.9.

news items. Some researchers suggest that there exists sort of an ideological hegemony where a few elite would impose their opinion on the greater majority and
help diffuse this opinion. Others suggest that there are limits to the influence of
the media on public opinion. They attribute these limitations to the fact that individuals are different in their need for orientation, in their dependence on the
media for orientation purposes, and in their perceived relevance of the issue presented to them by the media.

3.3. The Crisis of Objectivity

The media can be said to be passing through what amounts to a crisis of objectivity. It is, indeed, often accused of not being objective in its coverage and, thus,
of not fulfilling one of its basic ethical functions. At this point of the research,
moreover, it would seem appropriate to focus on the notions and factors that
indicate the existence of such a crisis and whether the media is the only one to be
blamed for such accusations of lack of objectivity in its coverage.

The first notion that would probably lend credibility to this crisis of objectivity
is the mere fact that the media has its own agenda. The word issue itself is interesting to explain. According to James Dearing W. and Everett M Rogers an agenda is
"a set of issues that are communicated in a hierarchy of importance at a point in
time"[1225]. Logically, when there is an agenda of issues, then there are mechanisms
set to achieve the desired objectives. It is, indeed, the mere fact of having objectives
that renders the notion of media objectivity quite obsolete. The placing and priority of placement of an issue on an agenda is alone a result of a conflict of interests.
Andrew O. Baolli explains, in this respect, that an issue is "a conflict between two
or more identifiable groups over procedural or substantive matters relating to the
distribution of positions or resources"[1226]. To take the analysis to a basic human
level, it can be said that when someone has his or her own agenda and objectives
then this person cannot be expected to be objective. Indeed, the mere existence of
such an agenda would negate the notion of objectivity.

References to the existence of this media agenda are many. Maxwell McCombs
and Daniel Shaw, for instance, conducted one of the first studies on the agenda-
setting function of the mass media. Their study reveals the degree of influence

---

1225 See James Dearing W. and Everett M Rogers, Agenda-Setting, Sage Publications
      Inc., Thousand Oaks, CA., 1996.
1226 See Andrew O. Baolli, The Effect of Ownership Structure on the Media Agenda",
      Online document found at http://www.funferal.org/essay/polecon.htm

and the existence of such an agenda-setting function, especially prior to elections. According to the findings of their study, voters in Chapel Hill (North Carolina) were asked to identify the most important issues that preoccupy them. Their responses revealed that they echoed the pattern of the news coverage they were exposed to through various media outlets one-month prior to obtaining the answers posed in their study[1227]. Others such as Noam Chomsky argue that only major media companies have the ability to be set and agenda, which he calls the "agenda-setting media". These are "major media outlets that end up setting a basic framework that other smaller units more or less have to adapt to"[1228]. Research on agenda-setting has also been conducted in Germany on the re-unification issue and its persuasion effects[1229]. Moreover, Agenda-Setting was also proven to exist on the community level in Japan, for instance[1230], as well as in larger communities, such as the legislative elections in (Buenos Aires) Argentina in 1997[1231]. Agenda-setting is, thus, not a monopoly of the major mass media outlets. It can also occur at a very narrow local level. Furthermore, the issues that this agenda-setting have vary from a city's local problems[1232] to general elections issues[1233], to its effects during an international crisis[1234], and more broadly to the media agenda-setting relation to the theory of communication as a whole[1235]. Thus, the existence of a media agenda and a media ability to set an agenda is a

---

1227 See Maxwell McCombs and Donald Shaw, "The agenda-setting function of mass media", <u>Public Opinion Quarterly</u>, vol.36, 1972, pp.176-187.

1228 See Noam Chomsky, Understanding Power, <u>op.cit.</u>, p.14.

1229 See Patrick Rossler and Michael Schenk, "Cognitive bonding and the German reunification: Agenda-setting and persuasion effects of mass media", <u>International Journal of Public Opinion Research</u>, vol.12, N°1, 2000, pp.29-47.

1230 See Toshio Takeshita, "Agenda-setting effects of the press in a Japanese local election", <u>Studies of Broadcasting</u>, vol.29, 1993, pp.193-216.

1231 See Federico Rey Lennon, "*Argentina: 1997 elecciones. Los diarios nacionales y la campana electoral*", <u>Report by The Freedom Forum and Austral University, 1998.</u>

1232 See Maria Jose Canel, Juan Pablo Llamas, and Federico Rey, Federico, "El primer nivel del efecto agenda setting en la informacion local: Los 'problemas mas importantes" de la ciudad de Pamplona ", <u>Comunicacion y Sociedad</u>, vol. 9, N°1&2, 1996, pp.17-38.

1233 See Maxwell McCombs, Esteban Lopez-Escobar and Juan Pablo Llamas, "Setting the agenda of attributes in the 1996 Spanish general election", <u>Journal of Communication</u>, vol. 50, N°2, 2000, pp. 77-92.

1234 See Shanto Iyengar and Adam Simon, "News coverage of the Gulf crisis and public opinion: A study of agenda-setting, priming and framing", <u>op.cit</u>

1235 See Eugene F. Shaw, "Agenda-setting and mass communication theory", <u>Gazette</u>, vol.25, N°2, 1979, p.10.

well-proven fact. It exists at every level from mass media to the smaller media outlets and its effects have been proven to exist from the most insignificant issue to the most important and sensitive one, such as the media agenda during the coverage of an international crisis, as well.

The second notion that lends credit to this idea of the existence of a crisis of objectivity in the media is one which is very much related to the previous notion of the existence of the media's own agenda. This notion is what is called the salience of issue in the media. Generally speaking salience can be seen as the importance given to various issues by the media and which can be measured by the amount and nature of coverage allocated to these issues. In this respect, Maxwell McCombs argues, "Newspapers provide a host of cues about the salience of the topics in the daily news—lead story on page one, other front-page display, large headlines, etc. Television news also offers numerous cues about salience—the opening story on the newscast, length of time devoted to the story, etc. These cues repeated day after day effectively communicate the importance of each topic"[1236]. The salience degree of an issue reflects its position on the media agenda. Andrew O. Baolli explains, "The position of an issue on the media agenda importantly determines that issue's salience on the public agenda. Salience measures the perceived relative importance of an item on an agenda. In other words, the amount and nature of coverage given to an issue within the media can determine how the public will treat that issue—and whether they will actually see it as worthy of being an issue"[1237]. The effects of this salience of issues in the media have been found to be quite important in the orientation of public opinion. In this respect, Maxwell McCombs states, "The salience of objects in the mass media is linked to the formation of opinions by the audience. With the increasing salience of public figures in the news, for example, more people move away from a neutral position and form an opinion about these persons"[1238]. This salience of certain issues over others has caused much criticism to the media. Noam Chomsky gives the example of the media's disregard of certain issues in spite of a large public support and consideration for those issues. He says, "The nuclear freeze movement had virtually no support in the media, no support among politicians and certainly no support by business-but nevertheless, 75 percent of the American population supported it"[1239]. Salience effect can easily be seen in the findings of the case study of this research. Indeed, the amount of the

---

1236 See Maxwelll McCombs, "The Agenda-Setting Role of the Mass Media in the Shaping of the Public Mind", op. cit., p.1

1237 See Andrew O. Baolli, op. cit.

1238 Ibid, p.11.

1239 See Noam Chomsky, Understanding Power, op. cit., p.21.

Bosnia conflict coverage and its priority placement in both *The New York Times* and Le Monde reflects the considerable importance and the priority of this conflict on the agenda of both newspapers compared to the Chechnya conflict. The result is that this concentrated salience of the Bosnia conflict gives it much more importance in the eyes of the public than other conflicts and crisis who receive little, minimizing, or no salience at all such as the crisis in Chechnya.

If the status of an issue on the media agenda is determined by its salience then this salience must have an effect on public opinion. Maxwell McCombs presents an explanation of such mechanism, according to which, this salience of issues functions as an orientating tool of public opinion His explanation is, however, particularly related to elections and performance in office of politicians and public figures. He argues that issues on the media agenda are objects. These objects are public issues or agendas of political candidates during election campaigns. Each of these objects has its own "attributes". These attributes are the characteristics of this object and its traits. Therefore, according to Maxwell McCombs, each object has an agenda of attributes that the media would choose to emphasize some and ignore others. For such issues and public figures, McCombs suggests the existence of what he called "the agenda of attributes"[1240]. This agenda has an important impact on people's perceptions. Maxwell McCombs states, in this respect, "The agenda of attributes presented for each of these issues, public figures, or other objects literally influences the pictures themselves that we hold in mind. Images held by the public of political candidates and other public figures are the most obvious examples of attribute agenda-setting by the news media[1241]".The idea that the media has the ability to set an agenda and to orient public opinion through manipulation of this agenda has even incited some researchers to argue that this mere fact (the power the media has to choose what is important or not) is a crisis in democracy itself and in the free market economy system as well. Agner Fog, argues, "The mass media constitute the backbone of modern democracy. This is the indispensable communication channel for the democratic process. The free press is often hailed as the cornerstone of democracy, but unfortunately the press is not free. It is controlled neither by the conscience of journalists and editors, nor by any democratically elected organization, but by the inescapable mechanisms of a free market economy. The unrestrained competition is forcing the media to select and frame their stories in ways that are counterproductive to an optimal political allocation of danger-fighting resources. Furthermore, it creates a distorted worldview in the audience that influences the

---

1240 See Maxwell McCombs, Maxwell McCombs, The Agenda-Setting Role of the Mass Media in the Shaping of the Public Mind, <u>op. cit.</u>, pp.1-5.
1241 Ibid.,p.5.

democratic process strongly in the regal direction[1242]". Hence, this power of the media, to define what is wrong or what is worth focusing public attention on in a society, is considered by some as a flow in the democratic system itself. This would make the media seem like an fully autonomous authoritarian entity that, alone, would determine what is good or not in a society, and when to focus on issues and when not to. This, however, is quite debatable as a notion. It is true that the media has an enormous ability to focus the public attention on issues that it considers worthy of being on its agenda. It is also true that, by consequence, what is on the media agenda has the greatest possibilities to be placed on the public agenda. On the other hand, it is not only the media that has an agenda. Other social actors have their own agendas as well. Such social actors include, amongst others, political parties, social movements, unions, the government,…etc. The attempts of the media to place its own agenda first can hence, always be considered as simply a competition to gain popularity for ideas and points of view in a democratic system, where every social actor has the ability to compete for the majority's support. In this line of thoughts is that the media, even if it is simply one of many social actors trying to impose their agendas to be adopted by the society, has, nevertheless, the greatest of possibilities to be much more diffused than the other social actors and, consequently, to by much more effective in imposing its agenda than the other social actors. The media has, moreover, more assets to enable it to present its agenda in a much more attractive and convincing manner than all the other social actors. To sum up, it can be said that if there is a flow in the fact that the media has an agenda, which it tries to impose for adoption by the public, then this flow is not in the fact that the media has an agenda to sell, but that it is has much more advantages than the other social actors for its agenda to be adopted.

The other notion that did probably contribute to this media crisis of objectivity is the numerous references to its "submission" to the free market conditions. Agner Forg explains, for example, how journalists end up being frustrated by such realities that they soon end up giving up their journalistic principles. He states," The economic competition between the media is so fierce that those who fail to push the right buttons will eventually perish, unless they have alternative sources of funding. This is survival of the fittest. But you can't blame the journalists. They leave the school of journalism with the highest ideals of fair and thorough journalism and consider this the hallmark of their trade. They soon get disappointed when discovering that the real world is different. Many journalists discuss the problems of journalism ethics in their media and in trade journals, but to no avail, because they can't change the logic of the free competition. The principle of *survival of the fittest* has

---

1242 See Agner Fog, Mass Media and Democracy Crisis, op. cit., pp.13-14.

never been compatible with altruistic ideals[1243]". For his part, Noam Chomsky explains how journalistic objectivity can be sacrificed for economic gain, especially in attracting advertisers. He states" I once asked another editor at the Boston Globe why their coverage of the Israeli/Palestinian conflict is so awful-and it is. he just laughed and said, "How many Arab advertisers do you think we have?"[1244]. Others such as C. E. Baker are of this opinion as well. He explains that the media's income depends largely on advertisers and that the media would, therefore, end up trying to satisfy those advertisers, even if their interests had nothing to do with those of the society as a whole[1245]. Noam Chomsky goes further in arguing that the products sold by the media are the audiences themselves, who are sold to the media's advertisers. He states that the media", like other corporations, have a product to sell and a market they want to sell it to: the product is audiences and the market is advertisers"[1246]. Noam Chomsky gives the example of prominent newspapers such as the Washington Post and the Wall Street Journal. He continues saying, "very often a journal that is in financial trouble will try to cut down its circulation, and what they'll try to do is to up scale their readership, because that increases advertising rates. So what they're doing is selling audiences to other businesses, and for the agenda-setting media like *The New York Times* and the *Washington Post* and the Wall Street Journal, they're in fact selling very privileged, elite audiences to other businesses-overwhelmingly their readers are members of the so-called "political class", which is the class that makes decisions in our society"[1247]. Some researchers also argue that it is not in the benefit of the media, commercially speaking, to be objective and show both sides of the coin. In this respect, Agner Fog explains, "The commercial media are not very inclined to cover controversial issues in a balanced way. People prefer to hear points of view that they agree with. It is therefore adverse to the media's economy to view a controversy from both sides and present alternative points of view. The media are prone to choose side in a controversy, and if later evidence should favour the opposite side they are likely to keep silent about the matter rather than loosing face. Disclaimers are not profitable. This is a self-amplifying process. The more the media create consensus about a particular issue through biased coverage, the fewer proponents of the opposite view will there be to balance the issue, and the more difficulties will these proponents have in gaining access to the media"[1248]. Indeed, the mega profits of some of the big media companies in the

1243 Ibid, p.10-11.
1244 See Noam Chomsky, Understanding Power, op. cit., p.22.
1245 See C. E. Baker, Advertising and a Democratic Press, Princeton University Press, Princeton, 1994.
1246 See Noam Chomsky, Understanding Power, op. cit., p.14.
1247 Idem.
1248 See Agner Fog, op. cit., p.9.

world can not but add to this assumption that journalism can be a very big business which would has high consideration for free market conditions and business values (See Table 40 below).

Table 41: Financial Data for Twenty-four Large Media Corporations (or Their Parent Firms) December 1986.

Company	Total Assets ($ Millions)	Profits before taxes ($ Millions)	Profits after taxes ($ Millions)	Total Revenue ($ Millions)
Advance Publications (Newhouse) 1	2,500	NA	NA	2, 200
Capital Cities/ABC	5,191	688	448	4,124
CBS	3,370	470	370	4,754
Cox Communications 2	1,111	170	87	743
Dow Jones & Co.	1,236	331	183	1,135
Gannett	3,365	540	276	2, 801
General Electric (NBC)	34,591	3,689	2,492	36,725
Hearst 3	4,040	NA	215 (1983)	2,100 (1983)
Knight-Rider	1,947	267	140	1,911
McGraw-Hill	1,463	296	154	1,577
News Corp. (Murdoch)4	8,460	377	170	3, 822
New York Times	1,405	256	132	1,565
Reader's Digest 5	NA	75-110 (1985)	NA	1,400 (1985)
Scripps-Howard 6	NA	NA	NA	1,062
Storer 7	1,242	68	(-17)	537
Taft	1,257	(-11)	(-53)	500
Time, Inc.	4,230	626	376	3,762
Times- Mirror	2,929	680	408	2,948
Triangle 8	NA	NA	NA	730
Tribune Co.	2,589	523	293	2,030
Turner Broadcasting	1,904	(-185)	(-187)	570
U. S. News and World Report 9	200+	NA	NA	140
Washington Post	1,145	205	100	1,215
Westinghouse	8,482	801	670	10,731

NA= not available.

1. The asset total is taken from *Forbes* magazine's wealth total for the Newhouse family for 1985; the total revenue is for media sales only, as reported in Advertising Age, June 29, 1987.
2. Cox Communications was publicly owned until 1985, when it was merged into another Cox family company, Cox Enterprises. The data presented here are for year-end 1984; the last year of public ownership and disclosure of substantial financial information.
3. Data complied in William Barrett," Citizens Rich," Forbes, Dec.14, 1987.
4. These data are in Australian dollars and are for June 30, 1986; at that date the Australian dollar was worth 68/100 of a U.S. dollar.
5. Data for 1985; as presented in *the New York Times*, Feb. 9, 1986.
6. Total revenue for media sales only, as reported in Advertising Age, June 29, 1987.
7. Storer came under the control of the Wall Street firm Kohiberg Kravin Roberts & Co. in 1986; the data here are for December 1984; the last period of Storer autonomy and publicly available information.
8. Total revenue for media sales only; from *Advertising Age*, June 29, 1987.
9. Total assets as of 1984-85, based on " Mon Zuckermann, Media's new Mogul", Forbes Magazine, Oct.14, 1985; total revenue from Advertising Age, June 29, 1987.

Source: Edward S. Herman and Noam Chomsky, Manufacturing Consent, <u>op. cit.</u>, pp 6-7.

As shown in the table above, the economic interests involved in some of the big media companies are sometimes so enormous that accusations of lack of objectivity can always be referred to the bias related to the economic interests involved. Advertising revenues and major shareholders, according to this free market conditions and competition logic, can always serve as a counterargument explaining the media's crisis of objectivity. Other evidence of the media becoming so subjected to the market values is the recent developments in the media market. These developments, which resulted from the liberalization of the media market, included convergence or merger operations in which a number of small media outlets have been merged together technically and economically. In this respect, Edward S. Herman and Noam Chomsky explain that this mainly occurred as a result of the globalisation trend in the beginning of the 1990s. They state, "Since 1990, a wave of massive deals and rapid globalisation have left the media industries further centralized in nine transactional conglomerates—Disney, Aol Time Warner, Viacom (Owner of CBS), News Corporation, Bertelsmann, General Electric (Owner of NBC), Sony, AT&T—Liberty Media, and *Vivendi Universal.* These giants own all the world's major film studios, TV networks, and music companies, and a sizable fraction of the most important cable channels, cable systems, magazines, major-market TV stations, and book publishers"[1249]. For his part, Agner Fog calls this process of mergers "concentration". He argues, "Media companies are being merged together and controlled by fewer owners. This concentration is horizontal (several media under the same owner) as well as vertical (several links in the "food chain" under the same company group). Different media bring news from the same sources"[1250]. The effects of such a concentration, concerning sources at least, are the same as indicated by Edward S. Herman and Noam Chomsky. They state, "Media centralization and the reduction in the resources devoted to journalism have made the media more dependent than ever on the primary definers who both make the news and subsidize the media by providing accessible and cheap copy. They now have greater leverage over the media, and public relations firms working for these and other powerful interests also bulk larger as media resources"[1251]. The cultural implication of such trends and the effects on society as a whole are very important as well. Agner Fog explains that due to this commercialisation of the media industry, "Advertisements are sneaked into entertainment as well as news stories. The distinction between advertisements, news and entertainment are increasingly blurred. Audience

---

1249   See Edward S. Herman and Noam Chomsky, Manufacturing Consent, op. cit., p. xiii.
1250   See Agner Fog, op. cit., p. 8.
1251   Ibid., p. xvii

groups with less spending money are not considered"[1252]. This gives both advertisers and owners rights on the editorial decisions. It also leads to what Agner Fog calls "trivialization", which he largely describes as being "more sex and violence"[1253]. Agner Fog elaborates, "More prying into the private lives of celebrities. The media avoid controversial issues and serious debates. Debates are reduced to an entertaining clash between personalities, resembling a boxing match, where the issue of controversy has only secondary importance"[1254]. Edward S. Herman and Noam Chomsky are also of this opinion. They explain that the culture and ideology fostered in this globalisation process relate largely to "lifestyle" themes and goods and their acquisition; and they tend to weaken any sense of community helpful to civic life"[1255]. Hence, one of the criticisms which is directed to the media and which constitutes one of the pillars of this crisis of objectivity is the fact that the media have, as a result of liberal globalisation, been mostly mutated into very lucrative business enterprises which follow the free market rules. On the other hand, it can always be argued that the media did not have any other choice but to adopt to the globalisation rules and to the free market in order to survive.

The last notion that seems to contribute to the media's crisis of objectivity is the accusation that the media is always reflecting elite opinion. Noam Chomsky explains, in this respect, that on major issues popular opinion might be very different from elite opinion and, in spite of that, it is only elite opinion that is advanced by the media. He states, "On major issues there is a very noticeable split between elite and popular opinion, and the media consistently reflect elite opinion. So for example, on things like sex, dismantling welfare state programs; or on a nuclear weapon freeze; or the U.S. policies in Central America in the 1980s; or on the nature of the Vietnam War, the views expressed in the media have always been very different from public opinion, and in line with elite opinion[1256]". Anne-Marie Gingras and Jean-Pierre Carrier present a similar description of the way this elite opinion is hegemonic over popular opinion. They state, "A parliamentary reporter used the word hegemony to explain that dominant social actors try to *create public opinion* that is favourable to their economic interests, thus associating domination with a leadership of ideas. These social actors use very specific strategies: they promote their special interests by presenting them as public interest and as the ideal way to solve public policy problems. He referred to the

---

1252 See Agnder Fog, op.cit., p. 8.
1253 Idem
1254 Idem.
1255 Edward S. Herman and Noam Chomsky, Manufacturing Consent, op. cit.,p.xvi.
1256 See Noam Chomsky, Understanding Power, op. cit., p.19.

example of deficit reduction, which became desperately urgent at the very moment social program budgets were being called into question. According to him, the sudden growth in importance of deficit reduction was generated by the elites' desire to cut social programs and was intentionally targeted as the main reason for the lack of control over public funds"[1257]. Other than being called elite opinion, such a notion has been referred to as "primary definers in a society", and as the "dominant ideology". Some researchers, such as Pierre Bourdieu, have explained that even the questions asked in an opinion poll are designed in a way that would always reflect the opinion of the political class[1258]. Noam Chomsky is of a similar opinion. He explains, "What are called opinions "on the left" and "on the right" in the media represent only a limited spectrum of debate, which reflects the range of needs of private power—but there's essentially nothing beyond those" acceptable" positions[1259]". Hence, there is a criticism to be directed to the media in reflecting the "elite opinion" and even if there are debates to be advanced by the media on certain issues, then the points of view presented in such debates are not totally objective. In fact, the media seems to be obliged to choose sides even in such debates or at least to remain silent about the correctness of the other point of view in order not to contradict its own agenda or to alienate influential advertisers.

The media's crisis of objectivity seems to be an unquestionable reality. The indicators of the existence of such a crisis are many. They have to do with notions related to the media's function itself, as well as to its organization. The media's ability to set its own agenda and the advantage that it has in diffusing this agenda is one of the main notions that contribute to giving credibility to this crisis of objectivity. Moreover, the media's ability to frame the selected news and information in a manner that is beneficial to its interests is another notion lending credibility to this crisis of objectivity. Market related developments such as globalisation and liberalisation of the media market have also contributed to these accusations of lack of objectivity. These developments have subjected the media to the free market values of competition and have given investors and shareholders priority over objectivity. Furthermore, the accusations that the media sets a frame for its debates and that the questions in opinion polls are designed to obtain the desired answers give rise to the accusation that the media simply reflects the elite opinion or is simply a tool of diffusion for such primary definers in a society.

1257   See Anne-Marie Gingras and Jean-Pierre Carrier, Op.Cit.,
1258   See Pierre Bourdieu, « *L'opinion publique n'existe pas* », Les Temps Modernes, 1973, pp. 1292-1309.
1259   See Noam Chomsky, Understanding Power, op. cit., p.13.

Yet, and particularly at the time of the coverage of an international crisis, there are what can be called objective limitations to media coverage. In order, to better examine this crisis of objectivity, it is useful to reflect on two main ideas relating to this issue. These are the existing limitations that might prevent the media from being objective in its coverage and the issue of the media(s independence and how much role does this independence play in setting the limit for the media's objectivity.

3.3.1. Objective Limitations on The Media's Coverage of Certain International Crises

There exist a number of what might be called "objective limitations" on the media coverage of certain international crisis. They are labelled as objective limitations precisely because they fall under the category of elements that the media cannot fully control in order to perform a totally objective coverage of a given international crisis. The purely objective limitations being discussed in the following section are mainly those that have much more to do with the technicalities related to the media coverage of an international crisis. There exists, however, other factors that can affect the media's objectivity in the coverage of an international crisis. These are principally related to the organizational structure and function of the media itself. They can be grouped under two main classifications. There are those that some people such as Edward S. Herman and Noam Chomsky call" Filters on Reporting"[1260] in addition to what is labelled as "Functional Subjectivity[1261]". It is, hence, important to discuss these two organizational impediments to a totally objective media coverage of an international crisis or conflict. Prior to discussing the objective limitations that prevent a fully objective coverage of an international crisis and on which the media has little or no control, it is important to discuss the limitations, or "filters", on objectivity that relate to structural organisation of the media.

The most interesting and related filters on media objectivity discussed by Edward S. Herman and Noam Chomsky are the limitations on the ownership of

---

1260 See Edward S. Herman and Noam Chomsky, Manufacturing Consent, op. cit.
1261 See Lise Garon, "A Case Study of Functional Subjectivity in Media Coverage: The Gulf War on TV", op. cit.

the media, advertising benefits, and mass media sourcing[1262]. Functioning together and as part of a multilevel system, these filters render the media subjective in its news coverage.

The first of these filters on media coverage is the limitations on the ownership of the media outlets and companies themselves. These limitations are mainly the result of the considerable size and wealth, interconnection, and interdependence of the biggest media companies and outlets, which makes it extremely difficult for a "renegade" voice to contradict the majority. In this respect, Edward S. Herman and Noam Chomsky explain that this concentration of the media in the hands of a minority is mainly due to free market policies that started to condition the media, as far back as the nineteenth century[1263]. This has been particularly true in the U.K. at that time where efforts were made to suppress the working class press by introducing high taxes on media ownership[1264]. At that time the cost of starting a profitable national weekly in the U.K in 1837, for instance was almost a thousand pounds and in 1867 a daily newspaper would cost around 50,000 bounds to be established[1265]. The same tendency was also found in the United States. Edward S. Herman and Noam Chomsky explain, for instance, "The start-up cost of a newspaper in New York City in 1851 was $69,000; the public sale of the St. Louis Democrat in 1872 yielded $ 456,000, and city newspapers were selling at $6 to $18 million in the 1920s. The cost of machinery alone, of even very small newspapers, has for many decades run into the hundreds of thousands of dollars; in 1945 it could be said that even small newspaper publishing is big business…and is no longer a trade one takes up lightly even if it has substantial cash or takes up at all if he doesn't…the limitations on the media with any substantial outreach by the requisite large size of investment——was applicable a century ago, and it has become increasingly effective over time. In 1986 there were some 1,500

1262 See Edward S. Herman and Noam Chomsky, Manufacturing Consent, op. cit., pp 1-35. The other filters discussed by Edward S. Herman and Noam Chomsky are "Flak" and its effect which has been discussed in a previous section of this book. The other two filters "Anticommunism as a Control Mechanism" and "Dichotomization and Propaganda Campaigns" are left out of discussion here because of the irrelevance of time (the book was first printed in 1988) and because Edward S. Herman and Noam Chomsy support in these two last filters a theory of a Propaganda Model. Thus, only the filters relevant to this research are included. Noam Chomsky in Understanding Power, Op.Cit., pp.24-30 discusses further these filters that he calls "Filters on Reporting".

1263 See Edward S. Herman and Noam Chomsky, Manufacturing Consent, op.cit., p.3.

1264 See James Curran and Jean Seaton, Power Without Responsibility: The Press and Broadcasting in Britain, (2nd ed.), Methuen, London, 1985.

1265 Ibid. pp. 38-39.

daily newspapers, 11,00 magazines, 9,000 radio and 1,500 TV stations, 2,400 book publishers and seven movie studios in the United States—-over 25,000media entities in all. But a large proportion of those among this set who were news dispensers were very small and local, dependent on the large national companies and wire services for all but local news. Many more were subject to common ownership, sometimes extending through virtually the entire set of media variants"[1266]. For his part, Agner Fog argues that the rationale behind liberalizing the media market was to produce more diversity but that this market principal didn't come up with such a result, as far as the media is concerned. He explains, "The main rationale for liberalizing the media market has been to assure diversity. However, this strategy has often failed because increased competition does not necessarily lead to increased diversity. Assume, for example, that a country has two competing TV-stations with each one channel. In this case they will both try to maximize their market share by sending the same kind of programs that appeal to the broadest possible audience. But if, on the other hand, both channels are owned by the same TV-station, then the owner will seek to minimize competition between the two channels by sending different types of programs on the two channels. The conclusion is that reduced competition may lead to increased diversity"[1267]. Thus, the free market system has concentrated the media ownership, or the biggest media firms, in the hands of a minority. This has of course its effects on the content of the media coverage of events. For instance, Ben H. Bagdikian explains how it is difficult for a small media outlet to have content in its coverage that would harm the bigger media organization, on which it is dependent[1268]. This is quite similar to the view of Noam Chomsky on this "parental" dependency effect of the ownership structure. He states that "there are a number of major media outlets that end up setting a basic framework that other smaller media units more or less have to adopt to"[1269]. The result of these ownership limitations is the emergence of an interdependence and inter-cooperation between the media owners. In this respect, Edward S Herman and Noam Chomsky explain that "the control groups of the media giants are also brought into close relationships with the mainstream of the corporate community through boards of directors and social links"[1270]. Some researchers attribute a considerable determining weight to this relationship. Ben H. Bagdikian, for example, explains

1266   See Edward S. Herman and Noam Chomsky, Manufacturing Consent, op.cit., p.4.

1267   See Agner Fog, Mass Media and Democracy Crisis, op.cit., p.7.

1268   See Ben H. Bagdikian, The Media Monopoly (2nd ed.), Beacon Press, Boston, 1987.

1269   See Noam Chomsky, Understanding Power, op. cit., p14.

1270   See Edward S. Herman and Noam Chomsky, Manufacturing Consent, op. cit., p. 8.

that these close relationships between the media owners amount to a "Private Ministry of Information and culture" which is able to set the agenda for a whole country[1271]. Moreover, it is quite common that the ownership of such mega media companies is transmitted from generation to another within the same family[1272]. Even with the public ownership and trading of stocks of the média companies, these concentrations of the media ownership don't seem to have been greatly affected. In this respect, Edward S. Herman and Noam Chomsky insist that "while the stock of the great majority of large media firms is traded in the securities market, approximately two thirds of these companies are either closely held or still controlled by members of the originating family who retain large stocks of stock"[1273]. These limitations on the media ownership produce other related effects. Indeed, due to such a situation, the few who own and control the media have to maintain an interdependent relation between them and between them and the political and economic power centres as well because they have a goal of profitability and of satisfying market demands. Edward S. Herman and Noam Chomsky explain the complexity and dimension of the relationship emerging from such a limitation on media ownership. They state, "The dominant media firms are quite large businesses; they are controlled by very wealthy people or by managers who are subject to sharp constraints by owners and other profit-oriented forces, and they are closely interlocked, and have important common interests, with other major corporations, banks, and government"[1274]. These free market rules are also being pointed at as the cause of frustration for journalists themselves, especially by those who seek the ethical ideals of journalism. Agner Forg, for example, explains, "journalists leave the school of journalism with the highest ideals of fair and thorough journalism and consider this the hallmark of their trade. They soon get disappointed when discovering that the real world is different. Many journalists discuss the problems of journalism ethics in their media and in trade journals, but to no avail, because they can't change the logic of the free competition. The principle of *survival of the fittest* has never been compatible with altruistic ideals"[1275]. Hence, one of the general organizational deficiencies of the media's ability to be fully objective resides in the limitations on the media ownership and control and in the demands and conditions of the free market economy.

1271 See Ben H. Bagdikian, <u>The Media Monopoly</u>, op. cit. p.,xvi.

1272 See for example the classification of wealth of the 24 largest media companies in the United Tsates for instance in 1986 in Edward S. Herman and Noam Chomsky's Manufacturing Consent(pp. 9-10, discussed I a previous section of this part. According to this table one family may own one or two mega média outlets.

1273 Ibid., p. 8

1274 Idem, p.14.

1275 See Agner Fog, <u>op. cit</u>, pp10-11.

The second of these organizational obstacles to the media's objectivity is that which has to do with the place of advertising and advertising benefits on the media's agenda. Indeed, many researchers and writers argue that advertising has an important effect on the media choices and conduct. Some also claim that advertising is one of the tools of suppressing unwanted or "dissident" opinions. Edward S. Herman and Noam Chomsky explain, for example, that "advertising did, in fact, serve as a powerful mechanism in weakening the working-class press"[1276]. They continue to say, "Before advertising became prominent, the price of a newspaper had to cover the costs of doing business. With the growth of advertising, papers that attracted ads could afford a copy price well below production costs. This put papers lacking in advertising at at a serious disadvantage; their prices would tend to be higher, curtailing sales, and they would have less surplus to invest in improving the stability of the paper (features, attractive format, promotions, etc.). For this reason, an advertising based system would tend to drive out of existence or into marginality the media companies and types that depend on revenue from sales alone"[1277]. The effect of advertising on the choices made by the media of its content and of its framing is more evident in other media forms and too much higher degrees than in the printed one. In his respect, Agner Fog explains that "advertising has a profound influence on the choice of programs. TV advertisers prefer to have their commercials shown in association with soft entertainment. Ideal from the advertisers' point of view are shows such as competitions where you can win sponsored merchandise, or soap operas that portray a privileged lifestyle where luxurious goods give status"[1278]. Indeed, the importance of advertising goes as far back as the mid-nineteenth century. James Curran and Jean Seaton explain, for instance, that in the U. K advertisers "acquired a de facto licensing authority since, without their support, newspapers ceased to be economically viable"[1279]. Other writers have also noted this significant power of advertising over Television programs' choices. Edward S. Herman and Noam Chomsky state, "The power of advertisers over television programming stems from the simple fact that they buy and pay for the programs—they are the "patrons" who provide the media subsidy. As such, the media compete for their patronage, developing specialized staff to solicit advertisers needs. The choices of these patrons greatly affect the welfare of the media,

---

1276   See Edward S. Herman and Noam Chomsky, Manufacturing Consent, op.cit., p.14.
1277   Idem.
1278   See Agner Fog, op. cit., p 9.
1279   See James Curran and Jean Seaton, op.cit, p 41

and the patrons become what William Evan calls "normative reference organizations"[1280]. Advertising is quite an important issue on the media's agenda. Its importance has, indeed, been proven in the printed and in audiovisual media. It can also be assumed that it is also important for modern forms of media such as Internet.

Indeed, the high priority given to attracting advertisers in order to serve the media's financial viability is a well-established fact. The effect of sacrificing journalistic values in favour of advertising related interests is also well established. Some writers go as far as saying that advertising has transformed the press into a tool for selling potential buyers or consumers to advertisers. Noam Chomsky is one of those. He states, "The press does not make money on people buying newspapers, they lose money on people buying newspapers. But the press is business interests—the major press is huge corporate interests, the small press is more local business interests, but either way it's kept alive by other business, through advertising"[1281]. This situation of competition for a bigger market share, which, consequently, would bring in more advertisers, has forced the media to concentrate on those topics that would appeal to the biggest audience regardless of whether or not those topics serve public interest or not. Agner Fog explains, in this respect, "Many papers and magazines therefore compete on news about celebrities and topics that appeal to the emotions. Everything that is dangerous, deviant or wrong has a prominent place, especially in those papers that are mainly sold from newsstands. They want to have a new scandal on the front page every day in order to tempt people to buy the paper. We may expect to see similar approaches when electronic pay-per-view media become common. Radio-and TV-channels based on advertising use fewer horror effects, because this would conflict with the principle of bringing the viewers into buying-mood"[1282]. The same tendency is also noted by Ben H. Bagdikian who explains that advertisers are selective of the programs that correspond to their own principals and to the objectives of their companies and organizations[1283]. The situation for audio-visual media is, indeed, much more sensible and attentive to advertisers' needs and market shares of audiences. Edward S. Herman and Noam Chomsky state that é for a television network, the audience gain or lose of one percentage point in the

---

1280 See Edward S. Herman and Nowam Chomsky, Manufacturing consent, op. cit., p16.
1281 See Noam Chomsky, Understanding Power, op. cit., p24.
1282 See Agner Fog, op. cit., p9.
1283 See Ben H. Bagdikian, op. cit., p160.

Nielsen[1284] ratings translates into a change in the advertising revenue from $80 to $100 million a year with some variation depending on measures of audience "quality". The stakes in audiences size and influence are thus extremely large, and in a market system there is a strong tendency for such considerations to affect policy profoundly"[1285]. The need for advertisers influences also the editorial choices and positions of the media. In this respect, Edward S. Herman and Noam Chomsky explain that "large corporate advertisers on television will rarely sponsor programs that engage in serious criticisms of corporate activities, such as the problem of environmental degradation, the working of the military-industrial companies, or corporate support of and benefits from Third World tyrannies"[1286]. Most efforts, hence, would be directed to having programs that attract audience rather than achieving objectivity. This is probably the reason behind the apparent lack of controversial programs and topics in the media. Agner Fog, for instance, states, "Advertising has a profound influence on the choice of programs. TV advertisers prefer to have their commercials shown in association with soft entertainment. Ideal from the advertisers' point of view are shows such as competitions where you can win sponsored merchandise, or soap operas that portray a privileged lifestyle where luxurious goods give status. This does not provide good conditions for the political debate. It is difficult to find sponsors for serious political debates because these do not make the viewers relax, and because some of the viewers will disagree with the points of view presented"[1287]. This, apparently, is due to psychological reasons relating to human behaviour, which the media has to take into consideration. Agner Fog continues to say, "The commercial media are not very inclined to cover controversial issues in a balanced way. People prefer to hear points of view that they agree with. It is therefore adverse to the media's economy to view a controversy from both sides and present alternative points of view. The media are prone to choose side in a controversy, and if later evidence should favour the opposite side they are likely to keep silent about the matter rather than loosing face. Disclaimers are not profitable[1288]". Edward S. Herman

---

1284 Nielsen Media Research is the world-famous TV Ratings company. Active in more than 40 countries, Nielsen Media Research provides television audience estimates for broadcast and cable networks, television stations, national syndicators, regional cable television systems, satellite providers, advertisers and advertising agencies. It also provides competitive advertising intelligence information through Nielsen Monitor-Plus in the U.S. and 30 other markets worldwide. Through a network of affiliates,

1285 See Edward S. Herman and Noam Chomsky, op. cit., p 16.

1286 Ibid., p. 17.

1287 See Agner Fog, op. cit., p.9.

1288 Idem.

and Noam Chomsky are also of this opinion. They state, "Advertisers would want, more generally, to avoid programs with serious complexities and disturbing controversies that interfere with the "buying mood". They seek programs that will lightly entertain and thus fit in with the spirit of the primary purpose of program purchases—the dissemination of a selling message"[1289]. It is logical to assume, therefore, that the media's coverage of an international crisis can also be affected by these advertising related interests. It can be first affected by the amount of coverage dedicated to this international crisis, especially if there were no national or economic interests involved. Advertising related considerations can also affect the content of the coverage and the positions taken vis-à-vis the international crisis or conflict. There is, indeed, a thin line between economic and political weights and interests. Advertisers are usually interested in their economic gains and in most cases the choices they impose on the media are more or less related to daily consumption of goods and services. However, being so close and interested by the political decisions and positions, they can also be assumed to be interested in the conduct of the media in its coverage of an international crisis. According to this logic, satisfying their interests can have an enormous influence on the media's objectivity tin its coverage of an international crisis.

The third organizational obstacle, which seems to contribute to the media's structural caused lack of objectivity is that which has to do with the media's sourcing. This need for reliable and for a continuous flow of sources incites the media to preserve a close and an friendly relationship with the various power centres in a country. This is particularly true at least as far as the mass media is concerned. In this respect, Edward S. Herman and Noam Chomsky explain, "The mass media are drawn into a symbolic relationship with powerful sources of information by economic necessity and reciprocity of interest. The media need a steady, reliable flow of row material of news. They have daily news demands and imperative news schedules that they must meet. They cannot afford to have reporters and cameras at all places where important stories may break"[1290]. This source dependency relationship has been particularly as far as the coverage of an international crisis is concerned where the fast pace of coverage competition made the media ignore the verification of the information supplied by its official sources. In this respect, Lise Garon, gives the example of the television coverage of the Gulf War of the beginning of the 1990s. She states that" official sources supplied the media news without effort and the race for the freshest news left no time for checking accuracy before broadcasting official materials"[1291]. Certain

---

1289 See Edward S. Herman and Noam Chomsky, op. cit., p17-18.
1290 Ibid., p. 18.
1291 See Lise Garon, op. cit.

writers suggest that the media would heavily use those official sources because the mass media advocate that they are merely "objective disseminators of the news", and partly because they want to protect themselves against libel suits[1292]. Moreover, this reliance on official sources does not come without a price. Edward S. Herman and Noam Chomsky argue that "because of their services, continuous contact on the beat, and mutual dependency, the powerful can use personal relationships, threats, and rewards to further influence and coerce the media"[1293]. This can take place by actively and openly presenting and supporting the political, economic, and other power centres' views or passively by denying or ignoring other points of view which are contrary to those of these power centres. Edward S. Herman and Noam Chomsky explain, in this respect, that "powerful sources may also use their prestige and importance to the media to deny critics access to the media"[1294]. The media's need for official sources seems to be one of the organizational obstacles that prevent this media from being totally objective in performing its functions. Such a need, however, seems to that of mere practical necessity due to various organisational and technical needs of the media machine.

Other than these organizational obstacles or "filters" on the media's objectivity, there seems to be another factor called "functional subjectivity" which also hinders the media's attainment of total objectivity. What underlies the concept of functional subjectivity is the assumption that absolute objectivity is an impossible goal and that subjectivity is a predetermined trait in both humans and institutions. Lise Garon explains, in this respect, "All sociologists generally agree that knowledge can never be objective because it is historically and individually determined by experience and socially determined by the functions it serves. Subjectivity has been considered inevitable and omnipresent in human knowledge by classical and neo-Marxist sociology as well"[1295]. What applies to knowledge in general can also be said to apply to news and information. Lise Garon elaborates on this process where the media cannot be but subjective because of this inherent trait of subjectivity in human beings. She states, "If objectivity is impossible in science and in ideologies, why should it be otherwise for the media? After all, processing the news is also processing knowledge. In this process, the media need only to decide what is worthy to be released to the audience. In doing so, they investigate, among all possible elements of reality, the more useful ones for attracting their audience.

1292 See Gaye Tuchman, "Objectivity as Strategic Ritual: An examination of Newsmen's Notions of Objectivity", <u>American Journal of Sociology</u>, vol.77, N°2, 1972, pp. 662-664.

1293 See Edward S. Herman and Noam Chmsky, <u>op. cit.</u>, p. 22.

1294 Idem.

1295 See Lise Garon, <u>op. cit.</u>

Therefore, their overall knowledge of facts can hardly be complete or balanced. Similarly, journalists are in search of information that is useful for their individual careers"[1296]. However, this view seems to be contested by people such as Edward S. Herman and Noam Chomsky who explain that the choice of what is news worthy and what is not is more determined by economic and political realties and not simply by a natural functional trait of the media as an institution that is built and run by naturally subjective humans[1297]. The hypothesis of Edward S. Herman and Noam Chomsky is aimed, nonetheless, towards the unveiling of a "propaganda model" which is in control of media behaviour.

On the other hand, the hypothesis of Lise Garon, concerning functional subjectivity, is based more on sociological explanations. Furthermore, for her, subjectivity in the media is not only natural but is also a survival technique. These basically are the main differences of perspective on the mechanism of news choices and presentation between Edward S. Herman and Noam Chomsky and the hypothesis of Lise Garon. At least concerning the television coverage of the second Gulf War (1990-1991), Lise Garon affirms the existence of such functional subjectivity. The study on the television coverage of the Gulf War included a comparison between the French, American, and Canadian television stations' coverage of the events of this war. Lise Garon argues, "Our data about the Gulf War coverage by television show that subjectivity, far from being a nuisance to the global media industry, may be designed to attract a worldwide audience. This hypothesis seems to work within each national context as well; from the U.S. and Canada to France, individual network subjectivity patterns seem to comply with the different national audience expectancies and the media search for higher ratings and improved positioning. This inspired the theory that subjectivity is functional and even instrumental in character. Media may claim to be objective. At times, they can perform not too badly in this point of view. However, if the functional subjectivity hypothesis holds, objectivity can never become an important characteristic of international information and/or crisis coverage"[1298]. For Lise Garon, functional subjectivity is nothing more than the reconstruction of reality by the media and, for that, the media has to be subjective in order to be competitive. In other words, in order for the media to survive, it has to be subjective and it does not do that by free choice. According to this hypothesis and for the media this is a natural survival function. Lise Garon goes on to say, "The main function of objectivity, or at least its assertion, may serve to protect the media's credibility

---

1296   Idem.

1297   See Edward S. Herman and Noam Chomsky, op. cit., in particular the chapter entitled "Worthy and Unworthy Victims" pp. 37-87.

1298   See Lise Garon, op. cit.

and maintain an audience in a competitive context. This hypothesis implies that the ethics of objectivity are subsumed by this vital and specific objective of the media: capturing the public eye. The media must reconstruct reality in ways, which will allow them to survive and become influential among the social actors. This process may imply considerable distortions of reality and variable dosages of subjectivity and objectivity. In extreme cases, such as wartime, objectivity may still be present but reduced to a ritual ornament of media discourse, at the expense of the informative function"[1299]. Moreover, functional subjectivity suggests that the media do not necessarily need to be objective but that they have to look objective in order to be more attractive to the public. Lise Garon adds, "Capturing the public eye belongs to a more general category that has little to do with objectivity: influence. In order to capture the public eye, each medium may try to convince the audience that its programs are the most entertaining, that it always tells the whole truth, that its editorial standpoint always provides new and deep insights into actuality, that it is useful and even essential to society, and so on. In order to reproduce such an image efficiently, the media do not have to be objective but they do have to look so. The media's power is essentially nothing but influence over its public (in the sense of persuading it to tune in)"[1300]. This seems to also relate to the psychological effects of the media on the public opinion, and the knowledge that the media has of the tendencies of this public opinion. Generally speaking, the public would be more attracted to what seems to be objective news or, at least, what this public, because of its affinities, heritage, culture, and interests perceives to be objective news coverage. Indeed, the hypothesis of functional subjectivity seems to suggest that, since the public is subjective by nature because of different sociological, historical, cultural, and economic particularities and affinities, the media is doing noting more than being what the public wants this media to be; Subjective.

The organizational obstacles or "filters" on the media's objectivity include the limitations on media ownership which would concentrate the media, or the most influential media at least, in the hands of an elite which has its own economic and political interests to protect. They also include the influence advertising related interests have on the conduct and content of the media. The attraction of advertisers and their satisfaction seems to force the media to submit to the conditions and demands of those advertisers in order to remain competitive and have a greater share of the market. Media dependency on official sources is also one of these organisational related or "filters" placed in the way of media's objectivity ideal. The media has to preserve a good relationship with the various power centres

---

1299 Idem.
1300 Idem.

in order to have a continuous flow of news items that it can present to the public. This is done for practical and economic reasons. It is practical because official sources lend more credibility to media coverage and, thus, can add to the media's quest to appear objective. Official sourcing is also economically useful because it protects the media against libel suits and because the media cannot have its own journalists and reporters everywhere.

Functional subjectivity suggests that the choice of news items and their presentation is merely a natural process that depends on competitive considerations and on a need to look objective but not to be really objective. If total objectivity is not a human trait then it will not be one in the human built and human run institutions such as the media. This is due to the difference in individual traits, preferences, beliefs, and environments between humans. If humans are subjective by nature, then the media is subjective too. In other words, in the subjective world of humans, the media has also to choose sides and be subjective as well. If people are subjective by nature, then the media is obliged to be functional and become subjective as well in order to satisfy this "subjective public" and remain in business. This is in short the concept of "functional subjectivity" developed by Lise Garon. It basically differs from the "propaganda model" behaviour theory advocated by Edward S. Herman and Noam Chomsky in that explanations given to functional subjectivity behaviour are more sociological and behavioural on the level of individuals while explanations crediting the propaganda model are on the level of media companies and governments and their effect on media behaviour in the United States'. Moreover, while Lise Garon's functional subjectivity of the media suggests that the media is obliged to be subjective in order to survive and respond to what the public actually needs, the propaganda behaviour model of Edward S. Herman and Noam Chomsky suggests that the media has the choice to be objective but does not and that the public actually expects "objectivity" and not "subjectivity" from its media.

It is important at this point, and after discussing the organisational related obstacles or "filters" on the media's objectivity in addition to the theories explaining the media's crisis of objectivity by concepts such as functional subjectivity and the propaganda model behaviour, it is important to discuss those purely "objective" limitations on the media's coverage of an international crisis or conflict. The difference between these limitations and the previously discussed obstacles on media'(s objectivity is that these "objective "limitations are ones over which the media has no or little control and are ones that concern media objectivity precisely during conflict reporting. Such "objective" limitations on media coverage of international conflicts and crisis are access to the crisis area, financial, and technological impediments hindering objective conflict reporting.

3.3.1.1. Access to the Conflict Area

The first important objective limitation on the media coverage of certain international crises and conflicts is the journalists' and reporters' free access to the conflict or crisis area. Indeed, if the media are not able to have free access to the crisis area, or if its access is conditioned by one party or another to the conflict, then its coverage would not be an objective. In this respect, the impediments to the media access to the crisis area can be classified in two main categories. The first one can be called the natural elements' impediments of access. These may include the nature of the crisis area concerned and the difficulty of the physical access to it. The other category of can be called the human related impediments to media access to the crisis area. This category includes any denial of access to the crisis area by human action such as the limitations imposed by the conflicting parties to accessing a conflict zone or reporting from it, and also security risks and threats to reporters.

The nature related limitations to journalists' access to the conflict area are often underestimated and even disregarded. Yet, these natural specificities of a conflict area can have an effect on the authenticity and objectivity of conflict reporting. In this respect, Malcolm W. Browne gives the example of a war reporter covering the Gulf War of 1990-1991 saying, "The Saudi hinterlands, unlike those of Vietnam, India or Central America, do not favour news coverage by stealth. Only a handful of roads cross the naked desert—mostly six lane highways on which traffic is sparse and a press vehicle is conspicuous"[1301]. Robert E. Denton explains, for his part, the effect of the natural environment on reporting from the conflict area. He states, "Indeed, the environment was dangerous, and a desert war makes it easy to control reporters. If an enemy tank or soldier can be easily spotted in a desert, so can a reporter"[1302]. The environment and geography of the conflict area can, indeed, be working with or working against a conflict reporter. Robert E. Denton, for instance, states, "Working in a largely treeless desert environment with few villages beyond the major cities, the press was left with a scarcity of safe outposts near forward military units. This problem was heightened by the fact that most journalists were officially unwelcome in units unless they were a part of a formally designated press pool. In other war zones ranging from Europe to Asia, reporters have often been able to retain some freedom of movement by using the protective cover of local villages and hamlets near

---

1301   Browne Malcolm W. "The Military vs. The Press". New York Times Magazine, March 3, 1991, p.45.

1302   Robert E. Denton, The Media and the Persian Gulf War, Praeger Publishers, Westport, CT, 1993, p.47.

the fighting. For example, Sydney Schanberg's insightful reporting on the fall of Cambodia in 1976—dramatized in the film The Killing Fields—would have probably been impossible without the protection of the forested terrain and his ability to gain the confidence and quiet access of many villagers"[1303]. One result of this harsh environment of the Gulf War area for journalists and reporters was that a number of those reporters covering the conflict preferred staying in their hotels or residences covering the conflict with the news items they received from the coalition forces. This was, however, also largely due to the technological advances in communication technologies[1304]. Others, nonetheless, explain that the desert environment for reporters of that conflict was an advantage for the deployment and use of journalists' communication material. Thownas A. Mccain and Leonard Shyles state, for example, "it was a war in the sand, not in the jungle. The implications of this were that highly efficient communication systems could quickly be put in place across the desert, allowing for rapid and immediate distribution of information"[1305]. The natural environmental elements of the conflict area's terrain can, hence, have a positive or a negative impact on the reporters' coverage of this conflict, or it can have both like it did in the case of the desert in the Gulf War of the beginnings of the 1990s.

The other category of access limitations to journalists' objective coverage of an international conflict or crisis is the much more common human related one. It mainly includes limitations on the media's free accessing of the crisis or conflict area set by the conflicting armed parties in the conflict. This type of limitations has much more impact on restricting the journalists' access to the conflict area than the previously mentioned nature related one.

To begin with it can be said that preventing or restricting media access to a conflict zone is a very common practice that is used quite often mostly for strategic or propaganda reasons by the conflicting parties. For strategic reasons, limiting media access to the conflict zone can have various reasons. It can be done to prevent the media from diffusing in its coverage of the conflict information about the military position, strategies, equipment, number of soldiers in the area, and so on. Propaganda related reasons explaining restricting media access to the conflict zone are those aimed at guarding against international human rights abuses accusations, which may result from the media's coverage of human tragedies in the conflict zone, or even to hide the discontent of the local populations in this zone with a foreign military occupation, for instance.

1303 Ibid., p. 21.
1304 See Robert E. Denton, op.cit.
1305 See Thownas A. Mccain and Leonard Shyles, The 1,000 Hour War: Communication in the Gulf, Greenwood Press, Westport, CT., 1994, p. xv.

Such restrictions are now quite often that reporters and journalists covering a conflict usually start by being acquainted with the degree of free access they are in the conflict zone. This is also true for the military institutions or warring parties in a conflict who, realising the impact of a media coverage of an international conflict or crisis on national and world opinion, developed strategies and set guidelines in order to use this media coverage to their advantage, or at least to limit its negative impact on them. Indeed, limitations and guidelines on media accessing of the combat zone are usually communicated to journalists in advance. This, for instance, was the case in the media coverage of the Gulf War of the 1990s. Robert E. Denton explains, in this respect, that "guidelines laid down by the Department of Defence greatly limited the access that the roughly 1,000 journalists gathered in Saudi Arabia would actually have to combat areas and military units[1306]". Such examples of military imposed limitations to accessing the conflict zone in the Gulf War of the 1990s are also mentioned by other writers, such as Hedrick Smith who states, "Our latest count shows that over 1,400 reporters, editors, producers, photographers, and technicians are now registered with the joint information bureaus in Dhahran and Riyadh, representing the U.S. and the international press. Not all of them want to go to the front. But more want to go than we can possibly accommodate".[1307] Restrictions on the media, however, are usually not one sided. Similar limitations were placed by the Iraqi military in that war. Robert E. Denton states, "Iraqi officials often delayed press conferences until CNN reporters arrived. The network enjoyed special treatment and access to Iraqi officials, events, and city locations. CNN reporters were the only ones allowed to stay in their hotel rooms early in the conflict. Peter Arnett became the world's window on Iraq"[1308]. Hence, physical access to the combat area by journalists and reporters is governed by the pre-set guidelines of the warring sides. Yet, the question is whether such a limitation of media accessing a combat zone is merely the result arbitrary decisions.

In this respect, some writers argue that such limitations imposed on the media are a mere reflection of the growing influence of war coverage on public opinion, and of the transformation of the conduct and the intensity of modern warfare. Hedrick Smith explains, for example, the difference between the coverage of the Gulf War of the 1990s and the coverage of the war in Vietnam, or that of the World War II, for reporters and journalists. He states" Unlike World War II, this will not be an operation in which reporters can ride around in jeeps going from one part of

---

1306   Ibid., p. 2.
1307   See Hedrick Smith, <u>The Media and the Gulf War, Seven Locks Press</u>, Washington, DC, 1992, p. 42.
1308   Ibid, p. 34.

the front to another, or like Vietnam where reporters could hop a helicopter to specific points of action. If a ground war begins on the Arabian Peninsula, the battlefield will be chaotic and the action will be violent. This will be modern, intense warfare"[1309]. For others limitations on the media access to combat zones are merely a realization of the media's ability to influence public opinion. Robert E. Denton, for instance, goes as far as using the term "telediplomacy" to describe this growing public opinion's sensitivity to the media coverage of combat zones, especially television coverage. He states, "For centuries wartime propaganda took months of preparation and execution. Today, thanks to modern technology and CNN, it takes mere minutes. Television provides instant access to the enemy's camp and into the public's psyche, ranging from troop manoeuvres to world opinion. Governments must be concerned about military information as well as public perceptions. There is a real danger of "telediplomacy" that may encourage leaders to become overemotional or may cause overreaction to foreign statements or actions"[1310].

The case of the restrictions set on journalists' access to the crisis area is certainly not a one-time case that is pertinent only to the Gulf War of the 1990s. Such restrictions and limitations of access actually exist vis-à-vis journalists' coverage of many other conflicts around the world. In Chechnya, for instance, "media coverage has also faced heightened restrictions from the Russian government"[1311] who "always tries to control the media coverage of the conflict"[1312]. In Chechnya's case, like in the Gulf War of 1990s, restrictions on the media's access became higher, compared to relatively free access of the media to the conflict zones in World War II. In this respect, Georgi M. Derluguian for instance states, "The footage of Chechen fighters, incidentally, was scarce and, in all instances, overtly propagandistic. Unlike the Chechen war of 1994-96, where hundreds of journalists roamed the battlefields and interviewed the warring sides with an almost bizarre freedom— which was chiefly responsible for the crop of journalistic books on Chechnya that had emerged by 1998—in 1999, no reporter or outside observer dared to approach the Chechen side for fear of the almost assured prospect of kidnapping"[1313]. Such

---

1309 See Hedrick Smith, op. cit., p. 41.

1310 See Robert E. Denton, op. cit, p. 35.

1311 See Tariq Yasin, Chechen Chagrin: Human Rights in Chechnya, Harvard International Review, Vol.24, N°.1, 2002,

1312 See Paul Bellamy, "Chechnya: The Russian Quagmire Paul Bellamy Reviews the Performance of the Russian Armed Forces in the Chechnya Conflict", New Zealand, International Review, Vol. 27, 2002. Online document found at http://www.questia.com/PM.qst?a=o&d=5000827350.

1313 See Georgi M. Derluguian, "Che Guevaras in Turbans", New Left Review, Vol. A., N° 237, 1999, p. pp. 3-27,

restrictions placed on media access by the warring sides were also quite evident in the conflict in Bosnia, where "foreign journalists, significantly, were prevented from crossing from Serbia into Bosnia-Herzegovina by Bosnian Serb border controls"[1314]. In general the Balkan recent conflicts are a good example of the importance warring parties hold for restricting the access of the media to the conflict zones. Susan Bryce, for example, states, "Many reporters have said access to the war zone was severely limited by the dominant military force on the ground in Serbia and Kosovo, and by NATO bombing raids. Travel restrictions in the Balkans war zone left reporters to cover daily press briefings at NATO headquarters in Brussels, Belgium, at the Pentagon and the White House in Washington"[1315].

The restrictions placed on journalists' access to the conflict zone seem to have become, indeed, a universal strategic practice. Restrictions would sometimes go as far as imposing restrictions on interviewing rebels. This was, for instance, the case of the Indonesian government who prevented foreign media interviews with the rebels of the Torn Aceh Province[1316]. The Indonesian government's practice was, however, not a new one. it did that before where Indonesian authorities "restricted "access by foreign journalists and human rights organizations to East Timor"[1317]. Similar restrictions on coverage were also evident in Rwanda, where "the fundamental law provides for freedom of speech and of the press"[1318] but yet, where "the Government restricted these rights in practice"[1319], "harassed journalists whose views were contrary to official views"[1320], and where "most journalists practiced self-censorship due to fear of government reprisals"[1321]. Such restrictions were also apparent in Haiti, where a foreign reporter can be

---

1314 See Norman Cigar, Genocide in Bosnia: The Policy of "Ethnic Cleansing, Texas A&M University Press, College Station, TX, 1995, p.51.

1315 See Susan Bryce, "The Public Relations of Modern Warfare", New Dawn, N°. 56, September-October 1999, Online Document found at http://www.agitprop.org.au/stopnato/19990928newdawn.htm.

1316 See "Indonesia Places Restrictions on Journalists in War-Torn Aceh Province", The Freedom of Information Center, June 11, 2003, Online document found at http://foi.missouri.edu/jourwarcoverage/indonesia.html

1317 See « Freedom in the World 1998-99 », report, Online Document found at http://freedomhouse.org/survey99/relterr/etimor.html

1318 See US Deprtment of State, "Rwanda Country Reports on Human Rights Practices—2002", March 31, 2003, P. 8, Online Document with pagination found at http://www.asylumlaw.org/docs/rwanda/usdos02_rwanda_cr.pdf

1319 Idem.

1320 Idem.

1321 Idem.

arrested for photographing a "corpse in the streets"[1322], and where "Several local "journalists reported experiencing rough treatment at the hands of the police"[1323]. In Tibet as well, journalists wanting to cover the situation there must first be aware of certain facts. Indeed, a World Tibet Network News report mentions, "Reporting has been hobbled by Chinese restrictions on foreign journalists wanting to visit Tibet. In the past, only a very few reporters were allowed in, invariably accompanied by officials who followed their every move, preventing them from speaking to ordinary Tibetans"[1324]. In another conflict area, Kashmir, one journalist, Martin Sugarman, explains the restrictions he had to go through to report from the region. He states, "In late November, 1993, I visited Kashmir to document the social and political turmoil and the massive human rights abuses there. Due to the government of India's restrictions on journalists visiting the area, I applied for tourist visa and found the means and assistance to work undercover for a month of so before the Indian authorities learned of my true purpose. Under very threatening conditions, I managed to escape with all my film and interviews"[1325]. Indeed, the list of restrictions and harassments to journalists in crisis or conflict areas goes on and on. Usually however, the restrictions and limitations are much higher on foreign journalists than on local ones. This is especially the case in non-democratic or totalitarian countries, where local journalists often have to go through censorship and are certain that they may put their lives in danger if they contradict too much their regime. Generally speaking, however, foreign journalists are considered by such totalitarian regimes as being more dangerous than domestic ones because, first, they usually have sophisticated and on the spot transmitting equipment and, second, because foreign journalists generally do not have the same fear of the regime that domestic journalists in a totalitarian regime have, and even if they do their fear is much less.

It is important, furthermore, to state that restrictions on the freedom of media to access the conflict area can take more subtle forms other than the complete physical prevention of access. Indeed, on many occasions access might be easily

---

1322 See "Haiti Country Reports on Human Rights Practices for 1996", Bureau of Democracy, Human Rights, and Labor U.S. Department of State, 30 January 1997, Online Document found at http://www.usis.usemb.se/human/1996/west/haiti.html.

1323 Idem.

1324 See World Tibet Network News, "End the Fairy-Tale Reporting of Tibet (LAT)", Wednesday, August 24, 1999, Online document found at http://www.tibet.ca/wtnarchive/1999/8/24-2_5.html

1325 See Martin A. Sugarman, "Kashmir: Paradise Lost", May 29, 1997. Online document found at http://www2.4dcomm.com/farookster30/kash1.htm.

granted to journalists but subjected to special conditions. The first of such conditions is imposing military escort on reporters wishing to access the combat zone. It
means that if a journalist wants to report from the conflict zone, he or she will have
to be accompanied by a military escort. Such a practice iss very much used and is
referred to by some writers as "the pool/escort reporting system[1326]. In this respect,
Hedrick Smith explains what this system is and how it developed. He states, "The
pool/escort reporting system was an outgrowth of reporters' earlier frustration at
being totally excluded from the assault on Grenada. The Pentagon's response was
to offer access to small "pools" of reporters as its only feasible means for moving
representatives of the press corps around hot battlefields, especially early in operations[1327]". Thus, imposed military escort largely means that a limited number of
journalists are chosen and allowed to accompany the troops in the conflict zone.
The result of such an arrangement is that the rest of the reporters would have to
depend in their coverage of the conflict on the information communicated to
them by those few chosen pool reporters. Robert E. Denton explains that in the
Gulf War of the 1990s "most of the approximately 1,000 journalists who wanted
to cover the war in the Persian Gulf were left at the Dhahran International Hotel
or the Riyadh Hyatt, able to receive only pool reports and the daily military briefings issued by representatives of the Joint Command[1328]".

The pool or escort system also hides another obstacles reporters face in their
coverage, which is that of direct and subtle censorship. Indeed, an escort military
unit's presence would sometimes discourage a reporter of being totally objective
on what he witnesses, can limit his choice of places he wants to cover[1329], and can
censor his work for military security reasons[1330]. Yet, for some writers explain

---

1326 See Robert E. Denton, op.cit., p.16.
1327 See Hedrick Smith, op.cit.,p. xviii.
1328 Ibid., p. 14.
1329 See Robert E. Denton, op.cit., p.13. Also see p. 15 where Robert E. Denton
      explaisn the three levels of filters that a pool reporter had to support. He states
      "They saw several levels of filters. First, reporters needed to obtain accreditation
      from the Pentagon. Second, they had to get into a pool—at best, a considerable
      long shot. Finally, if they managed that hurdle they were then dependent—as in
      Panama—on their escort's choice of a location for a story".
1330 Idem, p.14., Robert E.Denton states « Some journalists were bothered by the
      stipulation that "at U.S. tactical or field locations and encampments, a public
      affairs escort may be required because of security, safety, and mission require-
      ments, as determined by the host commander." 3 Reporters do not want to be
      told where they can go and to whom they may talk. But the decision to rely on
      censored pool reports as a primary conduit of battle and combat information was
      even more controversial".

that the pool system was better than being totally excluded from the coverage of the conflict, or worst of the reporters being unprotected during their conflict coverage. Robert E. Denton argues, for example, that in the coverage of the US invasion of Panama, the group of pool reporters accompanying the U.S. forces "was generally kept at some distance from the fighting in Panama City, and only escorted into an area after combat had mostly ceased."[1331]. On the other hand, "the few journalists who were already in Panama before the invasion began, found it difficult to do much more than provide phone reports from a Marriott hotel that was periodically raided by Noriega loyalists. Several were taken from the hotel as hostages"[1332]. Journalists fear for their own security should not be neglected, in this respect. After all, fear for one's own safety is legitimate and a natural human emotion. Sometimes, however, and even with the permission and escort to enter the combat zone, many journalists prefer not to enter the zone. A good example of this can be seen in the number of journalists who landed on the shores of France in the famous D-Day with the allied forces. Hedrick Smith states, in this respect, "461 reporters were signed up at the Supreme Headquarters, Allied Expeditionary Force to cove D-Day. Of that number, only 27 U.S. reporters actually went ashore with the first wave of forces"[1333].

Whether it is through denying physical access to the conflict area, imposing military escort, or military censorship for military security reasons, journalists' coverage of a conflict zone has to go through "filters", to borrow Robert. E. Denton's expression, that would reduce little by little the objectivity of their reports and coverage. In this sense, it can be assumed that journalists can sometimes and due to these filters be used by warring parties as propaganda diffusers in spite of themselves.

313.1.2. Financial Impediments

Financial impediments are another important element of these objective or neutral factors that contribute to the media's crisis of objectivity in its coverage of certain international conflicts and crises. Indeed, in many cases the ability to objectively be able to cover an international crisis might be limited by the media's own lack of financial resources. Being unable to allocate sufficient or any financial support to the coverage of an international crisis, the media might end up relying on other sources for its news coverage which can orient this media's crisis coverage. Financially, this small media or independent media outlet is neither able to verify the information it is buying or copying, nor is it able to disregard

---

1331   Ibid, p.10.
1332   Idem.
1333   Ibid, p. 42.

the entire coverage of the international crisis because it has to compete with other media outlets. In such a situation, this small media outlet has no other option but to cover this international conflict or crisis even with unverified information.

It is important to stress that not all media outlets, or small independent media, can afford the costs of a dispatching its own correspondents and obtaining direct coverage of an international conflict, or even sometimes of a domestic issue to relay the story. Noam Chomsky argues, in this respect, that "if the newspapers in Pittsburgh or Salt Lake City want to know about Angola, say, very few of them are going to be able to send their own correspondents and have their own analysts and so on"[1334]. It seems that there are two main reasons explaining this inability of small media outlets to cover objectively and have a first hand perception of an international conflict or crisis through its won correspondents and reporters. Yet, both explanations have to do with financial considerations. They are, first, the profitability of presenting news to consumers versus presenting advertisements and, second, the actual cost of news coverage.

The commercial considerations of the media business indicate that advertising is the backbone of a news company, and that the accompanying news are merely a by-product. Some views argue that, even at the beginning of its usage, the term "media" itself was not only limited to structures that gather and diffuse news but that it also included entertainment diffusion. More significantly, the significance is that the first connotations of the term were commercial and advertising related. In this respect, Leo Bogart states, "The 1909 edition of Webster's Dictionary included among its definitions of the word "medium, instrumentality, as in advertising medium." At about this time, the closely linked term "marketing" also came into use. In the context of the advertising business, media simply represented different methods by which advertisements could be delivered and products "marketed." Advertising agencies, beginning at the time of the first World War, set up media departments, to marshal facts and compare the channels— newspaper, magazine, billboard and car card space—through which their clients' messages could be disseminated. The Audit Bureau of Circulations was set up in 1915 to provide information that would facilitate the comparison and selection of publications"[1335]. Noam Chomsky, for his part, argues that newspapers, for instance, actually loose money in news production and diffusion. He states that "the press does not make money on people buying newspapers, they loose money on people buying newspapers[1336]". Leo Bogart is also a supporter of this view. He

---

1334   See Noam Chomsky, Understanding Power, op. cit., p. 14.

1335   See Leo Bogart, Commercial Culture: The Media System and the Public Interest, Oxford University Press, New York, 1995, p. 16.

1336   See Noam Chomsy, Understanding Power, Ibid., p. 24.

argues, "It is mainly "advertising chatter" that funds the media—themselves part of a marketing structure in which the production of goods is governed by manufacturers' perceptions of consumer demand. For advertisers, media are vehicles for diffusing their messages, not avenues of public enlightenment or cultural enhancement. This is to be noted, not to be deplored. Advertising appears to be a necessary element of a competitive business economy"[1337]. A distinction is made, however, between different media outlets, as far the impact of advertising is concerned. For instance, broadcasting media like television and radio broadcast are much more vulnerable to the impact of advertising on the programs than printed media[1338], since viewers have the choice of changing channels anytime to get news, and since "only one viewer in ten cites "news quality" as the reason for watching"[1339]. Indeed, it seems that the enormous news flow by different outlets have helped to loose interest in news itself and, consequently, make producing news only a non-profitable business. Leo Bogart explains "TV news-viewing, and network news ratings have dropped. The public at large once absorbed information inadvertently, serendipitously, by osmosis, through its almost universal reading of newspapers. Newspapers and news magazines continue to lose circulation and to intrude more fluff into their pages"[1340]. A similar view is expressed by Nicholas Burns who deplores, for instance, the "sorry minimum of foreign coverage, reflecting current prevailing public attitudes"[1341] in the U.S.

Perhaps the term "infotainment" is the most adequate to understand the commercial realities that govern news coverage. Infotainment simply signifies the combining of news with entertainment. Thus, news in this case would be a product presented, like entertainment, to consumers in a more and more consumer oriented culture. This has certainly helped distance journalism from its basic function of reflecting the truth. Leo Bogart states, in this respect, "The pursuit of audiences increasingly forces journalism to assume the guise of entertainment. Thus it departs from its proper functions, to report accurately on the world around us and to raise the issues that arouse public concern and require government action at every level"[1342]. The idea is that news nowadays has to be entertaining as well. If the news item is not entertaining or sensational, it will not draw public

---

1337 Ibid, p. 69.
1338 See leo Bogart, op.cit.
1339 Ibid., p. 181.
1340 Ibid., p. 11.
1341 See Nicholas Burns, "Talking to the World About American Foreign Policy", Harvard International Journal of Press/Politics, Vol. 1, No. 4, Fall 1996, p. 14.
1342 Ibid., p. 174.

attention which, consequently, means less consumers for advertisers and less ratings for the media outlet.

The result is that the chosen news has to capture, entertain, and maintain the audience the audience. The problem is to know what is more interesting to present, which explains the difference in priority given to the same news item by different media outlets. Indeed, most media would concentrate on domestic news as being more interesting to the audience and, thus, more susceptible of generating income. The determinant of choice for the media outlets is to distinguish if there is a domestic preference for coverage of certain types of news and to which degrees. In the case of an international crisis or conflict coverage, however, all seem to depend on the perceived national interests and distance involved. In this respect, Nik Gowing explains, "Treatment of stories will vary according to national and regional agendas. A crisis in one part of the world can easily be viewed elsewhere as irrelevant. The level of coverage (or refusal to cover) will often be a function of national interest and distance from the event. The lower the national interest and the greater the distance, the less likely it is that news organisations will have anything more than a passing interest in the developing story. There is no uniform media response that defies international borders and national identities"[1343]. For his part, Leo Bogart states, "When people are asked what they remember in the news, murders and murderers are mentioned far more than foreign wars. In fact, homicidal maniacs were seven times as memorable, at the time, as the bloody war between Iran and Iraq"[1344]. The competition between journalists' instincts and the media business's financial considerations and guidelines is quite evident. In this respect, Nik Gowing argues, "The conflict between journalistic instincts and commercial realities in the increasingly tough information marketplace will be profound. The relentless push for news that entertains ("infotainment") seems unstoppable, with a trend towards the "trivial and mediocre" and news that is predominantly domestic with scant reflection of foreign crises"[1345]. Hence, it can be said that the lack of profitability from covering an international conflict or crisis, especially if there is no domestic interest involved, is largely due to the dependence of media for commercial competition on ratings and advertising.

The second component of these financial impediments to the media's objectivity in covering an international conflict or crisis is that which has to do with the cost of coverage itself. Indeed, having a permanent correspondent in a far

---

1343 See Nik Gowing, "Media coverag: Help or Hinderance in Conflict Prevention", Online document found at
http://wwics.si.edu/subsites/ccpdc/pubs/media/media.htm
1344 See Leo Bogart, op. cit., p.160.
1345 See Nik Gowing, op. cit.

away country, sending a media outlets' own news staff to report on the conflict, or even buying the information of coverage from other news suppliers is a very expensive endeavour.

A media organisation or outlet that is prepared to employ a permanent correspondent with offices and staff in another country must be welling to pay an expensive amount of money. Salaries and expenses to maintain such correspondents can be quite costly for many media. These salaries vary naturally from one media organisation to another and from one journalist to another. Some like Barbara Walters, for example, are paid a very high salary, especially if their reputation as journalists or correspondents results in a transfer from the organisation they already work in to another. The example of Barbara Walters is interesting indeed. She was offered 1 million $ a year to be hired by ABC from NBC in 1976[1346]. Moreover, the wages got higher later on. Diane Sawyer, for instance, earned 7,5 million $ a year with ABC[1347].

As mentioned above, those salaries vary from one journalist to another and from one media outlet to another. They also vary from one country to another. According to the U.S. Department of Labour/Bureau of Labour Statistics' Occupational Outlook Handbook Survey, "Median annual earnings of news analysts, reporters, and correspondents were $29,110 in 2000. The middle 50 percent earned between $21,320 and $45,540"[1348], While "The lowest 10 percent earned less than $16,540, and the highest 10 percent earned more than $69,300"[1349]. There is also a difference between earnings of journalists working in printed media compared to those working in broadcast media outlets. According to the survey, "Median annual earnings of news analysts, reporters, and correspondents were $33,550 in radio and television broadcasting and $26,900 in newspapers in 2000"[1350]. In addition, some experienced journalists, such as news anchors, have salaries that are superior to those of other journalists, news analysts, or reporters. The survey mentions, "The annual average salary, including bonuses, was $83,400 for weekday anchors and $44,200 for those working on weekends. Television news reporters earned on average $33,700. Weekday sportscasters typically earned $68,900, while weekend sportscasters earned $37,200. Weathercasters averaged $68,500 during the week and $36,500

1346 Idem.
1347 Idem.
1348 See U.S. Department of Labor/Bureau of Labour Statistics' *Occupational Outlook Handbook survey,"* News Analysts, Reporters, and Correspondents" Online document found at http://www.bls.gov/oco/ocos088.htm.
1349 Idem.
1350 Idem.

on weekends"[1351]. According to the 2001 survey, "the annual average salary, including bonuses, was $55,100 for radio news reporters and $53,300 for sportscasters in radio broadcasting"[1352]. In the United Kingdom, the salaries paid to journalists also vary according to outlet and experience. For example, on August 2002, A UK specialised website survey mentions, "Starting salary range for a junior reporter on a local/regional paper: £11,000–£14,000. Junior reporters can expect rises of £2,000–£3,000 when qualified. Starting salary for a postgraduate trainee on a national paper is around £20,000 +"[1353], while the "range of salaries for senior reporters, feature writers and sub-editors on local/regional papers: £25,000–£40,000"[1354] and that the "range of salaries for senior editors on regional daily papers is £50,000–£80,000"[1355]. On the national papers, salaries can be £100,000 upwards"[1356]. Moreover, In broadcast journalism in the UK during the same period, starting salaries were between £10,000 and £20,000, while the "range of typical salaries at age 40" was between £24,000 and £45,000"[1357] This is why some media outlets would often be using the services of freelance journalists instead of permanent ones.

If a media outlet decides to open a permanent correspondence office in another country, then such an outlet must be able to bear the financial weight of such a decision. For example, "It cost $250,000 a year to maintain a correspondent in Tokyo, on top of the salary[1358]" for the correspondent. This is quite logical since such a office needs the allocation of lots of money for various technicalities such as staffing, equipment, salaries of local employees, if any, taxes…;etc. Even if a media outlet is able to open a correspondent office in other countries, the commercial realties would have It that, sometimes, to generate profit from such an office, the correspondent would be asked by the employing media outlet to sell information and reports to other media outlets or networks. This naturally would leave a correspondent less time to focus on the coverage of the events. Leo Bogart explains, in this respect, "The decline in network news ratings through the 1980s (they stabilized at the outset of the 90s) coincided with an economic turndown and placed great demands on news managements to cut costs. All three network news organizations underwent series of massive bloodbaths that thinned the ranks of senior

---

1351 Idem.
1352 Idem.
1353 See The Uk's Graduate Career Prospectus website found at www.prospects.ac.uk
1354 Idem.
1355 Idem.
1356 Idem.
1357 Idem.
1358 See Leo bogart, op. cit., p. 182

professionals. They closed many of their own bureaus at home and abroad and relied on their affiliates to cover domestic stories outside Washington and New York. The survivors on the staffs were pressed to become more productive. Correspondents were sometimes asked to supply material for so many network shows that they did not have time to cover stories"[1359]. Moreover, even if a news outlet that is not able to send its own correspondents to cover an international news item opts for buying the news about this international or sometimes even local event from a bigger news outlet, which is usually a news dispenser, not all media are able to pay some of the prices set as a price for quality news supply. These prices usually vary depending on the quality and, certainly, sensationalism of the news item that is being auctioned.

The financial impediments to journalists' objective coverage of an international conflict or crisis are simply another obstacle placed in the path of the desired journalistic objectivity goal. News production and diffusion in the current consumer oriented society seems to have mutated into becoming a mere by-product of the media's entertainment function. Advertising and ratings are the economic backbone of the media outlets. Journalists' objectivity has to be often modelled to the requirements of the media consumption marketplace. Furthermore, not all media can afford to bear the costs of having an independent first hand look of an international conflict or crisis. Indeed, the costs of such a venture is quite often economically unviable, especially to small media outlets. The determining consideration of whether an international conflict is economically interesting to the media is geographic proximity and national interests. If these elements were some or all of the significances of the international crisis or conflict for a country, then it would be interesting to the domestic consumer of the media and, hence, worthwhile to cover, sensationally of course for higher ratings.

3.3.1.3. Technological Impediments

Technological impediments are another obstacle placed in the path of the journalists' objectivity ideal. Indeed, the on-going advancement in communication and transmission technologies is quite remarkable. Technological advances for news coverage signify, however, two main difficulties. The first one, for certain media outlets and journalists, seems to be that it is financially costly and in some cases impossible to keep up with these technological advancements and innovations. For, even if they do acquire such modern technologies, new more efficient technologies are being developed everyday. The second problem that such advancements in communications technologies pose is that there is a parallel

---

1359 Idem.

advancement in the technology of instruments that can jam, intercept, prevent, and even falsify media transmission, diffusion, and reception.

The recent technological advances in communication technologies are indeed quite astonishing. In this respect, Stephen Jukes states, "It has been more than 150 years since Baron Julius von Reuter started using carrier pigeons to deliver news stories and stock prices from Brussels to Aachen in Europe. Within a year, technological advances and the introduction of the telegraph were already transforming his fledgling news business"[1360]. It is interesting to note that technological advances were not the same everywhere and that sometimes they resulted in media workers' protests. This, for example was the case of the UK when workers' unions protested against the introduction of new technologies in last two decades because such technologies would cause job losses[1361]. Indeed, the debate over ICT (International Communications technologies) continuing developments and effects is an on-going one. The continuity of such developments is a well-accepted fact. William H. Dutton and Malcolm Peltu state, for example, that "the rapid pace of ICT innovation and diffusion will be maintained well into the twenty-first century as computing, telecommunications, and broadcast and print media continue to converge on common digital-based techniques"[1362]. For his part, Christopher Freeman affirms the association of technological advances in this field with repercussions on human workers. He says, "interest in the role played by ICTs in shaping employment patterns grew during the 1980s and 1990s because the dramatic spread of ICTs coincided with rising underlying levels of unemployment in developed economies"[1363].

Technological advances in communications technologies can certainly facilitate a journalist's work of coverage during an international crisis or conflict. The times of writing in pens and carrier pigeons to transmit the news is over. Many news outlets have mobile TV satellite transmission systems that enables them to transmit news from anywhere on the globe in a more rapid and in a more efficient manner. Nonetheless, these transmitted pictures and precisely because they

---

1360   See Jukes States, "Real-time responsibility: journalism's challenges in an instantaneous age.", Harvard International Review, Vol. 14, N°. 2, 2002, pp. 14-18.

1361   Idem.

1362   See William H. Dutton, and Malcolm Peltu, Information and Communication Technologies: Visions and Realities, Oxford University Press, New York, 1996, p. v.

1363   See Christopher Freeman, "The Two-Edged Nature of Technological Change: Employment and Unemployment", in William H. Dutton, and Malcolm Peltu, Information and Communication Technologies: Visions and Realities, Oxford University Press, New York, 1996, pp. 19-36., p. 19.

are transmitted by telephone lines have become nowadays a bit slow[1364] and quite uncompetitive, as work instruments for a war reporter. For nowadays, many correspondents of more prestigious organisations have TV satellite transmission systems whose size is no bigger than that of an ordinary briefcase. They are, thus, more able and more mobile to cover conflicts events than other media. In fact, the technological revolution in this field has lead to what Nik Gowning calls "the supermarket of war videos"[1365]. A number of writers argue that such a revolution in communication technologies have had a positive effect on the coverage of conflicts simply because one reporter can "go in alone". In this respect, Stephen Jukes states, "Today, the laptop is hooked up to a satellite phone. Images from digital cameras are edited on a laptop and transmitted via the Internet within seconds from the site of a breaking story or sporting event to the reporter's central office. Wireless technology means court reporters can now type key verdicts into a Palm Pilot and transmit them back to editorial headquarters during a hearing. Miniature video cameras have transformed television news gathering, leading to the demise of big team camera crews and the opening of the news world to a generation of freelancers prepared to "go it alone" in dangerous conflict zones to secure footage. And as the tools of news gathering have become smarter, the relentless, insatiable 24-hour news cycle has become the norm"[1366]. Nik Gowing is of the same opinion regarding those smaller and more technically sophisticated cameras and transmission systems. He says, "The proliferation of Hi-8 video cameras (small, highly portable, and easily hidden) and a new generation of low-cost digital video (DVC) hand cameras, means that the information no longer has to be provided by expensive professional sources"[1367] Hence, these technological advances have helped in three main things as far as coverage is concerned. The first one is that they helped reduce the speed of transmission. The second is

---

1364 See Nik Gowing, op. cit., Nik Gowing states concerning these systems and the slowness of transmission that "In October 1996, BBC TV news and the TV agencies transmitted news videos of the Afghan civil war by satellite phone at a speed equal to one-thirtieth of real time. Each 2-minute news story took 1 hour to feed. The resulting video quality was adequate, but not perfect. The use of telephone instead of TV satellite dish (with its transport and transmission costs) contributed to a significant cost saving".

1365 See Nik Gowing, Lap-Top Bombardiers and the Media: Threat or Asset?" by Nik Gowing. Presentation to the Royal College of Defence Studies, London, 20 November 1995.

1366 See Stephen Jukes, op. cit.

1367 See Nik Gowing, "Media Coverage: Help or Hindrance in Conflict Prevention", op. cit.

that they helped increase the mobility of journalists in their coverage of different zones of the conflict or crisis areas. The third is that one reporter now has more of a chance to slip unnoticed to cover a conflict zone than to go in there with a big team for various technical reasons.

Yet such technological advances have also their negative effects for reporters and correspondents covering an international crisis or conflict. The most obvious of these disadvantages is that, first of all, a journalist has to be able to own such equipment. William H. Dutton and Malcolm Peltu state, in this respect, that one aspect of the debate concerning the advancements in communication technologies is the issue of those that have such technologies and those that do not. They state that "this technical revolution has generated vigorous debate around a number of 'hot button' issues, such as concerns over employment, privacy, and the growing gaps between information 'haves' and 'have nots"[1368]. Hence, a news organisation which does not have the ability to possess or keep up with these new technologies would not be able to perform as efficiently and rapidly as the other "richer" news organisations, to borrow Nik Gowing's expression,

The second of these disadvantages to an international conflict coverage caused by such new advances of communication technologies, is the dangers that such high-tech instruments can place the journalists in, precisely due to these gadgets speed of transmission. Dangers can also lie in the fact that such expensive equipment can be very tempting to some criminal elements in conflict zones. Yet, the principal danger remains in their speed of transmission, especially concerning filming and transmitting "undesired" images of human rights abuses. Indeed, a journalist can be quite threatening to warring sides of a conflict if he happens to catch a war crime on his camera, for instance. In this respect, Stephen Jukes gives the example of Daniel Pearl. He states "But the growing ease of reporting, aided by technology; has also made the work of foreign correspondents more dangerous. The average war criminal does not want to be caught red-handed on 24-hour cable television committing an atrocity. As seen most recently in the case of Daniel Pearl, the intimidation, abduction, and killing of journalists has become the norm in too many countries. As correspondents in Afghanistan have found, however, it is not just the ability to report in real time that makes them vulnerable. Expensive equipment has made them a target for attack, indeed, at the time of this writing nine correspondents—including two from Reuters—have been killed in the current conflict, several with robbery as the apparent motive"[1369]. The first danger concerning the use of these new communications technology

1368 See. William H. Dutton and Malcolm Peltu, op. cit., p. v
1369 Ibid.

appears, therefore, to be relating to the journalists and reporters own safety in combat or conflict zones.

It seems, however, that innovations do not only concern communications technologies but also journalistic practice itself. Indeed, a new type of reporters emerged mainly, due to these innovations in communications technologies in addition to the growing lucrative nature of the media sensationalism market. For, if permanent journalists or reporters are hesitant to expose themselves to danger by entering a conflict zone, another type of reporters has emerged to take their place. The new type are freelance reporters who now and due to technology have the ability to do all the reports needed using one small camera. In this respect, Stephen Jukes states, for example, "Thanks to cheap, lightweight video cameras, a new generation of "backpackers," or freelance journalists, is going into war zones and taking risks that few major media organizations would sanction. Those freelance journalists know that the closer they get to the front line, the more likely they are to get marketable footage"[1370]. Here, it seems again that the marketplace determines the type of coverage. For such freelance reporters, it can be logically assumed that the more sensational the stories they sell is the more money they will earn.

The third of these disadvantages brought on by the innovations in communication technologies is related to the enormous flow of images and stories that newsroom editors are bombarded with from all over the world and from everyone (Their own reporters, permanent correspondents, other news agencies and freelance reporters...etc). Nik Gowing states "From a matrix of incoming video on their desktop video-screens, journalists in a TV newsroom can pick and choose, just like walking down the supermarket aisles.... The task of filtering it all quickly is mind-boggling, given the mass of video and the short time usually available"[1371]. Naturally, lack of time in doing things would result in less perfection and, therefore, less objectivity. For instance, a news organisation that wants to diffuse a certain report may not have the time to investigate the context of its coverage and, thus, would be less objective in its coverage. Stephen Jukes, for his part, states, "Real-time news coverage also means that it is more important than ever to frame news events in their proper context. Several recent examples have revealed the confusion that stems from failing to obey one of the core principles of journalism. Television footage of a minority of Palestinians celebrating after the September 11 attacks was aired widely around the world. But that footage was often broadcast without commentary or any attempt to place it in the broader context of the Islamic world, which widely

---

1370 Idem.
1371 See Nik Gowing, "Media Coverage: Help or Hindrance in Conflict Prevention", <u>op. cit</u>

condemned the attacks[1372]". Here again, it is obvious that technological advances can be used as an asset in the fast pace inter media competition for a bigger market-share.

Another technological disadvantage, which is parallel to the innovations in the speed of transmission is that, ironically, technological innovations also help to jam the transmission of foreign correspondents in a conflict zone. The examples of such acts by certain governments and conflict parties in sabotaging the transmission of journalists are many. For instance, during a live studio debate in early December, the phone calls of two important guest speakers telephoning in from Turkey with the Kurdish Satellite Television were inexplicably drowned out for 10-20 minutes by Hezballah military march music, and electronic interference[1373]. In Bahrain, "In May the authorities jammed a satellite transmission of the British Broadcasting Corporation (BBC) program Assignment because it contained a report on the political unrest that was critical of the Government"[1374]. In China also, where "authorities frequently monitor telephone conversations, fax transmissions, electronic mail, and Internet communications of foreign visitors, businessmen, diplomats, residents, and journalists as well as Chinese dissidents, activists, and others"[1375]. Furthermore, same practices are also common in Syria and Vietnam[1376], and probably in many other countries including in the most democratic of them. The Echelon[1377] project is a very good example of this Big Brother is Watching situation carried out by democratic regimes.

The proliferation of technological innovations has rendered the work of journalists easier and faster, especially when they are covering conflicts or crisis. These technology advancements present the advantage of a more rapid transmission of news items, more mobility for journalists, and more discretion in their work, since

---

1372 Ibid.
1373 See Kurdish Satellite Television website at
       http://www.ib.be/med/med-tv/pr/jamming.htm
1374 See U.S. Department of State, "Country Reports on Human Rights Practices for
       1996", Online document found at
       http://www.privacyinternational.org/reports/hr96_privacy_report.html
1375 Idem.
1376 Idem.
1377 Echelon is perhaps the most powerful intelligence gathering organization in the
       world. Several credible reports suggest that this global electronic communications
       surveillance system presents an extreme threat to the privacy of people all over the
       world. According to these reports, ECHELON attempts to capture staggering
       volumes of satellite, microwave, cellular and fiber-optic traffic, including communications to and from North America. This vast quantity of voice and data
       communications are then processed through sophisticated filtering technologies.

it is no longer necessary in to send big crews for coverage purposes. Yet, technological innovations in communications and information transmission are a double-edged sword. It also has its disadvantages. First, keeping up with such
innovations creates a gap between the media outlets that can afford them and
those that cannot. Second, such innovations places journalists covering a conflict
in more danger, precisely because they can transmit atrocities and annoying images
fast, and also because of these instruments' tempting nature to outlaws. In addition, such innovations have helped create a marketplace competition of freelance
reporters and journalists who would compete even in risking their lives for a more
sensational news item in a conflict zones, because new technology provides them
with smaller and smaller equipment to perform their work, and because they have
to supply competitive news items that are both more sensational and more rapidly
transmitted than others. Finally, technological advances in communication systems can also be used by governments, or parties to a conflict, in order to sabotage
or jam a journalist's transmission of an annoying news item.

3.3.2. The Crisis of Objectivity and the Independence of Media

As explained in an earlier section, the media is going through a crisis of objectivity. The manifestations of this crisis, or its indications, are mostly related to the
media's functions and organisation. Indeed, the media's functional abilities, such
as its ability to set its own agenda, to frame news items, to diffuse its framed stories, and the organisational structure of the media and its relationship to the rules
of the information market place all contribute to this lack of objectivity accusations, the media's objectivity crisis. There exists, furthermore, objective or neutral
limitations to the media's objective coverage, which in their own way, both give
an excuse and at the same time contribute to the media's crisis of objectivity.
Notwithstanding, it should also be noted that this crisis of objectivity must be as
well examined against the notion of the media's independence itself. This independence can be analysed on two main levels. The first one is the individual
human level relating to journalists themselves, and the second is the one relating
to the independence of the media as an organisation. Undoubtedly, the first level
(the human level) can be said to influence the higher level (the organisation level
one), since, naturally, the characteristics of the whole is a refection and an outcome of the characteristics of its constituents.

The first and primary level of analysis in this discussion of the independence
of the media and its relation to its crisis of objectivity is that which is related to

the independence of journalists themselves. In this respect, most dictionaries would indicate that the word dependent largely means, "to be influenced by" or "decided by something"[1378]. The opposite of dependent would be found to mean either "not helped" or "not ruled"[1379]. The general idea that can be seen in the linguistic connotations of this "independence" is that in order to be "independent" one should not be helped or influenced in his ideas, opinions, or actions.

Indeed, the studies of human nature concerning objectivity indicate that objectivity, as a pure concept, is probably a utopia rather than a reality. Richard Streckfuss states, for instance, that "objectivity was founded not on a naive idea that humans could be objective, but on a realization that they could NOT"[1380]. Moreover, Laurent Derobert et al. argue, for their part, "no bridge is build. Objectivity has been opposed to subjectivism, even though objectivism would have been sufficient: It would have saved the subject. Because before we can tell what a "careful assessment" is, we must know by whom it is done"[1381]. Some, however, would label objectivity as simply being a "myth"[1382]. Others would refer to it as "a scientific ideal"[1383]. Human nature, surroundings and specificities have the greatest bearing on one's choices and actions. The difference between individuals also reflects a difference in specificities, surroundings and nature from one individual to another. Accordingly he determinants of choices and, consequently, acts can be interpreted against the different motives involved. Hence, "our actions have a constant union with our motives, tempers, and circumstances"[1384]. This is a quite logical assumption since to be totally objective, one has to be totally free from all motives, temperaments, and to has to be detached from all exterior predisposed environmental influences. This, naturally, is not possible. For such characteristics are what distinguishes humans from machines.

It can also be assumed that lack of objectivity can also mean lack of independence. Indeed, if dependent means "influenced by" or "decided by", then subjective

---

1378 See Cambridge Advanced Learner's Dictionary.

1379 Idem.

1380 See Richard Streckfuss, "Objectivity in Journalism: A Search and Reassessment", op. cit.

1381 See Laurent Derobert et al, "Human Nature and the Capability Approach", GREQAM, Université Aix-Marseille III, August 2003, Online document with pagination found at http://cfs.unipv.it/sen/papers/Teschl_Derobert_Luchini.pdf, p. 12.

1382 See Bernard K. Johnpoll and Robert Miraldi, Muckraking and Objectivity: Journalism's Colliding Traditions, Greenwood Press, New York, 1990, p. 15

1383 See Edmund Lambeth, Committed Journalism: An Ethic for the Press, op. cit., p.73.

1384 See Laurent Derobert et al, op. cit.,p. 12

would be understood to be largely the same. By consequence, if independent means, "not influenced by" or "not decided by", then objectivity would largely mean independence. According to this reasoning, if objectivity is a "utopia", a "myth", or an "ideal" then being independent is also an ideal or a "myth", since individuals are subjected to the influence of various inner and outer factors that influence their perceptions, choices, and actions.

Therefore, the first and primary level of analysis of the relationship between the media's objectivity crisis and its independence, is that of journalists and reporters being first humans and then journalists and reporters. Their human nature is bound, hence, to be reflected in the work they perform. It is completely utopian to expect them to be totally detached, objective, or independent. The idea of this influence of human nature on the desired objectivity of journalists is supported by many writers. Bernard K. Johnpoll and Robert Miraldi, for example, state, "To believe that bias can be excluded from news accounts written by human beings, concurs Washington Post reporter Lou Cannon, "perpetuates the most damaging bias of American journalism"[1385]. Others argue that a majority of journalists believe that objectivity is not an easily obtained goal because individual subjectivism more than being caused by the media institution's structural factors[1386]. For his part, Kevin Stoker explains, "Objectivity would place more responsibility in the trained intelligence of reporters and editors. This implies that the individual journalist would have the freedom not only to uncover the facts but also the intellectual tools necessary to make objective judgments"[1387]. Jay Rosen, for his part, argues, on another note, that not matter how much journalists try, they will not be totally objective. He says "What is insidious and crippling about objectivity is when journalists say: 'We just present you with facts. We don't make judgments. We don't have any values ourselves.' That is dangerous and wrongheaded[1388]". Thus, journalists will probably not be objective even if they want so much to be so. This inner human nature obstacle to attaining objectivity, which is caused by the differences between individuals' tempers, needs, and environment in all its forms (ethnic, social, religious, cultural, etc), is, unfortunately, accompanied by external pressures journalists are subjected to.

1385   See Bernard K. Johnpoll and Robert Miraldi, op. cit., p. 15.

1386   See R. Hackett, "Decline of a paradigm? Bias and objectivity in new media studies"., Critical Studies in Mass Communication, Vol.1, 1984, pp. 229-259.

1387   See Kevin Stoker, "Existential Objectivity: Freeing Journalists to Be Ethical", op. cit, p. 13.

1388   Jay Rosen is a press critic. Quoted in W. Glaberson, Fairness, "Bias and judgment: Grappling with the knotty issue of objectivity in journalism", New York Times, 12th December, 1994, p. D7

Indeed, being first and foremost humans, journalists are subjected to the outside pressures that affect the objectivity and sense of judgements of any human being regardless of his or her profession. These pressures can take various forms. They can be economic, social, political, or even fear, especially journalists working in non-democratic regimes. It can also take the form of legitimate natural fear for their safety while covering a conflict or a news item, where their lives might be in danger. All of these factors, whether combined or taken individually, limit journalists' independence and, consequently, affect their desired goal of objectivity.

Indeed, examples of such external factors, which limit journalists' independence and objectivity goal are many. The reliance on certain news sources and not exploring other points of view is a good example of such outside pressures. Meenakshi Gigi Durham argues, concerning this point, that "studies of journalists' reliance on elite sources indicate that the intense deadline pressures of modern-day print publication preclude them from expending the extra effort required to seek out non-traditional voices or use unorthodox reportorial methods"[1389]. Moreover, managerial pressures are quite often exerted on journalists to adopt certain pints of view or to abandon others. In the case of non-compliance to these managerial or editorial directives, journalists can be subjected to moral harassment, transfer to a less prestigious or important post or even dismissed, in certain cases. Such practices exist all over the world. Yet, they vary from one country to another depending on the political system in place and the margins of civil liberties applied.

Indeed, the examples of such pressures are abundant. For example, financial pressures and other subtle forms of government interference have become quite common posing a serious threat to media freedom in Albania[1390]. The same thing can be said about Nigeria. In this respect, a Human Rights Watch report mentions, "The media, like so many other sectors, is tainted by corruption, with many, though not all, journalists expecting to receive payment before agreeing to report, or not to report, an event. As in many other countries, deals are struck with individual politicians on whether, when or how to report particular events"[1391]. The problem is that the general perception is that such practices are only restricted to non-democratic countries when they are not. Indeed, It can be said that only "the Pakistani government has systematically violated the fundamental

---

1389 See Meenakshi Gigi Durham, "On the Relevance of Standpoint Epistemology to the Practice of Journalism: The Case for "Strong Objectivity". op. cit., p. 135

1390 See Human Rights Watch website found at
http://hrw.org/press/2002/11/albania1105.htm.

1391 See Human Rights Watch report "Nigeria: Renewed Crackdown on Freedom of Expression", online document found at
http://www.hrw.org/reports/2003/nigeria1203/index.htm

rights of members of the press corps through threats, harassment, and arbitrary arrests"[1392] and that, only in Pakistan, that many journalists "have been detained without charge, mistreated and tortured, and otherwise denied basic due process rights"[1393], and that only in that country, "the government has sought to, and in several cases succeeded in, removing independent journalists from prominent publications"[1394]. The most common assumption is that such harassments to the independence and objectivity of journalists only take place in freedom lacking political environments. Though this assumption might seem to be true, such pressures on journalists actually exist, although to lesser degrees and in less apparent forms, in even the most democratic of political systems. A good and prominent reporter, such as Peter Arnett, is, for example, dismissed from his post with NBC News because he "criticized the allied war (U.S. war on Iraq of 2003) plan on Iraqi television"[1395]. To intimidate other journalists from doing the same, NBC announced the news or Arnett dismissal "vividly on live television"[1396]. This happened in one of the most democratic systems of governance in the world, or at least in one that claims to be.

Indeed, press freedom in the world does not necessarily depend on the country's system of government. Moreover, one country might respect, to a good extent, journalistic freedoms on its own soil but abuse it outside its own territory. Perhaps the best illustration of this idea is the ranking of world countries concerning respect of press freedom, which was published by Reporters Without Borders in October 2003[1397]. According to this report, Finland ranked at the top of world countries respecting press freedom, while Cuba was second from last on the ranking list, ahead of North Korea. In Europe, for instance, Spain and Italy scored low amongst European Union countries, with Spain ranking 42nd, and Italy in the 53rd place. France occupied the 23rd position because of "its archaic defamation legislation, the increasingly frequent challenges to the principle of confidentiality of sources, and the repeated abusive detention of journalists by

---

1392   See Human Rights Watch report, "Pakistan: Threats to Journalists Escalate", online document found at http://www.hrw.org/press/2003/12/pakistan120303.htm
1393   Idem.
1394   Idem.
1395   See Jim Rutenberg," Arnett Dismissed After Remarks on Iraqi TV", <u>The New York Times</u>, April 1, 2003.
1396   Idem.
1397   See Reporters Without Borders, "Second World Press Freedom Ranking October 2003", Online document in pdf. Format found at http://www.rsf.org/article.php3?id_article=8247

police"[1398]. France, however, ranked better than the U.K., which occupied the 27th position. Surprisingly, countries such as Trinidad and Tobago, Latvia, and the Czech Republic were placed higher on the list even before such countries as the United States and Israel. Indeed, the above-mentioned report mentions a very interesting fact supporting the notion that respect of press independence and freedom is not linked to economic development or political liberalisation. The report states, "As in 2002, the ranking shows that a country's respect for press freedom is not solely linked to its economic development. The top 50 include countries that are among the poorest in the world, such as Benin (29th position), Timor-Leste (30th) and Madagascar (46th). Conversely, the 50 countries that respect press freedom least include such rich nations as Bahrain (117th) and Singapore (144th)"[1399]. More interestingly, the report indicates that some countries might preserve press freedom at home and abuse it abroad. This was, for instance, the case of the United States and Israel. the report mentions that" in the cases of the United States and Israel. They are ranked in 31st and 44th positions respectively as regards respect for freedom of expression on their own territory, but they fall to the 135th and 146th positions as regards behaviour beyond their borders"[1400]. Thus, even within their own borders, those two democratic model countries rank less on the list of world countries concerning press freedom than some countries, who are not "world models" for democracy such as Benin (29th position). It seems, thus, that pressures on journalistic independence are not necessarily governed by economic, political, or cultural nature of the country involved. This is due, perhaps, to a characteristic of the media, which is an advantage and a disadvantage for it at the same time. This characteristic of the media, which is a common trait for it everywhere, is an accepted perception of the media's power to influence public opinion. Indeed, something that has such a power needs to be controlled, even in the most democratic and liberal of societies.

The second level of analysis in this discussion of the media independence and its relationship with the crisis of objectivity is that which concerns the structural or organisational independence of the media as an enterprise. A careful analysis of the media's structure and business relations would reveal that the media, as an enterprise, are subjected to various pressures that would limit its independence and objectivity. The factors affecting the independence and, consequently, the can be grouped under certain general headings. These are structural, economic, political, and cultural factors.

1398 Idem.
1399 ibid., p. 1
1400 Idem.

The first of these is, hence, the structural factors that limit the independence of the media. These structural factors can be divided into two main categories: The effect of structural decision-making of the media, and the effect of the ownership structure on the media structure as a whole. Indeed, a number of scholars agree on the negative effect that the corporate news structure of the media can have on media objectivity and diversity. In this respect, David Demers and Debra Merskin argue, that quite a number of scholars have "major disagreements about the role and function of media in modern society" but that "on the issue of corporate structure they are all united by one common belief—that corporate media are destroying good journalism and democracy or the potential for democracy in modern society"[1401]. The idea here seems that profit maximization is a result of corporate media structure and that this profit objective is sought at the expense of more diversity and objectivity. David Demers, for his part, states that "most schol-ars and professionals believe media place greater emphasis on profits and less emphasis on non-profit goals, such as quality and information diversity, as they become more "corporatized"[1402]. One of the direct effects of this corporate struc-ture of the media is a managerial related one. For, with the increase of the size of an organization there comes an increase in the specialization of roles within this organisation, and an expansion of the division of labour[1403]. The result is that these structural forces would "increase the productive capacity of the organization and reduce costs"[1404], but, at the same time would "increase the complexity of the decision-making process"[1405]. Complexity can also be a synonym of bureaucracy. In this respect, David Demers mentions the studies of Max Webber, the sociology theorist, on structural organization. He argues, based on Webber's findings, that the "the most powerful kind of corporate organization is a bureaucracy—a corpo-rate organization in which behaviour is goal-directed and decision-making is rational"[1406]. In addition to rationality as a characteristic of a bureaucracy, it is also characterized by having a "hierarchy of authority, employment, and promotion based on technical qualifications, a set of rules and procedures that define job responsibilities and show how tasks are accomplished, formalistic impersonality, and a division of labour and role specialization"[1407]. Although bureaucracies are

---

1401 See David Demers and Debra Merskin, "Corporate News Structure and the Managerial Revolution", Journal of Media Economics, Vol. 13, N° 2., 2000, p. 104.

1402 See David Demers," Revisiting Corporate Newspaper Structure and Profit Making", Journal of Media Economics, Vol. 11, N° 2, 1998, p. 19,.

1403 Ibid. p. 115.

1404 Idem.

1405 Idem.

1406 See David Demers, op. cit., p. 21.

1407 Ibid., pp. 21-22.

efficient, according to Weber, they negatively affect "individual freedom", "auton-omy", and "democratic decision-making"[1408]. Interference in determining the content of news is probably the most important manifestation of the impact of corporate news organizational structure on the objectivity of media coverage. David Demers and Debra Merskin conducted a survey concerning corporate interference in editorial content of top-mangers (editors and publisher) in 269 daily newspapers in the United States. One of the findings of their survey is inter-esting. They state, "Editors and reporters would play a larger role in controlling news content as corporate structure increases. This finding applies to managing editors, editorial editors, and reporters. The only exception was top editors, for whom corporate structure does not make a difference, because most top editors at all newspapers play a major role in controlling editorial content"[1409]. Hence, it can be said that the internal organisation of a media enterprise limits the independence of the media in presenting various viewpoints, and, thus, limits its objectivity in the process. Furthermore, if the corporate objective is profit, then sacrifices on the expense of objectivity can be made.

Another aspect of this organizational structure of the media enterprises, which has an impact on, the independence of the media and its objectivity relates to the ownership structure. Indeed, many scholars indicate the effect of media owner-ship on its content and on its form as well. Edward S. Herman and Noam Chomsky, for instance, sets media ownership as first of the five filters on report-ing in the United States that affect news choices and constitute what they term as' propaganda model'[1410]. They continue to say that the "dominant media firms are controlled by very wealthy people or by managers who are subject to sharp con-straints by owners and other market-profit-oriented forces"[1411]. Edward S. Herman and Noam Chomsky conclude that this is "the first powerful filter that will affect news choices"[1412]. For his part, William Melody explains that the great-est danger to the liberty of expression is that owners would always be manipulat-ing the marketplace with ideas and concepts in the name of economic efficiency

---

1408   Idem, p. 22.

1409   See David Demers and Debra Merskin, op. cit., pp. 115-116.

1410   See Edward S. Herman and Noam Chomsky, Manufacturing Consent, op. cit., p. 4. The five filters constituting this propaganda model in the United States are 1-Size, ownership and profit orientation of the mass media, 2-The advertis-ing licence to do business, 3-Sourcing mass media news, 4-Flak and the enforcers, 5-Anticommunism as a control mechanism.

1411   Ibid., p. 14.

1412   Idem.

and profit[1413]. He explains that this concentration have also grown to include media related industries such as packaging and distribution which, according to William Melody, have "become a standardised production and marketing process in which the messages communicated are constrained and directed in both quantity and quality to meet the economic imperatives of that process"[1414]. The phenomenon of concentration of the media in more and more limited and elite ownership is the principal characteristics of the media ownership structure nowadays. This is an outcome of the free market conditions. Werner A. Meier, states in this respect, that "as a result of economic conditions or circumstances, access to the marketplace of ideas is restricted to a privileged few"[1415] and that "fewer owners have control over more newspapers and their circulation, and most of the media have been absorbed by large conglomerates, 'families' or chains"[1416]. This idea is quite close to that of Edward S. Herman and Noam Chomsky's who state, "Many of the large media companies are fully integrated into the market, and the others, too, the pressures of stockholders, directors, and bankers to focus on the bottom line are powerful. These pressures have intensified in recent years as media stocks have become market favourites"[1417]. Benjamin M. Compaine and Douglas Gomery are of a similar opinion to that of Edward S. Herman and Noam Chomsky concerning the concentration of media ownership to satisfy market conditions. To them, whether the media companies are owned publicly through stockholders or privately, the emphasis on profit generation has the highest priority. As far as the United States is concerned, they state, "Most of the largest companies are publicly held, meaning that anyone can buy stock and have a vote, however large or small, on major corporate decisions. Publicly owned firms have a fiduciary duty to their stockholders, meaning they must protect the value of their investment. Several of the largest companies, however, are privately held, closely controlled by families, who are usually founders or their decedents. Their responsibility is to private interests, rather than to public ones"[1418]. The

---

1413   See William H. Melody, 'Mass Media: The Economics of Access to the Marketplace of Ideas', in C. E. Aronoff (ed) <u>Business and the Media,</u> Goodyear, Santa Monica CA, 1978, pp. 216-226.

1414   Ibid., p. 219.

1415   See Werner A. Meier, "Media Ownership—Does It Matter?", in Robin Mansell et al. (eds.) <u>Networking Knowledge for Information Societies: Institutions & Intervention,</u> Delft University Press, Delft, 2002, pp 298-302, p. 298

1416   Idem.

1417   See Edward S. Herman and Noam Chomsky, Manufacturing Consent, <u>op. cit.,</u> pp. 7-8

1418   See Benjamin M. Compaine and Douglas Gomery, <u>Who Owns the Media? Competition and Concentration in the Mass Media Industry,</u> Lawrence Erlbaum Associates, Mahwah, NJ, 2000, p. 489.

result of this ownership structure whether corporate or privately owned is what Russell W. Neuman describes as being sort of a uniform production of content and same view of the world[1419]. This close to Noam Chomsky's idea of "elite opinion", where the media only reflects the opinion of the elite of the American society, for example.[1420]" For their part, Edward S. Herman and R. W. McChesney speak of the "ten colossal vertically integrated media conglomerates" which", dominate the global media market"[1421]. Nonetheless, some scholars argue that the effect of ownership in general on media content is still a subject to be researched more. In this respect, scholars such as Werner A. Meier, lament the lack of empirical studies concerning the impact of media ownership on media content and, consequently, on public opinion[1422]. Yet and even with such criticism, he admits, "Overall, the implications of media ownership and concentration on a global scale are as follows. The global interlocking of the media industry and traditional corporate power creates a powerful cartel, which in turn encourages the spread of certain values (for example, consumerism, shareholder value, individualism, egoism, etc.). There are strong incentives for the displacement of the public sphere with commercial infotainment, reality shows and trivialised news programmes. This strengthens a conservative 'common sense' view of the world, eroding local cultures and communities"[1423]. Any journalist's opposition to these administrative and ownership conditions is bound probably to failure. The reason is that "in most cases, journalists are directly affected but they do not report their own concerns (probably because of internal pressure)"[1424]. Hence, the implication of the media ownership structure whether privately held or publicly held (stockholders) seems to be an orientation for more profit and a reflection of the economic marketplace's hegemony over the media's independence and objectivity.

The relationship between the media's independence and its crisis of objectivity is an interesting one indeed. In order to be objective, the media has first to have enough independence. A careful analysis of the two main components of the media industry (the journalists and the media machine) would reveal that this independence is affected by various internal and external factors. On the primary human level of analysis, the independence of journalists can be said to be affected

---

1419 See Russell W. Neuman, The Future of the Mass Audience, Cambridge University Press, Cambridge, 1991, p. 131.

1420 See Noam Chomsky, Understanding Power, op. cit., pp 18-24.

1421 See Edward S. Herman and R. W. McChesney, The Global Media: The New Missionaries of Corporate Capitalism, London and Washington DC:1997, p. 52.

1422 See Werner A. Meier, op. cit., p. 299.

1423 Ibid, p. 300.

1424 See Werner A. Meier, op. cit., p. 301.

by various factors. The first of these factors is the characteristics of humans as being, by nature, more subjective than objective. Moreover, journalists' independence is affected by outside pressures that can be economic, social, political, or legitimate fear for their physical safety. The higher level of analysis is that of the media enterprise itself. In this respect, the issue of media ownership, whether privately or publicly owned, has a negative impact on the independence of media and, consequently, on its objectivity. Corporate media's bureaucracy can be said to result in lack of autonomy and in less democracy in decision-making, while elite ownership concentration results in a more uniform elite view of the world and a preference for maximising profit on the expense of objectivity.

Conclusion

Medius in Latin means intermediate. Today most dictionaries would give the word Medium or Method as the meaning of the word Media. The media, in its current form, is all of these meanings together. It is an intermediate between the public and its government, it is a medium through which the world is perceived by the public, and it is a method through which public opinion and society are observed and regulated.

Yet, the media was not always what it is today. It has developed, still developing, and will develop further both in its concept and in its form. Indeed, since its relatively modern beginnings as a vital institution of any human society and, as a social actor, the media has gone through various transformations and mutations making it the incredible powerful social actor it is today. These transformations were both in its forms, its role, its ethics, and its importance. Indeed, over the few past decades, not only the forms of the media has changed and multiplied but also its function and importance in influencing public opinion towards issues.

It was found that this change in the media's importance and functions is a result of various factors. Sometimes these factors only related to the international political context of the time. Sometimes they were the result of technological innovations in communications technologies and, sometimes, these changes were forced by the conditions of the free market competition; namely liberal globalisation. This change in the media's forms and functions can be seen all through the different periods of recent world history. Changes in media function brought about by the context of the prevailing international political conditions are those represented by the transformation of the media function corresponding to the international political atmosphere in place. Such transformation started with the partisan newspapers and the Penny press of the 19th century, passing by the clearly defined media propaganda function of the two global wars and the Cold-War era, up to the media of the New World Order or "Disorder" of today. As far as changes in media forms are concerned, these were brought about mainly by technological innovations and recently by the liberal globalisation wave. Changes due to technological innovations started with the Penny Press and its accessibility to the public and the separation of news and advertisements, passing by the invention of radio and television, up to the modern high-tech sophistication, speed, and multiplication of news and entertainment transmission gadgets and, most importantly, the personalised free access and transfer of information represented by Internet and other personal information and data transmitting and reception instruments (Mobile Phones, Satellite reception,...etc). Finally, changes due to market conditions and represented in the wave of mergers and acquisitions that started in the 1990s due to the intensive liberal globalisation fervour that swept the world in the immediate post-Cold War era and which resulted in less than a dozen mega media enterprises controlling the news and entertainment market and leaving no room for small and independent media outlets. Due to these transformations and changes, it can be concluded that nowadays there are two basic types of media. There is the institutional media, which is the current professional media enterprises and companies in all the forms of its outlets. Technological innovations and globalisation gave birth to the second type of media, which is the non-institutional one, represented by the individual free diffusion or reception of information via Internet and other forms of personal transmission and reception instruments. This research concerned that traditional and much more influential institutional media.

For its part, institutional or traditional media can be one of three forms: domestic or national, trans-national, and both national and trans-national. In other words, the demarcation line here is the physical frontiers of countries. If a media outlet only circulates within these frontiers then it's a national or a domestic media outlet. On the other hand if it circulates its news or products outside the frontiers as well, then it's a trans-national media outlet. If it can do both then its both national and trans-national. What is happening recently is that a lot of national media outlets are becoming both national and trans-national at the same time due to Internet and other communications innovations. Indeed, it is quite feasible for a small national newspaper in India, for instance, to establish a website for itself on the Internet that would be read by a subscriber in the other end of the world. Similarly, it is no longer difficult for citizens of a small village in Alaska, for example, to tune in via satellite reception to the national TV station in Australia.

Trans-national media discussed in this research is not, therefore, simply those media outlets that circulate outside national frontiers but those that are mega news gathering and dispensing enterprises. If a media outlet is the news dispenser to the public, then these trans-national news dispensers can be understood as being those enterprises that dispense news to this media outlet. In other words, it is those companies such as Reuters, Associated Press or *Agence France Press*.; etc which have offices and correspondents available all over the world and who's main function is to sell the news gathered to media outlets. These international news dispensers are also referred to sometimes as the TNMC's (Trans-National Media Cooperation's) or the TANA's (Trans-National News Agencies).

National media is a social actor, which interacts and responds to everything that exists in its environment. Basically, national media has to interact with internal national actors and elements and exterior ones. The interior national actors, includes the media's own audience, the politico-economic establishment, and Civil Society. Externally, those factors include national media's reaction to international political tendencies, as well as its relationship with trans-national news-gathering and dispensing media.

The relationship between national or domestic media and the political-economic establishment in a given country was found to be of a complementary nature and built around the interdependence between the needs and objectives of both institutions. This interdependence is first and foremost the outcome of the concordance of both institutions' agendas. The politico-economic establishment needs the media because of the media's ability to set the agenda of the public and because of its ability to manipulate public opinion. The media, for its part, needs the politico-economic establishment because of its need for official scouring and because of more technical needs such as licenses and permits…etc.

The issue of agendas and agenda setting effects is interesting. In democratic systems of government, three types of public policy agendas co-exist: the media agenda, the political-economic institution's agenda, and the public or citizens' agenda. Evidence found suggests that the concordance which exists between the media and the politico-economic establishment's agendas is much more higher and much more probable than between any of these two agendas and the public or citizens' agenda. In other words, it is much more difficult for an issue on the public agenda to be placed on that of the media agenda or the politico-economic establishment's agenda than the other way around. Moreover, issues on the public agenda are dependent in their designation, nature, and priority on the national media agenda and not vice versa. In other words, the politico-economic establishment can place an issue or upgrade its priority on the media agenda and, consequently, on the public agenda, the media can, for its part, place an issue or upgrade its priority on the politico-economic establishment, and both the media and the politico-economic establishment can easily place an issue or upgrade its status on the public or citizens' agenda. The politico-economic establishment can do that through its politico-economic decisions. The media can set the public agenda and upgrade the priority status of issues on this agenda through its privileged status as an agent of social change. It is much more difficult, on the other hand, that the public manages to place an issue on the action agenda of the politico-economic establishment. The public can only do this if it manages to place the issue on the agenda of the media (the intermediate) and create enough public pressure for this issue to gain more priority. The difficulty in doing this stems from the fact that the concordance between the media agenda and the politico-economic establishment's agenda is much stronger than the concordance between the public agenda with any of the two.

National media is, indeed, an irreplaceable social control agent through which a linkage with the public or the citizens is maintained in balance, particularly in democratic systems of government. This is probably why the media, as mentioned before, is not simply a method but is also an intermediate bridge between the public and the politico-economic establishment. For the politico-economic establishment, national media is some sort of a mirror in which national political and economic tendencies are reflected. In this respect, manifestations of national political tendencies are a normal and certainly an expected behavior of the national media and in any system of government. There exists, nonetheless, certain differences between the function of the media in both types of governments; i.e. in democratic and non-democratic ones. In non-democratic systems of government, national political manifestations in national media go no further than being a repetition of the regime's propaganda and of being a continuous collective brain washing process whereas, in democratic societies, national political manifestations in national media is a multitude of different national political points of view and convictions that do not necessarily favor the point of view of the regime in power. This does not mean that partisan media does not exist in democratic societies. On the contrary, in any given democratic country all daily newspapers, for instance, can be affiliated to support one political vision or party in the country or another. Yet, this is not done as aggressively and as openly as it was done in the 19th century where partisan newspapers openly and directly manifested their support for their respective parties. This is precisely why these national political tendencies are labeled as mere "manifestations of political tendencies, "and not as direct party propaganda. This suggests that national media, in democratic societies, has moved away from direct and open support for one political party or regime or another. This is, however, probably done because in order to gain more market shares or audiences, it is in the interest of the media not to show outright subjectivity. Subtle criticism is much more effective than direct aggressive one.

Two main notions can explain why the media has such an ability to set both the public and politico-economic agendas and why it has such a prestigious and effective social change and social control agent in any given society. The first notion relates to the advantages and disadvantages the media has in its relationship with the public, and the second relates to the advantages and disadvantages the public has in its relation with the media. Since the media is an enterprise, an economic analogy is best to illustrate these advantages and disadvantages. In simple economic terms, this prestigious status of national media is that where the media (the enterprise) distributes the news (products) to the public (the consumers). Accordingly, the advantages national media has are its ability to select, package, focus on certain products, create demand for its products, encourage consumption of certain products over others because it is more profitable, and to massively distribute these products. The disadvantages for the media in such a relationship is its own need to satisfy its public (consumers) and increase its market share of them, and the need to readjust its news (products) to constantly follow and respond to public tendencies and expectations. On the other hand, the disadvantage of the public in its relationship to the media is its growing need and dependence on these media products just as it depends on other products for almost every aspect of its daily life. The advantage the public has, in democratic societies, is that it can always have the possibility of sanctioning the media (the enterprise) and turning for its needs to another.

To set an agenda, issues have to be chosen and given priority. Since the public depends on the media to be informed of almost every aspect of the world around it, from international news to domestic traffic jams passing by national policies and events, then it is the media that presents the issues that this public depends on to set its agenda. In other words, the public, due to its dependence and need for orientation, sees the importance of issues through the importance given to these issues by the media. This is the effect of the media's advantage of being able to select what it presents to the public. But selection of issues to be presented alone is usually not enough to be effective in setting the public's agenda. To be more effective, the media has to choose also the adequate packaging of each issue presented. This is what is known as the media's framing function. Some believe framing to be the "conceptual tools, which the media and the public rely on to convey, interpret and evaluate information". Some consider framing to be that tool which helps audiences locate, perceive, identify, and label the information they receive. Roughly speaking, framing can be understood as the window frame through which the information is perceived. As far as types of frames used in media coverage are concerned, five main news frames have been identified in various studies. These frames are the Conflict Frame, the Human Interest Frame, the Economic Consequences Frame, the Morality Frame and the Responsibility Frame. The frame used in the presentation of a particular news usually governs the public's reaction to this news. If the Morality Frame is used, for instance, for a news item, then the result is that this news item would draw on the public's sense of morality and so on. Knowing what frame to use is also knowing what button to push in order to create the desired effect in the audience. In this respect, certain basic human emotions such as fear and empathy are more effective for the media to draw upon than others in order to capture and maintain the audience's attention and, most importantly, in order to manipulate public opinion towards issues. In a society, the definer and designator of what is dangerous or of what is to be feared is one that has a higher status as in the hierarchy of this society. Similarly, the media's ability to designate danger and deviance in a society gives it a high status in the hierarchy of this society as a prestigious social actor. What adds to the this ability of the media to set the public agenda, in addition to the ability to select and frame information, is the ability to focus on certain information or aspects of these information while ignoring others. Salience of issues has been proven to be quite effective in increasing the priority of these issues on the agenda of the public. Indeed, it has been seen that on many occasions what the media focused upon and repeated the most was also what the public considered to be important. Similarly, salience of attributes of issues at the expense of other attributes can have an enormous effect on public opinion orientations. The media can concentrate on a negative attribute of a political candidate, for instance, while ignoring other positive attributes and, consequently, define the place of this candidate in the public mind in terms of these negative attributes. Finally, the ability of the media to massively distribute this selected, framed, and salient information is another advantage that adds to this media's ability to set and manipulate the public agenda. These advantages or functions are the various steps in a mechanism through which the media is able to be a prestigious social actor in any society. Yet, the core reason behind this ability is not simply these advantages, which the media is endowed with. The core reason behind this influence the media has on its audience is this audience's own dependences on the media and its own need for orientation. The need for media orientation, however, is not the same for all individuals. In fact, it largely depends on the relevance an individual attaches to the information received and to this individuals confidence in his or her own knowledge about this information. This difference in individual need for media orientation is probably the only factor that limits the media's impact on public opinion. Additionally, satisfying the public's needs is one of the advantages the public has in its relationship with the media. Indeed, the media only exists because there is a public or an audience. Consequently, the media is conscience that not satisfying this audience means that it will alienate its own audience and loose market shares. To satisfy its public, the media has to be competitive. In order to be competitive, it has to be able not only to capture but also to maintain the attention of its audience and to increase it when possible. In order to capture, maintain, and increase its audience, and consequently, be able to stay in business and be more competitive than others, the media has to first sense what its own audience wants. In this respect, there are basically, three tasks the public expects the media to perform: Inform, Entertain, and Criticise.

The basic task expected from national media is that of informing the public of the events in the world in which this public exists. In other words, in addition to being an intermediate and a method, national media is expected to be the lenses through which the public perceives its own world. The second task this public needs the media to perform is to entertain it. Indeed, the public expects to find in the media an escape of daily reality. This can be done through programs and other media products that are specifically designed to entertain the public. It can also be done in combination with the other media function, i.e. providing information. For with no media outlet possibly able to have the exclusive right to a segment of the audience, due to the multiplication of media and other outlets through which this public is able to acquire the information it needs. The media, hence, have to be very competitive and to be very competitive; the media needs to respond to what the public psychologically needs. Indeed, psychologically, the public does not only have a need to be informed of news, but it also needs to be entertained while being informed. Physiologically speaking, being entertained while being informed provides a relief of and a distancing from the rigidity of the news received. This is the rationale underlying the concept of infotainment. To be more competitive, capture more audiences, maintain, and increase its market share of audiences, sensationalising of presented news is often used as a tool. The third task, the public, especially in democratic systems of government expects its national media to do is to be its number one horn blower and critic of the politico-economic establishment and society. Indeed, national media is not only expected to set the parameters for what is deviant or not inside a society but also to point out what is deviant in the national politico-economic establishment's behaviour. This is precisely the role of surveillance the media is expected to perform in democratic societies and precisely the one underlying its calling "the fourth estate". Some media outlets manage to set up products that enjoy considerable success with the audience, precisely because these products do the three things together; they inform, entertain, and criticize at the same time. For instance, a daily parody of politico-economic personalities actions and behaviour program on TV, such as the *Guignols* in France or the spitting Image in the UK, or a caricature in a newspaper, are examples of such media products that manage to inform, entertain, and criticize at the same time and which meet and have a high effect on public opinion.

In addition to its relationship to the politico-economic establishment and to its audience, national media interacts with other national non-state actors. These non-state social actors are the Civil Society and NGO's. The importance, for national media, of this relationship with these social actors stems from the fact that it is largely through these social actors that the pulse of national social movements can be sensed. National media cannot, thus, be indifferent to the tendencies of such non-state actors. For national media, these non-state social actors can help it pin point the public pulse regarding certain policies and, hence, identify what this public wants national media to criticize the politico-economic establishment for. On the other hand, for these non-state social actors, preserving a good relationship with the national media is important because it is through this media that their criticism and complaints are advocated, not just to the politico-economic establishment, but also to the public as well.

National news media does not only have to interact with national social actors and politico-economic forces, but it is also affected by the influence TNMCs (Trans-National Media Corporations) and TNNA's (Trans-National Media Agencies), as well as that of prevailing international political tendencies. TNMCs and TNNA's structure, extension, and trans-national nature endows these mega newsgathering and dispensing media with a great ability to influence national news media, and, consequently, domestic public opinion. Trans-national news gathering and dispensing media can do this because it has, on a much larger scale, the same advantages national media has in news production and distribution. In fact, the exact situation taking place at the national level between citizens of a country and its national news media can be said to be taking place at the international or trans-national level between these trans-national news gathering and dispensing media and national news media. Accordingly, If the public or the citizens in a country are the consumers of national media news products, then national news media is the consumer of trans-national newsgathering and dispensing enterprises' news. Trans-national newsgathering and dispensing media also selects, frames, salient, and massively distribute its products. The main difference is that, whereas the domain of national news media is national events and politics, the domain of these trans-national newsgathering and dispensing enterprises is international events and news.

There are, basically, two main notions characterising such a relationship between national news media and these trans-national newsgathering and dispensing enterprises: Dependence on and need for international news orientation and cultural hegemony of the Anglo-American culture. A small number of national news media are able to have their own correspondents to cover an international event or story, not to mention having their own permanent correspondence offices around the world or being available everywhere. On the national level, national news media needs to preserve a good relationship with the politico-economic establishment because it needs sourcing on events and policies and because, unlike the state, it cannot be everywhere whenever a news story breaks. Similarly, for its international news supply, national news media relies on professional trans-national news gathering and dispensing enterprises because it needs continuous feeds on international affaires, because it can not be physically there to have a first look view of events, and because it has to be competitive also in its international news coverage and depending on TNMCs and TNNAs is much cheaper than ~~~ correspondents to cover breaking events all over the world. This is why ~~~ ews media is said to be dependent on these trans-national newsgathering and dispensing enterprises. The impact of this dependence varies from orienting national news media towards a desired coverage of world events to a cultural impact. While coverage attitude orientation of national news media takes place due to the trans-national original selection, framing, and salience news items, the cultural influence trans-national newsgathering and dispensing enterprises project has two main manifestations. The first of these manifestations is the universalising of certain terms and adjectives to cover world events, which, later on, would be systematically adopted by national news media and re-used as the best terms to describe world events. The second is what can be called the Anglo-Americanisation of the world culture. Indeed, Anglo-American lexical dominance over the biggest trans-national media information and entertainment diffusion enterprises lends credibility to accusations of a systematic Anglo-American cultural and ideological imperialism process of the world. Indeed, quite a number of national news media outlets would employ Anglo-American terms to describe world events. What is more alarming is that most of the time these terms, if not kept in English in national news media coverage, are translated to give the exact meaning in the language of the country in question. The effect of this cultural influence varies, nonetheless; from one national news media to another. The reason of this variation in the impact of influence is that some national news media prefer to depend for their foreign news sourcing on trans-national newsgathering and dispensing enterprises that are linguistically, ideologically, and politically closer to them.

By definition, an international crisis is an unusual unexpected disruption of the natural course of affaires. If the event to be covered is unusual, would the behavior of national news media in its coverage of this international crisis or conflict be unusual as well and if it is then in what manner, to what end, and how can the coverage attitude of national news media of an international crisis affect national or domestic public opinion towards this crisis. These are roughly the questions the case study in this research attempted to answer. The outcome of the comparative case study of the French and U.S. national printed news media coverage (*Le Monde* and *The New York Times*) of the crisis of Bosnia-Herzegovina (15/10/1991-21/11/1995) and the crisis of Chechnya (1/11/1991-31/8/1996) reveled some interesting findings about national news media coverage attitudes of international crises and conflicts.

To begin with, the disruption in the usual course of events caused by the occurrence of an international crisis or conflict is important to states because of the factor of national state interests. The more the country has national interests in the region where the crisis or the conflict takes place the more its international relations policy conduct would be governed by its national interests. In other words, a disruption in the course of things brought about by the international crisis causes a corresponding disruption in the world countries' behavior within the international relations system. The degree of this disruption depends, logically, on the vitality of each country's national interests involved. If such an unusual event brings about a disruption and a change in the behavior of a state within the international system, then it is logical to assume that such an unusual event would bring about a disruption and a change in the social actors behavior within the country such as the media and the politic-economic establishment.

In addition to the factor of geographic proximity, five categories of national interests were identified: Cultural, Economic, Political, Regional; and Internal Social Interests. Similarities and differences were found concerning these national interests between the United States and France vis-à-vis the crisis of Bosnia and Chechnya. As far as national cultural interests are concerned, it was found that France seems to give much more importance to the promotion of its foreign cultural interests than the United States does. France is assisted in this task by a long cultural hegemonic history, recent pro-Third World political positions, and an impressive network of institutions and instruments. On the other hand, the United States' foreign policy seems to be the essential barrier inhibiting the acceptance and successful promotion of American culture in host countries. Indeed, since a culture of a country is often associated with its policies, the French concept of cultural shining fundamentally differs from the Americanisation efforts of the U.S. Moreover, foreign cultural promotion efforts of the United States are often regarded as a form of cultural imperialism, which is, even worst, camouflaging economic imperialist connotations (American culture exportation is represented by products such as MacDonald's, Movies,.etc). The similarity found is that both countries seem to have stronger cultural ties with those countries in which they have vital national interests, or with those countries that are geographically closer to them. For their part, the examination of the national economic interests of both countries in both crises revealed that both the United States and France have much more present and future prospects of economic interests to be considered in their economic relations with the Russian Federation than in their economic relation with the ex-Yugoslavia successor republics. The stability of the European continent was proven, however, to be quite vital for the economies of both countries. Moreover, the two countries were similar in having had much more national political interests involved in the crisis of Bosnia than they did in that of Chechnya. In addition, for both countries, exerting regional and world leadership in the post-Cold War world was imperative. France and the United States' national political interests vis-à-vis the two crises differed in certain points, nonetheless. For, whereas France was more interested in stabilising the newly constructed European bloc, the U.S. was mainly interested in stabilizing a continent, which is its most reliable partner, economically, politically, culturally, and ideologically. Furthermore, France aimed at containing a geographically close conflict through its leadership exhibition initiatives and, if possible, through the use of a European security organ which can limit the hegemony of the U.S. and NATO over Europe. The United States' political interests in the Balkans weighed against its past costly experience in European wars made it quite a reasonable and a feasible investment for the U.S. to take the lead in imposing a peace settlement to the conflict in Bosnia. Both countries, on the other hand, had little or no political interests in the Chechnya conflict. Additionally, the vitality of the United States and France's respective political interests with Russia was valued more than any critical political stands concerning Chechnya. Yet, they differed in the reasons for this vitality of preserving good political relations with Russia. For France, the insertion of Russia into the institutions of the European construction in the post-Cold War period meant the introduction of a counterweight to the United States and NATO's hegemony over Europe and,more importantly, having Russia's precious assistance in solving the more urgent nearby Balkan's conflict. On the other hand, the U.S. had no clear foreign policy line concerning Central Asia and the Caucasus because it had no previous experience in that region and because it never dealt with individual countries in there. Moreover, it was quite important for the United States to have a neutral Russia than to have it as an antagonist once again.

The same considerably higher status applies to both countries national regional interests in Bosnia as opposed to their interests in Chechnya. France was interested in experimenting with a European regional security organ, in guarding against a renewal of a re-unified Germany's hegemony, in guarding against the proliferation of independence and nationalistic tendencies in the European continent which can contaminate certain regions in the French Republic, and, finally, in taking into consideration its Mediterranean and Arab and Muslim relations in dealing with the crisis of Bosnia. For their part, the United States' national regional interests in the Balkans were based on core regional interests in Europe and by no means simply peripheral. In addition, the United States wanted to guard against a repetition of the historic errors resulting from the "appeasement policy" than to suffer much more costly involvement to stabilize a war ravaged Europe. The two countries also differ in their national regional interests in Chechnya. For its part, and other than energy related interests, France had no articulated vital regional interests in that region of the world. The same applies for the United States but with a much more U.S. articulated intention to dispute Russia's and other regional powers' hegemony in Central Asia and the Caucasus (U.S. strong ties with Armenia and Georgia), to guard against the proliferation of ethnic conflicts, and to support regional central governments against separatist movements. Guarding against the success and the proliferation of separatist tendencies in Central Asia and the Caucasus is, however, a regional interest of both the U.S. and France since it is much more easier to deal with a small number of countries for energy resource's routes and exploitation reasons than to deal with a much larger multitude of authorities and small newly born republics.

The importance of considering internal social factors when addressing an international crisis or conflict stems from the fact that foreign and domestic policy are interconnected and can affect each others behaviour. Internal social forces in a society represented by ethno-religious minority groups, national social movements, or the extended effects of trans-national social movements have all proved their effect on foreign policy options and decisions. France and the United States are no exception to this rule. In addition to ethno-religious minority groups and affinities in host countries, anti-war activism have been given a new mobilizing instrument represented in the use of non-institutional media (new technological innovations in personal and widely spread free information diffusion and transmission gadgets, such as SMS messages, and in the Internet). The innovation brought about by this non-institutional media is that it transformed anti-war and social protests activism to a preventive rather than a post-action activism due to the facility in informing, mobilizing, and informing brought about by this non-institutional media outlets.

To better understand the mechanism according to which media coverage of an international crisis or conflict is said to conform to national state interests and why such mechanism would have a bearing on domestic public opinion towards the crisis or conflict in question, a thorough dissection of the various elements involved in media coverage of an international crisis was done and then compared to the outcome of public opinion tendencies towards these crises in both countries in order to determine if, in its turn, national or domestic public opinion corresponded to national news media coverage of these international crises. Accordingly, the examination of the two newspapers' coverage included a dissection of the terminology and texts used, a dissection of the images used, an examination of the frequency of the occurrence of coverage and its volume, an analysis of the priority placement of coverage, and an examination of the involvement and attitudes of the journalists involved in the two cases, The main finding of this dissection of *The New York Times* and *Le Monde's* coverage of the two crises revealed that these two newspapers' coverage attitudes largely corresponded to their respective countries' positions and national interests involved. The outcome of this dissection of coverage, in all its aspects, (terminology, images, repetition, priority, journalists involved, reliance and influence of trans-national news gathering and dispensing enterprises on coverage) strongly supports this opinion.

As far as the analysis of the texts and the terminology used in coverage is concerned, the evidence found indicates that the two newspapers' shared a number of general characteristics in their coverage terminology but differed in others. They were both similar in using more negative terminology, which dehumanised and demonised both Serbs and Chechens. However, *Le Monde* was less intense in this in the case of the Serbs but more in the case of the Chechens. On the other hand, *The New York Times* was more intense in doing this in the case of the Serbs than in that of the Chechens. Moreover, there was an excessive dramatisation of the humanitarian tragedy in Bosnia as opposed to that of Chechnya by both newspapers. Finally, There was evidence that both newspapers, and in their coverage of both crises, re-employed terms employed by their sources. Evidence found also indicates that the general difference between the terminology of the two newspapers is that one adopted in its coverage a rigid clear-cut aggressor-victim terminology (*The New York Times*), while the other (*Le Monde*) opted for a more coloured terminology. The other differences found in the terminology used related to the general coverage attitude adopted. This general coverage attitude corresponded to a very high degree to the differences found in the national interests of France and the United States towards the two crises. It has been proven that each of the two newspapers' coverage attitude conformed to their respective country's national interests and positions cornering the crisis being covered. Dehumanisation of the Serbs, victimisation of Muslims, and excessive dramatisation of events characterised *The New York Times*' coverage of Bosnia. On the other hand, dehumanisation of Chechnya and its inhabitants and humanising the Russian forces action characterized its coverage of Chechnya. Insisting on the dangers of the spread of the conflict for Europe, indicating the U.N's failure to deal with the crisis, and projecting a more balanced designation of aggressors and victims in the conflict characterised *Le Monde's* coverage attitude of the Bosnia conflict. On the other hand, dehumanisation of Chechnya and its inhabitants, limiting the conflict to a power struggle within Chechnya, and dismissing the conflict as an internal Russian issue characterised *Le Monde's* coverage attitude of Chechnya.

Concerning the repetition of certain terms and adjectives in both newspapers' coverage of the two crises, the findings also support the opinion that both newspapers responded in their coverage to their respective countries' national interests involved. The first of these findings is that negative terms and adjectives were more repeated and associated with Serb actions by both newspapers than with Russian actions in Chechnya in general. Nonetheless, while *Le Monde* seems more critical of Russian actions in Chechnya, the opposite is true for *The New York Times* and its coverage of Bosnia. Moreover, the situation of Chechnya was more associated to a war of equal sides situation due to the repetition of certain terms to describe it as such, than it was the case of Bosnia. In addition, the repetition of negative degrading terms designating Serb and Chechen forces involved was much more frequent than the same designation for their rivals. In the case of Chechens, the degrading designation of their forces was much more obvious. Finally, repetition evidence suggested that Bosnians are more "Muslims" or

"Muslim Slavs" than Chechens who were quite rarely identified as Muslims, or even as a separate ethnicity. This last fact, in addition to indicating a hypocritical double-standard position, is interesting if it is taken in consideration with the Muslim public opinion.

As far as the images used in coverage is concerned, there was a basic difference in the nature of these images between the two newspapers. For whereas, *The New York Times* relied on photographs and maps to accompany its coverage of both crises, *Le Monde,* on the other hand, indicated its clear preference for the usage of caricatures. Use of caricatures can confer more objectivity on the media outlet since the caricature, unlike the photograph, leaves more freedom of interpretation for the audience and can always be considered as nothing more than humour. On the other hand, a caricature allows more expression of the desired message than a photograph since there is much more freedom in its creation. As far as the messages of these images is concerned, evidence indicates that *The New York Times'* images and their accompanying explanatory commentaries strongly supported its general coverage attitude of the Bosnia conflict (demonisation of Serbs, victimisation of Muslims, dramatisation of events) and of that of Chechnya (dehumanisation of the region and its inhabitants and humanising the action of the Russian troops). *Le Monde,* on the other hand, was less direct in the connection between its coverage content and the caricatures used. On the quantitive side of analysis, discrepancies in the frequency of the occurrence of these images were found between the two newspapers, in general, and in the coverage of each of the two crises, in particular. *The New York Times* used much more images in its coverage of the two crises than *Le Monde* did (a rate of one photograph for each article in the case of Bosnia against a rate of one caricature for every four articles for *Le Monde*). Moreover, both newspapers used much more images in their coverage of the crisis of Bosnia than they did for that of Chechnya.

The general importance of the two crises to the two newspapers was also reflected in the frequency of the occurrence of coverage and its volume (in words). Discrepancies found concerning this issue between the two crises are interesting. Generally speaking, it was found that priority of coverage was clearly given by the two newspapers to the Bosnia conflict. Indeed, in terms of the number of articles and news items published with a word in their title definitively indicating reference to the two crises, *The New York Times* published a total of 2264 articles on Bosnia against 342 articles only on Chechnya (a ratio of almost seven articles to one), while *Le Monde* published 3476 articles on Bosnia against only 590 articles on Chechnya (a ratio of approximately six articles to one). Moreover, In terms of the number of articles and news items with a clear reference to one of the two crises in their content but not in their title, *The New York Times* published 16027 articles and news items on Bosnia against only 2507 on

Chechnya (a ratio of approximately six to one), while *Le Monde* published 11586 articles and news items on Bosnia against only 3044 on Chechnya (a ratio of approximately four to one). Although *Le Monde* published slightly more news items and articles on Chechnya than *The New York Times*, the two newspapers generally published six to seven articles and news items on Bosnia against every article and news item they published on Chechnya. Moreover, *Le Monde* published more direct coverage articles and news items on Bosnia (3476) than *The New York Times* did (2264) due to geographic proximity and the immediacy of French national interests involved. Finally, significant discrepancies were also found in the volume of the articles and news items published by the two newspapers. In this respect, the two newspapers' volume of words of their coverage of Bosnia based on the examined sample (*Le Monde* used 28274 against a total of 19921 words for *The New York Times*) was significantly more than for their coverage of the crisis of Chechnya (*Le Monde* used 22751 words against only 17979 for *The New York Times*).

Significant discrepancies between the coverage of the two crises were also found in the priority placement given to each crisis's coverage by the two newspapers. Generally speaking, it was found that both newspapers gave much more priority placement to news items and articles on Bosnia than on Chechnya. In addition, the analysis conducted clearly indicated that higher priority placement was given to articles and news items supporting the general coverage attitude of each newspaper. In this respect and based on the sample examined, *Le Monde* published 9 front-page articles and news items on Bosnia against only one on Chechnya, while *The New York Times* published 6 front-page articles and news items on Bosnia against four for Chechnya. Moreover, all front-page articles and news items examined seem to support the two newspapers" respective general coverage attitude towards the two crises. Finally, it has been proven from a comparison of the frequency of coverage between the coverage of the two crises and that of other international conflicts and crises, which took place in more or less the same period of time, that the scale of humanitarian tragedy does not determine priority coverage. On the contrary, it was found that priority coverage is more driven by concrete factors, such as geographic proximity, direct involvement, and historical or ex-colonial ties rather than by mere humanitarian concerns. This finding suggests that for institutional national media, humanitarian concerns in an international conflict or crisis coverage seem to be nothing more than peripheral.

The examination of the journalists involved in the coverage indicated that both newspapers allocated double the number of journalists for the coverage of the conflict in Bosnia compared to those journalists sent to cover the Chechnya conflict. Moreover, it was found that both newspapers sent more experienced and qualified journalists to cover the conflict in Bosnia than to cover that of Chechnya (except for Sophie Shihab for *Le Monde* in Chechnya). Finally, some of these journalists involved in coverage were influenced by their environment such as Chuck Suedic of *The New York Times*, who was accused of impartiality due to his Croatian origins. It was also found that some journalists get personally attached to the conflict they cover. Some end up testifying in courts on war crimes (Florence Hartman of *Le Monde* in Bosnia), some write about the atrocities they witnessed (John F. Burns of *The New York Times* in Bosnia), and some write and defend, on various forums, the cause of one people in the conflict they cover (Sophie Shihab for *Le Monde* in Chechnya).

One of the main reasons for relying on trans-national newsgathering and dispensing enterprises is not having enough journalists because the conflict I not considered to be important, or not being able to send ones to cover the international conflict or crisis. Accordingly, the two newspapers were found to have relied much more in their coverage of the conflict of Chechnya on trans-national newsgathering and dispensing enterprises than they did in the case of their Bosnia coverage. Moreover, it seems that both newspapers preferred sourcing from trans-national news dispensers that are linguistically and politically closer to them. *Le Monde* indicated a clear preference for AFP as a source, while *The New York Times* preferred using Reuters and the Associated Press for sourcing purposes. Finally, both newspapers relied heavily on semi-official Russian agencies (Itar-Tass and Interfax) for their news items on Chechnya. Although, both newspapers, especially, *Le Monde*, tended to warn their readers of the doubtfulness of the sources sometimes (in the case of sourcing from Itar-Tass and Interfax). The danger is that such trans-national newsgathering and dispensing agencies can disseminate certain terms that will end up being adopted by the national media and taken for granted as being the most appropriate to use. It can also do this by selecting to disseminate certain facts or news and not others and, most importantly, by the original framing given to this disseminated news. Indeed, these two effects were proven to be true in the case of the two newspapers' coverage of the crisis in Chechnya. It is also important to mention that presupposing that a trans-national newsgathering and dispensing enterprise is more objective because its Western or bigger than others is a very dangerous assumption. In fact, evidence found after comparing *The New York Times*' sourcing from Reuters and the Associated Press in certain articles suggests that these two trans-national newsgathering and dispensing agencies offered a "unified" vision of the situation. Consequently, it is legitimate to assume that they might have did that simply because they project a unified vision of the world. This, however, is a hypothesis that requires further and totally specialized analysis.

News selection, framing, priority placement or priming, and salience of issues and attributes of issues constitute the general media mechanisms of orienting national or domestic public opinion. Other tools can also be used to influence public opinion such as the use or withholding of Mobilizing Information (Locational, Identificational, and tactical), Afghantinisation of issues (talking about other country's problems although the same problems exist in ones country) and the creation of relevance to the public. Out of these last three tools, the creation of relevance was found to be the most effective tool used by the national media to influence public opinion via its coverage of an international crisis or conflict. Indeed, in order to stress the importance of an international crisis in the public's mind or to negate the importance, or even the mere existence of others, the media can either choose to stress relevance or irrelevance of this international crisis to the general public. Moreover, repetition of the use of negative traits in the description of one crisis's events, while ignoring the same traits in others helps focus public opinion on the urgency of certain international crises and not others. This is how the media creates relevance of a given international crisis or conflict to the public. It was also found that one of the most effective manners of this relevance creating ability, as far as national media coverage of international crises and conflicts is concerned, is by creating relevance that draws on universal and basic human emotional and humanitarian concerns.

This creation of relevance effect, added to the other advantageous integrated media functions (selection, framing, priming, salience, massive distribution and facility of access) was seen in the result of the examination of public opinion tendencies in the United States and in France towards the two crises. Examination of public opinion tendencies in both countries revealed that while there were numerous public opinion polls conducted in the United States and in France on the conflict in Bosnia, practically none was found to sense public opinion tendencies in these two countries concerning Chechnya. This is not a surprising fact, since for the public of both countries the conflict of Bosnia is presented as a problem of general interest because of intensive media coverage and effective framing, while Chechnya simply did not exist. Indeed, no questions can be posed about a subject that does not exist in the first place. In addition, it was found that public opinion in the United States and in France conformed to the media coverage tendencies and attitudes of the two crises. Moreover, it was proven that public opinion did not remain static but that it changed radically sometimes, precisely when there were some sort of media coverage concentration or dramatisation of an event in the crisis. Finally, it was found that public opinion can change radically from one end of the scale to the other much more easily when there is no immediate vital national interests involved in this international crisis or conflict, especially after a media dramatisation of certain events. The evidence found suggests a correlation between the speed of public opinion changes and the existence or not of vital national interests.

To better understand media effect on public opinion during an international crisis or conflict, it was also important to discuss the nature of the notion of public opinion itself and its role in human society. It can be said, in this respect, that public opinion is something that exists in all human societies regardless of the political system adopted (authoritarian or democratic). Two basic differences relating to the nature and measuring mechanism of this public opinion were found however between these two basic systems of government. The first one of these differences relates to the importance given to measuring and satisfying public opinion in democratic societies as opposed to the disregard of this issue in authoritarian ones. Indeed, public opinion in democratic societies is becoming more and more important to understand because it is becoming more and more of a regulator of public policy (foreign and domestic policy). The second of these differences between public opinion in democratic and non-democratic societies is one that relates to the manner of its expression. For whereas public opinion in democratic societies is expressed pacifically through opinion polls and electoral votes, including when a government is sanctioned for its policies, public opinion in non-democratic societies is expressed violently, usually through revolutions, insurgencies,...etc.

Within democratic systems of government, three types of public opinion were identified. These are mass public opinion, majority public opinion, and effective public opinion. For its part, mass public opinion generally designates that segment of society whose members are more interested in consumer-oriented non-political issues of daily life. Members of this segment are those who do not vote in elections or are those commonly designated as *the silent majority*. Mass public opinion is important because it helps measure public interest in issues (abstention level) and is also dangerous to provoke for politicians. Majority public opinion, on the other hand, is the opinion of those who participate in voting on choices of policies or politicians. This type of public opinion is not reliable, however, because it excludes the opinion of those who did not take part in the voting. What politicians rely on to sense public opinion towards issues is what is known as effective public opinion. This type of public opinion is that which actually reaches politicians. Effective public opinion towards issues can be measured through the elections framework (voting outcome on elections or policies, ratio of abstention, exit poll interviews), and through the influence framework (the number and nature of received mail on issues for instance). While the elections framework is a public opinion measurement tool whose usage is limited to election periods, the influence framework is a continuous one.

Public opinion is not only domestic or national. Indeed, there seems to exist a moral hierarchy of world states according to what has come to be known as the World Opinion. There are two main reasons that gave birth to this new concept.

The first one is that hierarchy of states in terms of development has undergone a transformation from one that purely depended on economic advancement criteria to one that depends more on national characteristics. The second reason is that, in the aftermath of the Cold War and in a response to the New World order, a kind of consensus on acceptable behaviour amongst world countries has developed, which defines a countries moral status amongst other world nations mainly through its relations with other world nations, as well as its dealings with its own citizens. The importance of World Opinion is that a country's world image is becoming more and more of a national interest. Indeed, this growing importance of a country's world image can, and recently had provoked seduction campaigns conducted on the highest official levels in the political establishment of certain countries in order to improve their damaged world image. On the other hand, observing this interest can gain certain countries higher moral status in the eyes of the world opinion, due to these countries political leadership's stands.

One of the reasons why understanding public opinion's media influence mechanisms is that, on the national level, media coverage of an international crisis or conflict can be used as an effective political tool aimed at acquiring public opinion support for political foreign policy positions and actions. In authoritarian societies, mobilizing support for war effort and foreign military involvement in conflicts is a function of official regime propaganda. On the other hand, mobilizing a democratic society for war effort or a military involvement in an international conflict or crisis is found to be a function assumed by national institutional media. The behavioural similarities in mobilizing domestic support for war effort between national media in democratic societies and regime propaganda machines in authoritarian one suggests that national media in democratic societies tends to adopt a subtle propaganda behaviour, at least in the early stages of involvement in an international conflict or crisis. Two notions, however, support this hypothesis. The first one is that this mobilizing task is not that difficult to perform even in the most democratic and peace oriented of societies. Indeed, it was found, based on numerous cultural and sociological studies conducted, that the notion of risk is quite important for human beings and their behaviour. Emphasis or disregard of this notion makes it possible that a society can be directed in either the *regal* (war oriented) or the *kalyptic* (peace oriented) direction. It should be mentioned, on the other hand, that the speed of the transformation of a society from a peace to a war culture was found to be largely linked to the past history of conflicts and the environment in which this society exists. Moreover, war culture was found to be the product of a history and an environment of conflict, where conflict and war values become inherent in societal behaviour. Nonetheless, certain studies have indicated that because of the past conflicts and the Cold War experience the coverage of international crises in American and Europeans media seems to adopt a war discourse where polarization is emphasized. The second notion that supports such a hypothesis is that quite a number of researchers have advanced that the media is largely subjected to a propaganda model where the opinion of the elite is always advanced and where other "dissident" opinions are systematically suppressed. The third notion that credits this hypothesis of national media behaviour during an international crisis or conflict is that certain studies indicated that the introduction of PR—agencies in recent world conflicts and crises have resulted in a sort of privatisation of propaganda, where each journalist defends and stresses his or her point of view of the crisis and of the conflict as part of an inherent societal propaganda behaviour that can be found in every individual that lives within a culture of war. Nonetheless, it should be mentioned, that some studies indicated that that journalists, as individuals, are not capable of such privatisation of propaganda because they have to follow the direction of the bigger organisation which employs them. This is why it was found, in the case study of this research, that some journalists preferred to advocate their support of one party or another in a conflict they covered outside their own media outlet. The fourth notion which lends credibility to this hypothesis of a subtle propaganda national media behaviour during an international crisis or conflict coverage is the existence of a correlation between national interests of states and their national media's focusing or not on a given international crisis or conflict. The example of the extreme focusing of the coverage of Bosnia compared to Chechnya, as indicated in the case study supports this point of view. The fifth notion lending credibility to this subtle propaganda behaviour of national media in democratic societies is that it was found that it is not in the sole ability or best interest of national media to focus on an international crisis or conflict in which its country has no national interests. Two main reasons can explain why it is not in the media's interest to do this. The first one is that it was found that the media's coverage seems capable to trigger a change in foreign policy only if the politicians themselves were not certain of the action to take. In such a case, they would be compelled to satisfy the public protest resulting from the media's intensive coverage and framing, especially empathy framing. This, nonetheless, is particularly true in humanitarian crisis and humanitarian intervention. The second reason is that national media has to consider the fact that it needs to be competitive and, for that, it needs to have a good relationship with the political establishment and with the public in not appearing as being unpatriotic. The sixth reason lending credibility to such a hypothesis of a subtle propaganda behaviour of national media is that which has to do with the interdependence of interests between the media and the political machines. Such interdependence of interests can be seen in the concordance of interests between various interest groups which are placed at the higher hierarchical levels in both institutions.The most important milestone of this interdependence of interests between the two appears is the media-source relationship. The preservation of such a relationship seems to be quite important for both establishments. For the media this relationship allows it to have a continuous flow of information that would keep it spinning, and for the political establishment this flow of information it supplies would allow it to use the media as a an agent of social control and to manipulate it to its ends, when manipulation is needed. Moreover, it was found that based on such a source dependency relationship, two effective methods could be used by the political establishment to influence national media coverage of an international crisis or conflict. These methods are the bombardment or the withholding of information from national media and the use of selected experts as "neutral" and credible sources of opinion on the international crisis or conflict in order to disseminate the desired messages. Another notion that lends credibility to this hypothesis of national media behaviour during an international crisis or conflict, where national interests are at stake, is one, which has to do with the mutual surveillance behaviour between the media and the political establishment. For, in spite of the fact that the political establishment remains the most important and the highest authority in any given country, national media, in democratic societies, has over the years come close to rival with this privileged status of the political establishment. The growing importance of institutional national media in democratic societies is due to the constant need of both the public and the political establishment to be informed of issues on daily bases, to its ability to mobilize public opinion, as well as to the enormous economic weight. These advantages allow national media in democratic societies to assume the role of not only an observer of behaviour but of a regulator of this behaviour as well. it is this fact that justifies national media' surveillance of its political establishment. The political establishment, for its part, surveys national media to ensure that it doesn't harm its interests or that it doesn't deviate too much from the government's line of conduct. In order to do this, the political establishment can use pressures such as flaks, economic facilities, or access to sources to get the media back on track if needed. What is relevant to mention here is that during an international crisis or conflict the interests of both the media and the political establishment are accentuated and, hence, the degree of mutual surveillance is significantly higher.

The political establishment can, hence, use public opinion as sort of a legitimising means for its policies and actions. The best method to do this is not by direct propaganda, since the public can be doubtful and, hence, reject aggressive and direct propaganda campaigns, and since much more outlets other than those of the government can be used to get different information. To obtain consent and legitimacy from the public, interests and projects have to be presented as those primarily bearing interest to the public itself. They have to be presented, furthermore, as being those of the greater public and not of an elite. When people believe that the policy is what they want it to be, then they would be more supportive of this policy and the political establishment can, thus, have the necessary legitimacy for the pursuit of its projects. To influence public opinion and obtain this legitimacy, elite opinion or opinion definers play a central role. They do this in leading public opinion and imposing their own opinion in a manner that would make it be adopted by the wider public, which, consequently, would provide legitimacy for their actions. During an international crisis, this issue of securing supportive public opinion for the political establishment's action or inaction becomes more urgent. Fear is usually used to mobilize public opinion in support of an involvement in a crisis by convincing the public that its basic interests are at risk. On the other hand, ignoring the crisis or presenting inaction as the best means of maintaining the greater public interest can be used if the political establishment needs to legitimise its inaction vis-à-vis the international crisis or conflict at hand. This does not mean that national media helplessly follows propaganda indications of the political establishment because it cannot do otherwise. On the contrary, many studies indicated that the media has a propaganda machine of its own. This is very probable since the media has also its own agenda. What accentuates a national media propaganda behaviour is that, In many cases, the agendas of the national media and the politico-economic establishments would concord vis-à-vis an international crisis. When this happens, the official state propaganda and the media's own propaganda machine would both be moulded, due to shared interests, into one propaganda machine.

The behaviour of national media coverage was also found to be one that responds to market requirements, namely competition. Indeed, in order to be competitive in the market, the media has to find an audience for itself. It can do this by creating the interest and by presenting or framing this interest in a way that would preserve the audience and increase its number as well. The best means of creating an interest in the public is to play with the notion of fear. Indeed, it was found that If this basic human emotion is harnessed effectively, it can translate into higher ratings because of the increased need for information and news coverage of the international crisis or conflict. These choices are not without solid logic. In fact, human behaviour studies and sociological analysis suggests that humans react more to issues that disturb their natural and usual course of life. In this respect, danger and risk were found to be the most useful buttons the media can push for more audiences. On certain occasions, exaggeration of fear or the creation of a "moral panic" can be used to capture the audiences' attention and, consequently, increase ratings. Moreover, it was proven that the social actor that has the ability to determine what is deviant or not in a society would also have a high status in the hierarchy of the social system.

Two more important concepts, which are highly related to national media behaviour in its coverage of an international crisis or conflict, were examined in this research. These are the media's crisis of objectivity and its independence. The first finding was that the notion of journalistic objectivity, on the level of individual journalists, is one that never ceased to develop and mutate and one that is still an issue of controversy. Objectivity, as a notion, benefited from the innovations in the forms and in the concept of journalism itself. These innovations were essentially brought about by innovations in the forms of the media available to the public and by the growing facility of its accessibility to this public. It also developed due to the contributions of certain prominent journalists and researchers. In this respect, it was found that there are two main schools of thought concerning journalistic objectivity. These two schools are represented by Walter Lippmann and Nelson Crawford. For his part, Lippmann believes journalists should shape their own interpretations of the facts they have, while Crawford believes that journalists should only disseminate objective facts. Another difference found between these two schools of thought was that whereas Crawford thinks that institutions should be set up to monitor and preserve journalistic objectivity, while Lippmann believes in freeing journalists from the domination of such institutions. Other views consider objectivity as being simply a media tactic to increase audiences, while others dismiss journalistic objectivity as being simply a "myth" and an "ideal". The controversy, however, seem to be centred around the issue of whether journalists should be observers or regulators of their society, or whether they are able to be both at the same time. It also seems to stem out of the fact that truth can mean different things to different people.

On the institutional level of the media as an enterprise, a crisis of objectivity seems to be an unquestionable reality. Many indications supports the existence of such a crisis. They have to do with notions related to the media's function itself, as well as to its organization. Such indications were found to include the media's ability to set its own agenda, its ability to frame the selected news and information in a manner that is beneficial to its interests, its submission to the free market rules of competition and priority of advertising revenues, the accusations that the media sets a frame for its debates, and that the questions it poses in opinion polls are designed to obtain the desired answers. All of these indications and accusations give rise to the assumption that the media simply reflects the elite opinion in a society or that it simply serves as a tool of diffusion for such primary definers in a society.

Nonetheless, it was found that there exists objective or neutral obstacles to the media's objectivity goal attainment. Some of these obstacles can be said to apply in general to the media behaviour while the others are those factors that hinder media objective coverage of an international crisis or conflict and over which, the media, as an institution, has little or no control.

The generally observed obstacles to the media's objectivity goal are the organisational related obstacles or "filters" on the media's objectivity and functional ones such as functional subjectivity and the propaganda model. In this respect, three main organisational filters on media objectivity were found. These are the limitations on the ownership of the media, which concentrate a number of media companies in the hands of an elite, advertising benefits and the influence of advertisers on media attitudes and choices, and mass media sourcing.

Functional obstacles on media objectivity include concepts such as functional subjectivity and the propaganda model filters. For its part, what underlies the concept of functional subjectivity in media is the assumption that absolute objectivity is an impossible goal and that subjectivity is a predetermined trait in both humans and institutions Furthermore, subjectivity in the media is found not only to be a natural but also to be a survival technique. The propaganda model concept stipulates that certain functional obstacles are integrated in the media machine's mechanism, which makes it adopt a model of behaviour that is close to that of propaganda. This model was clearly identified in the United States media at least. It included five main filters on media objectivity. These are size, ownership and profit orientation of the mass media, advertising, sourcing, flak and the enforcers, and anticommunism as a control mechanism (particular to the U.S. media in the Cold War era but can be replaced by *unpatriotism* as well).

Three main categories of obstacles on media coverage objectivity that were found to particularly hinder the objectivity national media coverage during an international crisis or conflict were also found. These are access to the crisis area, financial, technological impediments. First, it was found that whether it is through denying physical access to the conflict area, imposing military escort, or military censorship for military security reasons, journalists' coverage of a conflict zone has to go through "filters" which would reduce little by little the objectivity of their reports and coverage. In this sense, it can be assumed that journalists can sometimes and due to these filters be used by warring parties as propaganda diffusers in spite of themselves. Second, the evidence found suggests that advertising and ratings are the economic backbone of the media industry. Accordingly, journalists' objectivity has to be often modelled to the requirements of the media consumption marketplace. Furthermore, not all media can afford to bear the costs of having an independent first hand look of an international conflict or crisis. Indeed, the costs of such a venture is quite often economically viable, especially to small media outlets. In this respect, the determining consideration of whether an international conflict is economically interesting to the media is geographic proximity and national interests. If these elements were some or all of the significances of the international crisis or conflict for a country, then it would be interesting to the domestic consumer of the media and, hence, worthwhile to cover, sensationally of course for higher ratings. Finally, It was found that the proliferation of technological innovations in communications certainly rendered the work of journalists much easier and faster, especially when they are covering conflicts or crisis. In fact, these technology advancements present the advantage of a more rapid transmission of news items, more mobility for journalists, and more discretion in their work, since it is no longer necessary to send big crews for coverage purposes. On the other hand, such advances and innovations are a double-edged sword because they were found to present certain disadvantages for the objectivity of media coverage of international conflicts and crises. The reasons for this assumption are many. First, keeping up with such innovations creates a gap between the media outlets that can afford them and those that cannot. Second, such innovations places journalists covering a conflict in more danger, precisely because they can transmit atrocities and annoying images fast, and also because of these instruments' tempting nature to outlaws. In addition, such innovations have helped create a marketplace competition of freelance reporters and journalists who would compete even in risking their lives for a more sensational news item in a conflict zone, because new technology provides them with smaller and smaller equipment to perform their work, and because they have to supply competitive news items that are both more sensational and more rapidly transmitted than others. Finally, technological advances in communication systems can also be used by governments or parties to a conflict to sabotage or jam a journalist's transmission of an annoying news item.

Finally, a correlation was found between the media's independence and its crisis of objectivity, since to be objective, the media has first to have enough independence. Indeed, the analysis of the two main components of the media industry (the journalists and the media institution or enterprise) revealed that this independence is affected by internal and external factors. On the primary human level of analysis, the independence of journalists seems to be affected by various factors such as the fact that humans are, by nature, more subjective than objective. It was also found to be affected by external pressures on journalists, which can be economic, social, political, or legitimate fear for their physical safety. On the level of the media as an institution or an enterprise, the issue of media ownership, whether privately or publicly owned, was proven to have a negative impact on the independence of the media and, consequently, on its objectivity. Moreover, corporate media's bureaucracy seems to result in lack of autonomy and in less democracy in the internal decision-making process, while elite ownership concentration results in a more uniform elite view of the world and a preference for maximising profit on the expense of objectivity.

It appears, therefore, that institutional national media is an intermediate between the public and its government, a medium through which the world is perceived, and a tool through which public opinion can be controlled and regulated. Furthermore, it seems that national institutional media, even in the most democratic of human societies, due to various functional and external factors and where national interests are involved, tends to adopt a subtle propaganda behaviour in its coverage of an international crisis or conflict. What would be quite interesting to reveal in further research is the role and effect of non-institutional media, such as Internet and other personal information and transmission innovations, on domestic public opinion in general, and on domestic and world opinion during an international conflict or crisis, in particular.

Bibliography

Books and Sections of Books

AANZULOVIC Branimir, Heavenly Serbia, New York, New York University Press, 1999.

AHEM (T. J., Jr.), "Determinants of Foreign Coverage in U.S. Newspapers". In R.L. Stevenson and D.L. Shaw (eds.), Foreign News and the New World Information Order, Ames, Iowa State University Press, 1984.

AKWULE (Raymond), Global Telecommunications, London, Focal Press, 1992.

ALDGATE (Anthony), The British Can Take It: The British Cinema in the Second World War, Edinburgh, Edinburgh University Press, 1994.

ALGER (D. E.), The Media and Politics, New Jersey, Prentice Hall, 1989.

ANDERSEN (Michael), "Russia and the Former Yugoslavia", in Mark Webber, Russia and Europe: Conflict or Cooperation?., New York, St. Martin's Press, 2000

ALTHEIDE (D.L.),.An Ecology of Communication: Cultural Formats of Control, New York, Aldine de Gruyter, 1995.

ARBATOV (Georgi), Re-Viewing the Cold War: Domestic Factors and Foreign Policy in the East-West Confrontation, Westport, CT, Praeger, 2000.

ARGYRIS (C.) & SCHON (D)., Theory in practice: Increasing Professional Effectiveness, San Francisco, Jossey-Bass, 1974.

BAKER (C. E.), Advertising and a Democratic Press, Princeton, Princeton University Press, 1994.

BAKER (James A. III), The Politics of Diplomacy: Revolution, War, and Peace, 1989-92, G.P. Putnam, New York, 1995.

BAILEY (Thomas A.), America Faces Russia: Russian-American Relations from Early Times to Our Day, Ithaca, NY, Cornell University Press, 1950.

BALTA (Paul) & RULLEAU (Claudine), La politique arabe de la France. De de Gaulle à Pompidou, Paris, Sindbad, 1973.

BARNEY (R.D.), "The Journalist and a Pluralistic Society: An Ethical Approach", in D. Elliott (Ed.), Responsible Journalism, Beverly Hills, CA. Sage, 1986, pp.60-80.

BELL (Martin), In Harms Way, London, Hamish Hamilton, 1995.

BENNETT (Lance W.) & PALETZ (David L.), (Eds.), Taken by storm: The media, public opinion, and U.S. foreign policy in the Gulf War, Chicago & London, University of Chicago Press, 1994.

BOGART (Leo), Commercial Culture: The Media System and the Public Interest, New York, Oxford University Press, 1995.

BURNETT (Ron), Cultures of Vision: Images, Media, and the Imaginary, Bloomington, Indiana University Press, 1995.

BEN-YEHUDA (Nachman), The Politics and Morality of Deviance, Albany, SUNY Press, 1990.

BERELSON (Bernard R.), LAZARSFELD (Paul F)., & MCPHEE (William N.), Voting, Chicago, University of Chicago Press, 1954.

BERMAN (Larry) & GOLDMAN (Emily O, "Clinton's Foreign policy at Midterm" in Colin Campbell and Bert A. Rockman, The Clinton Presidency: First Appraisals, Chatham, NJ., Chatham House Publishers, 1996, pp. 290-324.

BEST (Joel), Threatened Children, Chicago, University of Chicago Press, 1990.

BLOOMFIELD (Leonard), Language, New York, Henry Holt and Company, 1933.

BLUMER (Herbert), "The mass, the public, and public opinion". In A. M. Lee (Ed.), New outline of the principles of sociology, New York, Barnes and Noble, 1946, pp. 185-193.

BOULDING (Kenneth E.), Conflict and Defense, New York, Harper and Row, 1962.

BOYCE (George), CURRAN (James)., & WINGATE(Pauline), Newspaper History: From the 17th Century to the Present Day, London, Constable, 1978.

BRENNER (Michael) & DEAN (Jonathan), Terms of Engagement: The United States and the European Security Identity, Westport, CT., Praeger., 1998

BREWER (Marilynn B) & MILLER (Norman), Intergroup Relations., Buckingham, Open University Press, 1996.

BRODIE (Richard.), Virus of the mind: The new science of the meme, Seattle, Integral Press, 1996.

BROWN (Allison), Uniting Germany: Documents and Debates, 1944-1993, Providence, Berghahn Books, 1994.

BROWN (J. F.), Eroding Empire: Western Relations with Eastern Europe, Washington, DC., The Brookings Institution, 1987.

BRYCE (James), The American Commonwealth, London, Macmillan and Company, 1891.

CAHEN (Alfred), « L'Europe de la défense est-elle possible? », in Pascal Chaigneau, Les Grands Enjeux du Monde Contemporain, Paris, Ellipses, 1996.

CANTRIL (A.H.), The Opinion connection: Polling, Politics and the Press, Washington D.C., Congressional Quarterly press, 1991.

CAPPELLA (Joseph)., & JAMIESON (Kathleen), Spiral of cynicism, New York, Oxford University Press, 1997.

ALBRECHT-CARRIÉ (René), France, Europe, and the Two World Wars, New York, Harper, 1961.

CHAMPAGNE (Patrick), «Faire l'opinion», In Le nouveau jeu politique, Paris, Minuit, 1990, pp. 87-124.

CHILDS (Harwood L.), Public opinion: Nature, formation and role, Princeton, D. Van Nostrand., 1965.

CIGAR (Norman), Genocide in Bosnia: The Policy of "Ethnic Cleansing, College Station, TX, Texas A&M University Press, 1995.

COHEN (Bernard C.), The Press and Foreign Policy, Princeton, Princeton University Press, 1963.

COMPAINE (Benjamin M.) & DOUGLAS (Gomery), Who Owns the Media? Competition and Concentration in the Mass Media Industry, Mahwah N.J., Lawrence Erlbaum Associates, 2000.

CORNBEISE (Alfred E.), The Stars and Strips: Doughby's Journalism in World War I, West Port, CT, Greenwood Press, 1984.

CORNUT-GENTILLE (François) & ROZÈS (Stéphane), "La Réunification vue de L'Hexagone: les Français engourdis", in L'Etat de l'opinion 1991, Paris, Seuil, 1991, pp.75-91.

COTTAM (Richard W.), Nationalism in Iran, University of Pittsburgh Press, Pittsburgh, 1979.COX (Michael), US Foreign Policy after the Cold War, London, Pinter, 1995.

CHAIGNEAU (Pascal), Les Grands Enjeux du Monde Contemporain, Paris, Ellipses, 1996.

CHATFIELD (Charles) et al., Transnational Social Movements and Global Politics: Solidarity beyond the State, Syracuse, NY, Syracuse University Press, 1997.

CHOMSKY (Noam), Necessary Illusion: Thought Control in Democratic Society, Boston, South End Press, 1989.

CHOMSKY (Noam), Media Control: The Spectacular Achievements of Propaganda, New York, Seven Stories Press, 2002.

CHOMSKY (Noam), Understanding Power, New York, The New Press, 2002.

CHOMSKY (Noam), 9-11, New York, Seven Stories Press, 2002.

CHRISTIANS (Clifford), Propaganda and the technological system, In T. L. Glasser & C. T. Salmon (Eds.), Public opinion and the communication of consent. New York, Guilford Press, 1995, pp. 156-174.

CRARY (Jonathan), Modernizing Vision, Vision and Visuality, (ed.) Hal Foster, Seattle, Bay Press, 1988.

CRAWFORD (Nelson), The Ethics of Journalism, St. Claire Shores, MI: Scholarly Press, 1924.

CULL (Nicholas John), Selling War: the British Propaganda Campaign Against American "Neutrality" in World War II, New York, Oxford University Press, pp. 1-7., 1995.

CURRAN (J.), Capitalism and Control of the Press 1900-1975, London, Edward Arnold, 1977.

DEAN (John) & GABILLIET (Jean-Paul), European Readings of American Popular Culture, Westport, CT., Greenwood Press, 1996.

DEDIJER (Vladimir), «La route de Sarajevo», Paris, Gallimard, 1969.

DENTON (Robert E) & Rusciano (Frank Louis), The Media and the Persian Gulf War, Westport, CT, Praeger Publishers, 1993.

DONAHUE (G. A.) et al., "Media evaluations and group power". In A. Arno & W. Dissanayake (Eds.), The news media in national and international conflict, CO: Westview, Boulder, 1984, pp. 203-215

DOUGHERTY (James E.) & PFALTZGRAFF (Robert L.), Contending Theories of International Relations (3 rd ed), New York, Harper and Row, 1990.

DOUGLAS (Mary), Purity and Danger, London, Routledge, 1966.

DOUGLAS (Mary) & WILDAVSKY (A.), Risk and Culture: An essay on the Selection of Technical and Environmental Dangers, California, University of California Press, 1982.

Dutton (William H.) & PELTU (Malcolm), Information and Communication Technologies: Visions and Realities, New York, Oxford University Press, 1996.

DYE (Thomas R.), Understanding public policy (6th ed.), Englewood Cliffs NJ., Prentice-Hall, 1984.

ÉCHAUDEMAISON (Claude-Danièle), (Ed.), Dictionnaire d'économie et de sciences sociales, Paris, Nathan. 1989.

EDELMAN (Murray), The symbolic uses of politics, Urbana, University of Illinois Press, 1964.

EDELMAN (Murray), Constructing the political spectacle, Chicago, University of Chicago Press, 1988.

EDELMAN (Murray), Political language: Words that succeed and policies that fail, New York, Academic Press, 1977.

EDELMAN (Gerald M.), Bright Air, Brilliant Fire: On the Matter of Mind, New York, Basic Books, 1992.

ELDRIGE (John), Getting the Message: News, Truth and Power, London, Ruthledge, 1993.

ELDRIGE (John) et al, The Mass Media and Power in Modern Britain, Oxford, Oxford University, 1997.

ELGEY (Georgette), La République des Tourments, 1954-1959, Paris: Fayard, 1992, pp.165-259.

ENTMAN (Robert M.), Democracy without Citizens: Media and the Decay of American Politics, New York, Oxford University Press, 1989.

EVANS (Martin), The Memory of Resistance: French Opposition to the Algerian War (1954-1962), Oxford, Berg Publishers, Ltd., 1997.

FEIGERT (Frank B.) et al., Interaction, Foreign Policy and Public Policy, Washington, American Enterprise Institute, 1983.

FEHRENBACH (Heide) & POIGER (Uta G.), Transactions, Transgressions, Transformations: American Culture in Western Europe and Japan, New York, Berghahn Books, 2000.

FINE (B.), A giant of the press: Carr Van Anda, Oakland, CA, Acme Books, 1968.

FISHMAN (Mark), Manufacturing the News, Austin, University of Texas Press, 1980.

FRANKOVIC (Kathleen A.), News Media Polling in a Changing technological Environment, Evanston, Northwestern University, 1994.

FREEMAN (Christopher), "The Two-Edged Nature of Technological Change: Employment and Unemployment", in William H. Dutton, and Malcolm Peltu, Information and Communication Technologies: Visions and Realities, New York, Oxford University Press, 1996, pp. 19-36.

GALLUP (George) & SAUL (Forbes Rae), The Pulse of Democracy, New York, Simon & Schuster, 1940.

GANN (Peter) & DUIGNAN (L. H.), The Rebirth of the West: The Americanization of the Democratic World, 1945-1958, Cambridge, MA., Blackwell, 1992.

GARCIN (Thierry), les Grands Questions Internationales depuis la chute du mur de Berlin, Paris, Economica, 2001.

GAUNT (Philip), Making the Newsmakers: International Handbook on Journalism Training, Westport, CT, Greenwood Press, 1992.

GARDNER (Hall), Dangerous Crossroads: Europe, Russia, and the Future of NATO, Westport, CT, Praeger Publishers, 1997.

GARTHOFF (Raymond L.), The Great Transition. American-Soviet Relations and the End of the Cold War, Washington D.C., The Brookings Institution, 1994.

GILLIGAN (Carol), In a Different Voice: Psychological Theory and Women's Development, Cambridge, Harvard University Press, 1992.

GINSBERG (B.), "How polling transforms the public", In M. Margolis & G. Mauser (Eds.), Manipulating public opinion: Essays on public opinion as a dependent variable, Pacific Grove, CA: Brooks/Cole, 1989, pp. 271-293.

GITLIN (Todd), The whole world is watching: Mass media in the making and unmaking of the New Left, Berkeley, University of California Press, 1980.

GOFMAN (E.), Frame Analysis: An Assay on the Organization of Experience, New York, Harper & Row, 1974.

GOWER (Jackie), "Russia and the European Union", in Mark Webber, Russia and Europe: Conflict or Cooperation?, New York, St. Martin's Press, 2000

GOWING (Nik), Real-Time Television Coverage of Armed Conflicts and Diplomatic Crises: Does it Pressure or Distort Foreign Policy Decisions?; Cambridge, MA:, Harvard University, 1994.

GOWING (Nik), "Real-Time TV Coverage from War: does it make or break government policy", in J. Gow et al. (eds.), Bosnia by Television, London, British Film Institute, 1996, pp. 81-91.

GRABER (Doris), Mass media and American politics, Washington, DC, CQ Press, 1993.

GREEN (Daniel), Shaping political consciousness: The language of politics in America from McKinley to Reagan, Ithaca, Cornell University Press, 1987.

GREENFELD (Liah), Nationalism: Five Roads to Modernity, Cambridge, Harvard University Press, 1992.

HABERMAS (Jurgen), The structural transformation of the public sphere. (T. Burger & F. Lawrence, Trans.), Cambridge, MA, MIT Press, 1989.

HALLIN (Daniel C.) & GITLIN (Todd), "The Gulf War as popular culture and television drama". In W. Lance Bennett & David L. Paletz (Eds.), Taken by storm: The media, public opinion, and U.S. foreign policy in the Gulf War, Chicago & London, University of Chicago Press, 1994, pp. 149-163.

HALL (Stuart) et al., Policing the crisis: Mugging, the state, and law and order, London, Macmillan, 1978.

HAMPSON (Francoise), Incitement and the Media: Responsibility of and for the Media in Conflicts in the Former Yugoslavia, Essex, Colchester, 1993.

HAASS (Richard N.), Transatlantic Tensions: The United States, Europe, and Problem Countries, Washington, DC, The Brookings Institution, 1999.

HELMS (Robert F.) & DORFF (Robert H.), The Persian Gulf Crisis: Power in the Post-Cold War World, Westport, CT, Praeger, 1993.

HERBST (S.), "On the Disappearance of Groups: 19th-and Early 20th-Century Conceptions of Public Opinion", In T. L. Glasser & C. T. Salmon (Eds.), Public opinion and the commivnication of consent, New York, Guilford Press, 1995, pp. 89-104.

HERMAN (Edward S.) & MCCHESNEY (R. W.), The Global Media: The New Missionaries of Corporate Capitalism, London and Washington DC., Cassell, 1997.

HERMAN (Edward S.) & CHOMSKY (Noam), Manufacturing Consent: The Political Economy of Mass Media, New York, Pantheon Books, 2002.

HERRING (George C. Jr.), Aid to Russia, 1941-1946: Strategy, Diplomacy, the Origins of the Cold War, New York, Columbia University Press, 1973.

HOFFMANN (Stanley), Decline or Renewal? France since the 1930s, New York, Viking Press, 1974.

HOLBROOKE (Richard), To end a War, New York, Random House, 1998.

HYLAND (William G.), Clinton's World: Remaking American Foreign Policy, Westport, CT., Praeger, 1999

IRWIN (Will), The making of a reporter, New York, Putnam, 1942.

IYENGAR (Shanto) & KINDER (Donald R.), News That Matters!, Television and American Opinion, Chicago, University of Chicago Press, 1989

IYENGAR (Shanto), Is anyone responsible? How television frames political issues, Chicago, University of Chicago Press, 1991.

IYENGAR (Shanto) & SIMON (Adam), "News coverage of the gulf crisis and public opinion: A study of agenda-setting, priming, and framing". In W. Lance Bennett & David L. Paletz (Eds.), Taken by storm: The media, public opinion, and U.S. foreign policy in the Gulf War, University of Chicago Press, Chicago & London, 1994 pp. 167-185.

JACKAWAY (Gwenyth L.), The Media at War: radio Challenge to the Newspapers, 1924-1939, Westport, CT, Greenwood, 1995.

JAMIESON (Kathleen), Dirty politics: Deception, distraction and democracy, New York, Oxford University Press, 1992.

JENKINS (Philip), Intimate Enemies: Moral panics in contemporary Great Britain, New York, Aldine de Gruytes, 1992.

JOHNPOLL (Bernard K.) & (Robert), Muckraking and Objectivity: Journalism's Colliding Traditions, New York, Greenwood Press, 1990.

JOHNSON (B.B.), "The Environmentalist Movement and Grid/Group Analysis' in B.B. Johnson, & V.T. Covello (Eds.), The Social and Cultural Construction of Risk, Dordrecht Holland, D. Reidel, 1987, pp.147-175.

JOHNSTON (Carla) Brooks, Global News Access: The Impact of New Communications Technologies, Westport, CT., Praeger Publishers, 1998.

KATZ (Elihu) & SZECSKO (Tamas), (eds.), Mass Media and Social Change, Beverly Hills, CA., Sage, 1981.

KAIB (Marvin), The Nixon Memo: Political Respectability, Russia, and the Press, Chicago, The University of Chicago Press, 1994.

KASPI (André) & WIECK (Randolph), Ignorance Abroad: American Educational and Cultural Foreign Policy and the Office of Assistant Secretary of State, Westport, CT., Praeger Publishers, 1992.

KEANE (Fergal), Season of Blood: A Rwandan, London, Viking, 1995.

KERBEl (Matthew Robert.), Remote & Controlled: Media Politics in a Cynical Age, Boulder, CO., Westview Press, 1998.

KERTZER (David I.), Ritual, politics and power, New Haven, Yale University Press, 1988.

KEY (V.O., Jr.), "Public opinion and democratic politics". In B. Berelson and M. Janowitz (Eds.), Reader in public opinion and communication (2nd ed.), New York, Free Press, 1966, pp. 125-132.

KING (Pu-tsung), "The press, candidate images, and voter perceptions" in Communication and Democracy, eds. Maxwell McCombs, Donald Shaw and David Weaver, Mahwah, NJ., Lawrence Erlbaum Associates, 1997, pp.29-40.

KRAMER (Philip), Does France Still Count? The French Role in the New Europe, Westport, CT, Praeger Publishers, 1994.

KUZNICK (Peter J.) & GILBERT (James Burkhart), Rethinking Cold War Culture, Washington, Smithsonian Institution Press, 2001.

LAMBETH (Edmund.B.), Committed Journalism: An Ethic for the Profession (2nd ed.), Bloomington, Indiana University Press, 1996.

LANG (Kurt) & LANG (Gladys Engel), "The Mass Media and Voting", in Bernard Berelson and Morris Janowitz, eds., Reader in Public Opinion and Communication, 2d ed., New York, Free Press, 1966.

LANGER (William Leonard), The Franco-Russian Alliance, 1890-1894, Cambridge, Harvard University Press, 1929.

LAVRAKAS (Paul J.) & TRAUGOTT (Michael W.), The Election Polls, the News Media and Democracy, New York, Chatham House Publishers, 2000.

LAZARSFELD, (Paul F.), BERELSON (Bernard), & GAUDET (Hazel), The People's Choice, New York, Columbia University Press, 1948.

LEES (Lorraine M.), Keeping Tito Afloat: The United States, Yugoslavia, and the Cold War, University Park, PA., Pennsylvania State University Press, 1997.

LEBON (Gustav), The Crowd, New York, The Macmillan Company, 1922.

LAFEBER (Walter), The American Age: United States Foreign Policy at Home and Abroad since 1750, New York, Norton, 1994.

LEMERT (James B.), Does mass communication change public opinion after all? A new approach to effects analysis, Chicago, Nelson-Hall, 1981.

LEMERT (James B.), Criticizing the media: Empirical approaches, Newbury Park CA., Sage, 1989.

LEMERT (James B.), "Effective Public Opinion", in J. David Kennamer's, Public Opinion, the Press and Public Policy, Westport, CT., Praeger Publishers, 1992, pp. 43-44.

LEWIS (John Gaddis), Cold War Statesmen Confront the Bomb: Nuclear Diplomacy since 1945, Oxford, Oxford University Press, 1999.

LIPPMANN (Walter), Public Opinion, Free Press, New York, 1922.

LOOSELEY (David L.), The Politics of Fun: Cultural Policy and Debate in Contemporary France, Oxford, Berg Publishers Ltd., 1995.

LUHMANN (Niklas), Soziale Systeme: Grundriss einer allgemeinen Theorie, Frankfurt,/M: Suhrkamp, 1984.

LUHMANN (Niklas), The Reality of the Mass Media, Cambridge, Polity Press, 2000.

LYNCH (Dov), "Russia and the Organization for Security and Cooperation in Europe" in Mark Webber, Russia and Europe: Conflict or Cooperation?, New York, St. Martin's Press, 2000, pp. 99-124.

RUSCIANO (Frank Louis), Isolation and Paradox: Defining "the Public" in Modern Political Analysis, Westport, CT., Greenwood Press, 1989.

MADDUX (Thomas R.), Years of Estrangement: American Relations with the Soviet Union, 1933-1941, Tallahassee, FL., University Presses of Florida, 1980.

MANSFIELD (Michael D.) & NIMMO (Dan D.), Government and the News Media: Comparative Dimensions, Waco, TX., Baylor University Press, 1982.

MANDEL (Robert), The Changing Face of National Security: A Conceptual Analysis, Westport, CT., Greenwood Press, 1994, P. 15.

MAQUAIL (Denis), Mass Communication Theory: An Introduction, London, Sage, 1994.

MARBURY (Bladen Jr.), Public Opinion and Political Dynamics, Boston, Houghton Mifflin, 1950.

MAYER (William H.), Transnational Media and World Development: The Structure and Impact of Imperialism, New York, Greenwood Press, 1988.

MEDHURST (Martin J.), Cold War Rhetoric: Strategy, Metaphor, and Ideology, East Lansing, MI., Michigan State University Press, 1997

MEIER (Werner A.), "Media Ownership—Does It Matter?", in Robin Mansell et al. (eds.) Networking Knowledge for Information Societies: Institutions & Intervention, Delft, Delft University Press, 2002, pp 298-302.

MELODY (William H.), "Mass Media: The Economics of Access to the Marketplace of Ideas", in C. E. Aronoff (ed) Business and the Media, Santa Monica CA, Goodyear, 1978, pp. 216-226

MENARDIERE (Gilles de la), «Regards sur l'Imbroglio Yougoslave», in Pascal Chaigneau, Les Grands Enjeux du Monde Contemporain, Paris, Ellipses, 1996, pp. 96-100.

MERRILL (J. C.), The Imperative of Freedom. New York, Hastings House, 1974.

MEYER (William H.), Transnational Media and Third World Development: The Structure and Impact of Imperialism, New York, Greenwood Press, 1988

MCCAIN (Thownas A.) & SHYLES (Leonard), The 1,000 Hour War: Communication in the Gulf, Westport, CT., Greenwood Press, 1994.

MCCOMBS (Maxwell) & SHOW (Donald), (Ed. David L. Protess), Agenda Setting: Readings on Media, Public Opinion, and Policymaking, Hillsdale, NJ. Lawrence Erlbaum Associates, 1991.

MINEAR, (Larry) et al., The News Media, Civil War, and Humanitarian Action, Lynne, Boulder, CO, 1996.

MOELLER (Susan D,) Compassion Fatigue. How the Media Sell Disease, Famine, War and Death, New York, Routledge, 1999.

MOWLANA (Hamid), The new sovereigns: Multinational corporations as world powers, Englewood Cliffs, NJ, Prentice-Hall, Inc., 1975.

NEUMAN (Russell W.), The Future of the Mass Audience, Cambridge, Cambridge University Press, 1991.

NEUMAN (Russell W.) et al., Common knowledge, Chicago, University of Chicago Press, 1992.

Northcutt (Wayne), Mitterrand: A Political Biography, New York, Holmes & Meier, 1992.

OAKES (Guy), The Imaginary War: Civil Defense and American Cold War Culture, New York, Oxford University Press, 1994

ORWELL (George), Nineteen eighty four (critical introduction and annotation by Bernard Crick), Oxford, Clarendon Press, 1950.

ORWELL (George), "Politics and the English Language" in The Collected Essays of George Orwell, Harmondsworth, Penguin, 1968.

OWEN (David), Balkan Odyssey, New York, Harcourt Brace and Company, 1995.

PADIOLEAU (Jean), «De l'opinion publique à la communication politique». In Jean Padioleau (Ed.), L'opinion publique: examen critique, nouvelles directions, Paris, Mouton, 1980, pp. 13-60.

PATTERSON (Thomas), Out of Order, New York, Knopf, 1993.

PATERSON (Chris), "Global Battlefields", in Oliver Boyd-Barret, Terhi Rantanen, The Globalization of News, London, Sage, 1998. pp. 79-103.

POWASKI (Ronald E.), The Cold War: The United States and the Soviet Union, 1917-1991, New York, Oxford University Press, 1998,

PENNYCOOK (Alastair), Cultural Politics of English as an International Language, London, Longman, 1994.

POWASKI, Ronald E., The Cold War: The United States and the Soviet Union, 1917-1991, Oxford University Press, New York, 1998., 263 P.

PRITCHARD (David), "The News Media and Public Policy Agendas", in David J. Kennamer, Public Opinion, the Press and Public Policy, London, Praegar, 1992, pp. 103-112.

PRONAY (Nicholas) & SPRING (David. W) (eds.), Propaganda, Politics and Film 1918-45, London, Macmillan, 1982.

REEVES (Byron), "Hemispheres of scholarship: Pyschological and other approaches to studying media audiences". In Hay, J., Grossberg, L., and Wartella, E. (Eds.), The Audience and Its Landscape, Boulder, Westview Press, 1996, pp. 265-279.

RIDGEWAY (James) & UDOVI?KI (Jasminka), Burn This House: The Making and Unmaking of Yugoslavia, Duke University Press, Durham, NC, 1997.

RIVERS (William L.), "The Media as Shadow Government" in Protess, David L. (ed.) Agenda Setting: Readings on Media, Public Opinion, and Policymaking, Hillsdale, Lawrence Erlbaum Associates, 1991, pp. 153-160.

ROBERTS (Adam), "The Crisis in UN Peacekeeping" in A. Crocker and Fen Olster Hampson, Managing Global Chaos, Washington, DC., United States Institute of Peace Press, 1996, pp. 3-15.

ROBERTSON (Roland), Globalization: Social Theory and Global Culture, London, Sage, 1992.

ROMANYSHYN (Robert D.), Technology as Symptom and Dream, New York, Routledge, 1989.

ROSTOW (Eugene), The Stages of Economic Growth: A Non-Communist Manifesto, London, Cambridge University Press, 1971.

RUSCIANO (Frank Louis) & POLLOCK (John Crothers), "World Opinion During Times of Crisis" in World opinion and the emerging international order by Bosah Ebo et al., Westport, CT., Praeger Publishers, 1998.

RUSCIANO (Frank Louis) & BOSAH (Ebo), "National Consciousness, International Image, and the Construction of Identity" in World Opinion and the Emerging International Order by Bosah Ebo et al., Westport, CT., Praeger Publishers, 1998.

SCHUDSON (Michael). Origins of the Ideal of Objectivity in the Profession, New York, Garland, 1990.

SCOTT (William Evans), Alliance against Hitler: The Origins of the Franco-Soviet Pact, Durham, NC, Duke University Press, 1962.

SEVERIN (W. J.) & TANKARD, (J.W.), Communications Theories: Origins, Methods, and Uses in the Mass Media, New York, Longman, 1997.

SHAW (Martin), Civil Society and Media in Global Crises, London, St Martin's Press, 1996.

SCHILLER (Herbert I.), Mass Communications and American Empire, Boulder, Westview Press, 1992.

SCHLESINGER (Philip), Media, State and Nation: Political Violence and collective Identities, London, Sage Publications, 1991.

SCHMIDT (Alex) & DE GRAAF (Janny), Violence as Communication: Insurgent Terrorism and the Western News Media, London, Sage Publications, 1982.

SMITH (Anthony), (Ed.), British Broadcasting, London, Newton Abbott, David & Charles, 1974.

SMITH (Anthony), The Geopolitics of Information: How Western Culture Dominates the World, New York, Oxford University Press, 1980.

SMITH (Hedrick), The Media and the Gulf War, Washington, DC, Seven Locks Press, 1992.

SHAPIRO (Michael J.), "Textualizing Global Politics" In International/Intertextual Relations: Postmodern Readings of World Politics, eds. J. Der Derian and M. J. Shapiro. D.C. Heath, Lexington, MA., Lexington Books,1989, pp. 69-96.

SHULL (Steven A.), American Civil Rights Policy from Truman to Clinton: The Role of Presidential Leadership, Armonk, NY., M. E. Sharpe, 2000.

SIEBERT (Frederick S), PETERSON (Theodore)., & SCHRAMM (Wilbur), Four Theories of the Press, Urbana, University of Illinois Press, 1956.

STROBEL (Warren P.), "The Media and U.S. Policies Toward Intervention," in Chester A. Crocker and Fen Osler Hampson, Managing Global Chaos, Washington, DC., United States Institute of Peace Press, 1996, pp. 357-376.

TAYLOR (Phillip M.), Global Communications, International Affairs and the Media since 1945, London, Routledge,1997.

THOMSON (Charles A.) & LAVES (Walter H. C.), Cultural Relations and U. S. Forein Policy, Bloomington, Indiana University Press, 1963.

TRAGER (Frank), "Introduction to the Study of National Security" in Frank Trager and Philip Kronenberg, eds., National Security and American Society, Manhattan, KS., University Press of Kansas, 1973, pp 35-51.

TRENAMAN (Joseph) & MCQUAIL (Denis), Television and the Political Image, London, Methuen and Co., 1961.

THIONG'O (Ngugiwa), Decoliñizing the Mind: The politics of language in African Literature, London, James Carey, 1981.

TUCHMAN (Gaye), Making news, New York, Free Press, 1978.

TUATHAIL (GEARÓID.Ó) & Dalby (Simon), Rethinking Geopolitics, London, Routledge, 1998.

TURPIN (Jennifer), <u>Reinventing the Soviet Self: Media and Social Change in the Former Soviet Union</u>, Westport, CT., Praeger Publishers, 1995.

ULLMAN (Richard), The World and Yugoslavia's Wars, New York, Council on Foreign Relations Press, 1996.

VASQUEZ (John), The War Puzzle, Cambridge, Cambridge University Press, 1993.

VAUGHAN (Stephen L.), Holding Fast the Inner Lines, North Carolina, Chapel Hill University of North Carolina Press, 1980.

VOGEL (Charles), "L'Europe orientale depuis le Traité de Berlin", Paris, C. Reinwald, 1881.

VORYS (Karl Von), American Foreign Policy: Consensus at Home, Leadership Abroad, Westport, CT., Praeger Publishers, 1997.

WACHTEL (David), Cultural Policy and Socialist France, New York, Greenwood Press, 1987.

WEBBER (Mark), Russia and Europe: Conflict or Cooperation?, New York, St. Martin's Press, 2000.

WOLTON (Dominique), War game/L'information et la guerre, Paris, Flammarion, 1991.

WALZER (Michael), Toward a Global Civil Society, Providence R.I., Berghahn Books, 1998.

WILLIAMS (Kevin), Get me a murder a day. A History of Mass Communication in Britain. London, Arnold, 1998.

WOLFERS (Arnold)., Discord and Collaboration, Baltimore, John Hopkins University Press, 1962.

YERIC (Jerry L.) & TODD (John R.), Public opinion: Itasca, IL, The visible politics, F. E. Peacock. 1989.

YOUNG (John W.), Cold War Europe, 1945-1991: A Political History, London, Arnold, 1996.

Journals

ALBRITTON (Robert B.) & MANHEIM (Jarol B.), "News of Rhodesia: The Impact of a Public Relations Campaign", Journalism Quarterly, No. 60, 1983, pp. 6-22.

ALLPORT (F. H.), "Toward a science of public opinion". Public Opinion Quarterly, Vol.1, 1937, pp. 7-23.

BAKER (James A.III), "Report First, Check Later, interviewed by Marvin Kalb". Harvard International Journal of Press/Politics, Vol. 1, N° 2, Spring 1996.

BANKS (William C.) & STRAUSSMAN (Jeffrey D.), "A new imperial presidency? Insights from U.S. involvement in Bosnia", Political Science Quarterly, Vol.114, N°2, 1999, pp. 195-217.

Becker (Lee) & MCCOMBS (Maxwell),"The role of the press in determining voter REACTIONS to presidential primaries", Human Communication Research, N°4, 1978, pp.301-307.

BENNETT (Lance W.), "Myth, ritual, and political control". Journal of Communication, Vol. 30, N° 4, 1980, pp.166-179.

BENNETT (Lance, W.), "Toward a Theory of Press State Relations in the United States", Journal of Communication, N°40, 1990, pp. 103-125.

BENNETT (W. Lance.), "Constructing publics and their opinions", Political Communication, N°10,1993, pp. 101-120.

BELL (Martin), "Testament of an Interventionist", British Journalism Review, Vol. 4, N° 4, 1993,

BLECHMAN (Barry) & WITTES (Tamara M.), "Defining Moment: The Threat and Use of Force in America Foreign Policy", Political Science Quarterly, vol. 114, N°1, 1999,pp.1-30.

BOOT (W.), "Covering the gulf war: The press stands alone", Columbia Journalism Review, March/April1991, pp. 23-24.

BOURDIEU (Pierre), « L'opinion publique n'existe pas », Les Temps Modernes, N°318, 1973, pp. 1292-1309.

GAVIN (Bowd), "C'est la lutte initiale': Steps in the Realignment of the French Left", New Left Review, vol. a., N° 206, 1994, pp. 71-85.

BOYD (Charles), "Making peace with the guilty: The truth about Bosnia", Foreign Affairs, vol. 74, N° 5, 1995, pp.22-38.

BREED (Warren), "Mass Communication and Sociocultural Integration", Social Forces, N° 37, 1958, pp.109-116.

BREWER (Marilynn B.), "In-Group Bias in the Minimal Intergroup Situation: A Cognitive-Motivational Analysis, Psychological Bulletin, Vol. 86, N°2, 1979. pp. 307–324.

BROCK (Peter), "Dateline Yugoslavia: The Partisan Press", Foreign Policy, N° 93, Winter1994, pp. 152-172.

BROSIUS (Hans-Bernd) & KEPPLINGER (Hans Mathias), "Beyond agenda setting: The influence of partianship and television reporting on the electorate's voting intentions", Journalism Quarterly, N°69, 1992, pp.893-901.

BOWERS (J. W.), & OSBORN (M. M.), "Attitudinal effects of selected types of concluding metaphors in persuasive speeches, Speech Monographs, N°33, 1966, pp. 147-155.

BULARD (Martin), "Hors des Frontières, la France à la Recherche d'une Ambition Culturelle", Le Monde Diplomatique, June 2001.

BULMER (Simon) & PATERSON (William E), "Germany in the European Union : gentle giant or emergent leader?", International Affairs, Vol.72, N°1, 1996, pp. 9-32.

BURNS Nicholas, "Talking to the World About American Foreign Policy", Harvard International Journal of Press/Politics, Vol. 1, N° 4, Fall 1996.

CANEL (Maria Jose), LLAMAS (Juan Pablo), & FEDERICO (Federico Rey), "El primer nivel del efecto agenda setting en la informacion local: Los 'problemas mas importantes' de la ciudad de Pamplona", Comunicacion y Sociedad, Vol. 9, N°1&2, 1996, pp.17-38.

CHARLES (J.), SHORE (L.), & TODD (R.), The New York Times Coverage of Equatorial and Lower Africa, Journal of Communication, vol. 29,N°2, 1979, PP. 148-155.

COLLIER (Paul) & HOEFFLER (Anke), "On Economic Causes of Civil War," Oxford Economic Papers, 1998, Vol. 50, pp. 563-573.

CONNOR (Walker), "Beyond Reason: The Nature of the Ethnonational Bond." Ethnic and Racial Studies, 1983, Vol. 16: pp. 373-89.

Cook, F. et al., "Media and agenda setting: Effects on the public, interest group leaders, policy makers, and policy", Public Opinion Quarterly, N°47,1983, pp.16-35.

DAALDER (Ivo H.) & O'HANLON (Michael E.), "The United States in the Balkans: There to Stay", The Washington Quarterly, Vol. 23, N° 4, pp. 157-170.

DAKE (Karl), "Orienting Dispositions in the Perception of Risk", Journal of Cross-Cultural Psychology, Vol. 22, pp. 61-82.

DANNER (Mark), "The US and the Yugoslav Catastrophe", New York Review of Books, vol. 44, N° 18, 1997, pp. 56-64.

DAVIS (David R.) & MOORE (Will H.), "Ties that Bind? Domestic and International Conflict Behavior in Zaire", Comparative Political Studies, 1997, Vol. 31, pp. 45-71.

DERLUGUIAN (Georgi M.), "Che Guevaras in Turbans", New Left Review, Vol. A, N° 237, 1999, pp.16-17.

DEMERS (David), "Revisiting Corporate Newspaper Structure and Profit Making", Journal of Media Economics, Vol. 11, N° 2, 1998, pp. 19-45.

DEMERS (David) & MERSKIN (Debra), "Corporate News Structure and the Managerial Revolution", Journal of Media Economics, Vol. 13, N° 2, 2000, pp. 103-121.

DORMAN (William A.),"Peripheral Vision: U.S. Journalism and the Third World", World Policy Journal, Vol.3, N° 3., 1986, pp.419-445.

DU BOIS (Pierre), « La Question des Balkans », Relations Internationales, N° 103, Fall 2000, pp.271-277.

DURHAM (Meenakshi Gigi), "On the Relevance of Standpoint Epistemology to the Practice of Journalism: The case for "Strong Objectivity", Communication Theory, vol. 8, N° 2, 1998, pp. 117-140.

EASTERLY (William) & LEVINE (Ross), "Africa's Growth Tragedy: Policies and Ethnic Divisions." Quarterly Journal of Economics, vol. 112, N°4, 1997, pp. 1203–1250.

EDELMAN (Murray), "Contestable categories and public opinion. Political Communication, N°10, 1993, pp. 231-242.

ENTMAN (Robert M.), Framing: Towards the Clarification of a Fractured Paradigm, Journal of Communications, vol. 43, N° 3, 1993, pp. 51-58.

GALTUNG (J.) & RUGE (M.H.), "The Structure of Foreign News, Journal of Peace Research, N°2, 1965, pp. 64-91.

GERSHON (Richard A.), "The Trans-national Media Corporation: Environmental Scanning and Strategy Formulation"; Journal of Media Economics, vol. 13, N° 2, 2000, pp. 81–95.

GERBNER (George) & MARVANYI (George), "The Many Worlds of the World's Press", Journal of Communication, N° 27, 1977, pp. 52-61.

GIDEON (Rose), "The Exit Strategy Delusion", Foreign Affairs, N°77, 1998, pp. 56-67.

GREENFIELD (Liah,) "Nationalism and Class Struggle: Two Forces or One"?, Survey, N° 29, 1985, pp.153-174.

GINER-SOROLLA (Roger) & CHAIKEN (Shelley), "The causes of hostile media judgements", Journal of Experimental Social Psychology, N°30, 1994, pp.165-180.

FICO (Frederick) et al., "Fairness and balance of newspaper coverage of U.S. in the Gulf War", Newspaper Research Journal, vol.15, N°1, pp. 30-43.

HAFTENDORN (Helga), "The Security Puzzle: Theory-Building and Discipline-Building in International Security", International Studies Quarterly, N° 35, March 1991, pp. 3-17.

HACKETT (Robert A.), "Decline of a paradigm? Bias and objectivity in new media studies". Critical Studies in Mass Communication, Vol.1, 1984, pp. 229-259.

HERMAN (Edward S.), "The Institutionalisation of Bias in Economics", Media, culture and Society, N° 4, July 1982, pp. 275-291.

HIRSH (M.), "The Sins of Sears are not News in Chicago", Columbia Journalism Review, N° 5, 1976, pp. 29-30.

HILGARTNER (Stephen) & BOSK (Charles L.), "The Rise and Fall of Social Problems: A Public Arenas Model", American Journal of Sociology, N° 94, 1988, pp. 53-78

HOROWITZ, (Donald L.), "Democracy in Divided Societies, Journal of Democracy, vol.4, N°4, pp.18–38.

HUNTINGTON (Samuel), "The Clash of Civilizations", Foreign Affairs Vol. 72, No. 3, Summer 1993, pp. 22-69.

YOUNG (Marilyn J.) & LAUNER (Michael K.), "Redefining Glasnost in the Soviet Media", Journal of communications, Vol. 41, No. 2, 1991, pp. 102-105.

MORRISON (David C.), "How Bosnia Is Becoming a Priority", National Journal, N°. 26, August 1994, pp. 34-35.

MCANANY (Emile G.) & WILKINSON (Kenton T.), "From Cultural Imperialists to Takeover Victims", Communication Research, vol. 19, N°6, 1992, pp. 724-748.

MCCOMBS (Maxwell) & SHAW (Donald), "The agenda-setting function of mass media", Public Opinion Quarterly, vol. 36, 1972, pp.176-187.

MCCOMBS (Maxwell) & LOPEZ-ESCOBAR (Esteban) & LLAMAS (Juan Pablo), "Setting the agenda of attributes in the 1996 Spanish general election", Journal of Communication, vol. 50, N°2, 2000, pp. 77-92.

MIDLARSKY (Manus I.), "Mathematical Models of Instability and a Theory of Diffusion", International Studies Quarterly, N° 14, 1970, pp. 60-84.

MOORE (Will H.), "Ethnic Minorities and Foreign Policy", SAIS Review, Vol. 22, N°. 2, (Summer–Fall 2002), pp. 77-91.

MOST (Benjamin A.) & STARR (Harvey), "Diffusion, Reinforcement, Geopolitics, and the Spread of War", American Political Science Review, N° 74, December 1980, pp. 932-946.

MULLER (Edward N.) & SELIGSON (Mitchell A.), "Inequality and Insurgency," American Political Science Review, 1987, Vol. 8, pp. 425-452.

NEVILLE-JONES (Pauline), "Dayton, IFOR, and Alliance Relations in Bosnia", Survival, vol. 38, N°4, winter 1996-97, pp.46-47.

NNAEMEKA (T.) & Richstad (J.), "Structured Relations and Foreign News Flow in the Pacific Region", Gazette, N°26, 1980, pp. 235-258.

OGINANOVA (E.) & ENDERSBY (J.), "Objectivity Revisited; a Spatial Model for Political Economy and Mass Communication", Journalism and Mass Communication Monographs, N°159, October 1996.

JOHNSON (Melissa A.), "Predicting News Flow from Mexico", Journalism and Mass Communication Quarterly, vol.74, N°2, 1997, pp. 315-330.

KAHNEMAN (Daniel) & TVERSKY (Amos), "The Psychology of Preferences", Scientific American, N° 246, 1982, pp. 6-42.

KALB (Marvin), "The Pentagon and the Press", Harvard International Journal of Press/Politics, Vol. 1, N° 1, winter 1996.

KAREIL (H. G.), & ROSENVALL (L. A.), "Cultural affinity displayed in Canadian daily newspapers", Journalism Quarterly, N° 60, 1983, 431-436.

KARIEL (H.G.) & ROSENVALL (L.A.), "Factors Influencing International News Flow", Journalism Quarterly, N°61, 1984, pp. 509-516.

KNOPF (Jeffrey W.), "Domestic Society and International Cooperation: The Impact of Protest on US Arms Control Policy", American Political Science Review, Vol. 93, N°3, September 1999, pp. 759-760.

KOLODZIEJ (Edward A.), "Renaissance in Security Studies? Caveat Lector", International Studies Quarterly, N°36, December 1992, pp.421-438.

KONE (D.), & MULLET (E.), "Societal Risk Perception and Media Coverage", Risk Analysis, N°14, 1994, pp.21-24.

LAKE (David) & ROTHCHILD (Donald), "Containing fear: the origin and management of ethnic conflict", International Security, vol. 21, 1996, pp. 41-75.

LEMERT (J. B.) et al., "Journalists and mobilizing information", Journalism Quarterly, N° 54, 1977, pp. 721-726.

LEMKE (Douglas), "The Tyranny of Distance: Redefining Relevant Dyads", International Interactions, vol.17, N°1, 1995, pp. 113-126.

LENCZOWSKI (George), "Major Pipelines in the Middle East: Problems and Prospects", Middle East Policy, Vol.3. N° 4, 1995.

LIPARI (Lisbeth), "Polling as Ritual, Journal of Communication", Vol.49, N°1, 1999, pp. 83-102.

LIPPMANN (Walter), "Two revolutions in the American press", Yale Review, 1931, N° 20, pp. 437-440.

RICCHIARDI (Sherry), "Exposing Genocide", American Journalism Review, June 1993, pp. 32-36.

PAN (Zhongdang) & KOSICKI (Gerald) (1997), "Priming and media impact on the evaluations of the president's performance", Communication Research, Vol. 24, pp. 3-30.

PRICE (Vincent) et al," Switching Frames of Thought: The Impact of News Frames on Readers", Communication Research, vol.24, 1997,pp. 481-506.

Ricchiardi, Sherry. "Exposing Genocide...For What'?", American Journalism, Vol.15, N° 5, June 1993, pp.32-37.

PAVLOWITCH (Stevan K.), "Who is 'Balkanizing' whom? The misunderstandings between the debris of Yugoslavia and an unprepared West", Daedalus, Vol.123, N°2, 1994, pp. 203-223.

PROSS (Harry), "On German Identity", Media, Culture, and Society, N°13, 1991, pp. 341-356.

READ (S. J.) et al., "When is the federal budget like a baby? Metaphor in political rhetoric", Metaphor and Symbolic Activity, N°5,1990, pp 125-149

ROSE (Gideon), "The Exit Strategy Delusion", Foreign Affairs, N°.77, 1998, pp. 56-67.

ROSEN (Jay), "Beyond Objectivity", Nieman Reports, vol. 47, N°7, 1993, pp. 48-53.

ROSENGREN (K. E.), "Four Types of Tables", Journal of Communications, vol.27, N°1,1977, pp. 67-75.

ROSSLER (Patrick) & SCHENK (Michael), "Cognitive bonding and the German reunification: Agenda-setting and persuasion effects of mass media", International Journal of Public Opinion Research, vol.12, N°1, 2000, pp. 29-47.

SAMPDRO (Victor), "Grounding the Displaced: Local Media Reception in a Transnational Context", Journal of Communications, vol.48, N°2, 1998, pp. 125-144.

SEMETKO (Holli A.) & Valkenburg (Patti M.), "Framing European Politics: A Content Analysis of Press and Television News"; Journal of Communication, vol. 50.N° 2, 2000, pp. 93-109.

SERVAES (Jan), "European Press Coverage of the Grenada Crisis", Journal of Communication, vol. 41, N°4., 1991, pp. 29-41.

SHAW (Eugene F.), "Agenda-setting and mass communication theory", Gazette, Vol.25, N°2, 1979, pp.101-119.

Skurnik, (W.A.E.), "Foreign News Coverage in Six African Newspapers, The potency of national interests", Gazette, Vol.28, 1981, pp. 117-130.

SMITH (Tom W.), "Classifying Protestant Denominations", Review of Religious Research, N° 31, 1990, pp. 225-245.

STARR (Harvey) & MOST (Benjamin A.), "The Substance and Study of Borders in International Relations Research", International Studies Quarterly, N° 20, December1976, pp. 581-620.

STATES (Jukes), "Real-time responsibility: journalism's challenges in an instantaneous age", Harvard International Review, Vol. 14, N°. 2, 2002, pp. 14-18.

STOKER (Kevin), "Existential Objectivity: Freeing Journalists to be Ethical", Journal of Mass Media Ethics, vol.10, N°1, 1995, pp. 5-23.

STRECKFUSS (Richard), "Objectivity in journalism: A search and a reassessment", Journalism Quarterly, N°67, 1990, pp. 973-983.

STENSAAS (H.), "Development of the objectivity ethic in U.S. daily newspapers", Journal of Mass Media Ethics, vol.2, N°1, 1986-1987, pp. 50-60.

TAKESHITA (Toshio), "Agenda-setting effects of the press in a Japanese local election", Studies of Broadcasting, vol.29, 1993, pp. 193-216.

THOMAS (Alan M.), "Audience, Market and Public-An Evaluation of Canadian Broadcasting". Canadian Communications, vol. 1, N°1,1960, pp. 16-47.

TVERSKY (Amos) & Kahneman (Daniel), "Availability: A heuristic for judging frequency and probability", Cognitive Psychology, N°5, 1973, pp. 207-232.

UTLEY (Garrick), "The Shrinking of Foreign News", Foreign Affairs, Vol. 76, N°2, March/April 1997, pp. 2-10.

VULLIAMY (Ed.), "This War Has Changed My Life", British Journalism Review, Vol. 4, N° 2, 1993, pp. 5-11.

WESLEY (James P.), "Frequency of Wars and Geographical Opportunity", Journal of Conflict Resolution, Vol. 6, N° 4, pp. 387-389.

WILLNAT (Lars) & ZHU (Jian-Hua), "Newspaper coverage and public opinion in Hong Kong: A time-series analysis of media priming", Political Communication, N°13, 1996, pp. 231-246.

WU (Denis H.), "The Systematic Determinants of International News Coverage: A Comparison of 38 Countries", Journal of Communications, vol.50, N°2, pp.110-130.

ZELIZER (Barbie), "CNN, the Gulf War, and Journalistic Practice", Journal of Communications, Vol. 42, N°1, 1992, pp.66-99.

YAEL (Tamir), "The Right to National Self-Determination", Social Research, N°58, N° 3, Fall 1991, pp. 587.577-590.

YINGER (Milton J.), "Ethnicity", Annual Review of Sociology, 1985, Vol. 11, pp.151-80.

Magazines and Specialized Revues

BROWNE (Malcolm W.) "The Military vs. The Press". New York Times Magazine, March 3, 1991, pp. 44-45.

CHARMES (Francis), « Chronique de la Quinzaine », Revue des Deux Mondes, 1st of novembre 1912.

CALUDE (Cheysson), « La France doit avoir une politique arabe", France-Pays arabes, Eurabia, Paris, N°232, May 1997.

COUGHLIN (J.W.), "The great Mokusatsu mistake: Was this the deadliest error of our time", Harper's Magazine, vol. 206, N°1234, 1053, pp. 31-40.

HALIMI (Serge), "Réseaux", Le Monde Diplomatique, February 1995.

HERTSGUARD (Mark), "How Reagan Seduced Us: Inside the President's Propaganda Factory", Village Press, September 18, 1984.

LAURENS (Henry), «La politique musulmane de la France», Monde arabe. Maghreb-Machrek, N°152, April-June 1996.

REKACEWICZ (Jean), "Transport and Geostrategie in Southern Russia", Le Monde Diplomatique, Juin 1998.

STROBEL (Warren P), "TV Images May Shock But Won't Alter Policy", Christian Science Monitor, December 14, 1994.

The New York Times' Sample of Articles & News Items on Bosnia and Chechnya

BASSIR (Afsane), "L'adoption par le Conseil de sécurité des résolutions autorisant le recours à la force en Bosnie Les Occidentaux espèrent intimider les Serbes avant la conférence de Londres", Le Monde, 15 August 1992.

BASSIR (Afsane), "La querelle entre M. Boutros-Ghali et le Conseil de sécurité sur la Bosnie-Herzégovine Le secrétaire général de l'ONU juge excessive la part prise par la crise yougoslave", Le Monde, 26 July 1992.

DEBOVE (Alain),"L'adoption par le Conseil de Sécurité des résolutions autorisant le recours à la force en Bosnie Témoignages sur un cauchemar", Le Monde, 15 August 1992.

BRESSON (Henri De.), "La guerre en Tchétchénie empêche la Russie d'entrer au Conseil de l'Europe", Le Monde, 4 February 1996.

DEBOVE (Alain),"En permettant la sécession des Serbes et des Croates de la future Union Le nouveau plan de paix ouvre la voie à l'éclatement de la Bosnie-Herzégovine", Le Monde, 18 Septembre 1993.

HARTMANN (Florence), "Yougoslavie : Les Serbes de Bosnie-Herzégovine ont décidé de créer une huitième "République", Le Monde, 11 January 1992.

HARTMANN (Florence), "Tandis que des rassemblements pour la paix avaient lieu dans toute la République Le leader de la communauté serbe prône l'éclatement de la Bosnie-Herzégovine en trois Etats", Le Monde, 7 March 1993.

HARTMANN (Florence), "La Bosnie-Herzégovine entre paix et guerre La tension ne cesse de monter dans la République où milices serbes et musulmanes se préparent à l'épreuve de force", Le Monde, 3 March 1992.

HARTMANN (Florence), "Sur fond de guerre en Bosnie-Herzégovine Le premier ministre de la nouvelle Yougoslavie, s'entretient à Paris avec M. Mitterrand", Le Monde, 8 July 1992.

HELLER (Yves), "Yougoslavie: Tandis que lord Carrington tente d'obtenir un nouveau cessez-le-feu La Croatie met en garde contre l'extension de la guerre à la Bosnie-Herzégovine", Le Monde, 5 November 1992.

HELLER (Yves), "Le sort des Républiques de l'ex-Yougoslavie La Bosnie-Herzégovine se prononcera par référendum sur son indépendance Une poudrière ethnique menacée d'explosion", Le Monde, 19 January 1992.

HELLER (Yves), "Accord à Genève sur l'éclatement de la Bosnie-Herzégovine La présidence bosniaque a accepté" provisoirement "la création d'une" Union "de trois Républiques", Le Monde, 1 August 1993.

HELLER (Yves), "Bosnie: Un puzzle mal assemblé", Le Monde, 30 July 1994.

KRAUZE (Jan), "A la suite des pressions de la Russie Le président Djokhar Doudaïev a décrété la mobilisation générale en Tchétchénie", Le Monde, 13 August 1994.

KRAUZE (Jan), "Les forces russes subiraient de lourdes pertes dans Grozny", Le Monde, 3 January 1995.

NAUDET (Jean Baptiste), "Djokhar Doudaev, le général tchétchène qui défie l'" "empire russe", Le Monde, 15 September 1993.

NAUDET (Jean Baptiste), "Les guerriers de Tchétchénie fourbissent leurs armes", Le Monde, 11 September 1994.

NAUDET (Jean Baptiste), "Après un an de guerre en Tchétchénie, Moscou renonce à négocier avec les indépendantistes", Le Monde, 29 December 1995.

NAUDET (Jean Baptiste), "Les négociations de paix en Tchétchénie ont été ajournées", Le Monde, 2 August 1996.

JEGO (Marie), "Le général Lebed espère trouver un accord politique en Tchétchénie", Le Monde, 24 August 1996.

OURDAN (Remy), "Bosnie-Herzégovine : Entre Serbes et Serbes, un pont sur la Drina", Le Monde, 14 August 1993.

OURDAN (Remy), "Bosnie: Pale garde son calme", Le Monde, 13 August 1994.

OURDAN (Remy), "Le chef de la Forpronu en Bosnie menace de recourir aux frappes aériennes", Le Monde, 26 May 1995.

OURDAN (Remy), "Le massacre de Tuzla entraîne de nouveaux raids de l'OTAN Les artilleurs serbes ont ouvert le feu sur deux cafés de la ville bosniaque, faisant soixante et onze morts. Tandis que deux cents «casques bleus» étaient pris en otage à Sarajevo, les Occidentaux répliquaient par de nouvelles frappes aériennes", Le Monde, 27 May 1995.

ROLLIN (Jean), "Bosnie: Diamond Road", Le Monde, 4 September 1993.

SERVENTE (Pierre), "Bosnie : Sur une base alliée d'Italie, des pilotes se préparent", Le Monde, 18 August 1993.

SHIHAB (Sophie), "Anarchie en Tchétchénie Un an après la proclamation de son indépendance, la remuante République du Caucase, livrée à tous les trafics, va à vau-l'eau", Le Monde, 25 October1992.

SHIHAB (Sophie), "Russie: en Tchétchénie "indépendante" Les chars du président tirent devant le Parlement", Le Monde, 6 June 1993.

SHIHAB (Sophie), "La fuite en avant du Kremlin en Tchétchénie", Le Monde, 11 February 1995.

SHIHAB (Sophie), "M. Eltsine réaffirme son refus de négocier avec le président tchétchène", Le Monde, 20 January 1995.

SHIHAB (Sophie), "L'impasse est totale en Tchétchénie après un an de guerre et de massacres", Le Monde, 10 December 1995.

SHIHAB (Sophie), "La guerre en Tchétchénie est jugée conforme à la Constitution russe", Le Monde, 2 August 1995.

SHIHAB (Sophie), "Bill Clinton et Boris Eltsine ont constaté leurs divergences à Moscou Concession symbolique sur la coopération nucléaire avec l'Iran et promesse d'un vague cessez-le-feu en Tchétchénie sont les seuls résultats tangibles de cette rencontre", Le Monde, 12 May 1995.

SHIHAB (Sophie), "La fuite en avant du Kremlin en Tchétchénie", Le Monde, 11 February 1995.

SHIHAB (Sophie), "Boris Eltsine a annoncé la publication d'un statut pour la Tchétchénie", Le Monde, 30 May 1995.

SHIHAB (Sophie), "La trêve électorale a définitivement volé en éclats en Tchétchénie", Le Monde, 16 July 1996.

SHIHAB (Sophie), "M. Eltsine réélu, les bombardements reprennent en Tchétchénie", Le Monde, 11 July 1996.

TATU (Michel), "Bosnie: L'improbable "tempête des Balkans", Le Monde, 14 August 1992.

TATU (Michel), "Armer l'ONU Les échecs des Nations unies en Somalie comme en Bosnie soulignent la nécessité d'un renforcement des structures de l'organisation", Le Monde, 22 July 1993.

"Tchétchènie: Le retour de Rouslan Khasboulatov l'ancien rebelle de la" Maison Blanche", Le Monde, 11 September 1994.

"Russie: sur fond de combats en Tchétchénie Le traité de la Fédération a été signé", Le Monde, 2 April 1992.

The New York Times' Sample of Articles & News Items on Bosnia and Chechnya

BURNS (John F.), "Bosnia's Elderly Fall to a New Enemy: Cold: Bosnia Now Faces the Cruellest Enemy of the Siege: Winter's Cold", The New York Times, 6 January 1992.

BURNS (John F.), "Dim Hope For Bosnia: Geneva Pact Seen But No End to War", The New York Times, 22 January 1992.

BURNS (John F.), "U.N. General Warns Against an Airdrop for Bosnia: Concern that some may think aid flights are arms deliveries", The New York Times, 23 February 1992.

BURNS (John F.), "Bosnia Fights New War Against Croats", The New York Times, 20 April 1993.

COHEN (Roger), "A NATO Deadline in Bosnia Passes Without", The New York Times, 5 September 1995.

ERLANGER (Steven), "Russia's Army Seen as Failing Chechnya Test: Russia's Army, Deprived and Demoralized, Is Seen as Failing Chechnya Test", The New York Times, 25 December 1995.

ERLANGER (Steven), "Moscow Accepts Chechnya Talks", The New York Times, 19 June 1995.

ERLANGER (Steven), "Peace Talks In Chechnya Suspended", The New York Times, 26 May 1995.

ERLANGER (Steven), "Dissent on Chechnya: Word to the West", The New York Times, 14 April 1995.

ERLANGER (Steven), "Russia Sees Long Fight in Chechnya", The New York Times, 24 March 1995.

ERLANGER (Steven), "A Famous Victory: Russia Says It Has Won in Chechnya, But Evidence Contradicts the Claim", The New York Times, 10 February 1995.

GREENHOUSE (Steven), "U.S. Sharply Rebukes Russia For Its Offensive in Chechnya", The New York Times, 12 April 1995.

KIFNER (Johan), "Refugees Forced Out in Systematic Drive of Ethnic Hatred: Serbian Violence Rising in North Bosnia", The New York Times, 27 March 1994.

KINZER (Stephen), "Cease-Fire in Bosnia Starts, and Sides Meet on Details", The New York Times, 2 January 1995.

LEWIS (Paul), "U.N. Rules Out A Force to Halt Bosnia Fighting: U.N. Chief Rules Out Role For Peace Force in Bosnia", The New York Times, 14 May 1992.

LYONS (Richard D.), "Explosive Mix in Chechnya: History, Hatred and Oil", The New York Times, 14 December 1994.

ROANE (Kit R.), "Sarajevo Streets Are Humming Happily Again: With the uncertain peace in Bosnia, an immense task of reconstruction", The New York Times, 2 October 1995.

SARIRE (William), "Whom to Root for in Chechnya: Nothing succeeds like secession", The New York Times, 19 December 1994.

SCIOLINO (Elaine), "U.S. REJECTS PLEA TO ACT IN BOSNIA: Tells France Peace Cannot Be Won by Splitting a Nation", The New York Times, 25 January 1994.

SPECTER (Michael), "No Way Out On Chechnya: Yeltsin Takes Blame Despite Brutal Attack", The New York Times, 18 June1995.

SPECTER (Michael), "After Lull, War Revives in Chechnya's Ruins: After a Pause, War in Chechnya Revives Amid the Ruins", The New York Times, 26 November 1995.

STANLEY (Alexandra), "Russian General Halts His Tanks As Qualms Over Rebellion Grow: Russian General Halts Tanks in Chechnya", The New York Times, 17 December 1994.

STANLEY (Alexandra), "Chechnya: New Hope: Talks a First Hint Of Possible Peace", The New York Times, 23 June 1995.

STANLEY (Alexandra), "In the Provinces Russians Back Drive on Chechnya", The New York Times, 29 December 1994.

STANLEY (Alexandra), "Russian Assault Recaptures Police Station in Chechnya", The New York Times, 22 August 1995.

STANLEY (Alexandra), "24,000 Dead in Chechnya, Rights Group Tells Yeltsin", The New York Times, 22 February 1995.

STANLEY (Alexandra), "Russia Say sit Will Keep Army In Chechnya Permanently", The New York Times, 5 July 1995.

STANLEY (Alexandra), "Strains of Chechnya War Setting Russians on Edge: Strains of the War in Chechnya Put Russians on Edge First war, then rumours, and now even a little paranoia", The New York Times, 29 January 1995.

SUDETIC (Chuck), "Bosnia Prepares to Offer Pardons to Draft Dodgers", The New York Times, 14 July 1994.

SUDETIC (Chuck), "Serb Gang Expels 566 Muslims From Their Homes in Bosnia", The New York Times, 3 September 1993.

SUDETIC (Chuck), "Bosnia Is Using Islamic Funding For Serb Arms: Sale Perpetuates Battle Against Croat Forces", The New York Times, 17 January 1994.

SUDETIC (Chuck), "Serbs 'Militia Still Blocks U.N. Evacuation of Muslims: Stalemate in Bosnia, threats in New York", The New York Times, 10 March 1993.

SUDETIC (Chuck), "Serbs Attack Muslim Slavs and Croats in Bosnia", The New York Times, 4 April 1992.

SUDETIC (Chuck), "Ethnic Clashes Increase in Bosnia As Europe Recognition Vote Nears", The New York Times, 6 April 1992.

SUDETIC (Chuck), "Serb-Backed Guerrillas Take Second Bosnia Town", The New York Times, 10 April 1992.

SUDETIC (Chuck), "Breaking Cease-Fire, Serbs Launch Attacks Into Bosnia", The New York Times, 15 April 1992.

WEINER (Tim), "U.S. Vows to Carry On Work Of 3 Envoys Killed in Bosnia: U.S. Vows to Carry On Work Of 3 Envoys Killed in Bosnia",

"Serbs Reported to Recapture Town in Northwestern Bosnia", The New York Times, 24 September 1995.

"Death Toll in Battles in Chechnya Put at 600", The New York Times, 26 December 1995.

"Russia Pounds Rebel Positions Outside Capital of Chechnya", The New York Times, 21 March 1995.

Other Newspaper Articles (Author Identified)

AYERS (B. Drummond), "A Common Cry Across the U.S.: Its Time to Exist", The New York Times, October 9, 1993.

BONINO (Emma), "Bringing Humanitarian News Into Prime Time", International Herald Tribune, 28 June 1996.

COHEN (Roger), "In Bosnia, The War That Can't Be Seen" New York Times, December 25, 1994.

COWING (Nit), "Instant Pictures, Instant Policy: Is Television Driving Foreign Policy?", The Independent, July 3, 1994.

CHRISTOPHER (Warren), "Send Troops to Bosnia», USA Today, October 18, 1995.

GLABERSON (William), "Fairness, Bias and judgment: Grappling with the knotty issue of objectivity in journalism", New York Times, 12th December, 1994.

GORDON (Michael A.), "U.S. Finds Serbs Skim 25% of Bosnian Aid," New York Times, January13, 1993.

GORDON (Michael A.), The Africa Question: Should the U.S. Get Involved?, Los Angeles Times (November 3, 1996.

HURD (Douglas), "Why Foreign Policy Cannot Be Dictated by Blind Emotion", The Standard, 16 July 1996.

KENNAN (George), "'Somalia, Through a Glass Darkly", New York Times. 30 September, 1993.

MATHEWS (Jessica), "Policy Vs TV", The Washington Post, March 8, 1994.

Orr, David, "Hutu rage grows against Burundi's new Tutsi ruler", The Independent, 30 July 1996.

PERLMUTTER (Amos), "Squandering Opportunity in the Gulf", Wall Street Journal, October 3, 1983.

PILGER (Johan), "The Truth is Out", Broadcast, 10 May 1996.

RABINOVITCH (Dina), "The Million Dollar Action Woman", The Guardian, 6 July 1996.

RUTENBERG (Jim), "Arnett Dismissed After Remarks on Iraqi TV", The New York Times, April 1, 2003.

SONENSHINE Tara, "Clinton Makes Foreign Policy and Electoral Positive", International Herald Tribune, 15 May 1996.

STEINBERG (James), "Foreign Policy Myopia", Washington Times, January 19, 1996.

VULLIAMY (Ed.), "TV Giants Vie To Lure 'Brit Packer", The Observer, 19 May 1996.

TUNBRIDGE (Louise), "Killings by Tutsi-led-army fuel violence in Burundi: coup has provoked a vicious cycle of revenge", The Daily Telegraph, 30 July 1996.

UNGER (David C.), "Ferment in the Think Tanks: Learning to Live with No Global Threat", The New York Times, January 1991.

Newspaper Articles & News Items (Without Author)

"BBC Man Attacks Neutral War Reports," The Guardian, 23 November 1996.

"Burundi Slides Towards Civil War" by Michela Wrong, The Financial Times, 27 July 1996.

"Le conflit en Bosnie-Herzégovine Les Français hostiles à un retrait des" casques bleus", selon un sondage", Le Monde, 14 January 1994.

"Toll at 304 in Burundi attack," Agence France Press, International Herald Tribune, 22 July 1996.

Les Echos, 13 June 2003

Le Monde, Novembre 4, 1992

Le Monde, July 29, 1993

Le Monde, August 2, 1993

Le Monde, August 12, 1993.

Le Monde on June 17

The Financial Times, August 8, 1991

The New York Times, August 31, 1984.

The New York Times editorial, March 1, 1973.

The New York Times, August 9, 1952.

Time, January 7, 1952.

Washington Post, August 1, 1953.

Research Papers and Special Reports

ATWOOD (L.E.), "Old Colonial Ties and News Coverage in Africa", Paper presented to the International Communication Association annual convention, Honolulu, HI, US. May 1985.

CARMENT (David) et al., "Domestic Determinants of Ethnic Intervention: A Typology", A paper prepared for the 2001 Annual Meeting of the American Political Science Association, Francisco, CA., Aug. 29-Sept.2, 2001.

CATER (Nick), "Why does the media always get it wrong in disasters: Stereotypes, standards and free helicopter rides", research paper delivered to the review conference on 23 May 1996 launching World Disasters Report 1996 by the International Federation of Red Cross and Red Crescent Societies (IFRC). London: Oxford University Press, 1996.

FRANZBLAU (Kenneth J.), "Immigrations Impact on U.S. National Security and Foreign Policy", Research Paper for the US Commission on Immigration Reform, October 1997, pp. 1-48.

GNESOTTO (Nicole),"Lessons of Yugoslavia", Chaillot Paper 14, WEU Institute for Security Studies, March 1994; pp. 21-41.

GOWING (Nik), "Lap-Top Bombardiers and the Media: Threat or Asset?", Presentation to the Royal College of Defence Studies, London, 20 November 1995.

HINCKLEY (Ron), "World Public Opinion and the Persian Gulf Crisis", Proceedings of the American Association for Public Opinion Research, Phoenix, May 1991,pp. 16-19.

HILL (Fiona), "The Caucasus and Central Asia", Policy Brief N° 80, The Brookings Institution, May 2001.

HOROWITZ (Donald L.), "Structure and Strategy in Ethnic Conflict, Paper prepared for the Annual World Bank Conference on Development Economics, Washington, D.C., April 20–21, 1998.

KEMPF (Wilhelm), "De-escalation-oriented conflict coverage? The Northern Ireland and Israeli-Palestinian peace processes in the German press", Paper presented at the IAMCR Scientific Conference at Leipzig (Germany), July 26-31, 1999.

LENNON (Federico Rey), "Argentina: 1997 elecciones. Los diarios nacionales y la campana electoral", Report by The Freedom Forum and Austral University, 1998.

LINES (Trevor), "Liberia, who cares?", Letter from the field by Trevor Lines in a bulletin of UK Medecins sans Frontières, May 1996.

LOCKYER (Adam), "The Relationship between the Media and Terrorism", research paper for the Strategic and Defence Studies Centre, The Australian National University, 2003.

MOISY (Calude), "The Foreign News Flow in the Information Age, Discussion Paper N° D-23, Johan F. Kennedy School of Government, November 1996.

PIOTROWSKI (Ralph), "Recognising Croatia," Paper presented at the 3 Annual Graduate Student Workshop, The Kokkalis Program, Harvard University, 9-10 February 2001

RIGAUD (Jacuqes), "Les Relations Culturelles Extérieures", Report to the Ministry of Foreign Affaires, Documentation Française, Paris, 1979.

ROBINSON (Piers), "The News Media and Intervention: critical media coverage, policy uncertainty and air power intervention during humanitarian crisis", Paper for the Political Studies Association-UK 50th Annual Conference, London, 10-13 April 2000.

WALKER (Peter), "Disasters debate: Whose disaster is it anyway? Rights, responsibilities and standards in crisis", research paper delivered to the World Disasters Report 1996 review conference, 23 May 1996.

WALKER (Peter), "Should soldiers get off the humanitarian front line? Disasters, armies and the new world disorder", research paper delivered to the World Disasters Report 1996 review conference, 23 May 1996.

Woodward, Susan L., "Implementing Peace in Bosnia and Herzegovina: A Post-Dayton Primer and Memorandum of Warning", The Brookings Institution, Washington, DC:, 1996.

YOUNG (Christopher), "The Role of Media in International Conflict", Canadian Institute for Peace and Security, Working Paper no. 38, 1991.

"The International Response to Conflict and Genocide: Lessons from the Rwanda", Experience by the Steering Committee for Joint Evaluation of Emergency Assistance to Rwanda. Published by the Danish Foreign Ministry, Vol. E, 1996.

Internet Resources

BALDI (Catherine), "How oil Interests Play Out in US Bombing of Afghanistan", online document without pagination found at http://www.peacenowar.net/Nov%208%2001—Oil.htm.

BALTA (Paul), «La politique arabe et musulmane de la France», Confluences Méditerranée, N° 22, Summer 1997, Docmuent found onlin at e. http://www.ifrance.com/confluences/numeros/22.htm

BELLAMY (Paul), "Chechnya: the Russian quagmire Paul Bellamy reviews the performance of the Russian armed forces in the Chechnya conflict", New Zealand International Review, Vol. 27, 2002. Onoline document found at http://www.questia.com/PM.qst?a=o&d=5000827350.

BELKNAP (Margaret H.), "The CNN Effect: Strategic Enabler or Operational Risk?", Found on the Internet in Pdf. Form at http://carlisle-www.army.mil/usawc/Parameters.

BIDDLE (Stephen), "Role of the United States in Bosnia", online document found at http://www.unc.edu/depts/europe/articles/biddle_s010228.pdf.

BRYCE (Susan), "The Public Relations of Modern Warfare", New Dawn, N°. 56, September-October 1999, Online Document found at http://www.agitprop.org.au/stopnato/19990928newdawn.htm.

CARPENTER (Ted Galen), "The Domino Theory Reborn: Clinton's Bosnia Intervention and the "Wider War" Thesis", Cato Foreign Policy Briefing, No. 42, August 15, 1996, Online Document without pagination found at C:\windows\Bureau\Bosnia Clinton domino theory. htm.

COHEN (Ariel), "Ethnic Interests Threaten U.S. Interests in the Caucasus", Heritage Foundation Executive Summary N° 1222, 25 September1998.

DAALDER (Ivo H.), "The United States, Europe, and the Balkans *, The Brookings Institution, December 2000, Online document found at http://www.brook.edu/dybdocroot/views/articles/daalder/useurbalkch.htm

DEROBERT (Laurent) et al, "Human Nature and the Capability Approach", <u>GREQAM</u>, Université Aix-Marseille III, August 2003, Online document found at http://cfs.unipv.it/sen/papers/Teschl_Derobert_Luchini.pdf.

DOBRINSKY (Paula J.) & RIVKIN (David B.), "U.S. Policy Toward Russia: A Brief Critique", Online document found at http://www.watsoninstitute.org/bjwa/archive/7.1/Russia/Dobriansky.pdf

FONTAGNÉ (Lionel) & PAJOT (Michaël), "Foreign Trade and FDI Stocks in British, US and French Industries: Complements or Substitutes?", Found at http://team.univ-paris1.fr/trombi/fontagne/papers/ichapterpain.pdf,

GARON (Lise), "A Case Study in Functional Subjectivity in Media Coverage, The Gulf War on TV", Canadian Journal of Communications, Vol.21, N°3, 1996. Online Publication Without Pagination found at http://www.wlu.ca/~wwwpress/jrls/cjc/BackIssues/21.3/garon.html.

GINGRAS (Anne-Marie) & CARRIER (Jean-Pierre)· "Public Opinion: Construction and Persuasion", Canadian Journal of Communications, Found at http://www.wlu.ca/~wwwpress/jrls/cjc/BackIssues/21.4/gingras.html.

GOLDGEIER (James M.), "The United States And Russia", Policy Review, Oct-Nov 2001. Found at www.questia.com.

GOWING (Nik)," Media coverag: Help or Hinderance in Conflict Prevention", Found at http://wwics.si.edu/subsites/ccpdc/pubs/media/media.htm.

HILL (Fiona), "A Not-So-Grand Strategy: United States Policy in the Caucasus and Central Asia since 1991", Politique étrangère, February 2001, At http://www.brook.edu/dybdocroot/views/articles/fhill/2001politique.htm

HOLDEN (Kurt), "Public Opinion: American Public Would Intervene in Bosnia, But Not Unilaterally", Washington Report on Middle East Affaires, July/August 1993, found at http://www.washington-report.org/Washington-Report_org/www/backissues/0793/9307034.htm

KAHNEY (Leander), "Internet Stokes Anti-War Movement", Found at http://www.wired.com/news/culture/0,1284,57310,00.html.

KALIBER (Alper), "Securing Domestic Order through Securised foreign Policy: A critical Outlook to Turkey's Official Discourse on the Cyprus Issue", Found at http://www.ir.metu.edu.tr/conf/papers/kaliber.pdf.

KARLBERG (Michael) & HACKETT (Robert A.), "Cancelling each other out? Interest group perceptions of the mass media", Canadian Journal of Communication, Vol. 21, N° 4, 1996. Online publication without pagination found at http://www.cjc-online.ca/~cjc/BackIssues/21.4/karlberg.html.

LIVINGSTON (Steven), "Clarifying the CNN Effect: An Examination of Media Effect According to the Military Intervention", The Harvard Public Policy, Found at www.ksg.harvard.edu/presspol/publications/pdfs/70916_R-18.pdf

LOUIS (Rachal N.)" U.S. Strategy in Bosnia: Are We Really Committed?", 1997, At http://www.globalsecurity.org/military/library/report/1997/Rachal.htm

MANGEOT (Philippe) *"Cap au pire (Sophie Shihab)"*, April 2004, found at http://www.vacarme.eu.org/

MANTON (Hervé), « l'implantation des entreprises françaises en Russie », Information Report N° 955 Presented to the French National Assembly, 1st July, 2003. Found at http://www.assemblee-nat.fr/12/rap-info/i0995.asp.

MORGAN (Allison), "Running head: Beyond agenda setting Beyond Agenda Setting: The Media's Power to Prime", Middle Tennessee State University, found at http://mtsu32.mtsu.edu:11287/600/morgan_summary.pdf.

OBERSCHALL (Anthony), "The manipulation of ethnicity: from ethnic cooperation to violence and war in Yugoslavia", Found at http://www.unc.edu/courses/2002fall/soci/326/039/manipulation_of_ethnicity.pdf.

RADYUHIN (Vladimir), "A new Big Game in Central Asia", The Hindu, 18, July 2003, Found at http://www.cdi.org/russia/268-12.cfm.

ROBBINS (James S.), "The Balkans: A Time for Principled Action", Found at http://www.objectivistcenter.org/articles/jrobbins_balkans-time-principled-action-op-ed.asp

SAITO (Natsu Taylor), "Crossing the Border: The Interdependence of Foreign Policy and Racial Justice in the United States", Yale Human Rights & Development Law Journal., online document in pdf formatwth pagination found at http://www.yale.edu/yhrdlj/vol01/Natsu_Taylor_Saito_YHRDLJ.pdf

SHIHAB (Sophie), « Réponse A Un Anti-Tchéchene », Politique Internationale, N° 98, Winter 2002-2003. Fund at www. Politiqueinternationale.

SMITH (Tom W, "Religious Diversity in America: The Emergence of Muslims, Buddhists, Hindus, and Others", The American Jewish Committee, Found at http://www.ajc.org/InTheMedia/PublicationsPrint.asp?did=400.

SCHLESIGNER (James), "Quest for a Post-Cold War Foreign Policy," Foreign Affairs, Winter 1992. Online document Found at http://www.foreignaffairs.org/19930201faessay5916/james-schlesinger/quest-for-a-post-cold-war-foreign-policy.html.

SUGARMAN (Martin A.), "Kashmir: Paradise Lost", May 29, 1997, Online document found at http://www2.4dcomm.com/farookster30/kash1.htm.

WOODWARD (Susan L.), "Yugoslavia: Divide and Fall", Online document found at http://www.thebulletin.org/issues/1993/n93/n93Woodward.html.

WOODCOCK (Alexander E.R.) & HEATH (James E.), "Q-Analysis of Inter-Ethnic Relationships can Support Information Operations", found at http://www.dodccrp.org/1999CCRTS/pdf_files/track_3/woodc.pdf

YASIN (Tariq), "Chechen Chagrin: Human Rights in Chechnya", Harvard International Review, Vol.24, N°1, 2002. Found at http://www.hir.harvard.edu/search/category.html?category=region&regionid=5.

Internet Documents published by Official Websites With/or without Specified Author.

"Annual Report of 1996", French Central Bank, Official Website of the French Central Bank, document in pdf form with pagination found at http://www.banque-france.fr/

"BOSNIE-HERZEGOVINE : Situation économique Echanges bilatéraux et présence française", French Economic Mission in Bosnia, January 2003

"Bosnie : la question qui tue—La France doit-elle entrer en guerre en Bosnie, et si oui, pour quels objectifs. Sinon, pourquoi?, Réseau Voltaire Pour la Liberté D'Expression, found at http://www.reseauvoltaire.net/imprimer6839.html,and

"Country Reports on Human Rights Practices for1996", U.S. Department of State, At http://www.privacyinternational.org/reports/hr96_privacy_report.html

"Covering War", found at http://www.wpr.org/book/990131a.htm

Crimes of War Project page, Website of The Humanitarian Assistance Training Inventory found at http://www.reliefweb.int/

"Cubans react in anger to treatment of refugees", Online document without pagination found at http://www.fiu.edu/~fcf/anger63099.html.

"Democracy's Century: A Survey of the Global Political Change in the 20th Century", Freedom House survey "Online Document found at http://www.freedomhouse.org/reports/century.html

"End the Fairy-Tale Reporting of Tibet (LAT)", World Tibet Network News, "Wednesday, August 24, 1999, Online document found at http://www.tibet.ca/wtnarchive/1999/8/24-2_5.html

"Europinion n°6—Octobre 1995

Résultats des sondages "suivi continu" de l'opinion européenne (juillet à octobre 1995)", Opinion Publique, Online document found at http://europa.eu.int/comm/public_opinion/archives/europinion_cts/eo6/eo6_fr.htm.

"Europinion n°1—April 1995 Results of "Continuous Tracking" surveys of the European Union (January to April 1994)", Eurobarometer surveys, found at http://europa.eu.int/comm/public_opinion/,

"Freedom in the World 1998-99 Report", Online Document found at http://freedomhouse.org/survey99/relterr/etimor.html

"Foreign Direct Investment inflows, in individual countries", UNCTAD document website of UNCTAD found at http://www.unctad.org/Templates/StartPage.asp?intItemID=2068.

French Economic Mission in Serbia & Montenegro, Website found at http://www.france.org.yu

French Ministry of Foreign Affaires website found at http://www.france.diplomatie.fr/france/fr/politiq/11_2.html

"Haiti Country Reports on Human Rights Practices for 1996", Bureau of Democracy, Human Rights, and Labor U.S. Department of State, 30 January 1997, Found at http://www.usis.usemb.se/human/1996/west/haiti.html.

Human Rights Watch website found at http://hrw.org/press/2002/11/albania1105.htm.

"Indonesia Places Restrictions on Journalists in War-Torn Aceh Province", The Freedom of Information Center, June 11, 2003, Online document found at http://foi.missouri.edu/jourwarcoverage/indonesia.html

"International Press Freedom Awards 2003", CPJ (Committee to Protect Journalists) at http://www.cpj.org/awards03/burns.html

Interview with Bob Greene, Media Studies Journal, Vol.10, N°.4, Fall 1996,.

« Investissements Directs Etrangers et présence française en Croatie (1 er semestre 2003) », French Economic Mission in Zagreb, 16 October 2003. Online document in pdf form with pagination found at http://www.france.org.yu.

« Investissements directs étrangers et présence française en RFY », French Economic Mission in Belgrade, 18 October 2002. Online document found at http://www.commerce-exterieur.gouv.fr/economie/investissements.asp?sr=1.

Kurdish Satellite Television website at http://www.ib.be/med/med-tv/pr/jamming.htm

« Le commerce franco-russe en 2002 », French Economic Mission in Moscow, 30 June 2003. Online document in pdf form with pagination found at http://www.dree.org/russie/infopays.asp.

« Le stock des investissements directs français à l'étranger au 31 décembre 2001 », French Central Bank, Official Website of the french Central Bank, Document in Pdf. form with pagination found at http://www.banque-france.fr/

« Le stock des investissements directs étrangers en France au 31 décembre 2001 », French Central Bank, Official Website of the French Central Bank, Document in Pdf. Form with pagination found at http://www.banque-france.fr/

« Les échanges bilatéraux entre la France et la RFY au cours du premier semestre 2002 », French Economic Mission in Belgrade, 1 Octobre 2002. Online document with pagination found at http://www.commerce-exterieur.gouv.fr/economie/echanges.asp?sr=1.

"Nigeria: Renewed Crackdown on Freedom of Expression", Human Rights Watch Report online document found at http://www.hrw.org/reports/2003/nigeria1203/index.htm

"Occupational Outlook Handbook Survey: News Analysts, Reporters, and Correspondents".US. Department of Labor/Bureau of Labour Statistics, Online document found at http://www.bls.gov/oco/ocos088.htm

PACE "1055 Resolution 1055 (1995)1 on Russia's request for membership in the light of the situation in Chechnya", 2 February, 1995. Website at http://www.coe.int/DefaultEN.asp

PACE Document 7000, 24 January 1994, Found at http://www.coe.int/DefaultEN.asp

"Pakistan: Threats to Journalists Escalate", Human Rights Watch. found at http://www.hrw.org/press/2003/12/pakistan120303.htm.

« Procès Milosevic : la parole est aux « insiders », Le Courrier des Balkans, 7 Novembre 2002, found at http://www.balkans.eu.org/article1641.html

"Protests Around the World and at Home against US/NATO in Yugoslavia", Found at http://www.iacenter.org/yugdemos.htm.

"Rwanda Country Reports on Human Rights Practices—2002", US Department of State, March 31, 2003, P. 8, Online Document with pagination found at http://www.asylumlaw.org/docs/rwanda/usdos02_rwanda_cr.pdf

"Reconsidering Journalism Values", Report of the American Society of Newspaper Editors, 1995, Online document found at www. Asne. org.

"Religious Freedom in the United States of America", International Coalition for Religious Freedom, Online document without pagination found at http://www.icrf.com/wrpt/USrpt.htm

"Second World Press Freedom Ranking October 2003", Reporters Without Borders, Online document in pdf. Format found at http://www.rsf.org/article.php3?id_article=8247

Speech by National Security Adviser Anthony Lake to the Council on Foreign Relations, Washington, DC, 14 September 1994. Online document found at http://www-tech.mit.edu/V114/N40/haiti.40w.html.

"Stocks of Foreign Direct Investments on the 31 December 2001", French Central Bank Report, Official website of the French Central Bank, Document in pdf. Form with pagination found at http://www.banque-france.fr/

The United Kingdom's Graduate Career Prospectus website found at www.prospects.ac.uk

The California Poll 95-04, found at http://socrates.berkeley.edu:7503/sdadata/calpolls/cal9504/Doc/cbook001.html,

"World Investment Report: Trends and Determinants", UNCTAD, Geneva, 1998.

"EU-US Bilateral Economic Relations", European Union, Washington, 25 June 2003, online document with pagination in pdf form found at http://europa.eu.int/comm/external_relations/us/sum06_03/eco.pdf

The Economist Country Profile, at http://www.economist.com/countries/USA

United States Department of Commerce report on the U.S. Oil and Gas Mission to Russia, found at http://www.osec.doc.gov/obl/russiamission2003

The Business Information Services for the Newly Independent States Website found at http://www.bisnis.doc.gov/bisnis/bisnis.cfm

United States Bureau of Economic Analysis at www.bea.gov.

United States' International Trade Administration Website found at http://www.ita.doc.gov

Website of Comité Tchéchénie ar http://www.comite-tchetchenie.org/

Central and Eastern Europe Business Information Centre (CEEBIC), United States Department of Commerce website found at http://www.mac.doc.gov/ceebic/countryr/bosniah.htm

http://www.intelsat.int/cmc/bcaster/bc0996.html

PDD N° 25, 5 May 1994. Online Document

Website of the Fulbright Program found at
http://exchanges.state.gov/education/fulbright/.

Website of the Office of English Language Programs found at
http://exchanges.state.gov/education/engteaching/.

Website of Hubert H. Humphrey Fellowship Program found at
http://exchanges.state.gov/education/hhh/

Website of the Partnership Programs, found at
http://exchanges.state.gov/education/partnership/

Website of the Program, found at http://exchanges.state.gov/education/ivp/

Online Dictionaries & Encyclopaedias

Cambridge Advanced Learner's Dictionary

The Columbia Encyclopaedia (6th Edition), at
http://www.bartleby.com/65/li/LincolnA.html

Handbooks & Manuals

NATO Handbook, Brussels, NATO Office of Information and Press, 2001

0-595-32686-2

Printed in the United Kingdom
by Lightning Source UK Ltd.
102302UKS00001B/162